Theory and Interpretation of Narrative Series

Narrative Dynamics

Essays on Time, Plot, Closure, and Frames

Edited by BRIAN RICHARDSON

THE OHIO STATE UNIVERSITY PRESS
Columbus

Library of Congress Cataloguing-in-Publication Data

Narrative dynamics: essays on time, plot, closure, and frames / edited by Brian Richardson.
     p. cm. — (The theory and interpretation of narrative series)
   Includes bibliographical references and index.
   ISBN 0-8142-0895-9 (cloth : alk. paper)—ISBN 0-8142-5092-0 (pbk. : alk. paper)
   1. Narration (Rhetoric) I. Richardson, Brian, 1953– . I. Series

   PN212.N3735 2001
   808—dc21

                                                                    2001006168

Cover design by Melissa Ryan.
Text design by Jennifer Shoffey Carr.
Type set in Adobe Garamond.
Printed by Thomson-Shore.

The paper used in this publication meets the mimimum requirement of the American
National Standard for Information Sciences—Permanence of Paper for Printed Library
Materials. ANSI Z39.48-1992

9 8 7 6 5 4 3 2 1

This book is dedicated to my parents

Contents

Acknowledgments

I wish to thank James Phelan and Peter Rabinowitz for their excellent over-seeing of this project, from initial encouragement though numerous judicious interventions to the satisfaction of closure. I also wish to thank Gerald Prince, David Herman, and Emma Kafalenos for much extremely good advice along the way. I thank Hazard Adams, the one who first taught me narrative theory in a classroom. I greatly appreciate the diligent work of Bryan Herek, who assisted in the preparation of the manuscript. More generally, I wish to express my gratitude to the humanities faculty of the University of Maryland for their friendliness and professionalism, and to my many friends and colleagues in the Society for the Study of Narrative Literature for exemplary intellectual comradery. Special thanks, as always, go to my brother Alan for his astute advice and to my wife, Sangeeta Ray, for her insight, understanding, and love.

I gratefully acknowledge the following sources for allowing me to reprint essays in this book:

M. M. Bakhtin, from *The Dialogical Imagination: Four Essays,* edited by Michael Holquist, translated by Caryl Emerson and Michael Holquist, Copyright © 1981. By permission of the University of Texas Press.

Gérard Genette, "Time and Narrative in *À la recherche du temps perdu*," from *Aspects of Narrative,* edited by J. Hillis Miller. © 1971 Columbia University Press. Reprinted by permission of the publisher.

Acknowledgments

Paul Ricoeur, "Narrative Time," in *On Narrative*, ed. W. J. T. Mitchell. © 1981, University of Chicago Press. Reprinted by permission of the author and of the University of Chicago Press.

E. M. Forster, from *Aspects of the Novel.* © 1927. Reprinted by permission of Harcourt, Inc. (HBT) and The Society of Authors, London.

Vladimir Propp, "Fairy-Tale Transformations," from *Readings in Russian Poetics,* eds. Ladislav Matejka and Krystyna Pomorska, Michigan Slavic Publications, vol. 8, 1978. Reprinted with the permission of Michigan Slavic Publications.

Northrop Frye, "The Argument of Comedy," from *English Institute Essays, 1948,* ed. D. A. Robertson, Jr. © 1949 Columbia University Press. Reprinted by permission of the publisher.

R. S. Crane, "The Concept of Plot and the Plot of *Tom Jones,*" in *Concepts of Criticism,* ed. R. S. Crane. © University of Chicago Press, 1952. Reprinted by permission of the University of Chicago Press.

Nancy K. Miller, "Emphasis Added: Plots and Plausibilities in Women's Fiction." Reprinted by permission of the Modern Language Association from *PMLA* vol. 96 (1981).

Peter Brooks, from *Reading for the Plot* © 1984 by Peter Brooks. Reprinted by permission of Alfred A. Knopf, a division of Random House.

Susan Winnett, "Coming Unstrung: Women, Men, Narrative, and Principles of Pleasure." Reprinted by permission of the Modern Language Association from PMLA vol. 105 (1990).

Boris Tomashevsky, selections from "Thematics," reprinted from *Russian Formalist Criticism: Four Essays,* translated with an introduction by Lee T. Lemon and Marion J. Reis, by permission of the University of Nebraska Press. Copyright © 1965 by the University of Nebraska Press. Copyright © renewed 1993 by the University of Nebraska Press.

Jean Ricardou, "Nouveau Roman, Tel Quel," from *Surfiction,* 2nd edition, ed. Raymond Federman (Swallow Press/University of Ohio Press) © 1981. Reprinted with the permission of Ohio University Press/Swallow Press, Athens, Ohio.

Hayden White, "The Historical Text as Literary Artifact." © 1974. Reprinted by permission of the author.

Warhol, Robyn. "Making 'Gay' and 'Lesbian' into Household Words." *Contemporary Literature,* Vol. 40, No. 3. © 1999. Reprinted by permission of the University of Wisconsin Press.

Excerpt from *Beginnings* by **Edward Said,** © 1975, Columbia University Press. Reprinted by permission of the publisher.

Excerpt © **A. D. Nuttall** (1992). Reprinted from *Openings: Narrative Beginnings from the Epic to the Novel* by A. D. Nuttall (1992) by permission of Oxford University Press.

D. A. Miller, excerpts from *Narrative and Its Discontents,* © 1981 by Princeton University Press. Reprinted by permission of the publisher.

Rachel Blau DuPlessis, excerpts from *Writing beyond the Ending,* © 1984, by permission of the author.

Russell Reising, excerpts from *Loose Ends: Aesthetic Closure and Social Crisis,* © 1996, Duke University Press. Reprinted by permission of the publisher.

John Frow, "The Literary Frame," from *The Journal of Aesthetic Education* 16:2 (Summer 1982). Reprinted by permission of the University of Illinois Press and the author.

William Nelles, "Stories within Stories: Narrative Levels and Embedded Narratives," *Studies in the Literary Imagination* vol. 25:1, Spring 1992. Copyright 1992, Department of English, Georgia State University. Reproduced by permission.

Jacques Derrida, from *The Truth in Painting.* © 1987, University of Chicago Press. Reprinted by permission of the author and of the University of Chicago Press.

Marie-Laure Ryan, "Stacks, Frames, and Boundaries," *Poetics Today* vol. 11, no. 4, Winter 1990. Reprinted by permission of Duke University Press.

General Introduction

Time, plot, openings, endings, and frames are among the most important aspects of the study of narrative, and have been the subjects of numerous major critical investigations in the distant past, throughout the twentieth century, and during the last several years. Plot—the events of a story and the way those events are bound together to make the story—has historically been the single most discussed area of narrative theorizing. Narrative time has been a central critical concern since Horace advised authors to begin their recountings in the middle of the action being depicted rather than from its earliest origins—advice that many subsequent writers would follow, and many others, like Laurence Sterne, would flout. Recent criticism has pointed out the extreme importance attributed to the establishment of definitive beginnings and endings in all narratives, whether literary, popular, or religious, and the consequent scandal that disputed origins or the refusal of closure can cause. Similarly, how and by whom a story is told, for what purpose and to which audience, are concerns that cannot be taken for granted, since they themselves constitute so much of the narrative act: a narrative cannot be divorced from the contexts of its utterance without substantially altering the narrative itself.

Surprisingly, no anthology has attempted to bring together this rich and important body of work; existing collections have only a few articles devoted to these related subjects, subjects which are proving more significant each year in all fields that use narrative analysis: literature, cultural studies, gender studies, history, anthropology, and much else. The term "narrative dynamics" is used here to refer to the movement of a narrative from its opening to its end.

1

This includes the beginnings of both the story and the text, the temporality of the telling, the movement and shaping of the plot, and the functions of the ending. Of course, these aspects often flow into one another, and it can be difficult to disentangle and demarcate one from the other; as Henry James pointed out, "really, universally, relations stop nowhere, and the exquisite problem of the artist is eternally but to draw, by a geometry of his own, the circle within which they shall happily *appear* to do so."[1]

It is also true that each of these aspects of narrative dynamics generally has implications for all the others; the traditional well-made narrative is generally conceived of as having a particular type of beginning, development, temporal arrangement, and denouement. Until fairly recently, it has been a critical commonplace that the best plot depicted, as Aristotle observed, an action that was complete and whole, that is, one that possessed a beginning, a middle, and an end (*Poetics* 7.2).[2] The relative importance of each of these aspects has, however, been widely contested. For Edward Said, the choice of a beginning is crucial since it determines much of what follows; for Peter Brooks, on the other hand, it is the final climax of a narrative that determines everything that comes before and leads up to it. The notion of a single, final climax (and the language of male sexuality that Brooks uses to depict the narrative act) has been contested by a number of feminist writers and theorists, who argue against such a narrowly gendered and baldly teleological approach. Ejner Jensen also dissents from the theoretical aggrandizement of closure; he finds the recent critical emphasis on endings contrary to the spirit and design of comedy, which is better appreciated scene by scene.[3] This general stance can easily be extended to other genres, including romance or the serial, that seek to defer indefinitely or elude closure altogether, as Patricia Parker[4] and Robyn Warhol make clear. Finally, we may also consider Yuri Lotman's observation that different genres and historical periods privilege openings and endings differently: thus, the heightened role of the beginning as a fundamental boundary is typical of many myths and texts of the early Middle Ages.[5] Looking back at Aristotle's pronouncement on the best type of plot, we can clearly discern that many kinds of work do not aspire to the kind of interconnected form he preferred in tragedy; in many texts, some of the parts are greater than the whole.

The way a narrative is framed is also relevant to its interpretation; as Lotman and Rabinowitz point out, beginnings and endings help frame and direct the way we read the rest of the narrative; indeed, conventional ordering patterns can be foisted on a text despite its attempts to elude such reading. In addition, the motives, purpose, and context of the presentation of a particular narrative will greatly affect its reception and meaning. As Ross Chambers states, "consider, for example, a 'faggot' joke told by gay people among themselves, by straight people among themselves, [and] by a straight person to a gay person. . . . In each of these cases, the significance of the story is determined less by its actual content than by the point of its being told, that is, the relationships mediated by the act of narration."[6] The same of course is true for any narrative, and the way a story is framed or embedded will indicate how it is intended to be received. This is true regardless of whether the narrative in question is told by the wife of Bath, Br'er Rabbit, or one of the narrators within a novel by Faulkner.

The essays assembled below are intended to represent both enduring classic accounts and the most significant work recently done on time, plot, sequencing, beginnings, closure, and frames. Throughout, I have tried to present a variety of viewpoints as well as to show how some of the recurring theoretical positions develop over time and are applied to adjacent subjects. The reader is thus invited to follow out the century-old battle between analytical and dynamic notions of plot, or trace the contributions of formalist, psychoanalytic, or feminist approaches across different areas of narrative analysis. The introductions to each section are intended to place each contribution within the larger body of work in each field, sketch relevant historical antecedents, and suggest the directions that contemporary discussions seem to be heading toward. In doing so, they offer additional bibliographical resources for those interested in further study.

Narrative theory continues to embrace more areas of analysis, as seen by the proliferation of studies of autobiography and life writing, narratives of popular culture, and national and cultural narratives. The basic aspects of narrative dynamics are increasingly recognized as being prominent in an ever expanding number of disciplines. Indeed, according to cognitive scientists, narrative is the fundamental mode of human knowledge. A companion volume could easily be assembled with essays on narrative in philosophy, history, law, anthropology, psychology, politics, and popular culture. New subdisciplines continue to emerge, and even include narrative therapy and narrative theology. As the interest in narrative continues to proliferate, it is naturally important that the more capacious and sophisticated models of narrative analysis be the ones transported across the disciplines, and that issues under debate be recognized as such. Just as, in an earlier such migration, the importance of voice, unreliability, and the speaker's situation were emphasized by students of first-person historical and cultural accounts, so ought the contemporary investigator read carefully on the dynamics of plot production, the problematics of beginnings and closure, and the insistent push to keep reinscribing "the marriage plot" in patriarchal society and discourse. Indeed, a general—though not uncritical—sensitivity to ideological issues in the production of narrative is very important, as so many recent theorists have demonstrated.

Ideology has always been present in narrative theory, though its appearance is often disguised and its putative effects frequently mistaken. Here too we may begin with Aristotle, whose discussion of goodness of character is filled with the prejudices of his time, as he concedes that even a woman or a slave may be good, though the woman may be said to be an inferior being and the slave worthless.[7] Even the austere morphology of the folktale is inscribed with unfortunate scriptings of stereotypical gender role divisions; as Teresa de Lauretis points out, Propp identifies the attaining of a princess as a typical goal of the folktale hero,[8] as the passive woman is reduced to a token within an exclusively masculine economy. Christine Brooke-Rose notes a similar sexism built into the plot grammar of A. J. Greimas, as the cultural double standard for adultery is explicitly inscribed as an elementary structure of significance.[9]

Models derived from adjacent disciplines often carry with them stray pieces of ideological baggage as well. Using the metaphors of human sexuality as part of his fusion of Freudian psychology and narrative theory, Peter Brooks described narrative desire as "the arousal that creates the narratable as a condition of tumescence, appetency, ambition, quest, and gives narrative a forward-looking intention," and plot as "a postponement in the discharge which leads back to the inanimate."[10] But these are not metaphors of human sexuality, but merely male sexuality, as many feminists quickly pointed out. As Susan Winnett observes, female sexual response does not necessarily conclude with a single orgasm; female experience includes instead two different instances of tumescence and detumescence: giving birth and breast feeding. Their ends, however, are "quite literally, beginning itself. With this change in focus, the 'middle' and its repetitions must be conceptualized anew."[11]

Straightforwardly ideological claims are occasionally made for specific narrative techniques. John Dennis denounced episodic narratives as inherently heretical, since they seemed to call the order of providence into question. Georg Lukács condemned novels that limited themselves to the life or perceptions of a single individual, thereby obscuring the totality of social relations within which all individuals' acts occur. Under the aegis of conceptualizations formulated by Roland Barthes and others, Lukácsian directives were inverted, as the conventional realist narrative—relentlessly linear, causally connected, teleologically directed, formally closed, omnisciently narrated, and realistically feigned—was condemned as inherently conservative and repressive, while the innovative, politically progressive and artistically challenging text was claimed to be open-ended, multitemporal, fragmented, full of gaps and wayward movements, self-reflexive, and narrated by one or more decentered voices. Balzac, the preferred novelist of both Marx and Lukács, now seemed to incorporate every possible reactionary narrative technique. For a while, such conceptions held great authority in many circles (and certain facets of this opposition are still maintained by some). Recently, additional investigation however has tended to eat away at this dichotomous vision (see the introduction to the section on Time in this volume), and more simple or sweeping positions are being reformulated or abandoned. Theorists are increasingly inclined to follow the example of Michal Peled Ginsburg, who attempts "to dislodge the underlying assumption that a certain form has an inherent ideological content to it—that closed form, for example, is inherently conservative. . . . [N]o form is inherently 'conservative' or 'radical'—every form can be put to various uses."[12]

This anthology draws from every major tradition of narrative theory as well as more general critical theories that have been employed in narrative analysis in the twentieth century: Russian formalism, the Chicago School, archetypal criticism, structuralism, Freudian theory, feminist poetics, hermeneutics, deconstruction, and cognitive science. It should also be observed that in the introductions to the different sections below, I have tried to resist conventional narrative form with its regular linear trajectory, sleek plot lines, avoidance of messy subplots, and overall teleological shape. If the history of science includes long periods of "normal science" followed by a major revolution that definitively overthrows the dominant explanatory paradigm, then the history of literary criticism and theory is more like a never-ending series of coups d'état in an isolated province, in which deposed rulers and dynasties come back, decades later, in different guises and bearing new names and arms. Consequently, I have preferred to use the form of the chronicle to depict the often messy succession of leading ideas that are almost never deposed for good, but are instead being refashioned and reintroduced at repeated (if irregular) intervals.

This does not mean that significant patterns are not present in the development of modern narrative theory; a number of larger designs can definitely be made out. We may first remark that its origins coincide with the origins of modernist fiction, and many of its principal early practitioners—James, Ford, Wharton, Woolf, Forster—were innovative creative writers themselves (it might be further noted that this interaction continues to this day in the figures of Hélène Cixous, David Lodge, and Christine Brooke-Rose). Prominent attempts to make literary study less subjective and more scientific were launched by the Russian Formalists in the twenties and again in the fifties and sixties by a number of different groups. Political and other ideological approaches (also important in the thirties) become dominant from the late seventies to the early nineties. Feminism, the most significant intellectual movement of the second half of the twentieth century, transformed the study of literature and critical theory—and most other fields as well. Where narrative study will go next is impossible to predict, though several different types of telos seem to be beckoning.

A final general tendency needs to be pointed out, and that is the growth and development of narrative theory itself over the course of the century. It has not proceeded along a straight line, but traverses a more wayward path. Begun by creators and expositors of early modernist fiction, it has seen many backtrackings and golden ages, dead ends and rebirths. It is nevertheless safe to say that the last dozen years or so has produced a body of theoretical work on narrative that is unparalleled in its range, depth, subtlety, and sophistication. We now know more about narrative than at any other time; insofar as narrative is being recognized as fundamental to so many other basic disciplines, there has never been a better time to have and to use this knowledge.

In my introductions to the different sections I have tried to cast my net widely, situating the selections in this book within their critical and historical contexts, and pointing to many other significant contributors to the theoretical debates. I also should point out that many of the key terms deployed by major theorists below are not entirely synonymous, and may at times differ considerably from scholar to scholar. This is particularly true of the divergent meanings imposed on the term "plot" by those who emphasize entirely heterogenous aspects of the relation between events in a sequence. The term "frame" likewise can cover anything from a story within a story to conceptual or generic features that circumscribe a work or guide its interpretation. Rather than impose any single set of definitions, I have chosen to let the theorists speak for themselves and set forth their own best case for a particular definition. Those who wish to see such constructs compared may consult useful reference works like Wallace Martin's *Recent Theories of Narrative*, Gerald Prince's *A Dictionary of Narratology*, or the theorists themselves as they attempt to situate their own work within the existing critical discourse.

NOTES

1. Henry James, *Theory of Fiction: Henry James*, ed. James E. Miller Jr. (Lincoln: University of Nebraska Press, 1972), 17–72.

2. In Hazard Adams, ed., *Critical Theory Since Plato* (New York: Harcourt Brace Jovanovich, 1971), 48–66.

3. Ejner Jensen, *Shakespeare and the Ends of Comedy* (Bloomington: Indiana University Press, 1991), xi.

4. Patricia Parker, *Inescapable Romance: Studies in the Poetics of a Mode* (Princeton, N.J.: Princeton University Press, 1978), 31–39.

5. Yuri Lotman, *The Structure of the Artistic Text* (Ann Arbor, Mich.: Department of Slavic Language, 1977), 212–17.

6. Ross Chambers, *Story and Situation: Narrative Seduction and the Power of Fiction* (Minneapolis: University of Minnesota Press, 1984), 3.

7. In Adams, *Critical Theory Since Plato,* xv.

8. Teresa de Lauretis, "Desire in Narrative," in *Alice Doesn't: Feminism, Semiotics, Cinema* (Bloomington: Indiana University Press, 1982), 113.

9. Christine Brooke-Rose, *Stories, Theories, and Things* (Cambridge: Cambridge University Press, 1991), 237–40.

10. Peter Brooks, *Reading for the Plot: Design and Intention in Narrative* (New York: Random House, 1984), 103.

11. Susan Winnett, "Coming Unstrung: Women, Men, Narrative, and Principles of Pleasure," *PMLA* 105 (1990): 509.

12. Michal Peled Ginsburg, *Economies of Change: Form and Transformation in the Nineteenth-Century Novel* (Stanford, Calif.: Stanford University Press, 1996), 6.

■ PART I

TIME

Introduction: Narrative Temporality

Narrative time is barely discussed by Aristotle, who simply noted that "tragedy endeavors, as far as possible, to confine itself to a single revolution of the sun, or to but slightly exceed this limit" (V,4). This casual observation (which does not apply to Aristophanic comedy) was unfortunately reified by neoclassical theorists into a dogmatic stricture that held sway for several centuries in much of Europe. Fortunately, many dramatists ignored or eluded this decree. As Lope de Vega once boasted, "nobody can I call more barbarous than myself, since in defiance of art [critical strictures] I dare to lay down precepts. . . . But what can I do if I have written 483 comedies, along with the one I finished this week? For all of these, except six, gravely sin against art."[1]

Nevertheless, once it became established, the neoclassical ideal of an approximate equation between the time represented in the story and the duration of the performance on stage was rarely contested. Some accounts demanded still greater severity—the action of a play could stretch overnight only if characters stayed awake until daylight—while others found ways to wriggle through the critical confines. Corneille actually argued that the stage time of a play's final act could compress the exact time that would need to elapse for the events enacted to actually occur. Elsewhere, in *L'Illusion comique,* he devised a method (a magic mirror) to represent events occurring over several years and still conform to the "unity of time." The repudiation of this unfortunate theoretical stance was begun by Samuel Johnson and the iconoclastic examples of the romantic playwrights, whose innovations were then theorized by the Schelgels, Coleridge, Stendahl, and others.

In the modern period, the story begins again in the early twentieth century. Ford Maddox Ford described the deliberate chronological inversions he

9

and Joseph Conrad produced in the service of an aesthetic that they felt approximated human experience more closely than did a purely linear order. Boris Tomashevsky, in his essay, "Thematics," is the first to differentiate between *fabula* and *syuzhet* or story and text, that is, the chronological sequence of the events of the story and the sequence within which those events are presented to the reader. This is a foundational distinction that would be repeated and occasionally extended by several theorists throughout the century, most notably in Genette's *histoire* and *récit*.

Attempting to historicize the study of narrative forms, Mikhail Bakhtin advanced the notion of the chronotope, the kind of unified temporal movement, spatial setting, and narrative pattern typical of a given historical period. Bakhtin identified a number of major chronotopes, such as that of the Greek romance, with its abstract expanse of space, "adventure time" ("highly intensified but undifferentiated"), and numerous episodic events. Other chronotopes include "the adventure novel of everyday life" of Petronius and Apuleius (a time of exceptional and unusual events not localized in historical time), that of ancient biography and autobiography (specific, inseparable from historical time), the chivalric romance (characterized by a subjective playing with time), and the idyllic (possessing the implicit unity of folkloric time). Especially significant is the Rabelaisian chronotope in which time is presented in vast, exaggerated expanses which, along with other carnivalesque elements, ultimately purge and restore the material world through the destruction of all ordinary ties and false associations established by tradition and reinforced by religious and official ideology, thereby annihilating medieval temporal and historical orders. Also important is the chronotope of the road, where time "fuses together with space and flows in it,"[2] and which plays a prominent role in the history of the modern novel, as will be seen in the selection below. According to Bakhtin, a literary work's artistic unity in relation to an actual reality is defined by its chronotope, which is grounded in specific historical circumstances.[3]

Work on temporality proliferated after the end of World War II. Joseph Frank, using the term "spatial form," valorized distinctively modernist narratives that insistently slowed down, fragmented, or stopped altogether the chronological movement of the story. Günther Müller, in an article first published in 1948, elaborated on the distinction between *Erzählzeit* and *erzählte Zeit*, that is, the time it takes to tell a story and the time span covered *within* the story. In *Time and the Novel* (1952), A. A. Mendilow provided an extensive, philosophically informed analysis of the temporality of the modern novel as well as earlier, prototypical works like *Tristram Shandy*; this is an impressive volume that anticipates a number of issues that would later be developed by narrative theorists and is still worth consulting. A phenomenological account of the reader's experience of narrative temporality in a number of exemplary novels was offered by Georges Poulet in his *Studies in Human Time*. David Leon Higdon's *Time and English Fiction* proposed a poetics of fictional "time shapes," identifying what he called process time, retrospective time, barrier time, and polytemporal time to designate the major types of temporal organization in the English novel.

Käte Hamburger's linguistics-based theory of literature set forth in *The Logic of Literature* sought to identify key discursive features that were unique to literary fiction. Among these are what she terms the "epic preterite," or the past tense used in third-person fiction. This is a curious phenomenon since fictional events, she argues, are objectively "time-less," and only occur in a character's fictive and time-less present; fictional narration nullifies the temporal meaning of the tense in which a text is narrated. Harald Weinrich and Ann Banfield have also done significant work from the same general approach, Weinrich's often in opposition to Hamburger's. The most thorough development of the analysis of time in fictional discourse from the perspective of linguistics is Suzanne Fleischman's *Tense and Narrativity;* the most recent application of this kind of analysis is Dorrit Cohn's study of narratives written in the present tense (which she playfully designates "the fictional present") in her chapter, "'I Doze and I Wake': The Deviance of Simultaneous Narration."[4]

The most widely influential account of narrative time was developed by Gérard Genette. Building on the work of the Russian Formalists, he established and elaborated the principal categories of order, duration, and frequency. Order describes the relation between the events of the story and the sequence in which they are related (i.e., the same distinction as that demarcated by *fabula* and *syuzhet*); duration contrasts the time an event takes to occur in the story with the time it takes for it to be narrated; and frequency, the number of times an event occurs in a story as opposed to the number of times it is recounted in the text (a single event can be narrated several times; several repeated events can be depicted together in a single recounting). These categories and their subdivisions are elaborated and developed in *Narrative Discourse;* in *Narrative Discourse Revisited,* Genette further refines these analyses and answers objections. Other theorists have gone on to develop or extend this model: Genette, for example, divides the category of duration into four types of narrative movement to designate different "speeds" of the discourse relative to the story events being narrated: ellipsis, summary, scene, and pause [called "stasis" in the essay below]. Seymour Chatman adds "stretch" to this group to cover cases in which the time of narration is longer than the event narrated.[5] In a recent article on the reception of early serial narratives, Tom Keymer proposes the supplementary category of "reading time" to denote the specific duration of the original reading experience of serial fiction as paced by intervals determined by the author.

Paul Ricoeur draws on the traditions of philosophical hermeneutics and phenomenology in his account of temporality. For Ricoeur, the fundamentally temporal structure of human experience is entirely homologous with the temporality of narrative or, in his precise terminology, "I take temporality to be that structure of existence that reaches language in narrativity and narrativity to be the language structure that has temporality as its ultimate referent. Their relationship is therefore reciprocal."[6] Pointing out the mutually constitutive nature of temporality and plot, Ricoeur sets forth a complex, dynamic conception of time in narrative, arguing that it is never merely a linear sequence of discreet, successive instants, but an emplotted, dialectical whole that is projected toward a definite future and is envisaged though past experience. Fittingly, he insists on the additional category of "the fictive experience of time" devoted to readers's encounter with the chronology of the fictional work and their interpreting it through their own temporal experience.[7]

Different feminist accounts of narrative time have been set forth, Julia Kristeva's being the most influential. Drawing on concepts from Lacanian psychoanalysis, she situates the female within the Semiotic, or pre-Oedipal space. This in turn is linked to a notion of time as repetition and eternity, a conception that includes "cycles, gestation, [and] the eternal recurrence of a biological rhythm" as well as "extra-subjective time, cosmic time."[8] This concept is opposed to the patriarchal Symbolic order, which represents time as linear, teleological, and monumental, the time of history. Some feminists, inspired by Kristeva, Cixous, and Monique Wittig, have gone on to valorize circular or otherwise nonlinear plots; other feminists like Rita Felski have expressed strong doubts about such a binary opposition that ultimately remains ahistorical. Recent investigations of this subject, such as those made by Susan Stanford Friedman and Margaret Homans, have become considerably more nuanced and qualified.[9] Others have rejected the notion outright[10] or strongly contested more simple and sweeping formulations as part of a rethinking of the larger implications of linear, chronological sequences.[11] Elsewhere, Marianne Cave has pursued a different route, attempting to map the Bakhtinian chronotope to the female literary imagination.

Compelling accounts of postmodern temporal orderings are also beginning to emerge. Ruth Ronen discusses the contradictory story chronology of the later fiction of Robbe-Grillet and Tamar Yacobi provides a supple outline of unusual temporal movements in the postmodern poetry of Dan Pagis. In *Chronoschisms,* Ursula Heise analyzes several specimens of extraordinary chronological progression, following narrators who wander down "too many temporal dimensions, too many historical moments at the same time."[12] My own essay in this volume identifies several distinctively postmodern strategies of constructing narrative temporality, points out relevant antecedents of these constructions, and explains why such practices cannot be contained within earlier, mimetic-based theoretical frameworks like Genette's or Ricoeur's.

It is becoming increasingly apparent that we are in the middle of a new resurgence of theoretical investigation of temporality. In addition to the recent studies just mentioned, one may point to Homi K. Bhabha's postcolonial reflections on narrative time,[13] Gilles Deleuze's ambitious account of cinematic time, and Jesse Matz's attempt to identify a "tenseless" homosexual temporality. Uri Margolin offers a tense-aspect-modality approach grounded in general linguistics to circumscribe recent, unusual temporal constructions in fiction. In addition, new areas of critical investigation have been opened up in Catherine Gallagher's speculations on narrative length and in Gary Saul Morson's exploration of "tempics," or the variable, process-oriented temporality of contingent narratives that were not produced according to a preestablished design, but evolved while they were being created.

NOTES

1. Felix Lope de Vega, "The New Art of Writing Plays," in *European Theories of the Drama,* ed. Barrett H. Clark (Cincinnati, Ohio: Stewart and Kidd, 1918), 18.

2. Mikhail Bakhtin, *The Dialogical Imagination,* trans. Carol Emerson and Michael Holquist (Austin: University of Texas Press, 1981), 244.

3. Ibid., 243.

4. In Dorrit Cohn, *The Distinction of Fiction* (Baltimore, Md.: Johns Hopkins University Press, 1999), 96–108.

5. Seymour Chatman, *Story and Discourse: Narrative Structure in Fiction and Film* (Ithaca, N.Y.: Cornell University Press, 1978), 72–73.

6. Paul Ricoeur, "Narrative Time," in *On Narrative,* ed. W. J. T. Mitchell (Chicago: University of Chicago Press, 1981), 165; 35 in this volume.

7. Paul Ricoeur, *Time and Narrative,* trans. Kathleen McLaughlin and David Pellauer (Chicago: University of Chicago Press, 1984–87), 1: 80–85.

8. Julia Kristeva, "Women's Time," in *The Kristeva Reader,* ed. Toril Moi (New York: Columbia University Press, 1986), 191.

9. See, for example, Susan Stanford Friedman, "Lyric Subversion of Narrative in Women's Writing: Virginia Woolf and the Tyranny of Plot," in *Reading Narrative: Form, Ethics, Ideology,* ed. James Phelan (Columbus: Ohio State University Press, 1989), 162–85, and Margaret Homans, "Feminist Fictions and Feminist Theories of Narrative," *Narrative* 2 (1984): 3–16.

10. Meir Sternberg, "Telling in Time (1): Chronology and Narrative Theory," *Poetics Today* 11 (1990): 901–48.

11. See Jay Clayton, *The Pleasures of Babel: Contemporary American Literature and Theory* (Oxford University Press, 1993), 40–48; Honor McKitrick Wallace, "Desire and the Female Protagonist: A Critique of Feminist Narrative Theory," *Style* 34 (2000): 176–87;

Brian Richardson, "Linearity and Its Discontents: Rethinking Narrative Form and Ideological Valence," *College English* 62 (2000): 685–95.

12. Ursula K. Heise, *Chronoschisms: Time, Narrative, and Post-Modernism* (Cambridge: Cambridge University Press, 1997), 147.

13. Homi K. Bhabha, *The Location of Culture* (New York: Routledge, 1994), 139–70, 212–35.

1

Forms of Time and of the Chronotope in the Novel: Notes toward a Historical Poetics

M. M. BAKHTIN

The process of assimilating real historical time and space in literature has a complicated and erratic history, as does the articulation of actual historical persons in such a time and space. Isolated aspects of time and space, however—those available in a given historical stage of human development—have been assimilated, and corresponding generic techniques have been devised for reflecting and artistically processing such appropriated aspects of reality.

We will give the name *chronotope* (literally, "time space") to the intrinsic connectedness of temporal and spatial relationships that are artistically expressed in literature. This term [space-time] is employed in mathematics, and was introduced as part of Einstein's Theory of Relativity. The special meaning it has in relativity theory is not important; for our purposes we are borrowing it for literary criticism almost as a metaphor (almost, but not entirely). What counts for us is the fact that it expresses the inseparability of space and time (time as the fourth dimension of space). We understand the chronotope as a formally constitutive category of literature; we will not deal with the chronotope in other areas of culture.

In the literary artistic chronotope, spatial and temporal indicators are fused into one carefully thought-out, concrete whole. Time, as it were, thickens, takes on flesh, becomes artistically visible; likewise, space becomes charged and responsive to the movements of time, plot, and history. This intersection of axes and fusion of indicators characterizes the artistic chronotope.

The chronotope in literature has an intrinsic *generic* significance. It can even be said that it is precisely the chronotope that defines genre and generic distinctions, for in literature the primary category in the chronotope is time. The chronotope as a formally constitutive category determines to a significant degree the image of man in literature as well. The image of man is always intrinsically chronotopic.[1]

As we have said, the process of assimilating an actual historical chronotope in literature has been complicated and erratic; certain isolated aspects of the chronotope, available in given historical conditions, have been worked out, although only certain specific forms of an actual chronotope were reflected in art. These generic forms, at first productive, were then reinforced by tradition; in their subsequent development they continued stubbornly to exist, up to and beyond the point at which they had lost any meaning that was productive in actuality or adequate to later historical situations. This explains the simultaneous existence in literature of phenomena taken from widely separate periods of time, which greatly complicates the historico-literary process.

In the notes we are offering here toward a historical poetics, we will try to illustrate this process, taking our examples from the various histories of generic heterogeneity in the European novel, beginning with the so-called "Greek romance" and ending with the Rabelaisian novel. The relative typological stability of the novelistic chronotopes that were worked out in these periods permits us to glance ahead as well at various novel types in succeeding periods.

We do not pretend to completeness or precision in our theoretical formulations and definitions. Here and abroad, serious work on the study of space and time in art and literature has only just begun. Such work will in its further development eventually supplement, and perhaps substantially correct, the characteristics of novelistic chronotopes offered by us here.

THE CHRONOTOPE OF THE ROAD

A literary work's artistic unity in relationship to an actual reality is defined by its chronotope. Therefore the chronotope in a work always contains within it an evaluating aspect that can be isolated from the whole artistic chronotope only in abstract analysis. In literature and art itself, temporal and spatial determinations are inseparable from one another, and always colored by emotions and values. Abstract thought can, of course, think time and space as separate entities and conceive them as things apart from the emotions and values that attach to them. But *living* artistic perception (which also of course involves thought, but not abstract thought) makes no such divisions and permits no such segmentation. It seizes on the chronotope in all its wholeness and fullness. Art and literature are shot through with *chronotopic values* of varying degree and scope. Each motif, each separate aspect of artistic work bears value.

In these chapters we have analyzed only the major chronotopes that endure as types and that determine the most important generic variations on the novel in the early stages of its development. As we draw our essay to a close we will simply list, and merely touch upon, certain other chronotopic values having different degree and scope. In the first chapter we mentioned the chronotope of encounter; in such a chronotope the temporal element predominates, and it is marked by a higher degree of intensity in emotions and values. The chronotope of the *road* associated with encounter is characterized by a broader scope but by a somewhat lesser degree of emotional and evaluative intensity. Encounters in a novel usually take place "on the road." The road is a particularly good place for random encounters. On the road ("the high road"), the spatial and temporal paths of the most varied people—representatives of all social classes, estates, religions, nationalities, ages—intersect at one spatial and temporal point. People who are normally kept separate by social and spatial distance can accidentally meet; any contrast may crop up, the most various fates may collide and interweave with one another. On the road the spatial and temporal series defining human fates and lives combine with one another in distinctive ways, even as they become more complex and more concrete by the collapse of *social distances.* The chronotope of the road is both a point of new departures and a place for events to find their denouement. Time, as it were, fuses together with space and flows in it (forming the road); this is the source of the rich metaphorical expansion on the image of the road as a course: "the course of a life" "to set out on a new course," "the course of history" and so on; varied and multileveled are the ways in which road is turned into a metaphor, but its fundamental pivot is the flow of time.

The road is especially (but not exclusively) appropriate for portraying events governed by chance. This explains the important narrative role of the road in the history of the novel. A road passes through the ancient everyday novel of wandering, through Petronius's *Satyricon* and Apuleius's *Golden Ass.* Heroes of medieval chivalric romances set out on the road, and it often happens that all the events of a novel either take place on the road or are concentrated along the road (distributed on both sides of it).

And in such a novel as Wolfram von Eschenbach's *Parzival,* the hero's real-life course or path to Montsalvat passes imperceptibly into a metaphor of the road, life's course, the course of the soul that now approaches God, now moves away from Him (depending on the mistakes and failings of the hero and on the events that he encounters in the course of his real life). The road is what determined the plots of the Spanish picaresque novel of the sixteenth century (*Lazarillo* and *Guzman de Alfarache*). On the boundary line between the sixteenth and seventeenth centuries, Don Quixote sets out on the road in order that he might encounter all of Spain on that road—from galley-slaves to dukes. By this time the road had been profoundly, intensely etched by the flow of historical time, by the traces and signs of time's passage, by markers of

17

the era. In the seventeenth century, Simplicissimus sets out on a road rutted by the events of the Thirty Years' War. This road stretches onward, always maintaining its significance as major artery, through such critical works in the history of the novel as Sorel's *Francion* and Lesage's *Gil Blas*. The importance of the road is retained (although weakened) in Defoe's (picaresque) novels, and in Fielding. The road and encounters on the road remain important in both Wilhelm Meister's *Lehrjahre* and *Wanderjahre* (although here their ideological sense is substantially changed, since concepts of "chance" and "fate" have been radically reinterpreted). Novalis's Heinrich von Ofterdingen and other heroes of the Romantic novel set out on a road that is half-real, half-metaphorical. Finally, the road and encounters on it are important in the historical novel. Zagoskin's *Yury Miloslavsky*, for example, is structured around the road and road encounters. Grinev's meeting Pugachev on the road in a snowstorm determines the plot in *The Captain's Daughter*. We recall as well the role of the road in Gogol's *Dead Souls* and Nekrasov's "Who Lives Well in Russia."

Without touching here upon the question of the changing functions of the "road" and "encounter" in the history of the novel, we will mention but one crucial feature of the "road" common to all the various types of novels we have covered: the road is always one that passes through *familiar territory*, and not through some exotic *alien world* (Gil Blas's "Spain" is artificial and Simplicissimus's temporary stay in France is also artificial, since the foreignness of this foreign country is illusory: there is not a trace of the exotic); it is the *sociohistorical heterogeneity* of one's own country that is revealed and depicted (and for this reason, if one may speak at all about the exotic here, then it can only be the "social exotic"—"slums," "dregs," the world of thieves). This function of the "road" was exploited outside the novel as well in such nonnarrative genres as journalistic accounts of travel in the eighteenth century (the classic example is Radishchev's *Journey from Petersburg to Moscow*), and in the journalistic travel notes of the first half of the nineteenth century (for example, Heine's). The peculiarity of the "road" serves to distinguish these novels from that other line of development present in the novel of travel represented by such novelistic types as the ancient novel of wandering, the Greek Sophist novel (to whose analysis we have devoted the first part of this essay) and the Baroque novel of the seventeenth century. In these novels, a function analogous to the road is played by an "alien world" separated from one's own narrative land by sea and distance.

Toward the end of the seventeenth century in England a new territory for novelistic events is constituted and reinforced in the so-called "Gothic" or "black" novel—the castle (first used in this meaning by Horace Walpole in *The Castle of Otranto,* and later in Radcliffe, Monk Lewis and others). The castle is saturated through and through with a time that is historical in the narrow sense of the word, that is, the time of the historical past. The castle is the place where the lords of the feudal era lived (and consequently also the place of historical figures of the past); the traces of centuries and generations are arranged in it in visible form as various parts of its architecture, in furnishings, weapons, the ancestral portrait gallery, the family archives and in the particular human relationships involving dynastic primacy and the transfer of hereditary rights. And finally legends and traditions animate every corner of the castle and its environs through their constant reminders of past events. It is this quality that gives rise to the specific kind of narrative inherent in castles and that is then worked out in Gothic novels.

The historicity of castle time has permitted it to play a rather important role in the development of the historical novel. The castle had its origins in the distant past; its orientation is toward the past. Admittedly the traces of time in the castle do bear a somewhat antiquated, museum-like character. Walter Scott succeeded in overcoming the danger of excessive antiquarianism by relying heavily on the legend of the castle, on the link between the castle and its historically conceived, comprehensible setting. The organic cohesion of spatial and temporal aspects and categories in the castle (and its environs), the historical intensity of this chronotope, is what had determined its productivity as a source for images at different stages in the development of the historical novel.

In the novels of Stendhal and Balzac a fundamentally new space appears in which novelistic events may unfold—the space of parlors and salons (in the broad sense of the word). Of course this is not the first appearance of such space, but only in these texts does it achieve its full significance as the place where the major spatial and temporal sequences of the novel intersect. From a narrative and compositional point of view, this is the place where encounters occur (no longer emphasizing their specifically random nature as did meetings "on the road" or "in an alien world"). In salons and parlors the webs of intrigue are spun, denouements occur and finally—this is where *dialogues* happen, something that acquires extraordinary importance in the novel, revealing the character, "ideas" and "passions" of the heroes.

The narrative and compositional importance of this is easy to understand. In the parlors and salons of the Restoration and July Monarchy is found the barometer of political and business life; political, business, social, literary reputations are made and destroyed, careers are begun and wrecked, here are decided the fates of high politics and high finance as well as the success or failure of a proposed bill, a book, a play, a minister, a courtesan-singer; here in their full array (that is, brought together in one place at one time) are all the gradations of the new social hierarchy; and here, finally, there unfold forms that are concrete and visible, the supreme power of life's new king—money.

Most important in all this is the weaving of historical and socio-public events together with the personal and even deeply private side of life, with the secrets of the boudoir; the interweaving of petty, private intrigues with political and financial intrigues, the interpenetration of state with boudoir secrets, of historical sequences with the everyday and biographical sequences. Here the graphically visible markers of historical time as well as of biographical and everyday time are concentrated and condensed; at the same time they are intertwined with each other in the tightest possible fashion, fused into unitary markers of the epoch. The epoch becomes not only graphically visible [space], but narratively visible [time].

For the great realist writers, Stendhal and Balzac, parlors and salons are not, of course, the only places of intersection of temporal and spatial sequences. They constitute only one such place. Balzac's ability to *"see"* time in space was extraordinary. We need mention only Balzac's marvelous depiction of houses as materialized history and his description of streets, cities, rural landscapes at the level where they are being worked upon by time and history.

We will merely touch upon one more example of the intersection of spatial and temporal sequences. In Flaubert's *Madame Bovary* the *provincial town* serves as the locus of action. The petty-bourgeois provincial town with its stagnant life is a very widespread setting for nineteenth-century novels (both before and after Flaubert). Such towns occur in several different variants, including a very important one, the idyllic (in the works of the provincialists). We will deal with the Flaubertian category alone (which was not, of course, created by Flaubert). Such towns are the locus for cyclical everyday time. Here there are no events, only "doings" that constantly repeat themselves. Time here has no advancing historical movement; it moves rather in narrow circles; the circle of the day, of the week, of the month, of a person's entire life. A day is just a day, a year is just a year—a life is just a life. Day in, day out the same round of activities are repeated, the same topics of conversation, the same words and so forth. In this type of time people eat, drink, sleep, have wives, mistresses (casual affairs), involve themselves in petty intrigues, sit in their shops or offices, play cards, gossip. This is commonplace, philistine cyclical everyday time. It is familiar to us in many variants in Gogol, Turgenev, Gleb Uspensky, Saltykov-Shchedrin, Chekhov. The markers of this time are simple, crude, material, fused with the everyday details of specific locales, with the quaint little houses and rooms of the town, with the sleepy streets, the dust and flies, the club, the billiards and so on and on. Time here is without event and therefore almost seems to stand still. Here there are no "meetings," no "partings." It is a viscous and sticky time that drags itself slowly through space. And therefore it cannot serve as the primary time of the novel. Novelists use it as an ancillary time, one that may be interwoven with other noncyclical temporal sequences or used merely to intersperse such sequences; it often serves as a contrasting background for temporal sequences that are more charged with energy and event.

We will mention one more chronotope, highly charged with emotion and value, the chronotope of *threshold;* it can be combined with the motif of encounter, but its most fundamental instance is as the chronotope of *crisis* and *break* in a life. The word "threshold" itself already has a metaphorical meaning in everyday usage (together with its literal meaning), and is connected with the breaking point of a life, the moment of crisis, the decision that changes a life (or the indecisiveness that fails to change a life, the fear to step over the threshold). In literature, the chronotope of the threshold is always metaphorical and symbolic, sometimes openly but more often implicitly. In Dostoevsky, for example, the threshold and related chronotopes—those of the staircase, the front hall and corridor, as well as the chronotopes of the street and square that extend those spaces into the open air—are the main places of action in his works, places where crisis events occur, the falls, resurrections, renewals, epiphanies, decisions that determine the whole life of a man. In this chronotope, time is essentially instantaneous; it is as if it has no duration and falls out of the normal course of biographical time. In Dostoevsky these moments of decision become part of the great all-embracing chronotopes of *mystery-* and *carnival-*time. These times relate to one another in Dostoevsky in a highly distinctive way; they are interwoven with one another much as they had been intermingled for centuries on the public squares of the Middle Ages and the Renaissance (and in essence as they had been intermingled on the ancient squares of Greece and Rome, although in somewhat different forms). It is as if Dostoevsky's landscape is animated and illuminated by the ancient public square's spirit of carnival and mystery: in the streets (outside) and in his mass scenes, especially the parlor scenes (inside).[2] This does not, of course, exhaust the range of chronotopes in Dostoevsky; they are complex and multifaceted, as are the traditions that they infuse with new life.

In Tolstoy as distinct from Dostoevsky the fundamental chronotope is biographical time, which flows smoothly in the spaces—the interior spaces—of townhouses and estates of the nobility. In Tolstoy there are, of course, also crises, falls, spiritual renewals, and resurrections, but they are not instantaneous and are not cast out of the course of biographical time; in fact, they are welded firmly to it. For example, Ivan Ilyich's crisis and dawning awareness drags on for the whole duration of the final phase of his illness, and comes to a close only at the very end of his life. Pierre Bezukhov's spiritual renewal is also a lengthy and gradual one, fully biographical. Less lengthy but still not instantaneous is the renewal and repentance of Nikita ("The Power of Darkness"). We find in Tolstoy only one exception: Brekhunov's radical spiritual rebirth at the last moment of his life ("Master and Man"), something that is in no way prepared for, completely unexpected. Tolstoy did not value the moment, he did not strive to fill it with something fundamental and decisive: one rarely encounters the word "suddenly" in his works, and it never ushers in a significant event. In contrast to Dostoevsky, Tolstoy loves duration, the stretching-out of time. After biographical time and space, Tolstoy attached most significance to the chronotope of nature, the family-idyllic chronotope and even the chronotope of the labor idyll (in his descriptions of peasant labor).

What is the significance of all these chronotopes? What is most obvious is their meaning for *narrative*. They are the organizing centers for the fundamental narrative events of the novel. The chronotope is the place where the knots of narrative are tied and untied. It can be said without qualification that to them belongs the meaning that shapes narrative.

We cannot help but be strongly impressed by the *representational* importance of the chronotope. Time becomes, in effect, palpable and visible; the chronotope makes narrative events concrete, makes them take on flesh, causes blood to flow in their veins. An event can he communicated, it becomes information, one can give precise data on the place and time of its occurrence. But the event does not become a figure [*obraz*]. It is precisely the chronotope that provides the ground essential for the showing-forth, the representability of events. And this is so thanks precisely to the special increase in density and concreteness of time markers—the time of human life, of historical time—that occurs within well-delineated spatial areas. It is this that makes it possible to structure a representation of events in the chronotope (around the chronotope). It serves as the primary point from which "scenes" in a novel unfold, while at the same time other "binding" events, located far from the chronotope, appear as mere dry information and communicated facts (in Stendhal, for instance, informing and communicating carry great weight; representation is concentrated and condensed in a few scenes and these scenes cast a light that makes even the "informing" parts of the novel seem more concrete—cf., for example, the structure of *Armance*). Thus the chronotope, functioning as the primary means for materializing time in space, emerges as a center for concretizing representation, as a force giving body to the entire novel. All the novel's abstract elements—philosophical and social generalizations, ideas, analyses of cause and effect—gravitate toward the chronotope and through it take on flesh and blood, permitting the imaging power of art to do its work. Such is the representational significance of the chronotope.

The chronotopes we have discussed provide the basis for distinguishing generic types; they lie at the heart of specific varieties of the novel genre, formed and developed over the course of many centuries (although it is true that some of the functions of the chronotope of the road, for example, change in the process of this development). But any and every literary image is chronotopic. Language, as a treasure-house of images, is fundamentally chronotopic. Also chronotopic is the internal form of a word, that is, the mediating marker with whose help the root meanings of spatial categories are carried over into temporal relationships (in the broadest sense). This is not the place to deal with this more specialized problem. We refer the reader to the appropriate chapter in Cassirer's work (*The Philosophy of Symbolic Forms*), where his analysis of the ways time is reflected in language (the assimilation of time by language) provides a rich fund of factual material.

It was Lessing in the *Laocoön* who first made clearly apparent the principle of chronotopicity in the literary image. He established the temporal character of the literary image. Those things that are static in space cannot be statically described, but must rather be incorporated into the temporal sequence of represented events and into the story's own representational field. Thus, in Lessing's familiar example, the beauty of Helen is not so much described by Homer as it is demonstrated in the reactions of the Trojan elders; these come to light simultaneously in the sequence comprised by the activities and deeds of the elders. Beauty is drawn in to a chain of represented events and yet at the same time is not the subject of static description, but rather the subject of a dynamic story.

Despite the fundamental and seminal way he posed the problem of time in literature, Lessing nevertheless posed this problem primarily on the formal and technical plane (not, of course, in the formalistic sense). The problem of assimilating real time, that is, the problem of assimilating historical reality into the poetic image, was not posed by him, although the question is touched upon in his work.

The distinctiveness of those generically typical plot-generating chronotopes discussed by us above becomes clear against the background of this general (formal and material) chronotopicity of the poetic images conceived as an image of temporal art, one that represents spatially perceptible phenomena in their movement and development. Such are the specific novel-epic chronotopes that serve for the assimilation of actual temporal (including historical) reality, that permit the essential aspects of this reality to be reflected and incorporated into the artistic space of the novel.

NOTES

1. In his "Transcendental Aesthetics" (one of the main sections of his *Critique of Pure Reason*) Kant defines space and time as indispensable forms of any cognition, beginning with elementary perceptions and representations. Here we employ the Kantian evaluation of the importance of these forms in the cognitive process, but differ from Kant in taking them not as "transcendental" but as forms of the most immediate reality. We shall attempt to show the role these forms play in the process of concrete artistic cognition (artistic visualization) under conditions obtaining in the genre of the novel.

2. Cultural and literary traditions (including the most ancient) are preserved and continue to live not in the individual subjective memory of a single individual and not in some kind of collective "psyche," but rather in the objective forms that culture itself assumes (including the forms of language and spoken speech), and in this sense they are inter-subjective and inter-individual (and consequently social); from there they enter literary works, sometimes almost completely bypassing the subjective individual memory of their creators.

2

Order, Duration, and Frequency

GÉRARD GENETTE

I suggest a study of *narrative discourse* or, in a slightly different formulation, of *narrative (récit) as discourse (discours)*. As a point of departure, let us accept the hypothesis that all narratives, regardless of their complexity or degree of elaboration—and Proust's *A la recherche du temps perdu,* the text I shall be using as an example, reaches of course a very high degree of elaboration—can always be considered to be the development of a verbal statement such as "I am walking," or "He will come," or "Marcel becomes a writer." On the strength of this rudimentary analogy, the problems of narrative discourse can be classified under three main headings: the categories of *time* (temporal relationships between the narrative [story] and the "actual" events that are being told [history]); of *mode* (relationships determined by the distance and perspective of the narrative with respect to the history); and of *voice* (relationships between the narrative and the narrating agency itself: narrative situation, level of narration, status of the narrator and of the recipient, etc.). I shall deal only, and very sketchily, with the first category.

The time-category can itself be divided into three sections: the first concerned with the relationships between the temporal *order* of the events that are being told and the pseudo-temporal order of the narrative; the second concerned with the relationships between the *duration* of the events and the duration of the narrative; the third dealing with relationships of *frequency* of repetition between the events and the narrative, between history and story.

ORDER

It is well known that the folktale generally keeps a one-to-one correspondence between the "real" order of events that are being told and the order of the

25

narrative, whereas literary narrative, from its earliest beginnings in Western literature, that is, in the Homeric epic, prefers to use the beginning *in medias res,* generally followed by an explanatory flashback. This chronological reversal has become one of the formal *topoi* of the epic genre. The style of the novel has remained remarkably close to its distant origin in this respect: certain beginnings in Balzac, as in the *Duchesse de Langeais* or *César Birotteau,* immediately come to mind as typical examples.

From this point of view, the *Recherche*—especially the earlier sections of the book—indicates that Proust made a much more extensive use than any of his predecessors of his freedom to reorder the temporality of events.

The first "time," dealt with in the six opening pages of the book, refers to a moment that cannot be dated with precision but that must take place quite late in the life of the protagonist: the time at which Marcel, during a period when, as he says, "he often used to go to bed early," suffered from spells of insomnia during which he relived his own past. The first moment in the organization of the narrative is thus far from being the first in the order of the reported history, which deals with the life of the hero.

The second moment refers to the memory relived by the protagonist during his sleepless night. It deals with his childhood at Combray, or, more accurately, with a specific but particularly important moment of this childhood: the famous scene that Marcel calls "the drama of his going to bed," when his mother, at first prevented by Swann's visit from giving him his ritualistic goodnight kiss, finally gives in and consents to spend the night in his room.

The third moment again moves far ahead, probably to well within the period of insomnia referred to at the start, or a little after the end of this period: it is the episode of the *madeleine,* during which Marcel recovers an entire fragment of his childhood that had up till then remained hidden in oblivion. This very brief third episode is followed at once by a fourth: a second return to Combray, this time much more extensive than the first in temporal terms since it covers the entire span of the Combray childhood. Time segment (4) is thus contemporary with time segment (2) but has a much more extensive duration.

The fifth moment is a very brief return to the initial state of sleeplessness and leads to a new retrospective section that takes us even further back into the past, since it deals with a love experience of Swann that took place well before the narrator was born.

There follows a seventh episode that occurs some time after the last events told in the fourth section (childhood at Combray): the story of Marcel's adolescence in Paris and of his love for Gilberte. From then on, the story will proceed in more closely chronological order, at least in its main articulations.

À la recherche du temps perdu thus begins with a zigzagging movement that could easily be represented by a graph and in which the relationship between the time of events and the time of the narrative could be summarized as follows: N(arrative) 1=H(istory) 4; N2=H2; N3=H4; N4=H2; N5=H4; N6=H1 (Swann's love); N7=H3. We are clearly dealing with a highly complex and deliberate transgression of chronological order. I have said that the rest of the book follows a more continuous chronology in its main patterns, but this large-scale linearity does not exclude the presence of a great number of anachronisms in the details: *retrospections,* as when the story of Marcel's stay in Paris during the year 1914 is told in the middle of his later visit to Paris during 1916; or *anticipations,* as when, in the last pages of *Du Côté de chez Swann,* Marcel describes what has become of the Bois de Boulogne at a much later date, the very year he is actually engaged in writing his book. The transition from the *Côté des Guermantes* to *Sodome et Gomorrhe* is based on an interplay of anachronisms: the last scene of *Guermantes* (announcing the death of Swann) in fact takes place later than the subsequent first scene of *Sodome* (the meeting between Charlus and Jupien).

I do not intend to analyze the narrative anachronisms in detail but will point out in passing that one should distinguish between *external* and *internal* anachronisms, according to whether they are located without or within the limits of the temporal field defined by the main narrative. The external anachronisms raise no difficulty, since there is no danger that they will interfere with the main narrative. The internal anachronisms, on the contrary, create a problem of interference. So we must subdivide them into two groups, according to the nature of this relation. Some function to fill in a previous or later blank (ellipsis) in the narrative and can be called *completive* anachronisms, such as the retrospective story of Swann's death. Others return to a moment that has already been covered in the narrative: they are *repetitive* or apparently redundant anachronisms but fulfill in fact a very important function in the organization of the novel. They function as *announcements* (in the case of prospective anticipations) or as *recalls* (when they are retrospective). Announcements can, for example, alert the reader to the meaning of a certain event that will only later be fully revealed (as with the lesbian scene at Montjouvain that will later determine Marcel's jealous passion for Albertine). Recalls serve to give a subsequent meaning to an event first reported as without particular significance (as when we find that Albertine's belated response to a knock on the door was caused by the fact that she had locked herself in with Andrée), or serve even more often to alter the original meaning—as when Marcel discovers after more than thirty years' time that Gilberte was in love with him at Combray and that what he took to be a gesture of insolent disdain was actually meant to be an advance.

Next to these relatively simple and unambiguous retrospections and anticipations, one finds more complex and ambivalent forms of anachronisms:

anticipations within retrospections, as when Marcel remembers what used to be his projects with regard to the moment that he is now experiencing; retrospections within anticipations, as when the narrator indicates how he will later find out about the episode he is now in the process of telling; "announcements" of events that have already been told anticipatively or "recalls" of events that took place earlier in the story but that have not yet been told; retrospections that merge seamlessly with the main narrative and make it impossible to identify the exact status of a given section, etc. Finally, I should mention what is perhaps the rarest but most specific of all instances: structures that could properly be called *achronisms,* that is to say, episodes entirely cut loose from any chronological situation whatsoever. These occurrences were pointed out by J. P. Houston in a very interesting study published in *French Studies,* January, 1962, entitled "Temporal Patterns in *À la recherche du temps perdu.*" Near the end of *Sodome et Gomorrhe,* as Marcel's second stay at Balbec draws to a close, Proust tells a sequence of episodes not in the order in which they took place but by following the succession of roadside-stops made by the little train on its journey from Balbec to La Raspelière. Events here follow a geographical rather than a chronological pattern. It is true that the sequence of places still depends on a temporal event (the journey of the train), but this temporality is not that of the "real" succession of events. A similar effect is achieved in the composition of the end of *Combray,* when the narrator successively describes a number of events that took place on the Méséglise way, at different moments, by following the order of their increasing distance from Combray. He follows the temporal succession of a walk from Combray to Méséglise and then, after returning to his spatial and temporal point of departure, tells a sequence of events that took place on the Guermantes way using exactly the same principle. The temporal order of the narrative is not that of the actual succession of events, unless it happens to coincide by chance with the sequence of places encountered in the course of the walk.

I have given some instances of the freedom that Proust's narrative takes with the chronological order of events, but such a description is necessarily sketchy and even misleading if other elements of narrative temporality such as duration and frequency are not also taken into account.

DURATION

Generally speaking, the idea of an isochrony *between* narrative and "history" is highly ambiguous, for the narrative unit which, in literature, is almost always a narrative text cannot really be said to possess a definite duration. One could equate the duration of a narrative with the time it takes to read it, but reading-times vary considerably from reader to reader, and an ideal average speed can only be determined by fictional means. It may be better to start out from a definition in the form of a relative quantity, and define isochrony as a uniform projection of historical time on narrative extension, that is, number of pages per duration of event. In this way, one can record variations in the speed of the narrative in relation to itself and measure effects of acceleration, deceleration, stasis, and ellipsis (blank spaces within the narrative while the flow of events keeps unfolding).

I have made some rather primitive calculations of the relative speed of the main narrative articulations, measuring on the one hand the narrative of the *Recherche* by number of pages and on the other hand the events by quantity of time. Here are the results.

The first large section, *Combray* or Marcel's childhood, numbers approximately 180 pages of the Pléiade edition and covers about ten years (let me say once and for all that I am defining the duration of events by general consensus, knowing that it is open to question on several points). The next episode, Swann's love-affair with Odette, uses approximately 200 pages to cover about two years. The Gilberte episode (end of *Swann,* beginning of *Jeunes filles en fleurs)* devotes 160 pages to a duration that can be evaluated at two or three years. Here we encounter an ellipsis involving two years of the protagonist's life and mentioned in passing in a few words at the beginning of a sentence. The Balbec episode numbers 300 pages for a three-month-long time-span; then the lengthy section dealing with life in Paris society *(Coté de Guermantes* and beginning of *Sodome et Gomorrhe)* takes up 750 pages for two and a half years. It should be added that considerable variations occur within this Section: 110 pages are devoted to the afternoon party at Mme de Villeparisis's that lasts for about two hours, 150 pages to the dinner of nearly equal length at the Duchesse de Guermantes's, and 100 pages to the evening at the Princesse de Guermantes's. In this vast episode of 750 pages for two and a half years, 360 pages—nearly one half—are taken up by less than ten hours of social life.

The second stay at Balbec (end of *Sodome)* covers approximately six months in 380 pages. Then the Albertine sequence, reporting the hero's involvement with Albertine in Paris (*La Prisonnière* and the beginning of *La Fugitive*), requires 630 pages for an eighteen-month period, of which 300 deal with only two days. The stay in Venice uses 35 pages for a few weeks, followed by a section of 40 pages (astride *La Fugitive* and *Le Temps retrouvé)* for the stay in Tansonville,_ the return to the country of Marcel's childhood. The first extended ellipsis of the *Recherche* occurs here; the time-span cannot be determined with precision, but it encompasses approximately ten years of the hero's life spent in a resthome. The subsequent episode, situated during the war, devotes 130 pages to a few weeks, followed by another ellipsis of ten years again spent in a resthome. Finally, the concluding scene, the party at the Princesse de Guermantes's, devotes 190 pages to a two- or three-hour-long reception.

What conclusions can be derived from this barren and apparently useless enumeration? First of all, we should note the extensive shifts in relative duration, ranging from one line of text for ten years to 190 pages for two or three hours, or from approximately one page per century to one page per minute. The second observation refers to the internal evolution of the *Recherche* as a whole. It could be roughly summarized by stressing, on the one hand, the gradual slowing down of the narrative achieved by the insertion of longer and longer scenes for events of shorter and shorter duration. This is compensated for, on the other hand, by the presence of more and more extensive ellipses. The two trends can be easily united in one formula: increasing discontinuity of the narrative. As the Proustian narrative moves toward its conclusion, it becomes increasingly discontinuous, consisting of gigantic scenes separated from each other by enormous gaps. It deviates more and more from the ideal "norm" of an isochronic narrative.

We should also stress how Proust selects among the traditional literary forms of narrative duration. Among the nearly infinite range of possible combinations of historical and narrative duration, the literary tradition has made a rather limited choice that can be reduced to the following fundamental forms: (1) the *summary,* when the narrative duration is greatly reduced with respect to the historical duration; it is well known that the summary constitutes the main connective tissue in the classical *récit;* (2) the dramatic *scene,* especially the dialogue, when narrative and historical time are supposed to be nearly equal; (3) the narrative *stasis,* when the narrative discourse continues while historical time is at a standstill, usually in order to take care of a description; and (4) *ellipsis,* consisting of a certain amount of historical time covered in a zero amount of narrative. If we consider the *Recherche* from this point of view, we are struck by the total absence of summarizing narrative, which tends to be absorbed in the ellipses, and by the near-total absence of descriptive stasis: the Proustian descriptions always correspond to an actual observation-time on the part of the character; the time-lapse is sometimes mentioned in the text and is obviously longer than the time it takes to read the description (three-quarters of an hour for the contemplation of the Elstir paintings owned by the Duc de Guermantes, when the description takes only four or five pages of the text). The narrative duration is not interrupted—as is so often the case with Balzac—for, rather than *describing,* Proust *narrates* how his hero perceives, contemplates, and experiences a given sight; the description is incorporated within the narrative and constitutes no autonomous narrative form. Except for another effect with which I shall deal at some length in a moment,

Proust makes use of only two of the traditional forms of narrative duration: scene and ellipsis. And since ellipsis is a zero point of the text, we have in fact only one single form: the scene. I should add, however, without taking time to develop a rather obvious observation, that the narrative function of this traditional form is rather strongly subverted in Proust. The main number of his major scenes do not have the purely dramatic function usually associated with the classical "scene." The traditional economy of the novel, consisting of summarizing and nondramatic narrative alternating with dramatic scenes, is entirely discarded. Instead, we find another form of alternating movement toward which we must now direct our attention.

FREQUENCY

The third kind of narrative temporality, which has in general received much less critical and theoretical attention than the two previous ones, deals with the relative frequency of the narrated events and of the narrative sections that report them. Speaking once more very schematically, the most obvious form of narration will tell once what happens once, as in a narrative statement such as: "Yesterday, I went to bed early." This type of narrative is so current and presumably normal that it bears no special name. In order to emphasize that it is merely one possibility among many, I propose to give it a name and call it the *singulative* narrative (*récit singulatif*). It is equally possible to tell several times what happened several times, as when I say: "Monday I went to bed early, Tuesday I went to bed early, Wednesday I went to bed early," etc. This type of anaphoric narrative remains singulative and can be equated with the first, since the repetitions of the story correspond one-to-one to the repetitions of the events. A narrative can also tell several times, with or without variations, an event that happened only once, as in a statement of this kind: "Yesterday I went to bed early, yesterday I went to bed early, yesterday I tried to go to sleep well before dark," etc. This last hypothesis may seem *a priori* to be a gratuitous one, or even to exhibit a slight trace of senility. One should remember, however, that most texts by Alain Robbe-Grillet, among others, are founded on the repetitive potential of the narrative: the recurrent episode of the killing of the centipede, in *La Jalousie*, would be ample proof of this. I shall call *repetitive* narrative this type of narration, in which the story-repetitions exceed in number the repetitions of events. There remains a last possibility. Let us return to our second example: "Monday, Tuesday, Wednesday," etc. When such a pattern of events occurs, the narrative is obviously not reduced to the necessity of reproducing it as if its discourse were incapable of abstraction or synthesis. Unless a deliberate stylistic effect is aimed for, even the simplest narration will choose a formulation such as "every day" or "every day of the week" or "all week long." We all

31

know which of these devices Proust chose for the opening sentence of the *Recherche*. The type of narrative in which a single narrative assertion covers several recurrences of the same event or, to be more precise, of several analogical events considered only with respect to what they have in common, I propose to call by the obvious name of *iterative* narrative (*récit itératif*).

My heavy-handed insistence on this notion may well seem out of place, since it designates a purely grammatical concept without literary relevance. Yet the quantitative amount and the qualitative function of the iterative mode are particularly important in Proust and have seldom, to my knowledge, received the critical attention they deserve. It can be said without exaggeration that the entire Combray episode is essentially an iterative narrative, interspersed here and there with some "singulative" scenes of salient importance such as the motherly good-night kiss, the meeting with the Lady in the pink dress (a retrospective scene), or the profanation of Vinteuil's portrait at Montjouvain. Except for five or six such scenes referring to a single action and told in the historical past (*passé défini*), all the rest, told in the imperfect, deals with what used to happen at Combray regularly, ritualistically, every night or every Sunday, or every Saturday, or whenever the weather was good or the weather was bad, etc. The narrative of Swann's love for Odette will still be conducted, for the most part, in the mode of habit and repetition; the same is true of the story of Marcel's love for Swann's daughter Gilberte. Only when we reach the stay at Balbec in the *Jeunes filles en fleurs* do the singulative episodes begin to predominate, although they remain interspersed with numerous iterative passages: the Balbec outings with Mme de Villeparisis and later with Albertine, the hero's stratagems at the beginning of *Guermantes* when he tries to meet the Duchess every morning, the journeys in the little train of the Raspelière (*Sodome,* II), life with Albertine in Paris (the first eighty pages of *La Prisonnière*), the walks in Venice *(La Fugitive),* not to mention the iterative treatment of certain moments within the singulative scenes, such as the conversations about genealogy during the dinner at the Duchess's, or the description of the aging guests at the last Guermantes party. The narrative synthesizes these moments by reducing several distinct occurrences to their common elements: "the *women* were like this . . . the *men* acted like that; *some* did this, *others* that," etc. I shall call these sections *internal iterations,* in contrast with other, more common passages, in which a descriptive-iterative parenthesis begins in the middle of a singulative scene to convey additional information needed for the reader's understanding and which I shall call *external iterations.* An example would be the long passage devoted, in the middle of the first Guermantes dinner, to the more general and therefore necessarily iterative description of the Guermantes wit.

The use of iterative narrative is by no means Proust's invention; it is one of the most classical devices of fictional narrative. But the frequency of the mode is distinctively Proustian, a fact still underscored by the relatively massive presence of what could be called *pseudo-iterations,* scenes presented (mostly by the use of the imperfect tense) as if they were iterative, but with such a wealth of precise detail that no reader can seriously believe that they could have taken place repeatedly in this way, without variations. One thinks for example of some of the conversations between Aunt Léonie and her maid Françoise that go on for page after page, or of conversations in Mme. Verdurin's or Mme. Swann's salon in Paris. In each of these cases, a singular scene has arbitrarily, and without any but grammatical change, been converted into an iterative scene, thus clearly revealing the trend of the Proustian narrative toward a kind of inflation of the iterative.

It would be tempting to interpret this tendency as symptomatic of a dominant psychological trait: Proust's highly developed sense of habit and repetition, his feeling for the *analogy* between different moments in life. This is all the more striking since the iterative mode of the narrative is not always, as in the Combray part, based on the repetitive, ritualistic pattern of a bourgeois existence in the provinces. Contrary to general belief, Proust is less aware of the specificity of moments than he is aware of the specificity of places; the latter is one of the governing laws of his sensibility. His moments have a strong tendency to blend into each other, a possibility which is at the root of the experience of spontaneous recollection. The opposition between the "singularity" of his spatial imagination and, if I dare say so, the "iterativity" of his temporal imagination is nicely illustrated in the following sentence from *Swann.* Speaking of the Guermantes landscape, Proust writes: "[Its] specificity would at *times,* in my dreams, seize upon me with almost fantastical power" ("lé paysage dont *parfois,* la nuit dans mes rêves, l'individualité m'étreint avec une puissance presque fantastique"). Hence the highly developed sense of *ritual* (see, for example, the scene of the Saturday luncheons at Combray) and, on the other hand, the panic felt in the presence of irregularities of behavior, as when Marcel, at Balbec, wonders about the complex and secret law that may govern the unpredictable absences of the young girls on certain days.

Narrative frequency / Marcel proust.

I have particularly stressed the question of narrative frequency because it has often been neglected by critics and by theoreticians of narrative technique, and because it occupies a particularly prominent place in the work of Marcel Proust. An essay that deals so sketchily and provisionally with a single category of narrative discourse cannot hope to reach a conclusion. Let me therefore end by pointing out that, together with the daring manipulations of chronology I have mentioned in the first part of my essay and the large-sized distortions of duration described in the second, Proust's predilection for an iterative narrative mode and the complex and subtle manner in which he exploits the contrasts and relations of this mode with a singulative discourse combine to free his narrative forever from the constraints and limitations of traditional narration. For it goes without saying that, in an iterative temporality, the order of succession and the relationships of duration that make up classical temporality are from the very beginning subverted or, more subtly and effectively, *perverted*. Proust's novel is not only what it claims to be, a novel of time lost and recaptured, but also, perhaps more implicitly, a novel of controlled, imprisoned, and bewitched time, a part of what Proust called, with reference to dreams, "the formidable game it plays with Time" ("Le jou formidable qu'il fait avec le Temps").

[handwritten annotations: "Why is illusion sequence a prob?" / "Sequence = chronological time / Illusion of sequence = illusion of chronology."]

3

Narrative Time

PAUL RICOEUR

My aim in this essay is to investigate the topic of narrative time. My approach to the problem of the "illusion of sequence" is derived from two complementary claims. If by sequence we mean chronological time, and if by illusion of sequence we mean the illusion of chronology, we may be correct; but such a critique of chronology does not dispose of the question of time. On the contrary, such a critique opens the way for a more authentic reflection on narrative time. The complementary claim is that there is another response to the illusion of sequence than the recourse to achronological models, such as nomological laws in history or paradigmatic codes in literary criticism. This other response consists in elucidating a deeper experience of time, one that escapes the dichotomy between the chronology of sequence and the achronology of models.

1. PRESUPPOSITIONS

[handwritten annotation: "Definition of temporality"]

My first working hypothesis is that narrativity and temporality are closely related—as closely as, in Wittgenstein's terms, a language game and a form of life. Indeed, I take temporality to be that structure of existence that reaches language in narrativity and narrativity to be the language structure that has temporality as its ultimate referent. Their relationship is therefore reciprocal.

This structural reciprocity of temporality and narrativity is usually overlooked because, on the one hand, the epistemology of history and the literary criticism of fictional narratives take for granted that every narrative takes place within an uncriticized temporal framework, within a time that corresponds to the ordinary representation of time as a linear succession of instants. Philosophers

35

writing on time, too, usually overlook the contribution of narrative to a critique of the concept of time. They either look to cosmology and physics to supply the meaning of time or they try to specify the inner experience of time without any reference to narrative activity. Narrative function and the human experience of time thus remain strangers. In order to show the reciprocity between narrativity and temporality, I shall conduct this study as an analysis with two foci: for each feature of narrative brought out by reflection on either history or fictional narrative, I shall attempt to find a corresponding feature of temporality brought out by an existential analysis of time.

A second working hypothesis intervenes here: starting from the pole of temporality, there are different degrees of temporal organization. While this idea stems from division II of Heidegger's *Being and Time*,[1] one will not find here a blind submission to Heidegger's analyses. Quite the contrary; on essential points, important and even fundamental corrections in the Heideggerian conception of time will result from applying a Heideggarian framework to the question of narrativity, along with some recourse to other great philosophers of temporality and historicality, from Aristotle to Augustine to Gadamer. From the outset, however, I agree with Heidegger that the ordinary representation of time as a linear series of "nows" hides the true constitution of time, which, if we follow the inverse order that presented in *Being and Time*, is divided into at least three levels.

At the level closest to that of the ordinary representation of time, the first temporal structure is that of time as that "in" which events take place. It is precisely this temporal structure that is leveled off by the ordinary representation of time. An analysis of narrative will help to show in what way this "within-time-ness" already differs from linear time, even though it tends toward linearity due to its datable, public, and measurable nature and as a result of its dependence on points of reference in the world.

At a deeper level, time is more properly "historicality." This term does not coincide with within-time-ness of which I have just spoken, nor with "temporality" as such, which refers to the deepest level. Let us restrict ourselves here to characterizing historicality in terms of emphasis placed on the weight of the past and, even more, in terms of the power of recovering the "extension" between birth and death in the work of "repetition." This final trait is so decisive that, according to Heidegger, it alone permits objective history to be grounded in historicality itself to the point at which temporality springs forth in the plural unity of future, past, and present. It is here that the analysis of time is rooted in that of "care," particularly as care reflecting on itself as mortal.

Joining this second working hypothesis to the first, I shall try to check the successive stages of the analysis of temporality itself against and analysis of narrativity, which is itself composed of several levels.

36

My third working hypothesis concerns the role of narrativity. The narrative structure that I have chosen as the most relevant for an investigation of the temporal implications of narrativity is that of "plot." By plot I mean the intelligible whole that governs a succession of events in any story. This provisory definition immediately shows the plot's connecting function between an event or events and the story. A story is *made out of* events to the extent that plot *makes* events *into* a story. A plot, therefore, places us at the crossing point of temporality and narrativity: to be historical, an event must be more than a singular occurrence, a unique happening. It receives its definition from its contribution to the development of a plot. Still the temporal implications of the plot, on which my whole essay focuses, are precisely those overlooked by antinarrativist writers in the field of historiography and by structuralists in the field of literary criticism. In both fields, the emphasis on nomological models and paradigmatic codes results in a trend that reduces the narrative component to the anecdotic surface of the story. Thus both the theory of history and the theory of fictional narratives seem to take it for granted that whenever there is time, it is always a time laid out chronologically, a linear time, defined by a succession of instants.

My suspicion is that both antinarrativist epistemologists and structuralist literary critics have overlooked the temporal complexity of the narrative matrix constituted by the plot. Because most historians have a poor concept of "event"—and even of "narrative"—they consider history to be an explanatory endeavor that has severed its ties with storytelling. And the emphasis on the surface grammar in literary narration leads literary critics to what seems to me to be a false dichotomy: either remaining caught in the labyrinthine chronology of the told story or moving radically to an achronological model. This dismissal of narrative as such implies a similar lack of concern in both camps for the properly *temporal* aspects of narrative and therefore for the contribution that the theory of narrative could offer to a phenomenology of time experience. To put it bluntly, this contribution has been almost null because *time* has disappeared from the horizon of the theories of history and of narrative. Theoreticians of these two broad fields seem even to be moved by a strange resentment toward time, the kind of resentment that Nietzsche expressed in his *Zarathustra*.

2. WHAT OCCURS HAPPENS "IN" TIME

I will now fashion together a theory of narrative and a theory of time and, by moving back and forth between them, attempt to correlate the stages of the analysis of narrative with the different depths in the analysis of time. If, in this effort at comparison, the analysis of time most often performs the role of guide, the analysis of narrative, in its turn, serves as a critical and decisive corrective to it.

At the first level of our inquiry, the relation to time expressed by the preposition "in"—to happen "in" time—serves as our guide. What is at stake in an existential analysis—such as Heidegger's—is the possibility of discerning those characteristics by which within-time-ness differs from the ordinary representation of time, even though it is easily leveled off into this representation. I shall compare this existential analysis of time with the analysis of what may seem most superficial in narrativity, that is, the *development* of a plot and its correlate, the ability to *follow* a story.

First, a brief review of the main features of the Heideggerian analysis of within-time-ness: this level is defined by one of the basic characteristics of care—our thrownness among things—which makes the description of our temporality dependent on the description of the things of our concern. Heidegger calls these things of our concern *das Vorhandene* ("subsisting things which our concern counts on") and *das Zuhandene* ("utensils offered to our manipulation"). Heidegger calls this trait of concern "preoccupation" or "circumspection." As we shall see later, concern has other traits that are more deeply hidden, and because of these hidden, deep traits, it has fundamental temporal modes. But however inauthentic our relationship to things, to ourselves, and to time may be, preoccupation, the everyday mode of concern, nevertheless already includes characteristics that take it out of the external domain of the objects of our concern, referring it instead to our concern in its existential constitution. It is remarkable that in order to point out these properly existential characteristics, Heidegger readily turns to what we say and do with regard to time. This method is, not surprisingly, very close to that found in ordinary language philosophy: the plane on which we are placing ourselves in this initial phase of investigation is precisely the one on which ordinary language truly is what J. L. Austin and others have said it is, namely a treasurehouse of expressions appropriate to what is specifically human in experience. It is therefore language, with its storehouse of meanings, that keeps the description of concern, in the modality of preoccupation or circumspection, from slipping back into the description of the things of our concern and from remaining tied to the sphere of *vorhanden* and *zuhanden*.

Within-time-ness, then, possesses its own specific features which are not reducible to the representations of linear time, a neutral series of abstract instants. Being in time is already something quite different from measuring intervals between limiting instants: it is first of all *to reckon with* time and so to calculate. It is because we do reckon with time and make calculations that we have the need to measure, not the other way around. It should therefore be possible to give an existential description of this reckoning before the measuring it calls for. It is here that expressions such as "having time to," "taking time to," "wasting time," and so on, are most revealing. The same is true of the grammatical network of verbal tenses, and likewise of the far-ranging network of adverbs of time: then, after, later, earlier, since, till, while, until, whenever, now that, and so forth. All of these extremely subtle and finely differential expressions point out the datable and public character of the time of preoccupation.

It is our preoccupation, not the things of our concern, that determines the sense of time. It is because there is a *time to do* this, a right time and a wrong time, that we can reckon *with* time. If within-time-ness is so easily interpreted in terms of the ordinary representation of time, this is because the first measurements of the time of our preoccupation are borrowed from the natural environment—first of all from the play of light and of the seasons. In this respect, a day is the most natural of measures. "Dasein," Heidegger says, "historizes *from day to day*" (466). But a day is not an abstract measure; it is a magnitude which corresponds to our concern and to the world into which we are thrown. The time it measures is that in which it is *time to* do something (*Zeit zu*), where "now" means "now that"; it is the time of labors and days. It is therefore important to see the shift in meaning that distinguishes the "now" belonging to this time of preoccupation from "now" in the sense of an abstract instant, which as part of a series defines the line of ordinary time. The existential now is determined by the present preoccupation, which is "making-present," inseparable from awaiting and retaining. It is because, in preoccupation, concern tends to contract itself into this making-present and to obliterate its dependency with regard to awaiting and retaining that the now isolated in this way can fall prey to the representation of the now as an abstract instant. In order to preserve the meaning of now from this reduction to an abstraction, it is important to attend to the way in which we "say now" (*Jetzt-sagen*) in everyday acting and suffering. "Saying 'now,'" says Heidegger, "is the discursive Articulation of a *making-present* which temporalizes itself in a unity with a retentive awaiting" (469). And again, "The making-present which interprets itself—in other words, that which has been interpreted and is addressed in the 'now'—is what we call 'time'" (460). So we see how, as a result of certain practical circumstances, this interpretation is bent in the direction of the representation of linear time. Saying "now" becomes for us synonymous with reading the hour on the face of the clock. As long as the hour and the clock are still perceived as derivations of the day that links concern with the light of the world, saying "now" retains its existential significance; but when the machines used to measure time are cut off from this primary reference to natural measures, saying "now" is turned into a form of the abstract representation of time.

39

Turning to narrative activity, I shall now attempt to show that the time of the simplest story also escapes the ordinary notion of time conceived of as a series of instants succeeding one another along an abstract line oriented in a single direction. The phenomenology of the act of following a story may serve as our point of departure.[2] Let us say that a story describes a series of actions and experiences made by a number of characters, whether real or imaginary. These characters are represented either in situations that change or as they relate to changes to which they then react. These changes, in turn, reveal hidden aspects of the situation and of the characters and engender a new predicament that calls for thinking, action, or both. The answer to this predicament advances the story to its conclusion.

Following a story, correlatively, is understanding the successive actions, thoughts, and feelings in question insofar as they present a certain directedness. By this I mean that we are pushed ahead by this development and that we reply to its impetus with expectations concerning the outcome and the completion of the entire process. In this sense, the story's conclusion is the pole of attraction of the entire development. But a narrative conclusion can be neither deduced nor predicted. There is no story if our attention is not moved along by a thousand contingencies. This is why a story has to be followed to its conclusion. So rather than being predictable, a conclusion must be acceptable. Looking back from the conclusion to the episodes leading up to it, we have to be able to say that this ending required these sorts of events and this chain of actions. But this backward look is made possible by the teleological movement directed by our expectations when we follow the story. This is the paradox of contingency, judged "acceptable after all," that characterizes the comprehension of any story told.

If we now compare this brief analysis of the development of a plot to the Heidegerian concept of within-time-ness, we can say that the narrative structure confirms the existential analysis. To begin, it is clear that the art of story telling places the narrative "in" time. The art of storytelling is not so much a way of reflecting on time as a way of taking it for granted. We can apply to storytelling Heidegger's remark that "factical *Dasein* takes time into is reckoning, without any existential understanding of temporality" (456). And it is indeed to factical *Dasein* that the art of storytelling belongs, even when the narrative is fictional. It is this art that makes all the adverbs enumerated above directly significant—then, next, now, and so on. When someone, whether storyteller or historian, starts recounting, everything is already spread out in time. In this sense, narrative activity, taken without further reflection, participates in the dissimulation both of historicality and, even more so, of the deeper levels of temporality. But at the same time, it implicitly states the truth of within-time-ness insofar as it possesses its own authenticity, the authenticity of its inauthenticity, if one may so put it, and it therefore presents an existential structure quite as original as the other two existential categories of time that frame it.

To take an example, the heroes of stories reckon *with* time. They have or do not have time *for* this or that. Their time can be gained or lost. It is true to say that we measure this time of the story because we count it and that we count it because we reckon with it. The time of the story retains this reckoning at the threshold of measurement, at the point where it reveals our thrownness, by which we are abandoned to the changing of day into night. This time already includes the sort of reckoning used in dating events, but it is not yet the time in which the natural measures of "days" is replaced by artificial measures, that is, measures taken from physics and based on an instrumentation that follows the progress of the investigation of nature. In a narrative, the measuring of time is not yet released from time reckoning because this reckoning is still visibly rooted in preoccupation. It is as true to say of narrative as of preoccupation that the "day" is the natural measure and that "*Dasein* historizes *from day to day.*"

For these reasons, the time of a narrative is public time, but not in the sense of ordinary time, indifferent to human beings, to their acting and their suffering. Narrative time is public time in the same sense that within-timeness is, before it is leveled off by ordinary time. Moreover, the art of storytelling retains this public character of time while keeping it from falling into anonymity. It does so, first, as time common to the actors, as time woven in common by their interaction. On the level of the narrative, of course, "others" exist: the hero has antagonists and helpers; the object of the quest is someone else or something else that another can give or withhold. The narrative confirms that "in the 'most intimate' Being-with-one-another of several people, they can say '*now*' and say it 'together.' . . . The 'now' which anyone expresses is always said in the publicness of Being-in-the-world with one another" (463).

This first side of public time is, in some sense, internal to the interaction. But the narrative has a second relationship to public time: external public time or, we might say, the time of the public. Now a story's public is its audience. Through its recitation, a story is incorporated into a community which it gathers together. It is only through the written text that the story is open to the public that, to borrow Gadamer's expression, amounts to anyone who can read. The published work is the measure of this public. But even so, this public is not just anyone at all, it is not "they"; instead, it is they lifted out of anonymity in order to make up an invisible audience, those whom Nietzsche called "my own." This public does not fall back into they—in the sense in which a work is said to fall into the public domain—except through a leveling off similar to that by which within-time-ness is reduced to ordinary time, knowing neither day nor hour, recognizing no "right" time because no one feels concerned by it.

A final trait of within-time-ness is illustrated by the time of the narrative. It concerns the primacy of the present in preoccupation. We saw that for Heidegger, "saying now" is interpreting the making-present which is accorded a certain preference by preoccupation, at the expense of awaiting and retaining. But it is when within-time-ness is leveled off that saying "now" slips into the mathematical representation of the instant characteristic of ordinary time. "Saying now" must therefore continually be carried back to making-present if this abstract representation is to be avoided.

Now narratives invite a similar, yet quite original, reinterpretation of this "saying now." For a whole category of narratives, in fact (those which according to Robert Scholes and Robert Kellogg stem from the epic matrix[3] and those which Vladimir Propp and Algirdas Greimas place under the title of the quest), narrative activity is the privileged discursive expression of preoccupation and its making-present. It is privileged because these narratives exhibit a feature that the Heideggerian analysis of saying "present"—an analysis that is too brief and too centered around "reading the hour"—does not encounter, namely, the phenomenon of "intervention" (which, by the way of contrast, is at the center of Henrik von Wright's analyses in action theory). These narratives, in fact, represent a person acting, who orients him- or herself in circumstances he or she has not created, and who produces consequences he or she has not intended. This is indeed the time of the "now that . . . ," wherein a person is both abandoned and responsible at the same time.

The dialectical character of this "now that . . ." appears, however, only as it unfolded narratively in the interplay between being able to act and being bound to the world order. This interplay accentuates both what distinguishes within-time-ness from abstract time and what makes the interpretation of within-time-ness lean toward the representation of abstract time. On the one hand, the narrative's making-present is the instant suffering and acting, the moment when the actor knowing, in a nonrepresentative way, what he or she can do, in fact does it. This is the moment when, according to Claude Bremond, possible action becomes actual, moving toward its completion.[4] This present of praxic intervention has, therefore, nothing in common with the mathematical instant; one could say of it, with Heidegger, that it "temporalizes itself in a unity with awaiting and retaining" (459). Yet the fall into the representation of ordinary time is, in a sense, also lodged in this very structure of intervention. Days and hours are, of course, as much intimate measures of action caught up in circumstances as they are external measures punctuating the sovereign firmament. Nevertheless, in the instant of acting, when the agent seizes hold of such circumstances and inserts his or her action into the course of things, the temporal guides provided by the chain of meaning attached to manipulable objects tend to make world time prevail over the time of action. So it is in the phenomenon of intervention, in which our powers of action are linked to the world order, that what could be termed the structure of intersection characteristic of within-time-ness is constituted, in the nether zone between ordinary time and true historicality. Thus in this sense, narrative shows how concern "interprets itself" in the saying "now." The heroic quest is the privileged medium for this self-presentation. It, more than any other form, is the narrative of preoccupation.

The time of the plot, however, provides much more than an illustration of the existential analysis of within-time-ness. We have already seen that the actor's intervention in the course of the world affords a more refined and more dialectical analysis than Heidegger's analysis of making-present and saying "now." Turning our investigation now from narrative theory back to the theory of time, we must deal with a basic characteristic of plot that I have up to now neglected.

If so many authors have hastily identified narrative time and chronological time at the level of surface grammar—or, in Greimas's terms, at the level of manifestation—it is because they have neglected a fundamental feature of narrative's temporal dialectic. This trait characterizes the plot as such, that is, as the objective correlate of the act of following a story. This fundamental trait, which was already implied in my definition of events made into story through the plot, may be described as follows: every narrative combines two dimensions in various proportions, one chronological and the other nonchronological. The first may be called the episodic dimension, which characterizes the story as made out events. The second is the configurational dimension, according to which the plot construes significant wholes out of scattered events. Here I am borrowing from Louis O. Mink the notion of a configurational act, which he interprets as a "grasping together."[5] I understand this act to be the act of the plot, as eliciting a pattern from a succession. This act displays the character of a judgment or, more precisely, a reflective judgment in the Kantian sense of this term.[6] To tell and follow a story is already to reflect upon events in order to encompass them in successive wholes. This dimension is completely overlooked in the theory of history proposed by anti-narrativist writers. They tend to deprive narrative activity of its complexity and, above all, of its twofold characteristic of confronting and combining both sequence and pattern in various ways. This antithetical dynamic is no less overlooked in the theory of fictional narratives proposed by structuralists, who take it for granted that the surface grammar of what they call the "plane of manifestation" is merely episodic and therefore purely chronological. They then conclude that the principle of order has to be found at the higher level of achronological models or codes. Antinarrativist historians and structuralists thus share a common prejudice: they do not see that the humblest narrative is always more than a chronological series of events and that in turn the configurational dimension cannot overcome the episodic dimension without suppressing the narrative structure itself.[7]

The temporal implications of this twofold structure of the plot are so striking that we may already conjecture that narrative does more than just establish humanity, along with human actions and passions, "in" time; it also brings us back from within-time-ness to historicality, from "reckoning with" time to "recollecting" it. As such, the narrative function provides a transition from within-time-ness to historicality.

The temporal dialectic, then, is implied in the basic operation of eliciting a configuration from succession. Thanks to its episodic dimension, narrative time tends toward the linear representation of time in several ways: first, the "then" and "and then" structure that provides an answer to the question "What next?" suggests a relation of exteriority between the phases of the action; second, the episodes constitute an open-ended series of events that allows one to add to the "then" an "and then" and an "and so on"; and finally, the episodes follow one another in accordance with the irreversible order of time common to human and physical events.

The configurational dimension, in turn, displays temporal features that may be opposed to these "features" of episodic time. The configurational arrangement makes the succession of events into significant wholes that are the correlate of the act of grouping together. Thanks to this reflexive act—in the sense of Kant's *Critique of Judgment*—the whole plot may be translated into one "thought." "Thought," in this narrative context, may assume various meanings. It may characterize, for instance, following Aristotle's *Poetics,* the "theme" (*dianoia*) that accompanies the "fable" or "plot" (*mythos*) of a tragedy.[8] "Thought" may also designate the "point" of the Hebraic *maschal* or of the biblical parable, concerning which Jeremias observes that the point of the parable is what allows us to translate it into a proverb or an aphorism. The term "thought" may also apply to the "colligatory terms" used in history writing, such terms as "the Renaissance," "the Industrial Revolution," and so on, which, according to Walsh and Dray, allow us to apprehend a set of historical events under a common denominator. (Here "colligatory terms" correspond to the kind of explanation that Dray puts under the heading of "explaining what.") In a word, the correlation between thought and plot supersedes the "then" and "and then" of mere succession. But it would be a complete mistake to consider "thought" as achronological. "Fable" and "theme" are closely tied together as episode and configuration. The time of fable-and-theme, if we may make of this a hyphenated expression, is more deeply temporal than the time of merely episodic narratives.

The plot's configuration also superimposes "the sense of an ending"—to use Kermode's expression—on the open-endedness of mere succession. As soon as a story is well known—and such is the case with most traditional and popular narratives as well as with the national chronicles of the founding events of a given community—retelling takes the place of telling. Then following the story is less important than apprehending the well-known end as implied in the beginning and the well-known episodes leading to this end. Here again, time is not abolished by the teleological structure of the judgment which grasps together the events under the heading of "the end." This strategy of judgment is one of the means through which time is brought back from within-time-ness to repetition.

Finally, the recollection of the story governed as a whole by its way of ending constitutes an alternative to the representation of time as moving from the past forward into the future, according to the well-known metaphor of the arrow of time. It is as though recollection inverted the so-called natural order of time. By reading the end in the beginning and the beginning in the end, we learn also to read time itself backward, as the recapitulating of the initial conditions of a course of action in its terminal consequences. In this way, a plot establishes human action not only within time, as we said at the beginning of this section, but within memory. Memory, accordingly, *repeats* the course of events according to an order that is the counterpart of time as "stretching-along" between a beginning and an end.

This third temporal characteristic of plot has brought us as close as possible to Heidegger's notion of "repetition," which is the turning point for his whole analysis of historicality (*Geschichtlichkeit*). Repetition, for Heidegger, means more than a mere retrieval of our most basic potentialities inherited from our past in the form of personal fate and collective destiny. The question, then, is whether we may go so far as to say that the function of narrative—or at least of some narratives—is to establish human action at the level of genuine historicality, that is, of repetition. If such were the case, the temporal structure of narrative would display the same hierarchy as the one established by the phenomenology of time experience.

NOTES

1. Martin Heidegger, *Being and Time*, trans. John Macquarrie and Edward Robinson (New York, 1962); all further references to this work will be included in the text.
2. Here I am borrowing from W. B. Gallie's *Philosophy and the Historical Understanding* (New York, 1964).

3. See Robert Scholes and Robert Kellogg's *The Nature of Narrative* (New York, 1966).

4. See Claude Bremond's "La Logique des possibles narratifs," *Communications* 8 (1966): 60–76.

5. See Louis O. Mink's "Interpretation and Narrative Understanding," *Journal of Philosophy* 69, no. 9 (1972): 735–37.

6. See also the work of William H. Dray on judgment.

7. In my "Narrative Function" (*Semeia* 13 [1978]: 177–202), I contend that "if history may have been grafted, as inquiry, onto narrative activity, it is because the 'configurational' dimension of story-telling and story-following already paved the way for an activity that Mandelbaum rightly characterizes as subsuming wholes. This activity is not a radical break with narrative activity to the extent that the latter already combines chronological and configurational order" (184).

8. It may be noted in passing that this correlation between "theme" and "plot" is also the basis of Northrop Frye's "archetypal" criticism.

4

Beyond Story and Discourse: Narrative Time in Postmodern and Nonmimetic Fiction

BRIAN RICHARDSON

Narrative temporality is perhaps the area in which there is still the greatest degree of general agreement among major theorists. The standard conceptual framework here is Genette's, with its basic concepts of order, duration, and frequency. These concepts build on and are consonant with the Russian Formalists' earlier distinction between *fabula* and *syuzhet* and theoretical dyad of *Erzählzeit* and *erzählte Zeit,* long present in several strands of the German critical tradition; Genette's model also shares the same general mimetic assumptions of virtually every other current theory of narrative time, a common ground that allows the theory to attempt to cover both fictional and nonfictional works.[1]

In most cases, this is all that is required. There is no question that Genette's account is generally adequate to describe the temporality of most nonfictional narratives, of the great majority of works of realist fiction, and of much modernist fiction. Indeed, it was quite possibly the strikingly antilinear yet naturalistically recuperable texts of the modernists that may have originally inspired these investigations in the first place. However, these categories do not work if applied to many late modernist and postmodern texts, since they are predicated on distinctions that experimental writers are determined to preclude, deny, or confound—and this is also true of some postmodern forays into nonfictional genres.[2] As Diane Elam has written, "postmodernism is the recognition of the specifically *temporal* irony within narrative" (217). Surveying the considerable body of avant-garde and postmodern narratives that have recently proliferated, we are now in a position to identify several significant varieties of temporal construction that have become fairly well established that nevertheless cannot be contained within a Genettean framework.[3]

Among the numerous violations of realistic temporality present in recent texts, there are six kinds of temporal reconstruction that stand out as sufficiently distinctive to warrant particular notice. These strategies, as we will see, are often present in earlier narratives as well; furthermore, insofar as they engage in logical contradictions, they are usually only possible in works of fiction. Though nonmimetic, they nevertheless bear a dialectical relationship to the concept of mimesis, since it is only through that concept that we can understand its violation. The strategies include the following:

1. CIRCULAR

Perhaps the best known type, this kind of fiction instead of ending returns to its own beginning, and thus continues infinitely. Its circular temporality partially mimes but ultimately transforms the linear chronology of everyday existence; it always returns to and departs from its point of origin—which is also its (temporary) conclusion. The *locus classicus* of this type is *Finnegans Wake;* other earlier examples include Queneau's *Le Chiendent* (1933) and Nabokov's *The Gift* (1937–38).[4] Brian McHale further points out that "[o]ther variants on the ouroboros-structure include Julio Cortazar's *Hopscotch* (1963/7), Gabriel Josipovici's 'Mobius the Stripper' (1974), and John Barth's minimalist Mobius-strip narrative, 'Frame-Tale' (from *Lost in the Funhouse)*" (1987, 111). Such texts also problematize Genette's notion of frequency as well, since they are infinitely repeated instances of otherwise singulative events.

2. CONTRADICTORY

A prominent type of many of the more extreme postmodern narratives is the self-contradictory story, in which incompatible and irreconcilable versions of the story are set forth. In real life, such contradictions are not possible: a man may have died in 1956 or he may have died in 1967, but he cannot have died in 1956 *and* in 1967. But this law of noncontradiction does not have to be followed in nonmimetic works like J. B. Priestley's *Dangerous Corner,* Robert Coover's "The Babysitter," Caryl Churchill's *Traps,* Jeanette Winterson's "The Poetics of Sex," the mutually incompatible dual endings of John Fowles's *The French Lieutenant's Woman,* and most famously (and egregiously) in Robbe-Grillet's later fiction.[5] Discussing *La Maison de rendez-vous,* Ruth Ronen has observed that "fictional worlds can contain time paradoxes where time is presented as reversible or bilateral" (202).[6] In these texts, there is no single, unambiguous story to be extrapolated from the discourse, but rather two or more contradictory versions that seriously vitiate the very notion of story (*histoire*) insofar as it is conceived as a single, self-consistent series of events that can be inferred from the discourse. For that matter, Genette's notion of frequency as well as his concept of story presupposes the existence of a fixed, retrievable, noncontradictory sequence of events, a sequence many postmodern writers refuse to provide. Ursula Heise, who deftly analyzes such contradictory temporalities in Pynchon and Robbe-Grillet (113–46, 179–219), explains this practice in terms derived from Borges: "Postmodernist novels thereby project into the narrative present and past an experience of time which normally is only available for the future: time dividing and subdividing, bifurcating and branching off continuously into multiple possibilities and alternatives" (55).[7]

3. ANTINOMIC

There are several narratives that move backward in time (Elizabeth Howard's *The Long View*, C. H. Sisson's *Christopher Homm*, Harold Pinter's *Betrayal*); most can be easily situated within the standard temporal concepts that inform almost all contemporary narrative theory—that is, the order of the *syuzhet* is simply the opposite of the order of the *fabula*. Other, more complexly retroverted narratives however present more recalcitrant conundrums. Ilse Aichinger's "Spiegelgeschichte" (1952) is a doubly linear story that simultaneously moves backward and forward in time, as do later texts like Alejo Carpentier's "Journey Back to the Source" (1963), the final pages of Angela Carter's *The Passion of New Eve* (1977), and Martin Amis's *Time's Arrow* (1984).[8] Aichinger's protagonist, that is, goes from her burial backward in time to her birth, all the while acting as if she is instead moving forward in time, looking ahead to that which has already occurred, as it were.

Thus, we get statements like: "Drei Tage später wagt er nicht mehr, den Arm um deine Schultern zu legen. Wieder drei Tage später fragt er dich, wie du heisst, und du fragst ihn. Nun wisst ihr voneinander nicht einmal mehr die Namen. . . . Ein Tag wird kommen, da siehst du ihn zum erstenmal. Und er sieht dich. Zum erstenmal, das heisst: Nie wieder" (71). ("Three days later he no longer dares to put his arm round your shoulder. And three days after that he asks you what your name is, and you ask him his. And now neither of you knows the other's name. . . . A day will come when you will see him for the first time. And he you. For the first time means: never again" [74–75]). The first meeting, from one temporal perspective, is also the last one from the other perspective.

With this kind of story, one can certainly have anachronies, though it's not clear whether—and why—they should be called prolepses or analepses. In a mimetic text, the narrator tells the story retrospectively (i.e., in the past tense), as the audience's reception of the story is prospective; the interested reader wants to learn what has already happened. In antinomic narration, both narrator and reader are moving prospectively (present tense, even future tense), though time's arrow is reversed.

Aichinger's story also includes jocular, tongue-in-cheek comments about this unusual temporal situation that emblematize its opposed chronological trajectories: "Vom Hafen heulen die Schiffe. Zur Abfahrt oder zur Ankunft? Wer soll das wissen?" (66) ("Over in the harbour the ships are hooting. Does it mean arrival or departure? Who can know that?" [68–69]).[9] This joke is one that conventional narratology is incapable of explaining, since it does not imagine that the time of the story, in a work of fiction, might move in two directions simultaneously.[10]

4. DIFFERENTIAL

A curious temporality can be found in Woolf's *Orlando,* in which the eponymous character ages at a different rate than the people that surround him (her), as one chronology is superimposed on another, larger one. Thus, twenty years pass for Orlando at the same time that three and a half centuries pass for those around her (him). This situation drives the narrator to some playful descriptions in which metaphorical statements about time take on a literal meaning when applied to *Orlando:* "It would be no exaggeration to say that he would go out after breakfast a man of thirty and come home to dinner a man of fifty-five at least. Some weeks added a century to his age, others no more than three seconds at most" (70). This strategy is repeated (perhaps in homage to Woolf) by Caryl Churchill in her play *Cloud Nine,* which has the characters age twenty years as the society they inhabit gains a century. Borges's "The Secret Miracle" also employs a similar construction, as time slows down for a man awaiting execution so that he is able to finish composing a play even as the bullets from the firing squad move imperceptibly toward him; he experiences a year while his killers perceive an instant. The opposite happens to the protagonist of Rushdie's *The Moor's Last Sigh,* as the protagonist ages faster than the people around him. A still more elaborate deployment of such disparate yet synchronized embedded chronologies can be found in Calderón's classic, *The Great Theater of the World,* where both the history of creation and the time span of a human life are collapsed into the actual duration of the play's performance. It should be noted that Bakhtin's account of the chronotope of the medieval dream vision, which "synchronize[s] diachrony" to produce a time in which all events coalesce into "pure simultaneous existence" (157), is entirely consonant with the differential temporalities of Calderón and intriguingly anticipates more recent postmodern practices.[11]

5. CONFLATED

A distinctively contemporary construction is that in which apparently different temporal zones fail to remain distinct, and slide or spill into one another.

As the story segments run into each other, so do their respective temporalities. We find this in Pinget's *Passacaille,* in some of later novels of Claude Simon, and in Juan Goytisolo's *Landscape After the Battle.* Accounts of one set of events fold into a different set of events, presumably occurring at another time, without any framing device to clarify the relations between the disparate groups of events. In Simon's *Les Corps conducteurs,* we find a retarded, minimal, and resolutely antiteleological temporality; the narrative moves from setting to setting, and invariably the "separate" times and spaces begin to melt or bleed into each other, as the distinctions between each cluster of events begin to collapse, and "now" and "then" no longer signify clearly disparate times. A Genettean analysis of story or frequency will rapidly lead to a series of contradictions and impasses, since there is no principle of identity at work that would establish what is and what is not the "same" event.

There are also interesting variants of·this practice, such as the contamination of the basic eighteenth-century setting of Carpentier's *Concierto Barroco* by a brief and unexplained interlude in the twentieth century, Ishmael Reed's superimposition of modern technology and time consciousness onto the 1860s narrative in *Flight to Canada,* or the impossibly scrambled historical references in Guy Davenport's "The Haile Selassie Funeral Train." Another blatant use of this technique appears in Milan Kundera's *Slowness,* as the protagonist of the main, contemporary narrative is brought face to face with the hero of the eighteenth-century novel that has partially inspired the later fiction—and both characters are then encountered by narrator/fabricator himself.

6. DUAL OR MULTIPLE

We are now perhaps in a position to finally situate that problem child of Shakespeare criticism: the notorious "double time" of many of his mature plays, in which different plotlines, though beginning and ending at the same moment, nevertheless take different numbers of days to unfold. In *A Midsummer Night's Dream* (a play replete with sly allusions to skewed chronology), four days and three nights pass for the duke and his entourage in the city while—at the same time—only two days and a single night pass for the lovers in the enchanted forest.[12] As the character Time himself explains between the acts of *The Winter's Tale,* "it is in my pow'r/ to o'erthrow law, and in one self-born hour/ To plant and o'erwhelm custom" (IV. i. 7–9). *The Fairie Queen,* as Rawdon Wilson has shown, also embodies similar temporal contradictions.[13] Such a situation is present as well (and explicitly remarked on) in Byron's *Cain:* after Lucifer returns Cain to Eden, Adah expresses her thanks that he has come back so soon, after only "two *long* hours" (III. i. 54) according to the movement of the sun. Cain, understandably confused, responds:

> And yet I have approached that sun, and seen
> Worlds which he once shone on, and never more
> Shall light; and worlds he never lit: methought
> Years had rolled o'er my absence. (III.i.56–59)

The temporally enchanted forests of Shakespeare and Spenser almost certainly inspired "the time-shifting sorcery" of the jungle in the Sundarbans chapter of Rushdie's *Midnight's Children*.

In addition to the types of currently untheorized temporal construction identified above, there are adjacent areas that need to be explored in greater depth. The most prominent, and the one that is now beginning to receive critical attention, is a contestation of the opposition between story time and discourse time. Such a distinction presupposes that it is possible to retrieve or deduce a consistent story (*fabula*) from a text (*syuzhet*); in many recent works, this simply is not the case.[14] Beckett's *Molloy*, to take a familiar example, can be said to have no recoverable story, and therefore no story time. Near the end of his narrative, Molloy wonders about an event he has just recounted: "Yes, it seems to me some such incident occurred about this time. . . . But perhaps I am merging two times in one, and two women, one coming towards me, shyly, urged on by the cries and laughter of her companions, and the other going away from me, unhesitatingly" (75). This question can never be definitively answered, either by Molloy or by a narratologist, since in this self-negating novel every putative event is suspect or called into question, and may never have occurred at all.[15]

In other works Beckett offers more strident and uncompromising challenges to the notion of a preexistent, recoverable story that is independent of the discourse, as his narrators "denarrate" or deny and cancel the events they had earlier affirmed to be the case (*The Unnamable*, "Cascando," *Fizzles, Ill Seen, Ill Said*).[16] This pattern continues until we come to *Worstward Ho*, where descriptions are negated right after they are uttered: "First the body. No. First the place. No. First both. Now either. Now the other. Sick of the either try the other. Sick of it back sick of the either. So on. Somehow on. Till sick of both. Throw up and go. Where neither. Till sick of there. Throw up and back. The body again. Where none. . . . Say it stands. Had to up in the end and stand. Say bones. No bones but say bones" (7–8). In these contexts, it doesn't make sense to talk about a story (and, by implication, an originary chronological sequence) that can be deduced or extracted from the discourse. In such texts, the discourse serves to erase the story.[17] The representational model of a writer transcribing a preexistent story is here dissolved and supplanted by one that stresses the act of invention and the free play of an author who invents what he claims to recount; or to put it another way, mimesis is here replaced by poiesis.

Salman Rushdie offers a potentially more radical erasure. *Midnight's Children,* in which Shandean narrative arabesques are fused with the history of modern India, contains a temporal contradiction which the narrator himself points out: "Rereading my work, I have discovered an error in chronology. The assassination of Mahatma Gandhi occurs, in these pages, on the wrong date. But I cannot say, now, what the actual sequence of events might have been; in my India, Gandhi will continue to die at the wrong time" (198). This work's *histoire* negates the historical timetable that otherwise structures much of the text; it becomes inseparable from the discourse that expresses it. This strategy is a typically postmodern reconstitution of history that simultaneously underwrites a distinct postcolonial political allegory—Gandhi's death will always be untimely for those on the subcontinent, as recent events continue to demonstrate.

Up to this point I have been discussing texts that construct impossible stories and thereby challenge the mimetically grounded distinctions of *fabula* and *syuzhet* and Genette's category of order. Contemporary literature also provides us with a number of texts the narration or presentation of which is either unusual or impossible. One deliberately contradictory postmodern practice is that of first person "simultaneous" or present tense narration, recently analyzed by Dorrit Cohn (96–108), in which events are narrated by the protagonist at the time they are occurring, thus producing impossible sentences such as "Face down . . . I try to compose myself for a day of hiding. I doze and I wake, drifting from one formless dream to another" from J. M. Coetzee's *Waiting for the Barbarians* (101). The events themselves may be reported in a simple chronological order, but they are completely "de-naturalized" or removed from possible real world, natural discourse, by being narrated in what Cohn has felicitously termed "the fictional present" (106). As Cohn points out, this "form remains narratologically in limbo: neglected (if not denied) in theory, mis- or unidentified in practice, its anomaly falls between the cracks of established discursive norms" (101).

Genette's notion of duration—that is, the relation between the amount of time it takes for an event to occur and the time it takes for that event to be recounted—has not been developed as fully as it might be. Genette himself is a little apologetic about the necessary imprecision of its measurement (since reading speed varies greatly between individuals), and resorts instead to the expedient of the number of pages devoted to an incident, though of course different editions vary considerably in the number of pages they allot the same text. Greater exactitude need not be despaired of, however: a word count will be much more accurate for fiction, while the duration of the production of a play can be quite precisely determined, and the time of a film or video measured to a fraction of a second.

Fictional play with duration has been around at least since Henry Fielding vowed he would not merely be the anameunsis of time: "if whole years should pass without producing anything worthy his notice, we shall not be afraid to add a chasm in our history, but shall hasten on to matters of consequence" (*Tom Jones,* bk. 2, chap. 1). The concept of duration is quite useful in describing certain postmodern practices, such as the equivalence Rushdie sets up between of an hour of the time represented and a second for its presentation, as he recreates the hours leading up to India's independence (and the birth of Saleem Sinai) in a manner generally associated with the launching of a rocket or the onset of New Year's Day: "But now the countdown will not be denied . . . eighteen hours; seventeen; sixteen . . . and already, at Dr. Narlikar's Nursing Home, it is possible to hear the shrieks of a woman in labour" (Rushdie's ellipses); after a vertiginous pause of a full paragraph, the countdown resumes ("fourteen hours to go, thirteen, twelve") before it's paused once more (129). Foregrounding duration in this manner points to the artificiality of the book's temporal construction even as it paradoxically enhances its dramatic effect.

Such extreme play with duration has numerous antecedents, including Heinrich Mann's "Three Minute Novel," in which an entire life is recounted in some 500 words, as well as in passages such as the following from Queneau's *Le Chiendent,* which shows the arbitrary nature of conventional novelistic observations once the time frame is expanded beyond its ordinary parameters: "At about 3 o'clock, the [man in] silhouette blew its nose; at about 4, it spat; at about 5, it bowed; at about 5:50 it was already hearing the squeak of the little gate of its headless house. At 6, the other man was there, on the dot, at his cafe table" (10).

In drama, one may find many works in which the represented time of the story is contradicted by the method of its presentation. To take one of the best known instances, the final hour of Faustus's life is presented on stage in a continuous soliloquy of fifty-eight lines, unpunctuated by any indication of temporal ellipsis, as the time of the story is radically shrunken. Shakespeare plays with this kind of construction as well, collapsing three hours of story time into a continuous twenty minutes of performance in the last scene of *A Midsummer Night's Dream,* or compressing the unnatural night during which Duncan is slain in *Macbeth.*[18] Similarly, in *Hamlet,* the appearance of the ghost "that usurp'st this time of night" (1.1.46) twice impels the clock to hurtle from midnight to dawn in temporally uninterrupted periods lasting only a few minutes each (I.1; I.4–5). Hamlet is more prescient than he imagines when he complains that "The time is out of joint" (1.5.188).

Interestingly, this kind of temporal contraction was theorized about by Pierre Corneille (who himself, through the device of the magic mirror in his *L'Illusion comique,* found a way to dramatize many years and still preserve the neoclassical "unity of time"). Breaking from appeals to verisimilitude that informed his positions in his essay on the unities, he states: "the fifth act, by special privilege, has the right to accelerate time so that the part of the action which it presents may use up more time than is necesary for performance" (224). The reason given for this rupture is the convenience of the audience, impatient to see the end of the play. Corneille explains he deliberately made use of this "privilege" at the admittedly cluttered ending of *Le Cid,* and also pointed to a classical precedent for this temporal telescoping in the final act of Terence's *Andria.*

Comparable instances in fiction can also be found, such as des Grieux's oral recounting of the central events of Prevost's *Manon Lescaut.* Shklovsky has pointed out that such a narration would have lasted at least sixteen hours— far longer than the text explicitly indicates (37). The precise time that many of the dialogues actually take to unfold in Andrey Biely's temporally skewed novel, *St. Petersburg,* is often blurred and largely indeterminable, while in Woolf's novel, Mrs. Dalloway's return to her house after shopping is improbably, perhaps impossibly rapid.[19] Still more obviously transgressive is the preternaturally fast death of Lolita's mother, who is said to have been killed by a car in the street while Humbert was mixing her a drink in their house (chap. 22). The "Circe" chapter of *Ulysses* abruptly collapses, expands, and distorts temporal duration; at one point, a fantasy sequence extending over eighteen pages is situated between two seemingly consecutive lines of dialogue (390–407). Finally, we may note an avowedly contradictory duration quite similar to that in *Dr. Faustus* appears in Paul Auster's *City of Glass,* as the delivery of an eight-page speech takes up an entire day—much to the surprise of the confused auditor of the monologue. Together, these examples should demonstrate the usefulness of the concept of duration, as well as suggest that it can be measured more accurately, manipulated more playfully, and controverted more brashly than is generally recognized by theorists of narrative temporality.

The text types identified above, though covering the most prominent varieties of nonmimetic temporality in narrative, nevertheless do not exhaust the entire range of experimental fiction. Some particularly interesting pieces deserve to be set forth; we may begin with those that, though undeniably innovative, can probably be contained within the Genettean model. These include narratives in which time is virtually immobilized, such as Calvino's "t zero," which freezes temporal progression to speculate discursively on the nature of time— though its duration is arguably infinite, since all of its pages are devoted to a single moment in time that does not move forward. Beckett's almost literally time-less "Ping," which has (perhaps) no real events, potentially challenges the concept of narrative itself, inviting us to speculate on whether a minimal narrative can exist without temporality. Similarly, we should note the achievement of Christine Brooke-Rose's *Amalgamemnon,* which largely consists of statements made about the future—a future that is not clearly sequenced, nor always certain to occur as predicted—though this text too can probably be contained within Genette's model.

Still other works however ask potentially harder questions. What are we to do with Gertrude Stein's cubist narratives that fragment and displace time, or Jean Ricardou's *La Prise de Constantinople,* which was designed to be read either front to back or back to front, or with unbound manuscripts like Marc Saporta's *Composition No. 1,* the chapters of which readers must physically place into a sequence?[20] And in "La Chambre secrete," Robbe-Grillet may have created a story that has no temporality: there are instead a series of slightly different descriptions of what may be the same melodramatic scene to which a reader may or may not supply temporal connections. The scenes also resemble possible descriptions of a series of paintings, all variations of a single original. These images challenge or defy the reader to make them into a narrative by supplying the absent temporality, thereby connecting the images into a single story—an alternative that few readers are able to resist.

Both interpretations however remain problematic, since some of the "pictures" contain minimal movement, while any story we fabricate around them will contain an impossible chronology. One solution to this interpretive puzzle is to start with a resolutely antimimetic approach and admit that the text is internally contradictory, while noting at the same time that many of the descriptions (the stairs, the cape, the smoke, etc.) portray a spiral shape—including the temporal "spiral" the reader may be expected to project onto the sequence of vignettes. Robbe-Grillet would thus be using a geometrical shape to pattern events that are impossible in the real world; this is perhaps an apt analogue for his aesthetic practice as well as for many of the more committed antimimetic authors.

Genette of course is aware of many of the texts that seem to elude his system. He admits that there are some narratives that will not allow a consistent story and its attendant temporality to be inferred: "Obviously, this reconstitution is not always possible, and it becomes useless for certain extreme cases like the novels of Robbe-Grillet, where temporal reference is deliberately sabotaged" (35). But such extreme cases continue to proliferate, and from certain vantage points may even suggest a new norm. As Elizabeth Deeds Ermarth has stated, "[w]hile all narrative is temporal by definition because its medium is temporal, postmodern sequences make accessible new temporal capacities that subvert the privilege of historical time and bind temporality in language" (11). It must be acknowledged that this new practice can only be understood by reference to the mimetic aesthetic it flouts; nevertheless, its rejection of conventional mimesis is occasionally depicted as an effective method to represent the contemporary world in all its contradictions. At this juncture in both the development of narrative theory and the history of literature, there is no justification for ignoring the non- and antimimetic fiction that surrounds us.

Alternative theoretical formulations that insist on temporal features unique to fiction have been advanced from time to time (especially in the last few years) and deserve to be better known. In the first decades of the twentieth century Viktor Shklovsky asserted that "'Literary time' is clearly arbitrary: its laws do not coincide with the laws of ordinary time" (36). Bakhtin, in his analyses of the chronotopes of the history of fiction, sets forth a number of concepts that still have not been fully incorporated into the theory of narrative temporality. This is particularly true of his discussion of the Rabelaisian chronotope, the distinctive method of which consists "in the general destruction of all ordinary ties, of all the *habitual matrices* of things and ideas, and the creation of unexpected matrices, unexpected connections" (169), a practice that of course continues today in the more playfully disruptive and contradictory chronological formations typical of postmodernism. Since Bakhtin, little significant theoretical work on nonmimetic temporalities was done until quite recently in the studies cited above, particularly those of Yacobi, Ronen, and Heise.[21]

These are important developments that can lead not only to a more comprehensive model of narrative temporality, but also perhaps to a better understanding of the nature of narrative itself. Instead of ignoring the anomalous or "impossible" chronological features or, what is practically speaking little better, indiscriminately lumping all such works together under a single general category, we would do well to identify several of the most significant varieties of antimimetic narrative temporality. We may use the term "metatemporal" to cover both unusual and impossible temporalities. A subdivision of this grouping we may, following Genette, call "achronic" narratives, which designate works that contain numerous events which "we must ultimately take to be dateless and ageless" (Genette, 84); we will add, however, that this category should be greatly expanded and further delineated to include the various unknowable, self-negating, or inherently indeterminate story times present in numerous recent texts.[22] Those other works that resist or defy Genettean orders can also be given a general name consistent with the existing nomenclature, that of "antichronies."

This latter group may include David Herman's recent notion of polychrony, "a kind of narration that exploits indefiniteness to pluralize and delinearize itself" (75), as well as types derived from the examples already adduced, namely the circular, the contradictory, the antinomic, the differential, the conflated, and the dual or multiple. We might also want to reserve some additional theoretical space for still other significant types of temporal construction—I'm sure there must exist some compelling varieties that still elude the framework outlined here—as well as for innovative works that will be written in the future. Finally, at the largest level of generalization, we may want to add some rough edges or admit deliberately blurred boundaries at the limits of this surprisingly flexible and protean category of narrative analysis by considering additional notions like the quasi-temporal or even pseudo-temporal to describe the kinds of works that simultaneously seem to invoke and resist a temporal analysis ("La Chambre secrète" and partially nonrepresentational texts by Stein, e.g., "What Happened").

Despite the large number of narratives whose temporality transcends merely human time, literary theory has for the most part limited itself to a narrowly mimetic framework. To some extent, this is due to some historical accidents and extraliterary interventions. Had Aristotle's lost work on comedy survived, and if it did contain an account of the collapsible chronologies of the dramas of Aristophanes (where those trips to Hades or Cloudcuckooland always happen much too rapidly[23]), perhaps some of the excesses of neoclassicism might have been avoided. Similarly, had the Russian formalists not been suppressed and Bakhtin's work on the chronotope left unpublished for several decades, we might have had a better appreciation of non- and antimimetic temporal construction. Or if modern writers' frequent claims of creating new worlds, rather than merely reproducing the old one, been more sympathetically investigated and theorized, we might now occupy a more capacious critical position.

In any event, there are and always have been two major literary traditions, one mimetic, the other antimimetic; one more concerned with the object of representation, the other with the act of invention. The nonmimetic tradition stretches from Aristophanes and Menippean satire (including Lucian's protopostmodern "A True Story") to Rabelais and the more unusual medieval tales to Ariosto and Shakespeare. Romanticism provides another rich body of relevant texts, as do the large, strange, and still prolific family of narratives claiming descent from *Tristram Shandy*.

Nevertheless, in the history of criticism and theory, mimetic thinking has dominated for centuries. More recently, there has been a widespread desire by structuralists and nonstructuralists alike for theoretical constructs that would cover all narrative, fictional and nonfictional, classic and contemporary, high and low. For decades, a universal narrative theory was considered a plausible aspiration; obvious counterexamples seemed too few, too new, too obscure, too unique, too distant, or too marginal to demand inclusion. But the achievement and persistence of postmodern temporal strategies now means that we can no longer afford to ignore this cache of outrageously antimimetic narrative material. Indeed, it can be considered something of a scandal that narrative theory cannot encompass the works of the most exciting and dynamic creators of narrative of this century. The most urgent task of narrative theory is to construct a poetics of nonmimetic fiction that can finally do full justice to the literature of our time. Paradoxically, by doing so we will be thereby able to recover and disclose the many premodern antecedents of strategies and techniques now identified as the most distinctively "post-."

NOTES

I wish to thank James Phelan, Ross Chambers, and Monika Fludernik for their generous comments on an earlier draft of this essay.

1. For a discussion of the subtle differences between Günther Müller's and Genette's conceptions, see Ricoeur, *Time and Narrative,* vol. 2, 77–88 and 178–82.

2. See, for example, Christian Moraru's insightful analysis of the temporal curiosities of Nabokov's autobiography, *Speak, Memory.*

3. My objections apply equally to accounts of narrative temporality deriving from philosophical hermeneutics. Ricoeur for example postulates a reciprocal relationship between narrativity and the structure of existence (165); 35 in this volume. The narratives I am about to discuss have never existed except on a printed page.

4. Toker prefers to designate Nabokov's temporal structure as an infinite spiral; see her discussion of this point (158–63).

5. Concerning the temporality of novels like *La Jalousie* or *La Maison de rendez-vous,* I must disagree with Ruth Ronen's claim that "chronology does not seem to condition narrative organization or to be relevant at all to the organization of the narrative world" (216). I suggest that it is more useful to affirm instead that the narrative world is ordered by (and indeed may be defined by) a contradictory chronology. Furthermore, its transgressive effects are dependent on the reader's perceiving and reflecting on the implications this chronology has on the fictional world.

6. In addition, Emma Kafalenos has stated that *La Maison de rendez-vous.* "contains multiple (fragmentary) *fabulas,* each of which shares common elements with at least one other fragmentary *fabula*" (396). See also Ursula Heise's theoretical analysis of the contradictory temporality of Robbe-Grillet's *Topologie d'une cité fantôme* (113–46), whose narrator "wanders down hallways and streets that always seem to give access to too many temporal dimensions, too many historical moments at the same time" (147).

7. More localized contradictions can also be found in the temporal loops presented in Tom Stoppard's *Travesties* or the comparable chronological irregularities in Angela Carter's *Nights at the Circus.*

8. Brian McHale identifies other examples of "reversal of process" in Pynchon's *Gravity's Rainbow:* "Slothrop's family history *(GR:203–204),* or of rocket production ('faired skin back to sheet steel back to pigs to white incandescence to ore, to Earth,' *GR:139)*—which seems to presuppose the extension to reality itself of film's capacity to be run backwards"

(1994, 110)—not, that is to say, of a sequence of linear story progressions arranged in an antichronological discursive order.

9. The narrator of Martin Amis's *Time's Arrow* finds himself similarly confused: "Wait a minute. Why am I walking *backward* into the house? Wait. Is it dusk coming, or dawn? What is the—sequence I'm on? What are its rules? Why are the birds singing so strangely? Where am I heading?"(6).

10. An important exception to this statement is Tamar Yacobi, who employs the category of "backward movements" to describe the following powerful antinomic sequence in a poem by Dan Pagis, a few lines of which can suggest the intensity of this work that verbally, subjunctively, "undoes" the Holocaust:

> The scream goes back into the throat.
> The gold teeth to the jaw.
> The fear.
> The smoke to the tin chimneys and further inside
> Back to the hollow of bones.
> And already you will be covered with skin and sinews and you will live,
> You will still be living,
>
> Sitting in the living room, reading the evening paper.
> Here you are! All in time. (112)

11. Another unexpected instance of this strategy can be found in Ben Jonson's masque, "A Vision of Delight," in which seasonal and diurnal temporalities are collapsed into the time of their enactment on stage. Though a notorious stickler for observing neoclassical temporal strictures in drama proper, Jonson utilized a very different poetics when constructing his masques.

12. For a discussion of the play's temporality from the perspective of narrative theory, see my paper, "'Time Is Out of Joint'" (1987, 302–304). That article also analyzes the unusual temporalities of a number of other dramas, many of them mentioned in this essay, and dicusses contradictions between the actual time of performance and the time said to elapse during that period.

13. Thus, characters like Redcrosse both languish for a long time in captivity and are rescued swiftly from that captivity.

14. Other theorists who have recently contested the story/discourse distinction include Ruth Ronen, who uses the example of Robbe-Grillet's *La Maison de rendez-vous* "to demonstrate the impossibility of divorcing the order of events from modes of telling" (216), and Patrick O'Neill (35–57), who has argued against the stability of this conceptual opposition: "Perhaps the most striking thing of all with regard to the world of story, as far as narrative theory is concerned, is that ultimately we *cannot* ever 'say what really happened,' for that world, because of its status as a narrated world, finally both evades and exceeds description" (38). For an excellent discussion of indeterminate *syuzhets* and ambiguous or multiple *fabulas,* see Kafalenos. Culler's earlier discussion of these terms is misleading; see Fludernik for a sound critique (320–21).

15. For a more extended discussion of this practice, see my article on denarration.

16. For a comparable analysis of the problematics of duration in *How It Is,* see Ursula K. Heise (147–75); on the oddities of the temporality of *Waiting for Godot,* see Schechner.

17. For more discussion and additional examples of postmodern fictional "worlds under erasure," see McHale, 1987, 99–111.

18. *Macbeth* is in fact still more innovative temporally. In the *fabula,* night stretches much longer than it should: "By th' clock 'tis day,/ And yet dark night strangles the travel-ling lamp" (II.4.6–7); in the presentation of this scene, an equal and opposite chronological violation has transpired, as the duration of the entire night is radically compressed. For a full discussion of this play's temporality, see my article, "'Hours Dreadful and Things Strange.'"

19. John Sutherland is forced to imagine an unmentioned ride in a cab to account for this anomaly (215–24).

20. Concerning this text, Kafalenos however astutely points out that the order of its presentation is indeterminate: "throughout the process of reading, the reader cannot fail to be aware that control of the *syuzhet* sequence lies, literally, in her hands" (385).

21. Partial exceptions to this statement include A. A. Mendilow's suggestive account of *Orlando* (228–31), and David Leon Higdon's discussion of what he called "polytemporal time" in his book, *Time and English Fiction*, which does draw attention to the "destroying, ignoring or reconstituting clock time" (12) done by authors like Sterne, Lewis Carroll, and Beckett.

22. As David Herman points out, "temporal indefiniteness should not be conflated with timelessness or achrony: not knowing the exact temporal positions of several events occur-ring within a larger narrative sequence does not make those events achronic. Further, both the achronic and the temporally indefinite should be distinguished from the temporally multiple" (75). These are precisely the kinds of distinctions narrative theory now needs to be making.

23. In the *Peace,* Trygaeus's flight on a giant dung beetle to the halls of the gods is so rapid that he metadramatically protests to the zealous prop man who is physically changing the scene.

REFERENCES

Aichinger, Ilse. "Life Story in Retrospect," translated by J. C. Alldridge. In *Ilse Aichinger,* by J. C. Alldridge. Chester Springs, Pa.: Dufour Editions, 1969.

———. *Werke.* Vol 2. *Der Gefesselte. Erzählungen.* Frankfurt am Main: S. Fischer Verlag, 1991.

Amis, Martin. *Time's Arrow.* New York: Harmony, 1991.

Aristotle, *Poetics.* In *Critical Theory Since Plato,* edited by Hazard Adams, 48–66. New York: Harcourt Brace Jovanovich, 1971.

Bakhtin, Mikhail. *The Dialogical Imagination,* translated by Caryl Emerson and Michael Holquist. Austin: University of Texas Press, 1981.

Bal, Mieke. *Narratology: An Introduction to the Theory of Narrative,* translated by Christine van Boheemen. Toronto: University of Toronto Press, 1985.

Beckett, Samuel. *Three Novels by Samuel Beckett:* Molloy, Malone Dies, *and* The Unnam-able. New York: Grove, 1965.

———. *Worstward Ho.* New York: Grove, 1983.

Byron, George Gordon, Lord. *The Poetical Works of Byron.* Boston: Houghton Mifflin, 1975.

Cohn, Dorrit. *The Distinction of Fiction.* Baltimore, Md.: Johns Hopkins University Press, 1999.

Corneille, Pierre. "Of the Three Unities of Action, Time, and Place." In *Critical Theory Since Plato,* edited by Hazard Adams, 219–26. New York: Harcourt, Brace, Jovanovich, 1971.

Culler, Jonathan. "Fabula and Sjuzhet in the Analysis of Narrative: Recent American Discussions." *Poetics Today* 1 (1980): 27–37.

Elam, Diane. "Postmodern Romance." In *Postmodernism Across the Ages,* edited by Bill Readings and Bennet Schaber, 216–31. Syracuse, N.Y.: Syracuse University Press, 1993.

Ermarth, Elizabeth Deeds. *Sequel to History: Postmodernism and the Crisis of Representational Time.* Princeton, N.J.: Princeton University Press, 1992.

Fludernik, Monika. *Towards a 'Natural' Narratology.* London: Routledge, 1996.

Genette, Gérard. *Narrative Discourse: An Essay in Method,* translated by Jane E. Lewin. Ithaca, N.Y.: Cornell University Press, 1980.

Heise, Ursula K. *Chronoschisms: Time, Narrative, and Postmodernism.* Cambridge: Cambridge University Press, 1997.

Herman, David. "Limits of Order: Toward a Theory of Polychronic Narrative." *Narrative* 6 (1998): 72–95.

Higdon, David Leon. *Time and English Fiction.* Totowa, N.J.: Rowman and Littlefield, 1977.

James, Henry. *Theory of Fiction: Henry James,* edited by James E. Miller Jr. Lincoln: University of Nebraska Press, 1972.

Joyce, James. *Ulysses,* edited by Hans Walter Gabler. New York: Random, 1986.

Kafalenos, Emma. "Toward a Typology of Indeterminacy in Postmodern Narrative." *Comparative Literature* 44 (1992): 380–408.

McHale, Brian. *Constructing Postmodernism.* London: Routledge, 1992.

———. *Postmodernist Fiction.* New York: Methuen, 1987.

Mendilow, A. A. *Time and the Novel.* New York: Humanities Press, 1965.

Moraru, Christian. "Time, Writing, and Ecstasy in *Speak, Memory:* Dramatizing the Proustian Project." *Nabokov Studies* 2 (1995): 173–90.

O'Neill, Patrick. *Fictions of Discourse: Reading Narrative Theory.* Toronto: University of Toronto Press, 1994.

Prince, Gerald. "The Disnarrated." *Style* 22 (1988): 1–8.

Richardson, Brian. "Denarration in Fiction: Erasing the Story in Beckett and Others." *Narrative* 9 (2001): 168–75.

———. "'Hours Dreadful and Things Strange': Inversions of Chronology and Causality in *Macbeth*." *Philological Quarterly* 68 (1989): 283–94.

———. "'Time Is Out of Joint': Narrative Models and the Temporality of the Drama." *Poetics Today* 8 (1987): 299–309.

Ricoeur, Paul. "Narrative Time." In *On Narrative,* edited by W. J. T. Mitchell, 165–86. Chicago: University of Chicago Press, 1981.

———. *Time and Narrative.* Vol 2. Translated by Kathleen McLaughlin and David Pellauer. Chicago: University of Chicago Press, 1985.

Rimmon-Kenan, Shlomith. *Narrative Fiction: Contemporary Poetics.* London: Methuen, 1984.

Ronen, Ruth. *Possible Worlds and Narrative Theory.* Cambridge: Cambridge University Press, 1994.

Rushdie, Salman. *Midnight's Children.* New York: Avon, 1982 [1980].

Schechner, Richard. "There's Lot's of Time in *Godot*." In *Aspects of Time,* edited by C. S. Patrides, 217–24. Toronto: University of Toronto Press, 1976.

Shklovsky, Victor. "Sterne's *Tristram Shandy:* Stylistic Commentary." In *Russian Formalist Criticism: Four Essays,* translated and edited by Lee T. Lemon and Marion J. Reis, 25–57. Lincoln: University of Nebraska Press, 1965.

Sutherland, John. "Clarissa's Invisible Taxi." In *Can Jane Eyre Be Happy? More Puzzles in Classic Fiction,* 215–24. Oxford: Oxford University Press, 1997.

Todorov, Tzvetan. *Introduction to Poetics,* translated by Richard Howard. Minneapolis: University of Minnesota Press, 1981.

Toker, Leona. *Nabokov: The Mystery of Literary Structures.* Ithaca, N.Y.: Cornell University Press, 1989.

Wilson, R. Rawdon. "Time." In *The Spenser Encyclopedia,* edited by A. C. Hamilton. Toronto: University of Toronto Press, 1990.

Woolf, Virginia. *Orlando.* Hammondsworth, England: Penguin, 1942.

Yacobi, Tamar. "Time Denatured into Meaning: New Worlds and Renewed Themes in the Poetry of Dan Pagis." *Style* 22 (1988): 93–115.

■ PART II

PLOT

Introduction: Plot and Emplotment

From the outset, plot has been a central concern of literary theory and practice. Even before the earliest extant treatise on rhetoric or aesthetic theory, Aristophanes mocks a number of rather lame plot devices used by Euripides in the course of his comedy, the *Thesmophoriazusae.* For Aristotle plot (*mythos*) is the first principle and the "soul" of tragedy; it needs to be complete and of a certain magnitude, and its beginning and end must not be arbitrary. A plot should have an organic unity and be free from irrelevant incidents; the events that compose it should be connected in a probable or necessary progression, rather than simply conjoined in an episodic sequence. Aristotle prefers a single plot for tragedy, rather than a double thread that provides different outcomes for the good and the bad.

Bharata, the theorist of classical Sanskrit drama whose *Natyashastra* is in many ways analogous to Aristotle's *Poetics,* refers to plot as the "body" of drama and differentiates between the principal and subsidiary storylines. He identifies five means of developing the plot: the "seed" (*bija*) of plot, which is scattered and will expand; the "vital drop" (*bindu*) which restores continuity after narrative interruptions; the episode (*pataka*) which, though not centered on the hero, ultimately aids him in attaining his goal; the more oblique incident (*prakari*) which may contribute to the central action but is not itself continued; and the "goal" (*karya*) which describes the efforts made by the characters to achieve their ends.

In the Renaissance, the reinstitution of classical poetics meant that plot would remain a major focal point of criticism and theory. Aristotle's preferences and Horace's advice to begin in the middle of the action soon led to a valorization of "poetic" order over the unduly simple "natural" chronology. A theoretical problem that rapidly emerged was how to mesh the Aristotelian dictum that plot be a unified whole with the obvious success of works with multiple plot lines whose strands were largely autonomous or that rarely intersected (significant examples of this practice include Ariosto's *Orlando Furioso,* Middleton and Rowley's *The Changeling,* and Shakespeare's *King Lear*). Interestingly, many of the more theoretically minded playwrights were unable to adequately articulate their own practice. Ben Jonson, whose immense dramatic talent, according to T. S. Eliot, was not so much a skill in plot as a skill in doing without a plot, tended to echo neoclassical strictures in his critical writings. On the multiple plot he is rather more innovative, affirming that a work composed of many diverse parts can still achieve a desired unity if "those parts grow, or are wrought together,"[1] and laid the groundwork for the defense of the subplot.

John Dryden, referring to it as the "underplot," cited Jonson on this subject, praised his practice in the theater, and extended his conceptualizations: "'Tis evident that the more the persons are, the greater will be the variety of the plot. If then the parts are managed so regularly, that the beauty of the whole be kept entire, and that variety become not a perplexed and confusing mass of accidents, you will find it infinitely pleasing to be led in a labyrinth of design, where you see some of your way before you, yet discern not the end till you arrive at it."[2] As the observance of neoclassical strictures on time and place began to weaken toward the end of the eighteenth century, critical emphasis on the "unity of action" remained in place; at times, as in the case of Samuel Johnson, Schlegel, or Samuel Taylor Coleridge, the dismissal of the demand for single, continuous settings was accompanied by a corollary insistence on a unified or organic plot.

As the nineteenth century progressed, new theoretical foci emerged. In 1863, Gustav Freytag propounded a thesis that would become quite well known, suggesting that the most effective drama followed a basic pyramidal structure consisting of the introduction, the rising action, the climax, and the catastrophe. Henry James helped transform the discourse of criticism by various pronouncements in his letters, essays, and prefaces where he explained the reasons behind a number of compositional choices he had made. Many of his discussions are still widely cited and some of the critical concepts used to describe the achievements of the modernists derive from his analyses. Most of us are familiar with his position on the dynamism of plot and its imbrication with character: "What is character but the determination of incident? What is incident but the illustration of character?"[3] Many will also recall his castigation of Tolstoy and Thackeray for their sloppy composition in the production of "loose, baggy monsters" like *War and Peace* and *The Newcomes.*

In 1927 E. M. Forster memorably differentiated story from plot; story was presented as a continuing, additive collection of episodes in a temporal sequence (e.g., "The king died and then the queen died"), while plot was described as a more complex, causally conjoined arrangements of events ("The king died, and then the queen died of grief"). The key difference is that a story simply consists of one event after another, designed to answer the question, "and then?" while plot with its emphasis on causality seeks to explain the "why?" Later, Seymour Chatman would effectively critique this distinction, noting that unless otherwise instructed, readers will tend to assume a causal link between the two deaths, and that at a deeper structural level the causal element is present in both.[4]

The mature work of Georg Lukács constitutes one of the apogees of Marxist aesthetics and of realist literary theory. In numerous works he argued for the representation of the typical in the totality of its social and historical relations, as found preeminently in Balzac and Tolstoy. Balzac, by depicting some catastrophe tensely concentrated in time and space (or a chain of such catastrophes) and recycling characters throughout his opus, thereby escapes the flabby shapelessness of modern bourgeois life reproduced in the subjective and fragmented plots of the major modernists.

Building on and extending the accounts of theme and motif set forth by Boris Tomashevsky elsewhere in this volume, Vladimir Propp applied this analysis to the Russian folktale and sought to derive a few basic, underlying formal structures that lay behind the welter of examples and variants that could be amassed. Propp believed these basic action patterns or "functions" are stable and constant, their sequence is fixed, and their number is limited: he identified thirty-one basic functions that may appear in any given folktale, and together form a system. The functions may vary individually, but the effect they achieve is constant: thus, in the two depictions, "The king sends Ivan after some marvel; he departs"; and "The sister sends her brother for medicine; he departs" every element is different, but the function—the dispatch and departure on a quest—remains the same. This underlying structure, like a grammar governing the infinite patterns of human speech, was what Propp attempted to uncover. In the essay included here, Propp outlines a wide range of possible types of transformation, noting historical and cultural factors as they prove relevant, and attempts to establish criteria for effectively differentiating between earlier and derivative forms.

For R. S. Crane, plot is indeed the most fundamental aspect of narrative, though it is insufficiently recognized as such. Crane offers an expansive conception of plot: "the particular temporal synthesis effected by the writer of the elements of action, character, and thought that constitute the matter of his invention."[5] It then follows, Crane continues, that plots will differ according to which of these elements is utilized as the synthesizing principle. "There are, thus, plots of action, plots of character, and plots of thought."[6] Crane goes on to develop the implications of this broad notion of plot, showing how thought and character (as well as an implicit ethical framework) interanimate each other and the structure of the action itself. The general approach employed by Crane was taken up, extended, and further developed by many others, including Sheldon Sacks and James Phelan.

Northrop Frye differentiated four basic types of general plot: the romantic, the tragic, the comic, and the ironic; each type favors a particular narrative movement, is prominent in different periods, and leads to the next form: the romantic is typically built around an adventure or quest involving legendary figures in a heroic age; this later yields to the individualized struggle of the fully human protagonist of tragedy, and so forth. Each such plot also produces a readjusted society; in tragedy, the offending protagonist is killed or banished, while the essential comic resolution is an individual release which is also a social reconciliation. This new social integration was for Frye a kind of moral norm and the pattern of a free society. Recently, Allen Tilley has attempted to extend and reanimate this approach in his book, *Plot Snakes.*

In the sixties and seventies, Propp's project was revived and extended by a number of prominent structuralists (Claude Bremond, A. J. Greimas, Tzevetan Todorov, Roland Barthes in his structuralist phase, and Gerald Prince) who attempted to outline the fundamental grammar of all narratives; Thomas Pavel, in *The Poetics of Plot,* employed a MOVE grammar to describe the patterns of events of several Renaissance dramas, including *King Lear.* In general, this approach failed to engage the interest of most mainstream critics, and, despite Pavel's efforts, it was not generally deemed successful at depicting in depth the plots of more subtle and complex texts. As Barthes later came to recognize, the drive to discover minimal units of narrative syntax tended to reduce discourse, to miniaturize it as an example of grammar, and thus to lose its distinctive difference. Recent work in artificial intelligence and cognitive science,[7] however, has revived interest in text grammars and promises to reanimate this approach and the debates that surround it; other accounts, such as those of Emma Kafalenos, apply the earlier model to unusual texts like those of Kafka.

Other relevant areas that have received analysis were the double plot by William Empson, multiple plots in Elizabethan drama by Richard Levin, and the dynamics of the Victorian multiplot novel by Peter Garrett. Robert Caserio, in *Plot, Story, and the Novel,* traced out the transformations in the use and construction of plot by prominent novelists of the nineteenth and twentieth centuries, chronicling the withering away of the conventional plot. Most recently, Michal Peled Ginsburg has investigated economies of transformation in the nineteenth-century novel and produced a theoretically informed and historically grounded analysis of plot and related forms that still does justice to the specificity of each work.

Peter Brooks, in *Reading for the Plot,* expresses his dissatisfaction with static structuralist models, arguing instead that plot is rather "the dynamic shaping force of the narrative discourse."[8] Plot starts from the moment at which story is "stimulated into a state of narratability, into a tension, a kind of irritation, which demands narration."[9] For Brooks, plot follows the pattern of sexuality described by Freud and present as well in the basic trajectory of life itself: "plot itself stands as a kind of divergence or deviance, a postponement in the discharge which leads back to the inanimate."[10] Brooks's rather loose notion of desire has been critically dissected by Jay Clayton, who also scrutinizes this concept in the narrative theories of René Girard, Teresa de Lauretis, Leo Bersani, and others.

Major feminist interventions appeared in the 1980s. Nancy K. Miller's article, "Emphasis Added: Plots and Plausibilities in Women's Fiction," shows how notable novels written by women often fail to conform to expected causal progressions, but often take abrupt turns, especially at the narrative's end, to elude the conventional social plot: "the peculiar shape of a heroine's destiny in novels by women, the implausible twists of plot so common in these novels, is a form of insistence about the relation of women to writing."[11] Teresa de Lauretis, in her impressive work on narrative and desire, follows out a number suggestive couplings: narrative and desire, narrative and the oedipal pattern, narrative and male dominance, and narrative and sadism. Her analysis of the way narrative theory has been constructed by Propp, Yuri Lotman, and Robert Scholes reveals that the discourse of theory, like the works it seeks to encompass, constructs the hero as the subject, as human and as male; he is the active principle of culture. By contrast, the female is cast as that which is not susceptible to transformation, "she (it) is an element of plot-space, a resistance, matrix and matter."[12] Her admonition finally is not to abandon narrative, but rather to enact the contradiction of female desire, and of women as social subjects, in the terms of narrative. Other important critical works in this tradition include Joanne Frye's complementary critique of the conventions of the traditional marriage plot, Molly Hite's telling of "the other side of the story," and Susan Winnett's witty exposure of the phallocentric nature of many current narratological perspectives on plot development and closure.

Looking back over this richly heterogenous terrain, a few salient narrative strands may be discerned. One is the desire for an analytical account of the basic types of story and story transformation, often based on the model of linguistics; this is a line that stretches from the more scientifically inclined of the Russian formalists through the golden age of structuralism and that continues today with the aid of concepts from cognitive science. Another strand, always distinct though always present, is the desire for a more dynamic concept of plot that shows how plot forms and shapes story material toward a particular end that one finds in James, Forster, Propp, Crane, Ricoeur, and Brooks. Historically grounded and ideologically inflected accounts appear in many of these theorists; these are necessarily in opposition to more ahistorical accounts of those that attempt to transcend the moment of their formulation. Some of the richest accounts belong to those who, like Bakhtin or Nancy Miller, scrupulously attempt to do justice to both aspects of the theory and analysis of plot. Another overlapping theoretical framework is systematic psychology, whether Freudian, Jungian, Irigarayan, or cognitivist, as the plots projected onto fictional characters are readily seen to be narrativized projections of our private fears and desires.

If we have not moved beyond many of the basic issues framed by Aristotle, we do at least have more complex and resonant versions of stances he advocated or opposed. If we are no closer to definitive answers, we can nevertheless affirm that the same questions are now asked with greater sophistication and nuance than ever before. At the same time, it is increasingly apparent that many postmodern and experimental texts cannot be comfortably situated within any single notion of plot now available. The most pressing current concern for the theory of plot may well be the incorporation of a much broader spectrum of narrative practices, particularly the numerous nonlinear, untraditional, or nonteleological sequences one finds in late modernist, postmodern, and *nouveau roman*-style text generation. Few of the existing approaches can fully explain the actual narrative progression of *To the Lighthouse* or *The Waves,* to say nothing of a text by Gertrude Stein or Robbe-Grillet. One would welcome fresh attempts at theorizing the wide range of antimimetic sequences that run counter to traditional modes of ordering events.

NOTES

1. Ben Jonson, "Timber, or Discoveries," in *Ben Jonson's Literary Criticism,* ed. James D. Redwine Jr. (Lincoln: University of Nebraska Press, 1970), 39.

2. John Dryden, "An Essay of Dramatic Poesy," in *Critical Theory Since Plato,* ed. Hazard Adams (New York: Harcourt Brace Jovanovich, 1971), 245.

3. In *Theory of Fiction: Henry James,* ed. James E. Miller Jr. (Lincoln: University of Nebraska Press, 1972), 37.

4. Seymour Chatman, *Story and Discourse: Narrative Structure in Fiction and Film* (Ithaca, N.Y.: Cornell University Press, 1978), 45–46.

5. R. S. Crane, ed., "The Concept of Plot and the Plot of Tom Jones," in *Critics and Criticism: Ancient and Modern,* abridged ed. (Chicago: University of Chicago Press, 1957), 620; p. 97 in this volume.

6. Ibid.

7. E.g., Marie-Laure Ryan, *Possible Worlds, Artificial Intelligence, and Narrative Theory* (Bloomington: Indiana University Press, 1991), and David Herman, "Scripts, Sequences, and Stories: Elements of a Postclassical Narratology," *PMLA* 112 (1997): 1046–59.

8. Peter Brooks, *Reading for the Plot: Design and Intention in Narrative* (New York: Random House, 1984), 13; p. 131 in this volume.

9. Ibid., 103.

10. Ibid.

11. Nancy K. Miller, "Emphasis Added: Plots and Plausibilities in Women's Fiction," *PMLA* 96 (1981): 44; p. 122 in this volume.

12. Teresa de Lauretis, "Desire in Narrative," in *Alice Doesn't: Feminism, Semiotics, Cinema* (Bloomington: Indiana University Press, 1982), 119.

5

Story and Plot

E. M. FORSTER

Let us define a plot. We have defined a story as a narrative of events arranged in their time-sequence. A plot is also a narrative of events, the emphasis falling on causality. "The king died and then the queen died" is a story. "The king died, and then the queen died of grief" is a plot. The time-sequence is pre-served, but the sense of causality overshadows it. Or again: "The queen died, no one knew why, until it was discovered that it was through grief at the death of the king." This is a plot with a mystery in it, a form capable of high devel-opment. It suspends the time-sequence, it moves as far away from the story as its limitations will allow. Consider the death of the queen. If it is in a story we say "and then?" If it is in a plot we ask "why?" That is the fundamental dif-ference between these two aspects of the novel. A plot cannot be told to a gap-ing audience of cavemen or to a tyrannical sultan or to their modern descendant the movie-public. They can only be kept awake by "and then— and then—" They can only supply curiosity. But a plot demands intelligence and memory also.

Curiosity is one of the lowest of the human faculties. You will have noticed in daily life that when people are inquisitive they nearly always have bad memories and are usually stupid at bottom. The man who begins by ask-ing you how many brothers and sisters you have is never a sympathetic char-acter and if you meet him in a year's time he will probably ask you how many brothers and sisters you have, his mouth again sagging open, his eyes still bulging from his head. It is difficult to be friends with such a man, and for two inquisitive people to be friends must be impossible. Curiosity by itself takes us a very little way, nor does it take us far into the novel—only as far as the story. If we would grasp the plot we must add intelligence and memory.

71

Intelligence first. The intelligent novel-reader, unlike the inquisitive one who just runs his eye over a new fact, mentally picks it up. He sees it from two points of view: isolated, and related to the other facts that he has read on previous pages. Probably he does not understand it, but he does not expect to do so yet awhile. The facts in a highly organized novel (like *The Egoist*) are often of the nature of cross-correspondences and the ideal spectator cannot expect to view them properly until he is sitting up on a hill at the end. This element of surprise or mystery—the detective element as it is sometimes rather emptily called—is of great importance in a plot. It occurs through a suspension of the time-sequence; a mystery is a pocket in time, and it occurs crudely, as in "Why did the queen die?" and more subtly in half-explained gestures and words, the true meaning of which only dawns pages ahead. Mystery is essential to a plot, and cannot be appreciated without intelligence. To the curious it is just another "and then—" To appreciate a mystery, part of the mind must be left behind, brooding, while the other part goes marching on.

That brings us to our second qualification: memory. Memory and intelligence are closely connected, for unless we remember we cannot understand. If by the time the queen dies we have forgotten the existence of the king, we shall never make out what killed her. The plot-maker expects us to remember, we expect him to leave no loose ends. Every action or word ought to count; it ought to be economical and spare; even when complicated it should be organic and free from dead-matter. It may be difficult or easy, it may and should contain mysteries, but it ought not to mislead. And over it, as it unfolds, will hover the memory of the reader (that dull glow of the mind of which intelligence is the bright advancing edge) and will constantly rearrange and reconsider, seeing new clues, new chains of cause and effect, and the final sense (if the plot has been a fine one) will not be of clues or chains, but of something aesthetically compact, something which might have been shown by the novelist straight away, only if he had shown it straight away it would never have become beautiful.

6

Fairy-Tale Transformations

VLADIMIR PROPP

1

The study of the fairy tale may be compared in many respects to that of organic formation in nature. Both the naturalist and the folklorist deal with species and varieties which are essentially the same. The Darwinian problem of the origin of species arises in folklore as well. The similarity of phenomena both in nature and in our field resists any direct explanation which would be both objective and convincing. It is a problem in its own right. Both fields allow two possible points of view: either the internal similarity of two externally dissimilar phenomena does not derive from a common genetic root—the theory of spontaneous generation—or else this morphological similarity does indeed result from a known genetic tie—the theory of differentiation owing to subsequent metamorphoses or transformations of varying cause and occurrence.

In order to resolve this problem, we need a clear understanding of what is meant by similarity in fairy tales. Similarity has so far been invariably defined in terms of a plot and its variants. We find such an approach acceptable only if based upon the idea of the spontaneous generation of species. Adherents to this method do not compare plots; they feel such comparison to be impossible or, at the very least, erroneous. Without our denying the value of studying individual plots and comparing them solely from the standpoint of their similarity, another method, another basis for comparison may be proposed. Fairy tales can be compared from the standpoint of their composition or structure; their similarity then appears in a new light.

We observe that the actors in the fairy tale perform essentially the same actions as the tale progresses, no matter how different from one another in shape, size, sex, and occupation, in nomenclature and other static attributes. This determines the relationship of the constant factors to the variables. The functions of the actors are constant; everything else is a variable. For example:

1. The king sends Ivan after the princess; Ivan departs.

2. The king sends Ivan after some marvel; Ivan departs.

3. The sister sends her brother for medicine; he departs.

4. The stepmother sends her stepdaughter for fire; she departs.

5. The smith sends his apprentice for a cow; he departs.

The dispatch and the departure on a quest are constants. The dispatching and departing actors, the motivations behind the dispatch, and so forth, are variables. In later stages of the quest, obstacles impede the hero's progress; they, too, are essentially the same, but differ in the form of imagery.

The functions of the actors may be singled out. Fairy tales exhibit thirty-one functions, not all of which may he found in any one fairy tale; however, the absence of certain functions does not interfere with the order of appearance of the others. Their aggregate constitutes one system, one composition. This system has proved to be extremely stable and widespread. The investigator, for example, can determine very accurately that both the ancient Egyptian fairy tale of the two brothers and the tale of the firebird, the tale of *Morozka,* the tale of the fisherman and the fish, as well as a number of myths follow the same general pattern. An analysis of the details bears this out. Thirty-one functions do not exhaust the system. Such a motif as "Baba-Jaga gives Ivan a horse" contains four elements, of which only one represents a function, while the other three are of a static nature.

In all, the fairy tale knows about one hundred and fifty elements or constituents. Each of these elements can be labeled according to its bearing on the sequence of action. Thus, in the above example, Baba-Jaga is a donor, the word "gives" signals the moment of transmittal, Ivan is a recipient, and the horse is the gift. If the labels for all one hundred and fifty fairy-tale elements are written down in the order dictated by the tales themselves, then, by definition, all fairy tales will fit such a table. Conversely, any tale which fits such a table is a fairy tale, and any tale which does not fit it belongs in another category. Every rubric is a constituent of the fairy tale, and reading the table vertically yields a series of basic forms amid a series of derived forms.

It is precisely these constituents which are subject to comparison. This would correspond in zoology to a comparison of vertebra with vertebra, of tooth with tooth, etc. But there is a significant difference between organic formations and the fairy tale which makes our task easier. In the first instance, a change in a part or feature brings about a change in another feature, whereas each element of the fairy tale can change independently of the other elements. This has been noted by many investigators, although there have been so far no attempts to infer from it all the conclusions, methodological and otherwise. Thus, Kaarle Krohn, in agreeing with Spiess on the question of constituent interchangeability, still considers it necessary to study the fairy tale in terms of entire structures rather than in terms of constituents. In so doing, Krohn does not (in keeping with the Finnish school) supply much in the way of evidence to support his stand. We conclude from this that the elements of the fairy tale may be studied independently of the plot they constitute. Studying the rubrics vertically reveals norms and types of transformations. What holds true for an isolated element also holds true for entire structures. This is owing to the mechanical manner in which the constituents are joined.

2

The present work does not claim to exhaust the problem. We will only indicate here certain basic guideposts which might subsequently form the basis of a broader theoretical investigation.

Even in a brief presentation, however, it is necessary before examining the transformations themselves to establish the criteria which allow us to distinguish between basic and derived forms. The criteria may be expressed in two ways: in terms of general principles and in terms of special rules.

First, the general principles. In order to establish these principles, the fairy tale has to be approached from the standpoint of its environment, that is, the conditions under which it was created and exists. Life and, in the broad sense of the word, religion are the most important for us here. The causes of transformations frequently lie outside the fairy tale, and we will not grasp the evolution of the tale unless we consider the environmental circumstances of the fairy tale.

The basic forms are those connected with the genesis of the fairy tale. Obviously, the tale is born out of life; however, the fairy tale reflects reality only weakly. Everything which derives from reality is of secondary formation. In order to determine the origins of the fairy tale, we must draw upon the broad cultural material of the past.

It turns out that the forms which, for one reason or another, are defined as basic are linked with religious concepts of the remote past. We can formulate the following premise: if the same form occurs both in a religious monument and in a fairy tale, the religious form is primary and the fairy-tale form is secondary. This is particularly true of archaic religions. Any archaic religious phenomenon, dead today, is older than its artistic use in a fairy tale. It is, of course, impossible to prove that here. Indeed, such a dependency in general cannot be *proved:* it can only be *shown* on the basis of a large range of material. Such is the first general principle, which is subject to further development. The second principle may be stated thus: if the same element has two variants, of which one derives from religious forms and the other from daily life, the religious formation is primary and the one drawn from life is secondary.

However, in applying these principles, we must observe reasonable caution. It would be an error to try to trace all basic forms back to religion and all derived ones to reality. To protect ourselves against such errors, we need to shed more light on the methods to be used in comparative studies of the fairy tale and religion and the fairy tale and life.

We can establish several types of relationships between the fairy tale and religion. The first is a direct genetic dependency, which in some cases is patently obvious, but which in other cases requires special historical research. Thus, if a serpent is encountered both in the fairy tale and in religion, it entered the fairy tale by way of religion, not the other way around.

However, the presence of such a link is not obligatory even in the case of very great similarity. Its presence is probable only when we have access to direct cult and *ritual* material. Such ritual material must be distinguished from a combination of religious and *epic* material. In the first case, we can raise the question of a direct kinship along descending lines, analogous to the kinship line of fathers and children; in the second case we can speak only of parallel kinship or, to continue the analogy, the kinship of brothers. Thus the story of Samson and Delilah cannot be considered the prototype of the fairy tale resembling their story: both fairy tale and the biblical text may well go back to a common source.

The primacy of cult material should likewise be asserted with a certain degree of caution. Nonetheless, there are instances when this primacy may be asserted with absolute confidence. True, evidence is frequently not found in the document itself but in the concepts which are reflected there and which underlie the fairy tale. But we are often able to form our judgment about the concepts only by means of the documents. For example, the Rig-Veda, little studied by folklorists, belongs to such sources of the fairy tale. If it is true that the fairy tale knows approximately one hundred and fifty constituents, it is noteworthy that the Rig-Veda contains no fewer than sixty. True, their use is lyrical rather than epic, but it should not be forgotten that these are hymns of high priests, not of commoners. It is doubtless true that in the hands of the people (shepherds and peasants) this lyric took on features of the epic. If the hymn praises Indra as the serpent-slayer (in which case the details sometimes coincide perfectly with those of the fairy tale), the people were able in one form or another to *narrate* precisely how Indra killed the serpent.

Let us check this assertion with a more concrete example. We readily recognize Baba-Jaga and her hut in the following Vedic hymn:

> Mistress of the wood, mistress of the wood, whither do you vanish? Why do you not ask of the village? Are you afraid then?
>
> When the hue and cry of birds bursts forth, the mistress of the wood imagines herself a prince riding forth to the sound of cymbals.
>
> Cattle seem to be grazing on the edge of the woods. Or is it a hut which stands darkly visible there? In the night is heard a squeaking and creaking as of a heavy cart. It is the mistress of the wood.
>
> An unseen voice calls to the cattle. An ax rings out in the woods. A voice cries out sharply. So fancies the nocturnal guest of the mistress of the wood.
>
> The mistress of the wood will do no harm unless alarmed. Feed on sweet fruits and peacefully sleep to full contentment.
>
> Smelling of spices, fragrant, unsowing but ever having plenty, mother of the wild beasts, I praise the mistress of the wood.

We have certain fairy-tale elements here: the hut in the woods, the reproach linked with inquiry (in the fairy tale it is normally couched in the form of direct address), a hospitable night's rest (she provides food, drink, and shelter), a suggestion of the mistress of the wood's potential hostility, an indication that she is the mother of the wild beasts (in the fairy tale she calls them together); missing are the chicken legs of her hut as well as any indication of her external appearance, etc. One small detail presents a remarkable coincidence: wood is apparently being chopped for the person spending the night in the forest hut. In Afanas'ev (No. 99)[1] the father, after leaving his daughter in the hut, straps a boot last to the wheel of his cart. The last clacks loudly, and the girl says: *Se mij baten'ka drovcja rubae* [Me pa be a-choppin' wood].

Furthermore, all of these coincidences are not accidental, for they are not the only ones. These are only a few out of a great many precise parallels between the fairy tale and the Rig-Veda. The parallel mentioned cannot, of course, be viewed as proof that our Baba-Jaga goes back to the Rig-Veda. One can only stress that on the whole the line proceeds from religion to the fairy tale, not conversely, and that it is essential here to initiate accurate comparative studies.

However, everything said here is true only if religion and the fairy tale lie at a great chronological distance from each other, if, for example, the religion under consideration has already died out, and its origin is obscured by the prehistoric past. It is quite a different matter when we compare a living religion and a living fairy tale belonging to one and the same people. The reverse situation may occur, a dependency which is impossible in the case of a dead religion and a modern fairy tale. Christian elements in the fairy tale (the apostles as helpers, the devil as spoiler) are *younger* than the fairy tale, not older, as in the preceding example. In point of fact, we really ought not to call this relationship the reverse of the one in the preceding case. The fairy tale derives from ancient religions, but modern religions do not derive from the fairy tale. Modern religion does not create the fairy tale but merely *changes* its material. Yet there are probably isolated examples of a truly reversed dependency, that is, instances in which the elements of religion are derived from the fairy tale. A very interesting example is in the Western Church's canonization of the miracle of St. George the Dragon Slayer. This miracle was canonized much later than was St. George himself, and it occurred despite the stubborn resistance of the Church. Because the battle with the serpent is a part of many pagan religions, we have to assume that it derives precisely from them. In the thirteenth century, however, there was no longer a living trace of these religions, only the epic tradition of the people could play the role of transmitter. The popularity of St. George on the one hand and his fight with the dragon on the other caused his image to merge with that of the dragon fight; the Church was forced to acknowledge the completed fusion and to canonize it.

Finally, we may find not only direct genetic dependency of the fairy tale on religion, not only parallelism and reversed dependency, but also the complete absence of any link despite outward similarity. Identical concepts may arise independently of one another. Thus the magic steed is comparable with the holy steeds of the Teutons and with the fiery horse Agni in the Rig-Veda. The former have nothing in common with Sivka-Burka, while the latter coincides with him in all respects. The analogy may be applied only if it is more or less complete. Heteronymous phenomena, however similar, must be excluded from such comparisons.

Thus the study of *basic* forms necessitates a comparison of the fairy tale with various religions.

Conversely, the study of *derived* forms in the fairy tale shows how it is linked with reality. A number of transformations may be explained as the intrusions of reality into the fairy tale. This forces us to clarify the problem concerning the methods to be used in studying the fairy tale's relationship to life.

In contrast to other types of tales (the anecdote, the novella, the fable, and so on), the fairy tale shows a comparatively sparse sprinkling of elements from real life. The role of daily existence in creating the fairy tale is often overrated. We can resolve the problem of the fairy tale's relationship to life only if we remember that artistic realism and the presence of elements from real life are two different concepts which do not always overlap. Scholars often make the mistake of searching for facts from real life to support a realistic narrative.

Nikolaj Lerner, for example, takes the following lines from Puškin's "Bova":

> This is really a golden Council,
> No idle chatter here, but deep thought:
> A long while the noble lords all thought.
>
> Arzamor, old and experienced
> All but opened his mouth (to give counsel,
> Perhaps, was the old greybeard's desire),
> His throat he loudly cleared, but thought better
> And in silence his tongue did bite
> [All the council members keep silent and begin to drowse.]

and comments:

> In depicting the council of bearded senility we may presume the poem to be
> a satire on the governmental forms of old Muscovite Russia. . . . We note
> that the satire might have been directed not only against Old Russia but
> against Puškin's Russia as well. The assembly of snoring "thinker'" could easi-
> ly have been uncovered by the young genius in the society of his own day.

In actual fact, however, this is strictly a *fairy-tale* motif. In Afanasév (for example, in No. 140) we find: "He asked once—the boyars were silent; a second
time—they did not respond; a third time—not so much as half a word." We
have here the customary scene in which the supplicant entreats aid, the
entreaty usually occurring three times. It is first directed to the servants, then
to the boyars (clerks, ministers), and third to the hero of the story. Each party
in this triad may likewise be trebled in its own right.

Thus we are not dealing with real life but with the amplification and specification (added names, etc.) of a folklore element. We would be making the
same mistake if we were to consider the Homeric image of Penelope and the
conduct of her suitors as corresponding to the facts of life in ancient Greece and
to Greek connubial customs. Penelope's suitors are *false suitors,* a well-known
device in epic poetry throughout the world. We should first isolate whatever is
folkloric and only afterward raise the question as to the correspondence between
specifically Homeric moments and factual life in ancient Greece.

Thus we see that the problem which deals with the fairy tale's relationship
to real life is not a simple one. To draw conclusions about life directly from
the fairy tale is inadmissible.

But, as we will see below, the role of real life in the *transformation* of the fairy tale
is enormous. Life cannot destroy the overall structure of the fairy tale, but it does produce a wealth of younger material which replaces the old in a wide variety of ways.

The following are the principal and more precise criteria for distinguishing the basic form of a fairy-tale element from a derived form:

1. A fantastical treatment of a constituent in the fairy-tale is older than its rational treatment. Such a case is rather simple and does not require special development. If in one fairy tale Ivan receives a magical gift from Baba-Jaga and in another from an old woman passing by, the former is older than the latter. This viewpoint is theoretically based on the link between the fairy tale and religion. Such a viewpoint, however, may turn out to be an invalid with respect to other types of tales (fables, etc.) which on the whole may be older than the fairy tale. The realism of such tales dates from time immemorial and cannot be traced back to religious concepts.
2. Heroic treatment is older than humorous treatment. This is essentially a frequent variant of the preceding case. Thus the idea of entering into mortal combat with a dragon precedes that of beating it in a card game.
3. A form used logically is older than a form used nonsensically.
4. An international form is older than national form.

Thus, if the dragon is encountered virtually the world over but is replaced in some fairy tales of the North by a bear or, in the South, by a lion, then the basic form is the dragon, while the lion and bear are derived forms.

Here we ought to say a few words concerning the methods of studying the fairy tale on an international scale. The material is so expansive that a single investigator cannot possibly study all the one hundred elements in the fairy tales of the entire world. He must first work through the fairy tales of one people, distinguishing between their basic and their derived forms. He must then repeat the same procedure for the second people, after which he may proceed to a comparative study.

In this connection, the thesis on international forms may be narrowed and stated thus: a broadly national form is older than a regional and provincial form. But, if we start along this path, we cannot refute the following statement: a widespread form predates an isolated form. However, it is theoretically possible that a truly ancient form has survived only in isolated instances and that all other occurrences of it are younger. Therefore great caution must be exercised when applying the quantitative principal (the use of statistics); moreover, *qualitative* considerations of the material under study must be brought into play. An example: in the fairy tale "Pretty Vasilisa" (No. 104 in Afanas'ev) the figure of Baba-Jaga is accompanied by the appearance of three mounted riders who symbolize morning, day, and night. The question spontaneously arises: is this not a fundamental feature peculiar to Baba-Jaga, one which has been lost in the other fairy tales? Yet, after a rigorous examination of special considerations (which do not warrant mention at this point), this opinion must be rejected.

4

By way of example we will go through all the possible changes of a single element—Baba-Jaga's hut. Morphologically, the hut represents the abode of the donor (that is, the actor who furnishes the hero with the magical tool). Consequently, we will direct attention not only to the hut but to the appearance of all the donor's abodes. We consider the basic Russian form of the abode to be the hut on chicken legs; it is in the forest, and it rotates. But since one element does not yield all the changes possible in a fairy tale, we will consider other examples as well.

1. Reduction

Instead of the full form, we may find the following types of changes:

i.   The hut on chicken legs in the forest.
ii.   The hut on chicken legs.
iii. The hut in the forest.
iv.   The hut.
v.   The pine forest (Afanas'ev No. 95).
vi.   No mention of the abode.

Here the basic form is truncated. The chicken legs, the rotation, and the forest are omitted, and finally the very hut is dispensed with. Reduction may be termed an incomplete basic form. It is to be explained by a lapse of memory which in turn has more complex causes. Reduction points to the lack of agreement between the fairy tale and the whole tenor of the life surrounding it; reduction points to the low degree of relevance of the fairy tale to a given environment, to a given epoch, or to the reciter of the fairy tale.

2. Expansion

We turn now to the opposite phenomenon, by which the basic form is extended and broadened by the addition of extra detail. Here is an expanded form: The hut on chicken legs in the forest rests on pancakes and is shingled with cookies. More often than not, expansion is accompanied by reduction. Certain features are omitted, others are added. Expansion may be divided into categories according to origin (as is done below for substitutions). Some expanded forms derive from daily life, others represent an embellished detail from the fairy-tale canon. This is illustrated by the preceding example. Examination reveals the donor to be a blend of hostile and hospitable qualities. Ivan is usually welcomed at the donor's abode. The forms this welcome may take are extremely varied. (She gave him food and drink. Ivan addresses the hut with the words: "We'd like to climb up and have a bite to eat." The hero sees in the hut a table laid, he samples all the food or eats his fill; he goes outside and slaughters some of the donor's cattle and chickens, etc.) This quality on the part of the donor is expressed by his very abode. In the German fairy tale *Hansel and Gretel,* this form is used somewhat differently, in conformance with the childlike nature of the story.

3. Contamination

In general, the fairy tale is in a state of decline today, and contamination is relatively frequent. Sometimes contaminated forms spread and take root. The idea that Baba-Jaga's hut turns continuously on its axis is an example of contamination. In the course of the action, the hut has a very specific purpose: it is a watchtower; the hero is tested to see whether or not he is worthy of receiving the magical tool. The hut greets Ivan with its closed side, and consequently it is sometimes called the "windowless, doorless hut." Its open side, that is, the side with the door, faces away from Ivan. It would appear that Ivan could very easily go around to the other side of the hut and enter through the door. But this Ivan cannot and in the fairy tale never does do. Instead, he utters the incantation: "Stand with your back to the forest and your front to me," or "Stand, as your mother stood you," and so on. The result was usually: "The hut turned." This "turned" became "spins," and the expression, "When it has to, it turns this way and that" became simply, "It turns this way and that." The expression thus lost its sense but was not deprived of a certain characteristic vividness.

4. Inversion

Often the basic form is reversed. Female members of the cast are replaced by males, and vice versa. This procedure may involve the hut as well. Instead of a closed and inaccessible hut, we sometimes get a hut with a wide-open door.

5 – 6. Intensification and Attenuation

These types of transformation only apply to the *actions* of the cast. Identical actions may occur at various degrees of intensity. One example of intensification: the hero is exiled instead of merely being sent on a quest. Dispatch is one of the constant elements of the fairy tale; this element occurs in such a variety of forms that all degrees of dispatch intensity are demonstrable. The dispatch may be initiated in various ways. The hero is often asked to go and fetch some unusual thing. Sometimes the hero is given a task. ("Do me the service.") Often it is an order accompanied by threats, should he fail, and promises, should he succeed. Dispatch may also be a veiled form of exile: an evil sister sends her brother for the milk of a fierce animal in order to get rid of him; the master sends his helper to bring back a cow supposedly lost in the forest; a stepmother sends her stepdaughter to Baba-Jaga for fire. Finally, we have literal exile. These are the basic stages of dispatch, each of which allows a number of variations and transitional forms; they are especially important in examining fairy tales dealing with exiled characters. The order, accompanied by threats and promises, may be regarded as the basic form of dispatch. If the element of promise is omitted, such a reduction may be simultaneously considered an intensification—we are left with a dispatch *and* a threat. Omission of the threat will soften and weaken this form. Further attenuation consists in completely omitting the dispatch. As he prepares to leave, the son asks his parents for their blessing.

The six types of transformations discussed so far may be interpreted as very familiar *changes* in the basic form. There are, however, two other large groups of transformations: substitutions and assimilations. Both of them may be analyzed according to their origin.

7. Internally Motivated Substitution

Looking again at the donor's dwelling, we find the following forms:

i.   A palace.
ii. A mountain alongside a fiery river.

These are not cases of either reduction or expansion, etc. They are not changes but substitutions. The indicated forms, however, are not drawn from without; they are drawn from the fairy tale's own reserves. A dislocation, a rearrangement of forms and material, has taken place. The palace (often of gold) is normally inhabited by a princess. Subsequently this dwelling is ascribed to the donor. Such dislocations in the fairy tale play a very important role. Each element has its own peculiar form. However, this form is not always exclusively bound to the given element. (The princess, for example, usually a sought member of the cast, may play the role of the donor, or that of the helper, etc.) One fairy-tale image suppresses another; Baba-Jaga's daughter may appear as the princess. In the latter case, appropriately enough, Baba-Jaga does not live in her hut but in a palace, that is, the abode normally associated with a princess. Linked to this one are the palaces of copper, silver, and gold. The maidens living in such palaces are simultaneously donor and princess. The palaces possibly came about as the result of trebling the golden palace. Possibly they arose in complete independence, having, for example, no connection whatsoever with the idea of the Ages of Gold, Silver, and Iron, etc.

Similarly, the mountain alongside the fiery river is no other than the abode of the dragon, an abode which has been attributed to the donor.

These dislocations play an enormous role in creating transformations. The majority of all transformations are substitutions or dislocations generated from within the fairy tale.

8. Externally Motivated Substitutions

If we have the forms:

i. An inn.
ii. A two-storied house,

it is apparent that the fantastic hut has been replaced by forms of dwelling normal to real life. The majority of such substitutions may be explained very easily, but there are substitutions which require a special ethnographic exegesis. Elements from life are always immediately obvious, and, more often than not, scholars center their attention upon them.

9. Confessional Substitutions

Current religion is also capable of suppressing old forms, replacing them with new ones. Here we are involved with instances in which the devil functions as a winged messenger, or an angel is the donor of the magical tool, or an act of penance replaces the performance of a difficult task (the donor tests the hero). Certain legends are basically fairy tales in which all elements have undergone supporting substitutions. Every people has its own confessional substitutions. Christianity, Islam, and Buddhism are reflected in the fairy tales of the corresponding peoples.

10. Substitution by Superstition

Obviously, superstition and local beliefs may likewise suppress the original material of a fairy tale. However, we encounter this type of substitution much more rarely than we might expect at first glance (the errors of the mythological school). Pushkin was mistaken in saying that in the fairy tale:

> Wonders abound, a wood-demon lurks,
> Rusalka sits in the boughs.

If we encounter a wood-demon in the fairy tale, he almost always replaces Baba-Jaga. Water nymphs are met with but a single time in the entire Afanas'ev collection, and then only in an introductory flourish of dubious authenticity. In the collections by Onchukov, Zelinin, the Sokolovs, and others, there is not a single mention of Rusalka. The wood-demon only finds its way into the fairy tale because, as a creature of the forest, it resembles Baba-Jaga. The fairy tale accepts only those elements which can be readily accommodated in its construction.

11. Archaic Substitutions

We have already mentioned that the basic forms of the fairy tale go back to extinct religious concepts. Based on this fact, we can sometimes separate the basic forms from the derived ones. In certain unique instances, however, the basic form (more or less normal in the fairy-tale epic) has been replaced by a form no less ancient which can likewise be traced back to a religious source, but whose occurrence is unique. For example, rather than the battle with the dragon in the fairy tale "The Witch and the Sun's Sister" (No. 93 in Afanas'ev), we have the following: the dragon's mate suggests to the prince, "Let Prince Ivan come with me to the scales and we'll see who outweights whom." The scales toss Ivan sky-high. Here we have traces of psychostasia (the weighing of souls). Where this form—well known in ancient Egypt—came from and how it came to be preserved in the fairy tale are questions which need study.

It is not always easy to distinguish between an archaic substitution and a substitution imposed by superstition. Both have their roots (sometimes) in deep antiquity. But if some item in the fairy tale is also found in a living faith, the substitution may be considered as a relatively new one (the wood-demon). A pagan religion may have two offshoots: one in the fairy tale and the other in a faith or custom. They may well have confronted each other in the course of centuries, and the one may have suppressed the other. Conversely, if a fairy-tale element is not attested to in a living faith (the scales), the substitution has its origin in deep antiquity and may be considered archaic.

12. Literary Substitutions

Literary material shows the same low degree of likelihood of being accepted by the fairy tale that current superstition does. The fairy tale possesses such resistance that other genres shatter against it; they do not readily blend. If a clash takes place, the fairy tale wins. Of all the various literary genres, that of the fairy tale is the most likely to absorb elements from legend and epic. On rare occasions the novel provides a substitution; but even in such a case, it is only the chivalric romance which plays a certain role. The chivalric romance itself, however, is frequently a product of the fairy tale. The process occurs in stages: fairy tale, romance, fairy tale. Therefore, works such as "Eruslan Lazarevich" are among the "purest" of fairy tales in terms of construction, despite the bookish nature of individual elements. The *Schwank,* the novella, and other forms of popular prose are more flexible and more receptive to elements from other genres.

13. Modification

There are substitutions whose origin is not readily ascertainable. More often than not, these are imaginative substitutions which came into being through the teller's own resourcefulness. Such forms defy ethnographic or historical specification. We should note, however, that these substitutions play a greater role in animal tales and other types of tales than in fairy tales. (The bear is replaced by the wolf, one bird by another, etc.) Of course, they may occur in the fairy tale, too. Thus, as the winged messenger, we find an eagle, a falcon, a raven, geese, and others. As the sought-after marvel, we find a stag with antlers of gold, a steed with a mane of gold, a duck with feathers of gold, a pig with bristles of gold, and so on. Derived, secondary forms are generally those most likely to undergo modification. This may be shown by comparing a number of forms in which the sought wonder is simply a transformation of the sought princess with golden locks. If a comparison of the basic and the derived forms exhibits a certain descending line, a comparison of two derived forms reveals a certain parallelism. There are elements in the fairy tale having a particular variety of forms. One example is the "difficult task." If the task does not have a basic form, it makes little difference to the fairy tale, in terms of the unity of its construction, what kind of task is assigned. This phenomenon is even more apparent when we compare elements which have never belonged to a basic type of fairy tale. Motivation is one such element. But transformations sometimes create the need to motivate a certain act. As a result, we see a wide variety of motivations for one and the same act. Thus the hero's exile (exile is a secondary formation) is motivated by widely varied circumstances. On the other hand, the dragon's abduction of the maiden (a primary form) is hardly ever motivated externally but is motivated from within.

Certain features of the hut are also subject to modification. Instead of a hut on chicken legs, we encounter a hut on goat horns or on sheep legs.

14. Substitutions of Unknown Origin

We have been discussing substitutions from the point of view of their origin, but their origin is not always ascertainable; it does not always appear as a simple modification. Therefore we require a category for substitutions of unknown origin. For example, the little sister of the sun from the fairy tale "Little Sister" (Afanasév No. 93) plays the donor's role and may be considered a rudimentary form of the princess. She lives in the "solar rooms." We cannot know whether this reflects a sun cult, or the creative imagination of the narrator, or some suggestion by the collector asking the storyteller whether he knows any fairy tales dealing with a particular subject, or whether thus and so can be found; in such a case, the teller sometimes fabricates something to please the collector.

This places a limitation on substitutions. We could, of course, set up several more varieties which might be applied to a given isolated case. However, there is no need for that now. The substitutions specified here are meaningful throughout the entire breadth of fairy-tale material; their application to isolated cases may be easily inferred and demonstrated by employing the transformational types cited.

Let us turn to another class of changes, that of assimilations. By assimilation we understand an incomplete suppression of one form by another, the two forms merging into a single form. Because assimilations follow the same classification scheme as the substitutions, they will be enumerated in brief.

15. Internally Motivated Assimilations

An example occurs in the forms:

i.   A hut under a golden roof.
ii. A hut by a fiery river.

In a fairy tale we often meet with a palace under a golden roof. A hut plus a palace under a golden roof equals a hut under a golden roof. The same is true in the case of the hut by the fiery river.

The fairy tale "Fedor Vodovich and Ivan Vodovich (Onchukov No. 4) provides a very interesting example. Two such very heterogeneous elements as the miraculous birth of the hero and his pursuit by the dragon's wives (sisters) have been drawn together by assimilation. The wives of the dragon, in pursuing the hero, usually turn into a well, a cloud, or a bed and situate themselves in Ivan's path. If he samples some fruit or takes a drink of water, etc., he is torn to pieces. For the miraculous birth, this motif is used in the following manner: the princess strolls about her father's courtyard, sees a well with a small cup, and by it a bed (the apple tree has been forgotten). She drinks a cupful and lies down on the bed to rest. From this she conceives and gives birth to two sons.

16. Externally Motivated Assimilations

Take the form:

i.   A hut on the edge of the village.
ii. A cave in the woods.

Here we find that the imaginary hut has become a real hut and a real cave, but the solitude of its inhabitant has been preserved. Indeed, in the second instance, the forest element is also preserved. Fairy tale plus reality produces an assimilation which favors real life.

17. Confessional Assimilations

This process may be exemplified by the replacement of the dragon by the devil; however, the devil, like the dragon, dwells in a lake. The concept of evil beings of the deep does not necessarily have anything in common with the so-called lower mythology of the peasants; it is often explained as simply one type of transformation.

18. Assimilation via Superstition

This is a relatively rare phenomenon. The wood-demon living in a hut on chicken legs is an example.

19–20. Literary and Archaic Assimilations

These are encountered even more rarely. Assimilations with the folk epic and legend are of some importance in the Russian fairy tale. Here, however, we are more likely to find suppression rather than the assimilation of one form by another, while the components of the fairy tale are preserved as such. Archaic assimilations require a detailed examination of each occurrence. They do occur, but identifying them is possible only after highly specialized research.

Our survey of the transformation of types can end at this point. It is impossible to assert that absolutely all fairy-tale forms will be accommodated by our classificatory scheme, but at any rate a significant number clearly are. It would have been possible to bring in still other types of transformations, such as specification and generalization. In the first case, general phenomena become particularized (instead of the thrice-tenth kingdom, we find the city

Xvalynsk); in the latter case, the opposite occurs (the thrice-tenth kingdom becomes simply a "different, other" kingdom, etc.). But almost all types of specification may also be regarded as substitutions, and generalizations, as reductions. This is true, too, for rationalization (a winged steed becomes an earthbound horse) as well as for the conversion of the fairy tale into an anecdote, etc. A correct and consistent application of the types of transformation indicated will give a firmer foundation to the study of the fairy tale in the process of its development.

What is true for the individual elements of the fairy tale is also true for the fairy tale as a whole. If an extra element is added, we have amplification; in the reverse case, we have reduction, etc. Applying these methods to the fairy tales is important for comparative studies on fairy-tale plots.

One very important problem remains. If we write out all the occurrences (or at least a great many of them) of one element, not all the forms of one element can be traced back to some single basis. Let us suppose that we accept Baba-Jaga as the basic form of the donor. Such forms are a witch, Grannie-Behind-the-Door, Grandma-Widow, an old lady, an old man, a shepherd, a wood-demon, an angel, the devil, three maids, the king's daughter, etc.—all may be satisfactorily explained as substitutions and other transformations of Baba-Jaga. But then we encounter a "fingernail-sized peasant with an elbow-length beard." Such a form for the donor does not come from Baba-Jaga. If such a form does occur in a religion, we have a form which has been coordinated with Baba-Jaga; if not, we have a substitution of unknown origin. Each element may have several basic forms, although the number of such parallel, coordinated forms is usually insignificant.

5

Our outline would be incomplete if we did not show a model for applying our observations. We will use more palpable material to exhibit a series of transformations; let us take the forms: .

> The dragon abducts the king's daughter—
> the dragon tortures the king's daughter—
> the dragon demands the king's daughter.

From the point of view of the morphology of the fairy tale, we are dealing here with an element which we will call *basic harm*. Such harm usually serves as the start of the plot. In accordance with the principles proposed in this paper, we should compare not only abduction with abduction, etc., but also with all the various types of basic harm as one of the components of the fairy tale.

Caution demands that all three forms be regarded as coordinated forms, but it is possible to suggest that the first is still the basic form. In Egypt we find death conceived of as the abduction of the soul by a dragon. But this concept has been forgotten, whereas the idea that illness is a demon settled within the body lives on today. Finally, the dragon's demand for the princess as tribute reflects a shadowy archaism from real life. It is accompanied by the appearance of an army, which surrounds the city and threatens war. However, we cannot be certain. Be that as it may, all three forms are very old, and each allows a number of transformations.

Let us take the first form:

The dragon abducts the king's daughter.

The dragon is viewed as the embodiment of evil. Confessional influence turns the dragon into a devil:

Devils abduct the king's daughter.

The same influence affects the object of abduction:

The devil abducts the priest's daughter.

The dragon figure has already become foreign to the village. It has been replaced by a dangerous animal that is better known (externally motivated substitution), the animal acquiring fantastic attributes (modification):

A bear with fur of iron carries off the king's children.

The villain merges with Baba-Jaga. One part of the fairy tale influences another part (internally motivated substitution). Baba-Jaga is the essence of the female sex, and, correspondingly, the person abducted is a male (inversion):

A witch abducts the son of an old couple.

In one of two forms constantly complicating the fairy tale, the hero's brothers carry out a secondary abduction of their brother's prize. The intent to do harm has now been transferred to the hero's kin. This is a canonical form of complicating the action:

His brothers abduct Ivan's bride.

The wicked brothers are replaced by other villainous relatives from reserve members of the fairy tale's cast (internally motivated substitution):

The king (Ivan's father-in-law) abducts Ivan's wife.

The princess herself may take over the same function, and the fairy tale may assume more amusing forms. Here the figure of the villain has been reduced:

The princess flees from her husband.

In all these cases, a human being was abducted, but, by way of example, the light of day may be abducted (an archaic substitution):

The dragon abducts the light of the kingdom.

The dragon is replaced by other monstrous animals (modification); the object of abduction merges with the imagined life of the court:

The mink-beast pilfers animals from the king's menagerie.

Talismans play a significant role in the fairy tale. They are often the only means by which Ivan can attain his goal. Hence it is understandable that they are often the object of abduction. If the action is thus complicated in the middle of the fairy tale, such an abduction is even obligatory as far as fairy-tale canon is concerned. This middle moment in the fairy tale may be transferred to the beginning (internally motivated substitution). The abductor of the talisman is often a cheat, or a landowner, and so on (externally motivated substitution):

A shrewd lad abducts Ivan's talisman.

A landowner abducts the peasant's talisman.

The firebird fairy tale represents a transitional stage leading to other forms; here the stolen apples of gold are not talismans (cf. orpine apples). We should add that the theft of the talisman is not possible as a complication at the fairy tale's midpoint unless the talisman has already been acquired. The talisman can be made off with at the beginning only if its possession is properly motivated, however briefly. It is for this reason that the stolen items which appear at the beginning of the tale are not often talismans. The firebird found its way from the middle section of the tale back to the beginning. The bird is one of the basic forms of transporting Ivan to the thrice-tenth kingdom. Golden feathers and similar features are usually attributed to the animal life of the fairy tale:

The firebird steals the king's apples.

In every case the abduction is preserved. The disappearance of a bride, a daughter, a wife, etc., is ascribed to a mythic substratum in the fairy tale. However, this explanation of such a disappearance is alien to modern peasant life, therefore an alien, imported mythology is replaced by sorcery. Disappearance is ascribed to magic spells cast by evil sorcerers and sorceresses. The nature of the villainous deed changes, but its result is still the same: a disappearance entailing a quest (substitution via superstition):

A sorcerer abducts the king's daughter.

Nursie bewitches Ivan's bride and forces her to flee.

Again we see the activity transferred to wicked relatives:

Sisters force the girl's groom to flee.

Turning to the transformations of our second base form (a dragon tortures the king's daughter), we encounter transformations on the same patterns:

The devil tortures the king's daughter, etc.

Here the torture assumes the nature of seizure and vampirism, which can be fully explained ethnographically. Instead of the dragon and the devil, we see again another of the fairy tale's evil beings:

Baba-Jaga tortures the mistress of the knights.

A third variation of the basic form poses the threat of forced marriage:

The dragon demands the king's daughter.

This reveals a number of transformations:

A water sprite demands the king's son, etc.

This same form, morphologically speaking, may lead to a declaration of war without any of the king's offspring being demanded (reduction); a transfer of similar forms to relatives produces:

The sister, a witch, seeks to devour the king's son (her brother).

This case (Afanas'ev No. 93) is of special interest. Here the prince's sister is called a dragoness. Thus we have a classical example of internal assimilation. It points up the need for caution in studying kinship ties in the fairy tale. The marriage of brother and sister and other forms are not necessarily remnants of an old custom; rather, they may be the results of certain transformations, as the above case clearly shows.

The objection may be raised against all of the preceding that anything at all could be fitted into a single phrase having but two components. This is far from true. How would the start of the plot of the fairy tale "Frost, Sun and Wind" and many others fit into such a form? Second, the observed phenomena represent the same constructional element with respect to the overall composition. Although differently stated, they result in identical patterns in the progress of the plots: a plea for help may be masked as a departure from home, as a meeting with a donor, etc. Not every fairy tale containing a theft produces this construction. If this construction does not follow, subsequent patterns, however similar, cannot be compared, for they are heteronymous. Otherwise, we have to admit that an element from the fairy tale has entered a construction foreign to the tale. Thus we return to the necessity of making juxtapositions on the basis of identical components and not external similarity.

NOTE

1. All references to Afanas'ev are to *Narodnye russkie skazki* (Moscow: Khudozh, 1957).

7

The Concept of Plot and the Plot of *Tom Jones*

R. S. CRANE

Of all the plots constructed by English novelists that of *Tom Jones* has probably elicited the most unqualified praise. There is "no fable whatever," wrote Fielding's first biographer, that "affords, in its solution, such artful states of suspence, such beautiful turns of surprise, such unexpected incidents, and such sudden discoveries, sometimes apparently embarrassing, but always promising the catastrophe, and eventually promoting the completion of the whole."[1] Not since the days of Homer, it seemed to James Beattie, had the world seen "a more artful epick fable." "The characters and adventures are wonderfully diversified: yet the circumstances are all so natural, and rise so easily from one another, and co-operate with so much regularity in bringing on, even while they seem to retard, the catastrophe, that the curiosity of the reader . . . grows more and more impatient as the story advances, till at last it becomes downright anxiety. And when we get to the end . . . we are amazed to find, that of so many incidents there should be so few superfluous; that in such variety of fiction there should be so great probability; and that so complex a tale should be perspicuously conducted, and with perfect unity of design."[2] These are typical of the eulogies that preceded and were summed up in Coleridge's famous verdict in 1834: "What a master of composition Fielding was! Upon my word, I think the *Oedipus Tyrannus, The Alchemist*, and *Tom Jones,* the three most perfect plots ever planned."[3] More recent writers have tended to speak less hyperbolically and, like Scott, to insist that "even the high praise due to the construction and arrangement of the story is inferior to that claimed by the truth, force, and spirit of the characters,"[4] but it is hard to think of any important modern discussion of the novel that does not contain at least a few sentences on Fielding's "ever-to-be-praised skill as an architect of plot."[5]

94

1

The question I wish to raise concerns not the justice of any of these estimates but rather the nature and critical adequacy of the conception of plot in general and of the plot of *Tom Jones* in particular that underlies most if not all of them. Now it is a striking fact that in all the more extended discussions of Fielding's masterpiece since 1749 the consideration of the plot has constituted merely one topic among several others, and a topic, moreover, so detached from the rest that once it is disposed of the consideration of the remaining elements of character, thought, diction, and narrative technique invariably proceeds without further reference to it. The characters are indeed agents of the story, but their values are assessed apart from this, in terms sometimes of their degrees of conformity to standards of characterization in literature generally, sometimes of the conceptions of morality they embody, sometimes of their relation to Fielding's experiences or prejudices, sometimes of their reflection, taken collectively, of the England of their time. The other elements are isolated similarly, both from the plot and from one another: what is found important in the thought, whether of the characters or of the narrator, is normally not its function as an artistic device but its doctrinal content as a sign of the "philosophy" of Fielding; the style and the ironical tone of the narrative are frequently praised, but solely as means to the general literary satisfaction of the reader; and, what is perhaps more significant, the wonderful comic force of the novel, which all have delighted to commend, is assumed to be independent of the plot and a matter exclusively of particular incidents, of the characters of some, but not all, of the persons, and of occasional passages of burlesque or witty writing.

All this points to a strictly limited definition of plot as something that can be abstracted, for critical purposes, from the moral qualities of the characters and the operations of their thought. This something is merely the material continuity of the story considered in relation to the general pleasure we take in any fiction when our curiosity about the impending events is aroused, sustained, and then satisfied to a degree or in a manner we could not anticipate. A plot in this sense—the sense in which modern novelists pride themselves on having got rid of plot—can be pronounced good in terms simply of the variety of incidents it contains, the amount of suspense and surprise it evokes, and the ingenuity with which all the happenings in the beginning and middle are made to contribute to the resolution at the end. Given the definition, indeed, no other criteria are possible, and no others have been used by any of the critics of *Tom Jones* since the eighteenth century who have declared its plot to be one of the most perfect ever planned. They have uniformly judged it as interesting story merely—and this whether, as by most of the earlier writers, "the felicitous contrivance and happy extrication of the story" is taken to be the chief "beauty" of the novel or whether, as generally nowadays, preference is given to its qualities of character and thought. It is clearly of plot in no completer sense than this that Oliver Elton is thinking when he remarks that, although some "have cared little for this particular excellence, and think only of Partridge, timorous, credulous, garrulous, faithful, and an injured man; of Squire Western, and of the night at Upton, and of wit and humour everywhere," still "the common reader, for whom Fielding wrote, cares a great deal, and cares rightly, for plot; and so did Sophocles."[6]

When plot is conceived thus narrowly, in abstraction from the peculiar characters and mental processes of the agents, it must necessarily have, for the critic, only a relatively external relation to the other aspects of the work. That is why, in most discussions of *Tom Jones,* the critical treatment of the plot (as distinguished from mere summary of the happenings) is restricted to the kind of enthusiastic general appreciation of which I have given some examples, supplemented by more particular remarks on various episodes, notably those of the Man of the Hill and of Mrs. Fitzpatrick, which appear to do little to advance the action. The plot, in these discussions, is simply one of several sources of interest and pleasure afforded by a novel peculiarly rich in pleasurable and interesting things, and the problem of its relation to the other ingredients is evaded altogether. Occasionally, it is true, the question has been faced; but even in those critics, like W. L. Cross and Oliver Elton, who have made it most explicit, the formulas suggested never give to the plot of *Tom Jones* the status of more than an external and enveloping form in relation to which the rest of the novel is content. It is not, as they see it, an end but a means, and they describe it variously, having no language but metaphor for the purpose, as a "framework" in which character (which is Fielding's "real 'bill of fare'") is "set"; as a device, essentially "artificial," for bringing on the stage "real men and women"; as a "mere mechanism," which, except now and then in the last two books, "does not obtrude," for keeping readers alert through six volumes.[7]

I do not believe, however, that it is necessary to remain content with this very limited and abstract definition of plot or with the miscellaneous and fragmentized criticism of works like *Tom Jones* that has always followed from it. I shall assume that any novel or drama not constructed on didactic principles[8] is a composite of three elements, which unite to determine its quality and effect—the things that are imitated (or "rendered") in it, the linguistic medium in which they are imitated, and the manner or technique of imitation; and I shall assume further that the things imitated necessarily involve human beings interacting with one another in ways determined by, and in turn affecting, their moral characters and their states of mind (i.e., their reasonings, emotions, and attitudes). If this is granted, we may say that the plot of any novel or drama is the particular temporal synthesis effected by the writer of the elements of action, character, and thought that constitute the matter of his invention. It is impossible, therefore, to state adequately what any plot is unless we include in our formula all three of the elements or causes of which the plot is the synthesis; and it follows also that plots will differ in structure according as one or another of the three causal ingredients is employed as the synthesizing principle. There are, thus, plots of action, plots of character, and plots of thought. In the first, the synthesizing principle is a completed change, gradual or sudden, in the situation of the protagonist, determined and effected by character and thought (as in *Oedipus* and *The Brothers Karamazov*); in the second, the principle is a completed process of change in the moral character of the protagonist, precipitated or molded by action, and made manifest both in it and in thought and feeling (as in James's *The Portrait of a Lady*); in the third, the principle is a completed process of change in the thought of the protagonist and consequently in his feelings, conditioned and directed by character and action (as in Pater's *Marius the Epicurean*). All these types of construction, and not merely the first, are plots in the meaning of our definition; and it is mainly, perhaps, because most of the familiar classic plots, including that of *Tom Jones,* have been of the first kind that so many critics have tended to reduce plot to action alone.[9]

If this is granted, we may go farther. For a plot, in the enlarged sense here given to the term, is not merely a particular synthesis of particular materials of character, thought, and action, but such a synthesis endowed necessarily, because it imitates in words a sequence of human activities, with a power to affect our opinions and emotions in a certain way. We are bound, as we read or listen, to form expectations about what is coming and to feel more or less determinate desires relatively to our expectations. At the very least, if we are interested at all, we desire to know what is going to happen or how the problems faced by the characters are going to be solved. This is a necessary condition of our pleasure in all plots, and there are many good ones—in the classics of pure detective fiction, for example, or in some modern psychiatric novels—the power of which depends almost exclusively on the pleasure we take in inferring progressively, from complex or ambiguous signs, the true state of affairs. For some readers and even some critics this would seem to be the chief source of delight in many plots that have obviously been constructed on more specific principles: not only *Tom Jones,* as we have seen, but *Oedipus* has been praised as a mystery story, and it is likely that much of Henry James's popularity is due to his remarkable capacity for provoking a superior kind of inferential activity. What distinguishes all the more developed forms of imitative literature, however, is that, though they presuppose this instinctive pleasure in learning, they go beyond it and give us plots of which the effects derive in a much more immediate way from the particular ethical qualities manifested in their agents' actions and thoughts vis-à-vis the human situations in which they are engaged. When this is the case, we cannot help becoming, in a greater or less degree, emotionally involved; for some of the characters we wish good, for others ill, and, depending on our inferences as to the events, we feel hope or fear, pity or satisfaction, or some modification of these or similar emotions. The peculiar power of any plot of this kind, as it unfolds, is a result of our state of knowledge at any point in complex interaction with our desires for the characters as morally differentiated beings; and we may be said to have grasped the plot in the full artistic sense only when we have analyzed this interplay of desires and expectations sequentially in relation to the incidents by which it is produced.

It is, of course, an essential condition of such an effect that the writer should so have combined his elements of action, character, and thought as to have achieved a complete and ordered whole, with all the parts needed to carry the protagonist, by probable or necessary stages, from the beginning to the end of his change: we should not have, otherwise, any connected series of expectations wherewith to guide our desires. In itself, however, this structure is only the matter or content of the plot and not its form; the form of the plot—in the sense of that which makes its matter into a definite artistic thing—is rather its distinctive "working or power," as the form of the plot in tragedy, for example, is the capacity of its unified sequence of actions to effect through pity and fear a cartharsis of such emotions.

But if this is granted, then certain consequences follow for the criticism of dramas and novels. It is evident, in the first place, that no plot of this order can be judged excellent *merely* in terms of the unity of its action, the number and variety of its incidents, or the extent to which it produces suspense and surprise. These are but properties of its matter, and their achievement, even to a high degree, in any particular plot does not inevitably mean that the emotional effect of the whole will not still be diffused or weak. They are, therefore, necessary, but not sufficient, conditions of a good plot, the positive excellence of which depends upon the power of its peculiar synthesis of character, action, and thought, as inferable from the sequence of words, to move our feelings powerfully and pleasurably in a certain definite way.

But this power, which constitutes the form of the plot, is obviously, from an artistic point of view, the most important virtue any drama or novel can have; it is that, indeed, which most sharply distinguishes works of imitation from all other kinds of literary productions. It follows, consequently, that the plot, considered formally, of any imitative work is, in relation to the work as a whole, not simply a means—a "framework" or "mere mechanism"—but rather the final end which everything in the work, if that is to be felt as a whole, must be made, directly or indirectly, to serve. For the critic, therefore, the form of the plot is a first principle, which he must grasp as clearly as possible for any work he proposes to examine before he can deal adequately with the questions raised by its parts. This does not mean that we cannot derive other relevant principles of judgment from the general causes of pleasure operative in all artistic imitations, irrespective of the particular effect, serious or comic, that is aimed at in a given work. One of these is the imitative principle itself, the principle that we are in general more convinced and moved when things are "rendered" for us through probable signs than when they are given merely in "statement," without illusion, after the fashion of a scenario.[10] Critical judgments, valid enough if they are not taken absolutely, may also be drawn from considerations of the general powers of language as a literary medium, of the known potentialities or requirements of a given manner of representation (e.g., dramatic or narrative), and of the various conditions of suspense and surprise. We are not likely to feel strongly the emotional effect of a work in which the worse rather than the better alternatives among these different expedients are consistently chosen or chosen in crucial scenes. The same thing, too, can be said of works in which the thought, however clearly serving an artistic use, is generally uninteresting or stale, or in which the characters of the agents, though right enough in conception for the intended effect, are less than adequately "done" or fail to impress themselves upon our memory and imagination, or in which we perceive that the most has not been made of the possibilities implicit in the incidents. And there is also a kind of judgment, distinct from any of these, the object of which is not so much the traits of a work that follow from its general character as an imitative drama or novel as the qualities of intelligence and moral sensibility in its author which are reflected in his conception and handling of its subject and which warrant us in ascribing "greatness," "seriousness," or "maturity" to some products of art and in denying these values to others no matter how excellent, in a formal sense, the latter may be.

Such criticism of parts in the light of general principles is indispensable, but it is no substitute for—and its conclusions, affirmative as well as negative, have constantly to be checked by—the more specific kind of criticism of a work that takes the form of the plot as its starting point and then inquires how far and in what way its peculiar power is maximized by the writer's invention and development of episodes, his step-by-step rendering of the characters of his people, his use and elaboration of thought, his handling of diction and imagery, and his decisions as to the order, method, scale, and point of view of his representation.

All this is implied, I think, in the general hypothesis about plot which I have been outlining here and which I flow propose to illustrate further in a reexamination of the "ever-to-be-praised" plot of *Tom Jones*.

2

It is necessary to look first at its matter and to begin by asking what is the unifying idea by which this is held together. Elementary as the question is, I have not read any answers to it that do not, in one way or another, mistake one of the parts of Fielding's novel for the whole. Doubtless the most common formula is that which locates the essence of the story in the sustained concealment and final disclosure of Tom's parentage. "It is pleasant," writes Oliver Elton, "to consider *Tom Jones* as a puzzle and to see how well the plan works out." For others the most important unifying factor is the love affair of Tom and Sophia; for still others, the conflict between Tom and Blifil; for others again, the quasi-picaresque sequence of Tom's adventures with women and on the road. The novel, it is true, would be quite different in its total effect if any of these four lines of action had been left out, but no one of them so subsumes all the rest as to justify us in considering it, even on the level of material action, as the principle of the whole. A distinctive whole there is, however, and I venture to say that it consists, not in any mere combination of these parts, but rather in the dynamic system of actions, extending throughout the novel, by which the divergent intentions and beliefs of a large number of persons of different characters and states of knowledge belonging to or somehow related to the neighboring families of the Allworthys and the Westerns are made to cooperate, with the assistance of Fortune, first to bring Tom into an incomplete and precarious union, founded on an affinity of nature in spite of a disparity of status, with Allworthy and Sophia; then to separate him as completely as possible from them through actions that impel both of them, one after the other, to reverse their opinions of his character; and then, just as he seems about to fulfil the old prophecy that "he was certainly born to be hanged," to restore them unexpectedly to him in a more entire and stable union of both affection and fortune than he has known before.

The unity of *Tom Jones* is contained in this formula, but only potentially; and before we can properly discuss the plot as an artistic principle we must examine, in some detail, the intricate scheme of probabilities, involving moral choices, mistaken judgments, and accidents of Fortune, which binds its many parts together from the time we first see Tom in Allworthy's bed until we leave him, calmly enjoying his double good luck, at the end of Book XVIII. . . .

NOTES

1. Arthur Murphy (1762), quoted in Frederic T. Blanchard, *Fielding the Novelist: A Study in Historical Criticism* (New Haven, Conn.: Yale University Press, 1927), 161.
2. *Dissertations Moral and Critical* (1783), quoted in Blanchard, 222–23.

3. Ibid., 320–21.

4. Ibid., 327.

5. The phrase is Oliver Elton's in *A Survey of English Literature, 1730–1780* (New York: Macmillan, 1928), 1:195. See also Wilbur L. Cross, *The History of Henry Fielding* (New Haven, Conn.: Yale University Press, 1918), 2:160–61; Aurélien Digeon, *Les Romans de Fielding* (Paris, 1923), 210–16; Elizabeth Jenkins, *Henry Fielding* (London: Denver, 1947), 57–58; and George Sherburn, in *A Literary History of England,* ed. Albert C. Baugh (New York and London: Appleton-Century-Crofts, 1948), 957–58; cf. his interesting introduction to the "Modern Library College Editions" reprint of *Tom Jones* (New York, 1950), ix–x.

6. Elton, *A Survey of English Literature,* 1:195.

7. Cross, *The History of Henry Fielding,* 2:159-61; Elton, *A Survey of English Literature,* 1:195–96.

8. See above, pp. 65–68, 588–92.

9. This accounts in large part, I think, for the depreciation of "plot" in E. M. Forster's *Aspects of the Novel,* and for his notion of a rivalry between "plot" and "character," in which one or the other may "triumph." For a view much closer to that argued in this essay see Elizabeth Bowen, "Notes on Writing a Novel," *Orion* 2 (1945): 18 ff.

10. The meaning and force of this will be clear to anyone who has compared in detail the text of *The Ambassadors* with James's preliminary synopsis of the novel (*The Notebooks of Henry James* [New York: Oxford University Press, 1947], 372–415). See also the excellent remarks of Allen Tate, apropos of *Madame Bovary,* in his "Techniques of Fiction" (*Forms of Modern Fiction,* ed. William Van O'Connor [Minneapolis: University of Minnesota Press, 1948], esp. 37–45).

8

The Argument of Comedy

NORTHROP FRYE

The Greeks produced two kinds of comedy, Old Comedy, represented by the eleven extant plays of Aristophanes, and New Comedy, of which the best known exponent is Menander. About two dozen New Comedies survive in the work of Plautus and Terence. Old Comedy, however, was out of date before Aristophanes himself was dead; and today, when we speak of comedy, we normally think of something that derives from the Menandrine tradition.

New Comedy unfolds from what may be described as a comic Oedipus situation. Its main theme is the successful effort of a young man to outwit an opponent and possess the girl of his choice. The opponent is usually the father (*senex*), and the psychological descent of the heroine from the mother is also sometimes hinted at. The father frequently wants the same girl, and is cheated out of her by the son, the mother thus becoming the son's ally. The girl is usually a slave or courtesan, and the plot turns on a *cognitio* or discovery of birth which makes her marriageable. Thus it turns out that she is not under an insuperable taboo after all but is an accessible object of desire, so that the plot follows the regular wish-fullfillment pattern. Often the central Oedipus situation is thinly concealed by surrogates or doubles of the main characters, as when the heroine is discovered to be the hero's sister, and has to be married off to his best friend. In Congreve's *Love for Love,* to take a modern instance well within the Menandrine tradition, there are two Oedipus themes in counterpoint: the hero cheats his father out of the heroine, and his best friend violates the wife of an impotent old man who is the heroine's guardian. Whether this analysis is sound or not, New Comedy is certainly concerned with the maneuvering of a young man toward a young woman, and marriage is the tonic chord on which it ends. The normal comic resolution is the surrender of the *senex* to the hero, never the reverse. Shakespeare tried to reverse the pattern in *All's Well That Ends Well,* where the king of France forces Bertram to marry Helena, and the critics have not yet stopped making faces over it.

New Comedy has the blessing of Aristotle, who greatly preferred it to its predecessor, and it exhibits the general pattern of Aristotelian causation. It has a material cause in the young man's sexual desire, and a formal cause in the social order represented by the *senex,* with which the hero comes to terms when he gratifies his desire. It has an efficient cause in the character who brings about the final situation. In classical times this character is a tricky slave; Renaissance dramatists often use some adaptation of the medieval "vice"; modern writers generally like to pretend that nature, or at least the natural course of events, is the efficient cause. The final cause is the audience, which is expected by its applause to take part in the comic resolution. All this takes place on a single order of existence. The action of New Comedy tends to become probable rather than fantastic, and it moves toward realism and away from myth and romance. The one romantic (originally mythical) feature in it, the fact that the hero or heroine turns out to be freeborn or someone's heir, is precisely the feature that trained New Comedy audiences tire of most quickly.

The conventions of New Comedy are the conventions of Jonson and Molière, and a fortiori of the English Restoration and the French rococo. When Ibsen started giving ironic twists to the same formulas, his startled hearers took them for portents of a social revolution. Even the old chestnut about the heroine's being really the hero's sister turns up in *Ghosts* and *Little Eyolf.* The average movie of today is a rigidly conventionalized New Comedy proceeding toward an act which, like death in Greek tragedy, takes place offstage, and is symbolized by the final embrace.

In all good New Comedy there is a social as well as an individual theme which must be sought in the general atmosphere of reconciliation that makes the final marriage possible. As the hero gets closer to the heroine and opposition is overcome, all the right-thinking people come over to his side. Thus a new social unit is formed on the stage, and the moment that this social unit crystallizes is the moment of the comic resolution. In the last scene, when the dramatist usually tries to get all his characters on the stage at once, the audience witnesses the birth of a renewed sense of social integration. In comedy as in life the regular expression of this is a festival, whether a marriage, a dance, or a feast. Old Comedy has, besides a marriage, a *komos,* the processional dance from which comedy derives its name; and the masque, which is a by-form of comedy, also ends in a dance.

This new social integration may be called, first, a kind of moral norm and, second, the pattern of a free society. We can see this more clearly if we look at the sort of characters who impede the progress of the comedy toward the hero's victory. These are always people who are in some kind of mental bondage, who are helplessly driven by ruling passions, neurotic compulsions, social rituals, and selfishness. The miser, the hypochondriac, the hypocrite, the pedant, the snob: these are humors, people who do not fully know what they are doing, who are slaves to a predictable self-imposed pattern of behavior. What we call the moral norm is, then, not morality but deliverance from moral bondage. Comedy is designed not to condemn evil, but to ridicule a lack of self-knowledge. It finds the virtues of Malvolio and Angelo as comic as the vices of Shylock.

The essential comic resolution, therefore, is an individual release which is also a social reconciliation. The normal individual is freed from the bonds of a humorous society, and a normal society is freed from the bonds imposed on it by humorous individuals. The Oedipus pattern we noted in New Comedy belongs to the individual side of this, and the sense of the ridiculousness of the humor to the social side. But all real comedy is based on the principle that these two forms of release are ultimately the same: this principle may be seen at its most concentrated in *The Tempest*. The rule holds whether the resolution is expressed in social terms, as in *The Merchant of Venice,* or in individual terms, as in Ibsen's *An Enemy of the People.*

The freer the society, the greater the variety of individuals it can tolerate, and the natural tendency of comedy is to include as many as possible in its final festival. The motto of comedy is Terence's "Nothing human is alien to me." This may be one reason for the traditional comic importance of the parasite, who has no business to be at the festival but is nevertheless there. The spirit of reconciliation which pervades the comedies of Shakespeare is not to be ascribed to a personal attitude of his own, about which we know nothing whatever, but to his impersonal concentration on the laws of comic form.

Hence the moral quality of the society presented is not the point of the comic resolution. In Jonson's *Volpone* the final assertion of the moral norm takes the form of a social revenge on Volpone, and the play ends with a great bustle of sentences to penal servitude and the galleys. One feels perhaps that the audience's sense of the moral norm does not need so much hard labor. In *The Alchemist,* when Lovewit returns to his house, the virtuous characters have proved so weak and the rascals so ingenious that the action dissolves in laughter. Whichever is morally the better ending, that of *The Alchemist* is more concentrated comedy. *Volpone* is starting to move toward tragedy, toward the vision of a greatness which develops *hybris* and catastrophe.

The same principle is even clearer in Aristophanes. Aristophanes is the most personal of writers: his opinions on every subject are written all over his plays, and we have no doubt of his moral attitude. We know that he wanted peace with Sparta and that he hated Cleon, and when his comedy depicts the attaining of peace and the defeat of Cleon we know that he approved and wanted his audience to approve. But in *Ecclesiazusae* a band of women in disguise railroad a communistic scheme through the Assembly, which is a horrid parody of Plato's Republic, and proceed to inaugurate Plato's sexual communism with some astonishing improvements. Presumably Aristophanes did not applaud this, yet the comedy follows the same pattern and the same resolution. In *The Birds* the Peisthetairos who defies Zeus and blocks out Olympus with his Cloud-Cuckoo-Land is accorded the same triumph that is given to the Trygaeus of the *Peace* who flies to heaven and brings a golden age back to Athens.

Comedy, then, may show virtue her own feature and scorn her own image—for Hamlet's famous definition of drama was originally a definition of comedy. It may emphasize the birth of an ideal society as you like it, or the tawdriness of the sham society which is the way of the world. There is an important parallel here with tragedy. Tragedy, we are told, is expected to raise but not ultimately to accept, the emotions of pity and terror. These I take to be the sense of moral good and evil, respectively, which we attach to the tragic hero. He may be as good as Caesar, and so appeal to our pity, or as bad as Macbeth, and so appeal to terror, but the particular thing called tragedy that happens to him does not depend on his moral status. The tragic catharsis passes beyond moral judgment, and while it is quite possible to construct a moral tragedy, what tragedy gains in morality it loses in cathartic power. The same is true of the comic catharsis, which raises sympathy and ridicule on a moral basis, but passes beyond both.

Many things are involved in the tragic catharsis, but one of them is a mental or imaginative form of the sacrificial ritual out of which tragedy arose. This is the ritual of the struggle, death, and rebirth of a god-man, which is linked to the yearly triumph of spring over winter. The tragic hero is not really killed, and the audience no longer eats his body and drinks his blood, but the corresponding thing in art still takes place. The audience enters into communion with the body of the hero, becoming thereby a single body itself. Comedy grows out of the same ritual, for in the ritual the tragic story has a comic sequel. Divine men do not die: they die and rise again. The ritual pattern behind the catharsis of comedy is the resurrection that follows the death, the epiphany or manifestation of the risen hero. This is clear enough in Aristophanes, where the hero is treated as a risen god-man, led in triumph with the divine honors of the Olympic victor, rejuvenated, or hailed as a new Zeus. In New Comedy the new human body is, as we have seen, both a hero and a social group. Aristophanes is not only closer to the ritual pattern, but contemporary with Plato; and his comedy, unlike Menander's, is Platonic and dialectic: it seeks not the entelechy of the soul but the Form of the Good, and finds it in the resurrection of the soul from the world of the cave to the sunlight. The audience gains a vision of that resurrection whether the conclusion is joyful or ironic, just as in tragedy it gains a vision of a heroic death whether the hero is morally innocent or guilty.

Two things follow from this: first, that tragedy is really implicit or uncompleted comedy; second, that comedy contains a potential tragedy within itself. With regard to the latter, Aristophanes is full of traces of the original death of the hero which preceded his resurrection in the ritual. Even in New Comedy the dramatist usually tries to bring his action as close to a tragic overthrow of the hero as he can get it, and reverses this movement as suddenly as possible. In Plautus the tricky slave is often forgiven or even freed after having been threatened with all the brutalities that a very brutal dramatist can think of, including crucifixion. Thus the resolution of New Comedy seems to be a realistic foreshortening of a death-and-resurrection pattern, in which the struggle and rebirth of a divine hero has shrunk into a marriage, the freeing of a slave, and the triumph of a young man over an older one.

As for the conception of tragedy as implicit comedy, we may notice how often tragedy closes on the major chord of comedy: the Aeschylean trilogy, for instance, proceeds to what is really a comic resolution, and so do many tragedies of Euripides. From the point of view of Christianity, too, tragedy is an episode in that larger scheme of redemption and resurrection to which Dante gave the name of *commedia*. This conception of commedia enters drama with the miracle-play cycles, where such tragedies as the Fall and the Crucifixion are episodes of a dramatic scheme in which the divine comedy has the last word. The sense of tragedy as a prelude to comedy is hardly separable from anything explicitly Christian. The serenity of the final double chorus in the St. Matthew Passion would hardly be attainable if composer and audience did not know that there was more to the story. Nor would the death of Samson lead to "calm of mind all passion spent" if Samson were not a prototype of the rising Christ.

New Comedy is thus contained, so to speak, within the symbolic structure of Old Comedy, which in its turn is contained within the Christian conception of *commedia*. This sounds like a logically exhaustive classification, but we have still not caught Shakespeare in it.

It is only in Jonson and the Restoration writers that English comedy can be called a form of New Comedy. The earlier tradition established by Peele and developed by Lyly, Greene, and the masque writers, which uses themes from romance and folklore and avoids the comedy of manners, is the one followed by Shakespeare. These themes are largely medieval in origin, and derive, not from the mysteries or the moralities or the interludes, but from a fourth dramatic tradition. This is the drama of folk ritual, of the St. George play and the mummers' play, of the feast of the ass and the Boy Bishop, and of all the dramatic activity that punctuated the Christian calendar with the rituals of an immemorial paganism. We may call this the drama of the green world, and its theme is once again the triumph of life over the waste land, the death and revival of the year impersonated by figures still human, and once divine as well.

When Shakespeare began to study Plautus and Terence, his dramatic instinct, stimulated by his predecessors, divined that there was a profounder pattern in the argument of comedy than appears in either of them. At once—for the process is beginning in *The Comedy of Errors*—he started groping toward that profounder pattern, the ritual of death and revival that also underlies Aristophanes, of which an exact equivalent lay ready to hand in the drama of the green world. This parallelism largely accounts for the resemblances to Greek ritual which Colin Still has pointed out in *The Tempest.*

The Two Gentlemen of Verona is an orthodox New Comedy except for one thing. The hero Valentine becomes captain of a band of outlaws in a forest, and all the other characters are gathered into this forest and become converted. Thus the action of the comedy begins in a world represented as a normal world, moves into the green world, goes into a metamorphosis there in which the comic resolution is achieved, and returns to the normal world. The forest in this play is the embryonic form of the fairy world of *A Midsummer Night's Dream,* the Forest of Arden in *As You Like It,* Windsor Forest in *The Merry Wives of Windsor,* and the pastoral world of the mythical sea-coasted Bohemia in *The Winter's Tale.* In all these comedies there is the same rhythmic movement from normal world to green world and back again. Nor is this second world confined to the forest comedies. In *The Merchant of Venice* the two worlds are a little harder to see, yet Venice is clearly not the same world as that of Portia's mysterious house in Belmont, where there are caskets teaching that gold and silver are corruptible goods, and from whence proceed the wonderful cosmological harmonies of the fifth act. In *The Tempest* the entire action takes place in the second world, and the same may be said of *Twelfth Night,* which, as its title implies, presents a carnival society, not so much a green world as an evergreen one. The second world is absent from the so-called problem comedies, which is one of the things that makes them problem comedies.

The green world charges the comedies with a symbolism in which the comic resolution contains a suggestion of the old ritual pattern of the victory of summer over winter. This is explicit in *Love's Labor's Lost.* In this very masque-like play, the comic contest takes the form of the medieval debate of winter and spring. In *The Merry Wives of Windsor* there is an elaborate ritual of the defeat of winter, known to folklorists as "carrying out Death," of which Falstaff is the victim; and Falstaff must have felt that, after being thrown into the water, dressed up as a witch and beaten out of a house with curses, and finally supplied with a beast's head and singed with candles while he said, "Divide me like a brib'd buck, each a haunch," he had done about all that could reasonably be asked of any fertility spirit.

The association of this symbolism with the death and revival of human beings, is more elusive, but still perceptible. The fact that the heroine often brings about the comic resolution by disguising herself as a boy is familiar enough. In the Hero of *Much Ado About Nothing* and the Helena of *All's Well That Ends Well,* this theme of the withdrawal and return of the heroine comes as close to a death and revival as Elizabethan conventions will allow. The Thaisa of *Pericles* and the Fidele of *Cymbeline* are beginning to crack the conventions, and with the disappearance and revival of Hermione in *The Winter's Tale,* who actually returns once as a ghost in a dream, the original nature-myth of Demeter and Proserpine is openly established. The fact that the dying and reviving character is usually female strengthens the feeling that there is something maternal about the green world, in which the new order of the comic resolution is nourished and brought to birth. However, a similar theme which is very like the rejuvenation of the *senex* so frequent in Aristophanes occurs in the folklore motif of the healing of the impotent king on which *All's Well That Ends Well* is based, and this theme is probably involved in the symbolism of Prospero.

The conception of a second world bursts the boundaries of Menandrine comedy, yet it is clear that the world of Puck is no world of eternal forms or divine revelation. Shakespeare's comedy is not Aristotelian and realistic like Menander's, nor Platonic and dialectic like Aristophanes', nor Thomist and sacramental like Dante's, but a fourth kind. It is an Elizabethan kind, and is not confined either to Shakespeare or to the drama. Spenser's epic is a wonderful contrapuntal intermingling of two orders of existence, one the red and white world of English history, the other the green world of the Faerie Queene. The latter is a world of crusading virtues proceeding from the Faerie Queene's court and designed to return to that court when the destiny of the other world is fulfilled. The fact that the Faerie Queene's knights are sent out during the twelve days of the Christmas festival suggests our next point.

Shakespeare, too, has his green world of comedy and his red and white world of history. The story of the latter is at one point interrupted by an invasion from the comic world, when Falstaff *senex et parasitus* throws his gigantic shadow over Prince Henry, assuming on one occasion the role of his father. Clearly, if the Prince is ever to conquer France he must reassert the moral norm. The moral norm is duly reasserted, but the rejection of Falstaff is not a comic resolution. In comedy the moral norm is not morality but deliverance, and we certainly do not feel delivered from Falstaff as we feel delivered from Shylock with his absurd and vicious bond. The moral norm does not carry with it the vision of a free society: Falstaff will always keep a bit of that in his tavern.

Falstaff is a mock king, a lord of misrule, and his tavern is a Saturnalia. Yet we are reminded of the original meaning of the Saturnalia, as a rite intended to recall the golden age of Saturn. Falstaff's world is not a golden world, but as long as we remember it we cannot forget that the world of *Henry V* is an iron one. We are reminded too of another traditional denizen of the green world, Robin Hood, the outlaw who manages to suggest a better kind of society than those who make him an outlaw can produce. The outlaws in *The Two Gentlemen of Verona* compare themselves, in spite of the Italian setting, to Robin Hood, and in *As You Like It* Charles the wrestler says of Duke Senior's followers: "There they live like the old Robin Hood of England: they say many young gentlemen flock to him every day, and fleet the time carelessly, as they did in the golden world."

In the histories, therefore, the comic Saturnalia is a temporary reversal of normal standards, comic "relief" as it is called, which subsides and allows the history to continue. In the comedies, the green world suggests an original golden age which the normal world has usurped and which makes us wonder if it is not the normal world that is the real Saturnalia. In *Cymbeline* the green world finally triumphs over a historical theme, the reason being perhaps that in that play the incarnation of Christ, which is contemporary with Cymbeline, takes place offstage, and accounts for the halcyon peace with which the play concludes. From then on in Shakespeare's plays, the green world has it all its own way, and both in *Cymbeline* and in *Henry VIII* there may be suggestions that Shakespeare, like Spenser, is moving toward a synthesis of the two worlds, a wedding of Prince Arthur and the Faerie Queene.

This world of fairies, dreams, disembodied souls, and pastoral lovers may not be a "real" world, but, if not, there is something equally illusory in the stumbling and blinded follies of the "normal" world, of Theseus's Athens with its idiotic marriage law, of Duke Frederick and his melancholy tyranny, of Leontes and his mad jealousy, of the Court Party with their plots and intrigues. The famous speech of Prospero about the dream nature of reality applies equally to Milan and the enchanted island. We spend our lives partly in a waking world we call normal and partly in a dream world which we create out of our own desires. Shakespeare endows both worlds with equal imaginative power, brings them opposite one another, and makes each world seem unreal when seen by the light of the other. He uses freely both the heroic triumph of New Comedy and the ritual resurrection of its predecessor, but his distinctive comic resolution is different from either: it is a detachment of the spirit born of this reciprocal reflection of two illusory realities. We need not ask whether this brings us into a higher order of existence or not, for the question of existence is not relevant to poetry.

We have spoken of New Comedy as Aristotelian, Old Comedy as Platonic, and Dante's *commedia* as Thomist, but it is difficult to suggest a philosophical spokesman for the form of Shakespeare's comedy. For Shakespeare, the subject matter of poetry is not life, or nature, or reality, or revelation, or anything else that the philosopher builds on, but poetry itself, a verbal universe. That is one reason why he is both the most elusive and the most substantial of poets.

9

Emphasis Added: Plots and Plausibilities in Women's Fiction

NANCY K. MILLER

> Nothing came down the street; nobody passed. A single leaf detached itself from the plane tree at the end of the street, and in that pause and suspension fell. Somehow it was like a signal falling, a signal pointing to a force in things which one had overlooked.
>
> —Virginia Woolf, *A Room of One's Own*[1]

If we take *La Princesse de Clèves* as the first text of women's fiction in France, then we may observe that French women's fiction has from its beginnings been *discredited*.[2] By this I mean literally and literarily denied credibility: "Mme. de Clèves's confession to her husband," writes Bussy-Rabutin to his cousin Mme. de Sévigné, "is extravagant, and can only happen [*se dire*] in a true story; but when one is inventing a story for its own sake [*à plaisir*] it is ridiculous to ascribe such extraordinary feelings to one's heroine. The author in so doing was more concerned about not resembling other novels than obeying common sense."[3] Without dwelling on the local fact that a similarly "singular" confession had appeared in Mme. de Villedieu's *Les Désordres de l'amour* some three years before the publication of Mme. de Lafayette's novel, and bracketing the more general fact that the novel as a genre has from its beginnings labored under charges of *invraisemblance*,[4] let us reread Bussy-Rabutin's complaint. In a true story, as in "true confessions," the avowal would be believable because in life, unlike art, anything can happen; hence the constraints of likeliness do not apply. In a made-up story, however, the confession offends because it violates our readerly expectations about fiction. In other words, art should not imitate life but reinscribe received ideas about the representation of life in art. To depart from the limits of common sense (tautologically, to be extravagant) is to risk exclusion from the canon.[5] Because—as Genette, glossing this same document in "Vraisemblance et motivation," puts it—"*extravagance is a privilege of the real*,"[6] to produce a work not like other novels, an original rather than a copy, means paradoxically that its literariness will be sniffed out: "The first adventure of the Coulommiers gardens is not plausible," Bussy-Rabutin observes later in his letter, "and reeks of fiction [*sent le roman*]."

Genette begins his essay with an analysis of contemporary reactions to *La Princesse de Clèves*. Reviewing the writings of seventeenth-century poeticians, Genette shows that *vraisemblance* and *bienséance*, "plausibility" and "propriety," are wedded to each other; and the precondition of plausibility is the stamp of approval affixed by public *opinion:* "Real or assumed, this 'opinion' is quite close to what today would be called an ideology, that is, a body of maxims and prejudices which constitute both a vision of the world and a system of values" (73). What this statement means is that the critical reaction to any given text is hermeneutically bound to another and preexistent text: the *doxa* of socialities. Plausibility then is an effect of reading through a grid of concordance:

> What defines plausibility is the formal principle of respect for the norm, that is, the existence of a relation of implication between the particular conduct attributed to a given character, and a given, general, received and implicit maxim. . . . To understand the behavior of a character (for example), is to be able to refer it back to an approved maxim, and this reference is perceived as a demonstration of cause and effect. (174–75)

If no maxim is available to account for a particular piece of behavior, that behavior is read as unmotivated and unconvincing. Mme. de Clèves's confession makes no sense in the seventeenth-century sociolect because it is, Genette underlines, *"an action without a maxim"* (75). A heroine without a maxim, like a rebel without a cause, is destined to be misunderstood. And she is.

To build a narrative around a character whose behavior is deliberately idiopathic, however, is not merely to create a puzzling fiction but to fly in the face of a certain ideology (of the text and its context), to violate a grammar of motives that describes while prescribing, in this instance, what wives, not to say women, should or should not do. The question one might then ask is whether this crucial barbarism is in any way connected to the gender of its author. If we were to uncover a feminine "tradition"— diachronic recurrences—of such ungrammaticalities, would we have the basis for a poetics of women's fiction? And what do I mean by women's fiction?

Working backward, I should say first that I do not mean what is designated in France these days as *écriture féminine*, which can be described roughly as a process or a practice by which the female *body*, with its peculiar drives and rhythms, inscribes itself as text.[7] "Feminine writing" is an important

theoretical formulation; but it privileges a textuality of the avant-garde, a literary production of the late twentieth century, and it is therefore fundamentally a hope, if not a blueprint for the future. In what is perhaps the best-known
statement of contemporary French feminist thinking about women's writing,
"The Laugh of the Medusa," Hélène Cixous states that, "with a few rare
exceptions, there has not yet been any writing that inscribes femininity."[8] On
the contrary, what she finds historically in the texts of the "immense majority" of female writers is "workmanship [which is] . . . in no way different
from male writing, and which either obscures women or reproduces the classic representations of women (as sensitive—intuitive—dreamy, etc.)" (878). I
think this assertion is both true and untrue. It is true if one is looking for a
radical difference in women's writing and locates that difference in an insur-
gence of the body, in what Julia Kristeva has called the irruption of the semiotic.[9] And it is true again if difference is sought on the level of the sentence,
or in what might be thought of as the biofeedback of the text. If, however, we
situate difference in the insistence of a certain thematic structuration, in the
form of content, then it is not true that women's writing has been in no way
different from male writing. I consider the "demaximization" wrought by
Mme de Lafayette to be one example of how difference can be read.

Before I proceed to other manifestations of difference, let me make a few
general remarks about the status of women's literature—about its existence, in
my view, as a viable corpus for critical inquiry. Whether one believes, as does
Cixous, that there is "male writing," "*marked* writing . . . run by a libidinal
and cultural—hence political, typically masculine economy" (879), or that
(great) literature has no sex because a "great mind must be androgynous," literary *history* remains a male preserve, a history of writing by men.[10] In England the history of the novel admits the names of Jane Austen, the Brontës,
George Eliot, and Virginia Woolf. In France it includes Mme de Lafayette,
although only for *La Princesse de Clèves* and always with the nagging insinua-
tion that La Rochefoucauld had a hand in that. Mme de Staël, George Sand,
and Colette figure in the national record, although mainly as the scandalous
heroines of their times. Nevertheless, there have always been women writing.
What is one to do with them? One can leave them where they are, like so
many sleeping dogs, and mention them only in passing as epiphenomena in
every period, despite the incontrovertible evidence that most were successful
and even literarily influential in their day. One can continue, then, a politics
of benign neglect that reads difference, not to say popularity, as inferiority. Or
one can perform two simultaneous and compensatory gestures: the archaeo-
logical and rehabilitative act of discovering and recovering "lost" women writers and the reconstructive and reevaluative act of establishing a parallel literary
tradition, as Elaine Showalter has done in *A Literature of Their Own* and Ellen

Moers in *Literary Women*.[11] The advantage of these moves is that they make visible an otherwise invisible intertext: a reconstituted record of predecession and prefiguration, debts acknowledged and unacknowledged, anxieties and enthusiasms.

Elizabeth Janeway, by way of T. S. Eliot, has suggested another way of thinking about women's literature. She cites the evolution in Eliot's attitude toward that body of texts we know as American literature. At first he held, as many critics have about women's literature, that it does not exist: "There can only be one English literature. . . . There cannot be British or American literature." Later, however, he was to acknowledge "what has never, I think, been found before, two literatures in the same language."[12] That reformulation, as Janeway adapts it to delineate the continent of women's literature, is useful because it locates the problem of identity and difference not on the level of the sentence—not as a question of another language—but on the level of the text in all its complexities: a culturally bound and, I would even say, culturally overdetermined production. This new mapping of a parallel geography does not, of course, resolve the oxymoron of marginality: how is it that women, a statistical majority in our culture, perform as a "literary subculture"?[13] But it does provide a body of writing from which to begin to identify specificities in women's relation to writing and the specificities that derive from that relation. Because women are both of the culture and out of it (or under it), written by it and remaining a largely silent though literate majority, to look for *uniquely* "feminine" textual indexes that can be deciphered in "blind" readings is pointless. (Documentation on the critical reception of *Jane Eyre* and *Adam Bede*, for example, has shown how silly such pretensions can be.[14]) There are no infallible signs, no fail-safe technique by which to determine the gender of an author. But that is not the point of the *post*-compensatory gesture that follows what I call the new literary history. At stake instead is a reading that *consciously* recreates the object it describes, attentive always to a difference—what T. S. Eliot calls "strong local flavor" (quoted in Janeway, 344) not dependent on the discovery of an exclusive alterity.

The difficulty of the reading comes from the irreducibly complicated relationship women have historically had to the language of the dominant culture, a "flirtatious" relationship that Luce Irigaray has called mimetic:

> To play with mimesis is . . . for a woman to try to recover the place of her
> exploitation by language, without allowing herself to be simply reduced to
> it. It is to resubmit herself . . . to ideas—notably about her—elaborated in
> and through a masculine logic, but to "bring out" by an effect of playful rep-
> etition what was to remain hidden: the recovery of a possible operation of
> the feminine in language. It is also to unveil the fact that if women mime so

well they are not simply reabsorbed in this function. *They also remain else-where.* . . .[15]

This "elsewhere"—which, needless to say, is not so easily pinpointed—is, she adds, an insistence of "matter" and "sexual pleasure" (*jouissance*). I prefer to think of the insistence Irigaray posits as a form of emphasis: an italicized version of what passes for the neutral or standard face. Spoken or written, italics are a modality of intensity and stress; a way of marking what has always already been said, of making a common text one's own. Italics are also a form of intonation, "the tunes," McConnell-Ginet writes, "to which we set the text of our talk." "Intonation," she continues, "serves to underscore the gender identification of the participants in certain contexts of communication," and because of differences in intonation, "women's tunes will be interpreted and evaluated from an androcentric perspective."[16] When I speak of italics, then, I mean the emphasis added by registering a certain quality of voice. And this expanded metaphor brings me back to my point of departure.

Genette codes the perception of plausibility in terms of silence:

> The relationship between a plausible narrative and the system of plausibility to which it subjects itself is . . . essentially mute: the conventions of genre function like a system of natural forces and constraints which the narrative obeys as if without noticing them, and a *fortiori* without naming them. (76)

By fulfilling the "tacit contract between a work and its public" (77) this silence both gives pleasure and signifies conformity with the dominant ideology. The text emancipated from this collusion, however, is also silent, in that it refuses to justify its infractions, the "motives and maxims of the actions" (78). Here Genette cites the silence surrounding Julien Sorel's attempted murder of Mme. de Renal and the confession of Mme. de Clèves. In the first instance, the ideologically complicitous text, the silence is a function of what Genette calls "plausible narrative"; in the second it is a function of "arbitrary narrative" (79). And the *sounds* of silence? They are heard in a third type of narrative, one with a motivated and *"artificial plausibility"* (79): this literature, exemplified by the "endless chatting" of a Balzaeian novel, we might call "other-directed," for here authorial commentary justifies its story to society by providing the missing maxims, or by inventing them. In the arbitrary narrative Genette sees a rejection of the ideology of a certain plausibility—an ideology, let us say, of accountability. This "inner-directed" posture would proclaim instead "that rugged individuality which makes for the unpredictability of great actions—and great works" (77).

Two remarks are in order here. Arbitrariness can be taken as an ideology in itself, that is, as the irreducible freedom and originality of the author (Bussy-Rabutin's complaint, *en somme*). But more specifically, the refusal of the demands of one economy may mask the inscription of another. This inscription may seem silent, or *unarticulated* in/as *authorial commentary (discours)*, without being absent. (It may simply be inaudible to the dominant mode of reception.) In *La Princesse de Clèves,* for example, "extravagance" is in fact accounted for, I would argue, both by maxims and by a decipherable effect of italicization. The maxims I refer to are not direct commentary; and it is true, as Genette writes, that "nothing is more foreign to the style [of the novel] than sententious epiphrasis: as if the actions were always either beyond or beneath all commentary" (78). It is also true that within the narrative the characters do comment on the actions; and although Genette does not "count" such comments as "chatting," I would suggest that they constitute an internally motivating discourse: an artificial plausibility *en abyme*. This intratext is maternal discourse; and its *performance* through the "extraordinary feelings" of Mme. de Clèves is an instance of italicization. The confession, to state the obvious, makes perfect sense in terms of the idiolect spoken by Mme. de Chartres: "Be brave and strong, my daughter; withdraw from the court, force your husband to take you away; do not fear the most brutal and difficult measures; however awful they may seem at first, in the end they will be milder in their effects than the misery of a love affair" (68).[17] Moreover, the confession qua confession is set up by *reference* to a "real life" precedent and is presented by the prince himself as a model of desirable behavior: "Sincerity is so important to me that I think that if my mistress, and even my wife, confessed to me that she was attracted by another . . . I would cast off the role of lover or husband to advise and sympathize with her" (76). Seen from this perspective the behavior of the princess is both *motivated* within the narration and supplied with a pretext: the conditions of *imitation*.

But the confession, which I may already have overemphasized, is not an isolated extravagance in the novel. It is a link in the chain of events that lead to Mme. de Clèves's decision not to marry Nemours, even though in *this* instance, the maxims of the sociolect might support, even expect, the marriage. As Bussy-Rabutin again observes, "And if, against all appearances and custom, this combat between love and virtue were to last in her heart until the death of her husband, then she would be delighted to be able to bring love and virtue together by marrying a man of quality, the finest and the most handsome gentleman of his time." Mme. de Lafayette clearly rejects this delightful denouement. Now, Stendhal has speculated that if Mme. de Clèves had lived a long life she would have regretted her decision and would have wanted to live like Mme. de Lafayette.[18] We shall never know, of course, but his comment raises an interesting question: why did Mme. de Lafayette keep Mme. de Clèves from living in fiction the life she herself had led? The answer to that question would be an essay in itself, but let us tackle the question here from another angle: what do Mme. de Clèves's "renunciation" and, before that, her confession tell us about the relation of women writers to fiction, to the heroines of their fiction? Should the heroine's so-called "refusal of love" be read as a defeat and an end to passion—a "suicide," or "the delirium of a pré-cieuse"?[19] Or is it, rather, a *bypassing* of the dialectics of desire, and, in that sense, a peculiarly feminine "act of victory"?[20] To understand the refusal as a victory and as, I believe, a rewriting of eroticism (an emphasis placed "else-where"—as Irigaray and, curiously, Woolf say), from which we might gener-alize about the economy of representation regulating the heroine and her authors, let us shift critical gear for a while.

Claudine Hermann describes the princess as a heroine "written in a lan-guage of dream, dreamt by Mme. de Lafayette."[21] What is the language of that dream, and what is the dream of that language? In the essay called "The Rela-tion of the Poet to Daydreaming" (1908), Freud wonders how that "strange being, the poet, comes by his material."[22] He goes on to answer his question by considering the processes at work in children's play and then moves to day-dreams and fantasies in adults. When he begins to describe the characteristics of this mode of creativity, he makes a blanket generalization about its impulses that should immediately make clear the usefulness of his essay for our pur-poses: "Unsatisfied wishes are the driving power behind phantasies; every sep-arate phantasy contains the fulfillment of a wish, and improves upon unsatisfactory reality" (47). What then is the nature of these wishes and, more to our point, does the sex of the dreamer affect the shaping of the daydream's text? Here, as might be expected, Freud does not disappoint:

> The impelling wishes vary according to the sex, character and circumstances of the creator; they may easily be divided, however, into two principal groups. Either they are ambitious wishes, serving to exalt the person creating them, or they are erotic. In young women erotic wishes dominate the phantasies *almost exclusively,* for their ambition is *generally comprised* in their erotic longings; in young men egoistic and ambitious wishes assert themselves plainly enough alongside their erotic desires (47–48; emphasis added).

Here we see that the either/or antinomy, ambitious/erotic, is immediately col-lapsed to make coexistence possible in masculine fantasies: "in the greater num-ber of ambitious daydreams we can discover a woman in some corner, for whom the dreamer performs all his heroic deeds and at whose feet all his tri-umphs are to be laid" (48).

But is this observation reversible? If, to make the logical extrapolation, romance dominates the female daydream and constitutes its primary heroine-ism, is there a *place* in which the ambitious wish of a young woman asserts itself? Has she an egoistic desire to be discovered "in some corner"? Freud elides the issue—while leaving the door open (for us) by his modifiers, "almost exclusively" and "generally comprised"—presumably because he is on his way to establishing the relationship between daydreaming and literary creation. The pertinence of difference there is moot, of course, because he conjures up only a male creator: not the great poet, however, but "the less pretentious writers of romances, novels and stories, who are read all the same by the widest circles of men and women" (50). Freud then proceeds to identify the key "marked characteristic" of these fictions: "They all have a hero who is the centre of interest, for whom the author tries to win our sympathy by every possible means, and whom he places under the protection of a special providence" (50). The hero in this literature is continually exposed to danger, but we follow his perilous adventures with a sense of security, because we know that at each turn he will triumph. According to Freud, the basis for this armchair security, for our tranquil contemplation, is the hero's own conviction of invincibility, best rendered by the expression "Nothing can happen to me!" And Freud comments, "It seems to me . . . that this significant mark of invulnerability very clearly betrays—His Majesty the Ego, the hero of *all daydreams* and *all novels*" (51; emphasis added). Now, if the plots of male fiction chart the daydreams of an ego that would be invulnerable, what do the plots of female fiction reveal? Among French women writers, it would seem at first blush to be the obverse negative of "nothing can happen to me." The phrase that characterizes the heroine's posture might well be a variant of Murphy's law: If anything can go wrong, it will. And the reader's sense of security, itself dependent on the heroine's, comes from feeling not that the heroine will triumph in some *conventionally* positive way but that she will transcend the perils of plot with a self-exalting dignity. Here national constraints on the imagination, or what in this essay Freud calls "racial psychology," do seem to matter: the second-chance rerouting of disaster typical of Jane Austen's fiction, for example, is exceedingly rare in France. To the extent that we can speak of a triumph of Her Majesty the Ego in France, it lies in being beyond vulnerability, indeed beyond it all. On the whole, French women writers prefer what Peter Brooks has described as "the melodramatic imagination," a dreamlike and metaphorical drama of the "moral occult."[23] There are recurrent melodramatic plots about women unhappy in love because men are men and women are women. As I said earlier, however, the suffering seems to have its own rewards in the economy of the female unconscious. The heroine proves to be better than her victimizers; and perhaps this ultimate superiority, which is to be read in the choice to go beyond love, beyond "erotic longings," is the figure that the "ambitious wishes" of women writers (dreamers) takes.

In the economy of Freud's plot, as we all know, fantasy scenarios are generated by consciously repressed content; and so he naturally assumes a motive for the "concealment" of "ambitious wishes": "the overweening self-regard" that a young man "acquires in the indulgent atmosphere surrounding his childhood" must be suppressed "so that he may find his proper place in a society that is full of other persons making similar claims" (48)—hence the daydreams in which the hero conquers all to occupy victoriously center stage. The content that a young woman represses comes out in erotic daydreams because "a well-brought-up woman is, indeed, credited with only a minimum of erotic desire" (48). Indeed. Now, there is a class of novels by women that "maximizes" that minimum, a type of fiction that George Eliot attacks as "Silly Novels by Lady Novelists": "The heroine is usually an heiress . . . with perhaps a vicious baronet, an amiable duke, and an irresistible younger son of a marquis as lovers in the foreground, a clergyman and a poet sighing for her in the middle distance, and a crowd of undefined adorers dimly indicated beyond."[24] After sketching out the variations of plot that punctuate the heroine's "'starring' expedition through life" (302), Eliot comments on the security with which we await the inevitably happy end:

> Before matters arrive at this desirable issue our feelings are tried by seeing the noble, lovely and gifted heroine pass through many *mauvais moments,* but we have the satisfaction of knowing that her sorrows are wept into embroidered pocket-handkerchiefs . . . and that whatever vicissitudes she may undergo . . . she comes out of them all with a complexion more blooming and locks more redundant than ever. (303).

The plots of these "silly novels" bring grist to Freud's mill—that is, the grist I bring to his mill—in an almost uncanny way; and they would seem to undermine the argument I am on the verge of elaborating. But as Eliot says:

> Happily, we are not dependent on argument to prove that Fiction is a department of literature in which women can, after their kind, fully equal men. A cluster of great names, both living and dead, rush to our memories in evidence that women can produce novels not only fine, but among the very finest;—novels too, that have a precious specialty, lying quite apart from masculine aptitudes and experience. (324).

(Let me work through her essay to my own.) What Eliot is attacking here is not only the relationship of certain women writers to literature but the critical reception given women's fiction. We might also say that she is attacking, the better to separate herself from, those women writers whose language is structured exactly like the unconscious that Freud has assigned to them, those writers (and their heroines) whose ambitious wishes are contained *entirely* in their erotic longings. And she is attacking these novelists, the better to defend, *not* those women who write *like* men (for she posits a "precious specialty" to women's production), but those women who write in their own way, "after their kind," and implicitly about something else. Silly novels are that popular artifact which has always been and still is known as "women's literature"—a term, I should add, applied to such fiction by those who do not read it.[25]

Women writers then, in contrast to lady novelists, are writers whose texts would be "among the finest" (to stay with Eliot's terminology) and for whom the "ambitious wish" (to stay with Freud's) manifests itself as fantasy within another economy. In this economy, egoistic desires would assert themselves paratactically alongside erotic ones. The repressed content, I think, would be, not erotic impulses, but an impulse to power: a fantasy of power that would revise the social grammar in which women are never defined as subjects; a fantasy of power that disdains a sexual exchange in which women can participate only as objects of circulation. The daydreams or fictions of women writers would then, like those of men, say, "Nothing can happen to me!" But the modalities of that invulnerability would be marked in an essentially different way. I am talking, of course, about the power of the weak. The inscription of this power is not always easy to decipher, because, as has been noted, "the most essential form of accommodation for the weak is to conceal what power they do have."[26] Moreover, to pick up a lost thread, when these modalities of difference are perceived, they are generally called implausibilities. They are not perceived, or are misperceived, because the scripting of this fantasy does not bring the aesthetic "forepleasure" Freud says fantasy scenarios inevitably bring: pleasure bound to recognition and *identification* (54), the "agrément" Genette assigns to plausible narrative. (Perhaps we shall not have a poetics of women's literature until we have more weak readers.)

In *Les Voleuses de langue,* Claudine Hermann takes up what I call the politics of dreams, or the ideology of daydreaming, in *La Princesse de Clèves:*

> A daydream is perpetuated when it loses all chance of coming true, when the woman dreaming *[la rêveuse]* cannot make it pass into reality. If women did not generally experience the love they desire as a repeated impossibility, they would dream about it less. They would dream of other, perhaps more interesting things. Nevertheless, written in a language of dream, dreamt by Mme de Lafayette, the Princesse de Clèves never dreams . . . for she knows that *love as she imagines it* is not realizable. What is realizable is a counterfeit she

does not want. Her education permits her to glimpse this fact: men and women exchange feelings that are not equivalent. . . . Woman's "day-dreaming" is a function of a world in which nothing comes true on her terms (77–79).

"Men and women exchange feelings that are not equivalent." Mme. de Clèves's brief experience of the court confirms the principle of difference at the heart of her mother's maxims. Mme. de Clèves's rejection of Nemours on his terms, however, derives its necessity not only from the logic of maternal discourse (Nemours's love, like his name, is negative and plural: *ne/amours)* but also from the demands of Mme. de Lafayette's dream. In this dream nothing can happen to the heroine, because she understands that the power and pleasure of the weak derive from circumventing the laws of contingency and circulation. She withdraws then and confesses, not merely to resist possession, as her mother would have wished, but to improve on it: to *rescript* possession.

The plausibility of this novel lies in the structuration of its fantasy. For if, to continue spinning out Hermann's metaphor, the heroine does not dream, she does daydream. And perhaps the most significant confession in the novel is neither the first (to her husband, that she is vulnerable to desire) nor the third (to Nemours, that she desires him) but the second, which is silent and entirely telling: I refer, of course, to her nocturnal *rêverie* at Coulommiers. Although all three confessions prefigure by their extravagance the heroine's retreat from the eyes of the world, it is this dreamlike event that is least ambiguous in underlining the erotic valence of the ambitious scenario.

At Coulommiers, her country retreat, Mme. de Clèves sits one warm evening, secretly observed by Nemours, winding ribbons of his colors around an India cane. (I take her surreptitious acquisition of his cane to be the counterpart of his theft of her miniature, in this crisscrossing of desires by metonymy.) As Michel Butor observes in his seductive reading of this scene, "the mind of the princess is operating at this moment in a zone obscure to herself; it is as if she is knotting the ribbons around the cane in a dream, and her dream becomes clear little by little; the one she is thinking of begins to take on a face, and she goes to look for it."[27] Thus, having finished her handiwork, she places herself in front of a painting, a historical tableau of members of the court that she has had transported to her retreat, a painting including a likeness of Nemours: "She sat down and began to look at this portrait with an intensity and dreaminess [*rêverie*] that only passion can inspire" (155). And Butor comments, "One hardly needs a diploma in psychoanalysis to detect and appreciate the symbolism of this whole scene" (76). Indeed, it is quite clear that the princess is seen here in a moment of solitary pleasure, in a daydream of "fetishistic sublimation." This autoeroticism would seem to be the only sexual performance she can afford in an economy regulated by dispossession.[28]

Her retreat to Coulommiers, though, must be thought of not as a flight from sexuality but as a movement *into* it. As Sylvère Lotringer has observed, Mme. de Clèves leaves the court not to flee passion but to preserve it.[29] To preserve it, however, on her own terms. Unlike Nemours—who is not content to possess the object of his desire in representation (the purloined portrait) and who pleads silently after this scene, "Only look at me the way I saw you look at my portrait tonight; how could you look so gently at my portrait and then so cruelly fly from my presence?" (157)—the princess chooses "the duke of the portrait, not the man who seeks to step out of the frame" (Lotringer, "Structuration," 519). Here she differs from Austen's heroine Elizabeth Bennet, who stands gazing before her lover's portrait and feels "a more gentle sensation towards the original than she had ever felt in the height of their acquaintance."[30] Elizabeth can accept the hand of the man who steps out of the frame; the princess cannot. For if, in the world of *Pride and Prejudice,* "between the picture's eyes and Elizabeth's hangs what will be given shape when the marriage of the lovers is formalized" (Brownstein), in the world of the court the princess's response to Nemours must remain specular. Her desire cannot be framed by marriage—*à l'anglaise.* If, however, as I believe, the withdrawal to Coulommiers is homologous to the *final* withdrawal, then there is no reason to imagine that at a remove from the world—or, rather, in the company of the world contained by representation in painting—the princess does not continue to experience her "erotic longings." But the fulfillment of the wish is to be realized in the daydream itself.

The daydream, then, is both the stuff of fairy tales ("Someday my prince will come") and their rewriting ("Someday my prince will come, but we will not live happily ever after"). The princess refuses to marry the duke, however, not because she does not want to live happily ever after, but because she does. And by choosing not to act on that desire but to preserve it in and as fantasy, she both performs maternal discourse and italicizes it as repossession. Her choice is therefore not the simple reinscription of the seventeenth-century convention of female renunciation, dependent on the logic of either/or, but the sign of both-and, concretized by her final dual residence: in the convent *and* at home. "Perverted convention," as Peggy Kamuf names it, writing of another literary fetishist (Saint-Preux in Julie's closet): "The scene of optimal pleasure is within the prohibition which forms the walls of the house. Just on this side of the transgressive act, the fetishist's pleasure . . . is still in the closet."[31] This form of possession by metonymy both acknowledges the law and short-circuits it. Nobody, least of all the Duc de Nemours, believes in her renunciation (just as her husband never fully believed her confession):

Do you think that your resolutions can hold against a man who adores you and who is fortunate enough to attract you? It is more difficult than you think, Madame, to resist the attractions of love. You have done it *by an austere virtue which has almost no example;* but that virtue is no longer opposed to your feelings and I hope that you will follow them despite yourself. (174–75; emphasis added)

Mme. de Clèves will not be deterred by sheer difficulty, by mere plausibility, by Nemours's *maxims.* She knows herself to be without a text. "No woman but you in the world," she has been told earlier in the novel, "would confide everything she knows in her husband" (116). "The singularity of such a confession," the narrator comments after the fait accompli, "for which she could find no example, made her see all the danger of it" (125). The danger of singularity precisely is sociolinguistic: the attempt to *communicate* in a language, an idiolect, that would nonetheless break with the coded rules of communication. An impossibility, as Jakobson has seen: "Private property, in the domain of language, does not exist: everything is socialized. The verbal exchange, like every form of human relation, requires at least two interlocutors; an idiolect, in the final analysis, therefore can only be a *slightly perverse fiction.*"[32] Thus in the end Mme. de Clèves herself becomes both the impossibility of an example for others "in life" and its possibility in fiction. "Her life," the last line of the novel tells us, which "was rather short, left inimitable examples of virtue" (180). The last word in French is the challenge to reiteration—*inimitables,* the mark of the writer's ambitious wish.

I hope it is understood that I am not suggesting we read a heroine as the clone of her author—a reductionist strategy that has passed for literary criticism on women's writing from the beginning. Rather, I am arguing that the peculiar shape of a heroine's destiny in novels by women, the implausible twists of plot so common in these novels, is a form of insistence about the relation of women to writing: a comment on the stakes of difference within the theoretical indifference of literature itself.

Woolf begins her essay on Eliot in the *Common Reader* by saying, "To read George Eliot attentively is to become aware how little one knows about her." But then, a few pages later, she comments:

For long she preferred not to think of herself at all. Then, when the first flush of creative energy was exhausted and self-confidence had come to her, she wrote more and more from the personal standpoint, but she did so without the unhesitating abandonment of the young. *Her self-consciousness is always marked when her heroines say what she herself would have said.* . . . The disconcerting and stimulating fact remained that she was compelled by the very power of her genius to step forth in person upon the quiet bucolic scene.[33]

What interests me here is the "marking" Woolf identifies, an underlining of what she later describes as Eliot's heroines' "demand for something—they scarcely know what—for something that is perhaps incompatible with the facts of human existence" (175). This demand of the heroine for something else is in part what I mean by "italicization": the extravagant wish for a *story* that would turn out differently.

In the fourth chapter of Book V of *The Mill on the Floss* Maggie Tulliver, talking with Philip Wakem in the "Red Deeps," returns a novel he has lent her:

> "Take back your *Corinne*," said Maggie. "You were right in telling me she would do me no good, but you were wrong in thinking I should wish to be like her."
>
> "Wouldn't you really like to be a tenth muse, then, Maggie?". . .
>
> "Not at all," said Maggie laughing. "The muses were uncomfortable goddesses, I think—obliged always to carry rolls and musical instruments about with them. . . ."
>
> "You agree with me in not liking Corinne, then?"
>
> "I didn't finish the book," said Maggie. "As soon as I came to the blond-haired young lady reading in the park, I shut it up and determined to read no further. I foresaw that that light-complexioned girl would win away all the love from Corinne and make her miserable. I'm determined to read no more books where the blond-haired women carry away all the happiness. I should begin to have a prejudice against them. If you could give me some story, now, where the dark woman triumphs, it would restore the balance. I want to avenge Rebecca, and Flora MacIvor, and Minna, and all the rest of the dark unhappy ones."
>
> "Well, perhaps you will avenge the dark women in your own person and carry away all the love from your cousin Lucy. She is sure to have some handsome young man of St. Ogg's at her feet now, and you have only to shine upon him—your fair little cousin will be quite quenched in your beams."
>
> "Philip, that is not pretty of you, to apply my nonsense to anything real," said Maggie looking hurt.[34]

Maggie's literary instincts are correct. True to the laws of genre, Corinne—despite, that is, because of, her genius and exceptionality—is made miserable and the blonde Lucile, her half sister, carries the day, although she is deprived of a perfectly happy end. But whatever Eliot's, or Maggie's, "prejudices" against the destinies of Scott's heroines, Maggie no more than Corinne avenges the dark woman in her own person. Even though, as Philip predicts, Maggie's inner radiance momentarily quenches her fair-haired cousin, Lucy, "reality"—that is to say, Eliot's novel—proves to be as hard on dark-haired women as literature is. What is important in this deliberate intertextuality, which has not gone unnoted (see, e.g., Moers, 174), is that both heroines revolt against the text of a certain "happily ever after." As Madelyn Gutwirth observes in her book on Mme. de Staël, Corinne prefers "her genius to the . . . bonds of marriage, but that is not to say she thereby renounces happiness. On the contrary, it is her wish to be happy, that is to be herself *and* to love, that kills her."[35] Maggie Tulliver, too, would be herself and love, but the price for *that* unscriptable wish proves again to be the deferral of conventional erotic longings, what Maggie calls "earthly happiness." Almost two hundred years after the challenge to the maxim wrought by the blonde (as it turns out) Princesse de Clèves, George Eliot, through the scenario of definitive postponement, "imitates" Mme. de Lafayette.

The last two books of *The Mill on the Floss* are called, respectively, "The Great Temptation" and "The Final Rescue." As the plot moves toward closure, the chapter headings of these books—"First Impressions," "Illustrating the Laws of Attraction," "Borne Along by the Tide," "Waking," "St. Ogg's Passes Judgment," "The Last Conflict"—further emphasize the sexual struggle at the heart of the novel. For, as Philip had anticipated, Maggie dazzles blonde Lucy's fiancé, Stephen Guest, in "First Impressions," but then, surely what Philip had not dreamt of, the pair is swept away. Maggie, previously unawakened by *her* fiancé, Wakem, awakens both to her desire and to what she calls her duty, only to fulfill both by drowning, attaining at last that "wondrous happiness that is one with pain" (545). Though I do great violence to the scope of Eliot's narrative by carving a novel out of a novel, the last two books taken together as they chart the culmination of a heroine's erotic destiny have a plot of their own—a plot, moreover, with elective affinities to the conclusion of *La Princesse de Clèves,* and to the conclusion of my argument.

Like Mme. de Clèves after her husband's death, Maggie knows herself to be technically free to marry her lover but feels bound, though not for the same reasons, to another script. And Stephen Guest, who like Nemours does not believe in "mere resolution" (499), finds Maggie's refusal to follow her passions "unnatural" and "horrible": "If you loved me as I love you, we should throw everything else to the winds for the sake of belonging to each other" (470). Maggie does love him, just as the princess loves the duke, passionately; and she is tempted: part of her longs to be transported by the exquisite currents of desire. But her awakening, like that of the princess, though again not for the same reasons, is double. She falls asleep on the boat ride down the river. When she awakens and disentangles her mind "from the confused web of dreams" (494), like Mme. de Clèves after her own brush with death, Maggie pulls away from the man who has briefly but deeply tempted her. She will not build her happiness on the unhappiness of others:

> It is not the force that ought to rule us—this that we feel for each other; it would rend me away from all that my past life has made dear and holy to me. I can't set out on a fresh life and forget that; I must go back to it, and cling to it, else I shall feel as if there were nothing firm beneath my feet (502)

What is the content of this sacred past? Earlier, before the waking on the river, when Maggie was tempted only by the "fantasy" of a "life filled with all luxuries, with daily incense of adoration near and distant, and with all possibilities of culture at her command," the narrator had commented on the pull of that erotic scenario:

> But there were things in her stronger than vanity—passion, and affection, and long deep memories of early discipline and effort, of early claims on her love and pity; and the stream of vanity was soon swept along and mingled imperceptibly with that wider current which was at its highest force today. (457).

Maggie's renunciation of Stephen Guest, then, is not so simple as I have made it out to be, for the text of these "early claims," this archaic wish, has a power both erotic and ambitious in its own right. That "wider current" is, of course, the broken bond with her brother. And the epigraph to the novel, "In their death they were not divided," is the telos toward which the novel tends; for it is also the last line of the novel, the epitaph on the tombstone of the brother and sister who drown in each other's arms.

Maggie, obeying what Stephen called her "perverted notion of right," her passion for a "mere idea" (538), drowns finally in an implausible flood. Maggie, no more than Mme. de Clèves, could be *persuaded* (to invoke Jane Austen's last novel); for neither regarded a second chance as an alternative to be embraced. Maggie's return home sans husband is not understood by the community. And the narrator explains that "public opinion in these cases is always of the feminine gender—not the world, but the world's wife" (512–13). Despite the phrase, Eliot does not locate the inadequacy of received social ideas in gender per se; her attack on the notion of a "master-key that will fit all cases" is in fact directed at the "men of maxims": "The mysterious complexity of our life is not to be embraced by maxims . . ." (521). This commentary seeks to justify Maggie's choice, her turning away from the maxim, and thus inscribes an internal "artificial plausibility": the text within the text, as we saw that function in *La Princesse de Clèves*. The commentary constitutes another *reading*, a reading by "reference," as Eliot puts it, to the "special circumstances that mark the individual lot" (521). Like Mme. de Clèves, Maggie has been given extraordinary feelings, and those feelings *engender* another and extravagant narrative logic.

There is a feminist criticism today that laments Eliot's ultimate refusal to satisfy her heroine's longing for that "something . . . incompatible with the facts of human existence":

> Sadly, and it is a radical criticism of George Eliot, she does not commit herself fully to the energies and aspirations she lets loose in these women. Does she not cheat them, and cheat us, ultimately, in allowing them so little? Does she not excite our interest through the breadth and the challenge of the implications of her fiction, and then deftly dam up and fence round the momentum she has so powerfully created? She diagnoses so brilliantly "the common yearning of womanhood," and then cures it, sometimes drastically, as if it were indeed a disease.[36]

It is as though these critics, somewhat like Stendhal disbelieving the conviction of Mme. de Clèves, would have Maggie live George Eliot's life. The point is, it seems to me, that the plots of women's literature are not about "life" and solutions in any therapeutic sense, nor should they be. They are about the plots of literature itself, about the constraints the maxim places on rendering a female life in fiction. Mme. de Lafayette quietly, George Eliot less silently, both italicize by the demaximization of their heroines' texts the difficulty of curing plot of life, and life of certain plots.[37]

Lynn Sukenick, in her essay "On Women and Fiction," describes the uncomfortable posture of all women writers in our culture, within and without the text: what I would call a posture of imposture. And she says of the role of gender in relation to the literary project: "Like the minority writer, the female writer exists within an inescapable condition of identity which distances her from the mainstream of the culture and forces her either to stress her separation from the masculine literary tradition or to pursue her resemblance to it." Were she to forget her double bind, the "phallic critics" (as Mary Ellman describes them) would remind her that she is dreaming: "Lady novelists," Hugh Kenner wrote not so long ago, "have always claimed the privilege of transcending *mere plausibilities*. It's up to men to arrange such things. . . . Your bag is sensitivity, which means knowing what to put into this year's novels" (emphasis added).[38] And a recent reviewer of a woman's novel in a popular magazine complains:

> Like most feminist novels [this one] represents a triumph of sensibility over plot. Why a strong, credible narrative line that leads to a satisfactory resolution of conflicts should visit these stories so infrequently, I do not know. Because the

ability to tell a good story is unrelated to gender, I sometimes suspect that the authors of these novels are simply indifferent to the rigors of narrative.[39]

The second gentleman is slightly more generous than the first. He at least thinks women capable of telling a good—that is, credible—story. The fault lies in their indifference. I would not have descended to the evidence of the middlebrow mainstream if it did not, with curious persistence, echo the objections of Bussy-Rabutin.

The attack on female plots and plausibilities assumes that women writers cannot or will not obey the rules of fiction. It also assumes that the truth devolving from verisimilitude is male. For sensibility, sensitivity, "extravagance"—so many code words for feminine in our culture that the attack is in fact tautological—are taken to be not merely inferior modalities of production but deviations from some obvious truth. The blind spot here is both political (or philosophical) and literary. It does not see, nor does it want to, that the fictions of desire behind the desiderata of fiction are masculine and not universal constructs. It does not see that the maxims that pass for the truth of human experience, and the encoding of that experience in literature, are organizations, when they are not fantasies, of the dominant culture. To read women's literature is to see and hear repeatedly a chafing against the "unsatisfactory reality" contained in the maxim. Everywhere in *The Mill on the Floss* one can read a protest against the division of labor that grants men the world and women love. Saying no to Philip *Wakem* and then to Stephen *Guest,* Maggie refuses the hospitality of the happy end: "But I begin to think there can never come much happiness to me from loving; I have always had so much pain mingled with it. I wish I could make myself a world outside it, as men do" (430). But as in so much women's fiction a world outside love proves to be out of the world altogether. The protest against that topographical imperative is more or less muted from novel to novel. Still, the emphasis is always there to be read, and it points to another text. To continue to deny the credibility of women's literature is to adopt the posture of the philosopher of phallogocentrism's "credulous man who, in support of his testimony, offers truth and his phallus as his own proper credentials."[40] Those credentials are more than suspect.

NOTES

1. Although what is being pointed to ultimately is an "elsewhere" under the sign of an androgyny I resist, I respond here to the implicit invitation to look again. The quote should be replaced both in its original context and within Carolyn Heilbrun's concluding argument in *Toward a Recognition of Androgyny* (New York: Knopf, 1973), 167–72, which is where I (re)found it.

2. If one must have a less arbitrary origin—and why not?—the properly inaugural fiction would be Hélisenne de Crenne's *Les Angoysses douloureuses qui procèdent d'amours,* 1538. But *La Princesse de Clèves* has this critical advantage: it also marks the beginning of the modern French novel.

3. Bussy-Rabutin's oft-cited remarks on the novel are most easily found in Maurice Laugaa's excellent volume of critical responses, *Lectures de Mme de Lafayette* (Paris: Armand Cohn, 1971), 18–19. The translation is mine, as are all other translations from the French in my essay, unless otherwise indicated.

4. On the function and status of the confession in Mme. de Villedieu's novel and on the problems of predecession, see Micheline Cuénin's introduction to her critical edition of *Les Désordres de l'amour* (Geneva: Droz, 1970). The best account of the attack on the novel remains Georges May's *Le Dilemme du roman au XVIIIe siècle* (New Haven: Yale University Press, 1963), esp. his first chapter.

5. I allude here (speciously) to the first definition of "extravagant" in *Le Petit Robert* (Paris: Société du Nouveau Littré, 1967), 668: "C'est dit de textes non incorporés dans les recueils canoniques" 'Used to refer to texts not included in the canon.'

6. I refer here, as I indicate below, to Gérard Genette's "Vraisemblance et motivation," included in his *Figures II* (Paris: Seuil, 1969), 74. In my translation-adaptation of Genette's analysis I have chosen to render *vraisemblance* by "plausibility," a term with a richer semantic field of connotations than "verisimilitude." Page references to Genette's essay are hereafter given in the text.

7. For an overview of the current discussion about women's writing in France, see Elaine Marks's fine piece "Women and Literature in France," *Signs* 3 (1978): 832–42.

8. Cixous, "The Laugh of the Medusa," trans. Keith Cohen and Paula Cohen, *Signs* 1 (1976): 878.

9. For a recent statement of her position on a possible specificity to women's writing, see "Questions à Julia Kristeva," *Revue des Sciences Humaines,* no. 168 (1977): 495–501.

10. The opposition between these positions is more rhetorical than actual, as Woolf's gloss on Coleridge in *A Room of One's Own* shows. See esp. chap. vi.

11. Showalter, *A Literature of Their Own* (Princeton, N.J.: Princeton University Press, 1977), and Moers, *Literary Women* (New York: Doubleday, 1976). I understate the stakes of recognizing and responding to an apparently passive indifference. As Edward Said has written in another context: "Any philosophy or critical theory exists and is maintained in order not merely *to be there, passively around everyone and everything,* but in order to be taught and diffused, to be absorbed decisively into the institutions of society or to be instrumental in maintaining or changing or perhaps upsetting these institutions and that society" ("The Problem of Textuality," *Critical Inquiry* 4 [1978]: 682).

12. As quoted by Elizabeth Janeway in her insightful essay on women's writing in postwar America, "Women's Literature," *Harvard Guide to Contemporary American Writing,* ed. Daniel Hoffman (Cambridge, Mass.: Harvard University Press, 1979), 344.

13. See in particular Showalter's first chapter, "The Female Tradition," 3–36.

14. See Showalter's chapter "The Double Critical Standard and the Feminine Novel," 73–99.

15. Irigaray, *Ce Sexe qui n'en est pas un* (Paris: Minuit, 1977), 74.

16. McConnell-Ginet, "Intonation in a Man's World," *Signs* 3 (1978): 542.

17. My translations from *La Princesse de Clèves* are deliberately literal; page references to the French are from the readily available Garnier-Flammarion edition (Paris, 1966) and are incorporated within the text. The published English translation (New York: Penguin, 1978) is, I think, rather poor.

18. Stendhal, "Du Courage des femmes," *De L'Amour* (Paris: Editions de Cluny, 1938), chap. xxix, 111.

19. Serge Doubrovsky, *"La Princesse de Clèves:* Une Interprétation existentielle," *La Table Ronde,* no. 138 (1959): 48. Jean Rousset, *Forme et signification* (Paris: Corti, 1962), 25.

20. A. Kibédi Varga, "Romans d'amour, romans de femme à l'Epoque classique," *Revue des Sciences Humaines,* no. 168 (1977): 524. Jules Brody, in *"La Princesse de Clèves* and the Myth of Courtly Love," *University of Toronto Quarterly* 38 (1969): 105–35, esp. 131–34, and Domna C. Stanton, in "The Ideal of *Repos* in Seventeenth-Century French Literature," *L'Esprit Créateur* 15 (1975): 79–104, esp. 95–96, 99, 101–102, also interpret the princess's final refusal of Nemours (and her renunciation) as heroic and self-preserving actions within a certain seventeenth-century discourse.

21. Hermann, *Les Voleuses de langue* (Paris: Editions des Femmes, 1976), 77.

22. Freud, *On Creativity and the Unconscious,* trans. I. F. Grant Duff (New York: Harper, 1958), 44. Subsequent references to this edition are given in the text.

23. Brooks, *The Melodramatic Imagination* (New Haven, Conn.: Yale University Press, 1976), 20.

24. *The Essays of George Eliot,* ed. Thomas Pinney (London: Routledge and Kegan Paul, 1963), 301–302. Hereafter page references to this edition are included in the text.

25. On the content of popular women's literature and its relationship to high culture, see Lillian Robinson's "On Reading Trash," in *Sex, Class and Culture* (Bloomington: Indiana University Press, 1978), 200–22.

26. Barbara Bellow Watson, "On Power and the Literary Text," *Signs* 1 (1975): 113. Watson suggests that we look instead for "expressive symbolic structures."

27. Butor, "Sur *La Princesse de Clèves,"* *Repertoire* (Paris: Minuit, 1960), 76–77.

28. David Grossvogel, *Limits of the Novel* (Ithaca, N.Y.: Cornell University Press, 1971), 134. In Doubrovsky's terms, love in this universe means "being dispossessed of oneself and bound to the incoercible spontaneity of another" (47).

29. Lotringer, "La Structuration romanesque," *Critique* 26 (1970): 517.

30. The importance of this scene from Austen is underscored by Rachel Mayer Brownstein in *Becoming a Heroine: Reading about Women in Novels* (New York: Viking, 1982).

31. Kamuf, "Inside *Julie's* Closet," *Romanic Review* 69 (1978): 303–304.

32. Roman Jakobson, *Essais de linguistique générale* (Paris: Minuit, 1963), 33; quoted by S. Lotringer, "Vice de Forme," *Critique* 27 (1971): 203; italics mine.

33. Woolf, *The Common Reader* (New York: Harcourt, 1953), 166, 173; emphasis added.

34. Eliot, *The Mill on the Floss* (New York: NAL, 1965), 348–49. Subsequent references to the novel are to this edition and are given in the text.

35. Gutwirth, *Madame de Staël, Novelist: The Emergence of the Artist as Woman* (Urbana: University of Illinois Press, 1978), 255.

36. Jenni Calder, e.g., in *Women and Marriage in Victorian Fiction* (New York: Oxford University Press, 1976), 158.

37. I echo here, with some distortion, the terms of Peter Brooks's analysis of the relations between "plot" and "life" in his illuminating essay "Freud's Masterplot," *Yale French Studies,* no. 55–56 (1977): 280–300, esp. 298.

38. Sukenick's essay is quoted from *The Authority of Experience: Essays in Feminist Criticism,* ed. Arlyn Diamond and Lee R. Edwards (Amherst: University of Massachusetts Press, 1977), 28; Kenner's observation is quoted in the same essay, 30. Mary Ellman's term is taken from *Thinking about Women* (New York: Harcourt, 1968), 28–54.

39. Peter Prescott, in *Newsweek,* 16 October 1978, 112.

40. Jacques Derrida, "Becoming Woman," trans. Barbara Harlow, *Semiotext(e)* 3, no. 1 (1978): 133.

10

Narrative Desire

PETER BROOKS

Plot as we need and want the term is . . . an embracing concept for the design and intention of narrative, a structure for those meanings that are developed through temporal succession, or perhaps better: a structuring operation elicited by, and made necessary by, those meanings that develop through succession and time. A further analysis of the question is suggested here by a distinction urged by the Russian Formalists, that between *fabula* and *syuzhet*. *Fabula* is defined as the order of events referred to by the narrative, whereas *syuzhet* is the order of events presented in the narrative discourse. The distinction is one that takes on evident analytic force when one is talking about a Conrad or a Faulkner, whose dislocations of normal chronology are radical and significant, but it is no less important in thinking about apparently more straightforward narratives, since any narrative presents a selection and an ordering of material. We must, however, recognize that the apparent priority of fabula to *syuzhet* is in the nature of a mimetic illusion, in that the *fabula*—"what really happened"—is in fact a mental construction that the reader derives from the *syuzhet,* which is all that he ever directly knows. This differing status of the two terms by no means invalidates the distinction itself, which is central to our thinking about narrative and necessary to its analysis since it allows us to juxtapose two modes of order and in the juxtaposing to see how ordering takes place. In the wake of the Russian Formalists, French structural analysts of narrative proposed their own pairs of terms, predominantly *histoire* (corresponding to *fabula*) and *récit,* or else *discours* (corresponding to *syuzhet*). English usage has been more unsettled. "Story" and "plot" would seem to be generally acceptable renderings in most circumstances, though a structural and semiotic analysis will find advantages in the less semantically charged formulation "story" and "discourse."

"Plot" in fact seems to me to cut across the *fabula/syuzhet* distinction in that to speak of plot is to consider both story elements and their ordering. Plot could be thought of as the interpretive activity elicited by the distinction between *syuzhet* and *fabula,* the way we *use* the one against the other. To keep our terms straight without sacrificing the advantages of the semantic range of "plot," let us say that we can generally understand plot to be an aspect of *syuzhet* in that it belongs to the narrative discourse, as its active shaping force, but that it makes sense (as indeed *syuzhet* itself principally makes sense) as it is used to reflect on *fabula,* as our understanding of story. Plot is thus the dynamic shaping force of the narrative discourse. I find confirmation for such a view in Paul Ricoeur's definition of plot as "the intelligible whole that governs a succession of events in any story." Ricoeur continues, using the terms "events" and "story" rather than *fabula* and *syuzhet:* "This provisory definition immediately shows the plot's connecting function between an event or events and the story. A story is *made out of* events to the extent that plot *makes* events *into* a story. The plot, therefore, places us at the crossing point of temporality and narrativity" ("Narrative Time," 167 [37 in this volume]). Ricoeur's emphasis on the constructive role of plot, its active, shaping function, offers a useful corrective to the structural narratologists' neglect of the dynamics of narrative and points us toward the reader's vital role in the understanding of plot.

The Russian Formalists presented what one might call a "constructivist" view of literature, calling attention to the material and the means of its making, showing how a given work is put together. "Device" is one of their favorite terms—a term for demonstrating the technical use of a given motif or incident or theme. Typical is Boris Tomashevsky's well-known illustration of the technical sense of "motivation": if a character in a play hammers a nail into the wall in Act 1, then he or another character will have to hang himself from it in Act 3. The work of Tomashevsky, Victor Shklovsky, Boris Eichenbaum is invaluable to the student of narrative since it so often cuts through thematic material to show the constructed armature that supports it. Perhaps the instance of the Russian Formalists' work most compelling for our purposes is their effort to isolate and identify the minimal units of narrative, and then to formulate the principles of their combination and interconnection. In particular, Vladimir Propp's *The Morphology of the Folktale* merits attention as an early and impressive example of what can be done to formalize and codify the study of narrative. . . .

Plot as we have defined it is the organizing line and intention of narrative, thus perhaps best conceived as an activity, a structuring operation elicited in the reader trying to make sense of those meanings that develop only through textual and temporal succession. Plot in this view belongs to the reader's "competence," and in his "performance"—the reading of narrative—it animates the sense-making process: it is a key component of that "passion of (for) meaning" that, Barthes says, lights us afire when we read. We can, then, conceive of the reading of plot as a form of desire that carries us forward, onward, through the text. Narratives both tell of desire—typically present some story of desire—and arouse and make use of desire as dynamic of signification. Desire is in this view like Freud's notion of Eros, a force including sexual desire but larger and more polymorphous, which (he writes in *Beyond the Pleasure Principle*) seeks "to combine organic substances into ever greater unities."[1] Desire as Eros, desire in its plastic and totalizing function, appears to me central to our experience of reading narrative, and if in what follows I evoke Freud—and, as a gloss on Freud, Jacques Lacan—it is because I find in Freud's work the best model for a "textual erotics." I am aware that "desire" is a concept too broad, too fundamental, almost too banal to be defined. Yet perhaps it can be described: we can say something about the forms that it takes in narrative, how it represents itself, the dynamic it generates.

Desire is always there at the start of a narrative, often in a state of initial arousal, often having reached a state of intensity such that movement must be created, action undertaken, change begun. The *Iliad* opens with Agamemnon and Achilles locked in passionate quarrel over the girl Briseis, and the *Odyssey* with Odysseus, detained on Calypso's island, expressing the longing of his nostos, the drive to return home. To cite an explicitly erotic instance, Jean Genet's *Notre-Dame des fleurs* opens on an act of masturbation, and the narrative and its persons are called forth as what is needed for the phantasies of desire. One could no doubt analyze the opening paragraph of most novels and emerge in each case with the image of a desire taking on shape, beginning to seek its objects, beginning to develop a textual energetics. A rock-bottom paradigm of the dynamic of desire can be found in one of the very earliest novels in the Western tradition, *Lazarillo de Tormes* (1554), where all of the hero's tricks and dodges are directed initially at staying alive: Lazaro, the ragged, homeless *picaro,* must use his wits, his human ingenuity, to avoid the ever-present threat of starvation. Each chapter develops as a set of tricks and stratagems devised to overcome a specific form of the threat, and thus literally to enable life, and narrative, to go forward: the most telling illustration may be the second chapter, where Lazaro must simulate the actions of a mouse and a snake to work his way into his master the priest's locked bread chest. The resistance to desire in this novel is simply, and brutally, total deprivation of what sustains life; while the traditional comic structure—in theater and then in novel—presents the resistance of an older generation of "blocking figures" to the plotting of the younger generation, seeking erotic union. As in a great many folktales—the example of "Jack the Giant Killer" and its permutations comes to mind—the specifically human faculty of ingenuity and trickery, the capacity to use the mind to devise schemes to overcome superior force, becomes a basic dynamic of plot. If the giants of folktale are always stupid, it is because they stand opposed to human wit, which is seen as a capacity for leverage on the world, precisely that which overcomes inert obstacles, sets change in motion, reformulates the real.

By the nineteenth century, the *picaro's* scheming to stay alive has typically taken a more elaborated and socially defined form: it has become ambition. It may in fact be a defining characteristic of the modern novel (as of bourgeois society) that it takes aspiration, getting ahead, seriously, rather than simply as the object of satire (which was the case in much earlier, more aristocratically determined literature), and thus it makes ambition the vehicle and emblem of Eros, that which totalizes the world as possession and progress. Ambition provides not only a typical novelistic theme, but also a dominant dynamic of plot: a force that drives the protagonist forward, assuring that no incident or action is final or closed in itself until such a moment as the ends of ambition have been clarified, through success or else renunciation. Somewhat in the manner of the traditional sequence of functions in the folktale analyzed by Propp, ambition provides an armature of plot which the reader recognizes, and which constitutes the very "readability" of the narrative text, what enables the reader to go about the construction of the text's specific meanings. Ambition is inherently totalizing, figuring the self's tendency to appropriation and aggrandizement, moving forward through the encompassment of more, striving to have, to do, and to be more. The ambitious hero thus stands as a figure of the reader's efforts to construct meanings in ever-larger wholes, to totalize his experience of human existence in time, to grasp past, present, and future in a significant shape. This description, of course, most obviously concerns male plots of ambition. The female plot is not unrelated, but it takes a more complex stance toward ambition, the formation of an inner drive toward the assertion of selfhood in resistance to the overt and violating male plots of ambition, a counterdynamic which, from the prototype *Clarissa* on to *Jane Eyre* and *To the Lighthouse,* is only superficially passive, and in fact a reinterpretation of the vectors of plot.[2]

The ambitious heroes of the nineteenth-century novel—those of Balzac, for instance—may regularly be conceived as "desiring machines" whose presence in the text creates and sustains narrative movement through the forward march of desire, projecting the self onto the world through scenarios of desire imagined and then acted upon. Etymology may suggest that the self creates a circle—an *ambitus*—or aureola around itself, mainly in front of itself, attempting ever to move forward to the circumference of that circle and to widen it, to cast the nets of the self ever further. A most obvious example would be Eugène de Rastignac, hero of Balzac's *Le Père Goriot,* who, as the action of that novel begins, has just returned from his first soirée in Parisian high society and has discovered the uses of ambition:

> To be young, to have a thirst for society, to be hungry for a woman, and to see two houses open to oneself! to place one's foot in the Faubourg Saint-Germain with the Vicomtesse de Beauséant, and one's knee in the Chaussée d'Antin, with the Comtesse de Restaud! to plunge with one's glance into the salons of Paris all in a line, and to believe oneself a handsome enough young man to find there aid and protection in the heart of a woman! to feel oneself ambitious enough to give a proud stamp of the foot to the tightrope on which one must walk with the assurance that the acrobat won't fall, and to have found the best of balancing poles in a charming woman![3]

The disarming directness, even crudity, of the quotation suggests how Rastignac is conceived as a bundle of desires which need only be given a field for their exercise—the topography of which is suggested in the quotation—for the narrative to move forward.

The novel will indeed unfold as an anatomy of human desire, where the introduction of the professional master-plotter, Vautrin, will serve explicitly to theorize desire and the logical consequences of its full enactment. In a world so charged with desire, the central drama becomes—as in the Christian arch-drama—one of temptation. If Rastignac is able to resist the specific terms of Vautrin's plot, which offers the dowered maiden as the direct consequence of murder—a temptation that makes *too* clear a certain logic of desire—it is because he has found a more nuanced system for the realization of ambition in the conjunction of erotic and financial power represented by another woman, Delphine de Nucingen. Rastignac negotiates a path between the absolutes of plot expounded by his two would-be fathers, Vautrin and Goriot. It is sign and condition of his success that he gives absolute allegiance to neither and goes beyond both, escaping the constraints of paternity, moving forward with the hyperbolic rapidity typical of Balzacian narratives of ambition, accelerating toward a goal that here is represented in the famous final scene in which the hero, from his vantage point on the rise of Père-Lachaise cemetery, can view the *beaux quartiers* of Paris as ready for his possession: a world charged with meaning and possibility because it is charged, like the glance that takes visionary possession of it, with desire. In other cases (for instance, in the career of Lucien de Rubempré, across the two novels *Illusions perdues* and *Splendeurs et misères des courtisanes*) the narrative of ambition accelerates to the overheating and loss of energy of the desiring machine, indeed sometimes to its explosion.

But to characterize desire as a machine may be inadequate. As Michel Serres has argued, the eighteenth century's preoccupation with the machine, as a system for the transmission of forces outside itself, gives way in the nineteenth century to fascination with the motor, containing its source of movement within itself, built on the three principles of difference (of temperature), reservoir (of fuel), and circulation. The self-contained motor, working through combustion—typically, the steam engine—also corresponds to the emerging conception of human desire. If with La Mettrie in the eighteenth century we had *l'homme machine,* by the time of Freud we have moved to *l'homme moteur.*

Following Stendhal, many writers seized upon the engines and motors of nascent industrialism as central thematic and symbolic forces in their work. An early paradigm appears in the first paragraph of Balzac's *Illusions perdues,* a novel that begins by evoking the coming to France of the mechanical Stanhope press, these "devouring presses," the narrator calls them, which in turn will be supplanted by the steam-driven press, producing an enormous new demand for cheap paper that will drive David Séchard to the monomaniac obsession of the inventor, and to his ultimate exploitation by a new breed of industrial printers—and creating also the possibility of modern mass journalism, which will be the medium of the brief triumph and dismal failure of Lucien de Rubempré. In fact, the very production of the novel *Illusions perdues,* and more acutely its sequel, *Splendeurs et misères des courtisanes,* was caught up in the dynamic of the new journalism, as Balzac sought, unsuccessfully, to publish in the new medium of the *roman-feuilleton,* the novel published in installments in the mass-circulation daily newspaper. The devouring presses chewed up paper, ideas, and would-be poets, powering the way to what the critic Sainte-Beuve contemptuously labeled an "industrial literature."

Like Rastignac, Lucien de Rubempré is a bundle of appetencies that will motivate and animate the plot of his novels. But *Illusions perdues* appears at its outset to lay bare not only the desiring subject, but also the general dynamic subsuming and even controlling all specific forms of human desire, the very motor force of its plot. The thematic cluster of Lucien the poet, printing, and journalism makes particularly evident the intimate relations of desire, narrative, and the dynamics of plot. Through the key experience of journalism, the novel will set up a system of potentially unlimited energetic transformations and exchanges, a system where money, erotic desire, and language become interchangeable factors in an overheated circuit of power and signification. Subjacent to the circulatory system of signs, financial and linguistic, is indeed what might be called a libidinal economy, which in Balzac's world may always be the ultimate system of energies. . . . Corresponding to a France sick by way of the father stands the action of the devouring presses, the movement toward mass journalism, publicity, democracy, the reign of public opinion:

everything that for Balzac constituted the very antithesis of legitimate author-ity. The motor of the presses comes to represent an inevitable historical dynamic. It represents as well the dynamic of the modern narrative text, itself inevitably historical, caught in an irreversible and ever-accelerating process of change, a plot of energy and devourment which Balzac, as a dissenter from his time, perceives with particular clarity even as his own text succumbs to its dynamic. Life in the text of the modern is a nearly thermodynamic process; plot is, most aptly, a steam engine. . . .

"If only you knew my life," Raphaël has said to Emile [in Balzac's *La Peau de chagrin*], in a phrase that could stand for most tellings of the life's story, where the claim that intelligibility, meaning, understanding depend on a fully pred-icated narrative sentence, on a narrative totality, never is and never can be real-ized. Yet the performance of the narrative act is in itself transformatory, predicating the material of the life story in a changed context—subordinating all its verbs to the verb "I tell"—and thus most importantly soliciting the entry of a listener into relation with the story. The narrative act discovers, and makes use of, the intersubjective nature of language itself, medium for the exchange of narrative understandings. Here in the dialogic dynamic of the narrative transference—a topic for later elaboration—we may make our near-est approach to the antique dealer's notion of *savoir,* the knowledge wrested from the doomed dialectic of *vouloir* and *pouvoir,* in the transformatory func-tion of narrating itself.

The paradigm of what I have in mind would be the *Thousand and One Nights,* Balzac's inspiration as he sought to make the magic of an "oriental tale" unfold within the frame of contemporary Paris. In the *Thousand and One Nights,* Shahrazad's storytelling takes a desire that has gone off the rails—the Sultan's desire, derailed by his wife's infidelity, becomes sadistic and discon-tinuous, so that the mistress of the night must have her head chopped off in the morning—and cures it by prolonging it, precisely by narrativizing it. Desire becomes reinvested in tellings of and listenings to stories, it is recon-stituted as metonymy—over a thousand and one nights—until the Sultan can resume a normal erotic state, marrying Shahrazad, who thus fulfills her name as "savior of the city." Narration, in this allegory, is seen to be life-giving in that it arouses and sustains desire, ensuring that the terminus it both delays and beckons toward will offer what we might call a lucid repose, desire both come to rest and set in perspective.

Narratives portray the motors of desire that drive and consume their plots, and they also lay bare the nature of narration as a form of human desire: the need to tell as a primary human drive that seeks to seduce and to subjugate the listener, to implicate him in the thrust of a desire that never can quite speak its name—never can quite come to the point—but that insists on speaking over and over again its movement toward that name. For the analyst of narrative, these different yet convergent vectors of desire suggest the need to explore more fully the shaping function of desire, its modeling of the plot, and also the dynamics of exchange and transmission, the roles of tellers and listeners.

NOTES

1. Sigmund Freud, *Beyond the Pleasure Principle,* in *The Standard Edition of the Complete Psychological Works of Sigmund Freud,* ed. James Strachey (London: Hogarth Press, 1953–74), 18:50. Subsequent references to Freud are to this edition.

2. On women's plots, see Nancy K. Miller, *The Heroine's Text* (New York: Columbia University Press, 1980). One might recall here that the folktale "All-Kinds-of-Fur" in some measure represents the female plot, a resistance and what we might call an "endurance": a waiting (and suffering) until the woman's desire can be a permitted response to the expression of male desire.

3. Honoré de Balzac, *Le Père Goriot,* in *La Comédie humaine* (Paris: Bibliothèque de la Pléïade, 1976–81), 3:77–78.

11

Coming Unstrung: Women, Men, Narrative, and Principles of Pleasure

SUSAN WINNETT

> Here are two sides, and only half the argument.
> —Athena, in *The Eumenides* [line 428]

I would like to begin with the proposition that female orgasm is unnecessary. I am not, of course, saying that it is unnecessary to any particular woman that she experience orgasm or, for that matter, to any particular man that his female partner do so; rather, I mean that women's orgasm and, by extension, women's pleasure can be extraneous to that culmination of heterosexual desire which is copulation. Women's pleasure can take place outside, or independent of, the male sexual economy whose pulsations determine the dominant culture, its repressions, its taboos, and its narratives, as well as the "human sciences" developed to explain them. Considering the last decade's preoccupations with sexual difference and the pleasure of the text, it is surprising that theories concerned with the relation between narrative and pleasure have largely neglected to raise the issue of the difference between women's and men's reading pleasures. But this question seems to require critical tools that, for reasons I explore in this essay, have not been available. Indeed, the same analytic paradigms that give us professional access to texts have already determined the terms in which we accede to, comply with, or resist the coercions of a cultural program for pleasure that is not interested in—and whose interests may be threatened by—the difference of women's pleasure. If this paper does no more than get us as far as the giddy brink of an alternative to this cultural program, it will, I hope, suggest the magnitude of the resistances to this alternative as well as possible strategies for engaging them.

1

But, first, let us return to the question of orgasm. We all know what male orgasm looks like. It is preceded by a visible "awakening, an arousal, the birth of an appetency, ambition, desire or intention." The male organ registers the intensity of this stimulation, rising to the occasion of its provocation, becoming at once the means of pleasure and culture's sign of power. This energy, "aroused into expectancy," takes its course toward "significant discharge" and shrinks into a state of quiescence (or satisfaction) that, minutes before, would have been a sign of impotence. The man must have this genital response before he can participate, which means that something in the time before intercourse must have aroused him. And his participation generally ceases with the ejaculation that signals the end of his arousal. The myth of the afterglow—so often a euphemism for sleep—seems a compensation for the finality he has reached.

Before I proceed to hypothesize the pleasure of his female mate, I must account for the quotation marks in the previous paragraph. The words used to describe the trajectory of male arousal ("awakening, an arousal, the birth of an appetency, ambition, desire or intention" on the one hand and "significant discharge" on the other) are taken from Peter Brooks's influential "Freud's Masterplot" (*Reading*, 90–112), which examines the relation between Freud's plotting of the life trajectory in *Beyond the Pleasure Principle* and the dynamics of beginnings, middles, and ends in traditional narrative. Brooks's articulation of what are ultimately the oedipal dynamics that structure and determine traditional fictional narratives and psychoanalytic paradigms is brilliant, and it reminds us, in case we had forgotten, what men want, how they go about trying to get it, and the stories they tell about this pursuit. But it seems clear that a narratology based on the oedipal model would have to be profoundly and vulnerably male in its assumptions about what constitutes pleasure and, more insidiously, what this pleasure looks like; even Freud was troubled by his theory's inadequate explanation of female experience. Yet the gender bias of contemporary narratology seems not to have troubled our profession's most prominent practitioners of narrative theory and advocates of textual pleasure. Is it that the assumptions about narrative theory and the pleasure of the text that seem obvious to me are somehow not available to them? If they were conscious that the narrative dynamics and the erotics of reading they were expounding were specifically tied to an ideology of representation derivable only from the dynamics of male sexuality, would they not at least feel uncomfortable making general statements about "narrative," "pleasure," and "us"?

When I came upon the following passage—thanks to Teresa deLauretis, who cites it in *Alice Doesn't*—I realized that the problem was not that the narratologists were blind but that I was naive. In "The Orgastic Pattern of Fiction," Robert Scholes writes:

> The archetype of all fiction is the sexual act. In saying this I do not merely to remind the reader of the connection between all art and the erotic in human nature. . . . For what connects fiction—and music—with sex is the

fundamental orgastic rhythm of tumescence and detumescence, of tension and resolution, of intensification to the point of climax and consummation. In the sophisticated forms of fiction, as in the sophisticated practice of sex, much of the art consists of delaying climax within the framework of desire in order to prolong the pleasurable act itself.

(Scholes, *Fabulation,* 26; deLauretis, 108)

It comes as no surprise that Scholes, after reminding us that all fictional romance conforms to this model, crowns the novel as the "high art" manifestation of this universal pattern and claims for that genre the task of adapting the "'low atavistic' form, the orgastic story, to the job of spreading the news, telling the truth about man in society" (27). A refresher course in the fundamentals of structuralism should suffice to remind us that the "erotic in human nature" has to be understood within its various determining contexts if the concept is to be productive (what is "the erotic"? how do we define the "human nature" in which we locate "the erotic"? is "human nature" a cultural ["human"] or a biological ["nature"] construct?). And even if we have become wary of the generic "man in society," we still might need to be reminded that such generalizations in such contexts indicate that the pleasure the reader is expected to take in the text is the pleasure of the man. This would seem to be true even when—as Calvino's great novel of reading, *If on a winter's night a traveler,* suggests—the pleasure of the (projected) male author (or his surrogate, the critic) is heightened by the fantasy that the reader is a woman. Scholes continues:

Like the sexual act, the act of fiction is a reciprocal relationship. It takes two. Granted, a writer can write for *his* own amusement, and a reader can read in the same way [note the finesse with which the male generic is suspended here]; but these are acts of mental masturbation, with all the limitations that are involved in narcissistic gratification of the self. . . . The meaning of the fictional act itself is something like love. The writer, at *his* best, respects the dignity of the reader. . . . (27; my emphasis)

Figures, of course, will insist on their own economies, and it is not long before Scholes's reader becomes a man, and the act of pleasure becomes, despite the orgastic language of his foreplay, a "marriage of true minds," a platonized, legalized, entirely male circuit of desire:

The reader . . . respects the dignity of the writer. He does not simply try to take *his* pleasure and *his* meaning from the book. He strives to mate with the writer, to share the writer's viewpoint, to come fully to terms with the sensibility and intelligence that have informed this particular work of fiction. When writer and reader make a "marriage of true minds," the act of fiction is perfect and complete. (27; *his* emphasis)

I doubt that Scholes is conscious of or celebrating the profound homoerotic—or homoaesthetic—subtext in these passages, although its emergence in his discussion precisely at the moment when he articulates the relation between his reading and sexual pleasures might explain why the issue of women's reading pleasure has not attracted the attention it should: for the male critic, the sexual pleasure of reading would seem to take place within a nexus of homosocial arrangements in which "the marriage of true minds" is an affair "between men," as Eve Sedgwick has put it. In this system, woman is neither an independent subjectivity nor a desiring agent but, rather, an enabling position organizing the social fiction of heterosexuality. In its honest outrageousness, Scholes's erotics of reading makes clearer than does Brooks's more subtle articulation that the patriarchy has a simultaneously blind and enlightened investment both in the forms of its pleasure and in its conscious valorization and less conscious mystification of them.[1] And this realization does nothing but make it all the more frightening to contemplate the obstacles our own education has placed in the way both of women's conceiving (of) their own pleasure and of men's conceding that female pleasure might have a different plot.

For if we do now pursue the analogy between the representability of the sex act and a possible erotics of reading, we find a woman's encounter with the text determined by a broad range of options for pleasure that have *nothing to do* (or can choose to have nothing to do) with the notions of representability crucial to the narratologies of Brooks, Scholes, and, I dare say, others. I might point out, however, that it is exactly what I see as a potentially—but not necessarily—liberating relation to representability that has allowed the entire issue of female pleasure to go unacknowledged or to be entirely misconstrued for as long as it has. Everything that the last two decades have taught us about human sexual response suggests that the female partner in intercourse has accesses to pleasure not open to her male partner. It is, of course, a commonplace that she can fake pleasure. But she can also (like Mme. de Merteuil in Laclos's *Les Liaisons dangereuses*) fake frigidity. Without endangering her partner's ultimate "success," she can begin her own arousal at whatever point in the intercourse her fantasy finds exciting. She can even take as her point of arousal the attained satisfaction of her mate. Without defying the conventions dictating that sex be experienced more or less together, she can begin and end her pleasure according to a logic of fantasy and arousal that is totally unrelated to the functioning and representation of the "conventional" heterosexual sex act.

141

Moreover, she can do so again. Immediately. And, we are told, again after that.

While the reader completes or continues this fantasy as desired, I would like to review how pleasure is defined and generated in Brooks's version of Freud's "Masterplot," a scheme that has no place for such "unruly" sexual dynamics as the ones I have just sketched. According to Brooks, Freud's discussion of the pleasure principle charts the route an organism takes when, stimulated out of quiescence, it strives to regain equilibrium by finding the appropriate means of discharging the energy invested in it. According to this scheme, desire would be, even at its inception, a desire for the end; birth (the moment at which the organism begins to dispose of its energies) would be evaluated proleptically through the significance it acquires in the light of the death that consummates and totalizes the life history. And pleasure would involve the recognitions and reproductions of the dynamics "of ends in relation to beginnings and the forces that animate the middle in between" (Brooks, *Reading*, 299). In short, the pleasure principle seeks to overcome birth, to attain the quiescence that preceded the organism's delivery onto the stage of life. We remember, for example, how Mary Shelley describes the coming to life of Frankenstein's Monster, the moment when a being composed of inanimate matter—assembled, significantly, from pieces of dead bodies—receives the dangerous spark of life: "I saw the dull yellow eyes of the creature open, it breathed hard, and a convulsive motion agitated its limbs" (56). The *Master*plot of the novel would, according to the pleasure principle, be the chain of events that restores the creature to death while accounting for all the significances of its having come to life.

2

But just as *Frankenstein* does not get the Monster quite dead, it also seems not to account satisfactorily for all the significances that can be attributed to the creature's life. We need only to consider the kinds of major questions the novel raises to realize how successfully it avoids resolving any one of them.[2] This lack of resolution is often attributed to the young author's lack of skill, her inability, for all her imagination, to write a coherent plot (Rieger, xxiv). And indeed, *Frankenstein*'s narrative dynamics are not at all well explained by analogy with the pleasure principle, although both the problem of this model and its underlying oedipal scenario might be regarded as among the novel's most important thematic concerns. In its mise-en-scène of the fantasy of the pleasure principle, *Frankenstein* dramatizes the monstrosity of the relation the Freudian scheme posits between beginnings and endings; the detours and repetitions that a Freudian narratology would associate with the bindings (and sublimations) of life energy toward appropriate resolution pose and repose a question that traditional narrative is not plotted to answer.

I have been arguing that male narratology conceptualizes narrative dynamics in terms of an experience it so swiftly and seamlessly generalizes that we tend to forget that it has its source in experience—in fact, in experience of the body. Although I have stressed male and female sexualities' different relations to representability, I of course do not think that textual production and narrative dynamics are matters of sexuality alone; nor do I mean to trivialize Brooks's work by emphasizing its dependence on a physiological model. Yet this demonstration enables us to speculate about how another set of experiences might yield another set of generalizations, another theory as vulnerable to the introduction of a counterexample as the Masterplot itself. I would like to explore what would happen if, having recognized the Masterplot's reliance on male morphology and male experience, we retained the general narrative pattern of tension and resolution ("tumescence and detumescence," "arousal and significant discharge") and simply substituted for the male experience an analogously representable female one. I do not propose the hypothetical model that follows as *the* alternative to what I have called male narratology—indeed, it does not even hold up as a model for all "female" narrative. Rather, I see it as *an* alternative that, however useful in explaining *Frankenstein* (and perhaps other texts), is ultimately more valuable for its relativizing function than as a scheme competing for authority with the Masterplot. The existence of two models implies to me the possibility of many more; neither the schemes I am criticizing nor the one I develop here exhausts the possibilities offered by the psychoanalytic model.[3] Work, class, law, politics, ambition, domination, power, and geography—issues that involve gender but not necessarily sexuality—represent compelling and theoretically productive motivations for narrative outside a psychoanalytic paradigm that sees them as dramatizations of sexual drives (see, e.g., Beer, *Darwin's Plots;* Chambers; Gates; Jameson; and D. A. Miller).

Any narrative model can be shown to privilege a particular explanatory paradigm and thereby a particular thematics. Yet if my model, based on uniquely female experience, is to represent only a shift in *thematic* emphasis, we will not be meeting the Masterplot on the terrain it has staked out for itself—that of form. We will have to return to an examination of how the distinction between form and theme is drawn. First, I want to explore the different narrative logic—and the very different possibilities of pleasure—that emerge when issues such as incipience, repetition, and closure are reconceived in terms of *an* experience (not *the* experience) of the female body.

Female experience does indeed include two highly representable instances of "tumescence and detumescence," of "arousal and significant discharge," whose very issue might suggest why they have been ignored in conceptualizations of narrative dynamics.[4] Both birth and breast feeding manifest dynamic patterns not unlike those described in the various orgastic sequences I cite above. Yet because they do not culminate in a quiescence that can bearably be conceptualized as a simulacrum of death, they neither need nor can confer on themselves the kind of retrospective significance attained by analogy with the pleasure principle. Indeed, as sense-making operations, both are radically prospective, full of the incipience that the male model will see resolved in its images of detumescence and discharge. Their ends (in both senses of the word) are, quite literally, beginning itself. With this change of focus, the "middle" and its repetitions too must be conceptualized anew. Breast feeding involves much repetition without, I am told, all that much difference. Furthermore, it is stimulated by the demand of a very dependent other rather than by one's own desire. And its pleasure—which, I hear, is considerable—may well be why women keep doing it, but not why they are encouraged to.

Both breast feeding and birth involve the potentially—but not necessarily—satisfying presence of an other, and not simply the other who makes intercourse perhaps more gratifying than, but not essentially different from, masturbation. Now a woman whose mothering of this other was governed by an acute awareness of "ends in relation to beginnings" or, for that matter, beginnings in relation to ends would probably be both depressed and inefficient, whereas a man whose awareness of the logic of the pleasure principle inspired him to perfect his foreplay would be considered both a wise man and a good lover. We seem to have arrived at a crucial asymmetry in our analogy. While the male scheme fantasizes a scene of coupling, it then privileges a simultaneity of sensation and representability that is appropriate to one partner only (assuming, of course, that we are still talking about a heterosexual couple). In neither of the scenes of female experience in which a bodily part gets visibly larger and then smaller again can we fail to recognize that these changes are governed by the will, desire, and rhythms of another human being. The woman's will or desire may play a role in these processes, but it need not. A pregnancy may be willed (the result of reproductive lovemaking) or not (the result of rape or defective contraception); the onset of birth, too, is out of the mother's conscious control, unless one regards a representative of the medical profession and its chemical apparatus as an extension of her control; and a mother whose baby is asleep or sated is going to have trouble satisfying a desire to nurse it. Most important for our narratological purposes, however, both childbirth and breast feeding force us to think forward rather than backward; whatever finality birth possesses as a physical experience pales in comparison with the exciting, frightening sense of the beginning of a new life. (We should also not forget that birth is *painful;* its promise is so powerful that women often seem to forget what they have been through.)

Keeping in mind the possibility of some relation between female experiences of "tumescence and detumescence" and a narrative sense-making operation, we can now return to the narrative dynamics of *Frankenstein* and the particular quality of its irresolution. Critics have called attention to the thematics of birth in *Frankenstein,* noting poignantly that Shelley was pregnant, nursing a child, or mourning its death during the entire gestation of the novel.[5] Ellen Moers sees *Frankenstein* as "distinctly a *woman's* mythmaking on the subject of birth precisely because its emphasis is not upon what precedes birth, not upon birth itself, but upon what follows birth: the trauma of the afterbirth" (93). She reminds us that Shelley's experience as a mother was preceded by her experience as the daughter of a mother who died of poisoning when the placenta that had nourished the baby was not expelled and became septic. So Shelley's own experience of "beginnings in relation to ends" might itself be well described as the "trauma of the afterbirth."

Although Moers's analysis of the novel's focus on unsentimentalized motherhood is extraordinarily helpful, I am not sure I agree that Shelley set out to write a "horror story of maternity" (95). Moers overlooks that Frankenstein is a *male* mother; unlike the women in the novel, he is entirely unwilling to nurture the creature(s) dependent on him, although he all too readily sentimentalizes the creatures on whom he has been dependent. In other words, his indulgence in the retrospective mode of "male" sense making keeps him from acknowledging his ongoing responsibility to the birth he clones as well as from seeing that henceforth his plot inevitably involves the consequences of an act of creation that he regards as a triumph in and of itself. That creation would demand anything of him beyond the moment when scientific genius culminates the trajectory of its intellectual self-stimulation seems never to have occurred to him. Instead, in his fantasy of motherhood (which he calls fatherhood), he dwells exclusively on his own demands: "A new species would bless me as its creator and source; many happy and excellent natures would owe their being to me. No father [!] could claim the gratitude of his child so completely as I should deserve theirs" (53). The text suggests that Frankenstein has got things backward when, unlike a pregnant woman, he becomes increasingly pale and emaciated as his "creation" nears completion. And as if in anticipation of all the alienations his creature's alienation will cause him to share, he cuts himself off from friends and family for the duration of the project:

> I wished, as it were, to procrastinate all that related to my feelings of affection until the great object, which swallowed up every habit of my nature, should be completed. . . . [T]he energy of my purpose alone sustained me; my labours would soon end, and I believed that exercise and amusement would then drive away incipient disease; and I promised myself both of these when my creation should be complete. (54–55)

What Shelley's text makes appallingly clear is that the end of Frankenstein's "labours" effects a change in "all that related to [his] feelings of affection," if not in the feelings themselves. The postpartum nightmare in which "Elizabeth, in the bloom of health, walking in the streets of Ingolstadt" becomes "the corpse of my dead mother in my arms" is, of course, a neat foreshadowing of disasters to come, but it is also a parody of the kinds of retrospection Frankenstein has been promising himself as a reward for completing his act. The dream identifies Frankenstein with his mother and Elizabeth, so that the moment of retrospection fantasized by the pleasure principle becomes a nightmarish identification with the object of that fantasy. Frankenstein's completed feat, "read . . . in anticipation of the structuring power of those endings that will retrospectively give [it] the order and significance of plot" (Brooks, *Reading,* 94), is thus part of the wrong story, because it represents a beginning instead of an end. The dream concludes with an image of labor ("a cold dew covered my forehead, my teeth chattered, and every limb convulsed . . .") and culminates in a vision of the Monster: "I beheld the wretch—the miserable monster whom I had created" (57). The Monster's story not only emphasizes the disastrous consequences of confusing the accomplishment of fatherhood with the prospective relation of motherhood but involves them directly with issues of representability: it is the hideousness of his creation that triggers Frankenstein's abandonment of the Monster and leads to the series of brutal rejections that transform the creature's beautiful soul into a murderous one. The chain of monstrous acts that critics have had so much trouble accounting for within a traditional narratology seems to me to be about the inability of a male scheme to account for something it refuses to acknowledge. Shelley's use of the rhythms and dynamics of the experience of birth criticizes the culture's association of detumescence and "significant discharge" with ending and sense making. In its unrelenting insistence on the demands made by the figure whose existence turns the scientist's triumphant *consummatum est* into a new beginning, Shelley's narrative poses questions not accommodated in a *Master*plot and gestures toward an economy in which another consideration of the relations among beginnings, middles, and ends would yield radically different results.

3

From the way that both Brooks and Scholes implicate the scenario of male pleasure in the processes that determine narrative sequence as well as the narrative's aesthetic, erotic, and ethical yield, it would seem that the pleasure of the text depends on the gratification of the reader's erotic investment. Once we recognize how a psychoanalytic dynamics of reading assumes the universality of the male response, we have little difficulty noticing how arbitrary the foundations of its universalizations are. To examine how these assumptions make their way into critical practice, I want to return to Brooks's "dynamic model" for narrative and to the distinctions his discussion implies between properties of narrative that are formal (and that continue to be matters of form even when Brooks calls for a narrative "dynamics") and those that remain merely thematic. He specifically takes issue with a

> feminist criticism that needs to show how the represented female psyche (particularly of course as created by women authors) refuses and problematizes the dominant concepts of male psychological doctrine. Feminist criticism has in fact largely contributed to a new variant of the psychoanalytic study of fictive characters, a variant one might label the "situational-thematic": studies of Oedipal triangles in fiction, their permutations and evolution, of the role of mothers and daughters, of situations of nurture and bonding, and so forth. It is work often full of interest, but nonetheless methodologically disquieting in its use of Freudian analytic tools in a wholly thematic way, as if the identification and labeling of human relations in a psychoanalytic vocabulary were the task of criticism. ("Idea," 335)[6]

I especially like the "so forth." What it indicates is the writer's sense of the inessentiality ("situationality") of the feminist critic's concerns; Brooks seems not to be able to imagine that the study of, for instance, mothers and daughters in fiction could generate anything as compellingly theoretical as the study of fathers and sons. And such issues do indeed remain irrelevant to a narrative model that speaks to and of male experience. But they are more than irrelevant to Brooks's system; they threaten it and its hegemony. Feminist scholarship has been particularly and systematically critical of traditional psychoanalysis and self-consciously uncomfortable when it invokes the Freudian apparatus. Moreover, having recognized the extent to which any theory remains blind to its own thematics, much feminist criticism strikes me as being far less thematic than Brooks's. In attending to other versions of the issues traditionally referred to as "man's place in the world," "man's narratives," "man's fate," and so on, feminist scholarship calls into question the authority of many of the assumptions that enable Brooks to write it off as he does.

It is, then, only in the context of the androcentric paradigm that Brooks's Freudian reading of the crisis of paternity articulated by male nineteenth-century novelists can be considered the model for all narrative—or even for all "traditional narrative." Yet this "situational-thematic" swiftly becomes a paradigm, and we are asked to regard it as an issue of form rather than of theme. It is easy to fall into the trap such a move represents, since traditional narrative and criticism generally assume the universality of the male paradigm. And it is correspondingly difficult to map a way out of this trap, since this effort requires paying attention to interpretational details that could easily be written off as "merely" thematic ("studies of Oedipal triangles in fiction, their permutations and evolution, of the role of mothers and daughters, of situations of nurture and bonding, and so forth"), as quibbles about a part rather than statements about the whole.

Nevertheless. In a passage reflecting on the plots of Stendhal's novels, Brooks sees what he considers the major issues of nineteenth-century narrative:

> It is a fault inherent to fatherhood that to act toward the son, even with the intent of aiding him in *la chasse au bonheur* is inevitably to exercise an illegitimate (because *too* legitimate) control, to impose a model that claims authoritative (because authorial) status. All Stendhal's novels record the failure of authoritative paternity in his protagonists' lives, and at the same time demonstrate the narrator's attempt to retrieve the failure by being himself the perfect father, he who can maintain the conversation with his son. (*Reading,* 76)

This is, indeed, a formidable agenda, and Brooks's use of this situational-thematic to illuminate what is going on in *Le Rouge et le noir* is masterful. But his analysis proceeds at the expense of precisely the figures at whose expense Stendhal's novel—and Julien Sorel's plot—proceeds: the women. Hence, it reproduces, rather than acts critically on, the cultural assumptions encoded into the narrative form. Brooks comments, "[N]o longer interested in ambition, [Julien] judges his whole Parisian experience to have been an error; no longer interested in [the pregnant] Mathilde and his worldly marriage, he returns to the explicitly maternal embrace of Mme. de Renal" (*Reading,* 86). This passage has an endnote, and when I turned to the back of the book, hoping for a statement of discomfort about this sense-making operation, I found instead a long authorization, complete with references to the fathers of psychoanalysis and structural anthropology, of Julien's enactment of the oedipal story: "not only does Julien want Mme. de Renal to be mother to his unborn child, Mme. de Renal herself earlier expresses the wish that Julien were father to her children . . ." (337 n.25). By accepting such a hornet's nest as an issue of form instead of as a particular situation and a particular thematic, however powerfully they may govern what gets told in our culture, Brooks seems to vitiate rather than to enhance the power of his interpretation. If he claims for the novel the project of cultural criticism—of the nineteenth-century ideology of pleasure and its intersection with political institutions and narrative practices—then it would seem necessary to interrogate what becomes the uninterrogated ground of this vast cultural project, the woman's body and a particular myth of her pleasure and power that Brooks lays bare and then refuses to examine critically.[7] In the erotics of oedipal transmission, the woman is always a stage (in both senses of the word) for or in the working out of a problem of paternal interdiction, toward the moment of "significant discharge" when the son frees himself from the nets of paternal restriction and forges a self-creation—however ironized this process may be.

Like Scholes's homoaesthetic erotics of reading, then, Brooks's Masterplot occults the woman in such a way that the desire negotiated in the tug-of-war between men (here, fathers and sons) is played out, pleasured in, at her expense, without any acknowledgment of what her value outside this circuit of exchange might have been. *Le Rouge et le noir, La Peau de chagrin,* and *Nana* offer ample material for counterreadings, in which the text could be shown to be self-critically aware of the woman's presence as a function of its fantasy of the pleasure principle (Schor, *Breaking* and *Zola's Crowds*). Instead of undertaking such a counterreading, I would like to turn to a narrative of oedipal struggle written by a woman. George Eliot's *Romola* responds directly to such narratives as *Le Rouge et le noir* and *Great Expectations* by setting its central interests (if you will, its situational-thematic) in self-conscious opposition to its form (that is, the oedipal ideology of the nineteenth-century narrative trajectory).

4

When *Romola* appeared in 1863, it enjoyed considerable critical and popular success. In the course of the next century, however, it seems to have ceased to deliver reading pleasure, and if my students' responses are reliable indicators, the novel continues to baffle and annoy where Eliot's other works delight. Although a fascination with the Italian exotic might indeed have won readers in the 1860s, the novel's decline in popularity does not seem adequately explained by the density and heaviness that are Eliot's hallmarks. *Middlemarch,* for instance, has more pages and less action. Perhaps the modern resistance to *Romola* can best be understood as a measure of the novel's own resistance to its pleasure principle, for what Brooks would call its narrative desire and what the title indicates as its narrative interest turn out to occupy different and antagonistic trajectories.

Henry James called *Romola* "a kind of literary tortoise" (*"Deronda,"* 976). The image is particularly nice, since it enables us to envision the plot as a living organism encumbered by a burden it seems not to have been constructed to bear. *Romola* begins with the entrance into Florence of its ostensible hero, Tito Melema, and its plot traces his political rise and fall not only as a function of his ambition and desire but as a direct response to the oedipal challenge posed by his adoptive father, Baldassare Calvi. In other words, *Romola* is driven by precisely the dynamics Brooks describes in *Reading for the Plot.* But, I would contend, all its virtuoso plotting is but the tortoise without the shell.

The burden that so oppresses the novel and some of its readers is the subject announced in the title. *Romola* is ultimately not about Tito Melema, or even about his counterpart in the novel's other oedipal plot, Savonarola, but about its eponymous heroine (for a discussion of the novel that complements mine, see Homans, 189–222). The story of Romola is to some extent that of almost every George Eliot heroine: the struggle of an intelligent woman to live a life that does justice to her intelligence and to the vision it affords her. When Romola leaves Tito after his sale of her father's library, it is to seek out "the most learned woman in the world, Cassandra Fedele, at Venice, and ask her how an instructed woman could support herself in a lonely life there" (393). When she returns to Florence at Savonarola's behest, it is to follow his precept to "[l]ive for Florence—for [her] own people, whom God is preparing to bless the earth," to enter "that path of labour for the suffering and the hungry to which [she is] called as a daughter of Florence in these times of hard need" (438). Now Savonarola understands this duty to be primarily that of a wife, but Romola does not, and the interesting and difficult challenge she and the novel set for themselves is to find a vocation that follows the spirit of Savonarola's exhortation without succumbing to its letter.

It should not surprise us that the accomplishment of this challenge takes place outside Florence as well as (practically) outside narrative. As long as Romola remains in Florence, everything she does is presented by the narrative as determined by the logic of either Tito's or Savonarola's plot. The good deeds Romola performs when she joins Savonarola's followers, the Piagnoni, inevitably and repeatedly involve her with Baldassare as well as with Tito's other wife, Tessa, and we know that narrative "chance" has her encounter these particular representatives of Florentine society at large because of their—and her—importance (we might even say, despite themselves) to Tito's plot. That is, although her selfless, anonymous actions toward the befuddled, ailing old man and the charmingly vain and naive *contadina* are meant to demonstrate Romola's intention to subject her personal energies to the commonweal, what these events show us is the extent to which Romola, as the novel's protagonist, is subject to the exemplary oedipal plot even when she thinks she is generating a plot of her own. However much she might be out of Tito's thrall, she is precisely not free of his plot. Indeed, her story seems to be nothing but the record of the extent to which this is so. In our first glimpse of her as a Piagnone, we discover, as does she, that the half-dead man she revives with her wine is Baldassare. As a result, then, of the decision that breaks with and even defies Tito, Romola finds herself on the track of his oedipal secret. A subsequent incident functions in a similar manner: when, in an act of defiance expressing her uneasiness with the Piagnoni's anticarnival, Romola rescues Tessa from the zealots who would sacrifice the young woman's necklace to the "pyramid of vanities," the narrative immediately connects this act, through Baldassare's perception of it, to Tito's story. Again and again, Eliot's narrative checks Romola's will to a plot by subsuming her actions in the plot of her husband.

Yet Romola does have a story that is precisely *not* what the study of narrative would train us to regard as the story *of Romola*. Romola leaves Florence a second time, making her way to the Mediterranean coast, where she puts off to sea in a small sailboat. Instead of perishing, Romola awakens into a plot that rapidly acquires the force of legend—so rapidly, in fact, that it almost sacrifices its force as plot: she discovers a village decimated by plague, buries the dead, cares for the living, succumbs to exhaustion, recuperates in the care of the people she saved, and then decides she must return to Florence. The chapter has an oddly unspecific and dreamlike character that contrasts sharply with the novel's usual obsession with historical and local detail. This apparent departure from the historical novel is not, however, meant to be read as a dream; Eliot is careful to locate "Romola's Waking" in a specific history and, furthermore, in a specific history of persecution. The child whose crying "awakens" Romola from her reveries of "rest[ing] and resolv[ing] on nothing" (641) is a Portuguese Jew whose family is in flight from the Inquisition. The story of how Romola rescues a village and introduces a Jewish child into the Christian community is by no means a respite from history; it registers the intersection of two historical trajectories, reminding us, perhaps, of all the untold stories generated but not accounted for by the official histories that do get told. At this obscure historical crossroads, the sequence that in relation to *Romola's* Florentine plot could be summarized as "Romola went away and came back" acquires the force of legend:

> Every day the Padre and Jacopo and the small flock of surviving villagers paid their visit to this cottage to see the blessed Lady. . . . It was a sight they could none of them forget, a sight they all told of in their old age—how the sweet and sainted lady with her fair face, her golden hair, and her brown eyes that had a blessing in them, lay weary with her labours after she had been sent over the sea to help them in their extremity.
>
> Many legends were afterwards told in that valley about the blessed Lady who came over the sea, but they were legends by which all who heard might know that in times gone by a woman had done beautiful loving deeds there, rescuing those who were ready to perish. (649)

By narrating the process through which a historical community takes possession of an event, Eliot enables us to feel both the force of legend and its difference from the force of plot.

The movement here from history to legend, from plot to what resembles a protostructuralist narrative scheme, plays an important hermeneutic role in Eliot's novelistic commentary on the oedipal plot. What is *Romola* if not a dramatization of the question of where to find for female experience the authoritative pattern that turns mere inconsistency and formlessness" into a narrative of the effort to "shape . . . thought and deed in noble agreement" (Eliot, *Middlemarch,* 25)? And what is the Oedipus legend but Western culture's exemplary narrative model for this struggle? Every narrative, Eliot seems to be saying, needs a founding legend to lend provisional legitimacy to the accidents it records. Like Tito's, the male narrative has borrowed from the Oedipus legend for its readability; like Romola's, the female narrative remains in search of a comparably authoritative legend, the fiction of a "coherent social faith and order which could perform the function of knowledge for the ardently willing soul" (Eliot, *Middlemarch,* 25).[8]

Romola must and does provide its own legend, one that will govern and legitimate both our rereading of the novel and Romola's reading of her life. We should note, however, that the immediate transformation into legend of the episode in which Romola generates her own plot remains entirely ambivalent. She achieves legendary status in a community that is ignorant of her motivations for acting the way she does, to which she herself is essentially indifferent, and that is oblivious and irrelevant to the history in which we have been immersed for over five hundred pages: "Her work in this green valley was done, and the emotions that were disengaged from the people immediately around her rushed back into the old deep channels of use and affection. . . . Florence, and all her life there, had come back to her like hunger"(650–52). Romola's appetite for her own future requires that she return to Florence and realize what she has rehearsed in legend. We should note, moreover, that the narrative presents the story of Romola's deeds and its assimilation into village lore before we read of her decision to return to Florence. Is there not something wrong with disappearing into the impersonality of legend in the course of the narrative of one's own life? The process in which Romola becomes first the "sweet and sainted lady" and then the "blessed lady"—a process that turns her back into the villagers' original misprision of her—ratifies her decision to return to Florence, to reenter a history in which she is still alive and flawed, rather than embalmed in the collective past perfect. In addition to motivating the continuation of the novel, Eliot's account of the genesis of legend makes an important point about the relations of the self to its history and of this history to a community. The narrative significance of a life history lies ultimately in the hands (ears, mouths, pens) of others; however we attempt to shape this tale according to our sense of its retrospective significance, its retelling is always beyond our control; like Frankenstein's Monster, the plot generated by the life history takes on a life of its own as soon as the protagonist dies or otherwise signs off.

What distinguishes legend from plot, then, is not simply its emphasis on the general over the particular but its use of the retrospective mode. Plot, at least in the discussions we have focused on here, sees a particular action in the light of what it *will have meant* at a future moment that it is simultaneously determining and resisting. Plot registers the extent to which the protagonist can, through any particular action or sequence of actions, take possession of the totality of a life yet unled. It is a mode, we might say, of individual proleptic retrospection. Legend tells a story that is over. Its significance has been established not by its protagonist but by the community whose retelling of the story has become the sole measure of the story's importance. The legend is the possession of a community to the extent that this community is possessed by a story that has, quite literally, outlived its protagonist. No longer the narrative of an individual's attempt at self-determination, the legend predetermines the way each individual in the narrative community will confer significance on the plot of his or her life. Legend, then, structures a community, thereby determining the future of its own reception.

Romola's (and Romola's) final gesture must be viewed in relation to Eliot's understanding that the narrative community needs new legends to rescue female experience from the margins of narrative and to render it intelligible in its own right. In the epilogue, when Tito and Tessa's son declares to Romola that he "would like to be something that would make [him] a great man, and very happy besides—something that would not hinder [him] from having a good deal of pleasure" (674), she replies first with an admonition to choose the common good over personal gains and then with an anecdote that has the dispassionate economy of legend:

> There was a man to whom I was very near, so that I could see a great deal of his life, who made almost every one fond of him, for he was young, and clever, and beautiful, and his manners to all were gentle and kind. I believe, when I first knew him, he never thought of anything cruel or base. But because he tried to slip away from everything that was unpleasant, and cared for nothing else so much as his own safety, he came at last to commit some of the basest deeds—such as make men infamous. He denied his father, and left him to misery; he betrayed every trust that was reposed in him, that he might keep himself safe and get rich and prosperous. Yet calamity overtook him. (675)

Romola chooses not to tell the version of her husband's life that *Romola* has just told; no doubt Eliot could have devised for her heroine another last word had she wanted Romola simply to warn Nello against a career like his father's. What does it mean that a woman with Romola's experience tells a young man growing up in an all-female household a version of the Oedipus legend that is hardly recognizable as such? The gesture shows us what sense Romola has made of the events in the novel we have just read, on what interpretation of the past she is basing her present and projecting a future. It suggests a reason beyond the sentimental for her adoption of Tito's family: the myths of Oedipus and Antigone, of Ariadne and Bacchus, have structured her life, but that life has been one of ignorance. These myths spoke so eloquently of her culture's plot for her life that she remained blind to the desires generated by her experience. But there is another way to tell the story, one that we, perhaps, are not ready (or have just been made ready) to hear. We are meant, I think, to mark the discrepancies between Eliot's narrative and Romola's; we are challenged to reread the novel in the light of the lesson Romola has learned and the way she has chosen to teach it. If we start, as Nello does, with a different legend (that is, the same story told a different way), will our communities of understanding generate different narratives? The other stories have already been written; we simply have to learn how to read them.[9]

5

If we set out to seek women's pleasure in the text, there seems to have been scant yield of pleasure in our pursuit. And, indeed, neither the readings I have criticized nor those I have proposed entertain female pleasure as a representable option, although the former would hold out, I suspect, for the possibility of an accident, never recounted, in which the woman's desire would coincide exactly with the desire of the male protagonist and his official surrogate, the male reader. The meanings generated through the dynamic relations of beginnings, middles, and ends in traditional narrative and traditional narratology never seem to accrue directly to the account of the woman. At best, they point toward a rereading that evaluates the ideology of narrative dynamics according to whose desire they serve, rendering us suspicious of our complicity in what has presented itself to us as the pleasure of the text. We have been taught to read in drag and must begin to question seriously the determinants that govern the mechanics of our narratives, the notion of history as a sense-making operation, and the enormous investment the patriarchy has in maintaining them.

I would like to close with statements, roughly contemporaneous, from three figures central to our understanding of our culture and its narratives. Each was capable, despite his investment and powerful role in perpetuating the narratives of patriarchy from the nineteenth century into the twentieth, of glimpsing the utter arbitrariness of these constructs as well as the crucial role of gender in their formation and perpetuation. In 1900 Mrs. Everard Cotes sent Henry James a copy of her novel *His Honour and a Lady* and suggested that her writing was "like" his; in reply, James wrote:

> I think your drama lacks a little *line*—bony structure and palpable, as it were, tense cord—on which to string the pearls of detail. It's the frequent fault of women's work—and *I* like a rope (the rope of the direction *and march of the subject,* the action) pulled, like a taut cable between a steamer and tug, from beginning to end. [Your plot] lapses on a trifle too liquidly. (*Letters* 131)

Certainly this passage deserves any giggles it might provoke. But by underlining the "I" ("*I* like a rope") and admitting, a week later in another letter, that he "doubt[ed] if any man *ever* understands any woman's critical bias and method," James calls attention to the personal, ultimately arbitrary, and male bias of his own strictures (*Letters* 135). And a reading of his last novel, *The Golden Bowl,* could show how he addresses just this question of sexual difference by juxtaposing a man's "critical bias and method" with a woman's, offering us a glimpse of the kinds of pleasure narrative provides when the "pearls of detail" are strung differently—or not strung at all.

In *The Education of Henry Adams,* a text whose mythical investment in the figure of the virgin cannot be overstated, we read, "The study of history is useful to the historian by teaching him his ignorance of women; and the mass of this ignorance crushes one who is familiar enough with what are called historical sources to realize how few women have ever been known" (Adams, 353). And even Freud, in a rare moment of total divestiture, when he acknowledges his own inability—and furthermore, his utter lack of desire—to "cure" a perfectly healthy lesbian, whose only problem it seems, is her father's violent opposition to her choice of object, is able to distance himself from the Masterplot so crucial to his—and his followers'—constructions of culture and its narratives. He writes:

> So long as we trace the development from its final outcome backwards, the chain of events appears continuous and we feel we have gained an insight which is completely satisfactory and even exhaustive. But if we proceed the reverse way, if we start from the premises inferred from the analysis and try to follow them up to the final result, then we no longer get the impression of an inevitable sequence of events which could not have been otherwise determined. We notice at once that there might have been another result, and that we might have been just as well able to understand and explain the latter. The synthesis is thus not so satisfactory as the analysis; in other words, from a knowledge of the premises we could not have foretold the nature of the result. (154–55)[10]

155

It is time to start again, to see what comes of unstringing the Masterplot that wants to have told us in advance where it is that we should take our pleasures and what must inevitably come of them.[11]

NOTES

1. This is the place to acknowledge Scholes's subsequent engagement with feminism; his "Reading like a Man" shows that he has paid careful attention to the feminist revolution in his field: "More than any other critical approach feminism has forced us to see the folly of thinking about reading in terms of a transcendental subject: the ideal reader reading a text that is the same for all" (206). It is interesting to note the continuities in his practice: "reading like a man," he still prefers to articulate his (feminist) position in dialogue with a man (Jonathan Culler). This approach is certainly preferable to trashing female feminists. Yet a question remains: Does such a dialogue place the question of feminism in the "traditional position of women in patriarchy—the ultimately expendable item of exchange that merely gets the conversation going" (Boone 170), or can it be seen as a welcome response to Alice Jardine's suggestions that men "read women's writing—write on it and teach it . . . recognize [their] debts to feminism in writing . . . critique [their] male colleagues on the issue of feminism" (60–61)?

2. George Levine, for instance, writes, "[T]he text announces clearly . . . the terms of our modern crises," and goes on to discuss the "seven elements of the Frankenstein metaphor": "Birth and Creation"; "The Overreacher"; "Rebellion and Moral Isolation"; "The Unjust Society"; "The Defects of Domesticity"; "The Double"; "Technology, Entropy, and the Monstrous" (3–16).

3. Leo Bersani's work represents a compelling reading of Freud in relation to questions of narrative dynamics. Edward Said's language often resembles Brooks's, although Said examines "incipience" within a broader philosophical context. Among the numerous excellent book-length feminist studies of the nineteenth-century novel, Margaret Homans's and Marianne Hirsch's invoke a specifically feminist psychoanalysis that, whatever its debts to traditional psychoanalysis, focuses on other experiences and relations.

4. I am grateful to Susan Stanford Friedman for calling my attention to these issues, which my own lack of experience made me overlook in earlier versions of this paper. Further thanks to Marilyn Fries, Carolyn Heilbrun, Marianne Hirsch, Heidi Kruger, and Elaine Winnett, who have lent the authority of their experience to my subsequent attempts to do justice to the subject.

5. See Moers, 90–99 and Rieger, xi–xxiv. Johnson discusses *Frankenstein* as a narrative about maternity and female authorship.

6. Earlier, in *Reading for the Plot,* Brooks had this to say: "The female plot is not unrelated to [male plots of ambition], but it takes a more complex stance toward ambition, the formation of an inner drive toward the assertion of selfhood in resistance to the overt and violating male plots of ambition, a counterdynamic which, from the prototype *Clarissa* to *Jane Eyre* and *To the Lighthouse,* is only superficially passive and in fact a reinterpretation of the vectors of plot" (39); p. 133 in this volume. Indeed. Brooks further describes the female plot as "a resistance and what we might call an 'endurance': a waiting (and suffering) until the woman's desire can be a permitted response to the expression of male desire" (*Reading,* 330 n.3; p. 137 in this volume). See Hirsch, "Ideology," as well as Nancy K. Miller, *The Heroine's Text* and "Emphasis Added" [pp. 110–29 in this volume].

7. If we take the time to look at her now, we discover that she is either "impervious to desire, a smooth surface on which desire cannot take hold" (Balzac's Foedora [Brooks, *Reading,* 57]) or a being (Zola's Nana) whose "sexual organ, which is nothing, absence, becomes a tool more powerful than all phallic engines, capable of supreme leverage on the world" (Brooks, *Reading* 47).

8. Eliot seems intent on emphasizing the inadequacy of the legends available for structuring women's lives and narratives. Like the "legends . . . told in that valley about the blessed Lady who came over the sea," the legend of Saint Theresa that begins *Middlemarch* is neither a successful enough précis of the forces impelling and driving women's lives nor a strong enough cultural force itself to guide Dorothea Brooke to a better understanding of her desires and to a more satisfying realization of the potential Eliot bestows on her.

9. In "Beyond Determinism," Gillian Beer examines Eliot's narrative responses to the question "[C]an the female self be expressed through plot or must it be conceived in resistance to plot?" (117). Because of her interest in non-Freudian determinism, Beer passes over *Romola* ("After *Romola,* in which a succession of fathers and father-figures are killed and rejected, fathers are notably absent from [Eliot's] work" [129]) to focus on Gwendolyn's survival of "the business of sexual selection" (131), her acceptance of a "heterogeneity" of her own that calls into question the integrity of a Darwinian narrative model. I am not certain, however, that the killing or rejecting of fathers does away with the problem of oedipal determination in Eliot's later works; it is, after all, when she confronts the oedipal plot head on that Eliot can conclude a novel with her female protagonist actively involved in the narrative project.

10. The German, "so kommt uns der Eindruck einer notwendigen und auf keine andere Weise zu bestimmenden Verkettung ganz abhanden" (276–77), expresses better than the English translation the notion both of the narrative "chain" and the threat of things getting "out of hand."

11. I should like to thank Joe Boone, Peter Brooks, Rachel Brownstein, Carolyn Heilbrun, Marianne Hirsch, Jann Matlock, Nancy Miller, Julie Rivkin, Dan Selden, Catharine Stimpson, and Margaret Wailer, whose careful readings of this article helped me see the many other "halves" of the argument.

REFERENCES

Adams, Henry. *The Education of Henry Adams.* Boston: Houghton, 1961.

Beer, Gillian. "Beyond Determinism: George Eliot and Virginia Woolf." *Arguing with the Past: Essays in Narrative from Woolf to Sidney,* 117–37, London: Routledge, 1989.

———. *Darwin's Plots: Evolutionary Narrative in Darwin, George Eliot and Nineteenth-Century Fiction.* London: Routledge, 1983.

Bersani, Leo. *The Freudian Body.* New York: Columbia University Press, 1982.

Boone, Joseph Allen. "Me(n) and Feminism." *Gender and Theory: Dialogues on Feminist Criticism,* edited by Linda Kauffman, 158–80, Oxford: Blackwell, 1989.

Brooks, Peter. "The Idea of a Psychoanalytic Literary Criticism." *Critical Inquiry* 13 (1987): 334-48.

———. *Reading for the Plot: Design and Intention in Narrative.* New York: Knopf, 1984.

Chambers, Ross. *Story and Situation: Narrative Seduction and the Power of Fiction.* Minneapolis: University of Minnesota Press, 1984.

deLauretis, Teresa. *Alice Doesn't: Feminism, Semiotics, Cinema.* Bloomington: Indiana University Press, 1984.

Eliot, George. *Middlemarch.* London: Penguin, 1985.

———. *Romola.* London: Penguin, 1980.

Freud, Sigmund. "The Psychogenesis of a Case of Homosexuality in a Woman." 1920. Translated by Barbara Low and R. Gabler. In *Sexuality and the Psychology of Love*, 133–59. New York: Collier, 1963.

———. "Über die Psychogenese eines Falles von weiblicher Homosexualität," 1920. *Studienausgabe*. Vol. 7, 255–81. Frankfurt: Fischer, 1982.

Gates, Henry Louis, Jr. *The Signifying Monkey: A Theory of African-American Literary Criticism*. New York: Oxford University Press, 1988.

Hirsch, Marianne. "Ideology, Form, and *Allerleihrauh:* Reflections on *Reading for the Plot.*" *Children's Literature* 14 (1986): 163–68.

———. *The Mother/Daughter Plot: Narrative, Psychoanalysis, Feminism*. Bloomington: Indiana University Press, 1989.

Homans, Margaret. *Bearing the Word: Language and Female Experience in Nineteenth-Century Women's Writing*. Chicago: University of Chicago Press, 1986.

James, Henry. "*Daniel Deronda:* A Conversation." *Literary Criticism*, 974–92. New York: Library of America, 1984.

———. *Letters*. Vol. 4. Edited by Leon Edel. Cambridge, Mass.: Harvard University Press, 1984. 4 vols. 1977–84.

Jameson, Fredric. *The Political Unconscious: Narrative as a Socially Symbolic Act*. Ithaca, N.Y.: Cornell University Press, 1981.

Jardine, Alice. "Men in Feminism: Odor di Uomo or Compagnons de Route?" Jardine and Smith, 54–61.

Jardine, Alice, and Paul Smith, eds. *Men in Feminism*. New York: Methuen, 1987.

Johnson, Barbara. "My Monster/My Self." *Diacritics* 12, no. 2 (1982): 2–10.

Levine, George. "The Ambiguous Heritage of *Frankenstein*." *The Endurance of Frankenstein: Essays on Mary Shelley's Novel*. Edited by George Levine and U. C. Knoepflmacher, 3–18. Berkeley: University of California Press, 1979.

Miller, D. A. *The Novel and the Police*. Berkeley: University of California Press, 1988.

Miller, Nancy K. "Emphasis Added: Plots and Plausibilities in Women's Fiction." In *Subject to Change: Reading Feminist Writing*, 25–46. New York: Columbia University Press, 1988.

———. *The Heroine's Text: Readings in the French and English Novel (1722–1782)*. New York: Columbia University Press, 1980.

Moers, Ellen. *Literary Women*. Garden City, N.Y.: Doubleday, 1976.

Rieger, James, ed. *Frankenstein: Or, The Modern Prometheus (the 1818 Text)*. New York: Bobbs, 1974.

Said, Edward. *Beginnings: Intention and Method*. New York: Columbia University Press, 1975.

Scholes, Robert. *Fabulation and Metafiction*. Urbana: University of Illinois Press, 1979.

———. "Reading Like a Man." Jardine and Smith, 204–18.

Schor, Naomi. *Breaking the Chain: Women, Theory, and French Realist Fiction*. New York: Columbia University Press, 1985.

———. *Zola's Crowds*. Baltimore, Md.: Johns Hopkins University Press, 1978.

Sedgwick, Eve Kosofsky. *Between Men: English Literature and Male Homosocial Desire*. New York: Columbia University Press, 1985.

Shelley, Mary. *Frankenstein; Or, The Modern Prometheus*. New York: Dell, 1974.

▮ PART III

NARRATIVE SEQUENCING

Introduction: Narrative Progressions and Sequences

From Aristotle to Forster, critics and theorists have generally favored a plausible, unified, causally connected plot over wayward strands of unconnected, arbitrary incidents. Indeed, many theorists have even written as if all narrative sequences were necessarily connected into a single plot. Nevertheless, the history of literature provides us with any number of irregular, disjunctive, or retrograde clusters of events that severely contest the ideas of unity and teleology. One can readily think of works by Rabelais, Sterne, Diderot, Jean Paul, and Celine that do not seem at all to have a readily identifiable story line or unitary trajectory; rather, they can be more accurately described as resisting any such totalization. Modernism gave us the attenuated sequences of virtually plotless works, *écriture féminine* takes episodic sequences to new levels of dispersal, while postmodern texts repeatedly challenge the very nature of narrative in ways that supercede even Tristram Shandy's ingenious graph of his own plot lines. It this area, the ingenuity of creative writers has largely outstripped the theoretical analysis of their extraordinary achievements.

Many of the basic tools for an analysis of narrative sequence were set forth by Boris Tomashevsky, who began by distinguishing *fabula* (story), or "the aggregate of mutually related events" in chronological sequence, from *syuzhet,* the actual arrangement of those events as presented by the text. In the translation below, *syuzhet* is rendered (perhaps somewhat misleadingly) as "plot." Tomashevsky makes a number of other distinctions that would regularly reappear in narrative theory for several decades. The irreducible elements of the story are termed motifs; those which are irreplaceable are termed "bound motifs," while those that could be omitted without disturbing the whole causal-chronological course of events are "free motifs." Tomashevsky goes on to discuss motivation, or the connection between different motifs, and identifies the very different practices of compositional, realistic, and artistic motivation.

Viktor Shklovsky (who had, incidently, first noted the distinction that Tomashevsky would subsequently formalize as *fabula/syuzhet*), discusses the use of nonmimetic sequences of events in an important but little known essay, "The Relationship between Devices of Plot Construction and General Devices of Style." In it, he identifies the significant role of formal (or as he sometimes terms it, "artistic") arrangements of narrative materials. These techniques include repetition, parallelism, antithesis, and triadic patterns; in such texts, the form is primary and the events themselves secondary. Much of the *Chanson de Roland,* for example, is composed around dualistic and triadic repetitions of actions and events. In fact, many of the events are present only because they complete the pattern that has been deployed, as realistic concerns become irrelevant and causal connection between such events is minimal or absent. In Shklovsky's words, "form creates for itself its own content."[1]

From the thirties to the fifties, Lukacsian socialist realism was significantly challenged by the dramatic theory and practices of Bertold Brecht, who did much to interject new ideas that would continue to circulate, to mention only a few sites, in the plays of Caryl Churchill, the films of Godard, and the narrative theory of Barthes and his successors. Brecht drew on Elizabethan drama and developed an "epic" theater that was deliberately episodic, curvilinear, resisted closure, employed narration, pointed to its own constructedness, and eschewed realism. Each scene exited for itself, was intended to be critically assessed, and foregrounded process at all points.

Since the end of the 1960s, important work on narrative sequencing and progressions has regularly been set forth. Hayden White has written extensively on the methods by which historical events are given narrative form. In one particularly useful article, "The Value of Narrativity in the Representation of Reality," he differentiates between annals, which show no necessary connection between the events they record, chronicles, which contain a greater degree of organization and comprehensiveness, and historical narratives proper, which are plotted along causally connected lines toward a recognizable closure. In the essay included in this volume, White explains how historians endow sets of past events with meaning by exploiting similarities between sets of real events and the conventional structures of our fictions. The emplotment of historical events into a narrative is essentially a literary, not to say fictionalizing, activity.

Benjamin Hrushovski examines the issues of segmentation and motivation in what he calls the text continuum of literary prose. Deriving his concepts from a meticulous analysis of the many different segments and junctions of the opening episode of *War and Peace,* he argues that a literary text is "an unfolded continuum which has its own logic and its own organization and from which a reader is led to construct both 'form' and 'meaning.'"[2] He notes that a motif need not always be chained together with others to form a *fabula;* instead, a portion of text may serve as motif for several heterogenous patterns. He also differentiates between immediate, long-range, and global motivations.

In the section below, James Phelan outines an equally comprehensive theory of narrative progression that seeks to show how authors generate, sustain, develop, and resolve readers' interest in narrative. Such movement is given shape by the various interpretive instabilities that arise in the text. Instabilities may occur in the story, either between characters or created by situations. Alternatively, they may exist between readers and authors or narrators; such instabilities, created by the discourse, often involve differences in value, belief, knowledge, or expectation. The reader's processing of an individual instability is based on and modified by the perceived resolution of previous instabilities; each text retains its difference and the theory itself is a dynamic one. Finally, Phelan insists that issues of narrative progression are inextricably tied both to issues of character and larger theoretical issues of interpretation.

Structuralist-inspired investigations turned up a number of revealing patterns in unexpected texts. Some of these were synthesized in R. G. Peterson's article, "Critical Calculations: Measure and Symmetry in Literature," which outlined numerological and symmetrical patterns in the structure and sequence of chapters, books, and episodes, thus supplanting in part the customary dictates of plot. William W. Ryding analyzed several basic inorganic and non-Aristotelian structures in medieval narrative. Elsewhere, Jonathan Culler attempted to reassess the relation of *fabula* and *syuzhet.* Theorizing some recent critical speculations on the dubious or seemingly contradictory aspects of the *fabulas* of *Oedipus Rex* and *Daniel Deronda* in which causal progression seems to be inverted, and a key event (e.g., Deronda's Jewishness) is the effect that seems to precede the cause that engendered it. At a certain point, that is, the requirements of the plot determine the events (and their antecedents) that must occur (and be discovered). Though the article generated considerable interest, it has been challenged by a number of theorists, including Monika Fludernik, who identifies a rhetorical sleight of hand at work in this analysis.[3] Though Culler was unable to prove that the *fabula* in these works is somehow unstable, he does draw important attention to the difference between an anticipated *fabula* and the one finally disclosed by the discourse.

The 1970s and 1980s saw an explosion of innovative narrative analysis of postmodern works that established theoretical frameworks had not been able to adequately circumscribe. Jean Ricardou was himself an ingenious artificer of unusual fictions who had constructed a novel, *La Prise de Constantinople,* that could be read either front to back or back to front. He rapidly emerged as a major spokesman for the revolutionary fiction being written in France; in the essay excerpted below, he painstakingly analyzes and distinguishes between the compositional techniques employed to produce the texts of representative *nouveaux romans* and *Tel Quel* novels. Though the language he uses, with its emphasis on mechanism and structure, may seem outdated, it was at the time a very effective antidote to the attacks of arbitrariness and pointlessness leveled by conservative critics who could not understand the new texts' *raison d'être.* Soon after, critics like Roland Barthes and Charles Caramello examined the alternative "alphabetical orderings" of texts like Butor's *Mobile,* Walter Abish's *Alphabetical Africa,* and Barthes's own *Roland Barthes.* David Hayman, in *Re-Forming the Narrative* (1986), contributed to this critical project with his timely accounts of different types of textual self-generation,[4] and of what he terms "nodality," in which repetitions, echoes, permutations, and interlocking patterns do the work conventionally done by plot, which is now displaced.[5] Additional essential work appeared in Brian McHale's *Postmodernist Fiction* (1987, esp. 99–130) and Roy Jay Nelson's *Causality and Narrative in French Fiction from Zola to Robbe-Grillet* (1990). The most recent theoretical attempt to cover many of these disparate possible sequencings is found in Fludernik.[6]

Feminist and lesbian theorists made important contributions to the study of narrative sequence. *Écriture féminine* suggested new modes of narrative composition and progression that featured streams of language, discursive ruptures, and unexpected trajectories. In an article "Piecing and Writing," Elaine Showalter used the metaphor of quilting to depict the nonlinear collocation of related and adjacent stories in women's fiction from the nineteenth century. Both Marilyn Farwell and Judith Roof[7] have gone on to examine our very understanding of narrative and narrative theory to explain why heterosexual, marital, reproductive plots are so pervasive and insistent; for Roof, "something in the way we understand what a story is in the first place or something in the way narrative itself operates produces narrative's 'heterosexually friendly' shape."[8] Susan Stanford Friedman, adapting Bakhtin's notion of the chronotope and Kristeva's concept of text, defines narrative as the representation of movement within the coordinates of space and time. She postulates two "axes" of a text, one vertical, the other horizontal, whose symbiotic intersections are reconstructed by the reader in the process of interpretation. Both represent a movement through space and time, the horizontal referring to the linear movement of the characters through the coordinates of textual space and time, while the vertical designates the space and time inscribed by the writer and reconstituted by the reader as they collectively produce the text.

The vertical axis can be further separated into the literary, the historical, and the psychic strands. Together, these axes map out both the movement of the narrative and the story of our processing of that narrative in all its varied layers. In the last essay in this section, Robyn Warhol brings together and reexamines a number of positions discussed by earlier theorists as she ingeniously examines the conventions of serialized domestic fiction. She argues that serial form, by its inherent resistence to closure, continually undermines the ideological imperative for a man to couple up with a woman and for the two to stay that way forever that is found in most popular fiction. Ironically, this most Victorian of narrative conventions propagates a profoundly anti-"Victorian," anticonventional vision of sexual life, she concludes.

Looking back at this diverse body of theoretical work, we can get a sense of the multiplicity of sequencing strategies, the potential ideological valences of certain kinds of sequencing, and also the corresponding difficulties in articulating a unified concept of narrative production. On the other hand, we can readily conclude that nonplot-based techniques of text generation, as variously outlined by Shklovsky, Barthes, Ricardou, Ryding, Peterson, and Hayman, finally need to be included within more general accounts of narrative dynamics.

NOTES

1. Victor Shklovsky, "The Relationship between Devices of Plot Construction and General Devices of Style," in *Theory of Prose,* trans. Benjamin Sher (Elmwood Park, Ill.: Dalkey Archive Press, 1990), 24.

2. Benjamin Hrushovski, *Segmentation and Motivation in the Text Continuum of Literary Prose: The First Episode of* War and Peace. Papers on Poetics and Semiotics, vol. 5 (Tel Aviv University: Porter Institute, 1976), 11.

3. Monica Fludernik, *Towards a 'Natural' Narratology* (London: Routledge, 1996), 320–21.

4. David Hayman, *Re-Forming the Narrative: Toward a Mechanics of Modernist Fiction* (Ithaca, N.Y.: Cornell University Press, 1987), 105–46.

5. Ibid., 73–104.

6. Fludernik, *Towards a 'Natural' Narratology,* 288–310.

7. Judith Roof, *Come As You Are: Sexuality and Narrative* (New York: Columbia University Press, 1996), 41–72.

8. Ibid., xxxii.

12

Story, Plot, and Motivation

BORIS TOMASHEVSKY

STORY AND PLOT

A theme has a certain unity and is composed of small thematic elements arranged in a definite order.

We may distinguish two major kinds of arrangement of these thematic elements: (1) that in which causal-temporal relationships exist between the thematic elements, and (2) that in which the thematic elements are contemporaneous, or in which there is some shift of theme without internal exposition of the causal connections. The former are *stories* (tales, novels, epics); the latter have no "story," they are "descriptive" (e.g., descriptive and didactic poems, lyrics, and travel books such as Karamzin's *Letters of a Russian Traveler* or Goncharov's *The Frigate Pallas*).

We must emphasize that a story requires not only indications of time, but also indications of cause. Time indicators may occur in telling about a journey, but if the account is only about the sights and not about the personal adventures of the travelers, we have exposition without story. The weaker the causal connection, the stronger the purely chronological connection. As the story line becomes weaker, we move from the novel to the chronicle, to a simple statement of the sequence of events (*The Childhood Years of Bagrov's Grandson*).[1]

Let us take up the notion of the story (*fabula*), the aggregate of mutually related events reported in the work. No matter how the events were originally arranged in the work and despite their original order of introduction, in practice the story may be told in the actual chronological and causal order of events.

164

Plot (*syuzhet*) is distinct from story. Both include the same events, but in the plot the events *are arranged* and connected according to the orderly sequence in which they were presented in the work.[2]

The idea expressed by the theme is the idea that summarizes and unifies the verbal material in the work. The work as a whole may have a theme, and at the same time each part of a work may have its own theme. The development of a work is a process of diversification unified by a single theme. Thus Pushkin's "The Shot" develops the story of the narrator's meetings with Silvio and the Count, and the story of the conflict between the two men. The story of life in the regiment and the country is developed, followed by the first part of the duel between Silvio and the Count, and the story of their final encounter.

After reducing a work to its thematic elements, we come to parts that are irreducible, the smallest particles of thematic material: "evening comes," "Raskolnikov kills the old woman," "the hero dies," "the letter is received," and so on. The theme of an irreducible part of a work is called the *motif;* each sentence, in fact, has its own motif.

It should be noted that the meaning of "motif," as used in historical poetics—in comparative studies of migratory plots (for example, in the study of the *skaz* [or yarn][3])—differs radically from its meaning here, although they are usually considered identical. In comparative studies a motif is a thematic unit which occurs in various works (for example, "the abduction of the bride," "the helpful beast"—that is, the animal that helps the hero solve his problem—etc.). These motifs move in their entirety from one plot to another. In comparative poetics, reduction to the smaller elements is not important; what is important is only that within the limits of the given genre these "motifs" are always found in their complete forms. Consequently, in comparative studies one must speak of motifs that have remained intact historically, that have preserved their unity in passing from work to work, rather than of "irreducible" motifs. Nevertheless, many motifs of comparative poetics remain significant precisely because they are also motifs in our theoretical sense.

Mutually related motifs form the thematic bonds of the work. From this point of view, the story is the aggregate of motifs in their logical, causal-chronological order; the plot is the aggregate of those same motifs but having the relevance and the order which they had in the original work. The place in the work in which the reader learns of an event, whether the information is given by the author, or by a character, or by a series of indirect hints—all this is irrelevant to the story. But the aesthetic function of the plot is precisely this bringing of an arrangement of motifs to the attention of the reader. Real incidents, not fictionalized by an author, may make a story. A plot is wholly an artistic creation.

Usually there are different kinds of motifs within a work. By simply retelling the story we immediately discover what may be omitted without destroying the coherence of the narrative and what may not be omitted without disturbing the connections among events. The motifs which cannot be omitted are *bound motifs;* those which may be omitted without disturbing the whole causal-chronological course of events are *free motifs.*

Although only the bound motifs are required by the story, free motifs (digressions, for example) sometimes dominate and determine the construction of the plot. These incidental motifs (details, etc.) are presented so that the tale may be told artistically; we shall return later to the various functions they perform. Literary tradition largely determines the use of free motifs, and each literary school has its characteristic stock; however, bound motifs are usually distinguished by their "vitality"—that is, they appear unchanged in the works of various schools. Nevertheless, literary tradition clearly plays a significant role in the development of the story (for example, the stories of typical novels of the 1840s and 1850s are about the disasters of a petty official—e.g., Gogol's "The Greatcoat," Dostoevsky's *Poor People;* in the 1820s the stories were usually about the unfortunate love of a European for a foreigner—e.g., Pushkin's *Captive of the Caucasus* and *The Gypsies*).

In "The Undertaker" Pushkin wrote pointedly about the use of free motifs within a literary tradition:

> Just at noon the next day, the coffin maker and his daughters left through the wicket side-gate of their newly purchased home and set off for a neighbor's. I shall not begin to describe either the Russian kaftan of Adrian Prokhorovich nor the European clothes of Akulina or Darya—differing in that respect from the usual notions of recent novelists. I suppose, however, that it is not superfluous to note that both children wore the yellow caps and red shoes that they customarily wear only on festive occasions.

The description of the clothes is remarked upon here as a traditional free motif of that period (the 1830s).

Among the various kinds of motifs we may distinguish a special class of introductory motifs which require specific supplementation by other motifs, as, typically, when the hero is given a task. For example: A father wants his daughter to marry; the daughter, to avoid the marriage, assigns an impossible task. Or the hero woos the princess who, to avoid the dreaded marriage, sets him a task which at first seems impossible; or, as in Pushkin's "Tale of Balda," the priest, in order to rid himself of a worker, commissions him to collect quit rent from the devil. Any embodiment of this task motif requires an account of the task itself, an account which also serves to introduce the story of the hero's exploits. The delay of the story is another such motif; in *The Arabian Nights* Scheherazade forestalls her execution by telling stories to the prince who threatens to take her life. This "story telling" motif is the device which introduces the tales. So also in adventure stories there are motifs of pursuit, and so on. Usually the introduction of a free motif occurs as a development of a previously introduced motif which is inherently bound up with the story.

Motifs may be also classified according to their objective functions. Usually a story is developed by introducing several characters (dramatis personae) related to each other by mutual interests or by other ties (kinship, for example). This interrelationship at any given moment is the *situation*. For example, the hero loves the heroine, but she loves his rival. We have three characters: hero, heroine, rival. These are the ties: the love of the hero for the heroine and her love for the rival. Also typical are situations in which the characters are related by opposition, in which different persons want to change a situation by different means. For example the hero loves the heroine and she loves him, but the parents prevent their marriage; they try to marry, the parents try to separate them.

A story may be thought of as a journey from one situation to another. During the journey a new character may be introduced (complicating the situation), old characters eliminated (for example, by the death of the rival), or the prevailing relationships changed.

Motifs which change the situation are *dynamic motifs;* those which do not are static. Consider, for example, Pushkin's "Mistress into Maid." Although Alexey Berestov loves Akulina, his father is arranging his marriage to Liza Muromskaya. Alexey, unaware that Akulina and Liza are one and the same person, objects to the marriage thrust upon him by his father. He goes to have it out with Liza and discovers that she is Akulina, so the situation changes—Alexey's objections to the marriage vanish. The discovery that Akulina and Liza are the same person is a dynamic motif.

Free motifs are usually static, but not all static motifs are free. Thus we assume that if a murder is necessary to the progress of the story, one of the characters must have a revolver. The motif of the revolver, as the reader becomes aware of it, is both static and bound—bound because without the revolver the murder could not be committed. This situation occurs in Ostrovsky's *The Poor Bride.*

Descriptions of nature, local color, furnishings, the characters, their personalities, and so on—these are typically static motifs. The actions and behavior of the main characters are typically dynamic motifs.

Dynamic motifs are motifs which are central to the story and which keep it moving; in the plot, on the other hand, static motifs may predominate.

From the point of view of the story, motifs are easily ranked according to their importance. Dynamic motifs are most important, then motifs which prepare their way, then motifs defining the situation, and so on. The relative importance of a motif to the story may be determined by retelling the *story* in abridged form, then comparing the abridgement with the more fully developed narrative.

The development of a story may generally be understood as a progress from one situation to another, so that each situation is characterized by a *conflict* of interest, by discord and struggle among the characters.[4] The dialectical development of the story is analogous to the development of social-historical processes in which each new historical stage is seen both as a result of the struggle of social groups in the preceding stage and as a battlefield for the interests of the new social group constituting the current social system.

The struggle among the characters (the conflicts of interests mentioned above) is accompanied both by the gathering of the characters into groups and by the agreement of each group upon the tactics to be used against the other. This conduct of the struggle— the aggregate of motifs which characterize it— is called the intrigue (the usual term in dramatic criticism).

The development of the intrigue (or, with complex groups of characters, parallel intrigues) leads either to the elimination of the conflicts or to the creation of new conflicts. Usually at the end of the story all the conflicts are reconciled and the interests harmonized. If a situation containing the conflict furthers the progress of the story, then, since the coexistence of two conflicting forces is impossible, one must inevitably prevail. The later harmonious situation, which does not require further development, will neither evoke nor arouse the reader's anticipation. That is why the condition at the end of a work is so static. This static condition is called the *ending*.[5] Thus the old moralistic novels usually have a double movement in which virtue is oppressed while vice triumphs (a moral conflict), but in the ending virtue is rewarded and vice punished.

Sometimes a harmonious situation is found at the beginning of stories in which, for example, "the hero had been living peacefully and quietly. Suddenly . . . etc." Here, in order to get the story going, a dynamic motif destroys the initial peaceful situation. The aggregate of such motifs, disturbing the tranquillity of the initial situation and provoking action, is called the exciting force. Usually the nature of the exciting force determines the whole course of the story, and all the intrigue is reducible only to the various motifs which determine the basic conflict introduced by the exciting force. This change is the *peripety* (the movement from one situation to another).

The more complicated the conflict within the situation and the stronger the opposing interests of the characters, the greater the *tension* of situation. The increase in tension is proportionate to the proximity of a great change of fortune. Tension is usually achieved by preparing for the change in the situation. Thus in the typical adventure novel the villain, seeking to destroy the hero, constantly has the odds in his favor. He prepares for the hero's defeat, but at the last possible moment, when the hero's downfall seems positively certain, he is unexpectedly saved and the machinations of his enemies frustrated. Such preparation increases the tension.

Tension usually reaches its highest point just before the ending. This culminating point of the tension is usually called the climax (*Spannung*). In the simplest system of dialectics relevant to the construction of a story, the climax is like the antithesis (the thesis is the exciting force, the antithesis the climax, and the synthesis the ending).

We must remember that the formation of a plot from the material of the story requires a narrative introduction to the initial situation. The presentation of circumstances determining the initial cast of characters and their interrelationships is called the exposition.

Not all narratives begin with an exposition.[6] In the simplest case—that in which the author opens by acquainting us with the elements of the story material—we have *immediate exposition*. But the quick start (*ex abrupto*), in which the presentation begins with previously developed events and we are only gradually acquainted with the situation of the hero, is also fairly common. In such cases we have *delayed exposition,* which is sometimes quite prolonged. We may distinguish among the introductory motifs which comprise the exposition. Sometimes we come to know the situation through hints, and only the assimilation of such seemingly incidental remarks forms a coherent impression; then we do not have exposition proper—that is, the expository motifs are not grouped into one complete narrative section.

But sometimes, when outlining a certain event whose general ramifications we do not yet understand, the author, in clarifying it (either through his own comments or through the speech of a character) will include expository material which tells us about what has already happened. Then we have *transposed exposition;* more specifically, we have a time shift in the elaboration of the story material.

Delayed exposition may be continued to the very end, so that throughout the whole narrative the reader sometimes does not know all that is necessary for understanding what happens. Usually the author withholds information about the circumstances involving a group of major characters, telling the reader only what one or the other of the characters knows. The information about these "unrevealed" circumstances is then given in the ending. Such an ending, including in itself elements of exposition and, as it were, casting light back on everything preceding the peripety, is called a *regressive ending*. Let us assume that neither the reader of Pushkin's "Mistress into Maid" nor the hero, Alexey Berestov, knows the identity of Akulina and Liza Muromskaya. In that event, information about that identity would have regressive force—that is, it would give a true and fresh understanding of all the preceding situations. "Snowstorm," also from Pushkin's *Tales of Belkin,* is so constructed.

Usually this delayed exposition begins as a series of hints. In that case, these combinations are possible: The reader knows, the main characters do not; some of the characters know, some do not; the reader and some of the characters do not know; no one knows (the truth is discovered by accident); the characters know, but the reader does not.

These hints may run throughout the narrative and may involve only some of the motifs. In such a case the same motif may appear several times in the construction of the plot. Consider a typical novelistic device: One of the characters, long before the time of the action, has been kidnaped (first motif). A character appears, and we learn from his biography that he was not raised by his parents and does not know them (second motif). Then we learn (usually by comparison of dates and circumstances, or by the motif of a sign—an amulet, a birthmark, etc.) that the kidnaped child and the hero are the same person. Thus the identity of the first and second motifs is established. This repetition of a motif in variant forms is typical of plots in which aspects of the story are not introduced in their natural chronological order. A repeated motif usually shows the connection which exists in the story between parts of the plot structure. Thus, if, in the typical example used above, the means of recognizing the lost child is an amulet, then this amulet motif accompanies both the narrative about the disappearance of the child and the biography of the new character. (See, for example, Ostrovsky's *The Guilty Are Without Blame.*)

Such connecting motifs make chronological displacements possible in narratives.[7] Exposition is not the only element that may be transposed; certain parts of the story may be narrated after the reader knows that they have already occurred. A coherent account of significant parts of an event which foretells what will happen in an episode before it is narrated is called foreshadowing (*Vorgeschichte*). Delayed exposition, or the presentation of the biography of a new character introduced into a new situation, are typical forms of foreshadowing. Many examples of the technique may be found in Turgenev's novels. "Premonition" (*Nachgeschichte*), an account of what will happen told prior to the approaching events to prepare the reader, is more rare. *Nachgeschichte* sometimes takes the form of auguries, predictions, or of more or less likely assumptions. . . .

In analyzing the plot structure of individual works, attention should also be given to the use of *time* and *place* in the narrative.

Story time and *reading time* are distinct in a work of art. Story time is the amount of time required by the events that are said to occur; reading time is the time required for reading the work (or witnessing the spectacle). The latter depends on the *"size"* of the work.

Story time is given in three ways: (1) The moment of action may be dated absolutely (when the chronological moment is simply stated—for example, "at two o'clock on January 8 in 18—" or "in winter"), or relatively (by indicating the simultaneity of events or their chronological relationship—e.g., "after two years," etc.); (2) the duration of events may be indicated ("the conversation lasted for half an hour," "the journey continued for three months," or indirectly, "after five days they arrived at the appointed place"); and (3) an impression of the duration of time may be given, so that we indirectly determine the passage of time by judging the length of the speech or the normal duration of the action. We may note that writers use the last most freely, cramming long speeches into short lines and, conversely, expanding short speeches and quick action into long durations of time.

The place of the action may be either *static* or *dynamic*. If static, all the characters gather in one place (which is why hotels or their equivalents so frequently figure in stories—they make unexpected meetings possible); if dynamic, the characters are moved from place to place for the necessary encounters (travel-type tales, for example).

MOTIVATION

The system of motifs comprising the theme of a given work must show some kind of artistic unity. If the individual motifs, or a complex of motifs, are not sufficiently suited to the work, if the reader feels that the relationship between certain complexes of motifs and the work itself is obscure, then that complex is said to be superfluous. If all the parts of the work are badly suited to one another, the work is *incoherent*. That is why the introduction of each separate motif or complex of motifs must be *motivated*. The network of devices justifying the introduction of individual motifs or of groups of motifs is called *motivation*.

The devices of motivation are so numerous and varied that they must be classified:

1. Compositional motivation

This principle refers to the economy and usefulness of the motifs. Separate motifs may characterize either objects (stage properties) brought to the reader's attention or the activities of the characters (episodes). Not a single property may remain unused in the telling, and no episode may be without influence on the situation. Chekhov referred to just such compositional motivation when he stated that if one speaks about a nail beaten into a wall at the beginning of a narrative, then at the end the hero must hang himself on that nail.

171

A prop, in this case a weapon, is used in precisely this way in Ostrovsky's *The Poor Bride.* The third act set includes "a revolver hung on the tapestry over the divan." At first this detail of the setting seems a simple, concrete feature characterizing Karandyshev's way of life. In the sixth scene attention is directed towards this detail:

> ROBINSON: (looking at the tapestry) What do you have here?
> KARANDYSHEV: Cigars.
> R: No, what's hanging up there? Is this real?
> K: What do you mean "real"? This is a Turkish weapon.

The dialogue continues and the speakers ridicule the weapon; then the motif narrows until a remark is made about the worthlessness of the pistol:

> K: But in what way is it worthless? This pistol, for example . . . (he takes the pistol from the wall).
> PARATOV: (taking the pistol from him) This pistol?
> K: Ah, be careful—it shoots.
> P: Don't be afraid. It's just as dangerous whether it fires or not. All the same, it won't fire. Shoot at me from five paces; I'll let you.
> K: Well—no. This pistol may be loaded.
> P: So—it will do to hammer nails into the wall.
>   (Throws the pistol on the table.)

At the end of the act the fleeing Karandyshev takes the pistol from the table; in the fourth act he shoots Larissa with it.

Here compositional considerations motivate the introduction of the pistol motif. Because it prepares the audience for the final moments of the play, the pistol is an indispensable part of the denouement. This is the first kind of compositional motivation. A second type of compositional motivation occurs when motifs are used as devices of characterization, but these motifs must be appropriate to the story. Thus in the same play, *The Poor Bride,* the motif of the burgundy prepared and adulterated by a shady wine merchant for cheap sale typifies the poverty of Karandyshev's daily life and prepares for the departure of Larissa.

Details which show character may be integrated with the action either by psychological analogy (e.g., moonlight nights for love scenes and lightning and thunder for scenes of death or evil in novels) or by contrast (the motif of indifferent nature). In *The Poor Bride,* when Larissa dies, the singing of a Gypsy chorus is heard from the restaurant door.

We have still to consider the possibility of misleading motivation; props and episodes may be used to distract the reader's attention from the real situation. This happens frequently in detective novels, where a series of details is given in order to lead the reader (and a group of characters—for example, Watson or the police in Conan Doyle) up a blind alley. The author forces the reader to expect an ending inconsistent with the facts of the case. Techniques of misleading motivation occur chiefly in works created against the background of a major literary tradition; the reader naturally interprets each detail according to the conventions of the tradition. The deception is discovered at the end, and the reader is convinced that all such details were introduced merely to support the final surprises.

Misleading motivation (the play upon generally known literary rules firmly entrenched in tradition and used by the author in other than their traditional ways) is indispensable for parody.

2. Realistic motivation

We demand an element of "illusion" in any work. No matter how convention-filled and artistic it is, our perception of it must be accompanied by a feeling that what happens in it is "real." The naive reader feels this with extraordinary force and may try to verify the authenticity of the statements, perhaps even to make certain that the characters existed. Pushkin, after completing *The History of the Pugachyov Rebellion,* published *The Captain's Daughter* in the form of the memoirs of Grinyov and concluded with this epilogue:

> The manuscript of Peter Andreyevitch Grinyov was given to us by one of
> his grandchildren who had learned that we were occupied with a work con-
> cerning the times his grandfather described. We decided, with the family's
> permission, to publish it separately.

Pushkin creates the illusion of a real Grinyov and his memoirs, supported in detail by a well-known personal fact of Pushkin's life—his historical study of the history of Pugachyov. The illusion is further supported by the opinions and convictions expressed by Grinyov, which differ in many ways from opinions expressed by Pushkin himself.

For more experienced readers the need for realistic illusion expresses itself as a demand for "lifelikeness." Although firmly aware of the fictitious nature of the work, the experienced reader nevertheless demands some kind of conformity to reality, and finds the value of the work in this conformity. Even readers fully aware of the laws of aesthetic structure may not be psychologically free from the need for such illusion. As a result, each motif must be introduced as a *probable* motif in the given situation. But since the laws of plot construction have nothing in common with probability, any introduction of motifs is a compromise between objective reality and literary tradition. We will not mention the utter absurdity of many of the more traditional techniques for introducing motifs. To show the irreconcilability of these absurd traditional techniques with realistic motivation we should have to parody them. See, for example, *Vampuk,* the famous parody of operatic productions which humorously presents a selection of lampoonable traditional operatic situations. This parody is still included in the repertory of The Distorted Mirror.[8]

Accustomed to the techniques of adventures, we overlook the absurdity of the fact that the rescue of the hero always occurs five minutes before his seemingly inevitable death, the audience of ancient comedy or the comedy of Molière overlooks the fact that in the last act all the characters turn out to be close relatives. . . .

3. Artistic motivation

As I said, the use of the motif results from a compromise between realistic illusion and the demands of the artistic structure. Not everything borrowed from reality is fit for the work of art, as Lermontov noted when he wrote about the journalistic prose of his contemporaries in 1840:

> Whose portraits do they depict?
> Where do they hear their conversations?
> *Yet if they had really happened—*
> *We simply would not want to hear them.*

Boileau said much the same in his play on words, *"le vrai peut quelquefois n'être pas vraisemblable"* ("Sometimes the truth may not seem true"), understanding by *"vrai"* realistic motivation, and by *"vraisemblable"* artistic motivation.

A system of realistic motivation quite often includes a denial of artistic motivation. The usual formula is, "If this had happened in a novel, my hero would have done such and such, but since it really happened, here are the facts. . . ." But the denial of the literary form in itself asserts the laws of artistic composition.

Each realistic motif must somehow be inserted into the structure of the narrative and be illuminated by a particular part of it. The very selection of realistic themes must be justified artistically.

Usually quarrels between new and old literary groups arise over artistic motivation. The old, tradition-oriented group generally denies the artistry of the new literary form. This is shown, for example, in poetic diction, where the use of individual words must be in accord with firmly established literary traditions (tradition, which produces the distinction between prosaic and poetic words, strictly forbids their use together).

I consider the device of *defamiliarization* to be a special instance of artistic motivation. The introduction of nonliterary material into a work, if it is to be aesthetic, must be justified by a new and individual interpretation of the material. The old and habitual must be spoken of as if it were new and unusual. One must speak of the ordinary as if it were unfamiliar.

Techniques of defamiliarizing ordinary things are usually justified because the objects are distorted through the mental processes of a character who is not familiar with them. A well-known example of Leo Tolstoy's use of the technique occurs in *War and Peace* when he describes the council of war at Fils. He introduces a little peasant girl who watches the council and, like a child, interprets what is done and said without understanding it. Tolstoy uses precisely the same method of interpreting human relationships in "Kholstomer," where he presents them through the hypothetical psychology of a horse. (See "Kashtanka," in which Chekhov gives as much of the psychology of a dog as is necessary to defamiliarize the narrative; Korolenko's "The Blind Musician," which interprets the life of the seeing through the psychology of the blind, is of the same type.)

Swift uses these methods of defamiliarization extensively in *Gulliver's Travels* in order to present a satirical picture of the European social-political order. Gulliver, arriving in the land of the Houyhnhnms (horses endowed with reason), tells his master (a horse) about the customs of the ruling class in human society. Compelled to tell everything with the utmost accuracy, he removes the shell of euphemistic phrases and fictitious traditions which justify such things as war, class strife, parliamentary intrigue, and so on. Stripped of their verbal justification and thereby defamiliarized, these topics emerge in all their horror. Thus criticism of the political system—nonliterary material— is artistically motivated and fully involved in the narrative. . . .

THE VITALITY OF PLOT DEVICES

Although the general devices of plot construction of all lands and all peoples are significantly similar, and although it is possible to speak about the unique logic of plot construction, it is nevertheless true that specific devices, their combinations, their use, and their functions have changed greatly in the course of literary history. Each literary period, each school, is characterized by the system of devices which are present in the common style (in the broad sense of "style") of its literary genres and preferences.

In this respect we must distinguish between *conventional* and *free* devices.

Conventional devices are devices required by a given genre and a given period; the French classicism of the seventeenth century, with its dramatic unities and petty regulation of various genre forms, produced the strictest system of conventional devices. Conventional devices are the trademarks of the works produced by a school that accepts that particular convention. In any typical seventeenth-century tragedy the place of action remains unchanged and the time is limited to twenty-four hours. All comedies end in marriage, and all tragedies in the deaths of the principal characters. Any convention establishes its own set of devices. Everything in literature—from the choice of thematic materials, the various motifs and their use together, to systematic pronouncements about language, diction, etc.—may be made into a compositional device. The use of one word and the proscription of another, and so on, may be subject to regulation. Conventional devices originate because they are convenient technically; their repetition becomes traditional, and, falling into the area of normative poetics, they are codified as compulsory rules. But no convention can exhaust all possibilities and foresee all the devices necessary for the creation of an entire work, so that along with the conventional devices there are always free devices—devices peculiar to individual writers, works, genres, movements, etc.

Conventional devices usually destroy themselves. One value of literature is its novelty and originality. In the struggle for regeneration, the orthodox, the traditional, the stereotyped devices are most attacked, and the obligatory becomes prohibited. The creation of new traditions and techniques does not, however, prevent the revival of prohibited devices after the passing of two or three literary generations. . . .

Two literary styles may be distinguished in terms of the perceptibility of the devices. The first, characteristic of writers of the nineteenth century, is distinguished by its attempt to conceal the device; all of its motivation systems are designed to make the literary devices seem imperceptible, to make them seem as natural as possible—that is, to develop the literary material so that its development is unperceived. But this is only one style, and not a general aesthetic rule. It is opposed to another style, an unrealistic style, which does not bother about concealing the devices and which frequently tries to make them obvious, as when a writer interrupts a speech he is reporting to say that he did not hear how it ended, only to go on and report what he has no realistic way of knowing. In such a case, the author has called attention to the device or—as they say—the technique is "laid bare." Pushkin, in the fourth chapter of *Evgeny Onegin,* writes:

> And here already sparkle the snows
> And they spread among silver fields—
> (The reader waits for a rhyme like rose;
> Let him take quickly what this poem yields.)

Here we have a clear and deliberate laying bare of the technique of rhyme.

In the early stages of Futurism (in the works of Khlebnikov) and in contemporary literature, the laying bare of techniques had become traditional (many of the tales of Kaverin contain examples of the laying bare of devices of plot structure).

Among works containing such devices, we must distinguish those which lay bare extraneous devices—either traditional devices or those belonging to another writer. If the laying bare of extraneous literary devices is humorous, we have parody. The functions of parody are many, but its usual function is to ridicule an opposing literary group, blasting its aesthetic system and exposing it.

Parodies are quite widespread; they were traditional in dramatic literature, when any more or less outstanding work called for an immediate parody. The background from which a parody takes off is always another literary work (or a whole group of works). A significant number of parodies may be found among the tales of Chekhov.

Some parodies, not primarily satiric, are developed freely for the sole purpose of showing off the techniques. Thus the followers of Laurence Sterne at the start of the nineteenth century formed their own school, which had developed out of parody, into a school which pursued parody as an art in its own right. In contemporary literature, Sterne's techniques have been revived and widely disseminated (the transposition of chapters, excessive and casual digressions, the slowing of the action, and so on, are typical).

Devices are laid bare because a perceptible device is permissible only when it is made creatively outstanding. When a device is noticed despite the author's attempt to conceal it, it produces a detrimentally comic effect. To prevent this, the author deliberately lays bare the device.

Thus devices are born, live, grow old, and die. To the extent that their use becomes automatic, they lose their efficacy and cease to be included on the list of acceptable techniques. Renovated devices with new functions and new meanings are required to prevent techniques from becoming mechanical. Such renovation is like the use of a quotation from an old author in a new application and with a new meaning.

[This monograph continues with a discussion of the concept of literary genres, followed by discussions of the dramatic, lyric, and fictional genres.]

NOTES

1. A volume of reminiscences by Segey Aksakov, published in 1858. *Tr. note.*

2. In brief, the story is "the action itself," the plot, "how the reader learns of the action."

3. Possibly the nearest equivalent of *skaz* is "yarn." Technically, a *skaz* is a story in which the manner of telling (the normal speech patterns of the narrator—dialect, pronunciation, grammatical peculiarities, pitch patterns, etc.) is as important to the effect as the story itself. For a description of the American equivalent of the *skaz*, see Samuel Clemens's widely reprinted "How to Tell a Story." *Tr. note.*

4. Quite the same happens if, in place of a group of characters, we have a psychological novel in which the internal psychic history of the hero is described. The various psychological motifs of his conduct, the various sides of his spiritual life, instincts, passions, etc., assume the role usually played by other characters. In this respect we can generalize about his whole past and future.

5. To put this in more familiar terminology, the ending occurs after all tensions have been eased. Tomashevsky's analysis of plot structure here follows closely Aristotle's analysis of dramatic structure. *Tr. note.*

6. From the point of view of the arrangement of the narrative material, the part beginning the narrative is called the *prologue*. The close is called the *epilogue*. The prologue may include neither the exposition nor the exciting force, just as the epilogue may not occur simultaneously with the outcome of the theme.

7. If the motif is repeated more or less frequently, and especially if it is a free motif—that is, not involved in the story, then it is called a *leitmotif*. Thus certain characters appearing in the narrative under various disguises are often accompanied by some kind of fixed motif so that the reader may recognize them.

8. The Distorted Mirror was a Petersburg theater which staged parodies. *Vampuk, The African Bride: A Formal Opera in All Respects* was staged there in 1908; the term *Vampuk* was later applied to anything outlandish. *Tr. note.*

13

Text Generation

JEAN RICARDOU

Those who confine themselves endlessly to mere labels thereby grant themselves the precarious privilege of manipulating peculiar syncretisms—such, as
Paul Valéry often observed, is the very common way of eluding singular texts.
Conversely, those who let themselves be captivated by the individuality of literary work thereby expose themselves to the mirage of originality—at the risk
of omitting the very precise relations that prevail between the texts. Avoiding
both those temptations, and citing the texts to document our case, we shall
examine the complementary play of their divergences and similarities. A small
number of specific problems shall constitute the basis for a classification of
several recent works of fiction. Considered in themselves, the eventual super-
positions will enable us to transcend the singular toward an outline of typical
procedures; their probable respective oppositions, on the other hand, will suggest some of the differences which distinguish two kinds of fiction. *La Maison de rendez-vous,* by Alain Robbe-Grillet (1965), *Le Libera,* by Robert Pinget
(1968), on the one hand and, on the other, *Personnes,* by Jean-Louis Baudry
(1967), and *Nombres,* by Philippe Sollers (1968) shall constitute the field of
inquiry. The problems of *character, formalization,* and *representation* shall be
the topics of investigation. Thus, starting from an essential aspect of fiction,
the technical and the ideological will ultimately be brought into relation.

[Ricardou's discussion of character is omitted.]

FORMALIZATION OF THE FICTION

Several authors have shown how, in a narrative, the fiction may be governed
by formal principles: Propp, for instance, in his analysis of Russian folktales.

Although they are undeniably at work, such procedures are usually imperceptible. If the "laws that govern the narrated universe . . . reflect the logical constraints that any series of events organized in narrative form must respect in order to be intelligible" (Claude Brémond, "La Logique des possibles narratifs" in *Communications,* no. 8), the reader's attention will hardly be aroused. Thus it is often necessary to resort to a corpus of similar texts, that the analyst contrives to superimpose, if the (common) formal factors are to be made to appear:

1. The king sends Ivan to find the Princess. Ivan leaves.
2. The king sends Ivan to find a singular object. Ivan leaves.
3. The sister sends her brother to find a remedy. The brother leaves.
4. The mother-in-law sends her daughter-in-law to find fire. The daughter-in-law leaves.
5. The blacksmith sends his apprentice to find the cow. The apprentice leaves.
Etc. The dispatch and the departure connected with the quest are constants. The dispatcher and the dispatched are variables. (V. Propp: "Fairy Tale Transformations" [reproduced in Section Two, "Plot and Emplotment"])

For the naive consumer, immersed in the exciting flow of the plot, an analysis such as Propp's is practically sacrilegious: it elucidates that which is supposed to remain obscure—the process of production. By writing poems so similar to each other that they obviously constitute a simple set of variants, Paul Valéry managed on occasion to insert that critical instrument within the production itself.

A. "The rest of the script proceeds mechanically"

By the use of a procedure that is quite visible in *Jealousy,* for instance, *La Maison de rendez-vous* exacerbates that scandalous experiment. Instead of giving us, as Valéry did, a collection of autonomous variants, Robbe-Grillet's novel integrates them with its plot. Here the superposition, with its aptitude for disclosing formal communities, is inexorably accomplished by the properties of the text itself. We shall call formalization the tendency whereby the activity of these formal principles, instead of being carefully dissimulated, is intensified, and even made the object of an undeniable ostentation. In fact, as the sequences unfold, similarities and divergences, both equally surprising, gradually appear. Beneath the profuse variety of variables, more general patterns begin to emerge. Thus, for instance, the countless events with connotations of homicide, suicide, accident, or torture reveal the systematic application of a pattern of aggression. Others, complying with the former, signal, through a similar phenomenon of superposition, the models of wandering, visit, or the repetitive number three.

This alignment of the disparate along the coordinating axis of a small number of basic schemas certainly removes us from the everyday world, and plays a decisive antinaturalist role. Curiously enough, the same effect can be obtained by the opposite procedure. Applied to an eminently unique act (death), the matrix of aggression multiplies it into a collection of contradictory occurrences. Edouard Manneret committed suicide (94), had his neck broken by Lady Ava's dog (159), was the victim of an accident (165), was murdered by a black policeman with a stiletto (175), with the stem of a broken cocktail glass by some strange official (176), by the Communists (202), by Johnson with a revolver (211).

Carried to extremes, that formalization would generate all the possible arrangements of a limited set of elements (characters, places, objects . . .) and models of combinations (attack, wandering, visit). But, as we can easily imagine, the possibilities are far too numerous to be thoroughly exhausted. The fiction is therefore required not only to comply with the order of a logical sequence, but also to operate a selection. It must therefore rely on some principle capable of determining the successive stages of its development. And in fact, beneath the layers of like and conflicting events, such a principle may be perceived: it determines a ballistic trajectory—growth, fall, disappearance. Various series amply confirm this: the statues, the comic-strip illustrations:

> Most of them illustrate the most famous episodes of Princess Azy's imaginary existence: "The Dogs," "The Slave," "The Promise," "The Queen," "The Kidnapping," "The Hunter," "The Murder." (57)
>
> . . . Each illustration is accompanied by a short caption in large Chinese characters that signify, respectively and in order: "Drugs are a companion that betrays you," "Drugs are a tyrant that enslaves you," "Drugs are a poison that will kill you." (82)

The same principle may be detected behind the evolution of Lady Ava (young and adulated, faded and abandoned, on her deathbed), or of Johnson (possessing Lauren, fighting to keep her, losing her). Once the formal principles are clearly established, it is indeed true that "the rest of the script proceeds mechanically."

B. "Setting the mechanism in motion"

Of all Pinget's books, it is doubtless in *Passacaille* that combinatorial techniques are practiced the most systematically: less numerous, the elements and situations are effectively more controllable. But *La Libera*'s use of them was already quite analogous to the one we found in *La Maison de rendez-vous*. From the first pages, it is already clear that "the mechanism set in motion" (7) is, among others, that of a pattern of aggression drawing attention to the victim and leaving the aggressor unspecified. Seven people are injured or killed in the first twelve pages, but only one by an identified assailant. The formula's anti-naturalist effect, emphasized by the deliberate clumsiness of several attempts to retrieve by logical explanation a thoroughly illogical function: "Calamities always occur in July—an automobile accident, a drowning, a fire" (20), is further increased, as in *La Maison de rendez-vous,* by the diversification of a supposedly unique event. Already perceptible with the versatile deaths of Louis Ducreux, this phenomenon especially concerns the accident in which La Lorpailleur is involved. On her bicycle, she is the victim of a truckdriver (10) or an epileptic attack (11). But perhaps she just faked the accident (16), or maybe nothing happened at all: she just passed the truck on the road (12). There is also a less spectacular version: her falling off a chair (15).

The fast pace at which the scenes materialize and follow one another in Pinget's book allows an extremely ample actualization of possibilities. This means that the notion of a trajectory is both more diffuse and less necessary. Yet, from the aggressive beginning:

> If La Lorpailleur is insane, it's not my fault

to the disillusioned and senile ending:

> The bunch of old gags, dumb mirages and the rest of the
> junk cluttering up our nutty beanbrains.
> Botched bewitchments.

we can nonetheless detect the installation of a process of decay and decrepitude. Prevented by its formalization from proposing a traditional story, the fiction tends instead to stage a production of the idea of its own beginning and ending.

FORMALIZATION OF THE NARRATION

That curious hybrid, part actor, part reporter, the narrator is one of the points where fiction and narration strangely intersect. Introduced in these formalized fictions, that role is bound to suffer some far-reaching consequences. Here, the narrative function no longer belongs, as it does in a classic story, to one character or another depending on the requirements of the plot; instead, it is distributed mechanically and with periodic, violent switches. This procedure gives rise to what we might call floating narrators. In fact, the relations between narrative and narrator are known to be commonly univocal: the two are, literally, as one voice. In Ulysses' tale to Alcinoos, for instance, a single narrator offers a single version: it is *the* tale of *Ulysses*. This of course does not prevent a host of narrators from arriving at any point in the story, bringing either the confirmation of a textual repetition or the invalidation of a new version. Yet, if in the latter case an ambiguity is brought to light, it is only on the level of the fiction as a whole, whereas the relation of each individual narrator to his own narrative remains unequivocal. All that occurs is that stable narratives, respectively related by stable narrators, are arranged in some sort of sequence. Equivocal relations, on the other hand, are produced by quite different devices: stable narrator and floating narrative; floating narrator and stable narrative; and, naturally, their product: floating narrator and floating narrative. Robbe-Grillet's *Jealousy* for instance is based on the systematic development of the first case: to a single narrator, the famous "husband," there corresponds a floating narrative consisting of a succession of contradictory versions. Conversely, rather than being the joint property of a corpus of unanimous narrators, a narrative may be captured by an abruptly alien narrator, with the predictable retroactive effects. Here, lacking a specific narrator, the stable narrative is provided with floating narrators instead. *La Maison de rendez-vous* is a case in point, particularly in the shift from *he* (Johnson) to an enigmatic *I,* by the omission of quotation marks:

> Johnson, who had time to prepare for that question, immediately begins his account of the evening: "I arrived at the Villa Bleue around 9:10 by taxi . . ." I'm also skipping the part about the noise of the insects, already mentioned, and the description of the statues. I'm going right on to the scene where Lauren breaks up with her fiancé. (ii. 96–97)

Le Libera is another example:

> According to Mademoiselle Rhonzière, Etiennette didn't go by the bakery until eleven, she was on her way back from town with a big box from Brivance's, a new dress . . . those women dying of impatience to see her open the box . . . I can still see those women all excited, feeling the fabric. (63–64)

With that kind of double shift, any attempt by one of the characters to appropriate the narrative becomes precarious. But what are the rules that govern that strange rotation of narrators? It seems that, far from obeying some systematic principle of distribution, the occurrence which, at that particular point in the novel, is likely to cause the most confusion, is selected every time. Here, then, the order of narrators is still in a sense subordinate to the development of the fiction.

It is true that, in *Nombres,* a certain order effectively underlies the fiction's distribution: the anonymous citation of the line from Lucretius, for instance, at the beginning of the book, is there to provide not the outmoded elegance of a Latin ornament, but rather a precise thematic matrix: each term of that formula is like a seed replanted indefinitely, maturing, blossoming out, eventually, on a number of pages according to a profound sum. Nevertheless, the formalization in *Nombres* works out mainly on the level of the narration. The same is true for *Personnes.*

A. "The mechanism is in motion"

The reader quickly turning the pages of Baudry's novel is immediately struck by the material evidence of a "mechanism in motion" (46). Unorganized in most novels, here the grays and blanks of the printed page alternate with a regularity that betrays the calculated nature of their sequence. Better still, the workings of the mechanism are displayed in a table on the last page of the novel [reproduced below].

	I	She	He	I	He	She	She	I	He
She	1	5	13	21	29	27	19	11	3
He	9	33	37	45	56	51	43	35	7
I	17	41	57	61	69	67	59	39	16
He	25	49	65	73	77	75	63	47	23
I	32	53	72	80	81	79	71	55	31
She	24	48	64	76	78	74	66	50	26
He	16	40	60	68	70	62	58	42	18
She	8	36	44	52	54	46	38	34	10
I	4	12	20	28	30	22	14	6	2

Figure 1

Here, then, we have the exact opposite of a capricious continuity: the narration is allowed to materialize only in obedience to a rigorous system of fragmentation. It is not a homogeneous substance that could be poured into the sequential grid of pronouns as into a mold: it has been strictly ordered to conform, in its production, to nothing other than the discontinuity of irreconcilable directives. Defined in this case as noncommutative, the product of the pronouns engenders nine distinct combinations. Five of them are simple: I/I, I/She, I/He, He/He, He/She. Four are complex: He/I (*I* is only possible between quotes), She/I (by a curious reversal, *I* is "interlocuted" into *you,* and *She* becomes *I*), She/She (the whole sequence is then put in quotes). Confronted with the sexed third-person pronouns, *I* is forced to choose between an acrobatic neutrality (censuring, in its attributes, all determinations of gender: since, in French, an unaccented *e* added to the adjective makes it feminine, the choice would be limited to adjectives which already end in *e* in the masculine, e.g., *triste* [sad], and are thus invariable), a determinate sex (masculine or feminine endings), or hermaphrodism (some masculine, some feminine endings). Instead, a fourth solution was selected. *I* does in fact change genders, but never in the course of a single sequence [the book has no chapters, but 81 "sequences," each one-and-a-half pages long—Trans. note]. In its relations with *you,* singular and plural, *I,* as we have seen, derived from *she,* is feminine:

> So now I am standing in front of the mirror, nude (*nue*), and you came to stand next to me.

In the other pairs, it is masculine:

> Masked (*masqué*), I advance through a silent chaos . . . I see him when he can no longer escape the vast white building. . . .

These inflexible coercive measures avoid the ambiguities that would ensue from a confusion of the sexes. On the other hand, since the order of the very different sequences is determined by the requirement that the combinatorial grid be covered methodically, all attempts to subsume the narrative movement's diversity under a unitary principle are blocked a priori.

B. "Once the first propositions are put in the mechanism"

In 1965, Sollers's novel, *Drame* (which there are good grounds for mentioning in connection with *Personnes*), organized its sixty-four sequences in checkerboard fashion: a systematic alternation of "he" sequences and "I" sequences. The narration of *Nombres* is engendered by an equally rigorous device: as the title signals from the start, measure is the basis of its formation. The book was assigned one hundred sequences in a cyclic pattern with a period of four. That "predetermined, arbitrary, numerical space" (*Logiques,* by Sollers) does not bother to avoid a certain ostentation. Except, obviously, for the first four, every sequence begins with a double numeric notation. "3.91," for instance, provides a triple indication: this is the ninety-first sequence; it is of type three; it belongs to the twenty-third cycle. In addition, various diagrams inserted in the text give the schemas of this mechanism. The first one, in sequence 4.8, at the end of the second cycle, once the idea of a circuit has been established differentiates all the fourth sequences from the other three:

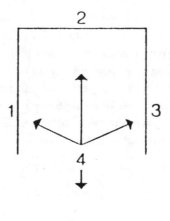

Figure 2

This because the grammar and even, tendentiously, the punctuation, according to this partition, follow a mandatory pattern of distribution: the first three sequences are in the imperfect tense; the fourth, in the present, between parentheses and almost always with the second person plural. Since the parenthesis creates an interruption and is concommitantly subject to an inclusion, the present, i.e. the time during which the book is read (by "you," the sequence means the reader), is defined as perfectly equivocal: it breaks with the imperfect of the narration while yet remaining caught in its circuit.

In addition, however they begin (upper or lower case, points of suspension), all the sequences are made to end with a dash of varying length. And, indeed, we soon find that narrational constraint becoming thematic: in 3.23 for instance it is "the line's simple, indestructible force." Thus a kind of symbolic strategy begins to evolve, where phonetic writing as the notation of a language is at grips with the line drawing on which a language may place its own interpretation. With the increasing number of Chinese ideograms at the ends of the sequences, and the permanent presence, at the beginning of each sequence, of arabic numerals that are independent of the languages in which they can be read, the written word is regularly gripped in the vise of spoken writing.

Within the limits of their common points, no doubt there is still reason to distinguish between *Personnes* and *Nombres*. Thus, whereas the former is content to exhibit *in extremis,* after the last word and, when all is said and done, by way of a table of contents [in France the table of contents is placed at the end of a book instead of the beginning as in the U.S.A.—Trans. note], the programmatic grid of its pronominal encounters, the latter inserts the schema in the text itself, and proposes, now and then (4.8, 4.24, 4.48, 4.52), various successive modifications. In the first case, separable, immutable, fundamental, the formalization prescribes the limits of the enclosure from which the narration cannot escape. In the second, this formalization becomes the plaything of the narration which by its laws it determines to the point of being transformed by that which it produces.

SELF-REPRESENTATION

It is common knowledge that the dogma which would reduce, in Sartre's words, "the verbal moment" to a "secondary structure," separates into two complementary doctrines: expression, representation. For the former, there is a given internal substance which is expressed; for the latter, there is a given external entity which is represented. To the expression of the Self corresponds the representation of the World. The essential, in both cases, is one and the same: the text is but the reflection of something prior to itself. The Stendhalian "mirror taken out for a walk" (*"un miroir qu'on promène le long d'une route"*) is echoed by the Romantic poem-mirror of the soul. It was Victor Hugo, in the preface to his *Contemplations,* who maintained: "If ever there was a mirror of the soul, this book will be it." Not only do the two principles not conflict, then, but in effect they act in perfect concert: anything that obviously disturbs the representation of the World is forthwith ascribed to the expression of the Self. The traditional fantastic tale, for instance, reads that way: it is not the World itself which is represented, but rather a world thoroughly infused with one of the major faculties of the Self: imagination. From the "objective" to the "subjective," the expression-representation creed sweepingly covers a vast field indeed.

The system of productive mechanisms, on the other hand, and directly in proportion to its ostentation, is irreducibly opposed to that comfortable belief. As we have seen, the Russian folktale, in its composition, is the result of a precise matrix. Yet it was only by resorting to a comparison transcending each individual tale that Propp was able to bring this fact to light. It is therefore advisable to discriminate between such purely external expedients, and the internal mechanisms exploited by *La Maison de rendez-vous* and *Le Libera*.

The fiction generated by the latter devices systematically diverges from any kind of reflection of the ordinary world, whose aspects they specifically attack. That which is commonly *unique* (a character, an event) suffers the *dislocation* of contradictory variants; that which is ordinarily *diverse* (several characters, several events) sustains the *assimilation* of strange resemblances. The fiction excludes perfect singularity as well as absolute plurality. In other words, it is ubiquitously invested with mirrors. Deforming mirrors to dislocate the unique; "forming" mirrors to assimilate the diverse.

The novel is thus no longer a mirror taken out for a walk; it is the result of internal mirrors ubiquitously at work within the fiction itself. It is no longer representation, but self-representation. Yet that is not to suppose it divided into two realms, the privileged one which would have the other as its representation. No, the novel is rather, tendentiously, everywhere a representation of itself. This means that, far from being a stable image of the ordinary world, the fiction, in its composition, is perpetually in the process of a double discomposition. The text's proliferation proceeds from the text itself: it writes by imitating what it reads. Whatever be the book containing it, any internal allegory [*mise en abyme:* a term borrowed from heraldry: marshaling of escutcheons, but here in addition the inset motif is defined as depicting or reinforcing its incorporating emblem—Trans. note] is already, of course, a larval case of these inherent mirror effects. André Gide quite rightly points out, as an instance of this, the tiny convex mirrors in the paintings of Memling and Metsys. Better still, this internal allegory often reflects the constitutive procedures of the text itself. Then if, in addition, it happens to reflect this reflection, it will form, quite literally, a figurative reduplication. This in fact is probably the way we are intended to read the following Byzantine allusion dropped on the very threshold of *La Maison de rendez-vous*:

> On the walls of the Byzantine cathedrals, the bilaterally symmetric sawed marble shapes before my eyes into female genitals, spread wide open.

where, in this evocation of the maternal orifice, what is stressed is naturally the productive aptitude proper to self-representation.

ANTIREPRESENTATION

If, with self-representation, the stability of the narrative is constantly undermined by a perpetual threat of fission, it is even more so, as we have seen in

Personnes and *Nombres,* by the systematic disruptions continually inflicted on it by a violent attempt at antirepresentation. In both instances, the fictional space becomes plural: in the former, by the rapid multiplication of similarities; in the latter, by the inordinate accumulation of differences. "The Way that can be told is not the constant Way": nothing, perhaps, might better serve as an emblem of the second activity than the first line of the Tao, also inscribed in *Nombres.* We have seen that, in order to achieve the most incisive ruptures, *Personnes* and *Nombres* both resorted to a very effective device. Since it was sufficient to bring irreconcilable levels into play and then to shift alternately from one to the other, their narratives were ordered to travel back and forth, from fiction to narration, and from the latter to the former. In this manner the two levels were made to challenge and engender each other reciprocally, in the course of a process of production constantly rendered perceptible. Whereas, in the pursuit of its ideal (to deceive the reader), the representative effort is aimed at a maximum dissimulation of the narration so that the fiction, with its illusionist resemblance, may be confused with that which it pretends to reflect; the system employed by *Personnes* and *Nombres,* on the other hand, insofar as it makes conspicuous by turns both fiction and narration, effectively forms the exact inverse of a representation.

The text's proliferation proceeds from the text itself: it is written by opposing what it reads. This plurality can be increased. By widening the extent of its multiplicity to include an ever greater number of other texts, *Nombres* accomplished that. This intertextual activity exerts a twofold criticism. Intervention of the text in the texts: reworked by the fabric into which it is received, the formula "the body of real numbers" assumes a volume of meaning which exceeds its strictly mathematical acceptation: torn from any scientific pretension to purity, it ends up inscribed within the semantic constellation that includes it: the previously cited line from the Tao is invested with a precise content (a particular scriptive organization) which deprives it of all appearance of pure paradox. Intervention of the texts in the text: the bringing into play, respectively, of precise references to the semantic activity and to a different civilization. In any antirepresentative perspective, the text is written in the plural.

REDUPLICATION, RUPTURE

From the various angles from which we have examined them, the four novels consistently paired off into steady couples. An outline of their typical methods has therefore been established. No doubt the reader of other such books will find them tendentiously characteristic of either the "New Novel" or "Tel Quel." A few short remarks concerning the treatment of the fictional character will confirm this. The similarization of two distinct protagonists, Lassalle and Lessing, is one of the operations accomplished, and initially by the assonance of their surnames, in Claude Ollier's *La Mise en scène* (1958). Conversely, the splitting up of a single entity 0 into irreconcilable characters, now masculine, now feminine, is effected by Claude Simon's *La Bataille de Pharsale* (1969). In *Imaginez la nuit,* by Jean Thibaudeau, a whole long sequence is built on the pronoun *elles* (they, feminine), without its ever receiving a stable identity. And it was on the basis of Marcelin Pleynet's *Comme* that Baudry evolved the system allowing for a continual variation of the content of personal pronouns.

Of course, all comparison oscillates between two extremes. The first has similitude for a principle, unification for an objective, Ecumenism for a name. The second is called sectarianism; its effect is that of dispersion, its agent is difference. According to the former, we may note that, in their common conflict with the representative dogma, the activity of the "New Novel" is reduplicated by that of "Tel Quel." The former subverts the category of character, the latter abolishes it. The former tends to formalize its fiction, the latter, with more violence, its narration. The former turns the process of representation against itself, the latter nullifies it.

According to the other extreme, Tel Quel's action breaks with that of the New Novel. The abolition of character makes its mere subversion look like the misadventure of a survival. Faced with the violent ruptures provoked by narrational formalization, the tendentious formalization of the fiction seems like an ultimate reprieve granted the narrative. For antirepresentation, self-representation is still too representative.

All proximity and distance, the radicalization of the New Novel's activity as operated by Tel Quel can thus only be epitomized by a contradictory figure. So, to conclude, we might evoke that paradoxical place where, the greater the weight given to the support, the farther the departure from it: the trampoline.

Translated from the French
by Erica Freiberg

14

The Historical Text as Literary Artifact

HAYDEN WHITE

One of the ways that a scholarly field takes stock of itself is by considering its history. Yet it is difficult to get an objective history of a scholarly discipline, because if the historian is himself a practitioner of it, he is likely to be a devotee of one or another of its sects and hence biased; and if he is not a practitioner, he is unlikely to have the expertise necessary to distinguish between the significant and the insignificant events of the field's development. One might think that these difficulties would not arise in the field of history itself, but they do and not only for the reasons mentioned above. In order to write the history of any given scholarly discipline or even of a science, one must be prepared to ask questions *about* it of a sort that do not have to be asked in the practice *of* it. One must try to get behind or beneath the presuppositions which sustain a given type of inquiry and ask the questions that can be begged in its practice in the interest of determining why this type of inquiry has been designed to solve the problems it characteristically tries to solve. This is what metahistory seeks to do. It addresses itself to such questions as, What is the structure of a peculiarly *historical* consciousness? What is the epistemological status of historical *explanations,* as compared with other kinds of explanations that might be offered to account for the materials with which historians ordinarily deal? What are the possible *forms* of historical representation and what are their bases? What authority can historical accounts claim as contributions to a secured knowledge of reality in general and to the human sciences in particular?

Now, many of these questions have been dealt with quite competently over the last quarter-century by philosophers concerned to define history's relationships to other disciplines, especially the physical and social sciences, and by historians interested in assessing the success of their discipline in mapping the past and determining the relationship of that past to the present. But there is one problem that neither philosophers nor historians have looked at very seriously and to which literary theorists have given only passing attention. This question has to do with the status of the historical narrative, considered purely as a verbal artifact purporting to be a model of structures and processes long past and therefore not subject to either experimental or observational controls. This is not to say that historians and philosophers of history have failed to take notice of the essentially provisional and contingent nature of historical representations and of their susceptibility to infinite revision in the light of new evidence or more sophisticated conceptualization of problems. One of the marks of a good professional historian is the consistency with which he reminds his readers of the purely provisional nature of his characterizations of events, agents, and agencies found in the always incomplete historical record. Nor is it to say that literary theorists have *never* studied the structure of historical narratives. But in general there has been a reluctance to consider historical narratives as what they most manifestly are: verbal fictions, the contents of which are as much *invented* as *found* and the forms of which have more in common with their counterparts in literature than they have with those in the sciences.

Now, it is obvious that this conflation of mythic and historical consciousness will offend some historians and disturb those literary theorists whose conception of literature presupposes a radical opposition of history to fiction or of fact to fancy. As Northrop Frye has remarked, "In a sense the historical is the opposite of the mythical, and to tell the historian that what gives shape to his book is a myth would sound to him vaguely insulting." Yet Frye himself grants that "when a historian's scheme gets to a certain point of comprehensiveness it becomes mythical in shape, and so approaches the poetic in its structure." He even speaks of different kinds of historical myths: Romantic myths "based on a quest or pilgrimage to a City of God or classless society"; Comic "myths of progress through evolution or revolution"; Tragic myths of "decline and fall, like the works of Gibbon and Spengler"; and Ironic "myths of recurrence or casual catastrophe." But Frye appears to believe that these myths are operative only in such victims of what might be called the "poetic fallacy" as Hegel, Marx, Nietzsche, Spengler, Toynbee, and Sartre—historians whose fascination with the "constructive" capacity of human thought has deadened their responsibility to the "found" data. "The historian works inductively," he says, "collecting his facts and trying to avoid any informing patterns except those he sees, or is honestly convinced he sees, in the facts themselves." He does not work "from" a "unifying form," as the poet does, but "toward" it; and it therefore follows that the historian, like any writer of discursive prose, is to be judged "by the truth of what he says, or by the adequacy of his verbal reproduction of his external model," whether that external model be the actions of past men or the historian's own thought about such actions.

What Frye says is true enough as a statement of the *ideal* that has inspired historical writing since the time of the Greeks, but that ideal presupposes an opposition between myth and history that is as problematical as it is venerable. It serves Frye's purposes very well, since it permits him to locate the specifically "fictive" in the space between the two concepts of the "mythic" and the "historical." As readers of Frye's *Anatomy of Criticism* will remember, Frye conceives fictions to consist in part of sublimates of archetypal myth-structures. These structures have been displaced to the interior of verbal artifacts in such a way as to serve as their latent meanings. The fundamental meanings of all fictions, their thematic content, consist, in Frye's view, of the "pregeneric plot structures" or *mythoi* derived from the corpora of Classical and Judeo-Christian religious literature. According to this theory, we understand *why* a particular story has "turned out" as it has when we have identified the archetypal myth, or pregeneric plot structure, of which the story is an exemplification. And we see the "point" of a story when we have identified its theme (Frye's translation of *dianoia*), which makes of it a "parable or illustrative fable." "Every work of literature," Frye insists, "has both a fictional and a thematic aspect," but as we move from "fictional projection" toward the overt articulation of theme, the writing tends to take on the aspect of "direct address, or straight discursive writing and cease[s] to be literature." And in Frye's view, as we have seen, history (or at least "proper history") belongs to the category of "discursive writing," so that when the fictional element—or mythic plot structure—is *obviously* present in it, it ceases to be history altogether and becomes a bastard genre, product of an unholy, though not unnatural, union between history and poetry.

Yet, I would argue, histories gain part of their explanatory effect by their success in making stories out of *mere* chronicles; and stories in turn are made out of chronicles by an operation which I have elsewhere called "emplotment." And by emplotment I mean simply the encodation of the facts contained in the chronicle as components of specific *kinds* of plot structures, in precisely the way that Frye has suggested is the case with "fictions" in general.

The late R. G. Collingwood insisted that the historian was above all a storyteller and suggested that historical sensibility was manifested in the capacity to make a plausible story out of a congeries of "facts" which, in their unprocessed form, made no sense at all. In their efforts to make sense of the historical record, which is fragmentary and always incomplete, historians have to make use of what Collingwood called "the constructive imagination," which told the historian—as it tells the competent detective—what "must have been the case" given the available evidence and the formal properties it displayed to the consciousness capable of putting the right question to it. This constructive imagination functions in much the same way that Kant supposed the *a priori* imagination functions when it tells us that even though we cannot perceive both sides of a tabletop simultaneously, we can be certain it has *two* sides if it has one, because the very concept of *one side* entails at least *one other.* Collingwood suggested that historians come to their evidence endowed with a sense of the *possible* forms that different kinds of recognizably human situations *can* take. He called this sense the nose for the "story" contained in the evidence or for the "true" story that was buried in or hidden behind the "apparent" story. And he concluded that historians provide plausible explanations for bodies of historical evidence when they succeed in discovering the story or complex of stories implicitly contained within them.

What Collingwood failed to see was that no given set of casually recorded historical events can in itself constitute a story; the most it might offer to the historian are story *elements.* The events are *made* into a story by the suppression or subordination of certain of them and the highlighting of others, by characterization, motific repetition, variation of tone and point of view, alternative descriptive strategies, and the like—in short, all of the techniques that we would normally expect to find in the emplotment of a novel or a play. For example, no historical event is *intrinsically tragic;* it can only be conceived as such from a particular point of view or from within the context of a structured set of events of which it is an element enjoying a privileged place. For in history what is tragic from one perspective is comic from another, just as in society what appears to be tragic from the standpoint of one class may be, as Marx purported to show of the 18th Brumaire of Louis Buonaparte, only a farce from that of another class. Considered as potential elements of a story, historical events are value-neutral. Whether they find their place finally in a story that is tragic, comic, romantic, or ironic—to use Frye's categories— depends upon the historian's decision to configure them according to the imperatives of one plot structure or mythos rather than another. The same set of events can serve as components of a story that is tragic *or* comic, as the case may be, depending on the historian's choice of the plot structure that he considers most appropriate for ordering events of that kind so as to make them into a comprehensible story.

This suggests that what the historian brings to his consideration of the historical record is a notion of the *types* of configurations of events that can be recognized as stories by the audience for which he is writing. True, he can misfire. I do not suppose that anyone would accept the emplotment of the life of President Kennedy as comedy, but whether it ought to be emplotted romantically, tragically, or satirically is an open question. The important point is that most historical sequences can be emplotted in a number of different ways, so as to provide different interpretations of those events and to endow them with different meanings. Thus, for example, what Michelet in his great history of the French Revolution construed as a drama of Romantic transcendence, his contemporary Tocqueville emplotted as an ironic Tragedy. Neither can be said to have had more knowledge of the "facts" contained in the record; they simply had different notions of the kind of story that best fitted the facts they knew. Nor should it be thought that they told different stories of the Revolution because they had discovered different *kinds* of facts, political on the one hand, social on the other. They sought out different kinds of facts because they had different kinds of stories to tell. But why did these alternative, not to say mutually exclusive, representations of what was substantially the same set of events appear equally plausible to their respective audiences? Simply because the historians shared with their audiences certain preconceptions about how the Revolution might be emplotted, in response to imperatives that were generally extra historical, ideological, aesthetic, or mythical.

Collingwood once remarked that you could never explicate a tragedy to anyone who was not already acquainted with the kinds of situations that are regarded as "tragic" in our culture. Anyone who has taught or taken one of those omnibus courses usually entitled Western Civilization or Introduction to the Classics of Western Literature will know what Collingwood had in mind. Unless you have some idea of the generic attributes of tragic, comic, romantic, or ironic situations, you will be unable to recognize them as such when you come upon them in a literary text. But historical situations do not have built into them intrinsic meanings in the way that literary texts do. Historical situations are not *inherently* tragic, comic, or romantic. They may all be inherently ironic, but they need not be emplotted that way. All the historian needs to do to transform a tragic into a comic situation is to shift his point of view or change the scope of his perceptions. Anyway, we only think of situations as tragic or comic because these concepts are part of our generally cultural and specifically literary heritage. *How* a given historical situation is to be configured depends on the historian's subtlety in matching up a specific plot structure with the set of historical events that he wishes to endow with a meaning of a particular kind. This is essentially a literary, that is to say fiction-making, operation. And to call it that in no way detracts from the status of historical narratives as providing a kind of knowledge. For not only are the pregeneric plot structures by which sets of events can be constituted as stories of a particular kind limited in number, as Frye and other archetypal critics suggest; but the encodation of events in terms of such plot structures is one of the ways that a culture has of making sense of both personal and public pasts.

We can make sense of sets of events in a number of different ways. One of the ways is to subsume the events under the causal laws which may have governed their concatenation in order to produce the particular configuration that the events appear to assume when considered as "effects" of mechanical forces. This is the way of scientific explanation. Another way we make sense of a set of events which appears strange, enigmatic, or mysterious in its immediate manifestations is to encode the set in terms of culturally provided categories, such as metaphysical concepts, religious beliefs, or story forms. The effect of such encodations is to familiarize the unfamiliar; and in general this is the way of historiography, whose "data" are always immediately strange, not to say exotic, simply by virtue of their distance from us in time and their origin in a way of life different from our own.

The historian shares with his audience *general notions* of the *forms* that significant human situations *must* take by virtue of his participation in the specific processes of sense-making which identify him as a member of one cultural endowment rather than another. In the process of studying a given complex of events, he begins to perceive the *possible* story form that such events *may* figure. In his narrative account of how this set of events took on the shape which he perceives to inhere within it, he emplots his account as a story of a particular kind. The reader, in the process of following the historian's account of those events, gradually comes to realize that the story he is reading is of one kind rather than another: romance, tragedy, comedy, satire, epic, or what have you. And when he has perceived the class or type to which the story that he is reading belongs, he experiences the effect of having the events in the story explained to him. He has at this point not only successfully followed the story; he has grasped the point of it, *understood* it, as well. The original strangeness, mystery, or exoticism of the events is dispelled, and they take on a familiar aspect, not in their details, but in their functions as elements of a familiar kind of configuration. They are rendered comprehensible by being subsumed under the categories of the plot structure in which they are encoded as a story of a particular kind. They are familiarized, not only because the reader now has more *information* about the events, but also because he has been shown how the data conform to an *icon* of a comprehensible finished process, a plot structure with which he is familiar as a part of his cultural endowment.

This is not unlike what happens, or is supposed to happen, in psychotherapy. The sets of events in the patient's past which are the presumed cause of his distress, manifested in the neurotic syndrome, have been defamiliarized, rendered strange, mysterious, and threatening and have assumed a meaning that he can neither accept nor effectively reject. It is not that the patient does not *know* what those events were, does not know the facts; for if he did not in some sense know the facts, he would be unable to recognize them and repress them whenever they arise in his consciousness. On the contrary, he knows them all too well. He knows them so well, in fact, that he lives with them constantly and in such a way as to make it impossible for him to see any other facts except through the coloration that the set of events in question gives to his perception of the world. We might say that, according to the theory of psychoanalysis, the patient has overemplotted these events, has charged them with a meaning so intense that, whether real or merely imagined, they continue to shape both his perceptions and his responses to the world long after they should have become "past history." The therapist's problem, then, is not to hold up before the patient the "real facts" of the matter, the "truth" as against the "fantasy" that obsesses him. Nor is it to give him a short course in psychoanalytical theory by which to enlighten him as to the true nature of his distress by cataloguing it as a manifestation of some "complex." This is what the analyst might do in relating the patient's case to a third party, and especially to another analyst. But psychoanalytic theory recognizes that the patient will resist both of these tactics in the same way that he resists the intrusion into consciousness of the traumatized memory traces in the *form* that he obsessively remembers them. The problem is to get the patient to "reemplot" his whole life history in such a way as to change the *meaning* of those events for him and their *significance* for the economy of the whole set of events that make up his life. As thus envisaged, the therapeutic process is an exercise in the refamiliarization of events that have been defamiliarized, rendered alienated from the patient's life-history, by virtue of their overdetermination as causal forces. And we might say that the events are detraumatized by being removed from the plot structure in which they have a dominant place and inserted in another in which they have a subordinate or simply ordinary function as elements of a life shared with all other men.

Now, I am not interested in forcing the analogy between psychotherapy and historiography; I use the example merely to illustrate a point about the fictive component in historical narratives. Historians seek to refamiliarize us with events which have been forgotten through either accident, neglect, or repression. Moreover, the greatest historians have always dealt with those events in the histories of their cultures which are "traumatic" in nature and the meaning of which is either problematical or overdetermined in the significance that they still have for current life, events such as revolutions, civil wars, large-scale processes such as industrialization and urbanization, or institutions which have lost their original function in a society but continue to play an important role on the current social scene. In looking at the ways in which such structures took shape or evolved, historians refamiliarize them, not only by providing more information about them, but also by showing how their developments conformed to one or another of the story types that we conventionally invoke to make sense of our own life-histories.

Now, if any of this is plausible as a characterization of the explanatory *effect* of historical narrative, it tells us something important about the *mimetic* aspect of historical narratives. It is generally maintained—as Frye said—that a history is a verbal model of a set of events external to the mind of the historian. But it is wrong to think of a history as a model similar to a scale model of an airplane or ship, a map, or a photograph. For we can check the adequacy of this latter kind of model by going and looking at the original and, by applying the necessary rules of translation, seeing in what respect the model has actually succeeded in reproducing aspects of the original. But historical structures and processes are not like these originals; we cannot go and look at them in order to see if the historian has adequately reproduced them in his narrative. Nor should we want to, even if we could; for after all it was the very strangeness of the original as it appeared in the documents that inspired the historian's efforts to make a model of it in the first place. If the historian only did that for us, we should be in the same situation as the patient whose analyst merely told him, on the basis of interviews with his parents, siblings, and childhood friends, what the "true facts" of the patient's early life were. We would have no reason to think that anything at all had been *explained* to us.

This is what leads me to think that historical narratives are not only models of past events and processes, but also metaphorical statements which suggest a relation of similitude between such events and processes and the story types that we conventionally use to endow the events of our lives with culturally sanctioned meanings. Viewed in a purely formal way, a historical narrative is not only a *reproduction* of the events reported in it, but also a *complex of symbols* which gives us directions for finding an *icon* of the structure of those events in our literary tradition.

I am here, of course, invoking the distinctions between sign, symbol, and icon which C. S. Peirce developed in his philosophy of language. I think that these distinctions will help us to understand what is fictive in all putatively realistic representations of the world and what is realistic in all manifestly fictive ones. They help us, in short, to answer the question, What are historical representations *representations of*? It seems to me that we must say of histories what Frye seems to think is true only of poetry or philosophies of history, namely that, considered as a system of signs, the historical narrative points in two directions simultaneously: *toward* the events describe in the narrative and *toward* the story type or mythos which the historian has chosen to serve as the icon of the structure of the events. The narrative itself is not the icon; what it does is *describe* events in the historical record in such a way as to inform the reader *what to take as an icon* of the events so as to render them "familiar" to him. The historical narrative thus mediates between the events reported in it on the one side and pregeneric plot structures conventionally used in our culture to endow unfamiliar events and situations with meanings, on the other.

The evasion of the implications of the fictive nature of historical narrative is in part a consequence of the utility of the concept "history" for the definition of other types of discourse. "History" can be set over against "science" by virtue of its want of conceptual rigor and failure to produce the kinds of universal laws that the sciences characteristically seek to produce. Similarly, "history" can be set over against "literature" by virtue of its interest in the "actual" rather than the "possible," which is supposedly the object of representation of "literary" works. Thus, within a long and distinguished critical tradition that has sought to determine what is "real" and what is "imagined" in the novel, history has served as a kind of archetype of the "realistic" pole of representation. I am thinking of Frye, Auerbach, Booth, Scholes and Kellogg, and others. Nor is it unusual for literary theorists, when they are speaking about the "context" of a literary work, to suppose that this context—the "historical milieu"—has a concreteness and an accessibility that the work itself can never have, as if it were easier to perceive the reality of a past world put together from a thousand historical documents than it is to probe the depths of a single literary work that is present to the critic studying it. But the presumed concreteness and accessibility of historical milieu, these contexts of the texts that literary scholars study, are themselves products of the fictive capability of the historians who have studied those contexts. The historical documents are not less opaque than the texts studied by the literary critic. Nor is the world those documents figure more accessible. The one is no more "given" than the other. In fact, the opaqueness of the world figured in historical documents is, if anything, it increased by the production of historical narratives. Each new historical work only adds to the number of possible texts that have to be interpreted if a full and accurate picture of a given historical milieu is to be faithfully drawn. The relationship between the past to be analyzed and historical works produced by analysis of the documents is paradoxical; the *more* we know about the past, the more difficult it is to generalize about it.

But if the increase in our knowledge of the past makes it more difficult to generalize about it, it should make it easier for us to generalize about the forms in which that knowledge is transmitted to us. Our knowledge of the past may increase incrementally, but our understanding of it does not. Nor does our understanding of the past progress by the kind of revolutionary breakthroughs that we associate with the development of the physical sciences. Like literature, history progresses by the production of classics, the nature of which is such that they cannot be disconfirmed or negated, in the way that the principal conceptual schemata of the sciences are. And it is their nondisconfirmability that testifies to the essentially *literary* nature of historical classics. There is something in a historical masterpiece that cannot be negated, and this nonnegatable element is its form, the form which is its fiction.

It is frequently forgotten or, when remembered, denied that no given set of events attested by the historical record comprises a *story* manifestly finished and complete. This is as true as the events that comprise the life of an individual as it is of an institution, a nation, or a whole people. We do not *live* stories, even if we give our lives meaning by retrospectively casting them in the form of stories. And so too with nations or whole cultures. In an essay on the "mythical" nature of historiography, Lévi-Strauss remarks on the astonishment that a visitor from another planet would feel if confronted by the thousands of histories written about the French Revolution. For in those works, the "authors do not always make use of the same incidents; when they do, the incidents are revealed in different lights. And yet these are variations which have to do with the same country, the same period, and the same events—events whose reality is scattered across every level of a multilayered structure." He goes on to suggest that the criterion of validity by which historical accounts might be assessed cannot depend on their "elements"—that is to say—their putative factual content. On the contrary, he notes, "pursued in isolation, each element shows itself to be beyond grasp. But certain of them derive consistency from the fact that they can be integrated into a system whose terms are more or less credible when set against the overall coherence of the series." But his "coherence of the series" cannot be the coherence of the *chronological* series, that sequence of "facts" (organized into the temporal order of their original occurrence. For the "chronicle" of events, out of which the historian fashions his story of "what really happened," already comes preencoded. There are "hot" and "cold" chronologies, chronologies in which more or fewer dates appear to demand inclusion in a full chronicle of what happened. Moreover, the dates themselves come to us already grouped into classes of dates, classes which are constitutive of putative domains of the historical field, domains which appear as problems for the historian to solve if he is to give a full and culturally responsible account of the past.

All this suggests to Lévi-Strauss that, when it is a matter of working up a comprehensive account of the various domains of the historical record in the form of a story, the "alleged historical continuities" that the historian purports to find in the record are "secured only by dint of fraudulent outlines imposed by the historian on the record. These "fraudulent outlines" are, in his view, a product of "abstraction" and a means of escape from the "threat of an infinite regress" that always lurks at the interior of every complex set of historical "facts." We can construct a comprehensible story of the past, Lévi-Strauss insists, only by a decision to "give up" one or more of the domains of facts offering themselves for inclusion in our accounts. Our *explanations* of historical structures and processes are thus determined more by what we leave out of our representations than by what we put in. For it is in this brutal capacity to exclude certain facts in the interest of constituting others as components of comprehensible stories that the historian displays his tact as well as his understanding. The "overall coherence" of any given "series" of historical facts is the coherence of story, but this coherence is achieved only by a tailoring of the "facts" to the requirements of the story form. And thus Lévi-Strauss concludes: "In spite of worthy and indispensable efforts to bring another moment in history alive and to possess it, a clairvoyant history should admit that it never completely escapes from the nature of myth."

It is this mediative function that permits us to speak of a historical narrative as an extended metaphor. As a symbolic structure, the historical narrative does not *reproduce* the events it describes; it tells us in what direction to think about the events and charges our thought about the events with different emotional valences. The historical narrative does not *image* the things it indicates; it *calls to* mind images of the things it indicates, in the same way that a metaphor does. When a given concourse of events is emplotted as a "tragedy," this simply means that the historian has so described the events it as to *remind us* of that form of fiction which we associate with the concept "tragic." Properly understood, histories ought never to be read as unambiguous signs of the events they report, but rather as symbolic structures, extended metaphors, that "liken" the events reported in them to some form with which we have already become familiar in our literary culture.

Perhaps I should indicate briefly what is meant by the *symbolic* and *iconic* aspects of a metaphor. The hackneyed phrase "My love, a rose" is not, obviously, intended to be understood as suggesting that the loved one is *actually* a rose. It is not even meant to suggest that the loved one has the specific attributes of a rose—that is to say, that the loved one is red, yellow, orange, or black, is a plant, has thorns, needs sunlight, should be sprayed regularly with insecticides, and so on. It is meant to be understood as indicating that the beloved shares the *qualities* which the rose has come to *symbolize* in the customary linguistic usages of Western culture. That is to say, considered as a message, the metaphor gives directions for finding an entity that will evoke the images associated *with loved ones and roses alike* in our culture. The metaphor does not *image* the thing it seeks to characterize, *it gives directions* for finding the set of images that are intended to be associated with that thing. It functions as a symbol, rather than as a sign which is to say that it does not give us either a *description* or an *icon* of the thing it represents, but *tells us* what images to look for in our culturally encoded experience in order to determine how we *should feel* about the thing represented.

So too for historical narratives. They succeed in endowing sets of past events with meanings, over and above whatever comprehension they provide by appeal to putative causal laws, by exploiting the metaphorical similarities between sets of real events and the conventional structures of our fictions. By the very constitution of a set of events in such a way as to make a comprehensible story out of them, the historian charges those events with the symbolic significance of a comprehensible plot structure. Historians may not like to think of their works as translations of fact into fictions; but this is one of the effects of their works. By suggesting alternative emplotments of a given sequence of historical events, historians provide historical events with all of the possible meanings with which the literary art of their culture is capable of endowing them. The real dispute between the proper historian and the philosopher of history has to do with the latter's insistence that events can be emplotted in one and only one story form. History-writing thrives on the discovery of all the possible plot structures that might be invoked to endow sets of events with different meanings. And our understanding of the past increases precisely in the degree to which we succeed in determining how far that past conforms to the strategies of sense-making that are contained in their purest forms in literary art.

Conceiving historical narratives in this way may give us some insight into the crisis in historical thinking which has been under way since the beginning of our century. Let us imagine that the problem of the historian is to make sense of a hypothetical *set* of events by arranging them in a *series* that is at once chronologically *and* syntactically structured, in the way that any discourse from a sentence all the way up to a novel is structured. We can see immediately that the imperatives of chronological arrangement of the events constituting the set must exist in tension with the imperatives of the syntactical strategies alluded to, whether the latter are conceived as those of logic (the syllogism) or those of narrative (the plot structure).

Thus, we have a set of events

1. $a, b, c, d, e, \ldots\ldots, n,$

ordered chronologically but requiring description and characterization as elements of plot or argument by which to give them meaning. Now, the series can be emplotted in a number of different ways and thereby endowed with different meanings without violating the imperatives of the chronological arrangement at all. We may briefly characterize some of these emplotments in the following ways:

2. $A, b, c, d, e, \ldots\ldots, n$
3. $a, B, c, d, e, \ldots\ldots, n$
4. $a, b, C, d, e, \ldots\ldots, n$
5. $a, b, c, D, e, \ldots\ldots, n$

And so on.

The capitalized letters indicate the privileged status given to certain events or sets of events in the series by which they are endowed with explanatory force, either as causes explaining the structure of the whole series or as symbols of the plot structure of the series considered as a story of a specific kind. We might say that any history which endows any putatively original event (a) with the status of a decisive factor (A) in the structuration of the whole series of events following after it is "deterministic." The emplotments of the history of "society" by Rousseau in his *Second Discourse,* Marx in the *Manifesto,* and Freud in *Totem and Taboo* would fall into this category. So, too, any history which endows the last event in the series (e), whether real or only speculatively projected, with the force of full explanatory power (E) is of the type of all eschatological or apocalyptical histories. St. Augustine's *City of God* and the various versions of the Joachite notion of the advent of a millennium, Hegel's *Philosophy of History,* and, in general, all Idealist histories are of this sort. In between we would have the various forms of historiography which appeal to plot structures of a distinctively "fictional" sort (Romance, Comedy, Tragedy, and Satire) by which to endow the series with a perceivable form and a conceivable "meaning."

If the series were simply recorded in the order in which the events originally occurred, under the assumption that the ordering of the events in their temporal sequence itself provided a kind of explanation of why they occurred when and where they did, we would have the pure form of the *chronicle.* This would be a "naive" form of chronicle, however, inasmuch as the categories of time and space alone served as the informing interpretative principles. Over against the naive form of chronicle we could postulate as a logical possibility its "sentimental" counterpart, the ironic denial that historical series have any kind of larger significance or describe any imaginable plot structure or indeed can even be construed as a story with a discernible beginning, middle, and end. We could conceive such accounts of history as intending to serve as antidotes to their false or overemplotted counterparts (nos. 2, 3, 4, and 5 above) and could represent them as an ironic return to mere chronicle as constituting the only sense which any cognitively responsible history could take. We could characterize such histories thus:

6.   "$a, b, c, d, e. \ldots \ldots, n$"

with the quotation marks indicating the conscious interpretation of the events as having nothing other than seriality as their meaning.

This schema is of course highly abstract and does not do justice to the possible mixtures of and variations within the types that it is meant to distinguish. But it helps us, I think, to conceive how events might be emplotted in different ways without violating the imperatives of the chronological order of the events (however they are construed) so as to yield alternative, mutually exclusive, and yet, equally plausible interpretations of the set. I have tried to show in *Metahistory* how such mixtures and variations occur in the writings of the master historians of the nineteenth century; and I have suggested in that book that classic historical accounts always represent attempts both to emplot the historical series adequately and implicitly to come to terms with other plausible emplotments. It is this dialectical tension between two or more possible emplotments that signals the element of critical self-consciousness present in any historian of recognizably classical stature.

Histories, then, are not only about events but also about the possible sets of relationships that those events can be demonstrated to figure. These sets of relationships are not, however, immanent in the events themselves; they exist only in the mind of the historian reflecting on them. Here they are present as the modes of relationships conceptualized in the myth, fable, and folklore, scientific knowledge, religion, and literary art, of the historian's own culture. But more importantly, they are, I suggest, immanent in the very language which the historian must use to *describe* events prior to a scientific analysis of them or a fictional emplotment of them. For if the historian's aim is to familiarize us with the unfamiliar, he must use figurative, rather than technical, language. Technical languages are familiarizing only *to* those who have been indoctrinated in their uses and only of those sets of events which the practitioners of a discipline have agreed to describe in a uniform terminology. History possesses no such generally accepted technical terminology and in fact no agreement on what kind of events make up its specific subject matter. The historian's characteristic instrument of encodation, communication, and exchange is ordinary educated speech. This implies that the only instruments that he has for endowing his data with meaning, of rendering the strange familiar, and of rendering the mysterious past comprehensible, are the techniques of *figurative* language. All historical narratives presuppose figurative characterizations of the events they purport to represent and explain. And this means that historical narratives, considered purely as verbal artifacts, can be characterized by the mode of figurative discourse in which they are cast.

If this is the case, then it may well be that the kind of emplotment that the historian decides to use to give meaning to a set of historical events is dictated by the dominant figurative mode of the language he has used to *describe* the elements of his account *prior* to his composition of a narrative. Geoffrey Hartman once remarked in my hearing, at a conference on literary history, that he was not sure that he knew what historians of literature might want to do, but he did know that to write a history meant to place an event within a context, by relating it as a part to some conceivable whole. He went on to suggest that as far as he knew, there were only two ways of relating parts to wholes, by metonymy and by synecdoche. Having been engaged for some time in the study of the thought of Giambattista Vico, I was much taken with this thought, because it conformed to Vico's notion that the "logic" of all "poetic wisdom" was contained in the relationships which language itself provided in the four principal modes of figurative representation: metaphor, metonymy, synecdoche, and irony. My own hunch—and it is a hunch which I find confirmed in Hegel's reflections on the nature of nonscientific discourse—is that in any field of study which, like history, has not yet become disciplinized to the point of constructing a formal terminological system for describing its objects, in the way that physics and chemistry have, it is the types of figurative discourse that dictate the fundamental forms of the data to be studied. This means that the *shape* of the *relationships* which will appear to be inherent in the objects inhabiting the field will in reality have been imposed on the field by the investigator in the very *act of identifying and describing* the objects that he finds there. The implication is that historians *constitute* their subjects as possible objects of narrative representation by the very language they use to *describe* them. And if this is the case, it means that the different kinds of historical interpretations that we have of the same set of events, such as the French Revolution as interpreted by Michelet, Tocqueville, Taine, and others, are little more than projections of the linguistic protocols that these historians used to prefigure that set of events prior to writing their narratives of it. It is only a hypothesis, but it seems possible that the conviction of the historian that he has "found" the form of his narrative in the events themselves, rather than imposed it upon them, in the way the poet does, is a result of a certain lack of linguistic self-consciousness which obscures the extent to which descriptions of events *already* constitute interpretations of their nature. As thus envisaged, the difference between Michelet's and Tocqueville's accounts of the Revolution does not reside only in the fact that the former emplotted his story in the modality of a Romance and the latter his in the modality of Tragedy; it resides as well in the tropological mode— metaphorical and metonymic, respectively—with each brought to his apprehension of the facts as they appeared in the documents.

I do not have the space to try to demonstrate the plausibility of this hypothesis, which is the informing principle of my book *Metahistory*. But I hope that this essay may serve to suggest an approach to the study of such discursive prose forms as historiography, an approach that is as old as the study of rhetoric and as new as modern linguistics. Such a study would proceed along the lines laid out by Roman Jakobson in a paper entitled "Linguistics and Poetics," in which he characterized the difference between Romantic poetry and the various forms of nineteenth-century Realistic prose as residing in the essentially metaphorical nature of the former and the essentially metonymical nature of the latter. I think that this characterization of the difference between poetry and prose is too narrow, because it presupposes that complex macrostructural narratives such as the novel are little more than projections of the "selective" (i.e., phonemic) axis of all speech acts. Poetry, and especially Romantic poetry, is then characterized by Jakobson as a projection of the "combinatory" (i.e., morphemic) axis of language. Such a binary theory pushes the analyst toward a dualistic opposition between poetry and prose which appears to rule out the possibility of a metonymical poetry and a metaphorical prose. But the fruitfulness of Jakobson's theory lies in its suggestion that the various forms of both poetry and prose, all of which have their counterparts in narrative in general and therefore in historiography too, can be characterized in terms of the dominant trope which serves as the paradigm, provided by language itself, of all significant relationships conceived to exist in the world by anyone wishing to represent those relationships in language.

Narrative, or the syntagmatic dispersion of events across a temporal series presented as a prose discourse, in such a way as to display their progressive elaboration as a comprehensible form, would represent the "inward turn" that discourse takes when it tries to *show* the reader the true form of things existing behind a merely apparent formlessness. Narrative *style,* in history as well as in the novel, would then be construed as the modality of the movement from a representation of some original state of affairs to some subsequent state. The primary *meaning* of a narrative would then consist of the destructuration of a set of events (real or imagined) originally encoded in one topological mode and the progressive restructuration of the set in another tropological mode. As thus envisaged, narrative would be a process of decodation and recodation in which an original perception is clarified by being cast in a figurative mode different from that in which it has come encoded by convention, authority, or custom. And the explanatory force of the narrative would then depend on the contrast between the original encodation and the later one.

For example, let us suppose that a set of experiences comes to us as a grotesque, i.e., as unclassified and unclassifiable. Our problem is to identify the modality of the relationships that bind the discernible elements of the formless totality together in such a way as to make of it a whole of some sort. If we stress the similarities among the elements, we are working in the mode of metaphor; if we stress the differences among them, we are working in the mode of metonymy. Of course, in order to make sense of any set of experiences, we must obviously identify both the parts of a thing that appear to make it up and the nature of the shared aspects of the parts that make them identifiable as a totality. This implies that all original characterization of anything must utilize *both* metaphor and metonymy in order to "fix" it as something about which we can meaningfully discourse.

In the case of historiography, the attempts of commentators to make sense of the French Revolution are instructive. Burke decodes the events the Revolution which his contemporaries experience as a grotesque by recoding it in the mode of irony; Michelet recodes these events in the mode of synecdoche; Tocqueville recodes them in the mode of metonymy. In each case, however, the movement from code to recode is narratively described, i.e., laid out on a timeline in such a way as to make the interpretation of the events that made up the "Revolution" a kind of drama that we can recognize as Satirical, Romantic, and Tragic, respectively. This drama can be allowed by the reader of the narrative in such a way as to be experienced as a progressive revelation of what the *true* nature of the events consists of. The revelation is not experienced, however, as a restructuring of perception so much as an illumination of a field of occurrence. But actually what has happened is that a set of events originally encoded in one way is simply being decoded by being recoded in another. The events themselves are not substantially changed from one account to another. That is to say, the data that are to be analyzed are not significantly different in the different accounts. What is different are the modalities of their relationships. These modalities, in turn, although they *may* appear to the reader to be based on different theories of the nature of society, politics, and history, ultimately have their origin in the figurative characterizations of the whole set of events as representing wholes of fundamentally different sorts. It is for this reason that, when it is a matter of setting different interpretations of the same set of historical phenomena over against one another in an attempt to decide which is the best or most convincing, we are often driven to confusion or ambiguity. This is not to say that we cannot distinguish between good and bad historiography, since we can always fall back on such criteria as responsibility to the rules of evidence, the relative fullness of narrative detail, logical consistency, and the like to determine this issue. But it is to say that the effort to distinguish between good and bad interpretations of a historical event such as the Revolution is not as easy as it might at first appear when it is a matter of dealing with alternative interpretations produced by historians of relatively equal learning and conceptual sophistication. After all, a great historical classic cannot be disconfirmed or nullified either by the discovery of some new datum that might call a specific explanation of some element of the whole account into question or by the generation of new methods of analysis which permit us to deal with questions that earlier historians might not have taken under consideration. And it is precisely because great historical classics, such as works by Gibbon, Michelet, Thucydides, Mommsen, Ranke, Burckhardt, Bancroft, and so on, cannot be definitely disconfirmed that we must look to the specifically literary aspects of their work as crucial, and not merely subsidiary, elements in their historiographical technique.

What all this points to is the necessity of revising the distinction conventionally drawn between poetic and prose discourse in discussion of such narrative forms as historiography and recognizing that the distinction, as old as Aristotle, between history and poetry obscures as much as it illuminates about both. If there is an element of the historical in all poetry, there is an element of poetry in every historical account of the world. And this because in our account of the historical world we are dependent, in ways perhaps that we are not in the natural sciences, on the techniques of *figurative language* both for our *characterization* of the objects of our narrative representations and for the *strategies* by which to constitute narrative accounts of the transformations of those objects in time. And this because history has no stipulatable subject matter uniquely its own; it is always written as part of a contest between contending poetic figurations of what the past *might* consist of.

The older distinction between fiction and history, in which fiction is conceived as the representation of the imaginable and history as the representation of the actual, must give place to the recognition that we can only know the *actual* by contrasting it with or likening it to the *imaginable*. As thus conceived, historical narratives are complex structures in which a world of experience is imagined to exist under at least two modes, one of which is encoded as "real," the other of which is "revealed" to have been illusory in the course of the narrative. Of course, it is a fiction of the historian that the various states of affairs which he constitutes as the beginning, the middle, and the end of a course of development are all "actual" or "real" and that he has merely recorded "what happened" in the transition from the inaugural to the terminal phase. But both the beginning state of affairs and the ending one are inevitably poetic constructions, and as such, dependent upon the modality of the figurative language used to give them the aspect of coherence. This implies that all narrative is not simply a recording of "what happened" in the transition from one state of affairs to another, but a progressive *redescription* of sets of events in such a way as to dismantle a structure encoded in one verbal mode in the beginning so as to justify a recoding of it in another mode at the end. This is what the "middle" of all narratives consist of.

All of this is highly schematic, and I know that this insistence on the fictive element in all historical narratives is certain to arouse the ire of historians who believe that they are doing something fundamentally different from the novelist, by virtue of the fact that they deal with "real," while the novelist deals with "imagined," events. But neither the form nor the explanatory power of narrative derives from the different contents it is presumed to be able to accommodate. In point of fact, history—the real world as it evolves in time—

is made sense of in the same way that the poet or novelist tries to make sense of it, i.e., by endowing what originally appears to be problematical and mysterious with the aspect of a recognizable, because it is a familiar, form. It does not matter whether the world is conceived to be real or only imagined; the manner of making sense of it is the same.

So too, to say that we make sense of the real world by imposing upon it the formal coherency that we customarily associate with the products of writers of fiction in no way detracts from the status as knowledge which we ascribe to historiography. It would only detract from it if we were to believe that literature did not teach us anything about reality, but was a product of an imagination which was not of this world but of some other, inhuman one. In my view, we experience the "fictionalization" of history as an "explanation" for the same reason that we experience great fiction as an illumination of a world that we inhabit along with the author. In both we recognize the forms by which consciousness both constitutes and colonizes the world it seeks to inhabit comfortably.

Finally, it may be observed that if historians were to recognize the fictive element in their narratives, this would not mean the degradation of historiography to the status of ideology or propaganda. In fact, this recognition would serve as a potent antidote to the tendency of historians to become captive of ideological preconceptions which they do not recognize as such but honor as the "correct" perception of "the way things *really* are." By drawing historiography nearer to its origins in literary sensibility, we should be able to identify the ideological, because it is the fictive, element in our own discourse. We are always able to see the fictive element in those historians with whose interpretations of a given set of events we disagree; we seldom perceive that element in our own prose. So, too, if we recognized the literary or fictive element in every historical account, we would be able to move the teaching of historiography onto a higher level of self-consciousness than it currently occupies.

What teacher has not lamented his inability to give instruction to apprentices in the *writing* of history? What graduate student of history has not despaired at trying to comprehend and imitate the model which his instructors *appear* to honor but the principles of which remain uncharted? If we recognize that there is a fictive element in all historical narrative, we would find in the theory of language and narrative itself the basis for a more subtle presentation of what historiography consists of than that which simply tells the student to go and "find out the facts" and write them up in such a way as to tell "what really happened."

In my view, history as a discipline is in bad shape today because it has lost sight of its origins in the literary imagination. In the interest of *appearing* scientific and objective, it has repressed and denied to itself its own greatest source of strength and renewal. By drawing historiography back once more to an intimate connection with its literary basis, we should not only be putting ourselves on guard against *merely* ideological distortions; we should be by way of arriving at that "theory" of history without which it cannot pass for a "discipline" at all.

BIBLIOGRAPHICAL NOTE

The quotations from Claude Lévi-Strauss are taken from his *Savage Mind* (London, 1966) and "Overture to *Le Cru et le cuit*," in *Structuralism,* ed. Jacques Ehrmann (New York: Anchor, 1966). The remarks on the ironic nature of metaphor draw upon Paul Henle, *Language, Thought, and Culture* (Ann Arbor, Mich.: Ann Arbor Paperbacks, 1966). Jakobson's notions of the tropological nature of style are in "Linguistics and Poetics," in *Style and Language,* ed. Thomas A. Sebeok (New York and London, 1960). In addition to Northrop Frye's *Anatomy of Criticism* (Princeton: Princeton University Press, 1957), see also his essay on philosophy of history, "New Directions from Old," in *Fables of Identity* (New York: Harcourt, Brace, and World, 1963). On story and plot in historical narrative in R. G. Collingwood's thought, see, of course, *The Idea of History* (Oxford: Oxford University Press, 1956).

15

Narrative Progression

JAMES PHELAN

Progression, as I use the term, refers to a narrative as a dynamic event, one that must move, in both its telling and its reception, through time. In examining progression, then, we are concerned with how authors generate, sustain, develop, and resolve readers' interests in narrative. I postulate that such movement is given shape and direction by the way in which an author introduces, complicates, and resolves (or fails to resolve) certain instabilities which are the developing focus of the authorial audience's interest in the narrative. Authors may take advantage of numerous variables in the narrative situation to generate the movement of a tale. In general, the story-discourse model of narrative helps to differentiate between two main kinds of instabilities: the first are those occurring within the story, instabilities between characters, created by situations, and complicated and resolved through actions. The second are those created by the discourse, instabilities—of value, belief, opinion, knowledge, expectation—between authors and/or narrators, on the one hand, and the authorial audience on the other. To recognize this difference in kind I reserve the term "instabilities" for unstable relations within story and introduce the term "tension" for those in discourse. Some narratives progress primarily through the introduction and complication of instabilities, whereas others progress primarily through tensions, and still others progress by means of both. In examining progression, we are also involved in considering narratives as developing wholes. In order to account for the effect of, say, a complication of one instability, we will need to consider the previous development of that instability and its relation to other instabilities or tensions as well as the way it is disclosed to the reader. To do a similar analysis for all such complications would lead one to an analysis of the whole narrative. The point, in other words, is not that all parts of a narrative are directly concerned with instabilities or tensions, but rather that all parts of a narrative may have consequences for the progression, even if those consequences lie solely in their effect on the *reader's understanding* of the instabilities, tensions, and resolution. Let me illustrate this conception of progression, and some of its consequences for the way in which I shall seek to develop my rhetorical theory of character by a look at a short narrative that progresses both by tension and instability. I choose Ring Lardner's "Haircut" in part because, as a narrative analogue to the dramatic monologue, it also fits in with the progression of examples in this chapter.

Just as the poet in a dramatic monologue seeks to create the illusion that his audience is not reading a poem but overhearing part of a conversation, so Lardner seeks to create the illusion that his audience is not reading a story but overhearing a barber's rambling monologue to a new customer. Lardner builds the illusion in large part by emphasizing the haphazardness of the barber's speech—Whitey frequently shifts topics with no more transition than a "Well" or a "But I was going to tell you." Like the poet in the dramatic monologue, Lardner needs to sustain the illusion of unartistically delivered speech even as he arranges it for maximum effect. But there is a significant difference between Whitey's narrative and most dramatic monologues: while the speaker in a dramatic monologue may or may not talk directly about himself, the movement of the poem is typically a movement toward the disclosure of his character, whereas the movement of Whitey's narration is toward the disclosure of events involving other characters, particularly Jim Kendall, Julie Gregg, Paul Dickson, and Doc Stair. Significantly, however, the first major instability among these characters is not introduced until after the halfway point of Whitey's narration, when he says that "Jim was like the majority of men, and women too, I guess. He wanted what he couldn't get. He wanted Julie Gregg and he worked his head off trying to land her."[1] Indeed, at this juncture, the narrative divides neatly into two parts; everything before this point serves to disclose information about the four chief actors and their environment, information that is necessary for the authorial audience's understanding of how and why they act as they do in the focused narrative of related events that follows this point. The apparently scattered information of the first half is brought into a coherent relationship as we draw upon it to infer the means and motives behind the central events of the story, Jim Kendall's humiliation of Julie Gregg and his subsequent death in what Whitey regards as an accident. This arrangement makes the second half of the story move with economy and power to its climax, but it raises some interesting questions about the first half: What does Lardner do there to propel the reader forward, and what happens to that principle of propulsion after the shift to a different principle just after the halfway point?

In the terms introduced above, the initial principle of movement in "Haircut" is the tension between Whitey and the authorial audience: Whitey's judgments of Jim Kendall as a "card" (25), as "kind of rough but a good fella at heart" (24), are at odds with our much harsher judgments, and we read on in part for the pleasure of communicating with Lardner behind Whitey's back, in part to take what he tells us about his small town, and in part to see how the portrait of our unreliable narrator develops. In other words, in the absence of any clear direction to the potential instabilities introduced in this first half of the narrative, Whitey becomes much like the speaker in a dramatic monologue: he is as much the focus of our interest as anything he tells us.

Now what emerges from the tension and our interest in Whitey is a clear, if limited, mimetic portrait: he is a small-town barber who is garrulous, loves a laugh, is well-liked, and most significantly, for this is the source of the tension, is morally obtuse. He is unable to detect the cruelty of most of Jim Kendall's practical jokes and unable to differentiate between such acts as Jim's kidding Milt Sheppard about the size of his Adam's apple, and Jim's falsely promising his wife and children that he would take them to the circus. In addition, Whitey has attributes that mark out a thematic potentiality: he is shown to be a representative of his own small town and thus of a small-town mentality. Whitey's occupation and personality make his shop the base of Kendall's operations, and indeed, the first joke of Jim's that Whitey tells about is directed at Whitey himself, and the barber is able to reply in kind. The occupation further identifies Whitey as a representative male—he is a man serving other men, talking and joking with them in a space where the women are excluded. In addition, Whitey seems to know and get on with everyone, and his nickname accentuates his status as one of the gang. Finally, Whitey's very role in the narrative, passing on the gossip of the town to its new inhabitant, emphasizes his place as representative male.

The initial movement by tension has many consequences for the narrative after it shifts to its movement by instability. First, our understanding of Whitey's obtuseness operates to create one of the dramatic ironies of the narrative: given what we know of Whitey, we have little trouble seeing that his report of Jim Kendall's death as accidental misses the truth of that event by a country mile. We are quickly able to discern that Paul Dickson, urged on by Doc Stair's angry remark that anyone who could pull anything like Kendall's trick on Julie Gregg "ought not to be let live" (32), had deliberately shot Kendall when they were out duck-hunting. We can discern further that Doc Stair as coroner took advantage of Paul's reputation as "cuckoo" (27) and "a half-wit" to declare the death accidental because that declaration would better serve the cause of justice than the truth would. The dramatic irony—and part of the effect of the story—arises, as Brooks and Warren say

213

in *Understanding Fiction,* from the fact that the biter is bitten[2] and from the fact that Whitey is blind to the complicated "trick" played on Jim by Paul Dickson and Doc Stair. But the effect produced by the ending is more than ironic satisfaction, and to describe the way that effect comes about I need to introduce one last distinction, that between completeness and closure.

Closure, as I use the term, refers to the way in which a narrative signals its end, whereas completeness refers to the degree of resolution accompanying the closure. Closure need not be tied to the resolution of instabilities and tensions but completeness always is. For example, in a narrative entitled "Diary of Disastrous December," which has 31 chapters, each of which is headed by the date and which follow each other in chronological order, the very inscription of 31 December at the head of the last chapter will be a strong signal of closure. Whether the narrative will have completeness will depend on how the instabilities and tensions are worked out in that (and of course previous) chapters. In a narrative in which a character sets out from home on a dangerous journey and returns at the end, the return itself will function as a sign of closure and the condition in which he returns will be a step toward completeness, indicating how the initial instability is resolved; the degree of completeness will depend upon whether and how the later instabilities have been resolved. In "Haircut," Lardner provides closure by signaling the end of the customer's turn in the chair. He provides completeness by using Whitey's final words, including the signal of closure, to provide final resolution to the instabilities by altering the authorial audience's understanding of the resolution that has already been narrated. This altered understanding is a result of Lardner using Whitey's final lines to convert the thematic dimension of Whitey's character into a thematic function. These lines create the second main consequence of the initial progression by tension as Lardner reemphasizes the tension between Whitey and the authorial audience and more subtly recalls his representative status:

> Personally I wouldn't leave a person shoot a gun in the same boat I was in unless I was sure they knew somethin' about guns. Jim was a sucker to leave a new beginner have his gun, let alone a half-wit. It probably served Jim right, what he got. But still we miss him round here. He certainly was a card.
>
> Comb it wet or dry? (33)

This ending creates an effect more chilling than satisfying first because Whitey's judgment of Jim ("It probably served Jim right, what he got") is made for a reason that misses the mark as widely as his judgments about Jim's character. The chill gets deeper when we reflect that Whitey as representative spokesman can confidently report Kendall's death as accidental and blithely talk about missing the old card only because Doc Stair's declaration has been accepted by the townspeople. And they have accepted the judgment because, like Whitey, they believe that Paul Dickson is a half-wit, a belief based not on Paul's recent behavior but on his having been given that label years ago. Whitey's final comments reveal that the whole sordid episode, begun with Kendall's pursuit and humiliation of Julie Gregg and ended by Paul Dickson's murder of Kendall, has transpired in front of the townspeople's eyes without their recognizing its sordidness. Because no one has been intellectually or morally sensitive enough to understand what happened in the case of Jim Kendall, it is not at all unlikely that a similar sequence of events could occur again. The insensitivity of the good-natured Whitey and by extension of the townsmen he represents is nicely underlined by the story's final sentence, or rather by the swift and matter-of-fact transition from the account of Kendall's death to the business at hand: "Comb it wet or dry?" Like Browning in "My Last Duchess," Lardner is able to make the final signal in the progression con-tribute to both its closure and completeness, that is, both indicate the narra-tive's end and reinforce its final effect. From this point, extrapolations to the significance of the story for Lardner's view of both the viciousness and stu-pidity of small-town life are rather straightforward. The more general point I want to emphasize is that Lardner uses both the initial movement by tension and its consequences for the characterization of Whitey to transform the pro-gression of the whole from the tale of a trickster tricked to a tale emphasizing the chilling implications of that event.

Indeed, Lardner's conversion of Whitey's thematic dimension into a the-matic function affects the authorial audience's understanding of the resolution still further. Given that Lardner has encouraged us to establish a general pat-tern of inverting Whitey's judgments, we may initially conclude that our obtuse friend is right for the wrong reason when he says that Jim got what he deserved. Once we begin thinking about how Lardner is using Whitey to reveal ideas about the American small town, we will soon reflect enough to question whether Jim's punishment fits his crimes: despite Jim's cruelties, murder in cold blood seems an excessive punishment. Furthermore, Whitey's representative obtuseness allows Lardner to leave murky the relation between Doc Stair's decision to call the death accidental and his own role as the agent, however unwitting, behind Paul's action: Is Doc simply protecting himself? Has he become another version of Kendall by playing upon the stupidity of the townspeople in his declaration that the death was accidental? Or is he a fit instrument of justice, someone who regrets what he said to Paul but also acknowledges, with Lardner's approval, that justice is better served through his lie than through putting Paul—and perhaps himself—on trial? Lardner's tech-nique does not allow us to answer these questions with any confidence, but this uncertainty adds to rather than detracts from the completeness of the story. The murkiness is appropriate because it contributes further to the unsettling, chilling experience of the narrative, especially the way its ending causes the authorial audience to reconsider its understanding of Whitey, Doc, Jim, Paul, Julie, and the town in which they live. Lardner's view of the viciousness and stupidity of the small town is not accompanied by any easy judgments about its simplicity or transparency.

This claim that the ambiguity about Doc's motives contributes to rather than detracts from the completeness of the story perhaps requires further explanation. With the conversion of Whitey's thematic dimension into a function, the progression gives new importance to the thematic sphere in the story as a whole. Thus, when the ambiguity about Doc contributes to our understanding of Lardner's view of small-town life it contributes to the completeness. If Doc Stair were the protagonist, if the progression centered on instabilities surrounding him and his motives, then this ambiguity would most likely be a sign of incompleteness: some major instability would not be resolved. In Lardner's story, however, the instabilities are resolved; it is the authorial audience's understanding of the resolution that is revised and completed in an appropriate way by our reflections on the residual ambiguity and Whitey's inability to resolve it.

NOTES

1. Ring Lardner, *The Best Short Stories of Ring Lardner* (New York: Scribner's, 1957), 29. Further citations will be given in page numbers in parentheses in the text.

2. To be sure, Whitey is not simply interchangeable with the other men: his nickname has a positive connotation and his general good nature sets him apart from the cruel group that accompanies Kendall in his effort to humiliate Julie Gregg.

16

Spatialization: A Strategy for Reading Narrative[1]

SUSAN STANFORD FRIEDMAN

In *Reading for the Plot,* Peter Brooks defines narrative as "the play of desire in time" (xiii) and identifies two sites for this play: first, the text itself, wherein desire to order compels the plot's unfolding; and, second, the space between text and reader, wherein the reader's desire for plot impels the reading (37–61). Analysis of these narrative desires involves seeing "the text itself as a system of internal energies and tensions, compulsions, resistances, and desires" (xiv). Like Paul Ricoeur in "Narrative Time," Brooks insists upon the temporal dimension of narrative, on narrative's essential relation to time. I want to extend Brooks's "dynamics of narrative" by reintroducing the issue of space into a discussion of narrative, by considering narrative, in other words, as the play of desire in space as well as time.

I define narrative most simply as the representation of movement within the coordinates of space and time.[2] Here, I adapt M. M. Bakhtin's concept of the chronotope, by which he means the special form in which the "intrinsic interconnectedness of temporal and spatial relationships" is expressed in literature (*Dialogic Imagination,* 84). Invoking Einstein's theory of relativity, Bakhtin argues for the "inseparability of space and time" (84) and resorts repeatedly to spatial tropes in his analysis of various chronotopes. I also want to develop Julia Kristeva's adaptations of Bakhtin's spatial tropes in two early essays, "Word, Dialogue, and Novel" (1966) and "The Bounded Text" (1966–1967), both of which are included in her collection *Desire in Language.* Here, in introducing her concept of intertextuality, she advocates a reading practice based in the "spatialization" of the word along vertical and horizontal axes in an intertextual grid. In this essay, I will adapt her spatial tropes to suggest that we can read narrative by interpreting the text's horizontal and vertical narrative movements and intersections.

Such interactions are events, I will argue, that take place at every moment in the text in a kind of interdependent interplay of surface and depth. Such moments may appear as juxtapositions, oppositions, conflations, convergences, or mirrorings of narrative coordinates. These moments in turn join to form a fluid "story" of a dynamic text ever in process, ever "narrated" by the reader.

KRISTEVA'S SPATIALIZATION OF THE WORD

For Kriesteva, spatialization—with its attendant graphic tropes of coordinates, axes, trajectory, horizontal, vertical, surface, intersection, linearity, loop, dimension, and so forth—allows for the visualization of the text-in-process, the text as a dynamic "productivity," an "operation" (*Desire*, 36–37). Spatialization does not mean the erasure of time by space, as it does for Joseph Frank, who, in his influential essay, "Spatial Form in Modern Literature," argues that avant-garde narrative techniques in modern literature created an illusory effect of simultaneity and unity. Rather, for Kristeva, spatialization constitutes the text as a verbal surface or place in which both space and time, synchrony and diachrony, function as coordinates for textual activity. Kristeva's earliest essays pose a critique of the static analysis of structuralism and a call for the identification of textual process. Invoking Bakhtin, Kristeva identifies this process as fundamentally dialogic and intertextual—at the level of word, sentence, and story. Bakhtin, she explains, "considers writing as a reading of the anterior literary corpus and the text as an absorption of a reply to another text" (*Desire,* 69). "Each word (text)," she continues, "is an intersection of word (texts) where at least one other word (text) can be read. . . . [A]ny text is constructed as a mosaic of quotations; any text is the absorption and transformation of another" (*Desire,* 66). She graphs these intersections by identifying the text's "three dimensions or coordinates" as the writing subject, the addressee, and exterior texts. What she calls the horizontal axis is a line drawn from writing subject across to the addressee, who is either a character to whom the speech is directed or, more generally, the reader. This horizontal axis represents the text as a transaction between writer and reader. The vertical axis is a line starting with the text and moving down to the exterior texts, or contexts, of the text in question. This vertical axis emphasizes the text as a writing in relation with other writings. In other words, a text's dialogic interaction operates along both horizontal and vertical axes, from writing subject to addressee, from text to contexts. What emerges from a text is not "a *point* (a fixed meaning)," but rather a dialogue of writer and reader, text and context (*Desire,* 65).

In her early work, Kristeva's insistence on spatialization, which embeds her critique of pure formalism, is part of her Bakhtinian project to (re)insert the social and historical context as a necessary dimension of a text. Reading, she suggests, should never be merely a "linguistic" process focused on an isolated text. Consequently, she advocates a reading of what she calls the "translinguistic," by which she means the text's dialogue along horizontal and vertical axes with its writer, readers, and context (*Desire*, 69). She coins the term "ideologeme" to identify the point of intersection between the text and its precursor texts. This ideologeme is "materialized" "along the entire length of its [the text's] trajectory, giving it its historical and social coordinates" (*Desire*, 36). Reading for the dialogic ideologeme means reading the text "within (the text of) society and history" (*Desire*, 37).

SPATIALIZING NARRATIVE

Kristeva's spatialization of the word has potential applications for narrative. I will alter her model of a text's vertical and horizontal axes at the same time as I maintain her insistence on historical and intertextual resonances. As an interpretive strategy (not as a narrative typology), I propose two kinds of narrative axes whose intersections are reconstructed by the reader in the interactive process of reading. Bakhtin's notion of the novel's double chronotope is useful:

> Even in the segmentation of a modern literary work, we sense the chronotope
> of the represented world as well as the chronotope of the readers and creators
> of the work. . . . . [B]efore us are two events: the event that is narrated in the
> work and the event of narration itself (we ourselves participate in the latter,
> as listeners or readers); these events take place in different time . . . and in
> different places. (255)

The totality of the work, he concludes, is made up of the interacting chronotopes of the writer, reader, and text. We can graph Bakhtin's two chronotopes along horizontal and vertical narrative axes. The horizontal narrative axis involves the linear movement of the characters through the coordinates of textual space and time. The vertical narrative axis involves the space and time the writer and reader occupy as they inscribe and interpret what Kristeva calls the "subject-in-process" constituted through the "signifying practice" of the text and its dialogues with literary, social, and historical intertexts.

Both axes represent a movement through space and time—the one (horizontal) referring to the movement of characters within their fictional world; the other (vertical) referring to the "motions" of the writer and the reader in relation to each other and to the text's intertexts. Where the horizontal movement exists in finite form within the bounded world of the text, the vertical movement exists fluidly as a writing inscribed by the writer and reconstituted by the reader more or less consciously and to a greater and lesser degree depending on the specific writers and readers. As different functions of narrative, these axes feed off each other symbiotically; neither exists by itself as a fixed entity. I separate them only for strategic purposes, for the insight that such a spatialization provides for interpreting the overdetermined complexities of narrative. A fully spatialized reading of a given narrative text, as narrative, involves an interpretation of the continuous interplay between the horizontal and vertical narrative coordinates. The "plot" of intersection, "narrated" by the reader, is a "story" based on a reading of the different forms that intersection takes through time, that is, how the horizontal and vertical narratives converge and separate, echo and oppose, reinforce and undermine each other.

Let me specify in more detail what I mean by horizontal and vertical narrative coordinates. The horizontal narrative is the sequence of events, whether internal or external, that "happens" according to the ordering principles of the plot and narrative point of view. Setting, character, action, initiating "problem," progression, and closure are its familiar components—the focus of much traditional narratology.[3] The horizontal narrative follows and is constrained by the linearity of language—the sequence of the sentence that moves horizontally in alphabetic scripts is repeated in the horizontal movement of the plot from "beginning" to "end," however the categories of start and finish are customarily understood. Determined in part by historically specific narrative conventions, the forms of the horizontal narrative differ particularly in their handling of chronology, teleology, and narrative point of view—from the "well-made" to the picaresque or "plotless" plot; from the omniscient to the multiple, unreliable, or first-person narrator; from the epistolary to the embedded and complexly framed narratives. But for all forms, reading the horizontal narrative involves interpreting the sequence inscribed in the linearity of sentence and story. In simplest terms, we ask, who is the story about? What happens? Where? Why? What does it "mean"? *Ulysses* and *Mrs. Dalloway*, for example, plot the movements of their characters through the cities of Dublin and London on a single day in June. Reading the horizontal narrative axis, we focus on the exterior and interior actions and thoughts of Clarissa and Septimus, Stephen, Bloom, and Molly (as well as a host of others). As readers, we may imaginatively inhabit their space and time, to become what Peter Rabinowitz and James Phelan variously call the "narrative audience" that participates in "the mimetic illusion" (Phelan, 5).[4] As with any text, the horizontal narrative is reconstituted in the process of reading. Its attendant meanings are consequently dependent on what Brooks calls the reader's "performance" of the text (37), what Ross Chambers refers to as the "performative force" of the narrative (4–5), and what Phelan identifies as "narrative dynamics." But in bringing the horizontal narrative to life, the reader (like the writer) nonetheless remains in a different space and time from that of the characters.

The vertical axis of narrative involves reading "down into" the text, as we move across it. The vertical does not exist at the level of sequential plot, but rather resides within, dependent on the horizontal narrative as the function that adds multiple resonances to the characters' movement through space and time. The palimpsest—a tablet that has been written on many times, with prior layers imperfectly erased—serves as an apt metaphor for the vertical dimension of narrative. Instead of the single textual surface of the horizontal narrative, the vertical narrative has many superimposed surfaces, layered and overwritten like the human psyche. Freud's image of the psyche as the "mystic writing-pad" serves equally well—for with this mechanism, the written impression remains embedded, but hidden, in the wax beneath the clean plastic slate ("A Note"). The point of these tropes is not to suggest a simple equation of the horizontal narrative with consciousness and the vertical narrative with the unconscious. Rather, they suggest that every horizontal narrative has an embedded vertical dimension that is more or less visible and that must be traced by the reader because it has no narrator of its own. Although not yet named as such, the vertical narrative has been the focus of much recent poststructuralist, feminist, Afro-Americanist, and Marxist narrative theory.[5]

Although interwoven, three distinct strands of the vertical narrative can be usefully separated for purposes of analysis: the literary; the historical; and the psychic. Both the literary and historical aspects of the vertical narrative involve reading the horizontal narrative's dialogues with other texts, interpreting, in other words, the various forms of intertextuality that Kristeva introduces in her tropes of spatialization. Whether consciously or unconsciously produced by the writer, these dialogues exist as "the mosaic of quotations" that traverse the text. They are the layered surfaces beneath and within the horizontal narrative, but they are not narrated by it and may seem tangential to it. When consciously intended by the writer, these intertextual resonances establish an indirect communication between writer and reader, with the characters and events of the horizontal narrative as points of mediation. Such resonances do not usually exist in the mind of the characters—in the space and time of the horizontal narrative. In *Mrs. Dalloway,* for example, it is the reader who "narrates" the story of Septimus as Shakespearean fool, as scapegoat, as sacrificial lamb and Christ figure within the anguished postwar landscape.

The literary aspect of the vertical narrative exists first of all in relation to genre. The writer's and reader's awareness of genre conventions exists as a chronotope, a space-time, within which the specific text is read—for its invocations and revocations, its uses and rescriptions, its repetitions and play. We read, for example, *The Voyage Out,* Woolf's first novel, within the grid of the *Bildungsroman* as a story of development that progresses conventionally through courtship and engagement, only to veer suddenly away from the marriage plot, in having its protagonist die at the end. More broadly, all literary texts exist—however centrally, ambivalently, or marginally—within one or more literary traditions or cultures. Horizontal narratives, consequently, have an indirectly narrated vertical dimension that accomplishes a dialogic engagement with what has been written before. In *The Signifying Monkey,* Henry Louis Gates proposes the term "signifyin(g)" to identify a culturally specific form of intertextuality, a mode tied to the African American oral and written traditions of speakers and writers self-reflexively and intentionally playing off the discourse of others in the tradition. The epistolary mode of Alice Walker's *The Color Purple,* in which Celie writes letters first to God and then to her sister, not only dialogues with such epistolary inscriptions of rape as Richardson's *Clarissa,* but also signifies on the oral frame of Hurston's *Their Eyes Were Watching God,* in which Janie narrates the events of the story to her friend Phoebe, and on the story of incest in Toni Morrison's *The Bluest Eye.* More generally, we recognize that intertextual reference may be highlighted or muted, intentionally or unintentionally present, collaborative or revisionist. But common to all intertextual resonances is a *story* of dialogue narrated by the reader that takes place outside the spatial and temporal coordinates through which the characters of the horizontal narrative move.

The historical aspect of the vertical narrative represents a similar mosaic of quotations, one that refers to the larger social order of the writer, text, and reader. Such a mosaic may involve reference to a specific historical event that the text reconstructs—such as Morrison's retelling in *Beloved,* with key departures, of Margaret Gamer's attempt to kill her children when faced with their and her own return to slavery in 1856. Or, more broadly, this historical mosaic may involve what Rachel Blau DuPlessis calls "cultural scripts" layered into the horizontal narrative (*Writing beyond the Ending* ix–xi, 1–19). DuPlessis's term acknowledges the part that "story" plays in both ideological and oppositional discourses. These political resonances that traverse the text might include interlocking narratives of race, gender, class, ethnicity, sexuality, religion, and so forth—stories, in other words, that reproduce, subvert, and otherwise engage with the dominant and marginalized cultural scripts of the social order. For Fredric Jameson, such narratives constitute what he calls the "political unconscious," by which he means the "buried and repressed" narrative of class struggle present in trace form on the surface of the text (20). His assertion that narratives of class struggle subsume all other stories is dangerously bounded, but his call for the critic to read the text for signs of its repressed political scripts is useful. In *Beloved,* the vertically embedded cultural scripts or textual unconscious include many "stories" of race and gender relations: for example, the master's right to violate slave women; western theories of black and African inferiority and bestiality; patterns of slave resistance; white women's liminal position between race privilege and gendered alterity. Whether these political and historical narratives are buried in the text or openly scripted, reading this aspect of the vertical narrative allows for an analysis of the text in dialogue with "its historical and social coordinates," as Kristeva advocates (*Desire*, 36).

Reading the psychic aspect of the vertical narrative involves recognizing that a text can be read as a linguistic entity structured like a psyche, with a conscious and an unconscious that interact psychodynamically. Freud's concept of the psyche as perpetually in the process of splitting suggests that nothing is ever lost, but only forgotten.[6] Analogically speaking, the text is, like a dream, the result of a negotiation in which the desire to express and the need to repress force a compromise that takes the form of disguised speech. The text, then, can be read as a site of repression and insistent return. Freud's grammar for the dream-work—the mechanisms of displacement, condensation, nonrational modes of representability, and secondary revision—is useful for decoding disguised expression (*Interpretation of Dreams*, 311–546). These mechanisms are often at work in the enigmatic textual sites that deconstruction unravels to subvert underlying binaries. As Shoshana Felman does in her reading of James's *The Turn of the Screw*, textual gaps, silences, knots, and aporias can be read vertically to gain some sort of access to the textual unconscious.

This is also, I would suggest, what Kristeva is doing in her integration of Lacanian psychoanalysis, Bakhtinian dialogics, and Barthesian semiotics in *Revolution in Poetic Language*.[7] Kristeva inverts Lacan's axiom that the unconscious is structured like a language to suggest that the text is structured like a psyche. Language, she argues, always engages in a dialectical interplay of two modalities, the semiotic and the symbolic. The semiotic—that oral and rhythmic dimension of language that exists prior to and outside a system of signification—harkens back to the pre-oedipal period of the child's desire for the maternal body. The symbolic—that meaning-centered, instrumental aspect of language that exists after the child grasps the principle of signification—reverts back to the oedipal period when (according to Lacan) the child's realization of sexual difference allows for the acquisition of language based on a system of differences governed by the Law of the Father ("Signification of the Phallus").[8] Reading for the interplay of the semiotic and the symbolic—newly and differently constituted in every text—is one form that reading the vertical narrative can take.

A relational reading strategy based on the compositional history of the text—the chronotope of the writer—offers another mechanism for reading the psychic dimension of the vertical narrative. Instead of privileging the "final" text as the "definitive" one, we can read the various versions of a text as an overdetermined palimpsest in which each text forms a distinct, yet inter-related part of a larger composite "text."[9] Freud's concept of dreams in a series as being part of a larger dream-text that can be interpreted is useful (*Interpretation of Dreams,* 369, 563). He suggests that the mechanisms of the dream-work govern the relation among the dreams and that "the first of these homologous dreams to occur is often the more distorted one and timid, while the succeeding one will be more confident and distinct" (369). Freud's gram-mar can be adapted to read what gets repressed on the one hand and worked through on the other in a series of drafts preceding a published text. Tracking the various versions of the same story can reveal a process of conscious or self-conscious self-censorship whereby textual revision of the horizontal narrative represses or further disguises certain forbidden elements that remain as part of the vertical narrative. Reading the composite "text" involves reconstructing the "story" of condensation, displacement, and secondary revision from one version to another. In short, earlier versions of a text can be read vertically as the textual unconscious of the horizontal narrative in the published text. For example, H. D.'s "Madrigal Cycle"—a triptych of three autobiographical nov-els about her life during the teens—forms a composite text in which the last one she wrote (*Bid Me to Live [A Madrigal]*) represses the stories of lesbian desire and illicit motherhood that are fully narrated in the earlier texts, *Paint It To-Day* and *Asphodel,* both of which she ultimately considered to be "drafts" for *Bid Me to Live.*[10]

Conversely, a writer's repeated return to the scene of writing a particular story can be read as a kind of repetition compulsion in which the earliest ver-sions are the most disguised, with each repetition bringing the writer closer to the repressed content that needs to be remembered. Here, I am adapting Freud's notion of analysis as a transference scene in which the analysand repeats the symptoms and dreams produced by repressed material in a process of "working through" that ultimately leads to conscious recollection of what has been forgotten ("Further Recommendations"). This analogy between ana-lytic and novelistic transference is especially cogent in autobiographical narra-tives, in which the split subject of the writing "I now" and the written about "I then" perform the different roles of analyst and analysand in a kind of "writing cure." Earlier or later versions of the horizontal narrative, in other words, can, when read together as a composite text, give us access to the psy-chic dimension of the vertical narrative. Joyce's autobiographical narratives about Stephen D(a)edalus, for example, (including "A Portrait of the Artist," *Stephen Hero, A Portrait of the Artist as a Young Man,* and *Ulysses*) constitute a composite "text" in which the death of Joyce's mother and the son's remorse remain unnarratable until the final text in the series—present only in trace forms that can be interpreted with Freud's grammar for the dream-work.[11]

WHY SPATIALIZE NARRATIVE?

What do we learn by conceptualizing narrative in spatial terms? In contrast to typological approaches, spatialization emphasizes the psychodynamic, interactive, and situational nature of narrative processes; it also provides a fluid, relational approach that connects text and context, writer and reader. Spatialization is not, of course, the only way to produce such readings. Other interpretative strategies have gained access to a text's literary and historical resonances without resort to spatial tropes. Other critics, such as Ross Chambers, have developed ways of reading what he calls "not the actual historicity of texts, but the markers, within them of historical situation" (10). His analysis of a text's contractual appeal and adaptation of Clifford Geertz's "thick description" represents a different route to reaching some of the same objectives. James Phelan's distinction between the mimetic and synthetic dimensions of character as the reader experiences it represents yet another. For Phelan, the mimetic aspect suppresses the reader's awareness of the character as authorial construction while the synthetic foregrounds this construction as part of a communication between author and reader (1–27, 115 [211–16 in this volume]). For him, it is the play between the mimetic and the synthetic that accounts for narrative progression, a theory that assumes, like spatialization of narrative axes, that the text operates on an interplay between two different chronotopes—the mimetic world of the characters, and the synthetic realm of the author and reader.

Spatialization can, however, go beyond these other methods by facilitating some new readings of narrative that might not otherwise exist. The notion of a vertical axis embedded in the horizontal suggests the way in which historical, literary, and psychic intertextualities constitute more than resonances attached to the text associatively, suggestively, or randomly. Instead, they initiate *stories* themselves—dialogic narratives "told" by the reader in collusion with a writer who inscribes them in the text consciously or unconsciously. This, I would argue, is the contribution made by Kristeva's graph of the writer/reader (horizontal axis) and text/context (vertical axis). Moreover, the concept of interactive horizontal and vertical narrative axes allows for a relational reading of the two that produces a "story" not present in either axis by itself. For example, the horizontal narrative of *The Voyage Out* is the story of failure, the *Bildung* that ends in death. The vertical narrative, reconstructed by the reader, is the story of rebellion, of Woolf's successful "voyage out" of the marriage plot, one that led out of the drawing room and into the world of letters, as an initial declaration of independence from the dominant literary and historical narratives of the early twentieth century. The confrontation in this case between the horizontal and vertical narratives constitutes a "story" of its own that is present in neither narrative axis by itself.

A "full" reading of narrative axes is not possible in a bounded text because, like the dream in Freud's psychoanalysis, the text's dialogism is unbounded, as is the story of the intersections between the horizontal and vertical coordinates. But a reading strategy based in the identification of horizontal and vertical narratives axes fosters relational readings, discourages "definitive" and bounded interpretations, and encourages a notion of the text as a multiplicitous and dynamic site of repression and return. Such spatialized readings also allow us as readers to construct a "story" of the fluidly interactive relationship between the surface and palimpsestic depths of a given text—taking into account all the historical, literary, and psychic resonances that are embedded within the horizontal narrative and waiting to become narrated in the reading process. Ideally such a story is made up of a sequence of relational readings that at every point in the horizontal narrative examines its vertical component. The richest insights produced by a spatialized reading strategy may well reside in the way it potentially produces interpretations of the textual and political unconscious of a given text or series of texts. But in general, spatializing narrative gives us a systematic way of approaching the various forms of narrative dialogism and of (re)connecting the text with its writer and world. In Kristeva's words, spatialization suggests an interpretive strategy that regards a text as "a dynamic . . . *intersection of textual surfaces* rather than a *point* (a fixed meaning), as a dialogue among several writings: that of the writer, the addressee . . . , and the contemporary or earlier cultural context" (*Desire,* 65).

NOTES

1. This essay presents the theoretical section of a much longer essay that includes a reading of Virginia Woolf's *The Voyage Out* in Kathy Mezei's *Ambiguous Discourse* (109–36). It was originally presented at the International Conference on Narrative in Nice, France, June 1991.

2. For my purposes here, I am not suggesting a masculine/feminine binary for time as space, as do Kristeva in "Women's Time" and de Lauretis in *Alice Doesn't* (143). See also Winnett's critique of Brooks's model [138–58 in this volume].

3. See for example Barthes's "Introduction to the Structural Analysis of Narratives"; Genette; Chatman; Phelan; and Brooks's discussion of spatialization in Russian Formalism and French structuralism (*Reading,* 16).

4. See their distinctions between the "narrative audience" (which accepts the story as "real") and the "authorial audience" (which covertly remains "aware of the synthetic"—that is, constructed—nature of the narrative) (Phelan, 5). Rabinowitz proposed the original

distinction, which Phelan develops extensively in relation to his work on the rhetorics of character and progression.

5. See, for example, DuPlessis, Brooks, Gates, Bersani, Chambers, and de Lauretis.

6. This is, of course, a founding principle of psychoanalysis, made as early as Josef Breuer's and Freud's jointly written *Studies on Hysteria* (1895). See also Freud's "Repression."

7. See especially *Revolution* (13–106), "From One Identity to an Other" (*Desire* 124–47) and "Motherhood according to Bellini" (*Desire,* 237–70). For other formulations of the textual unconscious, see Culler, Felman, Riffaterre, and Jameson.

8. See especially Kristeva, *Revolution* (13–106) and "From One Identity to an Other" (*Desire,* 124–47).

9. For a different attempt to move textual criticism beyond the teleological search for the "definitive" text, see Jerome McGann's *A Critique of Modern Textual Criticism.*

10. I have made this argument more fully in "Return of the Repressed in Women's Narratives."

11. Like H. D.'s Madrigal Cycle, the different versions of the Dedalus narratives can be read both ways, with both early and late texts serving as the textual unconscious for the others in the series. See my "(Self)-Censorship and the Making of Joyce's Modernity" in *Joyce: The Return of the Repressed.* The essays in this collection provide examples of reading the vertical narrative axis in its literary, historical, and psychic dimensions.

REFERENCES

Bakhtin, M. M. *The Dialogic Imagination.* Edited by Michael Holquist. Translated by Caryl Emerson and Michael Holquist. Austin: University of Texas Press, 1981.

Barthes, Roland. "Introduction to the Structural Analysis of Narratives" (1966). In *Image Music—Text,* translated by Stephen Heath, 79–124. New York: Hill and Wang, 1977.

Bersani, Leo. *A Future for Astyanax: Character and Desire in Literature.* New York: Columbia University Press, 1984.

Boone, Joseph Allen. *Tradition Counter-Tradition: Love and the Form of Fiction.* Chicago: University of Chicago Press, 1987.

Breuer, Josef, and Sigmund Freud. *Studies on Hysteria* (1895). Translated by James Strachey. New York: Basic Books, n.d.

Brooks, Peter. *Reading for the Plot: Design and Intention in Narrative.* New York: Vintage, 1984.

Chambers, Ross. *Story and Situation: Narrative Seduction and the Power of Fiction.* Minneapolis: University of Minnesota Press, 1984.

Chatman, Seymour. *Story and Discourse: Narrative Structure in Fiction and Film.* Ithaca, N.Y.: Cornell University Press, 1978.

Culler, Jonathan. "Textual Self-Consciousness and the Textual Unconsciousness." *Style* 18 (1984): 369–76.

de Lauretis, Teresa. *Alice Doesn't: Feminism, Semiotics, Cinema.* Bloomington: Indiana University Press, 1984.

DuPlessis, Rachel Blau. *Writing beyond the Ending: Narrative Strategies of Twentieth-Century Women Writers.* Bloomington: Indiana University Press, 1985.

Felman, Shoshana. "Turning the Screw of Interpretation." *Yale French Studies* 55/56 (1977): 94–207.

Frank, Joseph. "Spatial Form in Modern Literature" (1945), revised edition in *The Widening Gyre,* 3–62. New Brunswick, N.J.: Rutgers University Press, 1963.

Freud, Sigmund. "Femininity." In *New Introductory Lectures on Psychoanalysis,* translated by James Strachey, 112–35. New York: Norton, 1965.

———. Further Recommendations in the Technique of Psychoanalysis: Recollection, Repetition, and Working Through" (1914). In *Therapy and Technique,* edited by Philip Rieff, 157–66. New York: Collier, 1963.

———. *General Psychological Theory.* Edited by Philip Rieff. New York: Collier, 1963.

———. *The Interpretation of Dreams* (1900). Translated by James Strachey. New York: Avon 1965.

———. "A Note upon the 'Mystic Writing-Pad'" (1925). In *General Psychological Theory,* 207–12.

———. "The Psychogenesis of a Case of Homosexuality in a Woman." In *Sexuality and the Psychology of Love,* edited by Philip Rieff, 133–59. New York: Collier, 1963.

———. "Repression" (1915). *General Psychological Theory,* 104–15.

Friedman, Susan Stanford. "Return of the Repressed in Women's Narratives." *Journal of Narrative Technique* 19 (winter 1989): 141–56.

———. "(Self)-Censorship and the Making of Joyce's Modernism." In *Joyce: The Return of the Repressed,* edited by Susan Stanford Friedman. Ithaca, N.Y.: Cornell University Press, 1993.

Gates, Henry Louis, Jr. *The Signifying Monkey: A Theory of African-American Literary Criticism.* Oxford: Oxford University Press, 1988.

Geertz, Clifford. *The Interpretation of Cultures.* New York: Basic Books, 1973.

Genette, Gérard. *Narrative Discourse: An Essay in Method* (1972). Ithaca, N.Y.: Cornell University Press, 1980.

Jameson, Fredric. *The Political Unconscious: Narrative as a Socially Symbolic Act.* Ithaca, N.Y.: Cornell University Press, 1985.

Kristeva, Julia. *Desire in Language: A Semiotic Approach to Literature and Art.* Edited by Leon S. Roudiez. Translated by Thomas Gora, Alice Jardine, and Leon S. Roudiez. New York: Columbia University Press, 1980.

———. *Revolution in Poetic Language* (1974). Translated by Margaret Wailer. New York: Columbia University Press, 1984.

———. "Women's Time." Translated by Alice Jardine and Harry Blake. *Signs* 7 (1981): 13–35.

Lacan, Jacques. "Signification of the Phallus." In *Ecrits: A Selection.* Translated by Alan Sheridan, 281–91. New York: Norton, 1977.

McGann, Jerome J. *A Critique of Modern Textual Criticism.* Chicago: University of Chicago Press, 1983.

Mezei, Kathy, ed. *Ambiguous Discourse: Feminist Narratology and British Women Writers.* Chapel Hill: University of North Carolina Press, 1996.

Miller, D. A. *Narrative and Its Discontents: Problems of Closure in the Traditional Novel.* Princeton: Princeton University Press, 1981.

Miller, Nancy K. "Emphasis Added: Plots and Plausibilities in Women's Fiction." In *Subject to Change: Reading Feminist Writing.* New York: Columbia University Press, 1988. 25–46.

Phelan, James. *Reading People, Reading Plots: Character, Progression, and the Interpretation of Narrative.* Chicago: University of Chicago Press, 1989.

Rabinowitz, Peter. "Truth in Fiction: A Reexamination of Audiences." *Critical Inquiry* 4 (1977): 121–41.

Ricoeur, Paul. "Narrative Time." In *On Narrative,* edited by W. J. T. Mitchell, 165–86. Chicago: Chicago University Press, 1981.

Riffaterre, Michael. "The Intertextual Unconscious." *Critical Inquiry* 13 (1987): 371–85.

Winnett, Susan. "Coming Unstrung: Women, Men, Narrative, and Principles of Pleasure." *PMLA* 105 (1990): 505–18.

17

Queering the Marriage Plot: How Serial Form Works in Maupin's *Tales of the City*

ROBYN WARHOL

Tales of the City, Armistead Maupin's fictitious chronicle of gay, straight, lesbian, and bisexual life in San Francisco in the 1970s and 1980s, was the first—and arguably the most successful—of the late-twentieth-century bestselling novels to be published in serial installments.[1] Many genres of contemporary popular fiction deploy serial form (by which I mean the publication or broadcast and reception of a continuous fictional narrative in parts), including science fiction, detective novels, Westerns, maritime adventure novels, Hollywood movies with sequels, and even television commercials for long-distance phone companies or Taster's Choice coffee. Indeed, a significant portion of the narratives that circulate in mainstream popular culture today get composed and transmitted in parts, such as celebrity-centered news stories (the life and death of Princess Diana, or the continuing saga of Elizabeth Taylor's marriages and divorces, or the aftermath of the Bill Clinton-Monica Lewinsky affair, for instance), or the kind of serially published documentaries that appear regularly in such journals as *Rolling Stone* or the *New Yorker*.[2] *Tales of the City*, I will argue, is an example of a particular genre of serial narrative originating in the Victorian period and extending through the twentieth century in the form of radio and television soap opera. I am calling this genre "serialized domestic fiction." Combining formal features of a number of overlapping and interlocking nineteenth- and twentieth-century genres, serialized domestic fiction blends aspects of the satirical novel of manners, the sentimental novel, the social-problem novel, the melodrama, and the realist novel and distinguishes itself by being presented to its reading or viewing public in parts.

Beginning as a regular daily column in the "Style" section (at the time, just recently converted from "Women's Section") of the *San Francisco Chronicle* in

229

May 1976, *Tales of the City* employs the characteristic conventions of Victorian serialized domestic novels—wild coincidences, melodramatic events, open-ended plots, recurring characters, and cliff-hanger action—in its satirically pointed representation of upper- and middle-class social life in San Francisco through the late 1980s. Focusing on family, relationships, and the workplace and designed to be read or viewed in the home, serialized domestic fiction has, for almost two centuries, often worked to blur the lines between public and private discourse, social and familial concerns. *Tales of the City* is an especially interesting case in point, as it is the first serialized domestic novel addressed to a mainstream audience that explicitly attempts to reconfigure public and private assumptions about one of those topics that most insistently strains the boundaries between the public and the private at century's end: gay sexuality. In this respect it serves as an example of what Lauren Berlant and Michael Warner call, in "Sex in Public," "the queer project" whose goal is "not just to give access to the sentimentality of the couple for persons of the same sex, and definitely not to certify as properly private the personal lives of gays and lesbians. Rather, it is to support forms of affective, erotic, and personal living that are public in the sense of accessible, available to memory, and sustained through collective activity" (562).[3] Though Berlant and Warner are talking about public policy and zoning laws, not literary genres, their project imagines the possibility of changing received definitions of what is sexually and socially "normal." The genre of the serialized domestic novel—so deeply implicated in the history of establishing and reinforcing heterocentric norms for "intimacy," "family," "privacy," and "sex"—becomes in *Tales of the City* a vehicle for performing that "queer project," for contradicting and complicating the genre's own role in dominant culture.

Maupin's newspaper series survives as six novels that fit the genre of serialized domestic fiction, five of them lightly revised reprints of the original serial, the sixth a continuation, published in 1989, that never appeared in the newspaper. Because it appeared periodically over a dozen years, *Tales of the City* is the contemporary serial that most closely resembles the Victorian serials of an author like Anthony Trollope, whose Palliser series and Barsetshire series, for instance, each unfolded in multivolume form over twelve-year periods. Some of the novels in Trollope's series appeared originally in part-issue form, appearing monthly or bimonthly as separately published paperback pamphlets, including *Can You Forgive Her?* (1864–65), the first novel in the Palliser series, and *The Prime Minister* (1875–76), the penultimate volume in that series. Other volumes in the same series ran as serials in such periodicals as *St. Paul's Magazine* (*Phineas Finn* [1867–69], the second volume in the Palliser series), the *Fortnightly Review* (*The Eustace Diamonds* [1871–73]. the third volume), the *Graphic* (*Phineas Redux* [1873–74], the fourth volume), and *All the Year Round* (*The Duke's Children* [1879–80], the final volume). In Trollope's case, each novel appeared in volume form after its serial run had ended; sometimes the last installment of the serial would coincide with the publication of the entire novel.

Victorian readers of Trollopian serials, therefore, had to look to various sources for the next installments of the narratives they chose to follow: they did not have the luxury of tuning in to the same network at the same hour every weekday that soap-opera audiences enjoy, but they did have the advantage of being able to fill in episodes they had missed, as the volumes continued to be available through booksellers and circulating libraries. As with those Victorian novels that came out in periodicals, new installments of *Tales of the City* came out with predictable regularity in eight-hundred-word segments appearing daily in the *Chronicle*. Every two years between 1976 and 1982 another volume of *Tales* collected from the newspaper columns would appear, giving Maupin's audience the same opportunities to enter into the diegetic world that were enjoyed by the original readers of Trollope. Fans of Maupin, like fans of Trollope, could fill in the "backstory" by reading the published volumes if they joined the audience late; they could bridge any gaps in their idiosyncratic reading habits; and they could make the story even more vividly their own by rereading favorite episodes.

Though it moved from the *Chronicle* to the *San Francisco Examiner* during its decade-long Bay Area newspaper run, the serial's longevity testifies to its continuing popularity; in volume form, *Tales of the City* had sold over two million copies by 1996 (aided, in part, by a televised adaptation of its first volume, broadcast on PBS in the early 1990s). While I think that its innovative resuscitation of the print genre of serial domestic fiction can partly account for the popularity of *Tales of the City*, I will argue that serial formal conventions also enable the series to accomplish significant antihomophobic cultural work. In an ironic twist worthy of one of his own outrageous plots, Maupin appropriates serial form—arguably the most Victorian of narrative conventions—to propagate a profoundly anti-"Victorian," anticonventional vision of sexual life.

In accomplishing this, *Tales of the City* makes use of many formal features common to Victorian serial fiction and to the most popular twentieth-century version of serialized domestic fiction, the contemporary daytime soap opera. Maupin's series fits Jennifer Hayward's description of the conventions that have typified serial form from the 1830s to the present: "refusal of closure; intertwined sub-plots; large casts of characters (incorporating a diverse range of age, gender, class, and, increasingly, race representation to attract a similarly diverse audience); interaction with current political, social, or cultural issues; dependence on profit; and acknowledgment of audience response (this has become increasingly explicit, even institutionalized within the form, over time)" (3).[4] Hayward offers a detailed analysis of the features in common among the production and reception of serial narrative forms, surveying the genre from Dickens's part-issue novels, through newspaper comic strips, to soap operas on radio, daytime television, and the Web. Linda K. Hughes and Michael Lund have theorized that historical and philosophical circumstances peculiar to the British Victorian reading audience (ranging from dominant notions of personal development, to "uniformitarianism," to evolutionary theory [5–8]) made Victorians especially prone to enjoy serial fiction, but the persistent popularity of serial forms throughout the twentieth century in British and American culture suggests that the appeal of serials is less specifi-cally Victorian than Hughes and Lund argue. *Tales of the City* is a powerful case in point, as it reproduces so many of the narrative gestures that make Trollopian or Dickensian serials "serial."

Because of its subject matter and its particular historical and geographical placement, however, *Tales of the City* brings into view three additional features of seriality that can serve to complicate and enrich our understanding of how serial form works: (1) *Serial form defies the dominant "marriage plot" governing so much of popular fiction.* Due to its structurally mandated impulse to defer ending indefinitely, serialized domestic fiction has always tended to under-mine the heterocentric marriage plot by unraveling instances of closure that turn out to be only provisional and temporary (2). *Serial form infiltrates domestic space, blurring the boundaries between "public" and "private" discourse.* By its structuring of readers' time and its daily, habitual nature, serialized domestic fiction renders its fictional materials ordinary, quotidian—boring, even. The stuff of serial fiction becomes, to borrow the title of Dickens's peri-odical in which so many Victorian novels made their first appearance, "house-hold words"—famous but also familiar. (3) *Serial form interacts with events in "real time."* Serialized domestic fiction bears the marks of historical changes that happen during the period of composition; hence, narrative teleologies shift as the material circumstances of the producers and consumers of texts change over time. More strikingly, perhaps, than such other examples of con-temporary serialized domestic fiction as daytime soap opera, *Tales of the City* capitalizes on all three of these conventions of serial form not only to enlist its audience's readerly devotion (that is, to sell newspapers, ads, and books), but also to restructure readers' attitudes toward sexuality, and particularly toward what might be called "sexual diversity." In what follows, I will more fully define these three conventions and sketch out a few details of how they work in this particular serialized domestic fiction, with an eye to showing how the genre's form (in concert with its overt content) has the potential to subvert dominant ideologies of sexuality.

"It is impossible to think about narrative," Judith Roof contends, without engaging ideologies of sexuality" (24). In the excellent and provocative *Come As You Are* (1996), Roof has argued that there is something intrinsically straight, something essentially heteronormative about narrative—all narrative, any narrative that comes (as most narratives usually do) to closure. For Roof, narrative "as an organizing structure . . . plays a large part in the stubborn return of a particularly heterosexual normativity" (xxix), because "something in the way we understand what a story is in the first place or something in the way narrative itself operates produces narrative's 'heterosexually friendly' shape" (xxxii). This "something" turns out to be the way narratives governed by the marriage-plot convention always "come" to an "end" (with Roof, all puns are intended). In Roof's model, the same closure that directs conventional narratives' teleologies also lends them the orgasmic climax of their endings. Questioning "how [it is] that orgasm and the end are taken for one another, conflated in our narrative expectations" (6), Roof looks for alternatives to the hegemony of heteronormative closure.

Roof quite rightly emphasizes that the only way narratives could reflect and reinforce the pleasures of alternative sexualities would be for them to employ radical innovations in their discursive forms, not just to offer new or different subject matter for stories that follow the same old established patterns of closure. Although Roof's study surveys numerous unconventional examples of literary and popular texts, her search does not take her to that narrative form which most consistently, most doggedly, most addictively resists ending: serial fiction. While I agree with Roof's basic point about the heteronormative nature of stories that "come to an end," I would suggest that serialized domestic fictions—whether in the genre of Victorian novels, of daytime soap operas, or of long-running prime-time television series—are continually undermining the ideological imperative for a man to couple up with a woman and for the two of them to stay that way forever after in the unrepresented future toward which diegetic closure inevitably gestures. To be sure, in soaps, in Victorian serial fiction, and even, nowadays, on prime-time TV, story lines are still constantly being driven by the heterosexually defined desire for couples to get together, to make commitments to stay together, and so on, but in these serial genres the stories that are so powerfully propelled forward by the marriage plot are as readily unraveled as they are resolved. Sandy Flitterman-Lewis describes how this works through wedding scenarios in soap operas:

> Rather than resolving weeks of conflict which it has been the serial's function elaborately to spin out, the wedding provides a complex and fertile textual "knot," a matrix of disruption which instigates further narrative problems. In the wedding, new configurations of characters temporarily align as each

233

"knot" reveals new obstacles, new reasons for the deferral of completion. Underlying each wedding is thus a substratum of impermanence, a foundation of uncertainty reflecting the perpetually shifting complexities of soap opera relationships. (120)

These complexities may occur on- or offscreen; they may be consequences of diegetic or extradiegetic factors. For example, the day-time soap-opera "super-couple" can finally be getting married after years of obstacles and tribulations, but the audience can be sure that the secret affair the bride's half sister just had with the groom will become common knowledge soon enough to begin pulling the happy pair apart. Or, for a prime-time example, after multiple seasons of highly touted "sexual tension" in the long-running comedy series *Cheers,* Sam Malone and Diane Chambers could finally get engaged, but Shelley Long's career aspirations could take her character out of the marriage plot (and right out of the diegesis) without bringing the series to an end. And if, at the end of one of Anthony Trollope's Palliser novels, Phineas Finn finally settles on a bride from among the four women he has considered marrying over the course of that novel's story, that bride can die and his marriage plot can start all over again when his story line resumes, two volumes later in the series. In serials, the story never really comes to an end; the closure is always momentary; the climax—even if it is orgasmic—never has to mean the pleasure is over.[5]

For the past 150 years, then, serialized domestic fiction has played an important role in "queering" the closure of marriage plots, making it a significant exception to Roof's rule. Like Roof, I am more interested in examining the sexual and ideological implications of a narrative's form—the relation between its narrative discourse, in Gérard Genette's sense of the term, and its teleology—than in interpreting the details of its story.[6] Much of what I will say about the potentially transformative functions of the way serials resist closure would be equally true for heterocentric serials as it is for Maupin's assertively queer novels. I think, however, that the ways serial form can work to change culture can be brought most clearly into view through studying a serial like *Tales of the City* which is as overtly queer in its content as I would argue it is implicitly queer in its deployment of serial form.

Tales of the City takes the antiheterocentric impulse of serial fiction to its most extreme manifestation: the queer plot that reconfigures families, couples, and coupling in antitraditional and unpredictable patterns. Soap opera fans are familiar with a heterocentric version of this same pattern, as there is always something rather queer about soap opera families.[7] The received notion of soaps is that, as one scholar has recently asserted, "the nuclear family is alive and well" in their story lines; allegedly soaps uphold the structure of the bourgeois family with their almost obsessive reliance on individual lineage as the story line's deep background and on engagements and weddings as motors for the plot.[8] The truth is, though, that a close look at the family structure on a soap opera that has been running for three or four decades will reveal a highly idiosyncratic notion of "appropriate" families presented as the diegetic community's norm. For example, a man might recently have married a woman who is the niece of his former wife, and who was once sexually involved with another man who is now married to the bridegroom's daughter; his bride herself might have been previously married to a third man who (out of wedlock) fathered one of the sons of that same daughter of the bridegroom. In this particular case (I am thinking of John and Barbara on *As the World Turns*), the peculiarity of these combinations sometimes rises to the surface of the plot, as when the story line focused for six months or so on the need to keep that out-of-wedlock child ignorant of the fact that his ostensible father is not his birth father. After weeks of angst over whether the boy could handle the news, the story line ended with his matter-of-fact and cheerful acceptance of the advantages of having "two dads." Of course the boy's response invokes connotations of Lesléa Newman's lesbian-positive children's story *Heather Has Two Mommies,* but for the sake of argument I'll put this aside. That both those dads (Tom and Hal) had sex with the boy's mom (Margo) within the confines of her marriage to Tom, that both men had also in the past had sex with Barbara (John's bride in the anecdote I began with) exemplifies the way daytime soaps' serial plots subvert the structure of the nuclear family by doubling and trebling people's relationships to one another (now Barbara is Margo's stepmother as well as her sexual rival for both Tom's and Hal's attention, not to mention being also the niece of Margo's husband's stepmother). Within the diegetic frame of the soap, all these quasi-incestuous family groupings are naturalized, presented as (almost) perfectly normal—or, at least, only unusual enough to make the situations narratable. If you look closely enough at the relationships, though, and particularly at the way they kaleidoscope over time, they look like anything but nuclear families.

Tales of the City does the same kind of work, not for the incestuously multiplied family relations of daytime soaps but for family configurations that are in other respects "queer." To be sure, its multiple story lines begin with the predictably heterosexual search for partners that Mary Ann Singleton, the twenty-something protagonist; her stewardess friend from her high school in Cleveland, Connie; and Mary Ann's future husband, Brian Hawkins, undertake in late 1970s San Francisco. But the drive toward coupling up is already undermined by the social mores of the setting Maupin is satirizing, the "singles scene." The apartment building that centers the serial, 28 Barbary Lane, belongs to Anna Madrigal, a middle-aged woman who sees her four unmarried tenants as her "ersatz children" (*Further Tales,* 2). She (and they) always refer to the house's inhabitants as "a family," while the narrator continually asserts that "They weren't really her children, of course, but she treated them as such" (*Further Tales,* 2)—which means, in Anna Madrigal's case, that she listens to their troubles and often makes them presents of the especially nice marijuana she grows in the garden at 28 Barbary Lane. As it happens, one of the tenants—Mona—really *is* a daughter of Anna Madrigal's, but this is a secret, unknown to the narrative audience or to any of the characters other than Anna; this is a typical motif in daytime soap opera, and here, as there, although numerous hints and clues are offered, many extradiegetic weeks go by before the secret surfaces and the family structure adjusts to fit the revelation. Here, though, the revelation has a twist that "queers" the trope: when the secret comes out (in *More Tales of the City,* the second volume), we learn that though Mona is Anna Madrigal's child, Anna is not Mona's mother; she is her father, having undergone a transsexual operation after Mona's birth. This hilarious disruption of readerly expectations sets a pattern for queering the idea of what a "real" family might be, or how family members might "really" be related.[9]

Heterosexually based "nuclear families" don't exist in the universe of *Tales of the City,* at least not among the younger generation that centers the story lines. The twenty-something socialites DeDe and Beauchamp Day present the possibility of a "normal" heterosexual couple upon their first appearance, but that possibility quickly unravels, as DeDe becomes pregnant by the Chinese teenager who delivers her groceries, Beauchamp (after proving himself to be a faithless cad by seducing and dumping everyone from his secretary, Mary Ann, to his wife's gay gynecologist, Jon) dies horribly in a violent and well-deserved car crash, and DeDe proceeds to raise her twin babies with the help of her lesbian partner, D'Orothea. If the configuration of two lesbian parents raising twins looks too much like merely replacing heterosexual partners with a homosexual couple in the same old structure of a "nuclear family," consider the case of D'Orothea's former lover, Mona. After her breakup with D'Oro, Mona never places herself in another dyadic relationship with a lover, but in *Babycakes,* the fourth volume, she does get married to a gay British nobleman (giving him a visa to San Francisco and providing her with an English country house and an income) and creates her own distinctly nonnuclear family by legally adopting a black British gay teenage boy.

Even those characters who seem headed along the trajectory of traditional marriage plots end up taking detours. Until well into *Further Tales of the City,* the third volume (when Mary Ann and Brian get together), neither Connie nor Brian nor their many sexual partners are interested in anything more than a one-night stand, and Mary Ann's innocent assumption that a "commitment" is the desirable outcome of a date is consistently spoofed through the first two volumes, as her objects of desire turn out to be such inappropriate choices as a private investigator who trades in child pornography (whom Mary Ann inadvertently kills by pushing him over a cliff near the Palace of the Legion of Honor) and an amnesiac who is hopelessly embroiled in the notorious Episcopalian Cannibalistic cult. The predictably "normal" heterosexual marriage of Mary Ann and Brian eventually goes predictably sour, as Mary Ann's broadcasting career and her distaste for their adopted daughter, Shawna (whom Brian, as "househusband," has been raising since her birth mother, Connie, died), take Mary Ann (in *Sure of You*, the sixth volume) out of the family and away from San Francisco to the larger television market of New York. Significantly, what could have been figured as a *Kramer vs. Kramer* melodrama of maternal negligence works out to be good news for Brian and even for Shawna: the very last scene of the series shows him starting on another one of the just-for-fun sexual conquests he had specialized in for the first two volumes and looking forward with genuine paternal devotion to raising Shawna alone.[10]

The only character whose romantic ideas about committed coupling persist is the gay hero, Michael Tolliver, or "Mouse," whose entrance into the story line is precipitated by his breakup with one lover and whose pursuit of the ideal longtime companion propels his story through countless sexual liaisons over six volumes' worth of story lines. Michael declares throughout the series that he "believes in marriage"; early in their friendship, he tells Mary Ann, "I think about it every time I see a new face. I got married four times today on the 41 Union bus" (*Tales,* 236). When she laughs with "embarrassment," Michael explains that he's not thinking of weddings so much as marriage: "I know . . . a bunch of fairies in caftans, tripping through Golden Gate Park with drag bridesmaids and quotations from 'Song of the Loon.' . . . That's not what I mean. . . . It would be like . . . friends. Somebody to buy a Christmas tree with." Michael continues throughout the series to refine his ideal model of marriage, building in a distinctly antimainstream penchant for nonmonogamous coupling. In *Further Tales of the City,* Michael tells a friend he believes "some anonymous sex is so wonderful that it almost seems to prove the existence of God" (241), but he admits that for him, "that's just part of the time. As soon as the moon changes or something, I want to be married again. I want to sit in a bathrobe and watch *Masterpiece Theatre* with my boyfriend. . . . I want order and dependability and somebody to bring me NyQuil when I feel like shit" (242). In the end, Michael's relationship with his live-in lover, Thack ("the man who had made him happy" [*Sure of You* 254]), is the only coupling that looks anything like a "marriage," by Michael's definition or, for that matter, according to mainstream culture's model of what conjugal, domestic intimacy is supposed to be. That a gay couple would represent

237

the closest thing the novels present to a "normal" family is one of the effects of *Tales of the City's* reliance on serial structure to render the idea of lesbian and gay sex "ordinary" for a mainstream reading audience.

And yet there is nothing "ordinary" about *Tales of the City's* insistence on diverging from heterosexual norms of intimate relationship in the development of its plotlines. The contradictions implicit in Michael's simultaneous celebration of anonymous sex and his embrace of something that looks an awful lot like normal marriage combine with the structural imperatives of this serialized domestic fiction to point to the ways "heterosexual culture achieves much of its metacultural intelligibility through the ideologies and institutions of intimacy," as Berlant and Warner put it (553). As they explain, "intimacy is itself publicly mediated":

> First, its conventional spaces presuppose a structural differentiation of "personal life" from work, politics, and the public sphere. Second, the normativity of heterosexual culture links intimacy only to the institutions of personal life, making them the privileged institutions of social reproduction, the accumulation and transfer of capital, and self-development. Third, by making sex seem irrelevant or merely personal, heteronormative conventions of intimacy block the building of nonnormative or explicit public sexual cultures. Finally, those conventions conjure a mirage: a home base of prepolitical humanity from which citizens are thought to come into political discourse and to which they are expected to return in the (always imaginary) future after political conflict. Intimate life is the endlessly cited *elsewhere* of political public discourse.

Using the newspaper or the mainstream Harper-Perennial publishing house both to "publicize" queer models of intimate relationship and to bring them into the "private" spaces of heterocentric homes is one way to make that intimate "elsewhere" into the political here and now.

Michael's fantasy of watching *Masterpiece Theatre* in a regular, comfortable, and conjugal way is not just an example of the kind of bourgeois respectability his model of marriage is meant to appeal to; it is also an allusion to the role that serialized domestic fiction plays in structuring the emotional life that goes on in middle-class domestic spaces. *Masterpiece Theatre* is orderly and dependable; within a certain social and educational echelon, it is also intensely familiar. People who want to watch it know when and where to find it on the air; they can follow its continuing stories with predictable regularity; and they can count on having new episodes to talk about with one another. Like the eventual PBS dramatizations of Maupin's tales that Michael's remark presciently calls back from the future, *Tales of the City* uses the conventions of serial form to render gay and lesbian life familiar not just to those whose world is being represented in the series, but also to the homophobic mainstream audiences of the *San Francisco Chronicle* and of the nationally distributed reprinted novels.

This structuring of domestic spaces and familiar relationships is what makes the periodical nature of serialized domestic fiction so important. As Maupin remarked in a 1987 interview, "The daily form lets air in. . . . People have 24 hours to speculate on what's going to happen, so they remember it in a different way. It becomes part of their own experience" ("Talk," 54). What does it mean for a daily newspaper like the *Chronicle* or the *Examiner* to be a "periodical," after all? The period marked by the newspaper is twenty-four hours; the paper is literally quotidian, which means it's ordinary by definition: it's always there, every day, to be perused and discarded. If its headlines are always insisting on the special uniqueness of the events it reports, their very insistence only emphasizes how repetitious, how ordinary that uniqueness is. There are headlines every day, there is a newspaper every day. So what? So—here in the *San Francisco Chronicle,* the most ordinary of all ordinary daily papers, was this addictive, scandalous, hypersexual, hilarious serialized story. Having lived in the Bay Area during the early years of the serial's newspaper run, I can remember the shock and delight of finding in that notoriously superficial and bourgeois rag this continuing story full of "nudge-nudge, wink-wink" allusions to sex of so many kinds: not just straight but gay, bi-, and trans-; not just committed but promiscuous; not just vanilla but kinky.

For Richard Canning, *Tales* does not go far enough along this road, as "the radicalism of Maupin's liberal theft of family rhetoric in describing his performative family involves, simultaneously, a descriptive conservatism in relation to sex and the body" (165). Canning attributes Maupin's narrator's reticence about the bodily details of gay sex to the author's desire not to alienate the mainstream audience of the serial; as Canning sees it, Maupin's reluctance to represent gay sex acts means that "gay desire is suspended" in the text, and that homosexuality becomes a matter of essence (or even of mere "taste") rather than of (sexual) performance in Judith Butler's sense of the word. Canning's observation seems to me to be profoundly true of the representation of gayness in current mainstream popular culture, for instance in the spate of Hollywood movies featuring gay male characters in the late 1990s, from *My Best Friend's Wedding* to *The Object of My Affection. In and Out,* the most overt example of this phenomenon, begins with the premise that the Kevin Kline character has no idea that he is gay, but that everyone else in his hometown except his fiancée knows he is, because of the way he walks, dresses, speaks, and rides his bicycle. The Kline character "finds out" he is gay when the openly gay Tom Selleck character (brilliantly and wittily cast, I must admit, given the persistent gossip around Los Angeles about Selleck's own sexuality) gives him one big kiss, never to be repeated for the duration of the film. The implication is that Kline's being gay in the first place has nothing to do with homosexual desire and, in the long run, as the plot develops, very little indeed to do with acts of sex among men. Such a film exemplifies beautifully the current mainstream representation of gayness as an essence, a taste, a lifestyle—but not a matter of sexual practice.

Compared to what such films do to avert the gaze from gay sexuality, *Tales of the City* is remarkably frank. If Canning is right to point out the rhetorical limitations implicit in what Maupin's novels do not or cannot say about the specifics of gay sex, I think the formal structure of serialized domestic fiction has a performative force of its own, as it opens up an imaginative world of gay sex and desire that had not made its way into mainstream discourse before and would therefore have been literally unimaginable to many of the series' original readers—and indeed would still remain obscure, two decades later to mainstream audiences whose understanding of gay experience is circumscribed by films like *In and Out*. *Tales of the City* represents a world where sexual performance is central to identity. In this sense, *Tales of the City* can be understood as participating in what Berlant and Warner call queer culture's "world-making project" (558).

For subscribers to the San Francisco newspaper, following Mouse's sexual adventures meant entering diegetic realms that mainstream audiences rarely if ever encounter.[11] Readers regularly took in not just allusions to Michael's serially monogamous intercourse with Thack and, before him, Jon, but also to the string of sexual experiences in between these two relationships. These range from an S & M liaison with a gay cop to a fantasy of tasting "diesel fuel on a [truck driver's] sunburned neck and commit[ting] himself totally to the appetites of a stranger" while actually having sex with an aging matinee idol (identified as "——— ———," to be read as "Rock Hudson") and wondering whether some man, somewhere, was having sex with a truck driver while fantasizing about this movie star (*Further Tales* 118). (A former lover of Mouse's, taunting him about the cop and the movie star as well as a construction worker he's recently slept with, exclaims, "You're not having a life, Michael. You're fucking the Village People, one at a time!" [*Further Tales*, 328].) From the streets and bars of the Castro District, to the Reno Gay Rodeo, to all-male private Hollywood parties, to a women-only music festival and camp-out, *Tales of the City* brought countless diegetic spaces explicitly marked as exclusively gay or lesbian into the domestic spaces of all those *Chronicle*-reading households. As Maupin remarked in 1987, a decade after *Tales* got started, "The degree to which the subject of homosexuality has been opened for discussion is enormous. It has been demystified—it's less scary now. My goal is the day it becomes boring—the day it's just people and relationships, and we just leave it at that. That's what it comes down to, anyway" ("Talk," 54).

Of course, this strategy doesn't work for every reader, as a grouchy and cursory treatment of *Tales of the City* in the *Hudson Review* all too pointedly demonstrates. Dismissing *Tales* (along with Cyra McFadden's *The Serial,* set in Marin County) as an extended dirty joke that confirms every northeasterner's worst prejudices about California lifestyles, James P. Degnan offers his own list of what the characters in *Tales* are "into," including "SM bars, whips and chains, gold brocade cords and rubber batons, black leather sequined jock straps, cockrings, sex in men's rooms, sex orgies in steam rooms," and so on (147). He claims to find the series "tiresome," because he feels it "elects to deliver a message—a message that has become monumentally tiresome: that 'alienation'—e.g., homosexuality, hedonism, promiscuity—somehow is always preferable to 'conformity'—heterosexuality, marriage, fidelity, self-sacrifice—because the former is 'authentic,' the latter, hypocritical. In short, it is the same message we've been getting from books, movies, TV and stage plays for decades" (147). Degnan's stubbornly conservative misreading of Maupin's text comes through in his mysterious application of quotation marks (never do Maupin or any of his characters use the terms "alienation," "conformity," or "authentic" in the connections Degnan cites here), as well as in his false categorization of the plot's events ("marriage, fidelity, and self-sacrifice" are never dismissed from the values of Maupin's fictional world, just redefined). Degnan may claim to be bored, but his boredom is a response to something that is not actually present in Maupin's text; this boredom resembles the unconscious strategy for dealing with hysterical anxiety that D. A. Miller has so beautifully analyzed in his treatment of the tedium inspired by the Victorian serial form of Trollope's *Barchester Towers.*[12] The ideological deployment of boredom, tedium, repetition, and ordinariness is perhaps the most significant of the technical links between Maupin's project and those of the Victorian serialists.

When Charles Dickens gave the title *Household Words* to his Victorian periodical—the first place of publication for *Hard Times,* one of Dickens's most explicitly political interventions into prevailing social and economic attitudes—he was both establishing and pointing to the power of serial publications to make ideas and experiences familiar. Making "household words" out of phrases and concepts means more than just bringing them into the home through the vehicle of periodical publication. Through the domestic conversations serial fiction would presumably stimulate, the process of serial publication makes those ideas and experiences, phrases and concepts part of the discourse inside the household itself. Every week, from April to August of

1854, middle-class readers of *Household Words* took in another installment of events describing life among workers whose elbows they might brush in the street but whose private experience was made visible to them only through its rendition in social-problem novels like *Hard Times*.[13] Every day between 1976 and 1987, whenever they brought in the newspaper containing Maupin's column, every heterocentric middle-class household in the greater Bay Area was taking in words that might not have been spoken or heard in those households before, words that the story, over its remarkable decade-long newspaper run, made absolutely unremarkable: fag hags (*Tales*, 101); the Sutro Bath House (*Tales*, 127); the men's strip contest at the Endup (*Tales*, 221; *More Tales*, 250); the "A-Gays" (gay men of the highest San Francisco social class [*Further Tales*, 8]); the Gay Freedom Day Parade; the Sisters of Perpetual Indulgence (transvestite "nuns" on roller skates who show up from time to time in San Francisco, especially on Halloween); and—most significantly for the time and place of publication of *Tales of the City*, most dramatically in its impact on the characters in the series and on its initial audience—AIDS (*Significant Others*, 78 ff).

Throughout its long run, *Tales of the City's* plotlines reflect Bay Area preoccupations with current events, such as Queen Elizabeth II's highly publicized visit to San Francisco and the Peninsula (the background setting for *Babycakes*) and the Jonestown disaster that killed so many former Oakland residents in Guyana (a back-from-the-dead and surgically altered Jim Jones is the villain of *Further Tales of the City*). Most markedly in its last volumes, though, *Tales of the City* reflects the major shifts in gay culture and in individual relationships that accompanied growing public awareness of the AIDS epidemic in the Bay Area in the mid to late eighties. In the world of the text, AIDS becomes both another soap-opera-scale personal crisis (like the amnesia and the paralysis suffered temporarily by characters in the first volumes) and a community-wide disaster. At the same time, the text's serial form made AIDS into an ordinary, everyday event that happened to people who had become intimately familiar to the audience over the course of the series. "The result," as Tom Spain observes in the introduction to his interview with Maupin, "is a portrait of the devastating effects of the AIDS epidemic that achieves an intimacy that could scarcely be duplicated in any other format. Whether they read the newspaper series or the books, readers are faced with the prospect that someone they've 'known' for 10 years may be dying before their eyes" (Maupin, "Talk," 53).

In its deployment of serial conventions, *Tales of the City* works to make AIDS real for an audience comfortable with the genre of realist, sentimental fiction; if its ultimate aim is to make that audience more comfortable with homosexuality, it is also to make the reality of AIDS excruciatingly uncomfortable for a readership that might not be equally touched by the factual accounts running side-by-side in the newspaper with the series' installments. By becoming "household words" themselves, the familiar characters of a serial take on quasi-familial status: they enter the families of their readers as the newspaper enters their homes. This effect can also work, of course, for the audience who consumes the series in volume form. As one reader living in the Midwest put it in the context of a scholarly article on *Tales:*

> Upon the publication of each subsequent novel, I hurried to my local bookstore. I would devour each installment from cover to cover in one evening. During the intervening years, I would reread the novels, sometimes singly and sometimes the entire series in sequence. Maupin's characters were as real to me as my own closest friends; their travails and triumphs were mine, too. (Browning 86)[14]

In this way, Maupin's serial fiction has worked toward making AIDS a family matter, even in heterocentrically configured and otherwise emotionally (and—one presumed—medically) well-defended homes.

Reading *Tales of the City* retrospectively from the perspective of the nineties superimposes a teleology of doom on the mid-seventies stories of freewheeling sex that could not have been present in the minds of the original audience. When in the first volume (appearing in the newspaper in 1976) Mona says to Michael, on his way out for an evening of "trashing," "Be careful, will you? Don't do anything risky," and Michael replies, "You read the papers too much" (*Tales*, 110), the allusion might originally have invoked leather-bar machismo or gay bashing but would not have connoted AIDS. According to Randy Shilts's *And the Band Played On*, press coverage of the so-called gay plague began in the *Chronicle* (the only mainstream paper to treat the rising incidence of Kaposi's sarcoma among gay men as reportable news) in 1980, before the name acquired immunodeficiency syndrome was coined.[15] AIDS enters the story line of *Tales of the City* shortly thereafter, in the columns that comprise *Babycakes*, published in volume form in 1984. As that fourth volume in the series opens, Michael is grieving for his on-again, off-again lover Jon, with whom he had very romantically reconciled at the end of *Further Tales of the City*, the third volume, but who has been diagnosed with AIDS, sickened, and died—much like Phineas Finn's first bride, Mary—during the diegetic time elapsing between volumes. At the beginning of *Babycakes*, Jon has been dead for "over three months" (24), but it all has happened offstage: readers following the series were presented with the grief resulting from an AIDS death, but not with a representation of the anxiety and suffering of the disease itself.

The first central character in the series to be represented as experiencing an AIDS scare is not a gay man but rather the aggressively heterosexual Brian, who learns in *Significant Others,* the fifth volume, that one of his mistresses has contracted AIDS from a lover who uses intravenous drugs. Maupin capitalizes on the opportunity this plot situation offers to do some antihomophobic AIDS education. When Brian confesses his fear of being HIV-positive to Michael, he reveals his adherence to the heterocentric double standard controlling dominant discourse about AIDS, brushing off Michael's reminder that "I've been through this, remember?" with "Yeah, but . . . this is different. . . . Michael, there are innocents involved here," meaning Brian's wife, Mary Ann, and their daughter, Shawna. Michael bristles—"Innocents, huh? Not like me. Not like Jon. Not like the fags"—and when Brian backs off, Michael insists, "Lay off that innocent shit. It's a virus. Everybody is innocent" (79). By this time (around 1985–86), the serial had moved out of the *Chronicle* into its sister paper, the *Examiner,* but it was still a regular feature as the AIDS story moved into mainstream news, forcing devotees of the serial to come to terms with heterocentric prejudices about AIDS through their readerly attachments to Brian and Michael, protagonists since the beginning of the first volume. The next year, 1987, when this story line appeared in volume form, was also the publication date of Shilts's book; by 1987, ACT-UP had launched its "SILENCE=DEATH" campaign to make AIDS a household word in those vast American spaces inside and beyond the Bay Area where "AIDS" was still seldom if ever spoken.[16]

The impact of AIDS affects the action and settings of the story lines (for instance, all-out orgies give way to dreary safe-sex "jack-off" parties, and gay cruising among the central characters virtually disappears from the plot), but it also drastically alters the generic mode of the serial. What began in 1976 as a series of satirical novels of manners evolves into the more sentimental novels Maupin is writing in the late eighties, where the audience must ultimately come to terms with the gay hero's own HIV-positive status. Typically, novels of manners adhere to the marriage plot, and one of the definitions of the marriage plot is that the heroine's story can be resolved only by marriage or by death; there are no other options for ending the traditional feminocentric novel.[17] Significantly, if Michael Tolliver—the protagonist of this antimarriage plot—does not end up by following the comic heroine's narrative trajectory and literally getting married (no caftans in the park, no drag bridesmaids, no gay wedding), he does not die, either, as the protagonist of a dysphoric sentimental novel ought properly to do. Even though Maupin stopped writing it after publishing the last volume in 1989, the series does not end; just as it defies the heteronormative closure of the marriage plot, serial form resists both the settled, cathartic closure of tragedy and the redemptive telos of sentimentalism. This relieves the audience of the excruciating burden of watching a well-loved hero die a painful death, which could be understood as letting the mainstream readership off the hook of facing the reality of AIDS. At the same time, though, it leaves the story open-ended, unfinished, unsettled and unsettling, refusing to let death-by-AIDS determine the meaning of each of the details of Michael's life story up to "now," the point at which that story breaks off without reaching resolution.

Although I have been arguing for the transformative potential of the genre of serialized domestic fiction, I do not want to overstate the case, either for the radical effects of this particular serial or for the intrinsic subversiveness of the serial form in general. I realize the trajectory of my argument is heading for an assertion that the serial form of *Tales of the City* has somehow expedited a resolution to homophobia and to AIDS. Whatever the serial may have achieved in its newspaper run and its subsequently successful publication in volumes, it certainly wasn't adequate to the problems it addresses: AIDS still persists, underresearched, underfunded; homophobia prevails. To be sure, there is nothing necessarily radical about the manifest content of best-selling serial fiction in the late twentieth century, either: a comparison of the nostalgic, paternalist, racialist, and elitist politics of *Bonfire of the Vanities* with the "world-making" project of *Tales of the* City can show how the cliff-hanger endings, the wild but somehow predictable coincidences, and the interlocking subplots of serial narrative may serve conservative agendas, as well. As Armistead Maupin is to Charles Dickens, one might say, Tom Wolfe is to William Makepeace Thackeray: *Tales of the City* and *Hard Times* or *Bleak House* use audiences' emotional affinities for the characters of serialized domestic fiction as a tool for liberal social reform, while *Bonfire of the Vanities* and *Vanity Fair* eschew sentimentalism, inserting ironic distance between readers and characters to inspire a readerly aversion to "the way we live now." Still, if there is something indelibly bourgeois about the product of the sentimental social reformer, if there is something exploitative, even, in his uses of serial form and its emotional impact upon its audiences, at least—as with Dickens and Maupin—the project serves a vision of forward movement, a vision that resists either the backward glance of nostalgia or the final, slammed door of closure. As Maupin's novels continue to be adapted for television, and as the series is still circulating in volume form, the cultural work of *Tales of the City*—as well as work like this on how serial form works—remains "to be continued."

NOTES

1. To place it in the context of other best-sellers of those decades, *Tales of the City* predates Cyra McFadden's 1987 novel *The Serial* (which, like *Tales,* ran first in a San Francisco Bay Area newspaper), Tom Wolfe's 1987 blockbuster *The Bonfire of the* Vanities (first serialized in *Rolling Stone*), Stephen King's *The Green Mile* (which appeared in six monthly part-issues in 1995), and Pat Dillon's *The Last Best Thing* (serialized in the *San Jose Mercury News* and on the Worldwide Web before its publication in volume form in 1996).

2. Over a long term, such news stories unfold serially as the events of a celebrity's life occur. The mass dissemination of individual episodes in news stories, however, is structured very differently from serial narrative. Rather than stringing out a developing plot in parts, news coverage tends to give a brief, broad overview of a whole plot first, then to fill in details over time, in the initial article as well as in subsequent coverage and in sidebars. In the case of President Clinton's affair with an intern, for example, the bare outlines of a story were released first, then the details of the story got conveyed through various parallel but competing narratives (the Starr report, the president's videotaped testimony, Lewinsky's interview with Barbara Walters, and so on). Though the details of such narratives are transmitted over time, they do not engage their audiences in the same imaginative activity as serial narrative. The question for receivers of these news stories is not the serial-addict's insistent "What happens next?" It more closely resembles the theme of *Rashomon:* depending upon the perspective from which a story is told and retold, audiences' understanding of what happened and of what it means will vary. Serially published journalistic pieces, by contrast, share many of the formal features of composition and reception that I am attributing to serialized domestic novels.

3. I am grateful to the anonymous reader for *Contemporary Literature* who provided this citation and to both readers who gave me many insightful suggestions.

4. According to Tom Spain (Maupin, "Talk," 53) and to Barbara Kaplan Bass (255). Maupin kept ahead of the newspaper serial by only a few installments, taking readers' reactions and suggestions into account as he developed the details of the story line. Bass reports that Maupin "wrote none of his daily 800-word installments very far in advance because he liked responding to his readers' feedback about the characters and plot" (255).

5. This observation should serve as a reminder that, although Roof does not cite her, Susan Winnett has laid a foundation for Roof's argument in her important article analyzing the phallocentric bias of prevailing theories of readerly desire [138–58 in this volume].

6. Genette distinguishes among *story,* "the signified or narrative content," *narrative,* "the signifier, statement, discourse, or narrative text itself," and *narrating,* "the producing narrative action and, by extension, the whole of the real or fictional situation in which that action takes place" (27). I try to maintain these distinctions, though I share Genette's awareness that the oppositions ultimately break down in analysis of texts.

7. One of many insights into soap opera that I owe to conversations with Joseph Litvak.

8. For example, Gilah Rittenhouse asserts that "the expanding legion of soap opera fans can find in *As the World Turns* a view of the family unit that is stable and reassuring"; somewhat inexplicably, Rittenhouse describes the structure of the core families on that soap as "nuclear," although among the dozens of characters there are no examples of families fitting that description. Rittenhouse's argument imposes a false closure on the serial narrative plot by freezing family situations at the narrative moment of the essay's composition; since her essay was published (in 1992), many of the family configurations the essay describes have dissolved in the soap's continually evolving diegesis.

9. With reference to *Tales of the City,* folklorist Jimmy D. Browning comments: "Gay families can consist of as few as two persons, such as lovers or good friends, and, many times, former lovers. Not all members of the gay family are gay men, and sex and age are usually irrelevant factors in family membership. The structure of the gay family is based on levels of intimacy—more distant relationships are often the more short lived." Browning remarks that the gay hero of *Tales of the City,* Michael Tolliver, "estranged from the family into which he was born creates his own family by adapting the traditional family structure" (83).

10. I do not share Werner J. Einstadter's and Karen P. Sinclair's objection that "The transformation of Mary Ann is one of the nastiest and arguably the most misogynistic character portrayals of the series. Michael's defense of her, which in time even he cannot maintain, results from his fidelity to friendship rather than from Mary Ann's worthiness. It is Michael who sustains Brian during this difficult time. Brian in fact emerges as a hero in spite of himself; his nobility shines in the face of heterosexual treachery" (688). I note, however, how much of what they are saying in the second and third sentences of this quotation resembles comments one might make about "real people."

11. Maupin self-consciously specialized in representing uncharted territory. In a 1992 interview, he remarked, for instance, that *"Babycakes,* as far as I know, was the first fiction anywhere to deal with the AIDS epidemic" ("Interview," 8).

12. See "The Novel as Usual," *The Novel and the Police,* 107–45.

13. Maupin was fully aware of the parallels between his own project and Dickens's. He told Tom Spain: "The bottom line—the message—is acceptance, love and understanding. I try to celebrate difference through the books, the way nineteenth-century writers did, to show all the classes, the richness of humankind. . . . The reader is besieged by so many combinations that you just see them as relationships" (54).

14. The quotation comes from Jimmy D. Browning, who identifies himself as a gay reader (73), but speaking as a straight woman, I would describe my own feelings about *Tales* as very similar to his. In describing the breadth of the serial's appeal, Browning mentions several straight friends who have shared his enthusiasm for *Tales.*

15. Shilts's book borrows shamelessly, by the way, from Maupin's narrative method in its episodic accounts of individuals' experience with gay culture and with AIDS; it was itself originally serialized in the *New Yorker.* Unaccountably, given that Shilts was the AIDS reporter for the *Chronicle* during the same decade that Maupin's serial was appearing in that paper, it never mentions *Tales of the City.* Writing about the period when Shilts was composing his book, Frances FitzGerald says Shilts and Maupin were friends (55).

16. See Crimp and Rolston, 15. What Douglas Crimp and Adam Rolston say about anti-AIDS activists' rhetorical strategies applies also to Maupin: "ACT UP's humor is no joke. It has given us the courage to maintain our exuberant sense of life while every day coping with disease and death, and it has defended us against the pessimism endemic to other Left movements, from which we have otherwise taken so much" (20).

17. I borrow the force of this statement from Nancy K. Miller's *The Heroine's Text,* which charts the euphoric and dysphoric trajectories of plotlines in traditional French and British novels of the eighteenth century.

REFERENCES

Bass, Barbara Kaplan. "Armistead Maupin." in *Contemporary Gay American Novelists: A Bio-Bibliographical Critical Sourcebook,* edited by Emmanuel S. Nelson, 254–59.

Westport, Conn.: Greenwood, 1993.

Berlant, Lauren, and Michael Warner. "Sex in Public." *Critical Inquiry* 24 (1998): 547–66.

Browning, Jimmy D. "Something to Remember Me By: Maupin's *Tales of the City* Novels as Artifacts in Contemporary Gay Folk Culture." *New York Folklore* 19 (1993): 71–87.

Canning, Richard. "Tales of the Body? Problems in Maupin's Performative Utopia." In *American Bodies: Cultural Histories of the Physique,* edited by Tim Armstrong, 152–68. New York: New York University Press, 1996.

Crimp, Douglas, with Adam Rolston. *AIDS DemoGraphics.* Seattle: Bay, 1990.

Degnan, James P. "Cowboys and Crazies: The American West, Then and Now." Rev. of *The Serial,* by Cyra McFadden, and *Tales of the City,* by Armistead Maupin. *Hudson Review* 33 (1980): 146–50.

Einstadter, Werner J., and Karen P. Sinclair. "Lives on the Boundary: Armistead Maupin's Complete *Tales of the City.*" *Journal of the History of Sexuality* 1 (1991): 682–89.

FitzGerald, Frances. *Cities on a Hill: A Journey through Contemporary American Cultures.* New York: Simon, 1986.

Flitterman-Lewis, Sandy. "All's Well That Doesn't End—Soap Operas and the Marriage Motif." *Camera Obscura* 16 (January 1988): 119–27.

Genette, Gérard. *Narrative Discourse: An Essay in Method.* Ithaca, N.Y.: Cornell University Press, 1979.

Hayward, Jennifer. *Consuming Pleasures: Active Audiences and Serial Fictions from Dickens to Soap Opera.* Lexington: University Press of Kentucky, 1997.

Hughes, Linda K., and Michael Lund. *The Victorian Serial.* Charlottesville: University Press of Virginia, 1991.

Maupin. Armistead. *Babycakes* (1984). New York: Harper Perennial, 1994.

———. *Further Tales of the City* (1982). New York: Harper Perennial, 1982.

———. "An Interview with Armistead Maupin." With Scott A. Hunt. *Christopher Street* (23 November 1992): 8–12.

———. *More Tales of the City* (1980). New York: Harper Perennial, 1994.

———. *Significant Others* (1987). New York: Harper Perennial, 1994.

———. *Sure of You* (1989). New York: Harper Perennial, 1994.

———. *Tales of the City* (1978). New York: Harper Perennial, 1994.

———. "A Talk with Armistead Maupin." With Tom Spain. *Publishers Weekly* (20 March 1987): 53–54.

Miller, D. A. *The Novel and the Police.* Berkeley: University of California Press, 1988.

Miller, Nancy K. *The Heroine's Text: Readings in the French and English Novel.* New York: Columbia University Press, 1980.

Newman, Lesléa, and Diana Souza (illustrator). *Heather Has Two Mommies.* Boston: Alyson Wonderland, 1989.

Rittenhouse, Gilah. "The Nuclear Family Is Alive and Well: *As the World Turns.*" *Staying Tuned: Contemporary Soap Opera Criticism,* edited by Suzanne Frentz, 48–53. Bowling Green, Ohio: Bowling Green State University Popular Press, 1992.

Roof, Judith. *Come As You Are: Sexuality and Narrative.* New York: Columbia University Press, 1996.

Shilts, Randy. *And the Band Played On: Politics, People, and the AIDS Epidemic.* New York: St. Martin's, 1987.

Winnett, Susan. "Coming Unstrung: Women, Men, Narrative, and Principles of Pleasure." *PMLA* 105 (1990): 505–18.

■ PART IV

BEGINNINGS AND ENDS

Introduction: Openings and Closure

The critical discourse on beginnings has always been scant; that on closure has often been contradictory or strangely incomplete. Aristotle says simply that "a beginning is that which does not itself follow anything by causal necessity, but after which something naturally is or comes to be,"[1] an apparently simple idea that hides a number of potential points of disagreement. Horace modifies this prescription in his well-known counsel to begin *in medias res,* rather than *ab ovo,* at the absolute beginning.

In the 1970s, new energy in narrative theory brought attention to this long neglected and little understood aspect. Meir Sternberg comprehensively discusses the nature, extent, and place of exposition. Though generally assumed to occur entirely in the beginning of a work—indeed, it is often mistakenly assumed to be synonymous with the beginning—only the preliminary exposition in fact appears at the outset of a text. The remainder, the delayed exposition, can be provided judiciously at various points throughout the work, and thereby produce a range of dramatic effects. Thus, the detective story may be viewed as a "retardatory" structure that achieves its effects—sustained curiosity and suspense—by distributing the expositional material piecemeal throughout while postponing the concentrated, true exposition— the opening part of the *fabula*—to the end of the *syuzhet.*[2]

In *Beginnings,* Edward Said wrestles with the related problems of beginning, origins, and priority. He opposes the more active "beginning" to the relatively more passive "origin," and comments on the self-serving ficticiousness of most averred originary moments or events. He reflects on the apparently contradictory status of beginnings, which at once seem to be always already predetermined, and yet they also appear to effect a distinct break from that which precedes them. "Is the beginning simply an artifice, a disguise that defies the perpetual trap of forced continuity? Or does it admit of a meaning and a possibility that are genuinely capable of realization?" he asks.[3] Eschewing conventional notions of originality, Said nevertheless is able to point to "the intentional beginning act" which authorizes the text. This is not a simple authorial act, but one shaped by a multitude of social forces.

An essay by Steven Kellman, "Grand Openings and Plain: On the Poetics of Opening Lines," assembles an intriguing list of justly famous beginnings of literary works and seeks to identify larger principles governing their varied functions. For Kellman, openings generally tend to serve one of two functions, "either to thrust us immediately into the text or to retard our encounter until we are prepared for it."[4] In *Openings: Narrative Beginnings from the Epic to the Novel,* A. D. Nuttall outlines a different opposition within "the various tensions which exist between the formal freedom to begin a work of fiction wherever one likes and an opposite sense that all good openings are somehow naturally rooted, are echoes, more or less remote, of an original creative act: *in medias res,* as against 'In the beginning.'"[5] In the selection below, we will see that he finds both poles of this dyad (which he also refers to as "artificial" and "natural") to be distinctly problematic.

J. Hillis Miller, building on the work of Derrida and Said, states that "the paradox of beginnings is that one must have something solidly present and pre-existent, some generative source or authority, on which the development of a new story may be based," and that antecedent foundation itself in turn needs some prior foundation.[6] James Phelan, in his work on the subject, distinguishes usefully between four distinct aspects of openings: exposition (setting in its broadest sense), initiation (the opening instability that initiates the major action), introduction (initial rhetorical transactions among narrator, implied author, narrative audience, and authorial audience), and entrance (the actual reader's movement from outside the text to a specific location in the authorial audience). This concept of beginning means that it is a unit whose length will vary considerably from work to work. Additional critical interest on this subject is indicated by the publication of a volume addressing beginnings in classical literature, edited by Francis M. Dunn (*Yale Classical Studies* 29, 1992).

More ideologically oriented analyses of narrative beginnings can be expected to appear: in most public narratives, whether religious, political, or personal, stated origins are regularly arbitrary, misleading, or false. This confirms the necessity of critically examining beginnings in public discourse, particularly when they seem especially apt or utterly "natural." A conventionally satisfactory beginning in a work of nonfiction is usually a sure sign of its fictionality. Future investigations may well follow the direction set forth by Susanne Wofford who, in a recent essay,[7] contrasts origin tales in myths with those inscribed within traditional Western epics, and observes how the violent change at the founding of a nation is exposed in the origin myths but occluded in epic accounts.

The subject of endings has produced a considerably greater cluster of issues and approaches. One gets a sense of what is at stake in closure from Aristotle's numerous statements about how tragedies and epics should end. He acknowledges that concluding can be difficult: "many tie the knot well but unravel it ill."[8] He advocates a definitive, causally derived closure, and scorns the *deus ex machina;* condemns happy endings for evil protagonists and painful endings for virtuous ones; and he states that although a tragic ending is the superior one, many playwrights avoid this hard truth in order to cater to the weakness of the spectators. In ancient India, Bharata likewise prescribed an organic and connected conclusion in which the seed from which the drama developed is brought to fruition;[9] he also forbade the killing of the hero—whether onstage or off.

Neoclassical accounts of the "catastrophe" or denouement of a drama were quite demanding and probably contradictory; consider Dryden's formula for concluding: "there you see all things settling upon their first foundations; and the obstacles which hindered the design or action of the play once removed, it ends with that resemblance of truth and nature, that the audience are satisfied with the conduct of it."[10] Few plays would satisfy this prescription; it may well be an impossible stricture—the basic pattern of tragedy is fundamentally opposed to a strict application of poetic justice to the principal figures: Oedipus, Lear, and Andromache all suffer much more than they deserve. In later investigations, most aspects of this cluster of critical ideas will be untangled and opposed, as the complete resolution of events seems artificial and false rather than true or natural, while different, opposed audiences will each prefer a different type of conclusion (the notion of the removal of obstacles, however, recurs in a different form in Propp and D. A. Miller).

At the end of the nineteenth century, new energies were brought to bear on closure. Nietzsche's importance on subsequent literature should not be minimized, particularly his influential claim that most individuals (and societies) are too weak to endure tragedy. In his own words: "broadly speaking, a *preference for questionable or terrifying things* is a symptom of *strength;* while a taste for the *pretty and dainty* belongs to the weak and delicate. *Pleasure* in tragedy characterizes *strong* ages and natures. . . . It is the *heroic* spirits who say Yes to themselves in tragic cruelty; they are hard enough to experience suffering as a *pleasure.*"[11]

Henry James—himself no enemy of the dainty—produced a number of shrewd observations on this difficult subject, many of which continue to be widely cited. Of particular relevance is the following statement on the difficulty of finding natural stopping places: "We have, as the case stands, to invent and establish them, to arrive at them by a difficult, dire process of selection and comparison, of surrender and sacrifice,"[12] he observes in the preface to *Roderick Hudson*. E. M. Forster's famous quip, "Nearly all novels are feeble at the end. . . . If it was not for death and marriage, I do not know how the average novelist would conclude,"[13] echoed similar complaints by Shaw and Chekhov. Around this time Boris Eikhenbaum began to theorize the nature of the epilogue in fictional narratives ("O. Henry"). This period drew to an end with the valorizations of modernist open endings in the work of Robert Martin Adams and Alan Friedman.

Contemporary closure theory begins with Frank Kermode's *The Sense of an Ending* (1967), a study of the ubiquity of closure in all cultural productions; Barbara Herrnstein Smith's *Poetic Closure: A Study of How Poems End* (1968); and Umberto Eco's *The Open Work* (*Opera aperta,* 1962; published in English in 1989), which analyzed "works in motion" in several media that need to be completed by chance or by the audience. Several important studies devoted to the novel were published between 1974 and 1981, and a special issue of *Nineteenth-Century Fiction* on the subject (1978) which included an afterward by Frank Kermode also appeared. The first of the books, David H. Richter's *Fable's End: Completeness and Closure in Rhetorical Fiction* (1974), analyzes closure in narratives that are idea- or thesis-driven, such as *Rasselas,* and goes on to attack the easy assertions of uncritical advocates of open form. He importantly differentiates between "closure," where the sense of an ending is felt, and "completeness," in which all that needs to be included has been presented.

Marianna Torgovnick's *Closure in the Novel* identifies and analyzes a number of prominent strategies of arriving at the ending in novels from *Middlemarch* to *The Waves,* and develops the categories of circularity, parallelism, incompletion, tangential, and linkage to describe these practices. In *Narrative and Its Discontents: Problems of Closure in the Traditional Novel* (1981), D. A. Miller elaborates a theory of the narratable, that is, "the instances of disequilibrium, suspense, and general insufficiency from which a given narrative appears to arise," and goes on to investigate the invariably problematic and elusive "nonnarratable" state of quiescence that the novel attempts to recover at its end.[14] However, the narratable is stronger than the closure to which it is thus opposed, and can never generate the terms for its own arrest. Thus, George Eliot directs her text "toward a state of all-encompassing transcendence from which it is continually drawn back by the dispersive and fragmentary logic of the narrative itself."[15] In 1985, Armine Kotin Mortimer's *La Clôture narrative* appeared, a volume that traces ever changing closural strategies in French fiction from Mme de Lafayette to the *nouveau roman*.

252

Peter Rabinowitz identifies beginnings and endings as occupying privileged positions in nineteenth- and twentieth-century European prose narratives, whose conventions suggest such sites are especially pregnant with concentrated meaning. He also investigates the implicit "rule of conclusive endings" that assumes that material occupying this textual site is invested with especial significance, and may sum up the central concerns of the text. Rabinowitz further observes that such an assumption naturally produces the inevitable rupture of this rule; he also notes the ways that a convention like this one inevitably ensures that many readers will misread endings that fail to conform to their ideological expectations. These specifically ideological concerns would in turn be further interrogated by Russell Reising in his reflections on closure and its deferral in American literature and culture, as he examines the ways in which concluding moments ("loose ends") in representative American texts not only fail to resolve or conclude important narrative issues, but actually exacerbate and at times explode precisely the issues which generate the narrative in the first place. The formal imperative of concluding these works thus clashes with the impossibility of genuinely resolving the ideological tensions within them; these works can't close, precisely because they are so deeply embedded within the conflicted sociohistorical worlds of their genesis.

Ideological issues were prominent in the 1980s. Nancy K. Miller's concept of "the heroine's text," or conventional inscription of female destiny, outlined and attacked the limited closural options in traditional representations of women. This approach is considerably extended by Rachel Blau DuPlessis. In *Writing beyond the Ending,* she examines the endings of several twentieth-century texts whose authors replace the conventional fate of the female protagonist in death or marriage; "writing beyond the ending means the transgressive invention of narrative strategies, strategies that express critical dissent from dominant narrative" patterns.[16] In the section below, DuPlessis describes how, in the nineteenth-century novel, authors went to a great deal of trouble to ensure that *Bildung* and romance could not coexist and be integrated for the heroine at the resolution of the novel. Other important feminist analyses that contain significant discussions of closure include those of Joanne Frye, Susan Winnett, and Judith Roof.[17] In addition, Alison Booth's impressive anthology, *Famous Last Words: Changes in Gender and Narrative Closure,* assembles several theoretically informed essays on gender and closure in nineteenth- and twentieth-century British and American narratives; her introductory comments show the suppleness and importance of feminist theory as she examines, for example, feminist reinstatings of a closed form through the ironic quotation of famous last words.

The study of closure has continued to expand prolifically; there are important monographs or anthologies on several domains, including film

(Neupert), romance (Parker), ancient literature (Dunn; Roberts, Dunn, and Fowler), and Chaucer (Grudin). Drama has also received significant attention (Schmidt, Schlueter, Richardson; Schmidt includes an interesting discussion of plays whose original endings were altered).[18] Shakespeare's endings have also provided rich material for critical investigation, with individual studies devoted to the romances (R. S. White), some early comedies (Howard), the ever inconclusive histories (Hodgdon), and the notorious mature and "problem" comedies (Ejner Jensen). Jensen argues cogently against critics who overemphasize the significance of the end or unthinkingly attribute to it a privileged interpretive role; as Jensen puts it, "to crown the end rather than see it as a necessary and inevitable part of the total work is to . . . distort both the nature and function of Shakespeare's comedies."[19]

The critical discourse on closure continues to grow more varied, embracing ever new discursive practices and areas of concern. One expects more work on closure and its opposition in minority and non-Western texts and in the narratives of popular culture. It is clear that issues of closure are deeply entwined in the otherwise disparate arenas of genre, formal innovation, and ideological positioning, though the precise type of intersections between them remain opaque. One thing is certain: an easy correspondence between closed endings and conservative politics or open endings and progressive ideology is too facile and does violence to the texts it would thus evaluate; as Alison Booth observes in this context, "we do not find a clear correlation between disruption of formal convention and radical departure from social convention."[20] Furthermore, as Marianna Torgovnick points out, the insistently open ending is itself rapidly becoming thoroughly conventional.[21] A critical synthesis of this increasingly complex, ideologically laden, and expanding field is in all likelihood a long way off.

NOTES

1. Aristotle, *Poetics* 7.3, in *Critical Theory Since Plato,* ed. Hazard Adams (New York: Harcourt Brace Jovanovich, 1971).

2. Meir Sternberg, *Expositional Modes and Temporal Ordering in Fiction* (Baltimore, Md.: Johns Hopkins University Press, 1978), 182.

3. Edward Said, *Beginnings: Intention and Method* (New York: Basic Books, 1975), 43.

4. Steven G. Kellman, "Grand Openings and Plain: On the Poetics of Opening Lines," *Sub-Stance* 17 (1977): 146.

5. A. D. Nuttall, *Openings: Narrative Beginnings from the Epic to the Novel* (Oxford: Oxford University Press, 1992), vii–viii.

6. J. Hillis Miller, *Reading Narrative* (Norman: University of Oklahoma Press, 1998), 57.

7. Susanne Wofford, "Epics and the Politics of the Origin Tale: Virgil, Ovid, Spenser, and Native American Aetiology," in *Epic Tradition in the Contemporary World: The Poetics of*

Community, ed. Margaret Beissinger, Jane Tylus, and Susanne Wofford (Berkeley: University of California Press, 1999), 239–69.

8. Aristotle, *Poetics* 18, in *Critical Theory Since Plato,* ed. Adams, 59.

9. Bharata-Muni, *The Natyaśastra: A Treatise on Ancient Hindu Dramaturgy and Histrionics,* ed. and trans. Manohan Ghosh, rev. ed. (Calcutta: The Asiatic Society and Granthalaya, 1956–67), chap. 21, para. 42.

10. John Dryden, "An Essay of Dramatic Poetry," in *Critical Theory Since Plato,* ed. Adams, 234.

11. Friedrich Nietzsche, *Will to Power,* trans. Walter Kaufman and R. G. Hollingdale (New York: Random House, 1966), 450.

12. In *Theory of Fiction: Henry James,* ed. James E. Miller Jr. (Lincoln: University of Nebraska Press, 1972), 171.

13. E. M. Forster, *Aspects of the Novel* (New York: Harcourt, Brace Jovanovich, 1927), 95.

14. D. A. Miller, *Narrative and Its Discontents: Problems of Closure in the Traditional Novel* (Princeton, N. J. : Princeton University Press, 1981), ix.

15. Ibid, x.

16. Rachel Blau DuPlessis, *Writing beyond the Ending: Narrative Strategies of Twentieth-Century Women Writers* (Bloomington: Indiana University Press, 1985), 5; 285 in this volume.

17. Judith Roof, *Come As You Are: Sexuality and Narrative* (New York: Columbia University Press, 1996), 1–40.

18. H. J. Schmidt, *How Dramas End: Essays on the German Sturm und Drang* (Ann Arbor: University of Michigan Press, 1992), 35–61.

19. Ejner Jensen, *Shakespeare and the Ends of Comedy* (Bloomington: Indiana University Press, 1991), 21.

20. Alison Booth, ed., *Famous Last Words: Changes in Gender and Narrative Closure* (Charlottesville: University of Virginia Press, 1997), 9.

21. Marianna Torgovnick, *Closure in the Novel* (Princeton, N.J.: Princeton University Press, 1981), 204–206.

18

Beginnings

EDWARD SAID

As a problem for study, "beginnings" are attractive, first of all, because while one can isolate *a* beginning analytically, the notion of beginning itself is practically tied up in a whole complex of relations. Thus between the word *beginning* and the word *origin* lies a constantly changing system of meanings, most of them of course making first one then the other convey greater priority, importance, explanatory power. As consistently as possible I use *beginning* as having the more active meaning, and *origin* the more passive one.

I have tried to show that when the modern literary critic begins to write he cannot sustain himself at all well in a dynastic tradition. For not only is this tradition foreign to him by training and circumstance, but its repudiation is also the intention, the subject matter, and the method of most modern literature. He must therefore undertake his work with initiative. He, too, must seek a more suitable point of departure, a different topos, for his study. I have been hinting very broadly that such a topos is the "beginning" or "beginnings," which presents a problem at once more precise and more exigent than does the "New." Beginnings inaugurate a deliberately other production of meaning—a gentile (as opposed to a sacred) one. It is "other" because, in writing, this gentile production claims a status alongside other works: it is another work, rather than one in a line of descent from X or Y. Beginnings, as I treat them, intend this difference, they are its first instance: they make a way along the road.

A beginning, therefore, is a problem to be studied, as well as a position taken by any writer. For the critic a novel begins, as it does for the novelist who wrote it, with the intention to write a novel and not a play or a poem. As a problem, beginnings seem to have a sort of detachable abstraction, but unlike an idea about which one thinks at some distance from it, a beginning is already a project under way. Two examples to which I shall refer periodically are *Tristram Shandy* and *The Prelude:* each at the outset is only a beginning, each is preparatory to something else, and yet each amasses a good deal of substance *before* it gets past the beginning. How does this happen? Or more precisely: if the critic is studying beginnings, how does he go about bringing together material "for" his study? How is his material arranged? Where does it begin?

In the case of this book I have apparently begun with the present chapter, which anatomizes and intends what is to follow. But in fact my first formal step is taken in chapter 2, "A Meditation on Beginnings," about which I should like to speak briefly here. After the problem of beginnings first suggested itself to me it became fairly clear that my reading and teaching were increasingly addressing the question, sometimes directly and sometimes obliquely, but always in terms of auxiliary questions. I then sought a way to treat these auxiliary questions in and of themselves, as matters confronted in the practice of criticism. I also looked for a way of connecting them to the principal issues to which they are related. For example, every student of literature necessarily deals with originality and with the related subject of influences and sources; yet very few critics have systematically tried to examine originality in secular, as opposed to magical, language. I then found that critics like Paul Valéry, for whom the imaginative abstraction or the speculative generality was not an obstacle to thought but rather an enhancement and a provider of thought, suggested a kind of writing I might learn from directly. Valéry's critical prose, for all its sophistication, is virtually free of cynicism. It never resists purity as a subject, and yet it never refrains from submitting purity to a web of circumstances, most of them culled by Valéry from the immediate pressures upon him. In his relationships to Leonardo and to Mallarmé we can see how the weight of philosophical and personal intellectual pressures, respectively, bore down upon him. As a poet indebted to and friendly with Mallarmé, Valéry was compelled to assess originality and derivation in a way that said something about a relationship between two poets that could not be reduced to a simple formula. As the actual circumstances were rich, so too had to be the attitude. Here is an example from the "Letter about Mallarmé":

No word comes easier or oftener to the critic's pen than the word *influence,* and no vaguer notion can be found among all the vague notions that compose the phantom armory of aesthetics. Yet there is nothing in the critical field that should be of greater philosophical interest or prove more rewarding to analysis than the progressive modification of one mind by the work of another.

257

It often happens that the work acquires a singular value in the other mind, leading to active consequences that are impossible to foresee and in many cases will never be possible to ascertain. What we do know is that this derived activity is essential to intellectual production of all types. Whether in science or the arts, if we look for the source of an achievement we can observe that *what a man does* either repeats or refutes *what someone else has done*—repeats it in other tones, refines or amplifies or simplifies it, loads or overloads it with meaning; or else rebuts, overturns, destroys and denies it, but thereby assumes it and has invisibly used it. Opposites are born from opposites.

We say that an author is *original* when we cannot trace the hidden transformations that others underwent in his mind; we mean to say that the dependence of *what he does* on *what others have done* is excessively complex and irregular. There are works in the likeness of others, and works that are the reverse of others, but there are also works of which the relation with earlier productions is so intricate that we become confused and attribute them to the direct intervention of the gods.[1]

Valéry converts "influence" from a crude idea of the weight of one writer coming down in the work of another into a universal principle of what he calls "derived achievement." He then connects this concept with a complex process of repetition that illustrates it by multiplying instances; this has the effect of providing a sort of wide intellectual space, a type of discursiveness in which to examine influence. Repetition, refinement, amplification, loading, overloading, rebuttal, overturning, destruction, denial, invisible use—such concepts completely modify a linear (vulgar) idea of "influence" into an open field of possibility. Valéry is careful to admit that chance and ignorance play important roles in this field: what we cannot see or find, as well as what we cannot predict, he says, produce excessive irregularity and complexity. Thus the limits of the field of investigation are set by examples whose nonconforming, overflowing energy begins to carry them out of the field. This is an extremely important refinement in Valéry's writing. For even as his writing holds in the wide system of variously dispersed relationships connecting writers with one another, he also shows how at its limits the field gives forth other relations that are hard to describe from within the field.

Learning what I could from Valéry, I embarked on what I called a meditation on beginnings. Because the *topos* is neither a traditional nor a usual one, I could not geometrically define it beforehand. I undertook, however, to let it make possible a system of relationships, a field or constellation of significance in which my writing moved in order to gather in both the grosser and the more rarefied thoughts, images, and instances that crowd around beginnings. The logic of exposition I follow is not precursive; that is, my exposition follows no course determined in advance by convention, imitation, consecution, or thematics. The form of writing I chose was the meditative essay—first, because I believe myself to be trying to form a unity as I write; and second, because I want to let beginnings generate in my mind the type of relationships and figures most suitable to them.

Let me be more explicit. Every sort of writing establishes explicit and implicit rules of pertinence for itself: certain things are admissible, certain others not. I call these rules of pertinence *authority*—both in the sense of explicit law and guiding force (what we usually mean by the term) and in the sense of that implicit power to generate another word that will belong to the writing as a whole (Vico's etymology is *auctor: autos: sui ipsius: propsius: property*). The job of an initial meditation is to sketch this authority with regard to "beginnings" by allowing it to be set forth as clearly and in as much detail as possible. To do this as freely as possible, while preserving the necessary formalities of clarity, I did not confine myself to "the novel" or to "poetry." I make no claims of startling originality, and so far as possible I concern myself with works and figures of fairly wide currency. But it is no use looking in these pages for evidence arranged or amassed in familiar ways.

Since every beginning is different, and since there is no hope of dealing with every one, I arrange examples in series whose internal rule of coherence is neither a logic of simple consecutiveness nor random analogy. Rather, I adopt a principle of association that works, in a sense, against simple consecution and chance. For a subject like beginnings is more a structure than a history, but this structure cannot be immediately seen, named, or grasped. Moreover, as Roland Barthes has said of structure: "Tout concourt en effet à innocenter les structures que l'on recherche, à les absenter: le dévidement du discours, la naturalité des phrases, l'egalité apparente du signifiant et de l'insignifiant, les préjugés scolaires (ceux du "plan," du "personnage," du "style"), la simultanéité des sens, la disparition et la résurgence capricieuses de certain filons thématiques." ("Everything conspires to make the structures one looks for appear either innocent or absent: the unwinding of the discourse, the naturalness of the sentences, the apparent equivalence of signifier and signified, scholarly prejudices [those of *composition, character,* or *style*], the simultaneity of meanings, the capricious disappearances and re-appearances of certain thematic strands."[2] As I have said, there is no precursive model to follow. Most important, since the whole field of possibilities for a beginning is so vast and detailed—so irrational—and since I am basing my study upon what is rationally apprehensible, the links between steps in the argument are struck

259

according to what is allowable—according to what the subject of "beginnings" *authorizes.*

Much of this authorization is provisional, and even seems fortuitous in the meditation. But its value can be gradually established in the chapters that follow, chapters in which I will go on to make the association of ideas firmer. I want to insist that this is not a question of *proving* the meditation concretely, and still less of allowing the meditation to act as a "paradigm" for empirical study—unless by *paradigm* one very loosely adopts Thomas Kuhn's definition of the term as a "research consensus." For me it is rather a question of letting the structure multiply itself into more branches, into projects that I believe it makes especially interesting (and that in some cases even makes possible): fiction, the making of texts, and the criticism, analysis, and characterization of knowledge and language. . . .

Literature is full of the lore of beginnings despite the tyranny of starting a work *in medias res,* a convention that burdens the beginning with the pretense that it is not one. Two obvious, wide-ranging categories of literary starting point are the hysterically deliberate (and hence the funnier of the two) and the solemn-dedicated, the impressive and noble. The former category includes *Tristram Shandy* and *A Tale of a Tub,* two works that despite their existence cannot seem to get started; in each the beginning is postponed with a kind of encyclopedic, meaningful playfulness which, like Panurge taking stock of marriage before falling into the water, delays one sort of action for the sake of understanding another.

The latter category includes *Paradise Lost,* a prelude to portraying existence after the Fall, and *The Prelude,* which was to ready its author "for entering upon the arduous labour which he had proposed to himself." In both instances what was initially intended to be the beginning became the work itself. Although vastly different, both of these great English epics perform similar intellectual and psychological tasks. It is no accident, I think, that both poems are beginning poems—in the sense that each prepares for something more important to follow—and that both are therefore ways of delimiting, defining, and circumscribing human freedom. Of course, Milton and Wordsworth employ very distinctive frames of reference for understanding freedom; basically, however, each poet uses his poem to begin to *put* man in the world, to situate him. Thus in each case man at the outset faces, not an unlimited range of possibilities, but a highly conditioned set of circumstances in which his existence (that of Milton, Wordsworth, Adam, or *The Prelude's* narrator) is properly inaugurated. Both poems are radical in that they imagine human life as having a "beginning"; and in both an investigation of that beginning is the subject of the poem. Both poems open with several images of creatures in a free state—that is, unconstrained, wandering, extraterritorial. Compare Wordsworth's image of how he

> escaped
> From the vast city, where I long had pined
> A discontented sojourner: now free,
> Free, a bird to settle where I will,[3]

in Book 1 of *The Prelude* with Milton's Satan:

> Here at least
> We shall be free: th'Almighty hath not built
> Here for his envy, will not drive us hence:
> Here we may reign secure, and in my choyce
> To reign is worth ambition though in Hell:
> Better to reign in Hell, than serve in Heav'n[4]

In due course each poem develops correctives to such unrestrained sentiments. Wordsworth's are tied directly to the choice of a theme for the poem (this occurs at the end of Book 1), which in turn is associated with the decision to employ a vague, unbounded freedom for determinate ends:

> One end at least hath been attained; my mind
> Hath been revived, and if this genial mood
> Desert me not, forthwith shall be brought down
> Through later years the story of my life.
> The road lies plain before me;—'t is a theme
> Single and of determined bounds; and hence
> I choose it rather at this time, than work
> of ampler and more varied argument,
> Where I might be discomfited and lost. . .[5]

The choice of an autobiographical theme of course serves to evoke various phases and events in the poet's life. That this theme arises from a delimitation imposed at and for the sake of the beginning, however, accounts for the special type of vision which Wordsworth finally arrives at. I am referring not only to what he calls "the discipline/ And consummation of a Poet's mind" (that is, of one who will now be able to go on after such a prelude), but also the scene on Mount Snowdon and the commentary upon it in the fourteenth book. This vision of "mutual domination" is "the express resemblance" of Imagination,

that glorious faculty
That higher minds bear with them as their own.
This is the very spirit in which they deal
With the whole compass of the universe:
They from their native selves can send abroad
Kindred mutations; for themselves create
A like existence. . .[6]

As a poem of beginning, *The Prelude* sheds its unconditional early liberty for the purpose of forging the beginning—as distinguished from a narrator's mere initial enthusiasm. By the time we come to Book 14 and the lines quoted above, we recognize that Wordsworth's mind is capable of intention, production, determination—albeit with a sense of the loss of youthful, animal instincts thereby incurred. The "glorious faculty" is the power to begin poetry, which is itself not mere effusion but a meaning that is embedded in human circumstances. Together, these circumstances and imagination begin the fruitful, mutual domination of self and reality, of time and vision, that when articulated in language is poetry.

Milton's scheme is more complicated, but its resemblance with *The Prelude* is striking nevertheless. Milton is anxious to represent gradations of freedom in a continuum—God, His Son, the Angels, Adam, Eve—through which like a nomadic zero moves Satan, archangel and archfiend. Satan is the beginning—the cause of "Mans First Disobedience"—the *arche* in response to which the continuities of human history and destiny are arranged. Before the onset of Satan's machinations, Adam's earliest life had been a mystery to him:

For Man to tell how human Life began
is hard: for who himself beginning knew?[7]

Poised against this ignorance is, of course, Gabriel's knowledge, God's, Satan's, and Milton's. The whole of the poem in a sense is devoted to making intelligible to man his historical beginning after Paradise is lost and like Wordsworth's narrator (the "I" in *The Prelude*) "Man" in *Paradise Lost* discovers the commencement of history even as he loses the relatively untrammeled freedom of innocence. Milton's more heroic vision unashamedly weaves in the sexual drama, which more than any other image conveys the novelty, as well as the nexus of intention, circumstance, and force, that always characterizes the beginning. As Adam tells Michael, after the latter has explained Christ to him:

O Prophet of glad tidings, finisher
Of utmost hope! now clear I understand

> What oft my steddiest thoughts have searcht in vain,
> Why own great expectation should be call'd
> The seed of Woman: Virgin Mother, Haile,
> High in the love of Heav'n, yet from my Loynes
> Thou shalt proceed, and from thy Womb the Son
> Of God most High; So God with man unites.[8]

It is from such radical investigations as *Paradise Lost* and *The Prelude* that the pun in the title of Beckett's *Comment c'est* (*How It Is*)—a homonym of *commencez* (the command "Begin!") acquires its value. Yet not many writers would willingly combine the idea of a sort of universal beginning with the work's actuality; by the same token, in few works is the beginning so highly charged as in the two discussed here.

When a literary work does not dwell so self-consciously on its beginning as do the works just discussed, its actual start, as an intelligible unit, is usually deliberately formal or concessive. (I must put aside the question of whether it is really possible to begin unselfconsciously, though I am convinced that is not. The issue is one of degrees of self-consciousness: *Tristram Shandy* is uniquely sensitive about getting under way.) Specifying points of departure grew increasingly problematical during the eighteenth century, however, a trend as eloquently reflected by the titles of two modern works dealing with that period—Frank Manuel's *The Eighteenth Century Confronts the Gods* and W. J. Bate's *The Burden of the Past and the English Poet*—as by their contents. The search for such points not only is reflected in language, but is carried out in language and, as became evident to eighteenth-century thinkers like Vico, is necessary *because of* language. Polytechnical unlike any other human activity, language was discovered to be a suitable vehicle for posing questions of origin for purely linguistic as well as social, moral, or political reasons. Vico, miserable in his obscure position at Naples, sees the whole world of nations developing out of poetry; and Rousseau, for whom experience is clarified by words, feels he is entitled to use them simply because he is a man of sentiments and a member of the *tiers état:* these are two prominent examples. Kant's *Prolegomenon to Any Future Metaphysics,* to speak now of a beginning that really aims to strip away the accretions of academic philosophy, undertakes a description of those radical conditions which must be understood before philosophy can be practiced. Nevertheless, Kant's *Prolegomenon* fully anticipates his *Metaphysics of Ethics* and *Critique of Practical Reason*—it is coterminous with them—as well as the critical method with which he refashioned European philosophy. And Coleridge, in his essay "On Method" (in *The Friend*), echoes Descartes in taking up the theme as follows: Method, which reflects the noteworthy mind in its work, its discipline, its sustained intellectual energy and vigilance, requires an "initiative," without which things appear "distant, dis-jointed and impertinent to each other and to any common purpose." Togeth-er, initiative and the method that follows from it "will become natural to the mind which has been accustomed to contemplate not things only, or for their own sake alone, but likewise and chiefly the relations of things, either their relations to each other, or to the observer, or to the state, and apprehensions of the reader."[9]

All such investigations have in common what Wordsworth calls "a cheer-ful confidence in things to come,"[10] which is another way of describing what I have been calling *intention*. What is really anterior to a search for a method, to a search for a temporal beginning, is not merely an initiative, but a neces-sary certainty, a genetic optimism, that continuity is possible *as intended by* the act of beginning. Stretching from start to finish is a fillable space, or time, pretty much there but, like a foundling, awaiting an author or a speaker to father it, to authorize its being. Consciousness of a starting point, from the vantage point of the continuity that succeeds it, is seen to be consciousness of a direction in which it is humanly possible to move (as well as a trust in con-tinuity). Valéry's intellectual portrait of Leonardo divulges the secret that Leonardo, like Napoleon, was forced to find the law of continuity between things whose connection with each other escapes very nearly all of us.[11] Any point in Leonardo's thought will lead to another, for, Valéry says in a later essay, when thinking of an abyss Leonardo thought also of a bridge across it.[12] Consciousness, whether as pure universality, insurmountable generality, or eternal actuality, has the character of an imperial ego; in this view, the argu-ment *cogito ergo sum* was for Valéry "like a clarion sounded by Descartes to summon up the powers of his ego."[13] The starting point is the reflexive action of the mind attending to itself, allowing itself to effect (or dream) a construc-tion of a world whose seed totally implicates its offspring. It is Wagner hear-ing an E-flat chord out of which *The Ring* (and the Rhine) will rush, or Nietzsche giving birth to tragedy and morals by ascending a ladder of inner genealogy, or Husserl asserting the radical originality of consciousness which will support "the whole storied edifice of universal knowledge."

Husserl merits special attention because the nearly excessive purity of his whole philosophic project makes him, I think, the epitome of modern mind in search of absolute beginnings; he has rightly been called the perpetual *Anfänger* (beginner). The course of Husserl's development is, in the main, too controversial, too technical a subject to warrant extended analysis here. Yet the meaning of his philosophical work is that he accepted "the infinite goals of reason" while at the same time seeking to ground understanding of these goals in human experience. Interpretation, a major task in both Husserl's and Heidegger's enterprises, is thus committed to a radical undermining of itself, and not only because its goals are pushed further and further forward. For also its point of departure, no longer accepted as "naive"—that is, as merely given, or "there"—stands revealed to the scrutiny of consciousness; as a result, the point of departure assumes a unique place as philosophy itself, "essentially a science of true beginnings, *rizomata panton*," as well as an example of the science in action.[14] Putting this differently: Husserl tries to seize the beginning proposing itself *to* the beginning *as* a beginning *in* the beginning. Pierre Thevenaz describes it perfectly:

> In Husserl we see a circular movement which revolves around its point of departure, radicalizes it progressively without ever truly leaving it. This movement, by displaying itself simultaneously as reduction and intentionality, digs ever deeper, and in its exhausting "struggle for the beginning," for a beginning which is an end "situated at infinity," is consumed by a coming and going which Husserl himself characterized as zig-zag . . . . Obviously, it is inaccessible in fact and can only be aimed at. . . . The point of departure thus cannot be a *hold in being*.[15]

What emerges precisely is the sentiment of beginning, purged of any doubt, fully convinced of itself, intransitive, and yet, from the standpoint of lay knowledge which Husserl acknowledges to be "an unbearable spiritual need"[16]—thoroughly aloof, because always at a distance, and thus almost incomprehensible. It is to Husserl that Valéry's phrase "a specialist of the universal" is best applied.

What is important to modern ascetic radicalism of the kind that Husserl carries to an extreme is the insistence on a rationalized beginning even as beginnings are shown to be at best polemical assertions, at worst scarcely thinkable fantasies. Valéry's Leonardo is a construction, after all, and Husserl's phenomenological reduction temporarily "brackets" brute reality. The beginning—or the ending, for that matter—is what Hans Vaihinger calls a "summational fiction," whether it is a temporal or a conceptual beginning. But I want to shift Frank Kermode's emphasis in *The Sense of an Ending* by stressing the primordial need for certainty at the beginning over the usually later sense of an ending. Without at least a sense of a beginning, nothing can really be done, much less ended. This is as true for the literary critic as it is for the philosopher, the scientist, or the novelist. And the more crowded and confused a field appears, the more a beginning, fictional or not, seems imperative. A beginning gives us the chance to do work that compensates us for the tumbling disorder of brute reality that will not settle down.

NOTES

1. Paul Valéry, "Letter about Mallarmé," in *Leonardo, Poe, Mallarmé,* trans. Malcolm Cowley and James Lawler (Princeton, N.J.: Princeton University Press, 1972), 241.

2. Roland Barthes, "Par où commencer?" in *Le Degré zéro de l'écriture suivi de nouveaux essais critiques* (Paris: Editions du Seuil, 1972), 146 (Said's translation).

3. William Wordsworth, *The Prelude* in *Selected Poems and Prefaces,* ed. Jack Stillinger (Boston: Houghton Mifflin, 1965), 193.

4. John Milton, *Paradise Lost,* ed. Merritt Hughes (New York: Odyssey Press, 1962), 13.

5. Wordsworth, *The Prelude,* 206.

6. Ibid., 356.

7. Milton, *Paradise Lost,* 191.

8. Ibid., 310.

9. Coleridge, "On Method," in *The Friend,* ed. Barbara E. Rooke (Princeton, N.J.: Princeton University Press, 1969), 1:451.

10. Wordsworth, *The Prelude,* 194.

11. Valéry, "Letter about Mallarmé," 13.

12. Ibid., 79.

13. Valéry, *Masters and Friends,* trans. Martin Turnell (Princeton, N.J.: Princeton University Press, 1968), 31.

14. Husserl, *Phenomenology and the Crisis in Philosophy,* trans. Quentin Lauer (New York: Harper and Row, 1965), 146.

15. Pierre Thevenaz, *"What Is Phenomenology?" and Other Essays,* trans. James M. Edie (Chicago: Quadrangle Books, 1962), 104, 107, 108.

16. Husserl, *Phenomenology and the Crisis in Philosophy,* 140.

19

The Sense of a Beginning

A. D. NUTTALL

We saw in the openings of the *Aeneid,* the *Commedia,* and *Paradise Lost,* an ever-shifting process of imaginative negotiation between natural and formal inception. Virgil plunges *in medias res,* in Greek fashion, by beginning with Aeneas sailing before the wind, with his dispossessed followers. But in the preliminary invocation he obtrudes—in un-Homeric contrast with one another—his own personality and the declaration that the subject of his poem is the *real* beginning of the Latin race, the lords of Alba, the walls of towering Rome. If we accept from Donatus the restoration of four *preceding* lines, we have a syntactically odd 'opening-before-the-opening'; Virgil presents himself as emerging from a forest, leaving behind the flute (of pastoral *Eclogues*) to subdue the farmlands (*Georgics*), thereafter turning, at last, to arms and the man. The effect of this is greatly to strengthen the intuition of the personal significance of Virgil's placing *cano,* "I sing," before the Homeric "Tell, O Muse." The sentence thus restored is indeed strangely extended, producing a reduplicative effect through the tacking-on of relative clauses, first to the poet and then to the hero, who has likewise *emerged,* embarked upon a journey. Thus in Virgil the beginning of the *poem's* story is matched (and deliberately mismatched) with something Homer could never admit (or even, perhaps, conceive), with the beginning of a real, organized History, the true story of those then and there listening to the poem. Yet even as this deep engagement with the natural is proudly declared, the poet's sense of his own separate individuality is not healed but exacerbated, and the grand progression of Roman history is eerily pre-echoed by a sequence which is personal and literary.

Dante's poem is of course thoroughly medieval, unequivocally Christian, but even here the negotiation with the other, 'counternatural' opening is sustained.

267

The poem begins *in medias res,* in the middle of the journey of Dante's own life. Yet, as we have seen, Dante is here in one way the object, the matter of the poetry; we are asked to believe that the intervention is not the poet's but God's. *He* enters *in medias res* and in beginning the poem starts a transformation of Dante himself in which the poet grows into accord with the real shape of the universe. The ordinary march of events is broken in upon, not by something confessedly less real, an artful fiction, but by something more real, by that which is itself the beginning and end of all things, Alpha and Omega. We are as far as literature will permit, it would seem, from Valéry's formula for the weakly arbitrary novel-opening: "La marquise sortit à cinq heures." ["The marquise went out at five o'clock."] As with Virgil, so with Dante, we come to see that the circle is not closed. We are made aware, not only of the real story of the world, but of the real poet: as Virgil speaks of himself as *egressus silvis,* "emerged from the woods," so Dante finds himself in "una selva oscura," "a dark wood." *Mezzo* is moreover implicitly structured not only with reference to the real but also with reference to the structure of the poem. The word is indeed stiffened by a sense of symmetry which is fundamentally medieval (think of triptychs) and is wholly absent from the Horatian formula.

The narrative of *Paradise Lost* begins with Satan, now cast out from Heaven, staring wildly on the surrounding desolation. It begins *in medias res.* But, as with Virgil but still more radically, the preceding invocation joins the beginning of the poem to the beginning of the Story of Us All, as we are fallen creatures. As Johnson wrote more than a hundred years later, "All mankind will, through all ages, bear the same relation to Adam and Eve, and must partake of that good and evil which extend to themselves."[1] The first line, "Of man's first disobedience, and the fruit," tells of the first, constitutive act of humanity as we know it in ourselves. It is not, indeed, a Creation-of-the-World opening, but we are moving closer to that Hebraic extreme.

I am suggesting that an exclusively formalist account—an account which admits no concept of beginning other than that created by a fictive reading-in—will never be adequate for these canonical openings, for all their manifestly literary character. Even when we wish to register an appropriation of nature by art, we must notice the temporarily separate identity of that which is ineluctably appropriated. This feature of binary negotiation is continued, into the classic period of the novel. For all the elegant, self-referential wit of the opening chapter-heading, "I Am Born," the beginning of *David Copperfield,* is, with Victorian gusto, triumphantly fused with the natural beginnings of birth. Dickens is, to be sure, too intelligent to proceed without negotiation. It will be said by the Formalist that the wit here confesses what the narrative mode mendaciously denies, that all is art. This however will not quite do; where birth is once named, real beginning cannot be quite forgotten.

The wittiest of all openings is surely that of *Tristram Shandy*. Here the Horatian opposition between a despised beginning-from-the-egg and an admired plunge *in medias res* is joyously exploded. Tristram, the supposed teller of the story, begins indeed from his own insemination, invoking as he does so, with crack-brained inverse scholarship, the authority of Horace. But Sterne simultaneously bewilders the first-time reader, who is pitched *in medias res,* into the middle of an ill-conducted marital engagement, which is simply unintelligible until we know the *previous* history of those concerned.

Here the comedy works not simply by the incongruous juxtaposition of the formal and the natural, but by a sudden wilful movement (having, I think, real philosophical force) into the territory of the natural, which can be made to appear *inherently* opposed to the notion of a beginning. The ploy is to show, first, that there is something which appears to be a far more radical beginning than birth, namely conception, and *then* to show, in the same breath, that if you *look* at a conception you will find that you are not looking at a beginning but merely at a nodal point in a larger process. Frank Kermode (who was not, as far as I know, thinking of Sterne at the time) had the same thought: "We die," he says, *"in mediis rebus* and are born *in medias res."*[2] To show the conception of Tristram is to show two midlife persons in a relation which is, necessarily, only partly intelligible. They, not he, will fill the screen, if only because they are so much bigger! Sterne, as if in response to this very thought, switches his attention to the microscopic operations of spermatozoa, but here too we encounter not a clear inception but rather a baffled and baffling multiplicity of *process*. . . .

[T]he logical tendency of this insight is to abolish all beginnings from the order of nature . . . with one empty concession: the mystic, inherently uninspectable Genesis of the universe may stand as the sole permissible natural beginning . . . . [Nuttall goes on to point out other plausible "natural" beginnings.] My strong contrast between a confessedly fictional, interventionist opening (Homer) and a natural beginning (Genesis) begins to blur, to transform itself perhaps into a weaker antithesis: between culturally prominent, publicly baptized beginnings, and more fugitive, *shyer* beginnings, which the individual artist chooses to make prominent. . . .

Twentieth-century literature is full of variously elaborated authorial personae and in general a formalist criticism can be happy that this is so. But whenever we hear the beating of the Muse's wings, we shall be aware of the scandal of substance. In Joyce's *Ulysses* we are alerted by the suggestion (with Homeric overtones) of father-and-son relationship. Stephen Dedalus is Telemachus to Bloom's Odysseus. Bloom is a *fictional* parent-self, complicated and ironized by art. Because of the high quotient of distancing, objectifying elaboration he is more persona than Muse (outside not inside the poet's head). But even Bloom is touched by the mystery of subjective, generative power. With Stephen we are certainly nearer to the "I which is not I, but is nevertheless the source of the book." He is by several degrees more firmly objectified, more "wrought," than the Stephen of *Portrait of the Artist* (or, still more, of *Stephen Hero*), but a figure formed from autobiographical recollection, exalted by a name which means "craftsman" must be, in however vestigial a manner, some sort of Muse and not just a coldly controlled fictional persona. Similar things might be said about the shifting, variable figure of Marlow in Conrad's novels.

In the work of Joyce and Conrad there can of course be no question of the authorial double having the uncontested authority enjoyed by the Homeric Muse. That complete, joyously fruitful deference to the supervening voice was never recovered. Literary biographers often overplay the element of historical reference in poetry, but the New Critics and succeeding formalists, conversely, are mysteriously prevented, by the rules of the game they have chosen to play, from noticing that there is a necessary intersection with reality at this point of literary genesis. They are interested in the life of the book but cannot feel its inspiring breath, even when it is warm upon the reader's cheek.

The line I have traced in this book is heavily canonical: a sadly phallogocentric business, some would say, of fathers and sons (with some interference, however, from deviants like Sterne). It may be thought that the line is lost in the twentieth century, but that is not so. Joyce writes "out of" Homer and Eliot "out of" Virgil and Dante. In Eliot indeed we find an acute sense of an inherited poetic task; this American must reverse the pilgrimage of the Plymouth Fathers and, in a quest which seems to belong simultaneously to the worlds of Virgil and Henry James, must make his way through the chattering collage of the Jazz Age to the ancient source of literary strength. *Vergilium tantum vidi,* "I once caught sight of Virgil," wrote Ovid in his *Tristia* (iv. x. 51). Pope told Wycherley how at the age of eleven he sat in a coffeehouse and watched the great Dryden.[3] For Eliot there was no such glimpse, no unbroken sequence of the laying-on of hands. In some ways he was more like Milton (whom he at first instinctively disliked), straining in his proper darkness to hear the voices of a remote past. Like Milton he meditated his *Arthuriad* (*The Waste Land*). Everyone knows that in Eliot "tradition" is a word of power.

The Waste Land begins with the vernal word "April" and at once subjects it to an almost hysterical destruction. It is the cruellest month, breaking up the comfortable oblivion of winter. Then, as the voice of the poet becomes the voices of the poem, overheard fragments of asthenic complaint, after all, reconfirm our original intuition of life in 'April'. The warm forgetfulness under the snow is death and the cruelty of April is the hurt of life. The person who reads much of the night and goes south in winter is a person who, despite the memories of a sharper reality in the different winters of childhood ("hold on tight . . . there you feel free") is now "screening out" reality.

Chaucer's *Canterbury Tales* begins on the same note:

> Whan that Aprill with his shoures soote
> The droghte of March hath perced to the roote
>
> .   .   .   .
>
> Thanne longen folk to goon on pilgrimages

Here the reference to Spring is immediately and unproblematically linked to the notion of a holy pilgrimage to Canterbury. In Eliot the sense that the life implied at the opening may have religious character is simultaneously powerful and wholly indistinct. For those who relish improbable truths I would say that Chaucer's genuine pilgrimage is in some ways like a works' outing, while Eliot's disintegrative excursion is a real pilgrimage (Nevill Coghill would wish me to add, however, that in the long run the authentic character of Chaucer's pilgrimage is harmoniously clear). In *The Waste Land* as in the *Commedia* and *Paradise Lost* there is a negotiation between the disorientation and arbitrariness of art on the one hand and some sort of supernaturally authorized beginning on the other.

Ordinary people who think history and progress are real can sometimes be heard saying, "It was all fields here, when we first came." In Eliot the idea of linear progress is replaced by meaningless cycle or mere flux. It is already evident that we are far from the Virgilian notion of a progressively shaped history, expressing a divine order. We saw the Virgilian historical scheme break up in Dante, whose notion of *imperium* is beginning to betray its weakly retrospective character, leaving an absolute disjunction between the benighted world and the order of eternity. For Eliot, nourished (if that is the word) by the Bradleian Absolute, history can become wise only by confessing its futility. The voyage out becomes a circumnavigation, rotation becomes stillness. The road up and the road down are one and the same.

NOTES

1. Life of Milton, in Johnson's *Lives of the English Poets,* ed. G. Birkbeck Hill, 3 vols. (Oxford: Clarendon Press, 1905), 1:174–75.

2. *The Sense of an Ending* (London: Oxford University Press, 1967), 7.

3. See *The Correspondence of Alexander Pope,* ed. George Sherburn, 5 vols. (Oxford: Clarendon Press, 1956), 1:1–2. See also Joseph Spence, *Observations, Anecdotes, and Characters of Books and Men,* ed. James M. Osborn, 2 vols. (Oxford: Clarendon Press, 1966), 1:25.

20

Problems of Closure in the Traditional Novel

D. A. MILLER (Psychoanalytic critic)

> Que serait le récit du bonheur? Rien, que ce qui le prépare, puis ce le détruit, ne se raconte. [What would be the narrative of happiness? Nothing except that which prepares for it, then that which destroys it, is narrated.][1]
>
> —GIDE

The narrative of happiness is inevitably frustrated by the fact that only insufficiencies, defaults, deferrals, can be "told." Even when a narrative "prepares for" happiness, it remains in this state of lack, which can only be liquidated along with the narrative itself. Accordingly, the narrative of happiness might be thought to exemplify the unhappiness of narrative in general. Narrative proceeds toward, or regresses from, what it seeks or seems most to prize, but it is never identical to it. To designate the presence of what is sought or prized is to signal the termination of narrative—or at least, the displacement of narrative onto other concerns.

It is clear that the category of the nonnarratable cannot be limited to Gide's specification of it (as "le bonheur") in *my* epigraph. What leaves a novelist speechless is not always what makes him happiest, and there's a wide spectrum of ways in which a novel may characterize the function of the nonnarratable. In traditional fiction, marriage is a dominant form of this ne plus ultra, but death is another, and these are not the only ones. Narrative closure may coincide with the end of a quest, as in a story of ambition, or with the end of an inquest, as in a detective story. The closure, moreover, *may* be reinforced by other, secondary determinations, such as a proper transfer of property. But whatever the chosen privatives might be, it is evident that traditional narrative cannot dispense with the function that they motivate—namely, that of both constituting and abolishing the narrative movement. We might say, generally, that traditional narrative is a quest after that which will end questing; or that it is an interruption of what will be resumed; an expansion of what will be condensed, or a distortion of what will be made straight; a holding in suspense or a putting into question of what will be resolved or answered.[2]

272

What I have called the nonnarratable in a text should not be confused with what is merely unnarrated by it. In a broad sense, of course, every discourse is uttered against a background of all those things that it chooses, for one reason or another, not to say. Three subjects that Jane Austen's novels do not treat, for instance, are the Napoleonic wars, the sex lives of the characters, and the labor of the tenants who farm their estates. The first of these is only an unincluded subject of discourse; the second is an unincluded and also forbidden topic; the third is unincluded and perhaps (there are more than sexual taboos) forbidden as well. It is by no means a negligible fact that Jane Austen does not take up these subjects. To notice omissions of this order, however, seems to me mainly useful in establishing the level at which the novelistic representation is pitched (in Jane Austen's case, below the threshold of world history, above the threshold of primary biological functions and of work). This can help us to see the limits and lacunae of the novelistic representation, but it does not adequately account for the dynamics of the representation within the field so defined. Subjects like these have no place—not even the shadow of a place—in the novels, and the novels never invoke them to terminate their discourse. The marriage of the heroine in Jane Austen, on the other hand, does inhibit narrative productivity in this way. The "perfect union" of Emma and Mr. Knightley virtually *must* end the novel; otherwise, it would not be a "perfect" union. It would be brought back to the state of insufficiency and lack that has characterized the novelistic movement. What I am calling the nonnarratable elements of a text are precisely those that (like Emma's marriage) serve to supply the specified narrative lack, or to answer the specified narrative question. It is not the case that such elements cannot be designated by the text's language, or that they literally cannot be mentioned. The nonnarratable is not the unspeakable. What defines a nonnarratable element is its incapacity to generate a story. Properly or intrinsically, it has no narrative future—unless, of course, its nonnarratable status is undermined (by happiness destroyed, an incorrect solution, a choice that must be remade). . . .

In the last analysis, what discontents the traditional novel is its own condition of possibility. For the production of narrative—what we called the narratable—is possible only within a logic of insufficiency, disequilibrium, and deferral, and traditional novelists typically desire worlds of greater stability and wholeness than such a logic can intrinsically provide. Moreover, the suspense that constitutes the narratable inevitably comes to imply a suspensiveness of signification, so that what is ultimately threatened is no less than the possibility of a full or definitive meaning. Thus, novelists such as Jane Austen and George Eliot need to situate their texts within a controlling perspective of narrative closure, which would restore the world (and with it, the word) to a state of transparency, once for all released from errancy and equivocation.

One might say, of course, that this merely reformulates a truth generally acknowledged in every manual for aspiring writers—namely, that there must be conflict to generate a story and resolution to end it. Less simplistically, one might say that the traditional novelist gives play to his discontent only to assuage it in the end, much as the child in Freud makes his toy temporarily disappear the better to enjoy its reinstated presence. Charles Grivel has even argued that the novel's whole reason for being is precisely to *negate* the negativity that is its narrative. The traditional novel would therefore work on the principle of vaccination: incorporating the narratable in safe doses to prevent it from breaking out.

There is also need to deny the novel's attempt to master the narratable. The only real question is whether we can take it for granted that such an attempt perfectly succeeds. The novel may be a game of *Fort! / Da!,* turning on the disappearance and return of a full meaning, but in the cases we have considered, the game seems to have gone beyond this simple ground rule and begins to look like a symptom of the anxiety that its purpose was to master. In a sense, this is the case even in Freud. The seeming binary opposition on which the child's game is founded is in fact radically asymmetrical. The anxiety of disappearance is intrinsically stronger than the gratification of return, for the former is not merely a moment in the game, it is the underlying inspiration for the game itself. Even the gratification of return belongs to the logic of disappearance, since the toy stands in place of a primary, but irrevocably lost, satisfaction (total possession of the mother).

Similarly, I have implied, the narratable is stronger than the closure to which it is opposed in an apparent binarity. For the narratable is the very evidence of the narrative text, while closure (as, precisely, the nonnarratable) is only the sign that this text is over. It is significant that closure in Jane Austen takes the form of a dramatic conversion, a total abandonment of a nonnarratable world. In George Eliot, it takes the form of a mystical, quasi-miraculous experience of whose reality the novelist herself can hardly be sure. The otherness of closure suggests one of the unwelcome implications of the narratable—that it can never generate the terms for its own arrest. These must be imported from elsewhere, from a world untouched by the conditions of narratability. Yet as soon as such a world is invoked in the novels—its appearance is necessarily brief—its authority is put into doubt by the system of narrative itself. The closural world seems less like the absence of the narratable than its strategic denial or expedient repression. The problems of closure (suppression in Jane Austen, ambiguity in George Eliot) testify to the difficulty of ridding the text of all traces of the narratable, even—especially—at the moment when it is supposed to be superseded. Furthermore, just as the child's toy does not answer to what has really been lost, so too, closure, though it implies resolution, never really resolves the dilemmas raised by the narratable. In essence, closure is an act of "make-believe," a postulation that closure is possible. Although we have tried to make clear the moral advantages of this postulation, we have also been concerned to show its self-betraying inadequacy.

There is no more fundamental assumption of the traditional novel than this opposition between the narratable and closure. Even the devious endgames in which Stendhal defers or displaces the moment of closure are played within the orthodoxy of this assumption. The "perversity" we have found in his novels should not mislead us into thinking that they represent a radical break with the "normality" of Jane Austen or George Eliot. Perversity is no less dependent than normality upon the sanction of the law, with the difference, of course, that what the law in this case sanctions are the deliberate infractions on which perversity is founded. Though Stendhal overturns the opposition between the narratable and closure, one cannot say that he overthrows it, and the narrative regime organized by its polar terms proves just as relevant to an understanding of his fiction as it is to Jane Austen's. The appealingly libertarian ways in which Stendhal resists coming to closure, far from breaking this opposition down, may be the most subtle and persuasive means of keeping it in place. Sustained by the sheer insistence of Stendhal's dislike, closure ceases to be a positive ideal without ever surrendering its ideality per se, which is, moreover, rather enhanced than impugned by his attempts to render it unreachable. Yet if the regime of the traditional novel commands even the obedience of so evidently rebellious a subject as Stendhal, then the attractiveness of its governing opposition—between the narratable and closure—needs to be accounted for. To what advantage, we must finally ask, does such an opposition function in the novel? In the end, it may only be that it functions to prove its own possibility. For the most unwelcome implication of all carried by the narratable may well be that *there is nothing to oppose to it.* In this light, Stendhal's notorious resistance to closure would in fact only help him to believe—perversely—in the validity of its claims. His deepest strategy in evading closure would be to conceal the possibility that there is no closure to evade. Instead of the "freedom" that must always be won, there would only be a less joyful instability that could never be *lost.* The texts of all three of the novelists we have considered, then, would display a similar anxiety toward the narratable—an anxiety that Stendhal can turn into positive excitement only because he too believes in quiescence.

Jane Austen would say that conclusion is the moment when we should "have done with all the rest," but George Eliot would tell us instead that this is the moment for reflecting on the inadequacy of our "sample," which like any other risks being mistaken for an all-inclusive paradigm. I have implied, of course, precisely that Jane Austen, George Eliot, and Stendhal triangulate the field of the traditional novel in far more comprehensive ways than their interest as individual cases suggests. Psychoanalytically, the respective corners of the general topography that they typify may be conceived of as the normal, the neurotic, and the perverse; and ideologically, as the conservative, the liberal, and the libertarian. In terms, too, of the narratable and its closure, the three novelists project a triangular generalization, with the value emphases we have associated with Jane Austen reversed in those represented by Stendhal, and both mediated under the name of George Eliot. In defense of the schema, I should point out that the possibilities it fails to admit—psychotic desire, revolutionary politics, a fully effaced closure—are absent from the traditional novel as well. Yet lest, as triangles tend to do, this one persuade us that all the bases have been neatly covered, some cautions may be in order. For one thing, if I have proposed such divisions, I have also suggested that they divide each oeuvre from within itself as much as from one another. The triangle formed by Austen, Eliot, and Stendhal is ultimately only the most developed version of the triangle found in Austen, Eliot, *or* Stendhal. For another, I hope each case we have undertaken to study has been argued differently enough to warrant the inference that other novelists might have been included here with more profit than redundancy. In particular, I regret the absence of a few cases exemplifying special problems that might have complicated our geometry.

The narrative model we have derived from Jane Austen, for example, need not be confined within the small space and domestic scale of her "little bit (two Inches wide) of Ivory." On a far grander historical stage, the novels of Sir Walter Scott display a similar ambivalence toward narrative. On one hand, of course, the historical novel is based on a valorization of history and historical processes, and it might seem as if its attitude to narrative would be more positive. Yet on the other hand, it would be possible to show that the historical novel—at least as practiced by Scott—exists to deprive the course of history, as well as the course of narrative thus motivated, of its necessity. In a novel like *Old Mortality,* the narratable typically coincides with civil discord, which Scott not only deplores, but sees as ideally uncalled for. His reasonable narrator and his reasonable hero, Henry Morton, together offer a perspective in which, if sufficiently stressed, the entire conflict that has generated the novel must be seen as senseless waste. It is telling that Morton, the spokesman of reason, is neither corrupted nor transformed by his participation in the struggle of the novel. The balanced compromise that obtains at the end of the novel does not—*pace* Lukács—emerge from a dialectical process as the result of a conflict of social forces. Rather it is postulated a priori as a principle that *allows* us to see the narrative as at least theoretically dispensable. People make history in Scott only because people make mistakes: both can and should be avoided. Although one might well argue that such an ideology is contested and exposed by the narrative, Scott is Jane Austen's contemporary in a deeper sense than is usually recognized. In a similarly blinded dialectic, narrative remains a "development of every thing most unwelcome."

While the epic implications of this unwelcome development are most fully drawn in the novels of Scott, its erotic consequences are most extremely realized in the work of another, somewhat older contemporary, the marquis de Sade. Sade's reputation as the novelist of an endlessly inventive erotic excess may not seem to promise much in common with the more restrained libidinal economy that operates in Jane Austen. Yet when, as we have seen, desire in Jane Austen is consistently subject to a "repression" that not only intensifies its transgressive and dangerous character, but also (as in the cases of Elinor Dashwood and Fanny Price) positively *maintains* desire as such, then a rapprochement between her kind of fiction and Sadean pornography can no longer be thought outrageous. Moreover, if our reading of Jane Austen has brought her closer to Sade, it would also be possible to broach a reading of Sade that would place him nearer to Jane Austen. Specifically, such a reading would turn on the curious moralism that accompanies the portrayal of Sade's most egregious "crimes of love."

> To instruct man and reform his morals, is the sole motive that we intend in this anecdote. Let one be convinced, by reading it, of the magnitude of the peril that follows close on the heels of those who allow themselves anything to satisfy their desires. May they convince themselves that good education, wealth, talents and the gifts of nature are likely only to lead astray, whereas self-control, good behavior, wisdom and modesty support them and make them worthy: these are the truths that we are going to put into action. Pardon us the monstrous details of the hideous crimes of which we are constrained to speak; is it possible to make one hate similar misdemeanors, if we don't have the courage to offer them plainly?[3]

This is the opening paragraph of *Eugénie de Franval,* a short novel in which the eponymous heroine, seduced by her father, goes on at his instigation to murder her mother. Though the details of the "hideous crime" to which the narrator alludes will thus prove "monstrous" enough, they are apparently not so monstrous as to perturb the confidence with which he here installs his narration *dans le vrai.* Too moral not to have to be "constrained" to speak of such horrors, he is also too moral to need to fear that his laudable task of instructing man and reforming his morals might be undermined by the libidinal force of its own cautionary examples. Announced as a gross violation of natural order, the story is simultaneously kept from bringing the "truth" of this order into question. As matters turn out, moreover, the closure thus positioned at the start is perfectly confirmed at the end, both in Eugénie's self-punishing attack of conscience and in her father's contrite repentance.

If one is still likely to feel that *Eugénie de Franval* is more equivocal than the moral pretensions of its narrator, this is partly because a very different version of his situation occurs within the narrative itself. M. de Clervil, the spiritual director of Eugénie's much-abused mother, is at least as moral as the narrator, but when he is asked to publicize the incest, he declines on the grounds that "the narrative that one makes of it awakens the passions of those who are prone to the same kind of crimes." In his eyes, the narration of incest would give not a negative "leçon" as the narrator contends, but a positive "conseil" (440). This seems closer to our intuitions about the pandemically contagious nature of desire in pornography, but why Sade's narrator would wish to deny this here remains to be explained. Possibly his opening remarks merely make provision for the "redeeming social value" that permits the censorious reader to think he is reading a more edifying text than the one actually before him. Yet the outside evidence goes to show that Sade himself was convinced by the moral force of his story.[4] More plausibly, then, these lines offer only the purest statement of intention. Sade writes them as *an absolute moralist*, for only as such can he become the supreme pornographer, who invokes the law persuasively at every step and so secures for desire the full delectation of its flagrant delicta. The pornographic effect of *Eugénie de Franval* depends crucially on the eagerness of the text to retain all the closural sanctions of the law in the midst of the infractions that constitute it as a narrative. Thus, Sade's pornographic narrator is no less obliged to moralize than, from the other side of the mirror, a moralist like Jane Austen is compelled to narrate the dangerous course of erotic excitement. A radical incompatibility between desire (desire for narrative) and the law (the law of closure) determines the narrative structure that, for different reasons, accommodates both novelists. Jane Austen lets all the evidence of the incompatibility stand, knowing that her text will eventually pass over to the side of the law, where the rest doesn't count. Faced with the same incompatibility, Sade is profoundly more "cooperative": willing to inhabit permanently the (cruel? monstrous? sadistic?) universe in which desire and the law, narrative and closure, are as radically inseparable as they are absolutely at odds.

The limiting prestige of Jane Austen as a miniaturist does not encourage comparisons with Scott or Sade, but the typical character of George Eliot's closural practice in the nineteenth century will be more easily recognized. Balzac is a less persuasive intellect than the translator of Strauss and Feuerbach, but his work similarly exemplifies a closure at once enforced and effaced. Each novel in *La Comédie humaine* has a traditional enough ending (though often, as Roland Barthes points out in what is only the most literal case, taking the form of a mere cutting off of desire[5]), but what is left over is demonstrably capable of producing further narrative. Indeed, these further narratives are our best evidence that something *has* been left over. What better way of having, and not having, one's closure than the device of the *retour des personnages,* where what is most importantly "returned" are not the characters, but the narratable desires they have sponsored. Closure coexists with the possibility of going beyond it in Trollope's Barsetshire and Palliser novels as well. In both novelists, the double vision of closure projected by *Middlemarch* has simply been displaced into the structure of the novel *series.*

Displaced in still another way, the double vision determines the two endings of Dickens's *Great Expectations.* From our perspective, the chief interest of the endings—the first forever parting Pip and Estella, the second forever joining them—lies in the sheer fact that they both were possible. For if either ending wholly regulated the narrative leading up to it, Dickens would simply have been *unable* to change the original without substantially revising the rest of his novel. That the text can issue in either of two opposite resolutions points up the indeterminacy with which, in particular, the function of Estella has been invested. If, as there is reason to suppose, Estella embodies merely the most seductive of Pip's neurotic expectations, then his cure requires she be relinquished along with the others. But if, as there are also grounds for thinking, Estella represents a fairy princess whose worth is only temporarily and superficially obscured, then she is clearly destined to be Pip's reward for his mature self-understanding. The appropriateness of each ending is thus bound to bespeak a certain inappropriateness as well, Pip's sense of recovery in the original ending cannot allay the disappointment that the Estella for whom he was surely meant has married someone else. Neither, in the revised ending, can his happier vision of "no shadow of another parting from her" exclude the history of his blatantly obsessive attachment. One might, of course, dismiss such observations by arguing that, while each ending resolves opposite sides of a textual ambivalence, what counts—and what renders the text perfectly "readerly"—is the mere fact of resolution itself. Whether Pip loses or gains Estella must considerably affect the emphases of our reading, but not its fundamental stability. In either case, the narrative of Pip's cure (involving, as we should by now suspect, his being cured of narrative itself) would stand complete. Such memories of an unrealized "otherwise" as each ending seems to induce would only belong to what Barthes has called the "pensivity" of the traditional novel: the token gesture it makes, *once closure has taken place,* to imply that there may be more to tell.[6]

Yet while the anecdotal opposition between the two endings can be easily collapsed, a structural oscillation operates less vulnerably within each:

between the signs of Pip's cure, ensuring resolution, and the symptoms of his disease, requiring—if not providing—further development. In both endings, evidence of closure coexists, overlaps, and often coincides undecidably with counterevidence of the narratable. The conspicuous notice that the original ending takes of "little Pip," for instance, holds open the prospect of an irrecuperable process of repetition and difference. It is as though the text were underlining, by doubling, the self-contradictory name whose semantic content promises maturation even as its palindromic form threatens endless reversals. And when Estella wrongly takes little Pip for Pip's own child, her uncorrected error not only alludes (like the many other mistaken identities in the novel) to the mistaken *nature* of identity; it brings the allusion forward at the very moment when Pip may be most safely supposed to "know himself." The oscillation between cure and disease persists in the final sentence:

> I was very glad afterwards to have had the interview [with Estella]; for, in her face and in her voice, and in her touch, she gave me the assurance, that suffering had been stronger than Miss Havisham's teaching, and had given her a heart to understand what my heart used to be.[7]

Much as in the Finale of *Middlemarch,* the lines are filled by what they leave untold, as Pip skips from his melancholy last interview with Estella to a time "afterwards" when he can gladly assess it. The ambiguity of his heart as well as of his cure is perfectly maintained by the linguistic discretion of "used to be," which may be considered either a preterite ("used to be but is no longer") or an imperfect ("used to be and continues being"). In addition, this declaration of finality is what most immediately motivates a *further* narrative development, taking place even later than "afterwards": I mean Pip's decision, omitted but fully presupposed by the text, to write his autobiography. The end of narrative thus proves only its rebeginning, as the life concludes in a desire for the life story.

The revised ending deploys a more emphatic closural vocabulary, to which the act of autobiography, together with the need for narrative it implies, may appear irrelevant. Yet even here the details that lay stress on wholeness and quiescence are left ambiguous. "As the morning mists had risen long ago when I first left the forge, so the evening mists were rising now" (460). If we suppose that the evening inverts the morning, the text would clearly be suggesting that the forces of narratability have been turned back upon closure. But if, alternatively, we suppose that one rising simply repeats another, then the text would he telling a different story whose end is not in sight. In support of such a possibility, Estella's last words to Pip, telling him that they "will continue friends apart," bear the same burden as her language has always done; and Pip, who sees "no shadow of another parting from her," once more confers on her text the convenient legibility of his desires. Although one might bridge the gap between Estella's text and Pip's enraptured interpretation by reading the scene as a piece of romantic understatement, it remains the case that the romantic understatement takes the same form as the erotic delusion it ought to leave behind. In the oscillating perspective thus opened up, it becomes clear why Pip, repeating earlier projects, needs to embark on the autobiographical conquest of authority and control—and also why his passage (like the two I have been discussing) will not be altogether smooth.

NOTES

1. André Gide, *L'Immoraliste,* in *Oeuvres complètes,* ed. L. Martin-Chauffier, 15 vols. (Paris: Nouvelle Revue Française, 1932–39), 4:70.

2. See Roland Barthes, "Introduction à l'analyse structurale des récits," 23–25; and Tzvetan Todorov, "Le secret du récit," *Poétique de la prose* (Paris: Seuil, 1971), 151–85.

3. *Les Crimes de l'amour,* in *Oeuvres complètes du marquis de Sade,* ed. Gilbert Lély, 16 vols. in 8 (Paris: Cercle du livre precieux, 1966–68), 10:425. My subsequent comments on this passage are partly informed by Pierre Klossowski, preface to vol. 10 of the *Oeuvres complètes,* and *Sade, mon prochain* (Paris: Seuil, 1945); and by *Georges Bataille, L'Erotisme* (Paris: Minuit, 1957).

4. Sade's claim that "il n'y a ni conte ni roman dans toute le littérature de l'Europe où les dangers du libertinage soient exposés avec plus de force" may be found in his "Catalogue raisonné des oeuvres de M. de S*** à l'époque du 1er octobre 1788," *Oeuvres complètes,* 2:269.

5. According to Barthes, the castration in *Sarrasine* cuts with a double edge. Traditionally, it provides the "final nomination" that ends narrative discourse (*S/Z,* 193–94 and 215–16). Less traditionally, however, it also threatens to unmask the "repleteness" of the classical text, whose seemingly full forms in fact only reproduce the central deficiency of the castrato (pp. 204–206).

6. *S/Z,* 222–23. In a recent reading of *Great Expectations,* where the plot of Pip's cure is powerfully conceived as an attempt to "bind" (in Freud's sense) the mobile psychic energies behind it, Peter Brooks makes a similar point: "We may . . . feel that choice between the two endings is somewhat arbitrary and unimportant in that the decisive moment has already occurred before either of these finales begins. The real ending may take place with Pip's recognition and acceptance of Magwitch after his recapture—this is certainly the ethical denouncement—and his acceptance of a continuing existence without plot, as celibate clerk for Clarriker. The pages that follow may simply be *obiter dicta*" ("Repetition, Repression, and Return: *Great Expectations* and the Study of Plot," 521).

7. Charles Dickens, *Great Expectations* (London: Oxford University Press, 1953), 461.

21

Endings and Contradictions

RACHEL BLAU DUPLESSIS

Once upon a time, the end, the rightful end, of women in novels was social—successful courtship, marriage—or judgmental of her sexual and social failure—death. These are both resolutions of romance. Sometimes the ends of novels were inspirational, sublimating the desire for achievement into a future generation, an end for female quest that was not fully limited to marriage or death. These endings were dominant, related to real practices of sexuality, gender relations, kin and family, and work for middle-class women. The cultural conventions of narrative and depiction by which these relations were, in Raymond William's terms, "performed," were dominant also. No matter what notion of the sex-gender system one uses to explore the relation of women and men, and of women to society, the reproduction of these relations in consciousness, in social practice, and in ideology turns especially on the organization of family, kinship, and marriage, of sexuality, and of the division of all sorts of labor by gender. The point at which these basic formations cross, where family meets gender, where the division of labor meets sexuality, is the heterosexual couple. The "reproduction of the conventions of sex and gender" as well as the maintenance and production of new members of the social order centers on that couple. And depictions of that couple are socially maintained.

Romance plots of various kinds, the iconography of love, the postures of yearning, pleasing, choosing, slipping, falling, and failing are, evidently, some of the deep, shared structures of our culture. These scripts of heterosexual romance, romantic thralldom, and a telos in marriage are also social forms expressed at once in individual desires and in a collective code of action including law: in sequences of action psychically imprinted and in behaviors socially upheld. Romance as a mode may be historically activated: when middle-class

282

Duplesis— Female hero will turn into a heroine who has embraced positive female archetypes and ditties.

women lose economic power in the transition from precapitalist economies and are dispossessed of certain functions, the romance script may be a compensatory social and narrative practice.

Any social convention is like a "script," which suggests sequences of action and response, the meaning we give these, and ways of organizing experience by choices, emphases, priorities. The term offers to social analysis what "ideology" offers to cultural analysis: "a generic term for the processes by which meaning is produced, challenged, reproduced, transformed."[1] Indeed, sociologists and other students of social practices use terms like "scripts" to explain the existence of strongly mandated patterns of learned behavior that are culturally and historically specific, and that offer a rationale for unselfconscious acts. Scripts are also integrated; a whole "social script" is an interlocking group of cognitive and emotional structures.[2]

Simon and Gagnon's analysis, cited here, is particularly valuable because it argues that even so-called instinctual and physical acts like sex are not ever transparent, but are created in and by social life. "It is only because they are imbedded in social scripts that the physical acts themselves become possible."[3] This kind of analysis illustrates that all features of human life, even the most apparently impulsive—and love has sometimes been viewed this way—are organized.

So too literature as a human institution is, baldly, organized by many ideological scripts. Any literary convention—plots, narrative sequences, characters in bit parts—as an instrument that claims to depict experience, also interprets it. No convention is neutral, purely mimetic, or purely aesthetic.

All this is dramatically illustrated by an ironic letter by Virginia Woolf and E. M. Forster on the banning and prosecution of an "unexceptionable" melodramatic novel treating lesbians: Radclyffe Hall's *The Well of Loneliness* (1928). They comment pointedly that social values and, even more, legal apparatus decree that the subject of homosexuality in novels is actionable while "murder and adultery" remain "officially acceptable."

> May they mention it incidentally? Although it is forbidden as a main theme, may it be alluded to, or ascribed to subsidiary characters? Perhaps the Home Secretary will issue further orders on this point. And is it the only taboo, or are there others? What of the other subjects known to be more or less unpopular in Whitehall, such as birth-control, suicide, and pacifism? May we mention these? We await our instructions![4]

This study rests on the proposition that narrative structures and subjects are like working apparatuses of ideology, factories for the "natural" and "fantastic" meanings by which we live. Here are produced and disseminated the assumptions, the conflicts, the patterns that create fictional boundaries for experience. Indeed, narrative may function on a small scale the way that ideology functions on a large scale—as a "system of representations by which we imagine the world as it is."[5] To compose a work is to negotiate with these questions: What stories can be told? How can plots be resolved? What is felt to be narratable by both literary and social conventions? Indeed, these are issues very acute to certain feminist critics and women writers, with their senses of the untold story, the other side of a well-known tale, the elements of women's existence that have never been revealed.

One of the great moments of ideological negotiation in any work occurs in the choice of a resolution for the various services it provides. Narrative outcome is one place where transindividual assumptions and values are most clearly visible, and where the word "convention" is found resonating between its literary and its social meanings. Any artistic resolution (especially of a linear form that must unroll in time) can, with greater or lesser success, attempt an ideological solution to the fundamental contradictions that animate the work. Any resolution can have traces of the conflicting materials that have been processed within it. It is where subtexts and repressed discourses can throw up one last flare of meaning; it is where the author may sidestep and displace attention from the materials that a work has made available.

In nineteenth-century fiction dealing with women, authors went to a good deal of trouble and even some awkwardness to see to it that *Bildung* and romance could not coexist and be integrated for the heroine at the resolution, although works combining these two discourses in their main part (the narrative middle) are among the most important fictions of our tradition. This contradiction between love and quest in plots dealing with women as a narrated group, acutely visible in nineteenth-century fiction, has, in my view, one main mode of resolution: an ending in which one part of that contradiction, usually quest or *Bildung,* is set aside or repressed, whether by marriage or by death. It is the project of twentieth-century women writers to solve the contradiction between love and quest and to replace the alternate endings in marriage and death that are their cultural legacy from nineteenth-century life and letters by offering a different set of choices. They invent a complex of narrative acts with psychosocial meanings, which will be studied here as "writing beyond the ending."

Why are these endings in marriage and death both part of a cultural practice of romance? Marriage celebrates the ability to negotiate with sexuality and kinship; death is caused by inabilities or improprieties in this negotiation, a way of deflecting attention from man-made social norms to cosmic sanctions. This is a practice prominent in the novel from its inception on. For the eighteenth-century novel, Nancy Miller explores exactly these poles governing the heroine's ascent and integration into society and her descent into death. The "euphoric" pole, with its ending in marriage, is a successful integration with society, in which the gain is both financial and romantic success in the heterosexual contract; the "dysphoric" pole, with an ending in death, is a betrayal by male authority and aggression. Miller sees little definitive narrative change in nineteenth-century texts: "The ideological underpinnings of the old plot have not been threatened seriously: experience for women characters is still primarily tied to the erotic and the familial; . . . female *Bildung* tends to get stuck in the bedroom."[6] Even with the growing resistance from subtexts, traced, for example, in *The Madwoman in the Attic* by Sandra Gilbert and Susan Gubar, the "heroine's text" still persists until the ideological and material bases of that narrative choice are sharply modified, not just on an individual, but on a cultural level. This is my subject here. When women as a social group question, and have the economic, political, and legal power to sustain and return to questions of marriage law, divorce, the "couverte" status, and their access to vocation, then the relation of narrative middles to resolutions will destabilize culturally, and novelists will begin to "write beyond" the romantic ending.

In brief, this book argues that there is a consistent project that unites some twentieth-century women writers across the century, writers who examine how social practices surrounding gender have entered narrative, and who consequently use narrative to make critical statements about the psychosexual and sociocultural construction of women. For all the writers selected, the romance plot, as a major expression of these social practices, is a major site for their intrepid scrutiny, critique, and transformation of narrative. . . .

This concern enters their art works, not only in overt content and critical remarks but more drastically in the place where ideology is coiled: in narrative structure. As a narrative pattern, the romance plot muffles the main female character, represses quest, valorizes heterosexual as opposed to homosexual ties, incorporates individuals within couples as a sign of their personal and narrative success. The romance plot separates love and quest, values sexual asymmetry, including the division of labor by gender, is based on extremes of sexual difference, and evokes an aura around the couple itself. In short, the romance plot, broadly speaking, is a trope for the sex-gender system as a whole. Writing beyond the ending means the transgressive invention of narrative strategies, strategies that express critical dissent from dominant narrative. These tactics, among them reparenting, woman-to-woman and brother-to-sister bonds, and forms of the communal protagonist, take issue with the mainstays of the social and ideological organization of gender, as these appear in fiction. Writing beyond the ending, "not repeating your words and following your methods but . . . finding new words and creating new methods,"[7] produces a narrative that denies or reconstructs seductive patterns of feeling that are culturally mandated, internally policed, hegemonically poised.

Virginia Woolf once proposed that "there are only two ways of coming to a conclusion upon Victorian literature—one is to write it out in sixty volumes octavo, the other is to squeeze it into six lines of the length of this one."[8] Choosing approximately the latter course, I propose a brief survey of one main ideological dilemma of nineteenth-century fiction seen by the "Mary Carmichael" who will, in the rest of these pages, be responding to it. The fact that "love was the only possible interpreter" of most of the women in literature, rather than, say, "knowledge, adventure, art," led, Mary Carmichael felt, to a rigidity and inflexibility of social and expressive possibility, to a world that rebuffed women as she knew them, that, indeed, rebuffed herself.[9]

> From somewhere would come an adoring man who believed in heaven and eternal life. One would grow very good, and after the excitement and interest had worn off one would go on, with firm happy lips being good and going to church and making happy matches for other girls or quietly disapproving of everybody who did not believe just in the same way and think about good girls and happy marriages and heaven; keeping such people outside. . . . If Rosa Nouchette Carey [the author summarized] knew me, she'd make me one of the bad characters who are turned out of the happy homes. I'm some sort of bad unsimple woman. Oh damn, damn, she sighed. I don't know.[10]

Writing beyond the ending begins when authors, or their close surrogates, discover that they are in fact outside the terms of this novel's script, marginal to it. For the conventional outcomes of love, of quest, were strongly identified with certain roles for women. Thus Mary Carmichael will act to rescript the novel, so that one kind of narrative love is no longer the only interpreter of the lives she depicts.

The picture of the nineteenth-century novel proposed here has bracketed consideration of alternative circles of characters, such as Nina Auerbach's "communities of women," prefigurations of open form and the ethical and structural loosening of closure, analysis of the plots in which male characters are heroes, and possible distinctions between male and female authors' versions of the plot of romance. It is proposed here that Mary Carmichael was so intent on identifying that with which she disagreed and that by which she felt excluded as a potential character and as a writer that she saw no particular alternatives. We can even sense, without regarding her picture as being damagingly distorted, that she may have exaggerated slightly.

In nineteenth-century narrative, where women heroes were concerned, quest and love plots were intertwined, simultaneous discourses, but at the resolution of the work, the energies of the *Bildung* were incompatible with the closure in successful courtship or marriage. Quest for women was thus finite; we learn that any plot of self-realization was at the service of the marriage plot and was subordinate to, or covered within, the magnetic power of that ending.[11] Look, for example, at how even Elizabeth Barrett Browning, in a work celebrating female vocation, handles the dominating fact of female achievement in *Aurora Leigh:* she makes her hero's work facilitate the romance to be achieved. The famous "book" written by Aurora Leigh is mentioned at two key junctures: once when she talks of her enormous private loneliness, and once when her long-deferred suitor, Romney, talks of how his love for her has been awakened in reading it.

However, the resolution subordinating quest to love reveals much tension. For one, quest is often vital within a narrative, and the nature of the resolution, obeying, as it does, social and economic limits for middle-class women as a group, is in conflict with the trajectory of the book as a whole. So there is often a disjunction between narrative discourses and resolutions, which may be felt as the "patness" of a resolution, or as the ironic comment of an author at closure. There may also be a sense of contradiction between the plot and the character, where the female hero/heroine seems always to exceed the bounds that the plot delineates. Thus the tragic power of certain nineteenth-century female protagonists, the tension between selfless love and self-assertion. An ending in which one part of a structuring dialectic is repressed is a way of reproducing in a text the sense of juridical or social limits for females of one class, when that class ideology encourages striving behavior for males. Yet when that closure is investigated, the repressed element is present in shadowy form. The struggles between middle and ending, quest and love plots, female as hero and female as heroine, class and gender that animate many central novels of the nineteenth century can be posed as the starting point, the motivating inception for the project of twentieth-century women writers.

In *Emma* (1816), by Jane Austen, the problem and charm of the main character lie in the same traits: her resolute and aggressive assurance, making matches as if she were a thoroughly disinterested party, misreading the marital hopes of those she considers her entourage, and interferring with the rational self-interest of many people, but especially of the man in search of a wife. The engagement of Emma's strong will and desire to dominate occurs each time Austen proffers an eligible person; the author graduates the interest of each man and of Emma's involvement until, with Mr. Knightley's apparent attentions to Harriet Smith, Emma is shocked that her impetuous scheming may have hurt her own best interests. At the point when she is sincerely repentant for her assumed powers, she is marriageable, and is therefore proposed to. Her proper negotiation with class and gender makes the heroine from an improper hero.

In wedlock plots like *Pride and Prejudice,* because of the concentration on the heroine's force and her growing capacity for insight, her potential as a hero develops throughout the narrative; this paradoxically contributes to the force of the ending in marriage, by valorizing that social institution because it is the repository of so much personal energy. It is by the mediation of proper gender role that these passages occur. Gender proprieties are clearly implicated in Emma's acceptance ("What did she say?—Just what she ought, of course. A lady always does."), where the lack of dialogue produces discretion and reserve from what had been a babbling girl hero.[12]

Gender proprieties enter, too, into the allusions that the Elton and the Churchill engagements make to other kinds of romance plots—the feverish marriage-market tales of social advantage and the passionate stories of secret engagements. The parvenu economic vulgarity of Mrs. Elton's love of show is more than matched by the possessive romantic vulgarity of Frank Churchill's praise of his "angelic" fiancée, Jane Fairfax, to Emma: "Observe the turn of her throat. Observe her eyes . . . "(*E,* 331). The types of romance plots in these flanking relationships are not as promising for future happiness as is Emma's.[13]

The fact that the men married by these powerful female heroes are older, mature, temperate, and not indelicately passionate makes them trustworthy. The frequency with which such female heroes marry men so much "better" than they—in character sometimes, in wealth and class usually—is a way of using and occupying otherwise superfluous female energy. Rising up the imaginary ladder of maturity or class is a substitution for independent quest. In other cases, a male character is converted by the female, so that improvement of the man she will marry becomes the female's occupation. Often, there is an exchange of educative influence for class ascent. Soon after she accepts the man in the love plot, the female hero becomes a heroine, and the story ends. But despite the dissolving of heroics and the assimilation into community, the tempering of wanton female invention is preserved from dullness by the spritely, deft, and insistent wit of Austen's style. That style buys back into the texture of our experience what we are asked to exclude morally, and in this everlasting exchange between tone and judgment, an antimarriage of author and female hero opposes the marriage of patrician hero and newly invested heroine.

But the tension of achieving the resolution is palpable. The repressed term of the dialectic between love and quest may be readmitted in disguised form to the moment of resolution, because the energy and drive that once motivated the female hero are still powerful enough to be negatively acknowledged and displaced away from the (now) heroine. The last paragraph of *Emma* places that female energy in the jealous and disruptive chatter of Mrs. Elton, who has served the book throughout as an exaggerated and vulgarized picture of Emma's pretensions. Although she is out of keeping with a stability that need not call attention to itself, still she is evoked. So the energies of self-aggrandizement, displaced, can appear at the closure of the narrative, set in a character or a force that opposes the heroine precisely because it is the heroine's own trait factored out. St. John Rivers in *Jane Eyre,* the violent storm in *Villette,* and the flood in *The Mill on the Floss* also serve this crucial narrative and ideological function.

The problem of the resolution in *Jane Eyre* (1847) parallels that of its sister texts: a female character whose *Bildung* Charlotte Brontë made so dramatic and intense that it threatens the resolution in marriage, the "Reader, I married him," in which both *Bildung* and female hero are contained. Both quest and marriage plots form the basis of this work, which is structured as a novel of education and concerns the absorption of a marginalized character into kinship networks. Access to a fulfillment that reiterates the status quo is always facilitated by having a character begin so marginalized, so removed from common sources of satisfaction (family, friends, social situation), that if a plot simply provides such a character with access to what must usually be taken for granted, the atmosphere of gratitude will finally impede any criticism from occurring. The critique of social conditions that orphans symbolize (poverty, vulnerability, exclusion) will be muted by the achievement of the blessed state of normalcy, so thrillingly different from deprivation. Through the mechanism of orphans, novels can present standard family, kinship, and gender relations as if these were a utopian ideal.

The courtship of Jane by Rochester proceeds through a landmine of cunningly intertextual false marriages. There is a hidden wed*lock* with Bertha into which Rochester has been tricked and manipulated because of his former, now smoldering, lust, envy, and pride; that same entrapment he proposes to repeat in a far more subtle form on Jane. Rochester also has a charade "wife," Blanche Ingram, from a masquerade wedding tableau. We are present at a dramatically arrested false marriage ceremony, with Jane as fearful, decorated, enraptured bride. In this array of midbook "marriages," Brontë has created a critical context in which the normal activities of courtship (and the normal narratives as well) take on a lurid and foreboding quality. Jane's bridal veil is rent by the mysterious Bertha herself. But the falsest marriage of all those presented is Jane's complicit temptation to romantic thralldom with Rochester, which she purges through solitary suffering and the amazing discovery of a family cohort.

Jane Eyre may, in an individual or particularist tactic, change the material basis of marriage; when Jane becomes financially independent, the couple is socially interdependent. But Brontë does not change the emotional basis in romantic love. Jane still gives her life to serve Rochester in his humbled and mutilated state. The loss of his eye and his hand is a biblical retribution for adultery, and as such brings cosmic authority to the tempering of the overweening erotic male into a marked adult, more like a battered father than a potent lover. The mutilation also creates the path for Brontë to have Jane accede to a version of norms about wifehood, where husband and household are to receive all her care. When a man is totally confined to the private sphere (for all we are told by the narrative), then female confinement to the same sphere does not seem so narrow. Because he needs her, "as the one help meet for him," her booklong identity of intelligent, loving service, most keen when it is service for a family, is elaborated as her whole future identity. This despite the governessing and self-improvement skills of the female hero.

Her blasphemous energies are also contained because the spiritual blessing of the marriage is affirmed with God as a witness. Toward the end of the novel, as the resolution takes shape, there is a growing emphasis on coincidence, in preference to other more natural patterns of motivation. Brontë insists on providence, in the shape of a god-uncle's legacy, in the intuition for "home" that brings the wandering Jane to her very own cousins, and in the voices that transfix both Jane and Rochester. That Jane is the site at which supernatural forces collect enhances her heroic—even mythic—stature, but it also provides the only tempering structure short of ironic piercing of heroism. For the use of Providence in the latter third of the novel prepares for a resolution that will wean Jane from the cosmic—from St. John's self-idolatry—into the modest and tender feminine usefulness as "prop and guide." Providence, in short, is the only force compelling enough to displace Jane as quester from the heroic center of the novel, as it is the only force patriarchal enough to temper Rochester's earlier blasphemous claims that his Maker sanctioned his sexual schemes.

The second suitor and first cousin of Jane, St. John Rivers, is rejected because of his idolatry, his instrumentality, his pride and delusions of grandeur at the service of British and Christian imperial claims. His manipulative drive and legalistic turns attempting to entrap Jane are severely rejected. Yet the novel ends with an unironic peroration to St. John and his ambition. In the final paragraph, the very last words of the novel even allude to the very last words of the New Testament (Rev. [of St. John] 22:17 and 22:20). The apocalyptic union of the yearning spirit with Christ himself, and the matching cries "I come quickly" and "Even so come, Lord Jesus," mark the displaced reassertion of ambition, quest, and spiritual striving, which no longer reside in the character Jane Eyre. St. John represents the ecstatic trace of all the energies of pilgrimage, mastery,

Handwritten margin notes:

If Jane would give her life to take care of Rochester is this not as religious than daily the moral code of marriage Rochester and Jane

But is marriage religious?

True A HERO? But how much of this has to do w/ magic

Is St. John's proposal blasphemous?

and aggression that have been so central, the social and vocational dynamism rejected for the female hero as she assumes the mantle of heroine-wife.

Here as elsewhere, the female character is embarked on heroic endeavors of resistance, mastery, self-realization, and even personal independence in one of the very few available professions. Yet by the end of the story, the plot has created a heroine, a character whose importance in the society of the book lies in her status as an object of choice and as an educative influence. Her integration into kinship and family bonds is signaled by the production of the infant of the next generation, which ends the story in this one.

Lucy Snowe in Brontë's *Villette* (1853), an English teacher at a repressive boarding school in a foreign land, is launched into vocation by a series of desperate propulsive choices where standing still would have meant annihilation. Yet vocation as such is viewed with great suspicion, always seen as second best. Lucy's outsider's, even voyeur's, views of domestic warmth make her yearn for traditional feminine destinies of protection and Home, even as she abjures the deceitful images that teach proper female behavior in the museum scene and is aroused by female power in the Vashti scene. Yet work and independence are depicted as a "denial and Privation" in a passage in the latter part of the book: to be the headmistress of a pleasant school that she has created is still to have "no true home," and she questions why she will have "Nothing [i.e., husband or children] at whose feet I can willingly lay down the whole burden of human egotism, and gloriously take up the nobler charge of labouring and living for others."[14]

Romantic love is severely judged, as pandering, as hypocrisy, as exclusionary, and it is as severely desired. The heroes and heroines are not Lucy's to touch; in Tantalus fashion they recede, both the upper middle-class stable domesticity of Polly and Graham and the sexual scandal of Ginevra and de Hamel. Lucy tries to break into that circle of heroines, but she is incompletely formed for either saccharine darlingness or salty flirtation. Suffering her increasingly jealous marginalization from these "normal" narratives, she realizes that the plots of the romances that flank her (a sentimental and Gothic novel respectively, for the choice of plots is somewhat like *Emma*) are resistant to the depressive spoiler that she represents.

Thus Brontë has reserved the most complete vocation for her most neurotic character, and that equating of vocation and deprivation makes a textual undertow to the pilgrim's progress. This repressing of love is represented by the apparition of the nun, finally unmasked as a youth who enters the girls' school to seduce a willing student. The nun is the place where sexuality and repression meet, for the figure appears whenever Lucy must force down her already disguised passion. The nun is not used for any associations with spiritual calling, that is, as George Eliot will use St. Theresa, but rather to explore desire and entrapment.

But Lucy's negotiation with love does pose a richly textured alternative to the Gothic and the sentimental, the domestic and the scandalous romances. This alternative intertwines a quest for mastery and love, with Lucy the neophyte and M. Paul the guide, goad, and taskmaster. The relationship seems allusively erotic, with its games of dominance and submission, and full of the allusions to trial and torment, the tests of fortitude and purpose that one often has in quest. With this eroticized quest (and with the little school M. Paul sets up for Lucy as he proposed to her), the possibility for marriage linked with vocation has taken shape and has been sustained for the latter third of the book.

The deprivation and denial that follow express the ideology about narrative women that we are investigating. Even within the last paragraphs of the novel, the couple's forthcoming marriage is expected. But a dire change occurs suddenly. Lucy Snowe is denied the unprecedented resolution of marriage and vocation by a *coup d'auteur:* M. Paul drowns at sea. Readers of "sunny imaginations" who want the happy ending can be left, in the absence of the actual words announcing his death, "to conceive the delight of joy" (*V,* 451). The unprecedented utopian hope of marriage and vocation for the female hero is castigated as reader banality, the reductive yearning for a happy ending. Here too independence and quest have been punished with deprivation of love. The either/or choice between romance and vocation has been as forcefully maintained in this novel as it was in *Jane Eyre.*

The task of *Middlemarch* (1872) claims to be precisely illustrative of the proposition of its Prelude: that some people, women in particular, are born with aspirations and energy, desiring passionate service to an ideal, and yet social circumstances harness them in a narrower yoke. George Eliot speaks to the contradiction between vocation and role in its largest sense: the middling, threatened community of intricate webbings meets the inchoate drive of individual difference. The failure to transcend is stated at the beginning, for the book claims to depict a character or two who could have achieved greatness, but who will end "dispersed among hindrances."

With waste, compromised vocations, failures of marriages, life lived in modest normalcy, the novel's apparent lesson is that life is a necessarily flawed combination of sublime yearning with turgid institutions of all varieties—financial, romantic, social. It is Eliot's triumph in the Garth plot and its educative confrontations to make conventional middle-march wisdom sound both accurate and savory. The Dorothea and Lydgate plots overturn good sense by outrageous desire in varieties of tragicomic wedlock. The same impetuous drives that make for their high ambitions override the sounder processes of temperate choice. Both Lydgate and Dorothea leap into marriage, the one "marrying care, not help," the other marrying misogynistic pettiness, not large-souled breadth.[15] Eliot does not flinch as she works out the closure of possibility in the face of those marriages to Causaubon and Rosamond, the losses of desire and efflorescence in shame and bitterness, and then, with baleful tact, arranges the testing of the characters at that precise nadir.

Because of the misery of her first marriage, the narrative channels Dorothea's ambitions and desires for important action into her passionate declaration to Will Ladislaw, in defiance of Causaubon's last will and testament. The book asks us to applaud this shift from the desire for a grand autonomous life to a reasonable choice of life's companion. Indeed, in this second marriage, Dorothea even achieves fulfillment of part of her original dream "to help someone who did great works" (*M,* 251). So, for the most persuasive of reasons, female quest is rejected and the female helpmeet is again established at the resolution.

But at the end of the book, the narrator asks us to see Dorothea's life as a "sacrifice" and evokes, strangely, "many who knew her" for their opinions that her powers were not well used, or not fully engaged by being "absorbed into the life of another" (*M,* 576). These choral voices are curious, since community opinion and narrator sentiment had been running against the thought offered at the resolution: that Dorothea's strengths should have had a more glorious outlet. The fact that Dorothea herself half believes this is part of her yearning selfhood: "feeling that there was always something better which she might have done, if she had only been better and known better" (*M,* 575–76). That the narrator wants us to believe it seems to express an uncharacteristic reluctance to assent to the novel's tempering conditions. After having used her whole book to suggest with what we must be decently contented in the mellow "home epic" of middle range, Eliot reinserts discontent; the "epic life" suggested in the Prelude remains a permanent and sublime thorn in the side (*M,* 573, xii).

Thus Eliot is making contradictory statements, leaving the novel poised between the female hero's sublime scope, in the Dorothea/St. Theresa analogy, and her generally tragicomic moments, in the Dodo/Dorothea analogy. The contradiction we have identified appears again in the discrepancy between a narrator's opinion and an author's text, which shows that trace of female "ardour" exceeding "the common yearning of womankind" that will contain it (*M,* xiii).

Yet the quest part of the plots at the center of these books propounds something that the marriage plot with difficulty revokes: that the female characters are human subjects at loose in the world, ready for decision, growth, self-definition, community, insight. In the novels that end in marriage, and even some that end in death, there is a contradiction between two middle-class ideas—gendered feminine, the sanctified home, and gendered human, the liberal bourgeois ideology of the self-interested choice of the individual agent. This contradiction is most acutely visible in the voluntary and self-aware acceding of the protagonist to the received notion of "womanhood": "to live for others . . . to have no life but in the affections."[16] The highest expression of the female protagonist's moral and intellectual nobility and aspiration lies in her chosen understanding of her complex position—her influence, but her limits—as a woman. As a gendered subject in the nineteenth century, she has barely any realistic options in work or vocation, so her heroism lies in self-mastery, defining herself as a free agent, freely choosing the romance that nonetheless, in one form or another, is her fate. The female hero turns herself into a heroine; this is her last act as an individual agent.

A contemporary commentator in 1869 argues that there are two ideas about female character: woman is seen as an adjective, in service to man, or as a noun, "created for some end proper to herself."[17] Yet even as a modifier, she makes a statement. For although female narrative life will be structured by marriage, female power is, for a while, expressed in courtship. In the plots involving Jane Eyre, Aurora Leigh, Dorothea Brooks, and Elizabeth Bennet, the clear moment of desire and the female outspokenness that provokes the endgame incorporate back into romance some of the boldness and aggression of quest, making romance temporarily the repository of female will.

Further, as Igor Webb has argued, women have a social power in courtship, given the massive and irreversible social changes of industrial capitalism, changing parental authority, and family ties. The "maintenance of status, system and family has to be negotiated by means of courtship." As well, by the end of the eighteenth century, a middle-class home is neither a workplace nor a place of manufacturing; hence middle-class women have been "stripped of economic functions." Courtship choice then gets portrayed and valued as women's work.[18] Yet by the same token, the deepening division between work and home, and the use of love "with its implicit enfranchisement of women" were difficult to reconcile "with the evident exclusion of [middle-class] women from productive life."[19] Judith Newton's argument interlocks with Webb's: through the mid-nineteenth century, the confrontation of female powerlessness with male power grows more acute; male power is more overt at the same time it is seen as less "natural" and more imposed by community and social relations. Novels register the antonyms of female power in courtship, powerlessness in community, functional action in the love script, un- or underemployment in productive life.[20]

The plot of courtship as social and gender reconciliation begins to break by the latter half of the nineteenth century. The contradiction between love and vocation in plots centering on women is accentuated, and romance (whether marriage or courtship) is less able to be depicted as satisfying the urgencies of, inter alia, self-development, desire for useful work, ambition, and public striving.

If possession of a hero/husband in the romance story stands for possession of a world, the distortions that might lead to the death of the main female character are clearly related. In some cases, the nonpossession of a hero, the nonaccess to marriage will imply the loss of the world (in death); in other cases, possession by a nonhero—the erotic fall—will lead to death.

Flaubert knowingly puts Emma Bovary in her wedding gown at her funeral and then records how that once nubile beauty rots until it has presented itself as an unfillable, gaping hole—his trope for femaleness throughout. Death for the female protagonist in many nineteenth-century texts is the negative print of marriage—all the tones opposite, but the picture unmistakable. The relation of the rules of heterosexual romance to death is clear in a variety of texts. Death comes for a female character when she has a jumbled, distorted, inappropriate relation to the "social script" or plot designed to contain her legally, economically, and sexually. Death is the result when energies of selfhood, often represented by sexuality, at once their most enticing and most damaging expression, are expended outside the "couvert" of marriage or valid romance: through adultery (Mme. Bovary, Edna Pontellier), loss of virginity or even suspected "impurity" (Tess of the d'Urbervilles, Lily Bart), or generalized female passion (Maggie Tulliver, Monica Widdowson). When a character is undernourished and underemployed by the social rules defining her place, she may protest, but even a feeble protest may lead to her doom. Sometimes death comes to a female character who cannot properly negotiate an entrance into teleological love relations, ones with appropriate ends, a character whose marginalization grows concentrically as the novel moves to the end. Death in general is a more than economic arrangement, for the punishment of one desire is the end of all.

When social, familial, and internalized restraints lose their force, when the character, for sometimes the most subtle reasons, has been marginalized or herself chooses experimentally to step aside from her roles, death enforces the restrictions on female behavior. In narrative, then, death is the second line of defense for the containment of female revolt, revulsion, or risk. Death is the price exacted for female critique, whether explicit (*The Awakening*) or implicit (*The Mill on the Floss*). Death occurs as the price for the character's sometimes bemused destabilizing of the limited equilibrium of respectable female behavior—in her acceptance of a wrong man, a nonhero, or in her nonacceptance of a right one. And death occurs because a female hero has no alternative community where the stain of energy (whether sexual or, in more general terms, passionate) will go unnoticed or even be welcomed. This is why, in the twentieth-century critiques, community and social connectedness are the end of the female quest, not death. But in the nineteenth-century texts, death occurs as a "cosmic" or essentialist ending when a woman tests the social and historical rules governing the tolerable limits of her aspirations.

Yet her punishment is often treated as her triumph. Death itself becomes a symbolic protest against the production of a respectable female and the connivances of a respectable community. So in texts ending with death, there is often a moment of protest—social energy or a desiring life—just as in the marriage ending, the protest is autonomy or vocation. When the character wants more and more, certainly more than she is allowed, yet can get less and less, the flare of energy or desire surrounding the death is the trope of "more": the buzzing bees and flowers in Kate Chopin, the imaginary baby's nestling head in Edith Wharton, Tom's cry "Magsie" in George Eliot.

Lily Bart in Edith Wharton's *The House of Mirth* (1905) is an elegant marriageable woman, who is marginalized from a promising, dull marriage into greater depreciation and desperation. Never fully acquiescent, a little reluctant to settle, to obey the particular codes, although she is not ignorant of them, she always tries to gain a more favorable conjuncture and to keep every option open. She lacks an unquestioned complicity with the economic and social circumstances of the speculative marriage and divorce market, which she plays like a gambler. She is too daring for stolidness, yet too scrupulous for some of the more sordid exchanges of money and love in which she is, nonetheless, partially implicated.

Lily Bart is, in more ways than one, open to speculation. If gambling is one root metaphor, prostitution is another. Lily will never marry because she can't decide among the forms of prostitution and their various grades, from respectable to sordid, yet she cannot renounce the life altogether. She is an ornamental object to be purchased; she takes money for her charms. Yet she tries to gain without giving, a fact vulgarly, dangerously presented to her by Gus Tranor in his attempted rape. If never seduced, she is more and more compromised.

Lily's ambiguous suicide, occurring as a gambled side effect ("one chance in a hundred") of delivering herself from the temporary insanity of insomnia, is not willed; thus it is like all of Lily's decisions when she does not see that one option may genuinely foreclose another. In its coming, death is sensual, a seduction into the drug climaxing in her illusion of maternal bliss. Lily has been compromised by money, time, sexuality: all the high-risk components of female life. And yet she has arranged herself as a beautiful object so that her bier resonates with both narcissism and the failed community of the earlier tableaux scene.

The analogies with *The Awakening* are clear. The rules invented by a newly awakened but socially powerless individual cannot survive the impact of real power. When, at the end of Kate Chopin's *The Awakening* (1899), Edna Pontellier swims out to sea to commit suicide, she returns thereby to the scene of her double awakening into sexuality and autonomy. The death of Edna is her response to several kinds of possession—by husband, by lovers, by children: "They need not have thought that they could possess her, body and soul." She thereby expresses her opinion that she is her own to dispose of. Yet all avenues of apparent freedom—including adultery and the artist's life, which is itself half an expression of sexual freedom—had led to the dead end of oppressive ties. Feminine revolt comes up against the greater flexibility of society; her husband has face-saving strategies to declare that she has never really revolted. These being the rules of the world, her suicide is a protest of transcendent and acontextual—that is, impossible—autonomy. She has claimed for herself the script of death usually punitively accorded female characters in her position.

The laws governing marriage, sexuality, and dependence are so insistent in the nineteenth-century texts because the practices of gendering make them so, given the relative absence of historical possibility for women's public life. In *The Mill on the Floss* (1860), we begin at the beginning of women's narrative death: in childhood. Maggie Tulliver, like most female characters, is born into a code that calls for asymmetrical damage. She is warm, passionate, forceful, and even talented; she can do nothing with this but learn imperfectly to transfer her "wide hopeless yearning" for purpose and action into an almost depressive longing for dependency and love.[21]

As a sign of this limit to her energy, although Maggie would like to "read no more books where the blond-haired women carry away all the happiness," it isn't the love plot as a whole that she questions, just the convention that the dark-haired girl is always "the rejected lover" (*MotF,* 290–91). Maggie's hopeful substitution of dark for fair is just one more proof of the convention; she can rescript nothing. Her half-intended half-elopement with her cousin's fiancé is rejected too late for her to avoid suspicious taint.

Maggie has always been disruptive and intrusive while wanting never to be so. Repressing her power, she yearns for male approval, and during the scandals she creates by her need for love, she is torn between familial/fraternal and sexual love in ways she can barely negotiate, unequipped to choose between options for which her needs are all so intense. As a narrative idea, Maggie is Eliot's decisive measure of the degree to which only narrow norms of female behavior can be socially tolerated. The various situations in which she is caught are like the test for the witch on which Maggie is catechized early in the novel. If she drowns, she is proven innocent. At the end, Maggie will be so tried, proven innocent, but found dead.

But innocent of what? The simultaneous death of her brother, Tom, is a clue. Insofar as this novel concerns the double *Bildung* of the little brother and sister, it makes pointed comments about the values and rewards offered to the polarized sexes. The novel shows how gender is created in children, the differentials of behavior and values. Tom is without feeling and emotional depth, even cruel; Maggie is vulnerable to the point of masochism. Like other successful men, Tom has goals, skills of hard work, sublimation; he shares the dutiful, rigid, self-righteous character of male success. Women's talents are qualified out of existence; if Maggie is "quick" she must necessarily be "shallow" (*MotF,* 134). The flood, proof that quick water may also be very deep, is thus affiliated with the frustration of the female character.

The flood that carries the brother and sister to their deaths indicates all the capacities that they have repressed in order successfully to become male and female. The death is also Maggie's passion unrecognized, repressed, roiling up to bear them down; this is her dammed-up selfhood and her passionate desire for life, which cannot be repressed. A complex mixture of nature and culture combines to form the killing force. Tom and Maggie could almost navigate the flood with its currents, but the stuff made by people—the machinery—borne on that instinctual flood drags them under. For a brief moment the flood is the breaker of boundaries, the temporary end of gender scripts, creating the "undivided" embrace of two "daisy-field" children, with allusions to a *liebestod* almost incestuous. The flood also breaks the family mill, which ground them all exceedingly fine. In short, the flood briefly destroys the oedipal nexus of gender. But when the waters recede, the landscape has not changed all that much.

What we have discovered in the marriage/death closure in the romance plot is a "place" where ideology meets narrative and produces a meaning-laden figure of some sort. What we will study in the twentieth-century texts is the desire to produce several different figures at that place where text meets values.

NOTES

1. Michele Barrett, *Women's Oppression Today: Problems in Marxist Feminist Analysis* (London: Verso, 1980), 97.

2. John H. Gannon and William Simon, *Sexual Conduct: The Social Sources of Human Sexuality* (Chicago: Aldine, 1973), 19–26.

3. Ibid., 9.

4. Woolf and Forster, "The New Censorship," *Nation & Athenaeum,* September 8, 1928, 726.

5. Louis Althusser, *For Marx,* trans. Ben Brewster (London: New Left Books, 1977), 233.

6. Nancy K. Miller, *The Heroine's Text: Readings in the French and English Novel, 1722–1782* (New York: Columbia University Press, 1980), xi, 151, 157.

7. Virginia Woolf, *Three Guineas* (New York: Harcourt, Brace and World, 1938), 143.

8. Virginia Woolf, *Orlando* (New York: NAL, 1960 [1928]), 190.

9. Virginia Woolf, *A Room of One's Own* (New York, Harcourt, Brace and World, 1929), 87, 89.

10. Dorothy Richardson, *Backwater* (1916), in *Pilgrimage* (New York, Popular Library, 1976), 284.

11. A note on terms. What I mean by the female hero is a central character whose activities, growth, and insight are given much narrative attention and much authorial interest. When I mean heroine—the object of male attention or rescue—I will use that term. A quest plot may be any progressive, goal-oriented search with stages, obstacles, and "battles," which in general involves self-realization, mastery, and the expression of energy, where this may be at the service of a larger ideology (e.g., in *Pilgrim's Progress* or in *Percival*). What I call a romance or marriage plot is the use of conjugal love as a telos and of the developing heterosexual love relation as a major, if not the only major, element in organizing the narrative action. In its more virulent or purist strain, the romance plot asserts that *amor vincit omnia* [love conquers all].

12. Jane Austen, *Emma* (New York: Norton, 1972), 297. Further citations in the text, abbreviated as *E.*

13. The voluntary and profound good sense in marriage that comes to the female hero is often contrasted with a conventionally feminine character. For the female protagonists tend to triumph, by their moral depths and willed choices, over the shallow, superficial, and even designing versions of femininity depicted in the novels. This type of character may even extract a malicious or deceitful revenge for her powerlessness, while at the same time being incapable of nobility: Rosamond in *Middlemarch,* Ginerva in *Villette,* Blanche Ingram in *Jane Eyre.*

14. Charlotte Brontë, *Vilette* (London: Dent, 1974), 329.

15. George Eliot, *Middlemarch* (New York: Norton, 1977), 522. Further references in text, abbreviated as *M.*

16. John Stuart Mill and Harriet Taylor Mill, "The Subjugation of Women" (1869), in *Essays on Sex Equality,* ed. Alice S. Rossi (Chicago: University of Chicago Press, 1970), 141.

17. Frances Power Cobb, "The Final Cause of Woman," in *Women's Work and Women's Culture,* ed. Josephine E. Butler (London: Macmillan, 1869), 6.

18. Webb, *From Custom to Capital: The English Novel and the Industrial Revolution* (Ithaca, N.Y.: Cornell University Press, 1981), 171, 168.

19. Ibid., 175.

20. Judith Newton, *Women, Power, and Subversion: Social Strategies in British Fiction, 1778–1860* (Athens: University of Georgia Press, 1981), 10–11.

21. George Eliot, *The Mill on the Floss* (Boston: Houghton Mifflin, 1961), 252. Further references in the text abbreviated *MotF.*

22

Reading Beginnings and Endings

PETER RABINOWITZ

PRIVILEGED POSITIONS

If you ask someone familiar with *Pride and Prejudice* to quote a line from the novel, the odds are that you will get the opening sentence. Similarly, most readers of *The Great Gatsby* have a stronger recollection of its final image than of most of the others in the text. This is not because those passages are inherently more brilliant or polished or interesting than their companions. Rather, out of all the aphorisms and images that these novels contain, these gain special attention because of their placement. For among the rules that apply quite broadly among nineteenth- and twentieth-century European and American prose narratives are rules that privilege certain positions: titles,[1] beginnings and endings (not only of whole texts, but of subsections as well—volumes, chapters, episodes), epigraphs, and descriptive subtitles. As Marianna Torgovnick puts it, "It is difficult to recall *all* of a work after a completed reading, but climactic moments, dramatic scenes, and beginnings and endings remain in the memory and decisively shape our sense of a novel as a whole."[2] Placement in such a position does more than ensure that certain details will remain more firmly in our memory. Furthermore, such placement affects both concentration and scaffolding: our attention during the act of reading will, in part, be concentrated on what we have found in these positions, and our sense of the text's meaning will be influenced by our assumption that the author expected us to end up with an interpretation that could account more fully for these details than for details elsewhere.

The concentrating quality of a detail in a privileged position can be demonstrated by looking at *Anna Karenina*. The novel has a large cast of characters—

300

so large that we might hardly notice Anna's arrival were the novel not named for her. But because of the title, we know from the beginning that we should look at the other characters in their relationship to her, rather than vice versa. Since they are the ground and she the figure, we pay more attention to her appearance and to the initial description of her character than we do to Dolly's. Of course, one could well argue that the novel is structured so that even without the title, we would eventually concentrate on Anna rather than on Dolly. That is undoubtedly true, but it does not contradict the importance of the title; it merely suggests that the title does more to orient our reading at the beginning of the book than in the middle and the end. And even so, our reading experience would be quite different if the title were *Levin.* Similarly, we know we are expected to pay special attention to the dog that Gerasim rescues halfway through Turgenev's "Mumu" because she is the title character. The effect is all the stronger because until this point, the title has been a source of puzzlement.

One way to highlight how titles concentrate the process of reading is to consider cases where novels have alternate titles, or where alternate titles were seriously considered. When a novel's cover proclaims *Pride and Prejudice,* we are immediately alert to certain contrasts. While the book incorporates a number of other oppositions as well (young/old, male/female, mother/daughter, rich/poor, light/dark, city/country), no reading could ever control them all—and Austen's choice of title makes it clear where she wanted us to put our attention first. The resulting experience is quite different from the one that would have been encouraged had the novel been published under the title that Austen used for her first version, *First Impressions.* With the early title, we would have been more alert to the elements *common* to Darcy and Elizabeth than to their differences (the fact that both exhibit pride *and* prejudice is beside the point; the published title encourages us to look initially for contrasts rather than for unity), and we would be more prepared on first reading to see Elizabeth's reaction to Wickham as part of the same package as her reaction to Darcy. In addition, the title *Pride and Prejudice* prompts us to concentrate on character, whereas *First Impressions* encourages us to concentrate on plot—more specifically, on change. Pride and prejudice are static qualities that may or may not be transformed, but first impressions imply the existence of second (and different) impressions.

Whatever one feels about the trial of *Madame Bovary,* therefore, the prosecutor Pinard had reasonable critical justification for starting with the title in order to get at the novel's central meaning.[3] First sentences operate in a similar way. "All happy families resemble one another, but each unhappy family is unhappy in its own way."[4] So begins *Anna Karenina,* and from the beginning, the authorial audience is encouraged to pay more attention to family life than, say, to politics, which in this novel is subsidiary to individual action. The reader is further advised to see the novel in terms of a basic opposition between "happy" and "unhappy," and, more explicitly, to see happiness as a form of one's unity with others and unhappiness as a form of difference. No one could argue that the first sentence is essential to the book in the sense that if it were not there we would feel its lack. But without that sentence, the didactic message of the novel would be slightly muted, and it would thus engender a different reading experience for the authorial audience.

Titles not only guide our reading process by telling us where to concentrate; they also provide a core around which to organize an interpretation. As a general rule, we approach a book with the expectation that we should formulate an interpretation to which the title is in fact appropriate. This retrospective process of interpreting a completed book will be discussed in more detail in chapter 5, but a few examples may be useful here. The title of James Cain's *Postman Always Rings Twice* does little to direct our attention as we are reading. There are no postmen in the novel, and while it is eventually obvious that the title is metaphoric, it is not immediately clear just what the import of the metaphor is. At the beginning of the novel, perhaps, after the first murder attempt fails, it might warn us to expect a second—as if the title were a twist on "Opportunity knocks but once." But by the end, we are encouraged to give a fatalistic reading of the text, because it is only in the context of such an interpretation that the title is appropriate. It is not only that Frank and Cora fail, but that they *had* to fail.

Ford Madox Ford's *Some Do Not . . .* provides a more elaborate example of how a title can serve as a skeleton on which to build an interpretation. As in all of the novels that make up *Parade's End,* the title has multiple meanings because the phrase is used in a number of different contexts. Its first appearance after the title comes in a privileged spot as well: a citation, at the end of a section, typographically set off:

> The gods to each ascribe a different lot:
> Some enter at the portal. Some do not.[5]

The phrase returns near the close of part I (chap. 7, also in a privileged position, half a page from the end), after General Campion has run into Tietjens and Valentine's horse. When Tietjens decides to stay with the animal, the fly driver says, "But I wouldn't leave my little wood ut nor miss my breakfast for no beast. . . . Some do and some . . . do not" (149; ellipses in original). Later, when a "dark man" offers to help keep Tietjens out of the war, Tietjens tells him that he really wants to join the army; the dark man says, "Some do.

Some do not" (229; pt. 2, chap. 3). At the end of part 2, in chapter 5, after Valentine agrees to become Tietjens's mistress, the phrase becomes explicitly sexual: "'That's women!' he said with the apparently imbecile enigmaticality of the old and the hardened. 'Some do!' He spat into the grass, said: 'Ah!' then added: 'Some do not!'" (284). But a few pages later, he realizes, "We're the sort that . . . *do not!*" (287, pt. 2, chap. 6; ellipses in original).

The primary function of Ford's technique is not to create linguistic paradox by showing the multiple meanings latent in the title's language (although it does do that). Rather, the repetition of the title pressures the authorial audience to tie together the contexts in which the phrase appears and to interpret a number of apparently separate concerns (optimistic hope for the future, proper care for animals, willingness to fight in the war, and sexual honor) as in fact variations on a single theme. One might argue that the unity would be there without the title. Still, without the title to predispose the reader to notice its repetitions in the text, he or she would not be so likely to see them at all, much less to see them as contributing to a thematic unity. To put it another way: without the title, a reader who claimed to find this linguistic web uniting these disparate passages might reasonably be criticized for stretching things; with the title, a reader who refused to accept the connections could reasonably be accused of denseness. But this accusation carries weight only in a community where there is a prior agreement to privilege titles.

Last sentences, of course, cannot serve to focus a reading experience (at least, not an initial reading experience). But they do often serve to scaffold our retrospective interpretation of the book. The final image of Dashiell Hammett's *Glass Key* is Ned Beaumont staring at an empty doorway. Anywhere else in the novel, we might well slide over such a bland detail. By putting it at the end, though, Hammett is urging his reader to privilege that blankness and to tie it to all the other doors and entryways into mysterious psychological blanks that give the book much of its character.

Not *all* novels privilege opening and closing sentences; different genres stress different points to different degrees. Still, it is telling that novels that do not privilege the opening often make some linguistic gesture to signal their departure from the general rule. *The Postman Always Rings Twice* is a case in point. The opening paragraph tells us how our narrator, Frank, has been thrown off a hay truck. It gives us a general sense of his character, but we can tell that it is intended as introductory material (like the introduction of a sonata-form movement), rather than as the beginning of the exposition, because of the way that Cain begins the second paragraph: "That was when I hit this Twin Oaks Tavern."[6] The syntactic device "that was when" serves to inform us that this is the important point of departure. . . .

RULES OF NAMING, BUNDLING, AND THEMATIZING

Once done reading a text, readers usually try to tie it up in some way. If a text is short and simple, especially if it has a clear point, this may not prove difficult, any more than it is difficult to get a quart of milk from the checkout counter to your car. But a major text in our tradition is apt to be more cumbersome—and readers need some kind of packaging that allows them to treat it conveniently as a whole, just as they need paper bags and carts when doing more elaborate shopping. There are a number of ways in which texts can be packed up. . . .

Perhaps the most important bundling technique, however, involves the rule of conclusive endings. The ending of a text is not only to be noticed; there is also a widely applicable interpretive convention that permits us to read it in a special way, as a *conclusion,* as a summing up of the work's meaning. Marianna Torgovnick puts it especially strongly: "An ending is the single place where an author most pressingly desires to make his points—whether those points are aesthetic, moral, social, political, epistemological, or even the determination not to make any point at all."[7] I would phrase it differently: readers *assume* that authors put their best thoughts last, and thus *assign* a special value to the final pages of a text. It is particularly easy for the reader to do so, of course, when the ending is apparently congruent with the text that precedes it—for instance, the moral of a traditional fable or the marriage of a traditional paperback romance. As E. M. Forster puts it, "If it was not for death and marriage I do not know how the average novelist would conclude."[8] Endings, however, are not always so neat, and when they are not, the reader is often expected to reinterpret the work so that the ending in fact serves as an appropriate conclusion. Take, for instance, Lucas Beauchamp's demand for a receipt at the end of Faulkner's *Intruder in the Dust.* We not only notice it because of its privileged position, we are also expected to interpret the novel in such a way that it serves as a satisfactory summing up. In particular, it serves to undercut Gavin's political pronouncements—for the only way to turn that ending into a summation is to assume that Gavin, in contrast to Chick, has failed to attain the wisdom that would make him worthy of Lucas's trust and friendship. Similarly, Huckleberry Finn's decision to "light out for the Territory" could, taken out of context, be read as an introduction to adventures to come, but its placement in the novel we have requires us to read it as a conclusion—a final response—to what he has already experienced.

This is the general reading strategy that allows readers to deal with the formal contradictions that I mentioned at the end of the previous section of this chapter. To exemplify the process, I would like to look at some of the ways that the expectations aroused by the second metarule of configuration—the metarule that leads us to expect balance in a text, to expect that the ending will somehow be prefigured in the beginning—can be apparently frustrated, and the interpretive operations that readers are likely to use to restore balance. Specifically, I will look at two ways in which balance can be upset: through violation (deceptive cadence) and through exaggeration (excessive cadence).

1. Kenneth Burke suggests that formal excellence requires that a work's ending fulfill—perhaps after considerable teasing—the promises with which it begins. But novels often have endings that do not simply surprise (to surprise, after all, is not necessarily to contradict) but that seem, when we get to them, flagrantly to defy what has come before—which end, as Ives's Second Symphony does, with what musicians call a deceptive cadence. Ambrose Bierce's "Dame Fortune and the Traveler" provides a transparent example:

> A weary Traveler who had lain down and fallen asleep on the brink of a deep well was discovered by Dame Fortune.
>
> "If this fool," she said, "should have an uneasy dream and roll into the well men would say that I did it. It is painful to me to be unjustly accused, and I shall see that I am not."
>
> So saying she rolled the man into the well.[9]

The fable's detour around the expected tag line—especially since it moves in the name of a kind of cynical realism—jolts the authorial audience into questioning the validity of the moral it expected. This is because, by the general rule of conclusive endings, readers are invited to revise their understanding of the beginning of the text so that the ending, which at first seems a surprise, turns out to be in fact prefigured. One common way of doing this is by "thematizing" the jolt so that it becomes the very subject of the text. Thus, Torgovnick argues about *Sentimental Education:*

> Any shift in time-scale at the end of a novel ordinarily involves a movement forward in time; Flaubert parodically inverts this traditional element by having the novel end with an "incident" that had occurred before the beginning of the novel's action. The inversion has thematic value, for it indicates that our heroes' journey through life is regressive rather than progressive.[10]

More generally, the undermining of a conventional ending tends to stress the conventionality of that closure, and hence makes us aware of the gap between the authorial and narrative audiences. In works that present themselves as jests—works, like S. J. Perelman's parodies, that are intended primarily to charm—it is possible to interpret the opening of the gap as an end in itself, as a source of surprise and hence amusement. But in works that have greater pretensions to seriousness, we assume, in the absence of instructions to the contrary, that the undermining of a convention is to be read at least in part as a critique of that convention.

There are, in general, two directions such a critique can take. If the primary subject of the work in question is art itself, then we can assume that the convention is being questioned from an aesthetic point of view. Pushkin's ostentatious refusal to wrap up the plot at the end of *Eugene Onegin,* for instance, seems—given the discussion of poetry throughout the text—to be a commentary on literary convention itself.

If, on the other hand, the work seems to be trying to make a statement about the world, we will start off assuming that the convention is being criticized for its falseness when held up to the outside world—at least, the outside world assumed by the authorial audience. Take, for instance, Mark Twain's *Pudd'nhead Wilson.* At first, the text may seem but a variant of the traditional Cinderella pattern. In this plot, an impoverished but deserving person is cruelly abused, even enslaved, but he or she endures and is eventually discovered (usually through some bizarre coincidence, often involving switched infants) and rewarded with wealth and rank. Twain's novel tells the story of a black woman who, to save her child (who looks white) from being sold down the river, substitutes him for the son of one of the local aristocrats. In a climactic courtroom scene, the deception is uncovered, and the true freeman, the virtuous Valet de Chambers, who has spent the first two decades of his life as a slave, discovers that he is heir to a fortune. But just as we are about to delight in his success, there is an unexpected twist.

> The real heir suddenly found himself rich and free, but in a most embarrassing situation. He could neither read nor write, and his speech was the basest dialect of the negro quarter. His gait, his attitudes, his gestures, his bearing, his laugh—all were vulgar and uncouth; his manners were the manners of a slave. Money and fine clothes could not mend these defects or cover them up; they only made them the more glaring and the more pathetic. The poor fellow could not endure the terrors of the white man's parlor, and felt at home and at peace nowhere but in the kitchen. The family pew was misery to him, yet he could nevermore enter into the solacing refuge of the "nigger gallery"—that was closed to him for good and all.[11]

This does more than joke about art; it forces the authorial audience to question the ideological assumptions behind the convention: the belief that if we could somehow make our fortunes, we could easily transcend any limitations in our upbringing.

One of the primary targets for many nineteenth- and twentieth- century novelists has been closure itself. The term *closure,* unfortunately, has been confused by its application to at least two radically different concepts. On the one hand, closure can refer to the way a text calls on readers to apply rules of signification; in this sense, a text is "open" if its symbolic meanings are not restricted. Maeterlinck's play *Pelléas and Mélisande,* with its vague but resonant symbols, is open in this way, and it is presumably in this way that Renée Riese Hubert is using the term when she argues that "the modern work of art is essentially open, proposing a dialectic between the work and its interpreter."[12] But closure can also refer to the way that a text utilizes rules of configuration; in this sense, a work is "open" when, for instance, the plot remains unresolved and incomplete even at the end. In this second meaning, *Pelléas,* where both the mismatch of Mélisande's marriage to Golaud and the oddly innocent passion of her adulterous/incestuous love affair with Pelléas are rounded out by the deaths of the lovers, is a fairly closed text.

In the argument that follows, I will be talking about this second kind of closure. More particularly, I would argue that many realistic writers prefer endings in which the full consequences of the events portrayed—even the consequences immediately pertinent to the narrative at hand—are neither worked out nor clearly implied. *Crime and Punishment,* as I've noted, ends with Raskolnikov looking toward the future.

> At the beginning of their happiness at some moments they were both ready to look on those seven years as though they were seven days. He did not know that the new life would not be given him for nothing, that he would have to pay dearly for it, that it would cost him great striving, great suffering.

Now it is true that such unresolved endings are sometimes rounded off with a desultory closing of the door, such as the final paragraph of *Crime and Punishment,* which follows the passage just cited.

> But that is the beginning of a new story—the story of the gradual renewal of a man, the story of his gradual regeneration, of his passing from one world into another, of his initiation into a new unknown life. That might be the subject of a new story, but our present story is ended.[13]

Similarly, Robert O'Brien's book for young readers, *The Secret of NIMH,* ends with important unanswered questions about what has happened to some of the major characters, as well as about what will happen in the future. But it still includes the final gesture that brings down the curtain in so many children's stories: "They went to sleep."[14] These easy assertions of well-roundedness, however, do not make these texts substantially different from texts that are more blatant in their failure to tell the whole story, such as Chekhov's "Lady with the Dog," which ends with the following paragraph:

> And it seemed to them that they were within an inch of arriving at a decision, and that then a new, beautiful life would begin. And they both realized that the end was still far, far away, and that the hardest, the most complicated part was only just beginning.[15]

It is important to realize that such lack of closure does not mean lack of *conclusion*. By the rule of conclusive endings, the authorial audience will take these open endings and assume that openness itself is part of the point of the conclusion.[16] It will not, however, treat these texts as it treats *Eugene Onegin,* for in *Crime and Punishment, The Rats of NIMH,* and "The Lady with the Dog," art itself is not the primary subject. Thus, the authorial audience is more likely to thematize the apparent incompleteness as an attempt by the author to cast doubt on the social and philosophical implications of the traditional well-made story—most specifically, the implication that stories really do have endings, that lives ever reach a state of rest. "That is the story," writes Alice Walker in "Advancing Luna—and Ida B. Wells." "It has an 'unresolved' ending. That is because Freddie Pye and Luna are still alive, as am I."[17]

Of course, different conventions have different ideological implications—and even the same convention (or its overturn) may have different meanings in different texts, depending on when, where, by whom, and for whom it was written. Thus, for instance, when W. S. Gilbert mocked the Cinderella story in *H.M.S. Pinafore,* he may have been ridiculing certain class pretensions, but he apparently did not see the power of those class pretensions to warp personality beyond redemption. He may have thought that the lucky break was unlikely, but there is no textual indication that he did not believe that with luck the individual could transcend class. Twain sees the convention in radically different terms, for he sees class as *forming* the individual to begin with. Attacks on well-roundedness, too, bear a different ideological weight in different contexts. "The Lady with the Dog," for instance, reflects Chekhov's sense that humans always have to deal with concrete particulars rather than generalities, and that the course of an individual's future is therefore always unpredictable. In Chandler's *Big Sleep,* as I will show in more detail . . . , the attack on well-roundedness reflects a political critique of a certain notion of crime promulgated by the classical detective story. The novel violates the primary conventions of the genre, and the rule of conclusive endings allows the reader to treat these violations as a statement, specifically as an attack on the vision of the world that the traditional conventions imply.[18]

2. So far, I have considered only deceptive cadences. Thematizing a text's conclusion is more complex still when a convention is undermined not by overthrowing it, but rather by following it in such an ostentatious way that it looks absurd—where the cadence is not deceptive, but excessive. Farce is particularly apt to use this mode. In Ludovic Halévy's libretto for Offenbach's *Ba-Ta-Clan,* which concerns a revolutionary conspiracy in China, tragedy is averted at the last moment when it turns out that all the major characters are secretly French. A more pointed example is the rescue of Macheath in Brecht's *Threepenny Opera.* Even without Peachum's explicit criticism of the falseness of the ending ("In reality, their end [i.e., that of the poor] is generally bad. Mounted messengers from the Queen come far too seldom"),[19] the intended reader would have little trouble concluding that he or she should take the arrival of the mounted messenger as a criticism of the lack of realism inherent in all such last-minute rescues.

But the technique can be subtler as well. Southworth's *Allworth Abbey* provides a telling case. Annella Wilder is one of those dashing Southworth heroines like Capitola in *The Hidden Hand*—courageous, spirited, prepared for action while the men wring their hands in despair unable to think of what to do. She seems destined for a life of independence. Yet when the romantic couples are being united in that culminating series of marriages that ends so many comic novels, we find that Annella, too, has been paired up—with Valerius Brightwell. Annella has had no heterosexual romantic attachments in the course of the novel (in part because the men are so far beneath her in character and fortitude); and Brightwell, neither so bright as a button nor so deep as a well, has been entirely incidental to the plot until this point (he utters hardly a word and performs no actions at all). Their union thus seems flagrantly contrived—the conventional configuration of final marriages is fulfilled to a degree that the plot itself does not demand, and the artificiality of the convention is thus foregrounded almost as much as it would have been if it had been reversed. The effect is that the reader begins to doubt *all* of the marriages—and perhaps the institution itself.

Or is that the intended effect? Like all interpretations, this one requires the application of rules that preexist the text and that may not be appropriate to it. Surely, whether a given actual reader sees the ending of *Allworth Abbey* (or, for that matter, the formally similar ending of *Sense and Sensibility*) as subversive will depend to a large extent on his or her politics and prior opinion of the author's talents and outlook. If one takes the current deprecatory attitude toward Southworth and assumes that she didn't know what she was doing, one can conclude that the book is merely conventional. Similarly, if a given actual reader thinks that Chandler was not a skilled novelist, he or she may not apply the rule of conclusive endings to his texts, and may, as Stephen Knight does, conclude that his novels are simply poorly plotted.[20] Indeed, it is specifically because of his refusal to apply certain kinds of rules—in part because he sees Chandler as a popular novelist—that Luke Parsons can conclude that his novels are *not* a "serious indictment" of American society (if they were, they would have been "a boon to the propagandists of the Kremlin"): "His books, after all, are detective stories. . . . Just because Mr. Chandler writes so well, we must take care not to apply to him inappropriate literary standards."[21]

Chandler closes the novel with a despairing meditation, in a privileged position.

> What did it matter where you lay once you were dead? In a dirty sump or in a marble tower on top of a high hill? You were dead, you were sleeping the big sleep, you were not bothered by things like that. Oil and water were the same as wind and air to you. You just sleep the big sleep, not caring about the nastiness of how you died or where you fell. Me, I was part of the nastiness now. Far more a part of it than Rusty Regan was. . . .

> On the way downtown I stopped at a bar and had a couple of double Scotches. They didn't do me any good. All they did was make me think of Silver-Wig, and I never saw her again. [213–14, chap. 32]

Yet from the first reviews that greeted the novel, most critics have missed its irresolution. Thus, instead of interpreting it as a critique of the politics upheld by the traditions of the genre, they have instead read it as a heroic text, seeing not Marlowe's final despair, but rather his knightly—albeit muted—triumph. In other words, the text has been misread in such a way that it appears to provide a resolution. Even John Cawelti touts Marlowe in *The Big Sleep* as an example of a hero who "confronts, exposes, and destroys this web of conspiracy and perversion."[22] Philip Durham similarly decides that he was "the traditional American hero bringing fair play and justice where it could not be or had not been administered."[23] Why have they done so? And how?

In part, the phenomenon can be explained by a tendency of readers to find what they expect and want in a text. As I. A. Richards puts it, "When any person misreads it is because, *as he is at that moment,* he wants to. . . . Every interpretation is motivated by some interest."[24] Readers are likely to expect and want this kind of resolution for a number of reasons. On one level, of course, experiences with previous detective stories have had their toll. In addition, as I have argued (and poststructuralist critiques of traditional reading practices would support this claim), there is a general tendency in most reading to apply rules of coherence in such a way that disjunctures are smoothed over so that texts are turned into unified wholes—that is, in a way that allows us to read so that we get the satisfaction of closure. This interpretative technique is taught explicitly in school; and it may be connected to an innate psychological drive for closure.

But there are political reasons as well. Even if the desire for closure is cross-cultural, its *particular* manifestations are always social. We cannot explain why children's stories so often end with characters going to sleep simply by trotting out a generalized desire for closure. This particular closure is common under these circumstances—but less so in adult fiction—because in our culture children's stories often serve the social function of preparing children to go to sleep. Similarly, Janice Radway has eloquently demonstrated how the particular forms of closure found in popular romances respond to tensions within the structure of contemporary patriarchy.[25]

I suspect that readers in our culture tend to seek out (or impose) this particular kind of resolution—explanation with punishment—in *The Big Sleep* for much the same reason that they read detective stories in the first place: they want to be soothed, not irritated, and they do not want to confront Chandler's abyss and its demand for radical social change. As George P. Elliott puts it, we all have a malaise about the order of the world, and we like "to read a story which produces in the reader a safe version of the same thing and which purges this induced tension";[26] and while this may be less true with so-called elite art, it is widely felt to be true of popular texts.[27] It is thus not coincidental that the earliest reviews not only passed over the novel's irresolution, but also ignored Chandler's *social* analysis of evil. Almost uniformly, they stressed the theme of personal degeneracy rather than social corruption. The *New Yorker,* for instance, called it a "pretty terrifying story of degeneracy"; Ralph Partridge referred to the "full strength blend . . . of sadism, eroticism, and alcoholism"; the *Times Literary Supplement* described the novel's plot as Marlowe's trying "to conceal from an aged general the misadventures of his two degenerate daughters."[28] Even the more astute critics tended to see *The Big Sleep* as a collection of characters—mostly vicious, but at least individuals—rather than as a portrayal of a social situation.

Most readers, in other words, seem to misread Chandler for the same reasons they misread most disturbing books—they want to defend themselves against unwelcome points of view. But the question of the readers' *motives* for reading the novel as they do is only half the question. Even if I am right about *why* they do so, we still have to confront the even more vexing question of *how* they do so. For while readers tend to find what they want to find in books, there are, for most readers, limits to the process. Behind any persistent interpretation must lie not only some persistent desire to read in that fashion; at the same time, there must also be some coherent interpretive strategy, some approach to the text that makes *that* reading seem a plausible, even inevitable, consequence of the words on the page. For any interpretation, in other words, it ought ideally to be possible to trace the steps that allow readers to transform the text in that particular way.

In this case, the process of interpretation involves treating the novel primarily as a popular novel (stressing the solution) rather than as a serious one (stressing the indecisive conclusion). In addition, it has to involve an act of scapegoating: in order to create a sense of resolution in a morally chaotic situation, someone must be seen as the wrongdoer and appropriately punished. . . .

NOTES

1. See also John Fisher's discussion of titles in "Entitling." In some ways, Fisher's arguments support mine: "The title tells us how to look at the work" (292), but he fails to deal with *why* this is so—that is, that we live in a community that has agreed to treat titles in certain ways, and that authors know this. See also Umberto Eco's enunciation of a rule that "(irony or other figure excepted), the title of a chapter usually announces the content of it" (*Role of the Reader,* 20).

2. Marianna Torgovnick, *Closure in the Novel* (Princeton, N.J.: Princeton University Press, 1981), 3–4. See also Gerald Prince's claim that "the beginning or the end of various sequences" are "strategically important points" (*Narratology* 72); and Barbara Gerber Sanders's justification of an analysis based primarily on the ends of chapters in *The Great Gatsby:* "Structurally, the beginnings and endings of chapters are strategic places for development of thematic images. . . . The reader's mind is, or should be, more alert at these transitions" ("Structural Imagery in *The Great Gatsby:* Metaphor and Matrix," *Linguistics in Literature* 1, no. 1 [1978]: 57–58). Films differ markedly from novels in this regard, perhaps because filmmakers must take late arrivals into account. People will start films in the middle, but they will rarely do the same with books.

3. Ernest Pinard, "Requisitoire de M. L'Avocat Imperial," in *Madame Bovary,* by Gustave Flaubert (Paris: Librairie de France, 1921), 382.

4. Leo Tolstoy, *Anna Karenina,* trans. Louise Maude and Aylmer Maude (New York: Norton, 1970).

5. Ford, *Some Do Not . . . ,* bound with *No More Parades* (New York: NAL/ Signet, 1964), 28 (pt. 1, chap. 1). Further page references are given in the text.

6. Cain, *The Postman Always Rings Twice,* in *Cain x 3* (New York: Knopf, 1969), 3 (chap. 1). For the rhetorical significance of the definite article in such contexts, see Walker Gibson, *Tough, Sweet, Stuffy,* esp. 37–40.

7. Torgovnick, *Closure in the Novel,* 19.

8. Forster, *Aspects of the Novel,* 66.

9. Bierce, "Fantastic Fables," in *The Collected Writings of Ambrose Bierce* (New York: Citadel, 1963), 640.

10. Torgovnick, *Closure in the Novel,* 115. I, of course, would prefer to reword that final sentence: the inversion indicates regression because it is *assumed* beforehand to have thematic value. See also Jonathan Culler's claim that "*The Waste Land* can be unified by thematizing its formal discontinuities" ("Prolegomena to a Theory of Reading," in *Reader in the Text,* ed. Suleiman and Crosman, 48; much of this essay ended up, in altered form, in chap. 3 of *Pursuit of Signs*). This interpretive technique is applied to ancient as well as to modern texts. See Alice M. Colby-Hall's analysis of the "double ending" of Renaut's *Bel Inconnu* in the special issue of *Yale French Studies* devoted to closure ("Frustration and Fulfillment: The Double

Ending of the *Bel Inconnu*," *Yale French Studies,* no. 67 [1984]: 120–34).

11. Mark Twain, *Pudd'nhead Wilson,* in *Pudd'nhead Wilson and Those Extraordinary Twins* (New York: Harper, 1899), 224 (Conclusion). It is, though, risky to talk about coherence in a work as textually tangled as this one; for a discussion of the problems, see Hershel Parker, *Flawed Texts and Verbal Icons,* chap. 5.

12. Hubert, "The Tableau-Poème: Open Work," *Yale French Studies,* no. 67 (1984): 43 Hubert's claim, of course, applies only to a fairly restricted text-milieu. See also Gerald Prince's distinction between hermeneutic, proairetic, and tonal closure later in that same issue (*"La Nausée* and the Question of Closure," 183).

13. Fyodor Dostoyevsky, *Crime and Punishment,* trans. Constance Garnett (New York: Random House/Vintage, 1950), 492 (Epilogue, chap. 2).

14. O'Brien, *The Secret of NIMH* (New York: Scholastic/Apple, 1982), 249 (Epilogue). The novel was originally entitled *Mrs. Frisby and the Rats of NIMH,* but was later renamed to conform to the title of the film version.

15. Anton Chekhov, "The Lady with the Dog," trans. Ivy Litvinov, in *Anton Chekhov's Short Stories,* ed. Ralph Matlaw (New York: Norton, 1979), 235.

16. Prince, although he uses almost the opposite terms, is describing the same paradox when he says that there can be "a closure of uncertainty (making sense of or exploiting inconclusiveness, hesitation, and contradiction)" (*"La Nausée* and the Question of Closure," 188).

17. Walker, "Advancing Luna—and Ida B. Wells," in *You Can't Keep a Good Woman Down* (New York: Harcourt Brace Jovanovich/Harvest, 1982), 98.

18. More generally, as Fredric Jameson puts it, the "contamination of the central murder" by the "random violence" of what he calls the "secondary plot" ("the search") in Chandler's novels in general is part of a strategy of "de-mystification of violent death" ("On Raymond Chandler," 648–49).

19. Bertolt Brecht, *The Threepenny Opera,* trans. Desmond Vesey and Eric Bentley (New York: Grove/Evergreen Black Cat, 1964), 96.

20. Knight, *Form and Ideology,* esp. 150–51.

21. Luke Parsons, "On the Novels of Raymond Chandler," *Fortnightly Review,* May 1954, 351. For a fuller analysis of this novel, see my "Rats behind the Wainscoting."

22. Cawelti, *Adventure, Mystery, and Romance,* 149.

23. Philip Durham, *Down These Mean Streets a Man Must Go: Raymond Chandler's Knight* (Chapel Hill: University of North Carolina Press, 1963), 33. See also his claim, about Chandler's novels in general, that "the action and violence more or less covered up the fact that everything came out alright in the end" (97).

24. Richards, *Practical Criticism: A Study of Literary Judgment* (New York: Harcourt, Brace, and World/Harvest, 1964), 229.

25. Radway, *Reading the Romance,* esp. chap. 4.

26. Elliott, "Country Full of Blondes," 356. For a different perspective on this problem, see Stephen Knight's claim that Chandler holds a "conservative and elitist position" (*Form and Ideology,* 136–38).

27. See Russel Nye's claim that "popular art confirms the experience of the majority, in contrast to elite art, which tends to explore the new" (*The Unembarrassed Muse: The Popular Arts in America* [New York: Dial, 1970], 4). See also Donald Dunlop, "Popular Culture and Methodology," *Journal of Popular Culture* 9 (fall 1975): 375/2–383/31; Dwight Macdonald, "A Theory of Mass Culture," in *Mass Culture: The Popular Arts in America,* ed. Bernard Rosenberg and David Manning White (Glencoe, Ill.: Free Press/Falcon's Wing, 1957), 59–73.

28. "Mysteries," *New Yorker,* 11 February 1939, 84; Ralph Partridge, "Death with a Difference," *New Statesman and Nation,* 10 June 1939, 910; "Detective Stories," *Times Literary Supplement,* 11 March 1939, 152.

23

Loose Ends: Aesthetic Closure and Social Crisis

RUSSELL REISING

> While the countless tribes of common novels laboriously spin vails of mystery,
> only to complacently clear them up at last; and while the countless tribe of com-
> mon dramas do but repeat the same; yet the profounder emanations of the human
> mind, intended to illustrate all that can be humanly known of human life; these
> never unravel their own intricacies, and have no proper endings; but in imperfect,
> unanticipated, and disappointing sequels (as mutilated stumps), hurry to abrupt
> intermergings with the eternal tides of time and fate
> —Herman Melville, *Pierre; or, The Ambiguities*

When Mark Twain stops *Adventures of Huckleberry Finn* by having Huck
decide to "Light out for the Territory" rather than return to "sivilization," he
"concludes" his work only nominally. The abruptness of the novel's stopping
is only slightly less jarring than that cessation Mark Twain must have felt
when, after having a riverboat smash Huck and Jim's raft, he earlier stopped
work on the novel, putting it aside for about three years, from 1876 to 1879.
This second stoppage provides no satisfactory conclusion to the narrative's
generative thematics, no clarification, no tense ambiguity, no protomodernist
frustration of easy solutions, no liberating (or puzzling) openness: it simply
ends. *Adventures of Huckleberry Finn* shapes a fictional narrative world and
navigates its various communities and stresses without completing its imaginative work. Given the ignorance, stupidity, brutality, hypocrisy, fraud,
heartlessness, and exploitation that Mark Twain's narrative posits as definitive
of the antebellum U.S. South as well as of his own Reconstruction era,
Huck's choice of running farther west is indicative not only of his own desire
to escape the world he has laid bare, but also of Mark Twain's unwillingness,
perhaps inability, fully to resolve the very issues his picaresque narrative has
conjured. While it might itself function as an emblem of the westward mania
that has driven isolatoes, idealists, and malcontents into newly occupied territories at least since the time Eric the Red decided that Greenland was too

crowded for his tastes and voyaged to Vinland, Huck's and Mark Twain's "lighting out," their refusal to address or to impose any effective resolution onto the social world the novel constructs, can equally be read as a failure. The arbitrariness and abruptness of Huck's decision *not* to struggle to right the wrongs he has experienced suggests Mark Twain's cynicism, perhaps, but it could equally suggest his honesty. *Adventures of Huckleberry Finn* stops without in any way ameliorating the moral, economic, cultural, juridical, racial, and political evils it has so pointedly represented; no changes of heart, of law, of ethics intervene into the sickness of the novel's world. The death of Pap Finn, the tarring and feathering of the King and the Duke, the clarification of Jim's actual status as a free man following his manumission by the widow on her deathbed, and Tom and Huck's safe return to their homes provide no catharsis, no metaphorical or conceptual counterforce to the systemic brutality of life under slavery. Buck Grangerford's murder, the emergence of other con men to replace the King and the Duke, and the narrative's exposing of the inhumanity and racism underwriting the consciousnesses of all but one or two of the novel's "good and kind" characters serve at least to neutralize the impact of any putatively "happy" implications of the work's more upbeat moments.

There are obviously various ways of accounting for Mark Twain's choices. His own deepening cynicism and misanthropy could surely produce a novel content to expose the absurdity of life in late-nineteenth-century United States. Exhaustion and/or some writerly crisis of confidence could again have proven too oppressive for him to work more rigorously through the issues he raises. We might even speculate that Mark Twain's failure to "resolve" the loose ends of his narrative constitutes his triumph as a realist who refuses to impose utopian closure onto his recalcitrant subject matter. Or we might pursue the possibility that no novel, no social text, can resolve in its imaginative work the crises, tensions, and vexations that characterize the social and cultural world of its genesis, that any appearance of having done so is tantamount to political, moral, and rhetorical bad faith. It is this possibility and some of its related issues that I examine in *Loose Ends: Closure and Crisis in the American Social Text*. I will be reading works as diverse as Phillis Wheatley's poetry, Charles Brockden Brown's *Wieland*, Herman Melville's underread and underrated *Israel Potter: His Fifty Years of Exile*, an Emily Dickinson poem, Henry James's late fiction, and the Disney Studio's animated classic *Dumbo*, works that span nearly the entire history of the United States of America, paying special attention to the ways in which these and other works struggle to cordon off their narrative worlds, and to how the moments of stoppage with which they conclude paradoxically function to exacerbate, to reopen, the very tensions they are meant (or are to appear to mean) to "conclude."

I hope I am not falling prey to some naive expectations about just how cultural works are supposed to conclude. I am certainly not advocating some neat, thorough, premature, or totalitarian imposition of an ending that clarifies the entirety of a narrative world. I am not proposing any prescriptive utopian agenda. As Frank Kermode cautions early in his still provocative *The Sense of an Ending,*

> we cannot . . . be denied an end; it is one of the great charms of books that they have to end. But unless we are extremely naïve, as some apocalyptic sects still are, we do not ask that they progress towards that end precisely as we have been given to believe. In fact, we should expect only the most trivial work to conform to pre-existent types. (24)

Loose Ends will instead examine moments of closure in works that are anything but trivial with an eye toward reading the significance of what I will call a particular kind of anticlosure. I am concerned, in other words, not with proposing that Phillis Wheatley should have written differently, but with what it means that she can stop a poem celebrating the rising of the morning sun with an image of herself blinded and violated by the appearance of that sun, the very moment her ode exists to represent.

No approach to closure in American literature has yet accounted for such conundrums. In fact, two recent considerations of closure in American literature concentrate on different issues entirely. Joyce A. Rowe, for example, attempts to define the essential difference between literature produced in the United States from "that produced by comparable writers abroad" by relating what she calls "equivocal endings" to the ostensibly visionary ambitions of literary production in the United States. According to Rowe, the endings of American works

> are equivocal in a special thematic sense, as they simultaneously promote and deny a visionary ambition already defeated in the body of the work. . . . Yet these endings all adhere to a similar convention: they redeem or rehabilitate the ideal by recasting it in alternative terms. However equivocally it is stated, the protagonist refuses either to reconsider or to abandon visionary hope. (1, 2)

The endings Rowe characterizes as "equivocal" are, as these remarks suggest, closely and coherently related to the thematics of the works they conclude. I would also add that the conventional approach governing both Rowe's identification of an "essentially" American theme and also her choice of texts (all mainstream, canonical works by white, male authors—*The Scarlet Letter,*

Adventures of Huckleberry Finn, The Ambassadors, The Great Gatsby, and, briefly, *Moby-Dick*) seems not a little anachronistic. In another consideration of "the politics of openness and closure in American literature," Milton Stern has thematized openness as utopian and closure as "a pulling in, tight control and gravitational centralization, compacted time and space," associating, even in 1991, such qualities with the cold war demons of totalitarian grayness: "conservative control and limitation" (4–6). Reminiscent of R. W. B. Lewis's alternatives of "the party of hope" and "the party of irony," Stern's model deals largely with the thematic binary opposition central to approaches to American literature popularized by D. H. Lawrence, William Carlos Williams, George Santayana, Van Wyck Brooks, and other early-twentieth-century thinkers, many of whom pitted some image of openness to possibilities of existence in a "new world" and the United States against "Puritanical" forces of resistance and denial. Interested as they are in advancing thematic definitions of American literature, neither of these studies concerns itself with the structural problems posed by what I am calling anticlosure and the "loose ends" associated with it.

Closure, whether poetic, narrative, cinematic, or other, can surely take many vexingly ambiguous and frustrating forms. Not only are we suspicious of a conclusion that appears to tie together most of a work's vagrant energies into some neat bundle, but effective and provocative conclusions often frustrate readerly expectations for the reconciliation or resolution of major tensions that have driven their narratives. The gigantic and enigmatic white presence at the conclusion of Edgar Allan Poe's *The Narrative of Arthur Gordon Pym* brings that work to an abrupt and puzzling halt, but its enigmatic appearance conjures up horrors more or less consistent with those of the entire narrative. Similarly, Melville's warning that "something more may follow of [the] masquerade" of *The Confidence-Man* projects that novel into an unknown, dystopian future of cynicism and hopelessness, but one largely anticipated and prepared for by the twists and turns of the entire work. Hester Prynne's return from Europe to counsel women against utopian desire and revolutionary praxis at the end of The *Scarlet Letter* may crush many readers' desires for Hester to emerge as a feminist heroine, but it merely consolidates the misogyny driving much of Nathaniel Hawthorne's fictional project, just as Miles Coverdale's "shocking" announcement that he loved Priscilla closes out *The Blithedale Romance* in an anticlimactic, almost hackneyed, exposé of his own horror before the feminine. Henry James strands Isabel Archer, who cannot but return on "the very straight path" to Gilbert Osmond at the end of *The Portrait of a Lady,* in what is not only an oppressive but also a problematic (but thematically consistent) conclusion to that novel. Carrie Meeber-Wheeler-Maddenda's rocking near the end of *Sister Carrie* posits a future of unfulfilled desire, though this lack of final fulfillment in no way challenges the logics of Dreiser's first novel. Nor does the unspoken word at the conclusion of Edith Wharton's *The House of Mirth* force us back into the novel to revisit some moment we aren't even aware of having missed or misread. Nick Carroway's rhapsodic conclusion to *The Great Gatsby* or Jake Barnes's cryptic "isn't it pretty to think so" at the end of *The Sun Also Rises* are both metaphorically and dramatically related to their respective novels, even though they interpose different types of ambiguity. Flannery O'Connor's story always ends with some superficially cryptic but ultimately coherent, violent epiphany consolidating her rigidly conservative religious beliefs. When he has Oedipa Maas await the "crying of lot 49" at the conclusion of his second novel, Thomas Pynchon strands the reader amidst wildly diverse speculations, but we can hypothesize either some clarifying climax or, more likely, an anticlimax consistent with the novel's own plays on paranoia, entropy, or some covert and totalizing alternative postal regime. The fact that we don't know what lot 49 (or, for that matter, what V) is, while tantalizingly frustrating, is fully consistent with Pynchon's thematics. Bob Dylan's concluding stanza to "All Along the Watchtower"—

> Outside in the cold distance
> A wildcat did growl.
> Two riders were approaching,
> The wind began to howl

—resonates with apocalyptic mystery, though its ambiguity is fully consistent, not only within the song and with the rest of Dylan's work in *John Wesley Harding,* but with the Western apocalyptic tradition at least from the time of Revelations. We might not know where we are or what impending doom we face, but we've been there before. These works all pulse toward these final moments, which, however ambiguous or ironic, nonetheless crystallize many of their narratives' primary concerns. In all these cases, the openness and ambiguity of the conclusions are themselves versions of closural coherence, even when the coherence functions to conclude narratives without obvious or stable teleological end points.

Even such closural moments as these confirm standard theories of closure. Barbara Herrnstein Smith clarifies a still dominant structure of beliefs in *Poetic Closure:*

> The writer also wishes, however, that we have no further expectations at the end of the play, novel, or poem, no "loose ends" to be accounted for, no promises that go begging. The novelist or playwright is likely to end his work

at a point when either nothing could follow (as when the hero dies) or everything that could follow is predictable (as when the hero and heroine get married). The poet ends his work at some comparable point of stability, but unless (as sometimes happens) the poem follows a temporal sequence, this point will not be something we could call "the end of the story." It will, however, be a point of stability that is either determined by or accommodates the poem's formal and thematic principles of structure.

Closure occurs when the concluding portion of a poem creates in the reader a sense of appropriate cessation. It announces and justifies the absence of further development; it reinforces the feeling of finality, completion, and composure which we value in all works of art; and it gives ultimate unity and coherence to the reader's experience of the poem by providing a point from which all the preceding elements may be viewed comprehensively and their relations grasped as part of a significant design. (35–36)

Thus, even when the final passage of a work, Pynchon's *The Crying of Lot 49*, for example, projects the reader into a completely unarticulated narrative space, that space and the relationship it opens between the reader and the preceding narrative is densely rooted in and prepared for by the narrative itself. Whether the conclusion finalizes its narrative by confirming an excessively teleological structure or by adumbrating the vaguest, most projective openness, and whether the narrative has propelled us to its concluding moments with or without sufficient textual data to render its ending immediately coherent, even the most experimental conclusions (Don DeLillo's, for example) most commonly confirm, extend, complicate, qualify, or at least resonate significantly with the rest of the works they conclude. It might even be problematic to attempt so thorough a demarcation between work and conclusion. Final passages must function in a conclusive structural sense, but they are often thematically inseparable from everything preceding them in any particular work. While *Moby-Dick*'s (or any work's) epilogue stands in an obviously "concluding" relationship with the bulk of Melville's narrative, even T. S. Eliot's "Till human voices wake us / And we drown," which concludes "The Love Song of J. Alfred Prufrock," emerges as the revealing culmination of the entire poem, both thematically and, almost coincidentally, structurally. To return to Barbara Herrnstein Smith, "closure . . . may be regarded as a modification of structure that makes *stasis*, or the absence of further continuation, the most probable succeeding event. Closure allows the reader to be satisfied by the failure of continuation, or, put another way, it creates in the reader the expectation of nothing" (34). Of course "the expectation of nothing" does not eliminate the common necessity for readers to pursue their thinking beyond the final moment of reading or viewing; the narratives have already provided the necessary components for that postexperiential interpretive work.

D. A. Miller has offered a powerful reading of closure in the nineteenth-century European novel which counters Smith's study of the various logics of poetic closural coherence, at least relative to traditional fictional narrative. Critical of the teleological compulsion common to traditional studies of closure, Miller suggests the definitive theoretical flaw driving prior investigations:

> once the ending is enshrined in an all-encompassing cause in which the elements of a narrative find their ultimate justification, it is difficult for analysis to assert anything short of total coherence. One is barred even from suspecting possible discontinuities between closure and narrative movement preceding it, not to mention possible contradictions and ambiguities from within closure itself. (xiii)

By thus reifying closural moments, traditional narrative theory has unnecessarily constructed endings as the embedded and fully coherent essence of the narrative act, which, given the numerous energies and agendas driving toward some perfectly revelatory, demystifying closural epiphany can only be imagined as fully sufficient as both origin and telos of narrativity. Miller, in fact, pushes the opposite extreme by arguing that no closure can fully and coherently extinguish the various energies driving the narratable, by which he means the very possibilities and conditions of narrative; that is, those "instances of disequilibrium, suspense, and general insufficiency from which a given narrative appears to rise" (ix). While granting the crucial differences of novelistic subject matter as well as the historical specificity of novelistic structure, Miller nonetheless locates the "failure" of novelistic closure in two "primary determinations," the psychoanalytic "drift of desire" and the linguistic "drift of the sign," both of which drive narrative away from "a full and settled meaning." As Miller sums it up, "the narratable inherently *lacks finality*. It may be suspended by a moral or ideological expediency, but it *can never be properly brought to term*" (xi; my emphasis).

Miller's readings of Austen, George Eliot, and Stendhal are subtle and often brilliant; I will refer to only one of them to suggest how his theory works when deployed in specific analytical acts. George Eliot cannot successfully close *Middlemarch* because, as Miller puts it,

> it is as if the novelist could not help seeing the persistence of the narratable even in its closure. As a consequence, closure appears to take place only through a strategic misreading of the data—a misreading that is at once shown to be expedient (expressing a moral command), efficacious (settling

the final living arrangements of characters), and erroneous (deconstructed as a repetition of what it is supposed to overcome). The resulting ambiguity, of course, is bound to make conclusion less conclusive. (188–89)

I would like to affirm Miller's demonstrations while still creating a space for both theory and practice at a different level of specificity. Miller may be quite correct in his demonstration of the mutually reinforcing erotic and semiotic restlessness of narrative praxis; perhaps no narrative (poetic, novelistic, cinematic, or oral) can ever finally and perfectly close. However, I will be examining a dimension other than the essentialist, totalizing perspective he brings to bear on traditional nineteenth-century fiction. Austen's, George Eliot's, and Stendhal's failures to bring their narratives to appropriate (or even acceptable) moments of quiescence are, according to Miller, essential, inevitable even, to the very act of narrative. That is, narrative as we know it is unimaginable without the very originary energies and deeply embedded ideological assumptions that both elicit the narrative act from a prenarrative silence and render futile any attempt effectively to conclude in the ways valorized by traditional narrative (and poetic) theory.

I will be pursuing an array of absences, excesses, and final passages which function very differently relative *both* to the thematic and structural dimensions of the works they conclude *and* to the extranarrative worlds with which these works have their most plausible relationships. Unlike Miller, I will argue that the works I discuss in *Loose Ends* collapse into anticlosure because of historically specific concerns and narrative agendas, not due to an essentialist given of narrativity as such. Perhaps it is possible to demonstrate alternative anticlosural moments within the same works by refocusing on either (or both) the psychoanalytic or semiotic drifts definitive, as Miller would have it, of all narrative praxis. But in *Loose Ends* I will be paying more attention to the ways in which these works construct narrative worlds and evoke narrative themes with historically determined parameters that, as aesthetic constructs, these works cannot bring to successful conclusions. The issue I am interested in is the ideology of cultural productivity as embodied within these works. My own perspective, then, will at least in part account for just how I perceive the conclusions of these works as anticlosural as well as how and why I pursue these texts' situatedness within particular social and historical contexts.

I also differ from both Smith and Miller with reference to the relationship of these works to the extranarrative contexts of their genesis and production. According to Smith, "one of the most significant ways in which form contributes to our sense of the integrity of a poem is by, in effect, drawing an enclosing line around it, distinctly and continuously separating it from less highly structured and nonmimetic discourse" (25). She further elaborates:

"one of the functions or effects of poetic form is to 'frame' the poetic utterance: to maintain its identity as distinct from that of ordinary discourse, to draw an enclosing line, in other words, that marks the boundary between 'art' and 'reality'" (238). Miller incorporates an awareness of the nonnarrative, referential realm within his own theory of the impossibility of closure:

> The otherness of closure suggests one of the unwelcome implications of the narratable—that it can never generate the terms for its own arrest. These must be imported from elsewhere, from a world untouched by the conditions of narratability. Yet as soon as such a world is invoked in the novels—its appearance is necessarily brief—its authority is put into doubt by the system of narrative itself. . . . In essence, closure is an act of "make-believe," a postulation that closure is possible. (266–67)

For both Smith and Miller the "world" beyond the parameters of the autonomous work of art oppose, almost threaten, the imaginary inviolability of the cultural product. The "enclosing line" for which Smith argues must remain utterly stable for poetic discourse to be perceived as poetic, that is, for it to be distinguished from what she calls "less highly structured and non-mimetic" or "ordinary" discourses. Given the rigidity of these generic-discursive police lines, closure must function as a liminal moment, a threshold subdiscourse which simultaneously provides closure to the poetic utterance and initiatory openness to the postpoetic world. For all the differences between Miller's work on the futility of closure and Smith's on the varieties of closure, both agree on the nature of the pre-, post-, or transnarrative. Miller assumes that narrative would, of its own inertia, be ceaseless were it not for the forceful imposition of imported conditions "from a world untouched by the conditions of narratability" In other words, both Smith and Miller draw equally rigid lines between the internal and external worlds of the work and its environs (we assume historical, social, political, economic, cultural). Whereas for Smith that "other world" must be kept at bay in order for the poetic utterance to evolve and conclude coherently, for Miller both the emergence of narrative and its impulsion throughout narrative space function to keep the nonnarrative world forever beyond the possibility of narrative imagining. For Smith, poetry must stop. For Miller, narrative cannot stop. But for both, that stoppage is parasitically dependent on the aesthetic negation of the nonaesthetic.

I will be reading works whose relationship with the "other world" of the nonnarrative is essential to the very construction of their inner, intratextual worlds. The poems, short stories, novels, and films addressed in *Loose Ends* (perhaps all representational praxis with a linear or temporal dimension) can't close, precisely because their embeddedness within the sociohistorical worlds of their genesis is so complex and conflicted. These are works that admit of no "enclosing lines," works that repeatedly problematize the very possibility of such lines. The loose ends which characterize the concluding moments of these works function largely as provocations for the reader to reproblematize the very assumptions brought to the aesthetic experience and to reimagine the entire world of the work of art, especially those gestures beyond the works that often disappear as quickly as they catch our attention. They force us to return to the beginnings of the works we've just completed, but they do so only by (and after) indirectly revealing shadow narratives that have been lying latent within the dominant thematics of the works from which they emerge. These works conclude either by eliciting, via their final passages, counterreadings to the narratives, or by eliding the very tensions that need to be addressed for the works satisfactorily to "conclude." Once the primary narrative themes of the works I will examine stray into the realm of the social world otherwise elided by their narrative drives, that social world and the tensions elicited by these works' referential gestures infiltrate and recast nearly every dimension of their intratextual environments. The dynamics established by such necessary interconnections between textual zone and interdiscursive contexts circulate within the works even as they open the works to the influx of issues and struggles beyond their particular borders.

I will refer to these recoverable counternarratives as "shadow narratives," and by them I mean something akin to Fredric Jameson's notion of the political unconscious. In these cases, however, I suggest that the shadow narratives configure a massive residue of sociohistorical reference, usually generated by the sociohistorical pressures on the cultural moment of a text's genesis and encoded within these narratives by elaborate systems of transtextual gesturing. In Phillis Wheatley, references to the economics of slavery (however unobtrusive they appear) disrupt the superficially accommodationist gestures of her poems. In *Israel Potter: His Fifty Years of Exile,* Melville's complicated attack on the popular visions of the American past frustrates (to the point of self-sabotage) his attempt to recover a popular readership by offering them "nothing of any sort to shock the fastidious." As when he refers to *Pierre; or, The Ambiguities* as "a rural bowl of milk," Melville surely protests too much when he adds, "there will be very little reflective writing in it; nothing weighty" (*Israel Potter* 182). In Henry James's "The Jolly Corner," the density with which James represents turn-of-the-century New York's worlds of social, economic, and gender instability inhabits his text so thoroughly as to refigure the overt claims of his protagonists to exist beyond such crypto-naturalist determinations, recontextualizing them to reveal precisely the opposite of their expressed meanings. Similarly, in *Dumbo,* the superfluity of sociohistorical referents (including child abuse, labor unrest, vicious class rivalry, racism, and World War II) represented within the narrative of the little elephant with the huge ears explodes any possibility this film has of successfully containing the volatility of its social issues within its explicit genre, that of children's feature.

In one sense, such details are tangential to the dominant narrative of each text, but in another sense, cultural production is virtually impossible without them. As Peter Rabinowitz remarks,

> no matter how fantastic a novel's premises, no matter how unrealistic the setting, the authorial audience and the narrative audience must share some beliefs about reality in order for the situations and actions to have the consequences they do and for the plot to get from point A to point B. That's because every fictional world, like every real world, requires a history, sociology, biology, mathematics, aesthetics and ethics. (100–101)

What is true, say, in Kafka, Borges, Garcia Marquez, Kobo Abe, Pynchon, or Haruki Murakami holds equally for the more superficially conventional works I address in *Loose Ends*. The structuring of their narratives requires a scaffolding within the recognizable world of material things, social issues and tensions, and historical recollections: these simply constitute the frame of any narrative, but, in the cases of the works I will examine, these frames refuse to remain marginal and, instead, infuse the works with the stresses inherent within their narratives. By scaffolding I mean something similar to traditional notions of "setting" or "background" or "environment," but I mean to suggest that we can pursue them even farther into a denser field of material referents which constitute the sociohistorical basis for narratives of all sorts, however tangential they may seem to the social world of their eras (or, for that matter, of ours). Of course, some elements of a narrative world's "setting" serve symbolic or allegorical functions, like the temple turned summer house in *Wieland,* the forests and prairies in Cooper's works, "the prison door" and rosebush at the beginning of *The Scarlet Letter,* the sailors' and ship's equipage and the whale's penis in *Moby-Dick* or Wall Street in "Bartleby the Scrivener," Walden Pond, the house Silas Lapham tries to build in Boston's Back Bay, Gilbert Osmond's bibelots in *The Portrait of a Lady* or Paris in both *The Princess Casamassima* and *The Ambassadors,* the tiny "pigeon house" into which Edna Pontellier moves in Chopin's *The Awakening,* the cash register at the conclusion of Crane's "The Blue Hotel," the Chicago fire in Dreiser's *The Financier,* bullfighting in *The Sun Also* Rises, the bear in Faulkner, the valley of ashes and billboard in *The Great Gatsby,* or the mass Unification Church wedding that opens DeLillo's *Mao II.*

Perhaps all narrative constituents carry figurative residue, but those narrative elements I will be focusing on are, in many ways, profoundly demetaphorized. Yet they are not neutral, not excess material baggage, not dead weight. Neither (strictly speaking) symbolic, nor neutral, these elements take on narrative significance by virtue of being charged with the social issues which they are instrumental in representing and which, as a result of their status in these narratives, exert transformative energies within each work. Charles Brockden Brown's references to the religious affiliation of the elder Wieland wouldn't necessarily have the weight I attribute to them unless Wieland dwelled obsessively on problematics of subjectivity attributable to early American Protestantism. Phillis Wheatley's mentions of Christianity and her utilization of conventional light and dark imagery cease being conventional and, in fact, assume dangerous volatility once Wheatley attempts to articulate the status of African American slaves living in "Christian" Boston. Melville's concluding throwaway remark about Israel Potter's original personal narrative going out of print might be merely innocuous were it not for his novel pursuing the interconnections between the reputations of the "founding fathers" and their manipulation of the economics and technologies of the emerging print culture. The scenes of the roustabouts working facelessly and shrouded in darkness and of the clowns deciding to lobby for better pay would merely be filler in Disney's *Dumbo* were it not for the fact that *Dumbo* was made during a bitter animators' strike at the Disney Studio. Similarly, the notion that Dumbo's flying results in the development of a prototype for "Dumbombers for Defense" might merely be another example of animated whimsy if *Dumbo* hadn't been released in the early years of World War II. However, by being the representational vehicles for such volatile energies within the narratives we will examine, these otherwise marginal scenes and allusions become charged with the tensions, authorial animus, and ruptures in the social fabric that they import into their narrative worlds.

As a virtual requisite for any representational scheme, these elements I refer to as scaffolding comprise the entire range of social, economic, historical, political, psychological, even architectural assumptions and moments without which narrative theme or plot would be impossible, hopelessly abstract. But while they provide the structuring and complexity of details that fatten up any narrative and make coherence possible, these elements also have the potential to take on a counternarrative life of their own and, paradoxically, to make coherence impossible. Once these texts open up channels outside of themselves via such necessary social gesturing, their intranarrative structures and logics are themselves opened up to possibilities probably impossible to foresee, and certainly impossible to contain. The discourses, events, objects, technologies, and histories to which they allude circulate within and among

themselves, accruing a self-reproducing inertia which, by virtue of its proliferation, not only consolidates the presence of these discourses, but also has the
potential to recast the dominant narrative, its issues and themes. Once textual borders are ruptured by such conduits, there is no justification and no way
again to arrest the mutually constitutive trafficking between intra- and extratextual realms. In other words, the "enclosing lines" which both Smith and
Miller accept as constitutive of "literary" discourse can't really exist, unless we
as consumers consent to the arbitrary (and theoretically impossible) demarca-
tions they impose.

When Spencer Brydon in "The Jolly Corner," for example, articulates his
own discomfort over the transformation of New York's material being by
architectural and technological innovations, he merges his being with rather
than distinguishes it from those very historically specific fractures. When
Melville closes *Israel Potter* with a reference to books going out of print, the
technologies and economies of both history and literature are smuggled into
a work concerned with precisely those issues, but in a way that remains
obscure until the actual evocation of such economic concerns in the novel's
penultimate sentence. For these writers, the sensitivity of the issues they
address (sensitive both within each creator's oeuvre but also within their social
moments) heightens the disruptive potential of such social referents until they
assume what amounts to a life of their own by the concluding moments of
their works. The shadow narratives they conjure have, in almost every case,
been suspended or suppressed by the drift of the dominant narrative, but they
have never been totally effaced. We may not even remember that Emily Dickinson begins her poem "I started Early—Took my Dog—" with a structurally significant reference to a dog, since the dog simply disappears after the first
line. But, by poem's end, the stresses and ambiguities of Dickinson's poem
require us to revisit its every unit, and the disappeared dog suddenly reemerges
with new importance. Such moments have existed parasitically (perhaps symbiotically is a better term, suggesting as it does the mutually constitutive
dynamic I am pursuing between dominant and shadow narratives) throughout their texts, but have remained submerged, in some cases as a result of over-
sight or conscious subordination, but more commonly by virtue of the
thoroughness with which they violate the ideological conventions which their
host narratives struggle to adhere to. They restage, in other words, a different
drama, a return of the repressed counterhegemonic residue that the dominant
narratives haven't quite erased.

The relationship between these dominant and shadow narratives is even
more conflicted than this formulation suggests, however. I am also suggesting
that this shadow narrative constitutes not only an alternative narrative to its
host, but one which, paradoxically, often carries an alternative intentionality

of the work itself. The works we will examine tend to be narratives of struggle, works of highly volatile ideological significance, most of which oppose some dimension of the dominant culture's hegemony but which also struggle to speak in a language compatible with that culture's ideological preeminence. The dilemma these works often confront is how to speak in a language that will simultaneously reinforce *and* dismantle a particular facet of the status quo of their cultures. In the case of Phillis Wheatley, I suggest that her conventional odes "signify"; that is, according to African American literary theory and practice, they speak from within while simultaneously reconfiguring the terms of the dominant culture's discourses. As I will consequently demonstrate, when she begins her best-known poem, "'Twas mercy brought me from my Pagan land," she is actually struggling to characterize the barbarity of the slave trade and the hypocrisy of the Christian culture that could countenance trafficking in human beings. Similarly, the apparent naïveté of Dickinson's speaker belies her poem's negotiation of issues of intense volatility, including sexual violence and the oppression of women.

Perhaps what I am offering throughout *Loose Ends* is an analysis of what oppositional discourses look like and how they function prior to their recognition and formalization within the dominant discourse of a culture. In Raymond Williams's familiar tripartite model of the "dominant," "residual," and "emergent" forces and structures inhabiting any sociohistorical epoch, these shadow narratives and the discourses from which they are constructed smuggle into these works the "emergent" implications of the tensions and representational struggles of their eras. The particular discourses I will investigate tend, not surprisingly, to constellate around issues pertaining to race, class, and gender, although it may well be that virtually any oppositional discourse (gay or lesbian, for example) initially struggles to occupy some similarly secretly coded, liminal space on the margins of the dominant culture. These cultural artifacts all carry shadow plots, some of which are smuggled in by their creators, some of which emerge by virtue of the fullness of their respective text's referential schemes, at times in violent opposition to their creator's likely plans. In other words, I am interested not only in how oppositional energies are consciously deployed by politically engaged artists but also in how they can erupt, seemingly of their own inertia, from within various narratives. To paraphrase a recurring theme from Steven Spielberg's *Jurassic Park,* the notion that "nature finds a way" to protect and advance itself in spite of the most careful attempts of civilization and science to control it, in these narratives I will argue that "resistance finds a way."

That these shadow narratives often remain invisible or are simply ignored as unimportant until the host narrative's desperate attempt at aesthetic closure is, very likely, no surprise. Marianna Torgovnick makes an appropriate point:

"It is difficult to recall all of a work after a completed reading, but climactic moments, dramatic scenes, and beginnings and endings remain in the memory and decisively shape our sense of a novel as a whole" (3–4). In his extraordinary anatomy of narrative structures, Rabinowitz concurs with Torgovnick when he suggests that "last sentences . . . cannot serve to focus a reading experience (at least not an initial reading experience). But they do often serve to scaffold our retrospective interpretation of the book" (62). The function of conclusions is often precisely to provide that end point which enables us finally to configure the narrative strands that may have remained frayed or unresolved prior to the text's final moment. In fact, we often only "see" the narrative from the perspective of its finale. Again, Rabinowitz offers a systematic reading of such functions. Focusing on various "rules of notice," those textual features which call our attention to any work's heightened moments, he notes that "the stressed features in a text serve as a basic structure on which to build an interpretation" (53). Not surprisingly, Rabinowitz includes in his catalog of such "privileged positions" "titles, beginnings and endings (not only of whole texts, but of subsections as well—volumes, chapters, episodes), epigraphs, and descriptive subtitles" (58). I would like to build on Rabinowitz's classificatory system by conflating his remarks on "privileged positions," especially endings, with his idea of "rules of rupture." While "we tend to skim over the even and the unbroken," he admits,

> disruptions attract our notice. This explains why we notice the pyramid rising above the desert, and also why we notice certain details in literary works. Specifically, textual features stand out both when they disrupt the continuity of the works in which they occur and when they deviate from the extratextual norms against which they are read. (65)

The conclusions that I will examine in *Loose Ends* literally conflate these two notions: the very concluding moments upon which we quite naturally focus simultaneously disrupt the expectations we bring to them. To be sure, the "loose ends" we will encounter "disrupt the continuity of the works in which they occur," but they do so not by violating "the extratextual norms against which they are read" but, paradoxically according to Rabinowitz's calculus, by taking those norms seriously and by invading the narrative (aesthetic) logic with the pressures that the very extratextual norms intrude upon the text in question. These works reinscribe what had appeared to function merely as conventional, referential scaffolding for their major thematics as themselves alternative, disruptive, and, quite remarkably, dominant themes.

∎ PART V

NARRATIVE FRAMES

Introduction: Narrative Frames and Embeddings

Victor Shklovsky discusses a wide range of narrative frames and embeddings at the end of his essay on plot construction and general stylistic devices[1] and comments on their functions within the plot as a whole. He draws attention to a number of challenging classical Indian collections that have not subsequently been adequately discussed, and identifies among them an unusual practice that sounds strangely postmodern: "The type of storytelling where the principal characters tell their stories in succession ad infinitum until the first story is completely forgotten."[2]

A flurry of formalist works on embedded narratives (which at first glance might seem most amenable to a structuralist typology) appeared between 1967 and 1972. Tzvetan Todorov, in his essay "Narrative Men" in *The Poetics of Prose*,[3] speculated on the apsychological nature of the various embedded tellers of tales in the *Arabian Nights* and Jan Potocki's *The Saragossa Manuscript*. Boris Uspensky pursued the relations between frames in visual and in verbal artworks. Genette outlined a basic approach to narrative levels that identifies discrete narrative levels: when a figure within a narrative (first degree) begins to tell a story, the narrative level shifts (second degree). If a character in this inner narrative then tells another story, we have an additional level (third degree). These concepts are much simpler than Genette's terminology might suggest (respectively, extradiegetic, intradiegetic, metadiegetic, meta-metadiegetic, etc).[4] He also identified "metalepses," that is, any transgression of narrative levels or intrusion by an external narrator into the world of the fiction (or vice versa, as when, in Cortázar's story "The Continuity of Parks," a character emerges from the fiction to murder the reader). These seminal essays would be extended, adjusted, and reformulated by Mieke Bal in her "Notes on Narrative Embedding" (1981), Katherine Galloway Young, and William Nelles, who provides a critical account of a number of earlier approaches as he articulates his own position. Nelles also stresses an important differentiation between two kinds of narrative embedding: "horizontal" embedding, in which texts at the same diegetic level, but recounted by different narrators, follow one another; and "vertical" embedding, in which narratives at different diegetic levels are inserted within each other. He discusses varieties of "metalepsis" and further points out that narrative embedding has the paradoxical effect of producing the illusion of a profound realism, and also, at the same time, of undercutting that illusion.

Additional structuralist work was done by Genette in his analysis of the "paratext," or the various forms of discursive material that frame the text proper (title, dedication, preface, etc.). Lucien Dällenbach, in *The Mirror in the Text,* provides a comprehensive account of the *mise en abyme,* or a miniature work within a larger work that mirrors some of its salient features (e.g., the play within the play in *Hamlet*). His analysis identifies three basic forms: simple duplication, aporetic duplication, and infinite duplication—these last two categories, as their names suggest, describe how paradoxical such self-framed narratives can be.

Despite the structuralists' original assumptions, frames in fact are inherently unstable. They invite their own deconstruction because they appear so definitive yet are obviously partially arbitrary and capable of being reconstructed or placed themselves within a larger, different frame; this can be easily demonstrated any painter who depicts a fly on the wood surrounding the painting proper, or any author who ends a story by saying, "At least that was one version. Of course, there are other, different ones." For more playful creators who are not averse to going beyond the customary limits prescribed by realism, the frame is there to be jostled, bent, or broken altogether; one might even postulate a "rule of the violated frame" that notes that in the more antimimetic texts, basic frames are always broken, and ontological boundaries between embedded worlds are regularly transgressed.

In many different works, Jacques Derrida has insistently drawn attention to what he sees as the fallacious opposition of outside and inside, center and margin, the frame and the framed. "The total inclusion of the frame is both mandatory and impossible. The 'frame' thus becomes not the borderline between the inside and outside, but precisely what subverts the applicability of the inside/outside polarity to the act of interpretation" as Barbara Johnson lucidly articulates this basic tenet of deconstruction.[5] Or in the somewhat obscurer words of Derrida, the frame is "a hybrid of inside and outside, but a hybrid which is not a mixture or half measure, an outside which is called to the inside of the inside in order to constitute it as inside."[6] In the selection

330

below, Derrida interrogates Kant's casual references in the *Critique of Judgment* to the *parergon,* i.e., all that is neither in the work (*ergon*) nor outside it. As soon as the *parergon* takes place, it dismantles the most reassuring conceptual oppositions, Derrida affirms.

John Frow, working along similar lines, developed the ideas of multiple frames, of frames that are both literal and metaphorical, and the dual status of the frame as a component of structure and a component of situation. Important theoretically grounded studies of individual texts were made by John T. Matthews, Beth Newman, Katharine Gittes, and Brian Macaskill; perhaps most compelling was John H. Pearson's survey of a number of framed works by Cervantes, Hawthorne, Seurat, Rossetti, and Henry James, in which he showed how the frame and the work that is framed collaborate with, interanimate, and interpenetrate each other.

Patrick O'Neill, in a compelling account of what he terms "nested frames,"[7] has argued for the fundamental instability of any narrative world framed by and contained within an ontologically superior world; in each such case, "the narrator and naratee both constitute the text and are simultaneously constituted by it";[8] every narrative level is profoundly relative, and is potentially subverted by the discourse that frames it. Ross Chambers, in *Story and Situation,* draws important attention both to the fundamental importance of interpretative context and narrative frame for any discursive act, and to the ways in which narratives frame, situate, and attempt to order their own reception.

Jeffrey Williams, building on Derrida and Chambers, further explores the paradoxical nature of framing; for him, frames "serve a tropological rather than referential function, naming the embedded narrative as fiction and marking it in the rhetorical context of storytelling";[9] at the same time, "frames seemingly efface their own status as narrative."[10]

In the final essay in this volume, Marie-Laure Ryan builds on and adapts for narratology recent work in artificial intelligence. She makes the useful distinction between frames (a static model of narrative embedding) and "stacks" (a dynamic model derived from the discourse of programming languages for computers). This formulation has already proven capable of further development in the work of cognitivist Manfred Jahn, who is attempting to construct a more reader-oriented poetics, and in David Herman's advocacy of a "lateral reflexivity" that can disclose how characters and events replicate themselves across storyworlds. In other recent analyses, Werner Wolf has attempted to embrace current work in linguistics in a very general account of framing and contextualization, while James Paxon theorizes what he calls excessive, abused, and vertiginous forms of narrative embedding from a post-Derridean rhetorical framework.

NOTES

1. Victor Shklovsky, "The Relationship between Devices of Plot Construction and General Devices of Style," in *Theory of Prose,* trans. Benjamin Sher (Elmwood Park, Ill.: Dalkey Archive Press, 1990), 42–46.

2. Ibid., 42.

3. Tzvetan Todorov, *Introduction to Poetics,* trans. Richard Howard (Minneapolis: University of Minnesota Press, 1981), 66–79.

4. Gérard Genette, *Narrative Discourse,* trans. Jane E. Lewin (Ithaca, N.Y.: Cornell University Press, 1980), 227–37.

5. Barbara Johnson, "The Frame of Reference: Poe, Lacan, Derrida," *Yale French Studies* 55–56 (1977): 481.

6. Jacques Derrida, *The Truth in Painting,* trans. Geoff Bennington and Ian McLeod (Chicago: University of Chicago Press, 1987), 63.

7. Patrick O'Neill, *Fictions of Discourse: Reading Narrative Theory* (Toronto: University of Toronto Press, 1994), 110–16.

8. Ibid., 110.

9. Jeffrey Williams, *Theory and the Novel: Narrative Reflexivity in the British Tradition* (Cambridge: Cambridge University Press, 1998), 102.

10. Ibid., 103.

24

The Literary Frame

JOHN FROW

The function of the aesthetic closure which marks off literary space is to establish the particular historical distribution of the "real" and the "symbolic" within which the text operates. The border of the text constitutes and defines its specific fictional status[1] and the kinds of use to which it can be put. This border is therefore in one sense an immaterial system of expectational norms. But I will argue that it is also always materially embodied and should not be conceived simply as a mental projection; in Erving Goffman's words, "A cup can be filled from any realm, but the handle belongs to the realm that qualifies as reality."[2]

I shall use the term *frame* to designate this limit, at once material and immaterial, literal and figurative, between adjacent and dissimilar ontological realms. The frame can be anything that acts as a sign of a qualitative difference, a sign of the boundary between a marked and an unmarked space. If this definition seems tautological, it is because since Mauss and, in a different way, since Duchamp we know that the aesthetic space is not an anthropological constant but is constituted by a cultural recognition: the toilet seat hung in a museum is an aesthetic object because the museum sanctions its situation as aesthetic.

Every aesthetic object or process has a frame or frames peculiar to it. Since the frame is not simply a material fact, it can be multiple—the frame of a painting, for example, may be reinforced by the broader frame of the museum—and we could think of the "edge" of the work as a series of concentric waves in which the aesthetic space is enclosed. Theatrical space is defined by the borders of the stage and by the theater situation (the relation of the auditorium to the stage and the convention that the space of the stage is a privileged space of illusion).[3] Cinematic space is defined by the screen—by the darkness that surrounds the screen, by the projection apparatus, by the theater situation, and by advertisements and billings which have created expectations that this is a movie and that it is a particular kind of movie; but there is also an internal frame, the title sequence, which supplements and narrows down the predefinition of the kind of aesthetic space being presented. For a literary text the frame is particularly complex: it is made up, first of all, of the covers of a book or the lines enclosing a poem in a journal (or by a recitation or reading situation); of the title pages, specifying genre expectations and the expectations created by the date, by the author's name, by dedicatory material, by the title, and perhaps by the publishing house.[4] Texts which have a special legitimacy often display special framing effects such as that of a collected or standard edition, editorial exegesis (which may frame individual pages), an introduction stressing the canonic status of the text, or expensive binding (corresponding to "the salient and richly ornamented enclosures that once . . . conveyed the idea of the preciousness of the work through its gilded mount").[5] On a general scale, they are framed by the publishing apparatus and by their position within the literary system. A poem is usually framed, at a more intensive level, by the white margin that marks off line lengths (and this margin can be stressed in particular ways, as in the calligrams of Herbert or Apollinaire or the attentive dispersal of the lines over the page of *Un coup de dés*). For a narrative, the most intensive frame is that constituted by the beginning and, especially, the end of the narration. Jurij Lotman has constructed a typology of narrative modes on the basis of a distinction between those texts (e.g., myths, medieval chronicles) which emphasize origins and those, like the novel, which emphasize ends. The beginning of a text is governed by the modelling of causality, whereas the end stresses goals,[6] and this would seem to be a valuable way of linking plot structure to the "edge" of the text, the point at which the text passes into, and is closed off from, nonaesthetic space. The beginning of a text, finally, is the point at which the distancing between author and narrator usually occurs; the fourfold frame in which Scott encloses *Heart of Midlothian,* for example, sets up a succession of redundant narrators in a strangely hesitant development of the narration which will be more fully exploited later in the century. This distancing, like that effected by a prologue and epilogue, both reinforces the difference between the realm of narration and the realm of the narrated and eases the reader into the fictive world, sparing him the abruptness of a sudden passage.

The frame holds literary discourse in a kind of suspension such that the framed word is, in Mikhail Bakhtin's terminology, a "represented word": the word represents itself, *cites* itself as a fictive word, a word which cannot be accepted directly.[7] It is in this sense (a sense which does not depend on a positivistic notion of "truth") that we could adopt I. A. Richards's concept of literary discourse as pseudostatement.[8] Bracketed discourse is fictional to the extent that it handles consciously as unrealities the unrealities, the mythical patterns and codes, which ideology deals in unconsciously. By delineating aesthetic space as an "unreal" space (an "imaginary garden with real toads in it"), the frame both neutralizes direct referentiality and calls attention to the concentration of meaning within this space: the absence of immediate meaning creates an expectation of *total* meaning. The tendency of bracketed discourse is, then, to a universality of connotation, although particular genres will attempt to play this down as much as possible. And since the frame has the force of law, it is impossible to break the fictionality of a genre through a simple change of intention—for example, through a politicization of its themes. Unless the *function* of the genre is radically altered,[9] the introduction of political elements will lead, not to an "activation" of the work, but to a formalization and neutralization of the political thematic.

The authority of the frame is equivalent to that of the genre expectations which it establishes, and the internal structure of the text may either confirm this authority or react dynamically to it, or at the extreme it may break it. In all of these cases, structure is only made possible by the presence of the frame, as norm or restriction and as the conventional sign of a closure which separates the limitedness of the aesthetic object from the unlimitedness of its environment.[10] As a limit, its importance lies precisely in this ambiguity of its threshold situation. Meyer Schapiro and Boris Uspensky both assign the frame of a painting to the space of the observer rather than the illusory three-dimensional space of representation, although Schapiro does concede that the frame may also function as a compositional device.[11] Goffman, on the other hand, is fully aware of the ambivalence of its function. He distinguishes two levels of the frame: "One is the innermost layering, wherein dramatic activity can be at play to engross the participant. The other is the outermost lamination, the *rim* of the frame, as it were, which tells us just what sort of status in the real world the activity has, whatever the complexity of the inner laminations."[12] The frame of course is unitary, neither inside nor outside, and this distinction of levels must be seen as a convenient fiction to express the frame's dual status as a component of structure and a component of situation. For a literary text, it works both as an enclosure of the internal fictional space and as an exclusion of the space of reality against which the work is set; but this operation of exclusion is also an inclusion of the text in this alien space. The text is closed and suspended, but as a constructional element the frame is *internal* to this closure, and through it the text signifies *difference*, signifies what it excludes. Within the field of vision are included both the aesthetic space and the edge of aesthetic space. The extra-aesthetic is manifested negatively at this moment of passage, where the text reaches the limit and starts to become non-text. The energy of the frame thus radiates in two directions simultaneously. On the one hand, it conducts the "trace" of the excluded nonaesthetic area inwards, so that the delimited space of the text is structured by its limit and becomes significant because of the *selection* operated by the frame. Thus the compositional structure of a painting—its perspective, the play of vectors, the foregrounding and backgrounding of motifs—is defined by the relation to the vertical and horizontal lines of the "edge," and these are not simply the farthest points to which the painting reaches, but are rather the dynamic moments which constitute the system and the semantic richness of the painting; similarly, the margin around a poem is not an empty support of the printed text but actively breaks the poem off from its continuity with everyday life, suspending the line in arbitrary rhythmic or typographic lengths and isolating the poetic flower as *l'absente de tous bouquets;* and the end of a narrative shapes the plot, not as a static sequence of events but as a teleologically structured movement which characterizes the time of the text as a significant time in relation to the nonsignificant time against which it is set and from which it differentiates itself.[13] On the other hand, the frame situates the work within nonaesthetic space and thus transforms it into a *function.* The text is "quoted" by and within its context—the context of a particular kind of speech situation. This situation is variable: a text may be situated in the "normal" space of an aesthetic function indicated by its frame (e.g., a play may be staged as an aesthetic object), or the frame may be ignored and the text "quoted" to nonaesthetic ends (the text of the play may serve as a moral or sociological example, or the play may be staged as a historical curiosity so that it becomes a citation in a larger written or unwritten text). The frame signifies only the norm (the text as an aesthetic object and the normative expectations governing the reception of this object); as a sign of a *conventionally* guaranteed use of the text it cannot account for deviant functions, i.e., for uses of the text which choose to ignore this norm.

But the mere fact of the convergence of the internal structure and the contextual function of the text at the "edge" of the text indicates that the frame does not simply separate an outside from an inside but mediates between the two. This is not to posit a constant relation between two constant factors but to indicate the way in which changes in the context of reception of a work alter the kinds of expectation governed by the frame and are thus translated into structural shifts in the work; and, conversely, the way in which structural changes (i.e., new interpretations of a work) become institutionalized as changes in the norm signified by the frame and so gradually alter the situation of the work in its context. In this dialectic, the frame internalizes the "external" function of the text. Attention to the frame, not as physical border but as the conventionally regulated index of a demarcation, should perhaps lead us to think in terms of the mediations between "intrinsic" structure and "extrinsic" function, but the precondition for this would be a conception of the text as a "play" of forces which is constantly restructured (reinterpreted) as its relation to the frame (to the historically shifting conventions which establish it as an aesthetic object and through which it is "seen") changes. The drama, where the frame is manifested largely as a visible architectural border and where genre expectations can be closely correlated with the material fact (at least in the long term), provides a particularly clear example of this. The change from the projecting Elizabethan stage to the pictorial space of the proscenium arch both corresponds to and reinforces a radically different kind of speech situation in which the whole nature of the scenic illusion is modified. The alteration of the frame, in direct relation to modifications in the literary system (to the distance and the closed rigidity of frame characteristic of a neoclassical system), alters the nature of dramatic reality (the nature of the fictional space), and this is illustrated in exemplary fashion by modifications in the aesthetic object itself (modifications in interpretation of existing plays: for example of Shakespeare through new canons of performance [Tate's *Lear*] or through editorial restructuring of the texts; and in the production of new texts: e.g., the change between *Antony and Cleopatra* and *All for Love*).

As the index of a conventional mode of appropriation of reality, the frame thus corresponds roughly to what George Kubler calls the "self-signal" of a work,[14] its signification of itself as a function with a differential relation to reality. But the difficulty of coping with the concept of frame is the near-*invisibility* of the frame. We have been taught to naturalize the artificial space of the aesthetic object, to lose ourselves in an inside which is as *unlimited* as the world,[15] and this means that our "natural" inclination is to see the work in the same way we see the world, without awareness of the edge of our eyes' scan. The white margin around a poem, the beginning and end of reading, the darkness around the stage disappear as we focus on the presence of the text; they become an unapprehended negativity. And in fact the frame *is* an absence insofar as it is a purely relational moment, the point of crystallization of the normative conventions of reception; like the nonexistent meridian line dividing night from morning, it exists only as a sign of difference, and without a special act of attention it is blotted out by the quasi-substantiality of its content. To "see" the frame is to account for the culturally determined *vraisemblance* by which the conventions determining the reception of the work are naturalized, become second nature; and the full social dimension of the literary sign can only be restored through a deliberate reconstruction of these conventions.

337

NOTES

1. Boris Uspensky, *A Poetics of Composition,* trans. V. Zavarin and S. Wittig (Berkeley: University of California Press, 1973), 140.

2. Erving Goffman, *Frame Analysis: An Essay on the Organization of Experience* (New York: Harper & Row, 1974), 249.

3. Ibid., 124–25.

4. Cf. Christopher Logue's accentuation of this most unnoticed of frames in *New Numbers.* The flyleaf begins:

> This book was written in order to change the world
> and published at 12/ - (softback), 25/ - (hardback)
> by Cape of 30 Bedford Square, London WC1
> (a building formerly occupied by the Czarist Embassy) in 1969.

> It is generously scattered with dirty words particularly on pages 9, 31, 37 and 45
> and was written by © Logue
> a sexy young girl living among corrupted villagers. . .

5. Meyer Schapiro, "On Some Problems in the Semiotics of Visual Art: Field and Vehicle in Image-Signs," *Semiotica* 1, no. 3 (1969): 227–28.

6. Jurij Lotman, *The Structure of the Artistic Text,* trans. R. Vroon, Michigan Slavic Contributions no. 7 (Ann Arbor: University of Michigan Press, 1977), 212–13; but cf. also Barbara Herrnstein Smith, *Poetic Closure: A Study of How Poems End* (Chicago: University of Chicago Press, 1968).

7. Mikhail Bakhtin, *Problems of Dostoevsky's Poetics,* trans. R. Rotsel (Ann Arbor, Mich.: Ardis, 1973), 154.

8. I. A. Richards, *Poetries and Sciences: A Reissue of "Science and Poetry" (1926, 1935) with Commentary* (New York: Norton, 1970), 60.

9. As usually happens when the technical basis of a genre is altered, or as happens in Bertolt Brecht's *Lehrstücke,* where the frame situation of the spectator is abolished.

10. Lotman, *The Structure of the Artistic Text,* 210; note, however, Goffman's caution (*Frame Analysis,* 46) that "keying," the modulation to a secondary framework, is a shift not from the unframed to the framed but from the imperceptible primary frame of everyday experience to a *perceptible* secondary frame.

11. Uspensky, *A Poetics of Composition,* 143; Schapiro, "On Some Problems in the Semiotics of Visual Art," 227.

12. Goffman, *Frame Analysis,* 82.

13. Frank Kermode, *The Sense of an Ending* (London: Oxford University Press, 1966), 46.

14. George Kubler, *The Shape of Time* (New Haven, Conn.: Yale University Press, 1962), 24.

15. Although it is also true that much of the defamiliarizing effort of modernist art has been directed to a foregrounding of the frame, to stressing the arbitrariness of the limit of the work: cf. Degas's *Tête-à-tête dîner,* where the frame cuts off half of the man's face, or Godard's technique of having his characters walk casually in and out of a "badly composed" frame.

25

Stories within Stories: Narrative Levels and Embedded Narrative

WILLIAM NELLES

The device of the "story within the story," variously labeled "frame," "Chinese box," "Russian doll," or "embedded" narrative, is so widespread among the narrative literature of all cultures and periods as to approach universality. While this ubiquity alone would justify considerable theoretical interest, an additional consideration for narratology is offered by Gérard Genette's recent suggestion that the presence of narrative embedding may be one of the very few formal criteria for differentiating fictional from factual narratives (*Fiction* 79), and hence of potential value in the narratological Grail quest for definitions of such fundamental terms as "literature" and "narrative." Despite these powerful scholarly attractions, however, embedded narrative is an underdeveloped resource in literary theory. In fact, there is no generally accepted model or terminology for the analysis or even discussion of the structure. My intention here is to sketch out a rough version of such a model, with the intention rather of raising issues than settling them.

My approach to embedded narrative . . . will resemble that of Bal and Lanser in practice if not in theory, assigning all direct discourse to a particular narrative level. All three of us broadly follow Genette's theory of narrative levels to this end, but all depart from that theory to some extent. Lanser departs from Genette for two reasons: "Because so many of my colleagues have found Genette's neologistic terminology counterproductive . . . and because my distinctions are not quite the same as Genette's" (*Narrative,* 133). Unfortunately, her system cannot be correlated precisely with his, and Lanser admits that this is a deficiency in her model because "his framework is more technically refined" in this regard than her own (*Narrative,* 133). She suggests an adaptation of her system of public and private narrators to allow for the description of narrative levels, but recognizes that the result is not entirely satisfactory: "In choosing to use these terms instead of Genette's I am risking the danger that they carry misleading connotations; Genette's language has the advantage of precision. Terms like 'public' and 'private' must be understood here as somewhat metaphoric terms" (*Narrative,* 137). I have argued elsewhere on other grounds that Lanser's categories present additional problems for the description of narrative levels ("Problems," 209–11), but her own critique of her model will suffice here.

Once a methodology is set out for describing the various levels in a text, it becomes possible to produce a variety of groupings and classifications of narratives and embedded narratives. One such classificatory model has been proposed by Genette (*Revisited,* 128). His table, which takes into account focalization, narrative level, and relation (whether or not the narrator appears as a character in the story he tells), produces six types of narrative structure at each narrative level. Although Genette presents tables for only extra- and intradiegetic narrators, one could easily produce such a table for the other possible levels (meta-, tetra-, and so on), though it does become increasingly difficult to find examples to fill every possible position. Indeed, Genette already has three blank positions at the intradiegetic level. But these blanks do represent theoretical possibilities, even if they have not yet been realized, and it is often of as much interest to specify what writers have not done as to specify what they have done. That the categories created by this table mark out valuable distinctions for literary study is confirmed by the affinities that these classifications show with those arrived at by different means by theorists such as Franz Stanzel, Dorrit Cohn, and Jaap Linvelt, as Genette demonstrates in detail (*Revisited,* 114–29).

Bal has argued that there are two different ways in which embedded narratives can be related to embedding narratives. She illustrates the two types of embedding by reference to *The Thousand and One Nights* and then to Balzac's *Le Lys dans la vallée:*

> As we know, in the main narrative, which incorporates the other narratives and which I will refer to as R1, one narrates that a sultan who, ever since his wife cheated on him, kills each of his new wives after the wedding night. To stop him from killing her, Sheherazade tells the sultan captivating stories. The stories narrated by Sheherazade are the embedded narratives and will be referred to as R2throughX, a formula that takes into account their unlimited number. The relation between R1 and R2throughX is one of double subordination on the level of the actors and on the level of the action. Sheherazade, actor of R1, narrates R2throughX; she is its narrator. Narrated by an actor of R1, R2throughX are therefore subordinate to R1. Moreover,

R2throughX have a function within the action of R1: as long as Sheherazade tells stories the sultan does not kill her. . . . Even though the term *embedding* is used for all works where there is *a narrative within the narrative*, I would like to propose, for the clarity of the analysis, reserving it for works where there is a double subordination comparable to that in *The Thousand and One Nights*. If the subordination is carried out only on one of the two levels, I propose using the term *framing* (*encadrement*) as used by Balzac in his *Lys dans la vallée*. In this novel, the one who narrates the embedded narrative R2 is the subject of the embedding narrative R1; therefore, there is subordination of actors. However, the function of R2 in relation to the action R1 is limited, in this case, to providing afterwards an explanation for the behavior of the subject in R1; this behavior is already predetermined. The very fact that R2 is narrated does not influence the course of R1: it does not open up an alternative as in *The Thousand and One Nights* (the life or death of Sheherazade). Here therefore, it is a matter of a simple subordination. (*Narratologie,* 61–62)

But an examination of these two texts does not confirm Bal's analysis. To take her second example first, it is not the case that the embedded narrative does not influence the conduct of its narratee and hence the future of its narrator. The novel begins and ends with letters that frame the embedded narrative, Felix's life story. Although Bal contends that the embedded narrative does not affect the course of the embedding narrative, the story in the letters of Felix's wooing of and rejection by Natalie, the text contradicts her. As the final letter unambiguously declares, it is as a direct result of having read his history, in which he inadvertently reveals his truly unattractive nature, that Natalie decides to renounce "la gloire laborieuse" of returning Felix's love (462, 463). She further informs him that his narrative will produce the same effect on any other woman he tells it to: "If you are determined to remain in the world, and enjoy dealings with women, take care to hide from them all that you told me: they like neither to sow the flowering seeds of their love on rocks, nor squander their caresses in order to bandage a sick heart" (468). Thus both aspects of Bal's dual function are explicitly present here.

Instead it is in the story of Sheherazade that this dual aspect becomes problematic. Bal's contention is that if Sheherazade ceases to tell the stories, the sultan will kill her. This argument is compromised by the fact that she does cease to tell stories and the sultan does not kill her. One might object that it is only the cumulative effect of the telling of 1001 stories that saves her life, but the sultan himself explicitly denies this interpretation. Sheherazade requests that her life be spared not on the basis of her storytelling but because of the three children she has had by the sultan:

"For their sake I implore you to spare my life. For if you destroy the mother of these infants, they will find none among women to love them as I would."

The King embraced his three sons, and his eyes filled with tears as he answered: "I swear by Allah, Shahrazade, that you were already pardoned before the coming of these children. I loved you because I found you chaste and tender, wise and eloquent." (Dawood, 239)

If we take the sultan at his word, then, and allow for the terms of three pregnancies, she had been pardoned after the first few stories, and not exclusively or even primarily on the basis of her storytelling. The relation therefore is not that Sheherazade will be killed if she stops narrating but that Sheherazade believes that she will be killed if she stops narrating. But this is to say only that Sheherazade has a motive for narrating, and this holds true for all narrators.

But my conclusion is not really that Bal's classification should be reversed, that *Le Lys dans la vallée* is an example of *enchassement* and *The Thousand and One Nights* is an example of *encadrement*. Instead I would argue that Bal's distinction points to no significant structural features and is not a useful method of classification. Sheherazade's motivation contributes to the suspense of the story during a naive first reading and perhaps to an illusion of realism (though one would be hard pressed to find a reader so near the zero degree as to find this work realistic), but this motive has no structural component relevant to any objectively verifiable classificatory criterion. Sheherazade's earlier stories, which until some unspecified point must indeed exhibit this dual relation, differ in no discernible way from her later stories. One might as profitably try to guess which stories were told on Wednesdays and classify them on that basis. Natalie does suggest that certain particular aspects of Felix's tale were responsible for her decision, but there would seem to be little profit in separating these matters from the rest of the narrative and classifying them differently.

Bal's approach may also be faulted here for its privileging of her response over the text. No matter how often she rereads the book, Sheherazade will not stop narrating too soon and the sultan will not kill her; the mistaken belief that if she stops, then she will be killed is proper to Sheherazade, but not to the critical reader. Valéry called these sorts of imaginings "superstitions littéraires": "J'appelle ainsi toutes croyances qui ont de commun l'oubli de la condition verbale de la litterature. Ainsi l'existence et psychologie des *personnages,* ces vivants *sans entrailles*" (2.569). Paul de Man made a related observation about such criticism of the debate conducted in *La nouvelle Heloïse:* "it would be naive to ask who wins the match since in this model Rousseau, as author, controls the moves of each of the antagonists. . . . All the interest focuses on how one fights (or seduces), on the how, the *poetics* of writing and of reading rather than the hermeneutics" (112–13). Thus the question to be studied is not whether Felix seduces Natalie (we know that he does not) but how his attempt fails. . . . As noted above, the impossibility of discerning any differences between the early stories, which do help save Sheherazade's life, and the later stories, which do not, makes Bal's criterion inappropriate for narratological criticism. There is, however, a profound structural difference between the two works she uses as examples that does provide the basis for distinguishing two types of embedding. In Balzac's novel the opening letter and the history are both written by Felix to Natalie; both are intrahomodiegetic narratives, as is Natalie's response. Bal dismisses this feature as irrelevant (*Narratologie,* 83, n. 4). In doing so she ignores perhaps the most important question for narratological analysis, "who speaks?"

In *The Thousand and One Nights* the stories of Sheherazade are told as intradiegetic narratives in the general narrator's extradiegetic narrative. In this case there is a shift in narrative level between Bal's R1 and R2; in *Le Lys dans la vallée* there is not (leaving aside here the point that there is an implicit extradiegetic level occupied by the effaced general narrator of *Le Lys dans la vallée;* the example is compromised in that I allow two levels here to Bal's one). We can thus postulate that there are two structurally distinct types of narrative embedding: with a shift in narrator but not in narrative level, and with a shift of both narrator and narrative level.

Bal has astutely pointed out that there is at least one type of narrative that common sense would call embedded that nevertheless would not be considered as such according to this model: the case of a narrative that contains a dream:

> To take *La Chatte* again as an example: Alain's dream in the first chapter is clearly felt by the reader to be an interpolated narrative, a "metadiegetic" narrative. It does not enter into the series of events constituting the story of the novel, and it contains in itself an independent series of events. Where is the transition that lets us characterize the dream as "metadiegetic"? Denying it that designation is absurd, since the consensus of readers proves, albeit intuitively, that the dream is "metanarrative." ("Narrating," 243)

One might object to certain details of this analysis. It is not clear on what basis she claims that the dream is not one of the events of the novel, and her valorizing of the intuitive consensus of readers (a consensus of how many?) over the definitions of Genette is a questionable methodology. She also fails to explain her contention that a "passage from one level to another" takes place here ("Narrating," 243). The general narrator does not necessarily yield the narrating to an intradiegetic narrator. It could, of course, be argued that Alain dreams the dream to himself, that in a sense he narrates the dream to himself. In this reading there is indeed a shift in narrative level, with Alain becoming an intradiegetic narrator (and narratee). A clearer example of a dream that is presented with no shift in narrative level is found in the case of a dream narrated subsequently rather than as it is dreamed. In Chaucer's *The Book of the Duchess* the general narrator relates his dream after it has occurred, at the same narrative level as the rest of the text: "Loo, thus hyt was; thys was my sweven" (334, line 290).

Granting for the sake of discussion that Bal is correct in stating that there is no shift of level in Genette's sense, her conclusion does not necessarily follow. What Bal intuits here as a shift in diegetic level is in fact a shift in the *diégèse,* "l'univers où advient cette histoire" (Genette, *Palimpsestes,* 342). The events of the dream are not supposed to be physically carried out in the spatial-temporal universe of the bulk of the narrative, but they are none the less events narrated at the same level as other events of the novel. We might characterize this type of structure by postulating a form of ontological shift that can be opposed to the epistemological shift of the other examples of embedding considered thus far. I use these terms not in any strict philosophical sense but in the metaphorical sense adopted by Brian McHale in his contrasting of Modernism and Postmodernism. Epistemological embedding by means of a shift in narrator is characterized by emphasis on the process of communicating knowledge: who imparts what to whom; ontological framing, as in dreams or science-fiction stories of alternate dimensions, is characterized by emphasis on modes of being, by the shifting of levels of reality or existence. Bal is correct here in remarking that narratological models are more useful in describing epistemological frames than ontological frames. It should be recalled, however, that many of the thematic relations examined later in this essay in connection with embedding may be set up by these ontological shifts as well.

By way of simplifying this cumbersome pair of terms, Scott Vaszily has proposed to me the adoption of "vertical" rather than "epistemological" and "horizontal" in place of "ontological." The concept of a series of narrative *levels* is already conveniently set up in terms of a vertical metaphor, and perhaps the connotations of the root "horizon" are appropriate to the shifting of ontological realms. I would hope to invoke particularly the OED's definition 2.a, "A boundary, the frontier or dividing line between two regions of being."

John Barth and Genette have proposed similar tripartite models for further classifying embedded narratives. The first version of Genette's system distinguished three principal types of relation between embedding and embedded narrative:

> The first type of relationship is direct causality between the events of the metadiegesis and those of the diegesis, conferring on the second narrative an *explanatory function.* . . .

> The second type consists of a purely *thematic* relationship, therefore implying no spatio-temporal continuity between metadiegesis and diegesis: a relationship of contrast. . . . or of analogy . . . .
>
> The third type involves no explicit relationship between the two story levels: it is the act of narrating itself that fulfills a function in the diegesis, independently of the metadiegetic content—a function of distraction, for example and/or obstruction. Surely the most illustrious example is found in the *Thousand and One Nights,* where Scheherazade holds off death with renewed narratives, whatever they might be (provided they interest the sultan). (*Narrative,* 232–33)

Part of my earlier analysis of Bal's own use of this final example might be reinvoked here; the narrative structure may not be quite as straightforward as Bal and Genette claim. An additional subtlety is offered by Todorov's suggestion that we "attempt to take the opposite point of view, no longer that of the embedding narrative but that of the embedded narrative, and inquire: why does the embedded narrative need to be included within another narrative?" (*Poetics,* 76). Todorov goes on to observe that "if we consider the narrative in this way, not as enclosing other narratives but as being enclosed by them, a curious property is revealed. Each narrative seems to have something excessive, a supplement which remains outside the closed form produced by the development of the plot. . . . This supplement takes several forms in the *Arabian Nights*" (*Poetics,* 76, 77). He then lists a number of consequences for interpretation and reader response which result from this supplement; this concept also has affinities with the notion of the metalepsis, another means of opening up an apparently closed form, which I will discuss presently.

Furthermore, assignment of a narrative to one of these thematic categories is a matter of literary interpretation, not a matter of the simple recognition of significant structural features. As a result, they are not mutually exclusive and hence are difficult to use for purposes of classification or description. The same objections would apply to Barth's system of dramaturgical, thematic, and gratuitous relationships, which, though independently arrived at, are quite similar to Genette's categories ("Tales," 56–57). It is probably the case that any extensively studied embedded narrative could be suitable for any or all of the three categories, depending on the literary judgment of the person doing the classification. As Genette himself has argued elsewhere, more in keeping with the spirit of his system as a whole, such a system of classification, "which in reality has to do with 'interpretation,' does not lie within the province of narratology" (*Revisited,* 87). Narratology should rather provide a set of objective criteria that can precede interpretation and help direct it along profitable paths or even operate relatively independently of direct interpretation.

Genette later critiques Barth's model and incorporates elements of it within his own, producing six types (*Revisited,* 92–94). But the revised model still does not address the problems noted above. Genette's discussions of these issues do, however, suggest in passing two objective criteria for the classification of embedded tales, one more useful than the other. The first is his distinction between analeptic and proleptic embeddings (*Revisited,* 93). His restriction of the relevance of this temporal relation to his explicative function is unnecessarily limiting, since time-shifts could always serve a thematic function (as can any element of any narrative), but this temporal relation is generally objectively determinable and hence a readily verifiable basis for differentiation.

Genette's other suggestion seems less promising. Considering that narrative level has been accorded exaggerated importance by critics of his system, he argues that embedding narratives of very slight extent may be disregarded as insignificant: "the intradiegetic character of a narrative is very often, as we see clearly in Maupassant and again in *Jean Santeuil,* only a stratagem of presentation, a conventionality that, in many respects, is insignificant" (*Revisited,* 95). But the initial reason for using narrative level as a basis for classification is not that it is necessarily the most subjectively important criterion for the literary criticism of embedded narratives but that it is the most significant common structural feature for the description of embedded narratives . . . . Genette's choice of Maupassant as the epitome of the author whose embeddings are without critical interest underscores emphatically the relativity of such judgments and the need in narratological theory to avoid building a model on them. Angela Moger has devoted a full chapter of her dissertation and a published article to close study of the ways in which Maupassant's framing devices are in fact among the most significant elements to be considered in analysis of his stories. As she notes at one point in her discussion of Maupassant, "Indeed, it is to a certain extent *because of* their apparent gratuitousness" that certain framing elements can be identified as meaningful ("Working," 66 n.22; my emphasis). Moger's explicit limitation of her studies of framed narrative to precisely this type of "seemingly gratuitous 'border'" offers a valuable corrective to the assumption that any embedding narrative may be inconsequential ("Working," 6). Sarah Kozloff has proposed an alternative means of classifying embedded narrations by their extent, labeling embedded narrators "micro-narrators" if their "story comprises less than 25 percent of the entire text" (49). Such stories would presumably be called, by analogy, "micro-narratives." While her interest lies specifically in voice-over narrators in films, the principle she suggests would appear to be readily transferable to written narratives. Kozloff's assertion that in such cases this "quantitative difference becomes qualitative," which would be the clearest justification for the terminological distinction, is not developed. The assertion is nevertheless plausible, and her suggestion points to an area that needs to be explored.

My rejection of the dramatic and thematic and, especially, the gratuitous categories as a basis for classification should in no way be interpreted as meaning that these do not reflect important functions or effects of the structures of narrative embedding. In fact, I would argue that all embedded narrative has a dramatic impact, if only that of deferring or interrupting the embedding narrative, and that all embedded narrative has a thematic function, if only one of relative contrast or analogy. Even discontinuity or apparently gratuitous relationships may be read as thematically significant. I insist on this irreducible minimum of potential dramatic and thematic weight only to cover unforeseen limit cases. In practice, a shift in narrator (*Le Lys dans la vallée*) or a shift in narrator and narrative level (*The Thousand and One Nights*) always produces effects of some consequence. One of the reasons for this was offered by Boris Uspensky, who observed in his analyses of the psychological, spatial-temporal, phraseological, and ideological microtexts that may be found within every narrative that it is often the case that "the frames of the microtexts on one level (on the plane of phraseology, let us say) do not concur with the frames which are manifested on another level (for example, on the plane of spatial-temporal characteristics). A text which is organized in this way cannot be broken down into its constituent microdescriptions, although the separations may be defined in terms of each level" (155).

The exception to this obscuring of the compositional elements of point of view is, precisely, the embedded narrative as marked by a shift in narrator: "in literature the phenomenon of conjoining microdescriptions or particular texts in a more general text is represented by a composition employing a story within a story. The most obvious and simplest instance may be found in framed novellas and other clear-cut cases in which the change in narrator is presented explicitly, and the reader clearly perceives the borders between the separate stories" (154–55). In such cases "the borders concur on all levels" (155); the shift of narrator is thus the most prominent marker of a range of other important shifts and the most obvious point to focus on in studying them. This boundary is most pronounced when the shift in narrator is accompanied by a shift in narrative level in that this automatically entails additional structural and dramatic considerations that may be the sources of meaning. Barbara Herrnstein Smith has suggested the reasons that such frames will always, inherently, have a structuring effect; the fact that a narrator yields to an embedded narrator means that the resumption of the narrative by the first narrator will affect the reading of the whole:

any terminal element that has been in some way predetermined will strengthen closure by fulfilling the reader's expectation of it. One may observe, however, that the occurrence of predetermined elements also increases the reader's experience of validity: that is, by conforming to his expectations, such an element becomes both stable and self-validating and extends these effects to the whole utterance of which it is a part. It would seem then, that any device that predetermines the occurrence or form of terminal elements will tend to strengthen both closure and the sense of validity. (154–55)

This structural effect of validity would seem to reinforce an independent effect of plausibility or believability that can be produced by embedding. As David Lodge has remarked, "The Rise of the English novel in the eighteenth century began with the discovery of new possibilities of mimesis in prose narrative, through the use of characters as narrators—the pseudo-autobiographers of Defoe, the pseudo-correspondents of Richardson—thus making the narrative discourse a mimesis of an act of diegesis, diegesis at a second remove. These devices brought about a quantum leap in realistic illusion and immediacy . . ." (95).

Erving Goffman has suggested that structural effects like those predicted by Smith will still be produced even if the text ends after an embedded discourse without an explicit return to the embedding frame:

Consider now the possibility that the bracket initiating a particular kind of activity may carry more significance than the bracket terminating it. For— as already suggested in regard to the notational system of mathematics—it is reasonable to assume that the beginning bracket not only will establish an episode but also will establish a slot for signals which will inform and define what sort of transformation is to be made of the materials within the episode. . . . Closing brackets would seem to perform less work, perhaps reflecting the fact that it is probably much easier on the whole to terminate the influence of a frame than to establish it. However, epilogues do try to summarize what has occurred and ensure the proper framing of it. (255–56)

This would explain why writers so often leave off the final explicit return to the embedding frame (*The Turn of the Screw*, for example): the opening frame has provided all of the context necessary for interpretation of the embedded narrative and the structure is felt as complete even though implicit. It may also be part of the reason that narratives which leave off the initiating part of the embedding narrative and reveal only at the end that the story has been embedded ("it had all been a dream") are sometimes perceived as poorly structured.

348

That is not to say that such a surprise ending may not be effectively handled in other cases, of course, as in the example of "An Occurrence at Owl Creek Bridge."

A further component of embedded narrative that tends to almost automatically generate significance is that, as Peter Brooks notes, "framed narration in general offers a way to make explicit and dramatize the motive for storytelling . . ." (259). The narratee also may have motives, of course, which may become identified to some extent with those of the reader. Tzvetan Todorov has analyzed this interaction, which he finds especially significant in the case of vertically embedded tales like those of the *Decameron,* which have dramatized intra- and meta-diegetic narratees.

Ross Chambers explains, making a related point in a more schematic way, that narrational embedding places "narrative act within narrative act, narrative situation within narrative situation: it implies the representation, internally to the fictional framework, of a situation involving the major components of a communicational act (emitter-discourse-recipient)—and very frequently the mirroring within a story of the storytelling relationship itself: narrator-narration-narratee" (33). This structure constitutes one of Dällenbach's three elementary types of *mise en abyme,* which he has termed, following Jakobsen's model, *mise en abyme de l'énonciation* (61, 74). Moger has suggested that narrative embedding also produces what Dällenbach would call a *mise en abyme du code:* "Since, moreover, the framing of a narrative constitutes the explicitation of the self-referential quality of narrative (the frame compels the understanding that the story is about the telling of the story), we perceive the complexity of the paradigmatic axis engendered by the interplay of thematic element and structural element" ("Obscure," 136). Her analysis leads to the thematic interpretation that "The function of the frame, then, would be to undercut the framed, to make clear that the central narrative's appearance of substantiality is an optical illusion, and to mock the pretensions of the conventional reading of such a story" (134). Thus narrative embedding has the paradoxical effect of producing the illusion of a more profound realism, as the analyses of Smith, Lodge, and Prince explain, but also of undercutting that illusion at the same time.

This survey is intended to be representative rather than exhaustive, and if it leads to any simple conclusion, it would be that of Gregory Bateson, that "a frame is metacommunicative. Any message, which either explicitly or implicitly defines a frame, *ipso facto* gives the receiver instructions or aids in his attempt to understand the messages included within the frame" (188). Every embedded narrative must be considered to have strong potential for structural, dramatic, and thematic significance by virtue of the sole fact of its being embedded. A similar range of effects arises from the most complex class of embedded narratives, those in which the most emphatically structured frame, vertical embedding, is violated by use of the trope of the metalepsis.

Since most narrative texts contain more than one narrative level, they have at least the potential for narrative metalepsis, the move by means of which a character, frequently a narrator, moves from one diegetic level to another. The term as used with this sense is another Genettian coinage, defined by him as "any intrusion by the extradiegetic narrator or narratee into the diegetic universe (or by diegetic characters into a metadiegetic universe, etc.), or the inverse . . ." (*Narrative*, 234–35). Genette provides an example of what I will define as the basic "unmarked" case of metalepsis with an illustration drawn from Balzac's *Illusions perdues:* "'While the venerable churchman climbs the ramps of Angouleme, it is not useless to explain . . . ' as if the narrating were contemporaneous with the story and had to fill up the latter's dead spaces" (*Narrative*, 235). In this case the metalepsis is not precisely either a movement by the extradiegetic narrator into the intradiegetic fiction nor a movement by the intradiegetic character to the extradiegetic level. There is rather a temporary sharing of a common level. Granting this as the unmarked case, then, two other possibilities that are distinctly marked may be identified.

The first may be illustrated by the incident in chapter 55 of John Fowles's *The French Lieutenant's Woman,* in which the twentieth-century extradiegetic narrator enters a nineteenth-century railway coach and observes (and is observed by) one of his intradiegetic characters (318). This movement from an "outer" embedding level to an "inner" embedded level might be termed intrametaleptic. The opposite movement may be seen in Virgil's *Aeneid* at the point where Aeneas exclaims "crudelis tu quoque" (line 407). This is a quotation of his own creator's *Eclogue* 8, in which the phrase is repeated as a refrain through lines 48–50. Later in the *Aeneid* (lines 603–605), Virgil has Aeneas allude to Catullus 76, lines 17–26, elaborating the device by giving his ancient character knowledge of another contemporary poet (Fordyce, 368). This movement, which gives a character in the diegesis knowledge of the other works of his historical author, in a movement "outward" as opposed to the movement "inward" of Fowles's narrator, might be termed extrametaleptic.

These examples suggest two other means by which metalepses may be classified. The first takes into account the temporal relation: Fowles's narrator goes back in time a hundred years, while the prehistorical Aeneas exhibits familiarity with the works of poets centuries before their births. The first possibility would thus constitute, by analogy with Genette's other definitions of temporal relations, an analeptic intrametaleptic shift. The second, extending his terminology by the same logic, would be a proleptic extrametaleptic shift. The two examples also differ in another way: Fowles's narrator moves physically to a different diegetic world, where Aeneas only displays knowledge of the other world. Here my distinction between ontological and epistemological emphases in embedding may be reinvoked to characterize these metalepses as, respectively, ontological (or horizontal) and epistemological (or vertical). Aeneas engages therefore in a vertical proleptic extrametalepsis, Fowles's narrator in a horizontal analeptic intrametalepsis. I am of course conscious of the unwieldy nature of these terms, but their awkwardness may be compensated for in some degree by their precision. The alternative, using simpler metaphorical terms, would attribute to Aeneas something like a "mental forward out" metalepsis, which makes my adaptation of Genette's terms perhaps the lesser of evils. There are, mercifully, no further categories to specify, and it is possible to turn to the less tortuous activity of suggesting in broad outline the major implications of metalepsis for interpretation.

Genette has observed that the use of metalepsis most often produces "an effect of strangeness that is either comical . . . or fantastic" (*Narrative*, 235). Robyn Warhol has used her model of the distancing and engaging narrator to explain how the metalepsis functions not only to produce comedy but also to emphasize the effect of realism, which, as noted above, is often produced by narrative embedding: "A distancing narrator uses metalepsis humorously, as Genette has pointed out. . . . An engaging narrator, though, uses the device to suggest that the characters are possibly as 'real' as the narrator and narratee, who are, in these cases, to be identified with the actual author and actual reader" (814).

But these generally comic or realistic effects are also accompanied by the structural demand for a more complex model of reading. The interpenetration or overlapping of levels forces the reader to make other connections between the characters and worlds of the different levels. The metalepsis leads the reader to cross narrative levels along with the discourse, to read the two connected levels in terms of each other. As Dällenbach has noted, such slippage between narrative levels has the function "de provoquer des collusions spéctaculaires entre les . . . niveaux narratifs" (44). Genette has argued that these interactions finally produce effects that are rather unsettling than comic:

> All these games, by the intensity of their effects, demonstrate the importance of the boundary they tax their ingenuity to overstep, in defiance of verisimilitude—a boundary that is precisely the narrating (or the performance) itself: a shifting but sacred frontier between two worlds, the world in which one tells, the world of which one tells . . . . The most troubling thing about metalepsis indeed lies in this unacceptable and insistent hypothesis, that the extradiegetic is perhaps always diegetic, and that the narrator and his narratees—you and I—perhaps belong to some narrative. (*Narrative,* 236)

Genette is drawn to this last remark about the metaleptic effect by Borges's well-known analysis of certain metalepses: "Why does it disquiet us to know that Don Quixiote is a reader of the *Quixote,* and Hamlet a spectator of *Hamlet?* I believe I have found the answer: those inversions suggest that if the characters in a story can be readers or spectators, then we, their readers and spectators, can be fictitious" (*Other,* 46). What Genette and Borges both fail to point out here is that their conclusions apply not only to metalepsis but to all embedded narrative. Hamlet views not *Hamlet,* after all, but "The Murther of Gonzago" (2.2.537–38) or "The Mouse-trap" (3.2.237). Properly speaking, there is no metalepsis involved in the play within a play. That thematic and dramatic parallels exist between the embedding and embedded plays is not a function of an explicit metalepsis but rather of the structure of embedding and its potential for the effects of mise en abyme, as argued above.

My conclusion is therefore that any narrative context within which a character reads or writes, hears or tells a narrative can produce these same relations between embedding and embedded narratives. The trope of metalepsis more directly foregrounds this interplay of narrative levels, but such interplay is implicitly active in all embedded narratives, and it may be said that all embedded narratives produce, in some degree, the effects of metalepsis.

REFERENCES

Bal, Mieke. "The Narrating and the Focalizing: A Theory of the Agents in Narrative." Translated by Jane E. Lewin. *Style* 17, no. 2 (1983): 234–69.

———. *Narratologie: Essais sur la signification narrative dans quatre romans modernes,* (1977). Utrecht: HES, 1984.

———. *Narratology: Introduction to the Theory of Narrative.* Toronto: University of Toronto Press, 1985.

Balzac, Honoré de. *Le Lys dans la vallée.* Paris: Librairie Générale Française, 1972.

Barth, John. "Tales Within Tales Within Tales." *Antaeus* 43 (1981): 45–63.

Bateson, Gregory. *Steps to an Ecology of Mind.* San Francisco: Chandler, 1972.

Borges, Jorge Luis. *Other Inquisitions: 1937–1952.* Translated by Ruth L. C. Simms. New York: Simon and Schuster, 1965.

Brooks, Peter. *Reading for the Plot.* New York: Knopf, 1984.

Chambers, Ross. *Story and Situation.* Minneapolis: University of Minnesota Press, 1984.

Chaucer, Geoffrey. *The Riverside Chaucer.* Edited by Larry D. Benson. Boston: Houghton, 1987.

Dällenbach, Lucien. *Le Récit spéculaire.* Paris: Seuil, 1977.

Dawood, N. J., trans. *The Thousand and One Nights* (1954). Edinburgh: Penguin, 1961.

de Man, Paul. *The Resistance to Theory.* Minneapolis: University of Minnesota Press, 1986.

Fordyce, C. J. *Catullus.* Oxford: Clarendon, 1961.

Fowles, John. *The French Lieutenant's Woman,* (1969). New York: Signet, 1970.

Genette, Gérard. *Fiction et diction.* Paris: Seuil, 1991.

———. *Figures 2.* Paris: Seuil, 1969.

———. *Narrative Discourse.* Translated by Jane E. Lewin. Ithaca, N.Y.: Cornell University Press, 1980.

———. *Narrative Discourse Revisited.* Translated by Jane E. Lewin. Ithaca, N.Y.: Cornell University Press, 1989.

———. *Palimpsestes.* Paris: Seuil, 1982.

Goffman, Erving. *Frame Analysis.* Cambridge, Mass.: Harvard University Press, 1974.

Kozloff, Sarah. *Invisible Storytellers: Voice-Over Narration in the American Fiction Film.* Berkeley: University of California Press, 1988.

Lanham, Richard A. *A Handlist of Rhetorical Terms.* Berkeley: University of California Press, 1968.

Lanser, Susan S. *The Narrative Act.* Princeton, N.J.: Princeton University Press, 1981.

———. "Toward a Feminist Narratology." *Style* 20, no. 3 (1987): 341–63.

Lodge, David. "Mimesis and Diegesis in Modern Fiction." *SPELL* 1 (1984): 89–108.

McHale, Brian. "Change of Dominant from Modernist to Postmodernist Writing." In *Approaching Postmodernism,* edited by Douwe Fokkema and Hans Bertens, 53–79. Amsterdam: John Benjamins, 1986.

Moger, Angels S. "That Obscure Object of Narrative." *Yale French Studies* 63 (1983): 129–38.

———."Working Out (of) Frame(d) Works: A Study of the Structural Frame in Stories by Maupassant, Balzac, Barbey, and Conrad." Ph.D. diss., Yale University, 1980.

Nelles, William. "Getting Focalization into Focus." *Poetics Today* 11, no. 2 (1990): 365–82.

———. "Problems for Narrative Theory: *The French Lieutenant's Woman.*" *Style* 18, no. 2 (1984): 207–17.

Oxford English Dictionary. 2d ed. Oxford: Clarendon, 1987.

Prince, Gerald. "Introduction à l'étude du narrataire." *Poétique* 14 (1973): 178–96.

Smith, Barbara Herrnstein. *Poetic Closure.* Chicago: University of Chicago Press, 1968.

Todorov, Tzvetan. *Grammaire du* Decameron. The Hague: Mouton, 1969.

———. *The Poetics of Prose.* Translated by Richard Howard. Ithaca, N.Y.: Cornell University Press, 1977.

Uspensky, Boris. *A Poetics of Composition.* Translated by Valentina Zavarin and Susan Wittig. Berkeley: University of California Press, 1973.

Valéry, Paul. *Oeuvres.* 2 vols. Paris: Gallimard, 1960. Vol. 2.

Virgil. *The* Aeneid *of Virgil, Books 1-6.* Edited by R. D. Williams. New York: St. Martin's, 1972.

———. *The* Eclogues *and* Georgics. Edited by R. D. Williams. New York: St. Martin's, 1979.

Warhol, Robyn R. "Toward a Theory of the Engaging Narrator." *PMLA* 101 (1986): 811–18.

26

The Parergon

JACQUES DERRIDA

|⎯   the
word *parergon* intervenes, precisely (paragraphs 13 and 24) at the moment
when Kant has just distinguished between *material* and *formal* judgments, the
latter alone constituting judgments of taste in the proper sense. It is not, of
course, a matter of a formalist aesthetic (we could show, from another point
of view, that it is the contrary) but of formality as the space of aesthetics in
general, of a "formalism" which, instead of representing a determinate system,
merges with the history of art and with aesthetics itself. And the formality-
effect is always tied to the possibility of a framing system that is both imposed
and erased.

The question of the frame is already framed when it appears at a certain
detour of the *Critique*.

Why framed?

The "Clarification by Examples" (paragraph 14) belongs to the "Analytic
of the Beautiful," book 1 of the "Analytic of Aesthetic Judgment." This analytic of the beautiful comprises four parts, four sides, four moments. The
judgment of taste is examined from four sides: (1) according to *quality;* (2)
according to *quantity;* (3) according to the *relation of the ends* (the *parergon*
finds its lodgings here); (4) according to *modality*. The definition of the beautiful according to quality is the object of a disinterested *Wohlgefallen;* according to quantity, what pleases universally without concept; according to the
relation of ends, the form of finality without the representation of an end
(finality without end[1]); according to modality, that which is recognized without concept as the object of a necessary *Wohlgefallen*.

Such is the categorial frame of the analytic of the beautiful. Now where does this frame come from? Who supplies it? Who constructs it? Where is it imported from?

From the analytic of concepts in the *Critique of Pure* [speculative] *Reason.* A brief reminder: this analytic of concepts is one of the two parts of the transcendental analytic (transcendental analytic and dialectic, a division reproduced in the third *Critique:* analytic and dialectic of aesthetic judgment). The transcendental analytic comprises an analytic of concepts and an analytic of principles. The former breaks down the power of understanding in order to recognize in it the possibility of *a priori* concepts in their "country of birth," namely the understanding, where they lie dormant and in reserve. Since (receptive) intuition alone relates immediately to the object, the understanding does so by the intermediary, precisely, of judgments. Judgment is the mediate knowledge of an object. And we can "refer all the acts of the understanding back to judgments, in such a way that the understanding in general can be represented as a power to judge (*Urteilskraft*)." The power to think as power to judge. One will thus find the functions of the understanding by determining the functions of unity in judgment. Concepts relate, as predicates of possible judgments, to the representation of an object. Consequently, by considering the simple form of the understanding, by abstracting the content of judgments, one can establish the list of the forms of judgment under *four* headings and twelve moments (four times three: the four-times-three also constructs the table [*Tafel*] of the superior faculties at the end of the introduction to the third *Critique.* Kant replies, in a note, to those who object to his "tripartite" [*dreiteilig*] divisions and to his taste for "trichotomy"; and the *three + one* informs the relationship of the faculties required by the fine arts— imagination, understanding, soul—with taste: "the first three faculties are united only thanks to the fourth," affirms the note to paragraph 50): *quantity* of the judgments (universal, particular, singular), *quality* (affirmative, negative, indefinite), *relation* (categorical, hypothetical, disjunctive), *modality* (problematic, assertoric, apodeictic). *Table of twelve.* Now there are as many pure concepts of the understanding, originary and nonderivable concepts, as there are logical functions in judgments. Whence the deduction of the table of categories (against the so-called grammatical empiricism of Aristotle) from the table of judgments.

Kant thus imports this table, this tableau (*Tafel*) this *board*[2] this *border* into the analytic of aesthetic judgment. This is a legitimate operation since it is a question of judgments. But it is a transportation which is not without its problems and artful violence: a *logical* frame is transposed and forced in to be imposed on a *nonlogical* structure, a structure which no longer essentially concerns a relation to the object as object of knowledge. The aesthetic judgment, as Kant insists, is not a knowledge-judgment.

355

The frame fits badly. The difficulty can be felt from the first paragraph of the book, from the "first moment of the judgment of taste considered from the point of view of quality." "The judgment of taste is aesthetic": in this single case, not foreseen by the analytic of concepts and judgments in the other *Critique,* the judgment is not a "knowledge-judgment." Hence it does not come under the transcendental logic whose *board* has been brought in.

The violence of the framing multiplies. It begins by enclosing the theory of the aesthetic in a theory of the beautiful, the latter in a theory of taste and the theory of taste in a theory of judgment. These are decisions which could be called external: the delimitation has enormous consequences, but a certain internal coherence can be saved at this cost. The same does not apply for another gesture of framing which, by introducing the *bord,* does violence to the inside of the system and twists its proper articulations out of shape. This must therefore be the gesture of primary interest to us if we are seeking a rigorously effective grip.

In the course of the final delimitation (theory of taste as theory of judgment), Kant *applies,* then, an analytic of logical judgments to an analytic of aesthetic judgments at the very moment that he is insisting on the irreducibility of the one kind to the other. He never justifies this framing, nor the constraint it artificially imposes on a discourse constantly threatened with overflowing [*débordement*]. In the first note to the first page, Kant says that the *logical* functions of judgment served him as a guide (*Anleitung*). This note touches on a difficulty so decisive that one cannot see why it does not constitute the principal text of which it forms the ground bass, that is, the unwritten or underwritten space, the supposed range of the harmonics. Here it is: "The definition of taste which here serves as a foundation is the following: taste is the faculty of judging the beautiful. But what is then required in order to call an object beautiful must be discovered (*entdecken*) by the analysis of judgments of taste. I [intervention of the first person in a footnote] have looked for the moments (*Momente*) raised by this judgment in its reflection, taking as a guide the logical functions (for in judgments of taste there is still always (*immer noch*) a relation to the understanding. It is the moment of quality that I have examined first, because it is the one that the aesthetic judgment of the beautiful takes into consideration first."

This note is to the title, "First Moment of the Judgment of Taste Considered from the Point of View of Quality." The note thus precedes, in a certain way, the text of the exposition; it is relatively detached from it. The same goes for the parenthesis it includes: "(for in judgments of taste there is still always [*immer noch*] a relation to the understanding)." This parenthesis (inserted in a note which is neither inside nor outside the exposition, neither inside nor outside its content) attempts to justify—and it is the only such attempt—the frame of the exposition, namely the analytic of judgment whose *bord* has been hastily imported at the opening of the exposition.

Before the note and its parenthesis (before, if one looks at the space of the page from bottom to top, but after if one keeps to the order of the exposition which places the note at the top of the page, at the place of its reference), another briefer parenthesis forms a pocket in the supposedly "main" text and is *invaginated* in it, in a sense: "In order to distinguish whether or not a thing is beautiful, we do not relate the representation to the object by means of the understanding, with a view to knowledge, but to the subject and to its feeling of pleasure or unpleasure, by means of the imagination (united perhaps with the understanding, *vielleicht mit dem Verstande verbunden*)."

The two parentheses, *parerga* inside and outside the exposition, have the same object, the same finality: the justification (which is visibly very awkward) of the imported frame, of the analytic imposed—an ill-assured recourse, in order to get the table by and make the board fit—on a hypothetical "liaison" with the understanding, to which the judgment of taste, although there is nothing logical about it, supposedly "always still" has a relation.

Like an old liaison difficult to break off or a second-hand frame one is having trouble selling and that one wants to unload at any price.

The frame of this analytic of the beautiful, with its four moments, is thus furnished by the transcendental analytic, for the sole and bad reason that the imagination, the essential resource of the relation to beauty, is *perhaps* linked to the understanding, that there is perhaps and *still* (*vielleicht, noch*) some understanding in there. The relation to the understanding, which is neither certain nor essential, thus furnishes the frame of this whole discourse; and, within it, of the discourse on the frame. Without forcing things, but in any case in order to describe a certain forcing on Kant's part, we shall say that the whole frame of the analytic of the beautiful functions, with respect to that the content or internal structure of which is to be determined, like a *parergon;* it has all its characteristics: neither simply internal nor simply external, not falling to one side of the work as one could have said of an exergue, indispensable to *energeia* in order to liberate surplus value by enclosing labor (any market and first of all the picture market thus presupposes a process of framing: and an effective deconstructive labor cannot here do without a theory of the frame), it is called up and gathered together as a supplement from the lack—a certain "internal" indetermination—in the very thing that it comes to frame. This lack, which cannot be determined, localized, situated, *arrested* inside or outside *before the framing,* is simultaneously—still using concepts which belong, precisely, to the classical logic of the frame, here to Kant's discourse—both *product* and *production* of the frame. If one applies to it the rule defined in the "Clarification by Examples," and if it becomes in its turn an example of what it allows us to consider as an example (frame described in the frame), then one can act as though the content of the analytic of judgment were a work of art, a picture whose frame, imported from the other *Critique,* would by virtue of its formal beauty play the role of *parergon.* And if it were simply an attractive, seductive, amusing exergue, not cooperating with what is proper to the work, a pure loss of value and waste of surplus value, then it would only be adornment. But it so happens that it is this analytic of judgment itself which, in its frame, allows us to define the requirement of formality, the opposition of the formal and the material, of the pure and the impure, of the proper and the improper, of the inside and the outside. It is the analytic which *determines* the frame as *parergon,* which both constitutes it and ruins it [*l'abîme*], makes it both hold (as that which causes to hold together, that which constitutes, mounts, inlays, sets, borders, gathers, trims—so. many operations gathered together by the *Einfassung*) and collapse. A frame is essentially constructed and therefore fragile: such would be the essence or truth of the frame. If it had any. But this "truth" can no longer be a "truth," it no more defines the transcendentality than it does the accidentality of the frame, merely its *parergonality.*

Philosophy wants to arraign it and can't manage. But what has produced and manipulated the frame puts everything to work in order to efface the frame effect, most often by naturalizing it to infinity, in the hands of God (one can verify this in Kant). Deconstruction must neither reframe nor dream of the pure and simple absence of the frame. These two apparently contradictory gestures are the very ones—and they are systematically indissociable—of *what* is here deconstructed.[3]

If the operations engaged and the criteria proposed by the analytic of the beautiful depend on this parergonality; if all the value oppositions which dominate the philosophy of art (before and since Kant) depend on it in their pertinence, their rigor, their purity, their propriety, then they are affected by this logic of the *parergon* which is more powerful than that of the analytic. One could follow in detail the consequences of this infectious affection. They cannot be local. The reflective operation which we have just allowed to make itself writing on the frame or have itself written on the frame (this is—writing/written on the frame):[4] a general law which is no longer a mechanical or teleological law of nature, of the accord or the harmony of the faculties (etc.), but a certain repeated dislocation, a regulated, irrepressible dislocation, which makes the frame in general crack, undoes it at the corners in its quoins and joints,[5] turns its internal limit into an external limit, takes its thickness into account, makes us see the picture from the side of the canvas or the wood, etc.

To note only the first consequence of the initial forcing, see the end of the first note (another *parergon* which frames both the text and, within it as within itself, the parenthesis). Just as Kant cannot justify in all rigor the importation of the analytic of judgment, he cannot justify the *order* he follows in the application of the frame, of the four categories of the analytic of concepts. No more than with the transport of the table (*Tafel*), i.e., the frame, does the order of exposition here manage to rationalize its interest philosophically. Its motivation hides behind the arbitrariness of philosophical decree. The exposition begins with the group of the two *mathematical* categories (*quantity and quality*). Why not begin with the two *dynamic* categories (*relation and modality*)? And why invert the order of the mathematical categories themselves, as it was followed in the original exposition (quantity before quality)? This latter reversal is explained, to be sure, by the fact that knowledge is neither the end nor the effect of the judgment of taste: quantity (here, universality) is not the *first* value of a judgment of taste. End of the note: "It is the moment of quality that I have examined first, because it is the one that the aesthetic judgment of the beautiful takes into consideration first." Why first (*zuerst*)? The priority is not prescribed by the table, by the order of judgment, by the logic proper to the frame. Nothing in the (logical) analytic as such can account for this priority. Now if a reversal of the logical order takes place here for reasons which are not logical, why should it not continue? What is the rule or critical limit here?

Quality (the disinterested character) is the very thing that determines the formality of the beautiful object: it must be pure of all attraction, of all seductive power, it must provoke no emotion, promise no enjoyment. The *opposition* between the formal and the material, design and color (at least insofar as it is nonformal), composition and sound (at least insofar as it is nonformal), the formal *parergon* and the *parergon* for show or adornment, the opposition between the good and the bad *parergon* (which in itself is neither good nor bad) thus depends on the framing of this quality, of this frame effect called quality, value of value, and with which, violently, everything seems to begin. Position: opposition: frame.

Likewise, in the "Clarification," the discourse on sound and on color is held in the angle of the two mathematical categories (quality and quantity) even as the whole analytic of the beautiful is undoing, ceaselessly and as if without wanting to, the labor of the frame.

The frame labors [*travaille*] indeed. Place of labor, structurally bordered origin of surplus value, i.e., overflowed [*debordée*] on these two borders by what it overflows, it gives [*travaille*] indeed.[6] Like wood. It creaks and cracks, breaks down and dislocates even as it cooperates in the production of the product, overflows it and is deduc(t)ed from it. It never lets itself be simply exposed.

The analytic of the beautiful thus gives, ceaselessly undoes the labor of the frame to the extent that, while letting itself be squared up by the analytic of concepts and by the doctrine of judgment, it describes the absence of concept in the activity of taste. "The beautiful is what is represented without concept as object of a universal *Wohlgefallen.*" This definition (second moment, category of quantity) derives from the qualitative definition (disinterestedness). The object of a disinterested pleasure does not depend on an empirical inclination, it therefore addresses itself to freedom and touches everyone—no matter who—where everyone can be touched. It is therefore universal. Now in explaining why this universality must be without concept, Kant exhibits in a sense the forcing—imposing an analytic of concepts on a process without concept—but he justifies his operation by an argument that one can consider to be the *constitution,* that which makes the whole edifice of the third *Critique* hold-together-and-stand-upright in the middle of its two great wings (the critique of aesthetic judgment and the critique of teleological judgment). This argument is *analogy.* It operates everywhere in the book, and one can systematically verify its effect. At the place where we are in the exposition—its crossroads—it *gathers together* without-concept and concept, universality *without* concept and universality *with* concept, the *without* and the *with;* it thus legitimates the violence, the occupation of a nonconceptual field by the grid [*quadrillage*] of a conceptual force. Without and with at the same time (*ama*). By reason of its qualitative universality, the judgment of taste *resembles* the logical judgment which, nonetheless, it never is, in all rigor. The nonconceptual resembles the conceptual. A very strange resemblance, a singular proximity or affinity (*Ähnlichkeit*) which, somewhere (to be specified later)[7] draws out of *mimēsis* an interpretation of the beautiful which firmly rejects imitation. There is no contradiction here which is not reappropriated by the economy of *physis* as *mimēsis.*

He who takes a disinterested pleasure (without enjoyment and without concept) in the beautiful "will speak of the beautiful as if (*als ob*) beauty were a quality (*Beschaffenheit*) of the object and the judgment logical (forming a cognition of the Object by concepts of it); although it is only aesthetic, and contains merely a reference (*Beziehung*) of the representation of the object to the Subject—because it still bears this resemblance [*Ähnlichkeit:* affinity, proximity, family tie] to the logical judgment, that it may be presupposed to be valid for all men. But this universality cannot spring from concepts. For from concepts there is no transition to the feeling of pleasure or displeasure (save in the case of pure practical laws, which, however, carry an interest with them; and such an interest does not attach to the pure judgment of taste)" [Meredith, 51].

The discourse on color and sound belongs to the "Clarification by Examples," in the course of the exposition of the third category: the dynamic category of finality. The judgment of taste relates to a purely formal finality, without concept and without end, without a conceptual and determinant representation of an end. The two mathematical categories are nonetheless indispensable: sound and color are excluded as *attractions* only to the extent of their nonformality, their materiality. As pure forms, sound and color can give rise to a universal appreciation, in conformity with the quantity of a judgment of taste; they can procure a disinterested pleasure, conforming to the quality of a judgment of taste. The sensations of sound and color can "quite rightly" be held beautiful to the extent that they are "pure": this determination of purity concerns only the form, which alone can be "universally communicable with certainty." According to Kant, there are two ways of acceding to formal purity: by a nonsensory, nonsensual reflection, and by the regular play of impressions, "if one assumes with Euler" that colors are vibrations of the ether (*pulsus*) at regular intervals, and if (formal analogy between sounds and colors) sounds consist in a regular rhythm in the vibrations of the disturbed ether. Kant had a great deal of difficulty coming to a conclusion on this point. But the fact remains that on this hypothesis one would be dealing not with material contents of received sensations but with formal determinations. That is why simple color is pure color and can therefore belong inside the beautiful, giving rise to universally communicable appreciations. Mixed colors cannot do this. The empiricist motif (that simple color does not give rise to a transmissible perception) seems to have been inverted, but it is here not a question of determinant perception but only of pleasure or unpleasure.

This ambivalence of color (valorized as formal purity or as relation, devalorized as sensory matter, beauty on the one hand, attraction on the other, pure presence in both cases) is raised to the second power (squared) when it is a question of the color of the frame (*goldene Rahmen,* for example), when the parergonal equivocity of the color comes to intensify the parergonal equivocity of the frame. What would be the equivalent of this square for music   ⎯
|

|

⎯   it will be said that not all frames are, or have been, or will be square, rectangular, or quadrangular figures, nor even simply angular. Tables and tableaux (*Tafel*) likewise not. This is true: a critical and systematic and typological history of framing seems possible and necessary.[8] But the angle in general, the quadrangular in particular will not be just one of its objects among others. Everything that is written here is valid for the logic of parergonal bordering *in general,* but the privilege of "cadre" [*frame*], though it seems more fortunate in the Latin than in the Germanic languages, is not fortuitous ⎯
|

|

⎯   Kantian question: the relation of the concept to the nonconcept (up/down, left/right), to the body, to the signature which is placed "on" the frame: in fact, sometimes; structurally, always. The prosthesis

which does not run along as though on wheels in the third *Critique* as soon as one looks a little more closely at the example, that example of an example which forms and is formed by the frame. If things run as though on wheels, this is perhaps because things aren't going so well, by reason of an internal infirmity in the thesis which demands to be supplemented by a prosthesis or only ensures the progress of the exposition with the aid of a wheelchair or a child's pushchair. Thus one pushes forward something which cannot stand up, does not erect itself by itself in its process. Framing always supports and contains that which, by itself, collapses forthwith, exc

this is demonstrated by example, by the problem of the example and the reflective judgment. Now what does the *Critique of Pure Reason* tell us? That examples are the wheelchairs [*roulettes*] of judgment. The French translators sometimes say the "crutches" of judgment: but it really is wheelchairs (*Gängelwagen*), not skateboards [*planches-à-roulettes*] but the little wheeled cars in which children, the old, or the sick are pushed, those who have not enough judgment, enough good sense, that faculty of natural judgment, the best-shared thing (this is not the *sensus communis* of the third *Critique*) that is called—this is Kant's word—*Mutterwitz*. Those who do not have enough of this maternal *Witz*, the sick, imbeciles, need wheelchairs, examples. "Examples are thus the wheelchairs of the faculty of judging (*Gängelwagen der Urteilskraft*) and those who lack (*mangelt*) this natural talent will not be able to do without them." The wheelchairs, however, do not replace judgment: nothing can replace the *Mutterwitz*, the lack of which cannot be supplied by any school (*dessen Mangel keine Schule ersetzen kann*). The exemplary wheelchairs are thus prostheses which replace nothing. But like all examples (*Beispielen*), as Hegel will have pointed out, they play, there is play in them, they give room to play. To the essence, beside the essence (*beiher*), Hegel goes on to make clear. Thus they can invert, unbalance, incline the natural movement into a parergonal movement, divert the energy of the *ergon,* introduce chance and the abyss into the necessity of the *Mutterwitz*: not a contrary order but an aleatory sidestep which can make one lose one's head suddenly, a Russian roulette if one puts into play pleasure without enjoyment, the death-drive and the mourning of labor in the experience of the beautiful—

362

of the parergon—get one's mourning done. Like the entirely-other of hetero-affection, in the pleasure without enjoyment and without concept, it provokes and delimits the labor of mourning, labor *in general as* labor of mourning

le travail à parer[9]

reserve, savings, parsimony, stock—the self-protection *of* the work (*ergon*), energy captured, hemmed (the "binding" [*Verbindung*] of energy, condition for the "mastery" [*Herrschaft*] of the pleasure principle: the result "is not simple"—to be continued)

the self-protection-*of*-the-work, of *energeia* which becomes *ergon* only as (from) *parergon:* not against free and full and pure and unfettered energy (pure act and total presence of *energeia,* the Aristotelian prime mover) but against what is *lacking* in it; not against the lack as a posable or opposable negative, a substantial emptiness, a determinable and bordered absence (still verifiable essence and presence) but against the impossibility of *arresting différance* in its contour, of arraigning the heterogeneous (*différance*) in a pose, of localizing, even in a meta-empirical way, what metaphysics calls, as we have just seen, *lack,* of making it come back, equal or similar to itself (*adaequatio-homoiosis*), to its proper place, according to a proper trajectory, preferably circular (castration as truth). Although apparently opposed—or because opposed—these two *bordering* determinations of what the parergon is working against (the operation of free energy and of pure productivity or the operation of the essential lack) are *the same* (metaphysical).[10]

that which is outside the frame (putting-into-lethargy and absolute value of the frame): naturalization of the frame. There is no natural frame. *There is* frame, but the frame *does not exist.*

The parergon—apotrope (decoration, show, parry) *of the* primary processes, of free energy, i.e., of the "theoretical fiction" (*Ein psychischer Apparat, der nur den Primärvorgang besässe, existiert zwar unseres Wissens nicht und ist insoferne eine theoretische Fiktion*). So only a certain practice of theoretical fiction can work (against) the frame, (make or let it) play (it) (against) itself. Don't forget, nonetheless, that the *content,* the *object* of this theoretical fiction

363

(the free energy of the originary process, its pure productivity) is metaphysics, onto-theology itself. The practice of fiction always runs the risk of believing in it or having us believe in it. The *practice* of fiction must therefore guard against having metaphysical truth palmed off on it once again under the label of fiction. There is fiction and fiction. Necessity here of the angle—diagonality—where things work and play and give, and of showing up the remnants of the angle in round frames (there are such things). Hegel: spirit linked to the appearance of the round form   ⎤

⎣   everything will flower at the edge of a deconsecrated tomb: the flower with free or vague beauty (*pulchritudo vaga*) and not adherent beauty (*pulchritudo adhaerens*). It will be, for (arbitrary) example, a colorless and scentless tulip (more surely than color, scent is lost to art and to the beautiful (paragraph 53): just try to frame a perfume) which Kant doubtless did not pick in Holland but in the book of a certain Saussure whom he read frequently at the time. "But a flower, *zum Beispiel eine Tulpe,* is held to be beautiful because in perceiving it one encounters a finality which, judged as we judge it, does not relate to any end"   ⎤

⎣   even

NOTES

1. We have preferred to translate Derrida's "finalité sans fin" literally as "finality without end," rather than revert to the standard "purposiveness without purpose": this allows us to preserve a certain sense of Derrida's exploitation of different senses of the word *fin* ("end"), and to avoid certain traditional assumptions about Kant which Derrida's essay suspends at the very least. "Purpose" would be more suitable for *but,* but we have tended to translate this as "goal" to avoid confusion.

2. In English in the text.

3. "De *ce qui* se deconstruit": the French pronominal verb retains both passive and reflexive values.

4. "Ceci est—écrit sur le cadre": *écrit* can also be "a piece of writing."

5. "L'abîme en coin dans ses angles et ses articulations": the translation loses a certain sense of slyness; cf. "un regard en coin," a sideways glance. Use of the idiom "on the side" would interfere too much with the insistence on corners.

364

6. This sense of the verb *travailler* (i.e., to give or warp, of wood or metal) communicates with an important sense of *jouer* (literally "to play," but also "to give" in the sense of there being "play" or "give" in a steering wheel, for example).

7. Cf. "Economimesis."—J.D.

8. When "Parergon" was first published, I had not yet read Meyer Schapiro, "Sur quelques problèmes de sémiotique de l'art visuel: champ et véhicule dans les signes iconiques," translated into French by Jean-Claude Lebensztejn, *Critique* 315–16 [(1973): 843–66; originally published in *Semiotica* 1, no. 3 (1969): 223–42].

The reader will find more than one indication concerning the "history" of framing, its "late invention," the not very "natural" character of the "rectangular frame," as well as "the frame that bends and turns inward into the field of the picture to compress or entangle the figures (the trumeau of Souillac, the Imago Hominis in the Echternach Gospels)" (p. 228).

I also refer, as goes without saying, to *all* of Lebensztejn's publications.—J.D.

9. This syntagm is untranslatable as it stands: depending on the sequence into which it was inserted, it could mean, "(the) work to adorn," "(the) work to parry," "(the) work to be adorned," "(the) work to be parried," etc.

10. "*Le même* (metaphysique)": also, "the (metaphysical) same," "the same (metaphysics)."

27

Stacks, Frames, and Boundaries

MARIE-LAURE RYAN

On the map of narrative, as on the map of the world, boundaries are everywhere: boundaries within the representing discourse, and boundaries within the represented system of reality; boundaries with gates to get across, and boundaries with only windows to look through. While geographic boundaries divide space in a random pattern, narrative boundaries present a concentric structure: each territory is contained within another, and as travelers cross the narrative space, they must reenter in reverse order each of the territories encountered on the way.

This concentric structure is reflected in the family of metaphors through which narratologists have traditionally attempted to deal with the divisions of discourse and story: framing, embedding, and Chinese boxes (cf. Todorov, Stewart, Chambers, Bal, Young, McHale). The concepts of the frame family have become so deeply ingrained in our thinking about narrative that we tend to forget their metaphorical nature. Together with this nature, we also tend to forget their relativity, and we feel no need to look any further for descriptive models. In the present chapter, I propose to complement the standard metaphors of framing and embedding with another way to talk about narrative boundaries: the metaphor of the stack, which comes from the computer field and is widely used in the discourse models of artificial intelligence. (See Reichman and Hofstadter for the first use of the concept of stack relevant to narratology.)

NARRATIVE BOUNDARIES: A TYPOLOGY

The widely accepted distinction between story and discourse generates two types of boundaries: ontological and illocutionary. Ontological boundaries delimit domains within the semantic universe, and their crossing is a recentering into a new system of reality. Illocutionary boundaries delimit speech acts within a text or a conversation, and their crossing introduces a new speaker or a new narrator. When the utterance of this new voice is a self-sufficient text, it generates its own semantic universe and its own textual actual world which may or may not be presented as a reflection of the primary reality from which the text is transmitted.[1] As the territories defined by boundaries differ in their nature, they also differ in their mode of access. A narrative can cross a boundary by selecting the "here" and "now" of the other side as a point of reference, or it may simply look through boundaries, by revealing what is beyond the line from the perspective of this side of the line. In this second case, the crossing of the boundary is only virtual. If we cross-classify the three dichotomies [+/- illocutionary], [+/- ontological], [+/- actual crossing], we obtain the table of possibilities shown in figure 1.

In case 1 there is no boundary, and the distinction between virtual and actual is not applicable. This category corresponds to the standard narrative case: contiguous sentences have the same speaker, and they describe the same level of reality.

In 2a, the boundary involves a change of speaker, but the first and second speaker are members of the same world, and their respective utterances refer to the same reality. On the micro-level, this case is illustrated by directly quoted dialogues. Macro-level instances include narratives of personal experience (such as a newly encountered character telling what circumstances have led to her present situation), or "gossip narratives" (a character telling a story about another member of the same world to satisfy the hearer's curiosity, as in Balzac's "Sarrasine"). In 2b the speech act of the character is presented through the

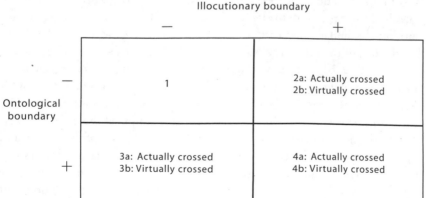

Illocutionary boundary

	−	+
Ontological boundary −	1	2a: Actually crossed 2b: Virtually crossed
Ontological boundary +	3a: Actually crossed 3b: Virtually crossed	4a: Actually crossed 4b: Virtually crossed

Figure 1

367

speech act of the narrator, as in indirect discourse. We are informed of the storytelling act of the character, but we are denied access to her actual discourse.

In 3a, the narrative transports the reader to a new system of reality without introducing a new speaker. An example of this situation is *Alice in Wonderland:* the text moves from the primary reality of an everyday world to the dream world of Wonderland, and back to the primary reality in a continuous speech act. Another example of this situation is the technique of the "animated picture" which is used in some novels by Claude Simon and Alain Robbe-Grillet (cf. McHale, chap. 8). A picture is described as an object contained within the primary reality; in the course of the description, the characters in the picture begin moving, their actions develop into a plot, and the world within the picture gradually emancipates itself from the primary reality. But there is no change in the reporting voice. The distinction between 3a and 3b is exemplified in this quote from Lewis Carroll: "'So, either I've been dreaming about Sylvie,' I said to myself, 'and this is reality' [case 3b]. 'Or else I've really been with Sylvie, and this is a dream!' [case 3a]." (*Sylvie and Bruno,* in Carroll 1976, 296). In the first part of the quote the report of the dream is anchored in reality and described from an external perspective, while in the second part the dream world is described from within its own confines, and temporarily takes the place of reality. Another example of 3b would be the description of a picture or a movie with repeated reminders of its object status in the primary reality.

Case 4a is the standard case of a fiction within a fiction: the stories told by Scheherazade in *The Arabian Nights,* or the series of novels begun but never finished in Italo Calvino's *If on a Winter's Night a Traveler.* The double crossing of boundaries is implicit to what I take to be the definition of fiction. In fictional discourse the author makes believe to relocate himself in a new system of reality by overtly pretending to be one of its members. Through this act of impersonation, the speech of the author in the real world transmits the speech of the narrator in the fictional world, and there is a crossing of an illocutionary boundary. Similarly, when Scheherazade begins telling what is for her the tale of the imaginary Ali Baba, she recenters reality around the world in which Ali Baba is a real person, and her voice fades into the speech act of the narrator who tells the story as true fact. In situation 4b, a fictional story is described rather than being actually narrated. (The description of a nonfictional narrative would fall in category 2b.) An example of this unusual situation occurs in a short story by Jorge Luis Borges, "Theme of the Traitor and the Hero." The primary narrator tells us that he plans some day to write a story, that the narrator's name will be Ryan, that Ryan will be engaged in writing the biography of an Irish hero, and that the hero will turn out to be a traitor; but the primary narrator never speaks as Ryan himself, and he never takes the step into the world of the projected story.

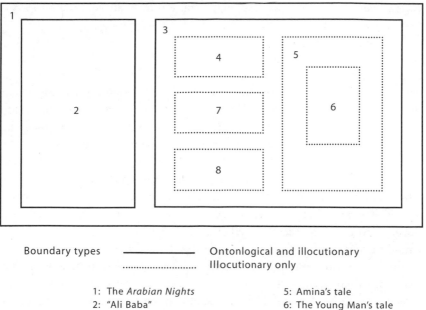

Boundary types ——————— Ontonlogical and illocutionary
.... Illocutionary only

1: The *Arabian Nights*   5: Amina's tale
2: "Ali Baba"   6: The Young Man's tale
3: "The Three Ladies of Baghdad" 7: Safia's tale
4: The Porter's tale   8: Zubaida's tale

Figure 2
The frame structure of *The Arabian Nights*

THE FRAMING/EMBEDDING MODEL

The analogical basis of the metaphors of the frame family is the idea of surrounding, transposed from the domain of the visual to the domain of the temporal. A narrative territory frames another territory when its verbal representation both precedes and follows the verbal representation of the framed territory. Figure 2 offers a concrete illustration of the frame structure of *The Arabian Nights*, a narrative known for the complexity of its system of boundaries. The different types of boundaries are represented by different kinds of lines. Scheherazade tells "Ali Baba" and "The Three Ladies of Baghdad" as fictions, and these stories are framed by a double illocutionary/ontological boundary. The porter, Amina, Safia, and Zuhaida are characters within "The Three Ladies of Baghdad," telling each other about their past, and the frame of their stories is of the illocutionary variety.

We see in figure 2 that the story of Scheherazade and the Sultan frames the stories told by Scheherazade, that "The Three Ladies of Baghdad" frames

Amina's tale, and so on. The mapping of fig. 2 is formally equivalent to a system of parentheses:

$$(( )(( )(( ))( )))$$

In order to be well formed the sequence must comprise the same number of left and right parentheses. The book of *The Arabian Nights* as a whole would not satisfy the conditions of narrative closure if it never returned to the story of Scheherazade and the Sultan. (Fig. 2 represents a semantic "deep structure," since in the actual narrative the return to the main story may precede the embedded stories: in some condensed versions of *The Arabian Nights,* we learn about the Sultan's decision to save the queen's life before we read the stories which motivated his decision.) The number of unmatched left parentheses crossed in order to reach a certain point is indicative of *narrative level:* "Ali Baba" is on the second level, together with "The Three Ladies of Baghdad," Amina's tale is on the third level, the Young Man's tale on the fourth, and so on. In the standard use of the metaphor, levels are considered to go down rather than up: narratologists will normally say that the Young Man's tale belongs to a deeper level than Amina's tale. The visual mapping of figure 2 not only provides an adequate account of narrative levels, it also predicts the range of acceptable transitions from a given point in the story. Boundaries must be crossed one at a time, either up or down. From Amina's story on level 3 the narrative can go to level 4 or level 2, but it cannot jump to level 1. The system also makes a distinction between "opened" and "closed" territories on the same level. A territory is closed when both its left and right border have been crossed. Boundary crossing can only lead into open territories: it would be illegal to step from Amina's tale on level 3 to "Ali Baba" on level 2, since at the point the narrative enters Amina's tale, the territory of "Ali Baba" has already been closed. The only legal transition from Zubaida's tale into level 2 is a return to "The Three Ladies of Baghdad," from where the step into level 3 had been taken.

The main limitation of the frame model lies in its inability to distinguish illocutionary from ontological boundaries. Representing the various types of boundaries with different kinds of lines, as I have done in figure 2, is only an ad hoc solution, since the meaning of the lines remains to be defined.

Another shortcoming stems from the system's implicit assumption that the ground level is the first encountered in the temporal sequence. This assumption underlies the procedure by which narrative level is calculated on the basis of the number of unmatched left parentheses. It turns out, however, that a narrative may begin on a level other than the first, and still appear well formed. An example of this situation is the play *The Maids* (*Les Bonnes*) by Jean Genet. The play begins with a play within the play, in which the two characters of level 1, Solange and Claire, impersonate respectively Claire and

Madame (their mistress). This play within the play belongs to level 2 because its semantic domain is ontologically supported by a reality in which Solange and Claire are simply Solange and Claire. This ground reality is first invisible, but it is retrospectively reconstructed by the spectator when Solange and Claire step out of their roles and return to what is for them the real world. From level 1, the play moves back to level 2, as Solange and Claire resume their act of impersonation. The same situation occurs in John Fowles's *The French Lieutenant's Woman:* the narrative begins in the world of Sarah and Charles, then crosses the ontological boundary into a world in which they are characters in a novel, and finally returns to the world in which they are real. In these two fictions, the temporal sequence leads from the second to the first and back to the second level, and the semantic level cannot be calculated on the basis of the number of boundary crossings. Since the action of level 2 surrounds the action of level 1, the system would wrongly regard the territory of level 2 as the frame of level 1. To predict levels adequately, the frame diagram should model the narrative in its logical deep structure, which inverts in this case the surface structure specified by the temporal order of presentation.

This conflict between semantic deep structure and dynamic order of presentation can be resolved by mapping narratives like *The Maids* or *The French Lieutenant's Woman* as shown in figure 3. This type of diagram is based on the metaphor of the stack. Frame diagrams and stack diagrams offer complementary views of the phenomenon of narrative boundaries: frames are static objects; stacks are dynamic; frames model a system of relations stretching over the entire semantic domain of the text; stacks capture the temporary states of this domain; frames provide a general map of boundaries; stacks model the mechanisms of the crossing of boundaries.

Stack a in figure 3 captures a provisory interpretation of the semantic domain of *The Maids* in its initial state. By virtue of an interpretive convention,

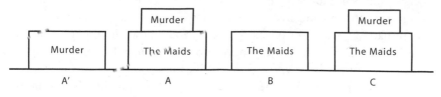

A': First situation, provisory interpretation
A: First situation, definitive interpretation
B: Second situation
C: Third situation

Figure 3
The stack structure of *The Maids*

371

the spectator believes that the dramatic action begins on the ground level. But the default specified by the convention can be overridden by an obvious transition to a lower level. This transition occurs when Solange and Claire put away their disguises and step into their true identities. The sequence of stacks a, b, c shows the definitive interpretation of the three states of the semantic domain. The operations through which the system passes from one state to another are known as pushing and popping: 2a becomes 2b through the popping of the top level of reality, 2b turns into 2c through the pushing of this level back on top of the stack. (This use of the verbs push and pop is itself metaphorical. The analogy derives from a stack of trays at a cafeteria. The stack is supported by a spring, and the top tray is always level with the counter. When a customer puts a tray on top of the stack, the structure must be pushed down in order to make the top tray even with the counter; when a tray is removed, the structure pops up, and the next tray on the stack is lifted to counter level. Being on top of the stack and level with the counter makes a tray the "current tray.")

The formalism of the stack works equally well with canonical narratives beginning on the ground level such as *The Arabian Nights*. Figure 4 gives two snapshots of the current state of the semantic universe, one from within the territory of "Ali Baba" and the other from within the Young Man's tale. The top level of a stack diagram represents the currently active narrative context, and the lower levels the narratives or realities whose verbal representation is waiting to he completed. The various levels must be popped in the reverse order of their pushing: stacks are known as a "last in, first out" structure (as opposed to queues, which are "first in, first out"). The principle "last in, first out" makes the formalism of the stack equivalent to the frame diagram in its ability to predict the sequence of boundary crossings and the range of legal transitions. From the Young Man's tale the narrative must return to Amina's tale, and from there to "The Three Ladies of Baghdad." A return to "Ali Baba" is impossible, since this semantic environment is no longer present on the narrative stack. When compared to frames, however, the stack inverts the direction of narrative transitions: what is seen as going down in a frame model is regarded as going up in a stack model. Amina's tale now belongs to a higher narrative level than "The Three Ladies of Baghdad."

How does the model of the stack address the two problems encountered by the frame model, namely, the need to explain how narratives can directly reach upper levels and to distinguish illocutionary from ontological boundaries? To answer these questions, I propose to draw an analogy between narrative and a computer language. The analogy maps the statements of a program onto the semantic constituents of a narrative. A computer program consists, broadly speaking, of three kinds of elements: the name of the pro-

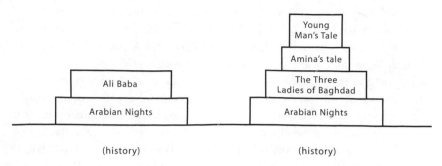

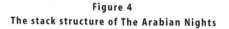

Figure 4
The stack structure of The Arabian Nights

gram, which identifies it uniquely to the computer; the list of variables; and the sequence of operations to be performed on the variables. These three components correspond, respectively, to the title of the narrative, the cast of characters, and the sequence of events that affect these characters. A further analogy resides in the fact that a computer program may activate other programs, just as a narrative may activate other narratives and other realities.

To demonstrate the mechanisms of the narrative stack, let us rewrite in the form of computer programs the history of the world, all the narratives ever written or told, and all the trips to other realities ever taken by human minds. Figure 5 shows the main program HISTORY OF THE WORLD, and the subprograms for THE ARABIAN NIGHTS and THE MAIDS. Some of the events in the program HISTORY OF THE WORLD are illocutionary and/or ontological boundary crossings. These events function as calls to subprograms. A calling statement consists of the name of the program to be activated, and of a list of variable names known in the programming jargon as the actual parameters. These parameters are variables of the calling program which will be passed into the subprogram and will become part of its semantic environment. The parameters thus establish a communication between the two units. The effect of the calling statement is to push a new semantic environment (i.e., a new set of variables) onto the top of the stack of currently active programs. When the execution of the top program terminates, its environment is popped, and control is returned to the program from which the call had been issued. We see in figure 5, for instance, that the program HISTORY OF THE WORLD contains a call to THE ARABIAN NIGHTS. The parameters of the call are the participants in the speech act: the historical author and the reader. These parameters are matched to the so-called formal parameters which appear in the title statement

subprogram THE ARABIAN NIGHTS, and they become members of the
ironment of THE ARABIAN NIGHTS under the name of these formal
arameters. When the call to THE ARABIAN NIGHTS is executed, the historical author becomes in make-believe the narrator, the reader becomes the narratee, and the environment specified in the cast of characters becomes the
currently active context. Adam and Eve, Hitler and Napoleon are no longer
valid discourse referents, since they do not belong to the current context. The
potential referents are Scheherazade and the Sultan, and all the characters of
this narrative level. The same substitution occurs when a call to THE THREE
LADIES OF BAGHDAD is issued from within THE ARABIAN NIGHTS, and from
there to AMINA'S TALE and THE YOUNG MAN'S TALE. Figure 4b shows the
configuration of the stack when the program THE YOUNG MAN'S TALE is

```
MAIN PROGRAM: HISTORY OF THE WORLD                          Title
Character: Adam, Eve, the author of                       Variable
The Arabian Nights, U.S.A., Soviet Union, etc.                list

Begin
        Adam and Eve are expelled drom Eden;              operations
        ( . . . )
        ARABIAN NIGHTS (author, reader);           Calling statement
        ( . . . )                                      with actual
        THE MAIDS ([Genet through] Actress 1,           parameters
                Actress 2, Actress 3, Spectator);
        Superpowers in nuclear war;
End.
ARABIAN NIGHTS (Narrator, Narratee)                   Subprogram title
Characters: Scheherazade, Sultan               with formal parameters

Begin
        Sultan marries Scheherazade;
        Sultan wants to kill Scheherazade at dawn;
        ALI BABA (Scheherazade, Sultan);
        THE THREE LADIES OF BAGHDAD (Scheherazade, Sultan);
        Sultan spares the life of Scheherazade;
End;

ALI BABA (Narrator, Narratee)
Characters: Ali Baba, his wife, forty thieves

Begin
        Ali Baba outsmarts: forty thieves with the help of his wife and is rich and
        happy ever after;
End;

THE THREE LADIES OF BAGHDAD (Narrator, Narratee)
Characters: Porter, three ladies: Amina, Safia, Zubaida
```

Figure 5

Narrative semantics as computer program

```
Begin
        The Porter meets the three ladies;
        THE PORTER'S TALE (the Porter, the three ladies);
        AMINA'S TALE (Amina, the Porter);
        SAFIA'S TALE (Safia, the Porter);
        ZUBAIDA'S TALE (Zubaida, the Porter);
        All spells broken, the Porter marries Amina and the other two ladies marry good men;
End;
```

AMINA'S TALE (Amina, the Porter)

```
Begin
        Amina looking for her lost husband walks into a palace where everybody
        looks like a statue. She finally meets a young man;
        THE YOUNG MAN'S TALE (the Young Man, Amina);
        Amina marries the Young man, but he is killed by her jealous sisters, who
        are turned into dogs;

End;
```

THE YOUNG MAN'S TALE (the Young Man, Amina)

```
Begin
        The Young Man was a son of a Shah and was the only one at the palace living
        by the laws of Islam;
        All those who did not obey the Koran were turned into stones;
End;
```

THE MAIDS (Claire/ Solange/ Madame, observer)
Characters not appearing onstage: Monsieur, the Milkman

```
Begin
        THE MURDER OF MADAME, Part I (Claire, Solange);
        Dialogue between Claire, Solange, and Madame;
        THE MURDER OF MADAME, Part II (Claire, Solange);
End;
```

THE MURDER OF MADAME I & II (Madame, Claire);
Characters: Counterparts of all the characters in THE MAIDS

```
Begin
        Dialogue between Madame and Claire, culminating
        (in part II) in the murder of MADAME

End;
```

Figure 5 (cont'd)

being executed. After the termination of THE YOUNG MAN'S TALE the sub-program is popped, and the execution of AMINA'S TALE resumes exactly where it had been interrupted. The same mechanism continues, changing the structure of the stack until the termination of THE ARABIAN NIGHTS and the popping of all levels except for the ongoing (and narratively always implicit) HISTORY OF THE WORLD.[2]

In the case of THE MAIDS, the impression that the action starts on the second level stems from the fact that the calls to the subprogram THE MURDER

MADAME (as I call it) are the first and last operation of the main play. As a result of this location, two levels are pushed in rapid succession, and one of them is purely transitory. Since the dramatic action proper is contained in the dialogue, it does not begin until THE MURDER OF MADAME has been pushed onto the stack. When part 2 of THE MURDER terminates, so does the script of THE MAIDS, and the last words uttered on stage belong, like the first ones, to the dialogue of level 2.

The different types of boundaries are represented in this programming pseudocode by the relations between the components of the subprogram and the calling statement. An ontological boundary crossing occurs when the subprogram has its own variable list. The characters of this list replace the inventory of the calling program, and we have a new reality. Some members of the list may have counterparts in the calling program: there is a Napoleon in the program HISTORY OF THE WORLD, and another Napoleon in the program WAR AND PEACE. In this case the character cast of the calling program and of the subprogram will contain identical names, but as the subprogram is pushed on top of the stack, its own referent for the name replaces temporarily the former referent. What happens to Napoleon in WAR AND PEACE has no influence on the Napoleon of world history.

Absence of a variable list in the subprogram means that a boundary-crossing has no ontological consequences. To make up for the lack of native characters, the subprogram borrows its population from the calling environment. As it borrows the characters, it also borrows their destinies: what happens to the characters in the subprogram should reflect what happens to them in the calling program. If a discrepancy occurs, the story told in the subprogram is an error or a lie.

Illocutionary boundary crossings are signaled by the formal parameters. When the names of the formal parameters match exactly the names of the actual parameters in the calling statement, the speaker and the hearer retain their identity across the boundary. This is the case of nonfictional embedded narratives. When the names differ, the actual participants in the communicative act engage in the role-playing of fictional communication: Scheherazade pretends to be an anonymous narrator, the Sultan becomes an anonymous narratee in a recentered reality.

An absence of formal parameters indicates an absence of illocutionary boundary. Since there is no distinct speech act, the name of the subprogram is not a story title, but a nonverbal reality such as "dream," "movie," "picture." Insofar as it contains its own variable list, this reality differs ontologically from the calling environment.

The three boundary-crossing categories of figure 1 are translated as follows into the programming pseudocode. (On the left is the calling statement with actual parameters, on the right the subprogram declaration with formal parameters and variable list.)

2: + illocutionary/ — ontological:
YOUNG MAN'S TALE
(Young Man, Amina)

YOUNG MAN'S TALE
(Young Man, Amina)
No variable list

3: — illocutionary/ + ontological:
WONDERLAND

WONDERLAND
Characters: Alice´, Queen of Hearts, Chesire, etc.

(Alice´ is a counterpart of Alice in the primary reality)

4: + illocutionary/ + ontological
ALI BABA (Scheherazade, Sultan)

ALI BABA (Narrator, Narratee)
Characters: Ali Baba, his wife, 40 thieves

The subprogram declaration of category 4 captures the standard case of impersonal third-person narration. Other types of fiction are represented by the following variations in the relation between calling statement and subprogram declaration:

Personal Narration
WUTHERING HEIGHTS
(Emily Brontë, Reader)

WUTHERING HEIGHTS
(Lockwood, Narratee)
Characters: Cathy, Heathcliff, etc.

Fictional self-impersonation
FUNES THE MEMORIOUS
(Borges, Reader)

FUNES THE MEMORIOUS
(Borges´, Narratee)
Character: Funes, etc.

Here Borges´ stands for a counterpart of the real Borges, linked to him through the principle of minimal departure: the properties of Borges´ are copied from the properties of Borges as far as the text of FUNES will allow, but FUNES has the last word in changing these properties.

Performed drama
THE MAIDS ([Genet through]
Actress 1, Actress 2, Actress 3, Spectator)

THE MAIDS (Solange, Claire, Madame, Observer)
Characters: Monsieur, the Milkman

The list of actual parameters translates the fact that drama is a communicative act between author and spectator through the mediation of the actors. The voiding of the authorial parameter in the subprogram expresses his or her absence from the stage. While the author takes no part in the performance, the spectator plays the passive role of an anonymous witness who looks through the transparent fourth wall of the classical stage. (For the spectator's role to be individuated, the script of the play would have to invite her to step on stage and to take an active part in the performance through improvisation.) The remaining parameters match the real-world identity of the actors to their respective roles. The call refers to an individual performance and *may* be repeated in HISTORY OF THE WORLD with different names filling the actor slots. As for the list of characters, it contains all the members of the semantic domain who are mentioned in the play but do not appear on stage.

Epistolary novel
LES LIAISONS DANGEREUSES
(Laclos, Reader)

LES LIAISONS DANGEREUSES
(Editor/Valmont/Merteuil, Witness)
Characters: mentioned individuals who
do not appear as letter writers
Begin
    Preface (Editor, Public)
    Letter (V, M)
    Letter (M, V)
    End.

The slashes in the subprogram declaration mean here that the formal parameter of the sender is split into various identities: Laclos pretends to he an editor addressing the public, then Valmont addressing Merteuil, then Merteuil answering Valmont, etc. In this analysis, each of the letters is itself a subprogram call of the illocutionary category, as is, on the microlevel, every turn in the performed dialogue of a play, or in the directly quoted dialogue of a novel. The same formalism of a slashed speaker parameter can be used for polyvocal fiction (such as *The Sound and the Fury*, where Faulkner speaks successively as Benjy, Jason, Quentin, and as an impersonal narrator), or for philosophical dialogues.

ADVENTURES OF THE STACK

In a canonical narrative, the building and unbuilding of the stack follows a rigid protocol which restricts the range of legal operations. This protocol requires that levels be kept distinct, that they be pushed or popped on the top of the stack exclusively; that pushing and popping be properly signaled; and that every boundary be crossed twice, once during the building and once during the unbuilding. At the end of the text, the only level left on the stack should be the ground level. This protocol is respected by all standard narrative texts, but not by all the texts of literary fiction. Far from being constrained by the conditions of narrativity, the fictional text may subvert the mechanisms of the stack, thus openly taking an antinarrative stance. This subversion take the following forms.

The Occulted Call

In the computer program representation of narratives, transitions to higher levels are effected by the calling statements. (A virtual crossing would be expressed by integrating the code of the subprogram into the body of the calling program.) Calling statements are typically manifested by boundary-signaling expressions: "'Once upon a time,' began the Queen"; "'This is what happened to me,' said the young man"; or "That night Joseph was visited by a dream. He saw the stars and the moon bowing in front of him." The popping of the stack is similarly signaled by specific textual devices: closing of quotation marks, description of the dreamer's awakening, reference to the story-status of the preceding section. These transition-signaling devices enable readers to properly construct the stack, identify the discourse referents, and orient themselves among the levels of the semantic domain. Like other semantic components of the plot, however, boundary-crossing events may be deleted from the narrative discourse. In *Alice in Wonderland,* the text slips without notice from Victorian England to the dream world of Wonderland: "She was considering whether the pleasure of making a daisy-chain would be worth the trouble of getting up and picking the daisies . . . when suddenly a white rabbit with pink eyes ran close to her" (Carroll 1975, 13). It is only when the rabbit takes a watch out of his waist pocket that the reader realizes what Alice will ignore until the end of the story: that she has crossed the boundary into a separate reality. This impression is confirmed when strange beings make their entrance on the scene, and when the laws of nature appear to lose their hold on the events. Because of the difference between the two realities, the occultation of the boundary crossing has no disorienting consequences for the reader.

   In striking contrast to *Alice in Wonderland* is the case of "The Adjourned Sorcerer" by Borges (an adaptation of a Spanish medieval text by the Infante Juan Manuel), included in the collection *A Universal History of Infamy:*

A dean in Santiago asks a magician, Don Illan, to teach him the magic arts, and promises him a reward. Don Illan first expresses doubts as to whether the dean will keep his promise, but finally agrees to the request. They both go down into a secret room located under the river bed. As the lesson is about to begin, two messengers arrive and announce that the dean has been named bishop in Santiago. Don Illan asks for his reward but the new bishop tells him to wait. Six months later the bishop becomes a cardinal in Toulouse. Don Illan asks for his reward but he is told to wait. Three years later the cardinal

.s elected pope in Rome. Don Illan asks for his reward but the new pope threatens to have him burned at the stake. As he pronounces these words, the pope finds himself back in the secret room, a simple dean in Santiago, and humbly apologizes to Don Illan for his ungrateful conduct.

In this story, the events of the rise of the dean to bishop, cardinal, and pope, as well as his refusal to reward the magician, are not actually lived on the ground level of reality, but hallucinated by the dean as the result of the magician's art. Through the occultation of the passage into the world of the hallucination—which takes place at the very moment the messengers enter the secret room—the reader is no less a victim of the magic than the unfortunate hero. The transition to the hallucinated events is not only camouflaged by the deletion of the calling statement, it is further hidden by the similarity of the casts of characters: all the members of the hallucination are counterparts of the members of the ground level of reality. It is only with the sudden and obvious return to reality at the end of the story that the ordinary reader realizes the true nature of the events and the configuration of the previous states of the narrative stack. Yet as Jean Ricardou has shown (26–29), an astute reader should have noticed a clue to the unreal character of the events: how could the messengers have reached the dean in Don Illan's secret underground room? The guilt expressed by the dean in the real world for what he was made to do in the world of the hallucination figures the guilt the reader should feel for missing the clues of the transition, and falling victim to the storyteller's magic.

The Endlessly Expanding Stack

When a computer program contains an unconditional recursive call to itself, or to any of its predecessors in the calling chain, the result is an ever-expanding stack of environments from which no return is possible. As soon as the same environment is pushed twice onto the narrative stack, the sequence of intermediate levels must be repeated indefinitely. The same effect can be achieved in narrative. We are all familiar with the interminable repetitions of folklore, such as:

> It was a dark and stormy night
> and Brigham Young and Brigham Old sat around the campfire.
> Tell us a story, old man!
> And this is the story he told:

> It was a dark and stormy night
> and Brigham Young and Brigham Old sat around the campfire.
> Tell us a story, old man!

And this is the story he told:
(Le Guin, 187)

Here the endlessly expanding stack is built by an open-ended, infinite text. If we do not step through the entire text, the possibility remains that on the next level Brigham will tell a different story, and that the whole stack will eventually tumble. This is indeed what happens in Le Guin's text: on the third recursion, we read:

> It was a dark and stormy night
> and Brigham Young and Pierre Menard, author of the *Quixote*
> sat around the campfire
> which is not quite the way my Great-Aunt Betsy told it
> when we said Tell us another story!
> Tell us, au juste, what happened
> And this is the story she told:

The appearance on the third level of a new environment suggests that in the program version of the narrative the first two calls are to different stories: BRIGHAM I calls BRIGHAM II, which reads exactly like BRIGHAM I, except that it calls BRIGHAM III, which in turn calls BETSY'S TALE. If the call in BRIGHAM I were to BRIGHAM I itself, there would be no way to stop the growth of the stack after the execution of the first recursive call. All it takes for a text to establish an indefinitely expanding stack is therefore explicit self-reference. According to an essay by Borges, this phenomenon occurs in the 602nd night of *The Arabian Nights:*

> On that night, the king hears from the queen her own story. He hears the beginning of the story, which comprises all the others and also—monstrously—itself. Does the reader clearly grasp the vast possibility of this interpolation, the curious danger? That the Queen may persist, and the motionless King hear forever the truncated story of *The Arabian Nights,* now infinite and circular. (Borges 1983, 195)

What Borges does not tell us, unfortunately, is how this self-referential narration is implemented. A literal enactment is out of the question, for if the text of *The Arabian Nights* actually retold the framing story and all the embedded tales, it would become physically infinite and formally open, like the Brigham Young segment.[3] The only way to generate infinite recursion in a closed and finite text is suggested by Italo Calvino's *If on a Winter's Night a Traveler.* The text opens with the sentence "You are about to read Italo Calvino's new novel, *If on a Winter's Night a Traveler*" (3). The title stands vicariously for the novel

, and if we want to know what exactly this fictional reader, who looks so
ch like us, is about to read, we must replace the words *If on a Winter's Night Traveler* with the text they refer to. Pretending that the above sentence is all there is to the novel, the text expands logically into

> You are about to read Italo Calvino's new novel, "You are about to read Italo Calvino's new novel, *If on a Winter's Night a Traveler*"

which in turn expands into

> You are about to read Italo Calvino's new novel, "You are about to read Italo Calvino's new novel, 'You are about to read Italo Calvino's new novel, *If on a Winter's Night a Traveler*'

and so on ad infinitum. The finite mirror of the self-referential title captures the virtual image of an infinite text, and we contemplate this text as a whole, without being caught in its endless repetition.

Strange Loops

In *Gödel, Escher, Bach,* Douglas Hofstadter defines the following violation of the stack's hierarchy: "The 'Strange Loop' phenomenon occurs whenever, by moving upwards or downwards, through the levels of some hierarchical system, we unexpectedly find ourselves right back where we started" (10). In *Postmodernist Fiction,* Brian McHale proposes several literary implementations of the strange loop. In Christine Brooke-Rose's *Thru* (1975), Larissa invents Armel, who in turn is the author of Larissa (McHale, 120). A push into the world of Larissa's invention, then another into the world of Armel's imagination—and we find ourselves back in the world where Larissa invents Armel. The strange loop is a vicious circle, a stack without a ground level, which prevents us from deciding which one, between Armel and Larissa, is "really real."

Another of McHale's illustrations is a short story by Cortázar, "Continuity of Parks" (1978): "A man reads a novel in which a killer, approaching through a park, enters a house in order to murder his lover's husband—the man reading the novel!" (120). For the strange loop effect to arise, the level we push into as the character begins to read must be identical, not just similar, to the primary level. If the two levels were simply similar, the man would be reading a novel about a counterpart of himself in an alternate possible world, and the fate of this counterpart would remain independent of his own. After finishing the story of his own murder, the reader would put down the book, pop out of its system, and resume his normal life. The text prevents this interpretation by ending abruptly, as the murderer reaches his prospective victim. Since the narrative technique makes us apprehend the story within the story through the consciousness of the reader on the ground level, the simultaneous and apparently arbitrary termination of both the embedded and the embedding text signifies the end of the mediating consciousness, the death of the reader.

The Contamination of Levels

In a computer language, the point of calling a subprogram is to modify the semantic environment of the main program. This communication is achieved through the parameters: the value acquired on the higher level by the formal parameters is transferred upon return to the actual parameters. In all other respects, however, the various levels of the stack constitute autonomous semantic environments separated by rigid boundaries. If a variable named x is declared in a calling program, and another variable by the same name in the called program, what happens to the x of the higher level has no influence on the value of the x on the lower level.

The same principles govern the functioning of the narrative stack. Whatever influence a higher level may exert upon a lower one occurs through the parameters. Telling a story is an act with a purpose and an effect, a consequential event for both participants. This consequentiality is showcased by Scheherazade saving her life through her storytelling magic, or by Mme. de Rochefide deciding to withdraw from the world after hearing the story of Sarrasine in Balzac's story by the same name (cf. Chambers 1984 on this topic). Aside from the changes effected in the narrator and narratee, the events of the upper level have no influence on the events of the lower level. A play about Napoleon escaping to New Orleans does not alter the fact that in the actual world Napoleon died on St. Helena. If there is an influence between levels, it runs from bottom to top: the textual world of a nonfictional story should ideally reflect reality, and the textual world of a fiction is assumed to be the closest possible to the actual world.

To reverse the direction of influence, the text must stage an event which denies boundaries and cuts across levels. In my two examples of level contamination, this privileged event is associated with death. In *The Maids,* the contamination of the lower level through the upper one is due to a transgression of standard acting behavior. In normal dramatic performance, the events of the actual world are protected from the events of the world of the play by a simulation of the gestures that would present lasting consequences for the actors. An action like combing a character's hair is actually performed, but a murder is represented on stage by merely going through the moves. In Claire and Solange's enactment of the murder of Madame, however, there is no simation: Claire poisons Madame in THE MURDER OF MADAME through olange's poisoning of Claire on the ground level of reality. Because Madame had to die in the world of make-believe, Claire must die in reality, and Solange must go to jail. But this price to pay is also a reward, since the dead Claire and the jailed Solange will be freed from their servile condition.

In *One Hundred Years of Solitude,* by Gabriel Garcia Márquez, Aureliano Buendia, last descendant of his line, deciphers the prophetic chronicle of the Buendia family by the gypsy Melquiades. As the narrative catches up with the present, it absorbs reality, and Aureliano realizes that he will never pop out of the world of the Book:

> Then he skipped again to anticipate the predictions and ascertain the date and circumstances of his death. Before reaching the final line, however, he had already understood that he would never leave that room, for it was fore-seen that the city of mirrors (or mirages) would be wiped out by the wind and exiled from the memory of men at the precise moment when Aureliano Buendia would finish deciphering the parchment. (422)

Why cannot Aureliano survive the narration of his own death? Because the book is not merely a prophetic but a performative utterance. Its text does not reflect the events—whether past or future—of a more basic level of reality; it makes events happen at the very moment of its own deciphering. The history of the Buendia family is the product of the book, or rather, it is the product of Aureliano's reading experience, which is as unrepeatable as the experience of his own death.

With this performative analysis, we are led back to the case of "Continuity of Parks," which can also be regarded as an instance of reverse contamination. If reality is produced by the text of the book, then by entering the textual universe we enter reality, and the fate of the reader cannot be dissociated from the fate of the reader's counterpart in the book.

The Reverse Push and the Bottomless Stack

The normal procedure for constructing the stack is to push new levels at the top exclusively. But when the hero of Borges's "Circular Ruins," after having dreamed a human being into reality, begins wondering whether he is not him-self "a mere appearance dreamt by another" (1983, 50), a level is inserted below the ground level. What we took for reality turns out to be a dream pro-jected from another reality, and the base of the system is shifted down one notch. This raises the question of whether the operation is repeatable (who dreamed the dreamer?), and whether the stack has a ground level at all.

384

Ontological Paradoxes and the Denial of Boundaries

The most fundamental act of self-consciousness situates the self on the ground level of reality: I am, therefore I am real, and the world I live in is the one and only actual world. The suspicion by Borges's hero of existing only in the alternate possible world of his creator's dream denies this fundamental experience, and constitutes an ontological paradox. So does the admission by characters of their own fictionality. Another form of the ontological paradox, common to modern fiction, is the meeting of author and characters (*Six Characters in Search of an Author, The French Lieutenant's Woman*). Since we can only meet face to face with members of our own level of reality, the encounter of author and characters denies the imaginary status of the latter, and abolishes the ontological boundary that defines their relation.

NOTES

1. The illocutionary boundary does not always coincide with the textual boundary of the story. If a speaker in a conversation narrates an anecote, after some preliminary statements, the illocutionary boundary is crossed when the speaker takes the floor, but the textual universe only comes into being when the story begins. I assume here that the illocutionary crossing is completed when the speaker has both taken the floor and set up the textual universe as an autonomous context, separable from the previous topics of the exchange. I recognize, however, a microlevel illocutionary boundary crossing, which occurs in a text—or in a conversation—at every turn of a dialogue. See Young (1987) on the question of delineating a narrative textual universe—what she calls a Taleworld—during the course of a conversation.

2. HISTORY OF THE WORLD functions like the operating system of a computer: it runs all the programs, and it remains active until the system crashes.

3. My checking of *The Arabian Nights* to see how the text resolves this paradox provided no clue to an answer: the two editions I consulted (translations by Burton and by Madrus) have different stories for the 602nd night, and none of them has to do with Scheherazade and the Sultan.

REFERENCES

Bal, Mieke. *Narratology: Introduction to the Theory of Narrative.* Translated by Christine van Boheemen. Toronto: University of Toronto Press, 1985.

Beebee, Thomas. "Recursivity in Narrative/Life." Unpublished manuscript, Pennsylvania State University, 1988.

Borges, Jorge Luis. *A Universal History of Infamy.* Translated by Norman di Giovanni. New York: Dutton, 1972.

———. *Labyrinths: Selected Stories and Other Writings.* New York: Modern Library, 1983 (1944).

Burton, Sir Richard, trans. *The Book of the Thousand and One Nights.* Vol. VI. The Burton Club, 1885–88.

Calvino, Italo. *If on a Winter's Night a Traveler.* Translated by William Weaver. New York: Harcourt Brace Jovanovich, 1981 (1979).

Carroll, Lewis. *Alice's Adventures in Wonderland* and *Through the Looking-Glass.* New York: Rand McNally, 1975 (1916).

———. *The Complete Works of Lewis Carroll.* New York: Vintage, 1976.

Chambers, Ross. *Story and Situation: Narrative Seduction and the Power of Fiction.* Minneapolis: University of Minnesota Press, 1984.

Chatman, Seymour. *Story and Discourse: Narrative Structure in Fiction and Film.* Ithaca, N.Y., and London: Cornell University Press, 1978.

Fowles, John. *The French Lieutenant's Woman.* Chicago: Signet/New American Library, 1981 (1969).

Genet, Jean. *Les Bonnes.* Collection Folio. Paris: Gallimard, 1984 (1947).

Garcia Márquez, Gabriel. *One Hundred Years of Solitude.* Translated by Gregory Rabassa. New York: Harper and Row, 1971 (1967).

Hofstadter, Douglas. *Gödel, Escher, Bach: An Eternal Golden Braid.* New York: Vintage, 1980.

Le Guin, Ursula K. "It Was a Dark and Stormy Night; or, Why Are We Huddling about the Campfire?" In *On Narrative,* edited by W. J. T. Mitchell, 187–98. Chicago: University of Chicago Press, 1981.

Madrus, J. C., trans. *The Book of the Thousand Nights and One Night.* Vol. III. London: Folio Society, 1980.

McHale, Brian. *Postmodernist Fiction.* New York and London: Methuen, 1987.

Reichman, Rachel. *Getting Computers to Talk Like You and Me.* Cambridge, Mass., and London: MIT Press, 1985.

Ricardou, Jean. *Problèmes du Nouveau Roman.* Paris: Seuil, 1967.

Riordan, James. *Tales from the Arabian Nights.* New York: Rand McNally, 1983.

Ryan, Marie-Laure. "Fiction, Non-Factuals, and the Principle of Minimal Departure." *Poetics* 9 (1980): 403–22.

Stewart, Susan. *Nonsense: Aspects of Intertextuality in Folklore and Literature.* Baltimore, Md., and London: Johns Hopkins University Press, 1970.

Todorov, Tzvetan. *Poétique de la prose.* Paris: Seuil, 1971.

Young, Katharine. *Taleworlds and Storyrealms.* Dordrecht, Boston, and Lancaster: Martinus Nijhoff, 1987.

Bibliography

Adams, Hazard, ed. *Critical Theory Since Plato.* New York: Harcourt Brace Jovanovich, 1971.

Aristotle. *Poetics.* In Adams, *Critical Theory Since Plato,* 48–66.

Bakhtin, Mikhail. *The Dialogical Imagination.* Translated by Caryl Emerson and Michael Holquist. Austin: University of Texas Press, 1981.

Bal, Mieke. "Notes on Narrative Embedding." *Poetics Today* 2 (1981): 41–59.

———. *Narratology: An Introduction to the Theory of Narrative.* Translated by Christine van Boheemen. Toronto: University of Toronto Press, 1985.

Banfield, Ann. *Unspeakable Sentences: Narration and Representation in the Language of Fiction.* Boston: Routledge and Keegan Paul, 1982.

Barthes, Roland. "Literature and Discontinuity." *Critical Essays,* translated by Richard Howard, 171–84. Evanston, Ill.: Northwestern University Press, 1972.

———. "Introduction to the Structural Analysis of Narratives." In *Image Music Text,* edited and translated by Stephen Heath, 79–124. New York: Hill and Wang, 1977.

Bhabha, Homi K. *The Location of Culture.* New York: Routledge, 1994.

Bharata-Muni. *The Natyásastra: A Treatise on Ancient Hindu Dramaturgy and Histrionics,* edited and translated by Manomohan Ghosh. 2 vols. revised edition, 1956–67. Calcutta: The Asiatic Society and Granthalaya.

Booth, Alison, ed. *Famous Last Words: Changes in Gender and Narrative Closure.* Charlottesville: University of Virginia Press, 1993.

Brecht, Bertold. *Brecht on Theatre.* Edited and translated by John Willett. New York: Hill and Wang, 1964.

Bremond, Claude. "The Logic of Narrative Possibilities." *New Literary History* 11 (1980): 387–411.

Brooke-Rose, Christine. *Stories, Theories, and Things.* Cambridge: Cambridge University Press, 1991.

Brooks, Peter. *Reading for the Plot: Design and Intention in Narrative.* New York: Random, 1984.

Caramello, Charles. *Silverless Mirrors: Book, Self and Postmodern American Fiction.* Tallahassee: University Press of Florida, 1983.

Caserio, Robert. *Plot, Story, and the Novel.* Princeton, N.J.: Princeton University Press, 1979.

Cave, Marianne. "Bakhtin and Feminism: The Chronotopic Female Imagination." *Women's Studies* 18 (1990): 117–27.

Chambers, Ross. *Story and Situation: Narrative Seduction and the Power of Fiction.* Minneapolis: University of Minnesota Press, 1984.

Chatman, Seymour. *Story and Discourse: Narrative Structure in Fiction and Film.* Ithaca, N.Y.: Cornell University Press, 1978.

Clayton, Jay. *The Pleasures of Babel: Contemporary American Literature and Theory.* Oxford: Oxford University Press, 1993.

Cohn, Dorrit. *The Distinction of Fiction.* Baltimore, Md.: Johns Hopkins University Press, 1999.

Corneille, Pierre. "Of the Three Unities of Action, Time, and Place." In Adams, *Critical Theory Since Plato,* 219–26.

Crane, R. S. "The Concept of Plot and the Plot of *Tom Jones.*" In *Critics and Criticism: Ancient and Modern,* edited by R. S. Crane, 62–83, abridged edition. Chicago: University of Chicago Press, 1957.

Culler, Jonathan. "Fabula and Sjuzhet in the Analysis of Narrative: Some Recent American Discussions." *Poetics Today* 1 (1980): 27–37.

Dällenbach, Lucien. *The Mirror in the Text.* Translated by Jeremy Whitely with Emma Hughes. Chicago: University Chicago Press, 1989.

de Lauretis, Teresa. "Desire in Narrative." In *Alice Doesn't: Feminism, Semiotics, Cinema,* 103–57. Bloomington: Indiana University Press, 1982.

Deleuze, Giles. *Cinema 2: The Time Image.* Translated by Hugh Tomlinson and Robert Galeta. Minneapolis: University of Minnesota Press, 1989.

Derrida, Jacques. *The Truth in Painting.* Translated by Geoff Bennington and Ian McLeod. Chicago: University of Chicago Press, 1987.

Dryden, John. "An Essay of Dramatic Poesy." In Adams, *Critical Theory Since Plato,* 228–57.

Dunn, Francis M. *Tragedy's End: Closure and Innovation in Euripidean Drama.* Oxford: Oxford University Press, 1996.

Dunn, Francis M., and Thomas Cole, eds. *Beginnings in Classical Literature. Yale Classical Studies* 29 (1992).

DuPlessis, Rachel Blau. *Writing Beyond the Ending: Narrative Strategies of Twentieth-Century Women Writers.* Bloomington: Indiana University Press, 1985.

Eco, Umberto. *The Open Work.* Translated by Anna Cancogni. Cambridge, Mass.: Harvard University Press, 1989.

Eichenbaum, Boris. "O'Henry and the Theory of the Short Story." In *Readings in Russian Poetics: Formalist and Structuralist Views,* edited by Ladislav Matejka and Krystyna Pomorska, 227–70. Ann Arbor: Michigan Slavic Publications, 1978.

Empson, William. "Double Plots." In *Some Versions of Pastoral,* 27–88. Norfolk Conn.: New Directions, 1960 [1935].

Farwell, Marilyn. *Heterosexual Plots and Lesbian Narrative.* New York: New York University Press, 1996.

Fleischman, Suzanne. *Tense and Narrativity.* Austin: University of Texas Press, 1990.

Fludernik, Monika. *Towards a 'Natural' Narratology.* London: Routledge, 1996.

Ford, Ford Madox. *The Critical Writings of Ford Madox Ford.* Edited by Frank MacShane. Lincoln: University of Nebraska Press, 1964.

Forster, E. M. *Aspects of the Novel.* New York: Harcourt Brace Jovanovich, 1927.

Frank, Joseph. "Spatial Form in Modern Literature." *Sewanee Review* 53 (1945): 221–46, 433–56.

Freytag, Gustav. *Technique of the Drama.* Translated by E. J. McEwan. Chicago: Scott, 1894.

Friedman, Susan Stanford. "Lyric Subversion of Narrative in Women's Writing: Virginia Woolf and the Tyranny of Plot." In *Reading Narrative: Form, Ethics, Ideology,* edited by James Phelan, 162–85. Columbus: Ohio State University Press, 1989.

————. *Mappings: Feminism and the Cultural Geographies of Encounter.* Princeton, N.J.: Princeton University Press, 1998.

Frow, John. "The Literary Frame." *Journal of Aesthetic Education* 16, no. 2 (1982): 25–30.

Frye, Joanne. *Living Stories, Telling Lives: Women and the Novel in Contemporary Experience.* Ann Arbor: University of Michigan Press, 1986.

Frye, Northrop. *Anatomy of Criticism.* Princeton, N.J.: Princeton University Press, 1957.

Gallagher, Catherine. "Formalism and Time." *Modern Language Quarterly* 61 (2000): 229–51.

Garrett, Peter K. *The Victorian Multiplot Novel: Studies in Dialogical Form.* New Haven, Conn.: Yale University Press, 1980.

Genette, Gérard. *Narrative Discourse: An Essay in Method.* Translated by Jane E. Lewin. Ithaca, N.Y.: Cornell University Press, 1980.

————. *Narrative Discourse Revisited.* Translated by Jane E. Lewin. Ithaca, N.Y.: Cornell University Press, 1988.

————. *Paratexts: Thresholds of Interpretation.* Translated by Jane E. Lewin. Cambridge: Cambridge University Press, 1997.

Ginsburg, Michal Peled. *Economies of Change: Form and Transformation in the Nineteenth-Century Novel.* Stanford, Calif.: Stanford University Press, 1996.

Gittes, Katharine. *Framing the* Canterbury Tales: *Chaucer and the Medieval Frame Narrative Tradition.* New York: Greenwood, 1991.

Greimas, A. J. "Narrative Grammar: Units and Levels." *Modern Language Notes* 86 (1971): 793–806.

Grudin, M. "Discourse and the Problem of Closure in the Canterbury Tales." *PMLA* 107 (1992): 1157–67.

Hamburger, Käte. *The Logic of Literature.* Translated by Marilyn Rose. Bloomington: Indiana University Press, 1973.

Hayman, David. *Re-Forming the Narrative: Toward a Mechanics of Modernist Fiction.* Ithaca, N.Y.: Cornell University Press, 1987.

Heise, Ursula K. *Chronoschisms: Time, Narrative, and Postmodernism.* Cambridge: Cambridge University Press, 1997.

Herman, David. "Lateral Reflexivity: Levels, Versions, and the Logic of Paraphrase." *Style* 34 (2000): 293–306.

————. "Limits of Order: Toward a Theory of Polychronic Narrative." *Narrative* 6 (1998): 72–95.

————. "Scripts, Sequences, and Stories: Elements of a Postclassical Narratology." *PMLA* 112 (1997): 1046–59.

Higdon, David Leon. *Time and English Fiction.* Totowa, N.J.: Rowman and Littlefield, 1977.

Hite, Molly. *The Other Side of the Story: Structures and Strategies of Contemporary Feminist Narrative.* Ithaca, N.Y.: Cornell University Press, 1989.

Hodgdon, Barbara. *The End Crowns All: Closure and Contradiction in Shakespeare's Histories.* Princeton, N.J.: Princeton University Press, 1991.

Homans, Margaret. "Feminist Fictions and Feminist Theories of Narrative." *Narrative* 2 (1994): 3–16.

Horace. "Art of Poetry." In *Critical Theory Since Plato,* edited by Adams, 68–75.

Howard, Jean E. "The Difficulties of Closure: An Approach to the Problematic in Shakespearean Comedy." In *Comedy from Shakespeare to Sheridan,* edited by A. R. Braunmiller and J. C. Bulman, 113–28. Newark: University of Delaware Press, 1986.

Hrushovski, Benjamin. *Segmentation and Motivation in the Text Continuum of Literary Prose: The First Episode of* War and Peace. *Papers on Poetics and Semiotics,* vol. 5. Tel Aviv University: Porter Institute, 1976. (Also in *Russian Poetics,* edited by Thomas Eekman and Dean S. Worth, 117–46. Los Angeles: UCLA Slavic Studies, vol. 4.)

Jahn, Manfred. "Frames, Preferences, and the Reading of Third-Person Narratives: Towards a Cognitive Narratology." *Poetics Today* 18 (1997): 442–67.

James, Henry. *Theory of Fiction: Henry James.* Edited by James E. Miller Jr. Lincoln: University of Nebraska Press, 1972.

Jensen, Ejner. *Shakespeare and the Ends of Comedy.* Bloomington: Indiana University Press, 1991.

Johnson, Barbara. "The Frame of Reference: Poe, Lacan, Derrida." *Yale French Studies* 55–56 (1977): 457–505.

Johnson, Samuel. "Preface to Shakespeare." In *Critical Theory Since Plato,* edited by Adams, 329–36.

Jonson, Ben. "Timber, or Discoveries." In *Ben Jonson's Literary Criticism,* edited by James D. Redwine Jr., 3–40. Lincoln: University of Nebraska Press, 1970.

Kafalenos, Emma. "Lingering Along the Narrative Path: Extended Functions in Kafka and Henry James." *Narrative* 3 (1995): 117–38.

Kellman, Steven G. "Grand Openings and Plain: On the Poetics of Opening Lines." *SubStance* 17 (1977): 139–47.

Kermode, Frank. *The Sense of an Ending: Studies in the Theory of Fiction.* Oxford: Oxford University Press, 1967.

Keymer, Tom. "Reading Time in Serial Fiction before Dickens." *Yearbook of English Studies* 30 (2000): 34–45.

Kristeva, Julia. "Women's Time." In *The Kristeva Reader,* edited by Toril Moi, 187–213. New York: Columbia University Press, 1986.

Levin, Richard. *The Multiple Plot in English Renaissance Drama.* Chicago: University of Chicago Press, 1971.

Lope de Vega, Felix. "The New Art of Writing Plays." In *European Theories of the Drama,* edited by Barrett H. Clark, 89–93. Cincinnati: Stewart and Kidd, 1918.

Lotman, Jurij [Yuri]. *The Structure of the Artistic Text.* Ann Arbor: Department of Slavic Languages, 1977.

Lukács, Georg. *Studies in European Realism.* New York: Grosset and Dunlap, 1964.

Macaskill, Brian. "Interrupting the Hegemonic: Textual Critique and Mythological Recuperation from the White Margins of South African Writing." *Novel* 23 (1990): 156–81.

Margolin, Uri. "Of What Is Past, Is Passing, or to Come: Temporality, Aspectuality, Modality, and the Nature of Literary Narrative." In *Narratologies: New Perspectives on Narrative Analysis,* 167–94. Columbus: Ohio State University Press, 1999.

Martin, Wallace. *Recent Theories of Narrative.* Ithaca, N.Y.: Cornell University Press, 1986.

Matthews, John T. "Framing in *Wuthering Heights.*" *Texas Studies in Language and Literature* 27 (1985): 26–61.

Matz, Jesse. "*Maurice* in Time." *Style* 34 (2000): 188–211.

McHale, Brian. *Postmodernist Fiction*. London: Methuen, 1987.

Mendilow, A. A. *Time and the Novel*. New York: Humanities Press, 1965 (1952).

Miller, D. A. *Narrative and Its Discontents: Problems of Closure in the Traditional Novel*. Princeton, N.J.: Princeton University Press, 1981.

Miller, J. Hillis. *Reading Narrative Discourse*. Norman: University of Oklahoma Press, 1998.

Miller, Nancy K. "Emphasis Added: Plots and Plausibilities in Women's Fiction." *PMLA* 96 (1981): 36–48.

———. *The Heroine's Text: Readings in the French and English Novel (1722–1782)*. New York: Columbia University Press, 1980.

Morson, Gary Saul. *Narrative and Freedom: The Shadows of Time*. New Haven, Conn.: Yale University Press, 1994.

Mortimer, Armine Kotin. *La Clôture narrative*. Paris: Corti, 1985.

———. "Narrative Finality." *Studies in Twentieth Century Literature* 5 (1981): 175–95.

Müller, Günther. *Morphologische Poetik*. Tübingen: Max Niemeyer, 1968.

Nelles, William. *Frameworks: Narrative Levels and Embedded Narrative*. New York: Peter Lang, 1997.

Nelson, Roy Jay. *Causality and Narrative in French Fiction from Zola to Robbe-Grillet*. Columbus: Ohio State University Press, 1990.

Neupert, Richard. *The End: Narration and Closure in the Cinema*. Detroit: Wayne State University Press, 1995.

Newman, Beth. "Narratives of Seduction and the Seductions of Narrative: The Frame Structure of *Frankenstein*." *ELH* 53 (1986): 141–63.

Nietzsche, Friedrich. *Will to Power*. Translated by Walter Kaufmann and R. G. Hollingdale. New York: Random, 1966.

Nuttall, A. D. *Openings: Narrative Beginnings from the Epic to the Novel*. Oxford: Oxford University Press, 1992.

O'Neill, Patrick. *Fictions of Discourse: Reading Narrative Theory*. Toronto: University of Toronto Press, 1994.

Parker, Patricia. *Inescapable Romance: Studies in the Poetics of a Mode*. Princeton, N.J.: Princeton University Press, 1978.

Pavel, Thomas. *The Poetics of Plot: The Case of the Case of English Renaissance Drama*. Minneapolis: University of Minnesota Press, 1985.

Paxson, James. "Revisiting the Deconstruction of Narratology: Master Tropes of Narrative Embedding and Symmetry." *Style* 35 (2001): 126–50.

Pearson, John H. "The Politics of Framing in the Late Nineteenth Century." *Mosaic* 23 (1990): 15–30.

Peterson, R. G. "Critical Calculations: Measure and Symmetry in Literature." *PMLA* 91 (1976): 367–75.

Phelan, James. *Reading People, Reading Plots: Character, Progression, and the Interpretation of Narrative*. Chicago: University of Chicago Press, 1989.

———. "Beginnings and Endings: Theories and Typologies of How Novels Open and Close." *Encyclopedia of the Novel*, edited by Paul Schellinger, 1:96–99. 2 vols. Chicago: Fitzroy Dearborn, 1998.

Poulet, Georges. *Studies in Human Time*. Translated by Elliott Coleman. Baltimore, Md.: Johns Hopkins University Press, 1956.

Prince, Gerald. *A Dictionary of Narratology*. Lincoln: University of Nebraska Press, 1987.

———. *A Grammar of Stories*. The Hague: Mouton, 1971.

Propp, Vladimir. *The Morphology of the Folktale.* Translated by L. Scott, revised Lewis A. Wagner. Austin: University of Texas Press, 1968.

Rabinowitz, Peter. *Before Reading: Narrative Conventions and the Politics of Interpretation.* Reprint. Columbus: Ohio State University Press, 1999.

Reising, Russell. *Loose Ends: Closure and Crisis in the American Social Text.* Durham, N.C.: Duke University Press, 1996.

Ricardou, Jean. "Nouveau Roman, Tel Quel." *Surfiction: Fiction Now . . . and Tomorrow,* 2d ed., edited by Raymond Federman, 101–33. Chicago: Swallow, 1981.

Richardson, Brian. "Closure and Its Violation: Dramatic Convention, Aesthetic Stance, and Ideological Critique." (forthcoming).

———. "Linearity and Its Discontents: Rethinking Narrative Form and Ideological Valence." *College English* 62 (2000): 685–95.

———. "'Time is Out of Joint': Narrative Models and the Temporality of the Drama." *Poetics Today* 8 (1987): 299–309.

Richter, David. *Fable's End: Completeness and Closure in Rhetorical Fiction.* Chicago: University of Chicago Press, 1974.

Ricoeur, Paul. "Narrative Time." In *On Narrative,* edited by W. J. T. Mitchell, 165–86. Chicago: University of Chicago Press, 1981.

———. *Time and Narrative.* 3 vols. Translated by Kathleen McLaughlin and David Pellauer. Chicago: University of Chicago Press, 1984–87.

Rimmon-Kenan, Shlomith. *Narrative Fiction: Contemporary Poetics.* London: Methuen, 1984.

Roberts, Deborah H., Francis M. Dunn, and Don Fowler, eds. *Classical Closure: Reading the End in Greek and Latin Literature.* Princeton, N.J.: Princeton University Press, 1997.

Roof, Judith. *Come As You Are: Sexuality and Narrative.* New York: Columbia University Press, 1996.

Ronen, Ruth. *Possible Worlds and Narrative Theory.* Cambridge: Cambridge University Press, 1994.

Ryan, Marie-Laure. *Possible Worlds, Artificial Intelligence, and Narrative Theory.* Bloomington: Indiana University Press, 1991.

Ryding, William R. *Structure in Medieval Narrative.* The Hague: Mouton, 1971.

Sacks, Sheldon. *Fiction and the Shape of Belief.* Berkeley: University of California Press, 1964.

Said, Edward. *Beginnings: Intention and Method.* New York: Basic Books, 1975.

Schlueter, June. *Dramatic Closure: Reading the End.* Madison, N.J.: Fairleigh Dickinson University Press, 1995.

Schmidt, H. J. *How Dramas End: Essays on the German* Sturm und Drang. Ann Arbor: University of Michigan Press, 1992.

Shklovsky, Victor. "The Relationship between Devices of Plot Construction and General Devices of Style." In *Theory of Prose,* translated by Benjamin Sher, 15–51. Elmwood Park, Ill.: Dalkey Archive Press, 1990.

Showalter, Elaine. "Piecing and Writing." In *The Poetics of Gender,* edited by Nancy K. Miller, 222–47. New York: Columbia University Press, 1986.

Smith, Barbara Herrnstein. *Poetic Closure: A Study of How Poems End.* Chicago: University of Chicago Press, 1968.

Sternberg, Meir. *Expositional Modes and Temporal Ordering in Fiction.* Baltimore, Md.: Johns Hopkins University Press, 1978.

———. "Telling in Time (1): Chronology and Narrative Theory." *Poetics Today* 11 (1990): 901–48.

———. "Telling in Time (2): Chronology, Teleology, Narrativity." *Poetics Today* 13 (1992): 463–541.

Tilley, Allen. *Plot Snakes and the Dynamics of Narrative Experience.* Gainesville: University of Florida Press, 1992.

Todorov, Tzvetan. *Introduction to Poetics.* Translated by Richard Howard. Minneapolis: University of Minnesota Press, 1981.

———. *Poetics of Prose.* Translated by Richard Howard. Ithaca, N.Y.: Cornell University Press, 1977.

Tomashevsky, Boris. "Thematics." *Russian Formalist Criticism: Four Essays,* translated by Lee T. Lemon and Marion J. Reis, 61–95. Lincoln: University of Nebraska Press, 1965.

Torgovnick, Marianna. *Closure in the Novel.* Princeton, N.J.: Princeton University Press, 1981.

Uspensky, Boris. *The Poetics of Composition,* translated by Valentina Zavarin and Susan Wittig. Berkeley: University of California Press, 1973.

Wallace, Honor McKitrick. "Desire and the Female Protagonist: A Critique of Feminist Narrative Theory." *Style* 34 (2000): 176–87.

Warhol, Robyn. "Making 'Gay' and 'Lesbian' into Household Words: How Serial Form Works in Armistead Maupin's *Tales of the City.*" *Contemporary Literature* 40 (1999): 379–402.

Weinrich, Harald. *Tempus, Besprochene und Erzählte Welt.* Stuttgart: W. Kohlhammer, 1964.

White, R. S. *Let Wonder Seem Familiar: Endings in Shakespeare's Romance Vision.* London: Althone, 1985.

White, Hayden. "The Value of Narrativity in the Representation of Reality." In *On Narrative,* edited by W. J. T. Mitchell, 1–23. Chicago: University of Chicago Press, 1981.

Williams, Jeffrey. *Theory and the Novel: Narrative Reflexivity in the British Tradition.* Cambridge: Cambridge University Press, 1998.

Winnett, Susan. "Coming Unstrung: Women, Men, Narrative, and Principles of Pleasure." *PMLA* 105 (1990): 505–18.

Wofford, Susanne. "Epics and the Politics of the Origin Tale: Virgil, Ovid, Spenser, and Native American Aetiology." In *Epic Traditions in the Contemporary World: The Poetics of Community,* edited by Margaret Beissinger, Jane Tylus, and Susanne Wofford, 239–69. Berkeley: University of California Press, 1999.

Wolf, Werner. "Framing Fiction: Reflections on a Narratological Concept and an Example: Bradbury, *Mensonge.*" In *Grenzüberschreitungen: Narratologie im Kontext,* edited by Walter Grünzweig and Andreas Solbach, 97–124. Tübingen: Narr, 1998.

Yacobi, Tamar. "Time Denatured into Meaning: New Worlds and Renewed Themes in the Poetry of Dan Pagis." *Style* 22 (1988): 93–115.

Young, Katherine Galloway. "Edgework: Frame and Boundary in the Phenomenology of Narrative Communication." *Semiotica* 41, no. ¼ (1982): 277–315.

Suggested Further Reading

TIME

Susan Stanford Friedman, "Lyric Subversion of Narrative: Virginia Woolf and the Tyranny of Plot," in *Reading Narrative: Form, Ethics, Ideology,* edited by James Phelan (1989), 162–85.

Meir Sternberg, "Telling in Time I: Chronology and Narrative Theory," *Poetics Today* 11 (1990): 901–48.

Dorrit Cohn, "'I Doze and I Wake': The Deviance of Simultaneous Narration," in *The Distinction of Fiction* (1999), 96–108.

PLOT

Claude Bremond, "The Logic of Narrative Possibilities," *New Literary History* 11 (1980): 387–411.

Teresa de Lauretis, "Desire in Narrative," in *Alice Doesn't* (1984), 103–57.

Michal Peled Ginsburg, "The Case against Plot in *Bleak House* and *Our Mutual Friend,*" in *Economies of Change* (1996), 138–56.

David Herman, "Scripts, Sequences, and Stories: Elements of a Postclassical Narratology," *PMLA* 112 (1997): 1046–59.

SEQUENCE

Viktor Shklovsky, "The Relationship between Devices of Plot Construction and General Devices of Style," in *Theory of Prose* (1929; 1990), 15–51.

Roland Barthes, "Literature and Discontinuity," in *Critical Essays* (1972), 171–83.

Elaine Showalter, "Piecing and Writing," in *The Poetics of Gender,* edited by Nancy K. Miller (1986), 222–47.

David Hayman, "Self-Generation, or The Process Text," in *Re-Forming the Narrative* (1987), 105–46.

Brian McHale, "Construction," in *Postmodernist Fiction* (1987), 99–130.

BEGINNINGS AND ENDINGS

James Phelan, "Beginnings and Endings: Theories and Typologies of How Novels Open and Close," *Encyclopedia of the Novel,* 1: 96–99.

Armine Kotin Mortimer, "Narrative Finality," *Studies in Twentieth-Century Literature* 5 (1981), 175–95.

Henry Schmidt, *How Dramas End* (1992), 1–34.

Judith Roof, "The End Is Coming," in *Come as You Are* (1996), 1–40.

FRAMES AND EMBEDDED NARRATIVES

Boris Uspensky, "The Frame of an Artistic Tex," in *A Poetics of Composition* (1973), 137–67.

Gérard Genette, "'Narrative Levels' and Related Topics," in *Narrative Discourse* (1980), 227–37.

Patrick O'Neill, "Discourse Discoursed: The Ventriloquism Effect," in *Fictions of Discourse* (1994), 58–66.

[See Bibliography for additional publication information.]

Relevant Short Narratives

TIME

Ilse Aichinger, "Mirror Story," from *The Bound Man and Other Stories.*
Ambrose Bierce, "Incident at Owl Creek," from *Collected Stories.*
Jorge Luis Borges, "The Secret Miracle," from *Labyrinths.*
Italo Calvino, "t zero," from *t zero and Other Stories.*
Alejo Carpentier, "Journey Back to the Source," from *War of Time.*
Vladimir Nabokov, "The Circle," from *Collected Stories.*
Jeanette Winterson, "The Politics of Sex," from *The Penguin Book of Lesbian Short Stories,*
    edited by Margaret Reynolds.

PLOT AND SEQUENCE

Samuel Beckett, "Ping," from *The Collected Short Prose;* "Worstward Ho," from *Nohow On.*
Jorge Luis Borges, "The Garden of Forking Paths," from *Labyrinths.*
Robert Coover, "The Babysitter," from *Pricksongs and Descants.*
Guy Davenport, "The Haile Selassie Funeral Train," from *Da Vinci's Bicycle.*
Lydia Davis, "Story," from *Break it Down.*
Clarice Lispector, "The Fifth Story," from *The Foreign Legion.*
Lorrie Moore, "How," from *Self Help.*
Vladimir Nabokov, "'That in Aleppo Once . . . ,'" from *The Complete Stories.*
Joyce Carol Oates, "Plot," from *Marriages and Infidelities.*
Tim O'Brien, "How to Tell a True War Story," from *The Things They Carried.*
Grace Paley, "A Conversation with My Father," from *Enormous Changes at the Last Minute.*
Alain Robbe-Grillet, "The Secret Room," from *Snapshots.*
Jeanette Winterson, "The Politics of Sex" [see above].
John Updike, "Problems," from *Problems and Other Stories.*

BEGINNINGS AND ENDINGS

Margaret Atwood, "Happy Endings," from *Murder in the Dark.*

Beckett, "*Fizzle* 8: For to end yet again," from *Fizzles*.
Maurice Blanchot, "The Madness of the Day" [twelve-page pamphlet].
Malcolm Bradbury, "Composition," from *Who Do You Think You Are?*
Alasdair Gray, "Fictional Exits," from *Ten Tales Tall and True*.
Joyce Carol Oates, "Nightmusic," from *Marriages and Infidelities*.

FRAMES AND EMBEDDED NARRATIVES

John Barthes, "Frame-Tale," from *Lost in the Funhouse*.
Jorge Luis Borges, "The Circular Ruins," "The Immortal," "The Theme of the Traitor and the Hero," "Partial Magic in the *Quixote*," from *Labyrinths*.
Julio Cortázar, "The Continuity of Parks," from *Blow Up and Other Stories*.
Gabriel Josipovici, "Moebius the Stripper," from *Steps*.
James Alan McPherson, "Elbow Room," from *Elbow Room*.
John Edgar Wideman, "Surfiction," from *Fever*.

THE THEORY AND INTERPRETATION OF NARRATIVE SERIES
James Phelan and Peter J. Rabinowitz, Editors

Because the series editors believe that the most significant work in narrative studies today contributes both to our knowledge of specific narratives and to our understanding of narrative in general, studies in the series typically offer interpretations of individual narratives and address significant theoretical issues underlying those interpretations. The series does not privilege any one critical perspective but is open to work from any strong theoretical position.

Bleak House Narrative
Present tense summary omniscient
Esther in past tense, third person.

Story time / discourse time
repetitive / normative
frequency

STATES

New Orleans

GULF OF
MEXICO

ATLANTIC

OCEAN

BAHAMAS

C U B A

C A R I B B E A N

JAMAICA

SEA

GUATEMALA

HONDURAS

SALVADOR

NICARAGUA

*Lake
Nicaragua*

MOSQUITO
COAST

COSTA
RICA

ISTHMUS OF PANAMA

NEW
GRANAI
(COLOME

THE CARIBBEAN FEDERATION
AS CONCEIVED BY
WILLIAM WALKER

THE WORLD AND WILLIAM WALKER

Books by Albert Z. Carr

JUGGERNAUT: THE PATH OF DICTATORSHIP

MEN OF POWER

AMERICA'S LAST CHANCE

NAPOLEON SPEAKS

TRUMAN, STALIN AND PEACE

THE COMING OF WAR

JOHN D. ROCKEFELLER'S SECRET WEAPON

THE WORLD AND WILLIAM WALKER

ALBERT Z. CARR

THE WORLD
AND
WILLIAM WALKER

HARPER & ROW, PUBLISHERS
NEW YORK, EVANSTON, AND LONDON

FIRST EDITION

G-N

LIBRARY OF CONGRESS CATALOG CARD NUMBER: 63-16504

68838

CONTENTS

v

PART TWO: The Shape of Destiny

PART THREE: All or Nothing

AUTHOR'S NOTE

In the years just prior to the Civil War, William Walker's name was read in countless headlines, and heard everywhere. Millions of Americans regarded him as their Man of Destiny, and a leading European periodical hailed him as "the rival of Washington"; while President James Buchanan ordered the United States Navy into action against him, and Horace Greeley attacked him with bitter invective. His prodigious career dazzled the country. Before he was twenty-five he had been a physician, a lawyer, and a crusading newspaper editor. At thirty-one he entered Nicaragua with only fifty-eight men, defeated armies of thousands, made himself general and dictator, and was elected president. People were thunderstruck by his temerity in challenging simultaneously the might of England, the power of the President of the United States, and the millions of Cornelius Vanderbilt.

This man with the pedestrian name painted his exotic adventures on so large a canvas, in such brilliant colors, and in so surrealistic a style that it is easy to miss their inner meaning. Through his story the politics of an age may be discerned. His achievements were intimately connected with great issues—whether the Civil War would be fought —where the canal connecting the Atlantic and Pacific oceans would be dug—whether Cuba and Central America would become part of the

United States. The pattern of America's present-day relations with the Latin-American countries was largely set in Walker's time, and in spite of him. There is even perhaps in the background of the strange Walker saga a kind of Neanderthal anticipation of the dilemma in which the world finds itself in the mid-twentieth century.

In the intense agitation that he created, Walker himself, his human essence, his personality, all but disappeared from view. He became a historical enigma. In the literature about him, as it deals with the crucial passages of his life, such words as "baffling," "inexplicable," "incredible," repeatedly occur. The great volume of extreme propaganda for and against him, the myths and the legends created a distorting fog around his character, motives, and intentions. Viewing him as a political phenomenon or as a knightly hero or as a ruthless power-seeker, men lost sight of the human passions that drove him to storm the citadels of power and to defy the great forces that dominated the world of the 1850's.

It was in an effort to dispel some of the uncertainties about him that I began years ago to investigate the surviving documents of his life in cities that had known and reacted to him—New Orleans, Nashville, San Francisco, León, Washington, New York, London. Gradually a coherent and remarkable personality emerged from the record. In these pages I have tried so far as possible to let that record speak for itself. Dialogue passages are as reported in newspapers and magazines of the period, or, in one or two instances, as reconstructed from clear indications in the historical accounts.

A. Z. C.

Truro, Massachusetts

"How far high failure overleaps
the bounds of low success!"
—SIR LEWIS MORRIS

PART ONE

Overture for Bugles

《《 》》

"A great idea springs up in a man's soul; it agitates his whole being, transports him from the ignorant present and makes him feel the future in a moment. . . . Why should such a revelation be made to him . . . if not that he should carry it into practice?"

WILLIAM WALKER

I

THE GALAHAD COMPLEX

In Nashville, Tennessee, where Walker was born and raised, every literate and prosperous home had in its bookcase, alongside the Bible, Webster's Dictionary, and Marshall's *Life of George Washington,* half a dozen books by Sir Walter Scott. "The Sir Walter disease," as Mark Twain called it, was then rampant throughout the South. In the 1830's and 1840's everyone read pirated editions of *The Lady of the Lake, Ivanhoe, Marmion, The Talisman, Quentin Durward,* and the rest. *Ivanhoe* especially, according to Mark Twain, set the South "in love with dreams and phantoms." But popularizations of Malory's Arthurian legends also had a great vogue, and the chastity and dedication of Galahad were as much admired as the strength and nobility of Ivanhoe. It was a period that gave to its favorite books a devotion approaching reverence, with the result that the dreams of a generation of Southerners were shaped by medieval romance.

The yearning for the ancient glories of chivalry was more than a literary passion. Almost certainly, young people of Walker's day and place turned to Scott and the *Morte d'Arthur* out of psychological need, as a response to social conditions then prevalent. Contrary to a popular impression, the puritanical austerity of life in most parts of the

3

South was more extreme than in the North, and this was especially true of inland communities, such as Nashville, where the Protestant sects vied with each other in repressing the normal impulses of youth. Millions of youngsters like Walker had the virtues of male "purity" drilled into them by countless preachments from adolescence on, and were brought up believing that the sexual impulse, outside of the marriage bed, was the prompting of the devil. In this strict moral environment, anything that evoked the romantic mood was bound to reach deeply into the lives of the young. They wanted to idealize the relations between the sexes so as to be better able to resist the natural temptations of sensual pleasure and conform to the mores of the community. In emulating Ivanhoe or Galahad, unmarried young men found a psychological crutch with which to bear the dislocation of the reproductive instinct. Many a Southern youth, compelled to remain virginal too long, filled his mind with all the high and impossible traditions of chivalry and learned to make a virtue of abstention. It was easier to endure sexual frustration if one was living up to a grand conception of knightly honor, however illusory.

II

During Walker's childhood an ailing mother was his special care. In a memoir of the time, a friend of the Walkers' wrote, "I used often to go to see his mother and always found him entertaining her in some way." The chief form of sickroom entertainment was a reading from a favorite book. Many an afternoon, while his mother lay back on her pillows, Walker, reading in his soft Tennessee voice, must have evoked and been carried away by the mood of chivalry, in which any damsel in distress had a claim on the true knight, in which no honorable chevalier permitted a woman to be wronged if he could help her, in which one willingly gave up one's life for a friend, in which the feat of derring-do had the greater fame if the odds against one seemed hopeless. These were attitudes that stayed with him all his life.

He was not taken in by the absurdities of the chivalric manner—he was impatient of grandiose expressions of sentiment, elaborate rituals of courtesy and the naïve ferocity displayed by many Southerners in the defense of narrow points of honor. But when it came to questions of soldierly behavior and the claims of womanhood he was the romantic unalloyed. During his heyday as a conquerer, when he was leading an army of hardened soldiers of fortune to whom the looting of conquered cities and the raping of women seemed altogether reasonable, he many times risked his popularity by imposing unheard-of standards of personal restraint on his men. "On entering a town," wrote the poet Joaquin Miller, who served under him in Nicaragua, "he as a rule issued a proclamation making death the penalty for insulting a woman, for theft, or for entering a church save as a Christian should." Drunkenness among soldiers on duty was more heavily punished than in the United States Army. When his own brother, Captain Norvell Walker, got drunk on the eve of a battle, Walker publicly reduced him to the ranks; and at the most desperate point of his military fortunes he was capable of warning his men that he intended "to see properly punished, socially as well as legally, the intemperance which is calculated to bring the army into contempt and disgrace." He himself did not need to drink. For him danger was wine enough; it made him glow.

His youth in Nashville was painfully good. In sophisticated New Orleans, where the lively Creole tradition was strong, glossy young bloods kept mistresses, bedded slave girls, seduced coquettes, and slept with widows, but in the Walkers' circle in Nashville even talk of such libertinism was unthinkable. There were, of course, Nashville men who made concubines of their female slaves, but they were not likely to be found among the Disciples of Christ, the stern sect to which the family adhered. In such an environment the only chance for the sexual education of an adolescent boy was seduction by some bold and amorous girl, and what girl would bother with a lad who was short, slight, towheaded, freckle-faced, shy, bookish, and over-sensitive?

Doubtless before he reached manhood he had some kind of sexual experience—he lived for a year as a medical student in Paris. But if, as seems not improbable, his friends took him once to a brothel, he would have been repelled by the experience. There was nothing in his background to prepare him for frank nudity, bawdy talk, and casual sex. One can imagine him, after his first hopeless encounter with a laughing Parisian prostitute, flinging his cloak around him, stalking out into the night, and pacing the cobbled streets of the Left Bank, indignant, disturbed, unwilling to admit his frustration even to himself, determined more than ever to maintain his knightly ideals.

By his early twenties, although he had emancipated himself from fundamentalist religion, the ascetic pattern was firmly fixed in him. He had dissected many a corpse, he knew the physiology of sex, he was drawn to women; but sex, love, and marriage were in his mind linked in a romantic chain to a conception of beauty virginal and distressed, which needed him to rescue it and defend it. Then, in New Orleans, he met Ellen Galt Martin* and found the beauty, the virginity, and the affliction. She was a year younger than himself, twenty-three, desirable, intelligent—but a deaf-mute. The sight of beauty cut off from all the sounds of life must have called forth every protective impulse in Walker, made him wish to hold his shield before Ellen and by his personal force keep her safe from the hurtful world. He fell deeply in love.

The only extant picture of Ellen, a stylized painting, suggests a considerable charm: a high forehead, searching dark eyes, a heart-shaped, piquant face, firmly molded features, and a delicate sensuality of figure, so far as petticoats and pantalettes permit judgment. There is an alert look about her that accords with other testimony to the effect that she was exceptionally well-read and deeply interested in the questions of the day. After an attack of scarlet fever at the age of five had robbed her of both voice and hearing, her parents sent her to a school near Philadelphia which specialized in the teaching of handicapped children. On her return to New Orleans she revealed a spirited quality of mind that enabled her to share in the social life of the Martins, who were a well-to-do and prominent family. Ellen, says a family account, "used to go to balls and parties, carrying a tiny pad and pencil which she used to exchange lively repartee with many beaux."

In 1848, when Walker met her, her brothers had married and left home, and she was living with her widowed mother, Clarinda Glasgow Martin, in a large house fashionably situated. Among their acquaintance was a young lawyer and man about town, Edmund Randolph, who coming as he did of the noted Virginia family (his grandfather had been George Washington's Attorney General) had entrée everywhere; and Randolph, who had become Walker's closest

---

* Her name erroneously appears as Helen Martin in most of the Walker literature. New Orleans *Times-Picayune,* Sept. 26, 1937.

friend, brought him to the Martins' home. The result might have been predicted. Ellen responded to his love. No doubt they could read each other's feelings in eyes and expressions, in shy embraces, but their frustration at inability to communicate in speech must have been overwhelming. A book on the manual sign language for the deaf and dumb had been published not long before, and Walker spent long hours practicing its spectral routines, until he could read Ellen's patient fingers and gesticulate his way letter by letter through brief replies. It was a courtship charged with tenderness, urgency, and intense concentration.

Randolph was able to give Mrs. Martin the necessary assurances as to Walker's background and respectability, but beyond this, Ellen would have learned from her mother the striking facts about him that all New Orleans knew: that before he was twenty he was a physician with a degree from the University of Pennsylvania Medical College; that for two years he had traveled in Europe, pursuing his studies in Paris, Edinburgh, and Heidelberg; that he had put aside medicine in order to study law in New Orleans, and had practiced briefly and brieflessly as Edmund Randolph's partner; and that he had just given up the law to become an editor of the city's youngest newspaper, the Crescent. But she needed answers to a thousand questions, too many to be conveyed by sign language. Many a night Walker must have sat at his desk and dashed off, with ink and quill, the long letters that she craved. The written word came naturally to him—he was always fluent on paper, laconic in speech.

III

His father, James Walker, was a Scotsman born, who emigrated to Nashville, Tennessee, for the good reason that he had inherited property there from an uncle, and notably a prosperous dry-goods store. Soon he made a constructive marriage with the daughter of a well-known Tennessee family, Mary Norvell, whose father had been an officer in George Washington's army. Thereafter James Walker founded a commercial insurance company and became its president; and as one of Nashville's rising men, lost no time in building a substantial brick house in Nashville's best district. William was born there, the eldest of the four Walker children.

The stern spirit of Calvin and Knox was strong in the Walker home.

The Disciples of Christ maintained that a primitive and stark simplicity of worship and a literal adherence to the Bible was the only route to godliness. Religious conviction may account for the fact that James Walker would not own slaves. Too canny a businessman to let himself be called an abolitionist in a Southern community, he yet made it a point to employ as servants free Negroes to whom he paid wages—a practice not uncommon in the border states, where the example of Washington and Jefferson in freeing their slaves had not been ignored. To be sure, the economic condition of the free Negro was generally little better and sometimes worse than that of the slave, but for Negroes freedom was nevertheless the only word of hope. In any event William was brought up in a home with a nonconformist attitude toward slavery, and without firsthand experience of slave owning.

James Walker was not an unkind man, but he was a pietistic and austere father. The relationship between him and his eldest son evidently followed a classical pattern of authority and rebellion. In his early years, William was a difficult child and a reluctant schoolboy —avid for learning, but impatient of discipline. One guesses that the pride, the silence, and the tenacity that characterized him in later years were conditioned in him early by the bullying of larger boys— and most boys of his age were larger than he. From the very beginning his chief weapon in life must have been his fighting spirit. There is a certain type of small boy who is an insoluble problem to the lads of superior muscle who knock him down, because he never knows when he is licked; they cannot make him stop coming at them; they can never have an easy moment until they make peace with him. Walker the man created the impression of having been such a boy.

His father similarly gave way before him. When he was twelve, and James Walker pressed him to study for the ministry, William successfully resisted. In a time when fathers customarily selected their sons' careers, and in a household deeply dedicated to religion, his stubbornness must have shocked the older Walker, while for William the triumph of this, his first rebellion, opened a whole new vista of possibilities in life. Later, when he determined to leave Nashville, he had his way again. Perhaps his father was glad to get the rebel out of the house. His other children yielded easily to his authority.

William's first choice of a career was strongly influenced by his intense feeling for his mother. He was one of those boys who wish that they had been immaculately conceived. Mary Walker was a quiet woman, and during his school years William saw her stoically endure persistent pain which her physician was unable to diagnose or to ease. He was seized by a boy's dream of returning home as a master physician and effecting her cure; and the same dream may well have been the spur that thereafter speeded him through his schooling. Before he was ten he turned a psychological corner and became an exceptional student; he entered the University of Nashville at twelve, and graduated at fourteen, *summa cum laude*. This was, of course, less prodigious a feat than it would have been at Harvard or Yale. Nevertheless, to qualify for admission at the University of Nashville, Walker had to be fluent in Latin through Caesar's *Commentaries* and Cicero's *Orations,* and in Greek through the New Testament; while the compulsory courses at the university included algebra, geometry, trigonometry, and calculus; surveying, navigation, and astronomy; chemistry, mineralogy, and geology; logic, experimental philosophy, and natural history; Greek and Latin classics, rhetoric and belles-lettres; history, political economy, international and constitutional law; composition, criticism, and oratory. The University of Nashville's claim "to rank among the first institutions of learning in the Republic" and its pride in its library of 3,500 volumes and "the best mineralogical collections in the United States" were perhaps excessive, but it took its obligations seriously.

Religion was strongly stressed, with classes in theology and "moral training." Walker's class of twenty prayed twice every day in chapel, attended church on Sundays, and rose to hear a long benediction before every meal in the dining hall. But the puritanical spirit showed itself even more in that which was banned. The light indulgences known to college students elsewhere—balls, horseraces, cockfights, theaters—and such luxuries as dogs, horses, carriages, and servants—were strictly forbidden at Nashville. Even the study of music was permitted only as a special dispensation. It seems that Walker was allowed to practice fencing under a private master; the longing to handle a sword had been in him since childhood, and he had a wiry physique well suited to the art.

After his graduation, some months spent in reading medical books in the office of the family's physician, Dr. Thomas Jennings, confirmed his desire to pursue a career in medicine. He had no difficulty in entering the Medical College of the University of Pennsylvania, at Philadelphia, and in 1843 he graduated with his degree in medicine. He was then nineteen years old—certainly one of the youngest qualified physicians in the country.

The subject of his doctoral essay was "The Iris," and there is some reason to believe that Walker at this period became interested in mesmerism. His extraordinary eyes, "which burned with a cold grey fire," and to which some later attributed hypnotic power, were enough in themselves to attract him to a study of what was then called "mesmeric phenomena." The vogue for hypnotism to which the work of the controversial Dr. Mesmer had given rise in Europe had not made much headway in the United States, but the possible pain-relieving power of hypnosis was much debated among medical students, at a time when no effective anesthetic for use in surgery was yet available.

Although a career was waiting for him in Nashville, he showed no interest in pursuing it. His heart was set on further study, this time in Europe. Edinburgh, the Mecca of aspiring American medicos, seemed the obvious choice among foreign universities, and James Walker's family was in Scotland, but William elected to go to Paris. The faculty of the Sorbonne, where he attended lectures, may have been of less importance in his decision than the immemorial appeal of France for romantic spirits.

IV

The disillusionment that led Walker to give up medicine began in the hospitals of Paris. Balzac's novels portray the materialism, corruption, and cynicism that flourished under the last Bourbon kings, and medicine, no less than business and government, had become hopelessly reactionary. Of all Frenchmen, a wry wit said, physicians shrugged best. Except in those hospitals which served the wealthy, facilities were medieval, sanitation negligible, and methods ruthless. Infant mortality was far higher than in London; epidemics of contagious disease within hospitals were frequent; and human suffering under the surgeon's scalpel was beyond description. The conditions observed by Walker at nineteen made a mockery of his Hippocratic ideals; and the mood of the city, for all its surface gaiety, must have been equally trying for a young puritan who did not patronize brothels, drink, or gamble. The chief values of Paris for him lay in his exposure to French literature. Victor Hugo became one of his idols. His political ideas especially leaped ahead. But Parisian *politesse* also left its mark on him; his manners took on a formality and a subtlety which many Americans considered "sissified," and which, in his filibustering* days, startled those who, meeting him for the first time, expected to find a roughhewn swashbuckler.

Leaving Paris after something over a year, Walker attended medical lectures at Heidelberg. He seems to have had a gift for language; later he learned Spanish. A German source relates that he participated in the compulsory duels, with two-edged swords, of the student societies at Heidelberg, and emerged unscarred—no small tribute to his Nashville fencing master, if true; but this may be apocryphal. What other European centers he visited is uncertain, but finally he headed north for study at Edinburgh, spending some time in London on the way. His stay there apparently prejudiced him against the British. *Martin Chuzzlewit* was just then putting an additional strain on Anglo-American relations; and Walker, who had none of the American habits caricatured by Dickens—he did not get drunk, spit, swear, boast, murder the language, or regard money as the main thing in life—would have resented the patronizing style in which most Englishmen of the period spoke of his countrymen.

After a long, rough, transatlantic crossing he returned to Nashville, where he was received with all the admiration that a widely traveled young man with university degrees evoked in those days. "The most accomplished surgeon that ever visited the city," he was called. But there was bitter irony in his situation, for he found his mother not very far from death, wasted away, grey before her time, in pain most of her waking hours from "rheumatism" and "neuralgia"; and he could not pretend to know, any more than the family physician, how she should be treated.

The profession of medicine now seemed futile to him. He made a brief attempt to practice, but without zest. Although he never lost his interest in medical theory or his respect for dedicated physicians, he quickly realized that the dispensing of calomel, the administering

---

* "Filibuster"—from the Dutch *vrijbuiter,* freebooter.

of purges, and the obstetrics which filled the doctor's daily round were not for him. That he was tossing aside the fruit of years of study and a large financial investment, and bitterly disappointing his father, made no difference.

After his long absence, he must have felt himself something of a stranger in his family, holding views sharply different from theirs, and perhaps displaced from the center of his mother's affections by his two younger brothers and his sister. In any event, he was determined not to remain in Nashville. Of all the cities in the United States, New Orleans attracted him most, with its Creole glamor, its international flavor, and its metropolitan culture. Nowhere else in the South could there be found in one city theaters, opera, publishers, literary clubs, a variety of newspapers, and a famous cuisine. And it was easy to find a reason for going there. Having long since rejected the ministry, and having no inclination, or so it seemed, for military life, he was left with only one "gentlemanly" profession still open to him, the law. He would study law, and in New Orleans; the superiority of the Code Napoléon, as established in Louisiana, was a favorite conviction of romantic young Southerners.

His father's assistance, if it was forthcoming at all, was on a meager scale, for William as a law student in New Orleans had very little money. Two years of reading for the bar saw him qualified for practice. He was then twenty-three years old, and although hardly gregarious, had formed a wide and useful acquaintance. Edmund Randolph, a few years his senior, and who was Clerk of the United States Circuit Court, was closest to him. In type they were sharply different. Randolph was a cheerful blade, with a pretty quadroon mistress in a house on Rampart Street and a proper collection of gambling debts and bar bills. He evidently saw in Walker qualities needed to complement his own, for at his urging they opened a law office, as partners. But the firm did not prosper. Randolph was more interested in the pursuit of pleasure than in his practice, and although Walker was a fluent and effective speaker when he chose, he tended to be silent and enigmatic with strangers. His style could not have been inviting to potential clients; he dressed without regard to fashion, and made an unimpressive appearance. Standing only five feet, five inches, weighing less than 120 pounds, he seemed even younger than his years. If one did not observe his eyes, his face gave no special indication of latent force. A high unwrinkled brow under lank, light-brown hair; a long straight nose; a wide mouth, not unfriendly, but with a hint of the satirical in the quirked corners; an angular jaw—all this was familiar American physiognomy. Only the heavy-lidded eyes suggested the possibilities within him. Grey, brilliant, luminous, they seemed to penetrate the skulls of the men he talked to; they quickened the interest of friends, arrested strangers, and threw antagonists off balance.

In all probability he had given up the law in his heart, as he had given up medicine, even before he began to practice it. It would not have taken him long to discover that practitioners in the courts of New Orleans had to have as thick a skin as did physicians in the hospitals of Paris. A tight cabal of politicians controlled the municipal government, rigged the elections, hand-picked the judges, packed the juries, ran the police force, had keys to the jails, and made a mockery of the Code Napoléon. New Orleans' men of wealth came to terms with the political bosses in the usual financial way, but there was little justice and less mercy for the citizen without money who came up against the civic authority. As for serious municipal administration, it was conspicuous by its absence. No money was forthcoming for sanitary improvements, the draining of marshes, construction of sewers, repairs of the levees, paving of muddy streets, and the regular garbage collections needed to protect the city against recurrent epidemics. Gambling and vice flourished, however. Brothels, protected by the police, openly distributed handbills advertising their "virgins just in from the country" and "*filles de joie* trained in Paris."

Randolph, with his realistic outlook, was able to play the game, but Walker could no more accommodate himself to the chicanery of the city's courts than he could have patronized Madame Fifi's Select Cabaret. He had no real interest in the ordinary run of legal business. It was only the drama of the courtroom that attracted him. It is as impossible to imagine him sending out bills and pocketing fees as, in his medical guise, prescribing placebos or cultivating a bedside manner. He tasted medicine and law as most young gentlemen of his time tasted a brace of bottles of dubious wine, found them sour, and turned away.

The excuse that he needed to throw aside his new profession came early in 1848, when he was approached by two experienced newspapermen, A. H. Hayes and J. C. McClure, who had just resigned from the staff of the conservative New Orleans *Delta*. They were planning to publish a paper of their own, to be called the *Crescent*, and they were looking for a man to edit news from abroad and write on foreign affairs. Walker, with his European experience, his several languages, his classical education, and his medical and legal training, struck them as hopeful for their purpose. He could not have hesitated long before accepting. A newspaper would give him needed opportunity for self-expression, enemies to tilt against, and above all the chance to make his reputation. Time was moving fast. Educated young men in those days liked to quote Schiller's *Don Carlos:* "Twenty-four years old and still nothing accomplished for immortality!" Napoleon, Pitt, and Bolívar were not long dead, and their gigantic careers had already been in movement at twenty-four.

For an additional spur to his new enterprise, there was his need for Ellen. The nature of their relationship can best be imagined in the context of the age. His great ambition and knightly ideals, far from striking Ellen as absurd, would have had her warm encouragement. Beneath his reserved style she would have recognized a warm and generous spirit, and would have loved his pride, his kindness, his gentle manner. But these inexperienced and silent lovers were caught "between ascetic rocks and sensual whirlpools." For them the seeking touch of hand to hand, the brief caress of lips, were novel and exquisite sensations, which taxed their restraint. The problem was compounded by their silence. Without words there was no way for them to express ardor and reveal pulsing desire except by such physical trespass as would have violated the code in which they had been reared.

Marriage was their need and their hope; but that would have to wait until Walker could offer a suitable home and reasonable prospects. It was essential for him to prove himself a man of substance, one to whom Mrs. Martin need have no fear of confiding her daughter. The offer from the *Crescent* came at a propitious time. Although his first pieces, signed with his initial, W, were contributed experimentally, he was soon a full-time member of the paper's small staff. By March, 1848, he had given up his uncliented law office to become a journalist, with a small income but large aspirations.

II

⚜

FAR TO THE LEFT

Eighteen-forty-eight was a great year for American newspapers. Sensation followed sensation. It seemed that year as if the entire human species felt a spontaneous urge to burst its bonds. Everywhere discontent and frustration were suddenly translated into violence. The revolutionary furor first revealed itself in Paris, where in three days of street fighting republican insurgents toppled King Louis Philippe from his throne. From France the contagion spread swiftly eastward. The King of Prussia, his hair standing on end as he heard rumors of a new and frightening creed called Communism, felt compelled to grant a constitution to appease the grim crowds of Berlin. In Vienna, the Hapsburg emperor was saved only when Cossack cavalry sent by the Czar of Russia came to his aid; but even the feared Russians could not prevent Hungary, led by Kossuth, from achieving independence, or the Balkans from blazing in rebellion, while the entire north of Italy shook off the Austrian yoke. Spain held its breath as Spanish exiles from a bloody rule established bases in France from which to launch a civil war against the Bourbon monarchy. Starving men in Ireland vented their panic and grief in riots against the British government as they counted one fifth of all the Irish, a million and

15

a half people, dead or emigrated in three years of potato blight and famine. Even in dispirited Asia men were challenging established authority. The anti-imperial rebellion called Taiping, or Great Peace, began to make itself felt in China. Hardly a month passed in India without action by British troops to punish states and tribes foolhardy enough to contest the might of Queen Victoria.

All this passionate turmoil would soon subside. France would return to Napoleonism, kings and dictators everywhere would continue to reign, and liberals pursued by the secret police of their native lands would seek sanctuary abroad. Soon the Russian writer Alexander Herzen would write with a sigh from Paris, "It is a strange thing: since 1848 we have all faltered and diminished, we have thrown overboard all that mattered, we have shrunk back into ourselves." But while the year ran its course, anything seemed possible. The managing editor of the New York *Herald,* Charles A. Dana, reported from France, "I find that . . . socialism has gained very greatly. A shrewd observer, who is not a socialist, remarked to me the other day that the ultimate triumph of the new ideas was certain. The future will show whether he was a true prophet."

Of the great powers of Europe one alone escaped the revolutionary temblor—England. Not that the British people lacked cause for anger. Describing their condition, the London *Inquirer* said, "Misery and degradation confront you at every step. . . . It is absolutely distressing to sit by your fireside on account of the piteous objects who place themselves before your windows, exhibiting every mark of wretchedness and woe. . . . We have no plan . . . to remedy this great evil which pervades English society. We can only lament its existence."

A few daring spirits went so far as to advocate the abolition of child labor and the shortening of the factory work week from eighty to seventy-two hours, and workers assembled under the Chartist banner tried to demonstrate in the streets. But the British as a whole, although they wept over the plight of Oliver Twist and Little Nell, were at the same time so charmed and stimulated by recent triumphs of British arms, diplomacy, and commerce that Monday's protests were drowned in Tuesday's cheers. India was yielding undreamed-of riches. From romantic Cathay, too, great revenues were coming as millions of Chinese contracted the opium habit; for a few years earlier England's artillery had compelled Peking to permit the importation of the previously forbidden drug. Not merely an empire but the entire globe was being tapped by British commercial enterprise, backed by the world's strongest navy. American rivalry in trade, while energetic, was by no means alarming. The Atlantic stood between the Yankee factories and the European market; while the Cape of Good Hope route to the Orient gave England a long advantage in distance and time over American vessels compelled to go around Cape Horn. Gold poured into London from all quarters, including the United States, where British manufacturers had a huge market. In so congenial a situation, the mood of England's governing class was benign.

As for the United States, its people could hardly have cared less about the fall of kings and the overturn of governments abroad—except to agree, in general, that it served them right. Great events close to home that year were exalting the American state of mind. The surrender of the Mexican army under Santa Anna had enabled President Polk's administration to wrest nearly half of Mexico's territory from her, on pretexts so thin that some leading Americans—Daniel Webster and Henry Clay among them—were apologetic. But many on the contrary berated the President as a "Slow-Polk" for his failure to make all of Mexico forthwith a territory of the United States. At any rate, what was done was done; and then came the breath-taking news of vast deposits of gold in California, making every American a millionaire in his dreams, and setting off a burst of speculative enthusiasm on Wall Street. At the same time, American industrial genius was displaying its power on all sides. In Chicago, Cyrus McCormick had begun to manufacture his revolutionary reaper. In Philadelphia, Richard Hoe's steam-powered rotary press was turning out newspapers four times faster than had ever been possible before. Samuel Morse's electric telegraph now ran the length of the American coast from Boston to New Orleans.

Especially there were the railroads. With the aid of British capital, tracks were being laid from New England to the Mississippi, from the Great Lakes to the Ohio. Asa Whitney that year appeared before Congress to urge the building of a transcontinental line. President Polk made a treaty with the South American country of New Granada (Colombia) for the construction of a railroad across the Isthmus of

Panama, to transport passengers between the Atlantic and Pacific oceans. The steam locomotive was hope, it was wealth, it was the future. Monied men were buying railroad stocks, and every child aspired to be an engineer—except those who longed to be captain of a China clipper or pilot of a Mississippi steamboat.

Such a year of good news, military, mineral, and industrial, the American people had never before experienced. The country was on the move, growing, surging, rushing. But as 1848 drew to its close, beneath the shimmering surface of events was a current of deep concern. Unemployment was high, wages were low, and crime was mounting in the cities. Bitter old John C. Calhoun of South Carolina was saying that the slavery question "must be brought to a final decision," and that if the government attempted to prevent the spread of slavery to the West the question of Southern adherence to the Union might soon be vital. He went so far as privately to threaten the President of the United States with immediate secession. Horace Greeley in the New York *Tribune* ominously demanded, "Men and Brethren, how shall this great question be decided?" Yet there were men both North and South who still looked for gradual emancipation of slaves, to be achieved by nonviolent means.

II

With so much excitement to be had for a penny, newspaper circulation soared and advertising revenue multiplied. All over the country papers sprang up, and educated young men turned to journalism in increasing numbers as they recognized in the press a shortcut to influence, fame, and wealth. There were in the nation over 2500 dailies, weeklies and periodicals, as compared with 1500 in 1840—this for a population of 23,000,000. In New York the *Herald* alone had a circulation of almost 17,000 daily, and the *Tribune* not much less. Never before had the press exerted so much power. Columns of telegraphed news made it possible for the first time to shape the opinions of the American people quickly on a national scale.

Of all the infant newspapers of the year none had a better beginning than the *Crescent*. New Orleans was the metropolis of the South, the heart of the all-important cotton trade, the chief port for south-bound shipping, and the focal point for news from Mexico. The

Crescent set out to offer its readers something more than they could find in the well-established *Picayune* or *Delta*—a broad and less specifically Southern view of the world. In their opening announcement, Hayes and McClure expressed the intention to establish "a general and accurate newspaper with enlarged and liberal views on subjects connected with commercial enterprise and agricultural industry." Here, for those able to read between the lines, was a daring hint of something less than enthusiasm for the institution of slavery. The *Crescent,* added the front-page editorial, "would discuss the great questions of State and National policy with impartiality and freedom"— or in other words, they would not necessarily support the prevailing Southern view of states' rights, among which the alleged right of secession was uppermost in men's minds. That so bold a stand might prove poor business the men who ran the *Crescent* recognized, but their venture, they said, would be "persevered in while there is any hope of success."

The generally lucid style of the *Crescent's* editorials stood in contrast to the murky and adjectival rhetoric then favored by many journalists in the South. Walker's contributions especially were distinguished by a certain intensity of feeling, indignation or enthusiasm. He respected facts—a trait instilled in him by his medical and legal training—but the main quality of his writing was its heat. At the same time, according to reporters who worked for him, he was a dependable and effective editor. One of them later described him as "very silent and very kind, with the look of a man bent upon a hard course of study, and a book always in his hand."

Almost from the first, the paper throve surprisingly, for its opinions were stimulating, its news coverage professional, its format creditable, and its writing superior. A New York journalist who visited New Orleans in 1848 remarked that "the *Crescent* is growing like Anak." After its first month it was able to thank its readers and advertisers "for support beyond what we had anticipated." A few months later one of the city's prominent lawyers and politicians, "Judge" J. C. Larue, bought an interest in the paper; and an editorial proudly said, "With a daily increasing subscription list and an advertising business which is extended with every number, the establishment of our paper is no longer an experiment: it is 'a fixed fact.' "

One of the *Crescent's* successful novelties was a first-page feature called "Sketches of the Sidewalks and Levees, with Glimpses into the New Orleans Bar (Rooms)." The author was a young journeyman printer—Walt Whitman—who had adventured to New Orleans from the North, and was entranced by the city. Although he earned his living in the *Crescent*'s pressroom, the abundance in him flowed constantly into reportage. He saw the colorful life around him with a poet's fresh and loving eye—the sensual excitement of the streets, the gay cries of the street vendors, the strong Negro women in their blue dresses and bright turbans, the beautiful quadroon girls paraded and guarded by watchful mothers, the half-starved grisettes of the seamstress shops, the elegant French restaurants with their noble wines, the drunken squalor of the rivermen's bars, the cotton, slave, and horse markets in and around the grand Hotel St. Louis, the love of Napoleonic glory, the streets named after Bonaparte's victories. All this he caught with a lightly satirical pen.

Perhaps Whitman's best piece for the *Crescent* was "Daggerdraw Bowieknife"—a violent lampoon of the professional duellist and bully whose type was then common in the city, and who, Whitman said, "would rather shoot a man than pay him what he owed him." Where Walker was preoccupied with large political issues, Whitman explored the troubled soul of the city, perceiving that its polite society of a few thousand people of means and education was merely a gloss over the broad, bawdy, and orgiastic life which teemed below. In no other large city in America—it was then third in rank after New York and Philadelphia, with a population, white and black, of 125,-000—did the ordinary citizen spend so much time in the pursuit of pleasure, in the forms of women, cards, alcohol, prize fighting, cock-fighting, and well-cooked food. Throughout its history, under Spanish, French, and American rule, New Orleans had always been a wide-open town. Perhaps its extreme sensual indulgence grew in part out of its acute sense of the chanciness of life. More than in most metropolises, to live in New Orleans was to live with peril—peril from Mississippi floods—peril from almost annual epidemics of cholera, the plague, and most dreaded of all, the yellow fever—peril from hooligans and thieves swarming in the dark streets at night—peril from brawling backwoodsmen and roistering boatmen on their drunken sprees—peril from venereal diseases that spread from scores of thriving brothels—economic peril from the violent movements of cotton and sugar prices—psychic peril from the corrupting effects of Negro slavery on the young of both races. Even the man of position was more vulnerable than in other cities, for social rank did not protect him from hot-eyed, pistol-carrying young bloods eager to mock the law that forbade duelling and risk their lives for what they considered points of honor.

As for the 60,000 Negroes of the city, of whom all but a few were slaves, their characteristic broad placatory smiles meant only that they had learned to live with their terrors and resentments. The great torchlit slave dances held to the beating of drums in Congo Square, and watched by Whites as an entertainment—where glistening black bodies shuffled, swayed, and pranced—and where the rhythms of jazz are said to have had their origin in American culture—these provided not merely recreation but more important, a way for the young Negro to work off in uninhibited physical movement his week's accumulation of frustration and hostility. Small slave mutinies on the plantations around New Orleans were sufficiently familiar so that no one, of either race, could long forget the danger implicit in the "peculiar institution." Even the seemingly gay little "Gombo" songs and sayings in French dialect that the Negroes made up almost daily, and sang in the streets, often had an undertone of bitterness and served as a kind of running social commentary. One was nothing more than a little musical sigh: "I don't die, I don't get well." Another made a social symbol out of the pocket: the Negro needed a pocket because he stole chickens, the mulatto used his pocket to carry stolen jewels, but the white man's pocket was for money with which to deceive women. The plight of the pretty quadroon girls was caught in a sardonic little song: "Ah, clever one, we know you—you're colored—there isn't any soap white enough to let you pass."

III

It was the *Crescent*'s loss and poetry's gain when Whitman's wander-lust, or it may have been the fact that he had drawn advances on his salary beyond hope of repayment, prompted him, in the summer of 1848, to make his farewells and catch a northbound riverboat. His departure left Walker as the only writer of outstanding ability on the newspaper. Almost certainly it was through his pen that the *Crescent* greeted the European revolutions. "The French republicans have difficulties to surmount before they can gratify their generous and noble aspirations. We hope they may overcome them all and secure the emancipation of their country." The pro-French and anti-British tone of the newspaper was unmistakable. An editorial on the suppression of the Chartist demonstrations in London assailed the British way of life. "Aristocracy may triumph now . . . but the day of the people must come at last; and the longer it is delayed, the more terrible will be the reckoning, and the more radical the reform. . . . Our sympathies are with the people."

As for national politics in the United States, the *Crescent* refused to be either Whig or Democratic. It pronounced itself "neither pleased nor grieved" on the election of that high military personage and intellectual nonentity, General Zachary Taylor, to the Presidency. But there was unmistakable heat and sincerity in its frequent outbursts of indignation at social injustice. When its own weapons of attack became blunted by overuse, it went out of its way to quote from other newspapers, even from Northern papers that shared its views. Thus, from Milwaukee: "Every true patriot will ask, is not the preponderating and crushing power of capital caused, in no small degree, by the partial and special legislation which blackens the Statute book of nearly every State, even in our own Republic?" Similarly, through a Boston paper, the *Crescent* endorsed the agrarian reforms of revolutionary European governments which were "taking the feudal estates from their owners without compensation."

Walker at this time unquestionably stood far to the Left, even among the advanced liberals of the time. The vein of compassion which revealed itself in his love for Ellen Martin carried also a strong flow of democratic principles. He began to wear a black, wide-brimmed Kossuth hat, named after the Hungarian revolutionary, who had become an idol of American democrats. It is perhaps a legitimate surmise that Ellen shared his dangerous idealism, and encouraged his bold thrusts in the *Crescent*. She must have been pleased when the newspaper one day risked the mockery of New Orleans' male population by advocating "the rights of women" to suffrage and property, and praised the example of a legislative measure which had then been introduced for these purposes in the French Chamber of Deputies. The *Crescent* even declared its willingness "to lay ourselves open to the accusation of radicalism, jacobinism, agrarianism and . . . other hard names." It jeered at "well-fed and well-clad propriety" for refusing to admit "that the poor man has rights which it is his duty to assert by all the means in his power—by reason or by force." The *Crescent*'s views on slavery were less overt than on other issues, for to exist in New Orleans it had to escape the deadly label of "abolitionist," but the knowledgeable reader could feel no doubt as to its stand. A front-page column praising Alexis de Tocqueville seems to have been written primarily for the inclusion of one sentence; *"Democracy in America* is one of the best works ever published on the institutions of this country." In this way the paper was able to endorse de Tocqueville's indictment of slavery without actually mentioning it. A similar policy was followed with respect to the controversy over the fugitive slave laws, which was reported without comment—a fact which was in itself a comment. The *Crescent* delighted, furthermore, in publishing from time to time in prominent positions macabre little items describing slave revolts, murders of slave owners, bloody insurrections on slave ships, and the like. Quotations from moderate Northern writers implied the hope that as the South's economic condition improved through the introduction of new industries, slavery would be gradually reduced and eventually abolished. "If these states [Virginia, Kentucky, and Tennessee] choose to abolish slavery within their own borders—and we confess that the signs of the times indicate they will do it—it is their own concern." Above all, nothing must be left undone that might help to avoid a civil war. "Before a people resort to it they will naturally inquire . . . is it [the grievance] sufficient to arm brother against brother? . . . Is the abstract right [of slave ownership] so certain that no disinterested man can doubt upon the subject? . . . There is another question which prudent men will put to themselves before they risk all upon the uncertain chance of war. What will be gained by victory?"

On only one main issue of the day did the *Crescent* stand with prevailing Southern opinion. It believed that Cuba should be part of the United States. Said one editorial, early in 1848, "Cuba *must* be independent of Spain, and as an ultimate consequence, a member of our union." But as to the means of acquisition, the *Crescent* differed with the Southern view. Most leaders of the South were unwilling to entrust the island's future to any federal administration dominated by

Northern politicians. Either Cuba would become a slave state, under Southern influence, or it was better left to its Spanish owners. The solution, as seen in New Orleans, was a Cuban revolution under leadership sympathetic to the Southern position. To foment such a revolution was a major objective of Southern expansionists, and a filibustering military expedition recruited in the South and financed by private gentlemen was their chosen means.

The *Crescent* would have none of this. As always where slavery was concerned, its position was against expansion. Cuba should certainly become an American state, but through legitimate purchase of the island from Spain or perhaps by a spontaneous revolution of its abused people, followed by the achievement of independence and voluntary application for admission to the Union. "Cuba . . . must win her own freedom." "If we wait a little the ripened plum will fall into our laps." Ostensibly the *Crescent* based its stand on the need to maintain the integrity of the Neutrality Laws, established thirty years earlier, which forbade unauthorized American military intervention in the affairs of friendly nations. This argument could not, however, disguise from readers the newspaper's lack of enthusiasm for Negro slavery.

Late in 1848, word came that Congress was debating a measure to abolish the slave trade in the District of Columbia, and that the Southern members, led by Senator Calhoun, had threatened to walk out in a body and dissolve the Union if the bill were passed. Popular sentiment in New Orleans was strongly in their favor. The *Picayune* advocated "risking everything on a collision," and assumed that "something more than ink would be shed." Alone among the city's papers, the *Crescent* urged caution. "Being friends of peace and good order, and devotedly attached to our Union, we thought it our duty to say a word in behalf of its preservation." This was almost a slap in the face to those in the South, and they were many, who regarded the Mason-Dixon line as the northern boundary of their country, except perhaps on the Fourth of July and Washington's birthday. Angry editors of newspapers in South Carolina and Mississippi openly branded the *Crescent* "a Yankee paper," a reputation that it never thereafter was able to shake off.

IV

The extent to which Walker influenced the total editorial policy of the *Crescent* must be conjectural, but to judge by the internal evidence of content and style, his individual mark was all over it. A series of studies of French philosophers, including Pascal, Montesquieu, and Chateaubriand is probably attributable to his influence. His advanced intellectual interests were a source of pride to the newspaper. When, in October, 1848, he was invited to Nashville to deliver the commencement address at his university, choosing as his subject "The Unity of Art," the *Crescent* reported the event with satisfaction, and quoted from the Nashville press to make the point that "Mr. W. acquitted himself with great ability in composition and delivery."

This address,* reprinted by the University but long lost from sight, throws a revealing light on Walker at the age of twenty-four. "Were I called upon to state succinctly the object of University education," he begins, "I should say that it is the cultivation of art. . . . On the university depends, in great measure, the maintenance of good taste which is a chief and essential element of what we denominate civilization." Art he conceived broadly as the outward manifestation of man's spiritual life, embodied in beauty, truth, and virtue. The study of science, he said, far from being antagonistic to art, could contribute to the development of artistic perceptions, for "science teaches the principles on which the worlds were made, as well as the great mathematical truths . . . pointing to the invisible world, the world of spirit."

Of all the arts, it was heroic poetry that touched him most deeply. He saw Shakespeare and Milton as the poets of heroism, Byron as the hero of poetry. Byron's life he considered to have been lived artistically—"although he died young, yet was he old in fame and deeds." Life itself was an art form. It was only through the pursuit of the art of living that man, "half worm and half angel," could rise above the primeval. Man's artistic self found an outlet even in war—"the strongest and fiercest expression of patriotism"—and the artist in life must strive to achieve the "perfect and radiant countenance" of courage.

---

* Library of the Tennessee State Archives, Nashville.

He cautioned against letting petty proprieties and conventional ideas stifle the impulse to art. Aiming an ironic shaft at those "who are afraid of philosophy," he urged the reading of the poetry of Milton, with its inquiry into man's inner nature; and he even went so far as to remind his pious Tennessee audience that in *Paradise Lost* the most interesting and attractive figure is Satan of the "unconquerable will" and "immortal hate."

Walker's entire subsequent career may in some sense be regarded as an expression of these ideas. They gave the directional thrust to his life's trajectory. He had already begun to formulate the principles of heroic conduct by which he tried to live; from the ideal of Galahad to the ideal of Byron was a natural evolution for him. In his time, for a young man to strive for a life of Byronic grandeur was not considered absurd. The striving was its own justification.

Perhaps equally important, "The Unity of Art" reveals him as fully aware of many of the great seminal ideas of the age then taking root in Europe. This same awareness came out repeatedly on the editorial page of the *Crescent*. Walker almost certainly wrote a striking article called "The Wars of the World," taking its text from Thomas Hobbes, and asking speculatively, "Must men remain forever the slaves of their purely destructive propensities? Or are we yet but in the germ of being, and is it necessary to pass through the lower grades of existence before we can arrive at the higher and nobler states that await us [mankind] in the future?" This was a decade before Darwin published the *Origin of Species;* it would appear that someone on the *Crescent* had been reading the works of the earlier French evolutionists. Similarly it is likely that Walker, with his medical training abroad, was responsible for the publication in the *Crescent* of some advanced and original articles written by other physicians on the prevention and treatment of cholera and yellow fever. Appearing long before the investigations of bacteria by von Helmholtz and Pasteur were published, these articles hinted at the existence of such microorganisms, plainly spoke of "the animalcular theory of cholera and all diseases, with very few exceptions," and urged that sanitary measures be taken in "places favoring the development of insects which spread disease."

Late in December, 1848, one of the *Crescent*'s editors, and not improbably Walker, set himself to the composition of an article, such as newspapers have immemorially presented to their readers, appraising the significance of the year. "The year which has just completed its course . . . is crowded with events which will cause it to stand out in such bold relief that posterity will look back on it as the beginning of a new era." Europe was convulsed by revolutionary and democratic agitation. The United States stood as victor in war and proud possessor of vast new territories. Incalculable possibilities for the country had been opened up by the gold of California. The dream of riches was causing thousands of starry-eyed Americans to leave their homes and journey westward. In New Orleans the mood of excitement was caught in a local witticism: "Last year it was yellow fever, this year it's gold fever." The entire front page of the *Crescent* that New Year's Day was given over to descriptions of California and a map of the mining regions.

But the editorial concluded on a sobering note. A severe epidemic of cholera had broken out in New Orleans. "In the midst of these golden dreams . . . the cup of happiness is dashed from our lips. The returning pestilence has invaded our land, carrying . . . misery to many a heart." Over a thousand deaths had already been reported. Many New Orleans families were fleeing northward. Walker must have worried deeply about Ellen and her mother, who remained in the city. "Thus ends the Old Year, and begins the New with the souls of men flamed with the desire for gain and the Asiatic plague recommencing its deadly and terrible march."

III

〰️

"LET IT COME"

It was while he edited the *Crescent* that Walker took the specific political position on which he based his subsequent career. Like the majority of Americans in his time, he believed ardently in the nation's "Manifest Destiny" to establish its institutions and its power throughout the Western Hemisphere. With him, however, this conviction was not merely the product of wild and thoughtless chauvinism. He felt, as did many of America's political leaders, that the best chance for preventing the nation from tearing itself apart over the slavery issue was to rally the people in a common cause, with a moral justification. That cause, that justification, as he saw it, lay in the Monroe Doctrine. In 1849, the country learned that England had been almost contemptuously flouting the Doctrine by its actions in Central America. The London *Times* openly boasted that almost half of the isthmus was in British hands.

The point of contention that arrested Walker lay in a broad strip of land along the Atlantic coast of Nicaragua, a territory known as Mosquitia, or Mosquito. Belatedly, the United States had awakened to its strategic importance. Europe, however, had long believed that Nicaragua was one of the main keys to the world empire of the future.

28

More than a hundred years earlier, in 1740, a French scientist, La Condamine, had said as much before the Academy of Sciences in Paris and had proposed the construction of a canal in Nicaragua to connect the Atlantic and Pacific oceans. His paper came to the attention of the British Foreign Office; and while the French were still considering the matter, England sent warships to Nicaragua, then a possession of declining Spain, and hoisted her flag on the swampy east shore. The primitive Mosquito Indians offered no opposition. Always careful, the British then justified their action in diplomatic terms. A document was solemnly produced to show that in 1720 the "King" of the Mosquitos had voluntarily put his territory under the protection of the governor of Jamaica.

Spain protested; England shrugged; and so the matter stood for a century. But when the Central American states shook off Spanish rule, and under Bolívar's inspiration formed a Federation, Nicaragua felt emboldened to ask by what right the British governed in part of her territory. England's representatives in Central America decided that the old Jamaican authority would no longer serve. Accordingly they dressed a descendant of one of the former Mosquito kings in the uniform of a British major, formally crowned him King Robert Charles Frederick of the "Mosquito Shore and Nation," surrounded him with a court of "noble lords," and solemnly asserted his sovereign powers.

Here arose an unforeseen development; King Robert took his role seriously, and since he was fond of whisky and bright clothing, began to give away large tracts of his country to Yankee traders, in return for liquor and gay cotton prints. The British intervened, spirited the King away, and imprisoned him for the rest of his life, but not before he had signed (with an "x") a document appointing an Englishman as his regent, "in recognition of all the favors heaped upon him and his people by the English." Thereafter the country was ostensibly governed by a native Council of State, who provided a diplomatic screen for the British officers in the background.

All this was part of a larger British plan—to get rid of the Central American Federation, which, being democratic in tendency, was already under heavy pressure from the large Nicaraguan landholders of Spanish descent. Its destruction took some years, but in 1838 the Federation fell apart in a welter of civil war and confusion. This was the moment England had been awaiting. First she seized the east coast of Guatemala, known as Belize, and which she thereafter called British Honduras; next, she took possession of Cape Honduras, which lay just to the north of Mosquito; and finally she pushed the Mosquito protectorate southward. For it had now become clear that the best canal route across Nicaragua would utilize the San Juan River, close to the boundary of Costa Rica. A drowsy little town of grass-thatched huts, San Juan del Norte, lying at the mouth of the river, had taken on strategic importance. There, one day, appeared a party of armed Englishmen. Raising the Mosquito flag (which had a small Union Jack in its corner) they formally claimed San Juan in the name of the Mosquito King, and ordered the Nicaraguan customs officer of the port to leave. When he refused, he was forcibly taken off in a boat and abandoned miles away on an uninhabited shore. The Mosquito Kingdom was threafter alleged to run to the southern limit of Nicaragua, and even beyond into Costa Rica. San Juan del Norte was renamed with the brisk English syllables of Greytown, and would be so called until Walker, as the ruler of the country, restored its original proud, sleepy name.

II

As he grasped the story, Walker was incensed by the ignominy of the American position. The Monroe Doctrine might never have existed. True, almost every administration had made a gesture toward Nicaragua. Andrew Jackson in 1836 had sent a special agent to study the possibility of a Nicaraguan canal, but the man became involved in a shady transaction in Panama, and never even stopped off at Nicaragua. President Van Buren's agent, although he thought the canal feasible, warned that "capitalists will not sink their money in an unsettled and revolutionary country." After England's seizure of San Juan, when the American press raised some small outcry, Daniel Webster, then Secretary of State for President Harrison, sent one of his men to Nicaragua to report, only to have him roundly snubbed by the British, and return with nothing to suggest. Webster himself was seeking to avoid war with England over the noisy Maine and Oregon boundary disputes, and the buzzing of the Mosquito affair was understandably faint in his ears.

But England, with her eternal vigilance for weeds in her diplomatic garden, knew that the issue was far from dead. With the outbreak of the Mexican War in 1846, talk of a transisthmian canal mounted. Sooner or later, the British realized, Washington would challenge their presence in Greytown. Early in 1847 Lord Palmerston, then Foreign Secretary, took the precaution of writing to all agents of the Crown in Central America, requiring them to report "what authentic information they could obtain as to the boundaries claimed by the King of Mosquito," and also what in their opinion was "the line of boundary which Her Majesty's Government should insist upon as essential for the security and well-being of the Mosquito State." It was not really surprising that the boundaries established by this procedure reached south from Cape Honduras through Nicaragua and into Costa Rica, in full accord with previous British claims.

Nicaragua protested that there had never been, and still was not, a Kingdom of Mosquito; and in a mood of recklessness, sent troops into Greytown, who took prisoner every Englishman they could find. The British reply was the arrival of a naval squadron on January 1, 1848, and the landing of a strong force of marines, who quickly recaptured Greytown, reasserted England's authority "in the name of the Mosquito Indians," and marched inland toward Lake Nicaragua. This development shook the Nicaraguan government into hasty appeasement. A parley was held, a treaty was drafted, Nicaragua apologized and recognized the existence of Mosquito, if not British authority there.

James Buchanan was then Secretary of State, and his response to the British action was altogether in character. In a letter to the American minister to Nicaragua, he said, "The object of Great Britain in these seizures is . . . to obtain control of the route for a railroad and canal between the Atlantic and Pacific oceans," but he warned that "the government of the United States is not as yet determined what course it will take." During the ensuing year Washington made no progress toward a decision, and when the Taylor administration took office in 1849, the country's sense of frustration in the Greytown issue had grown into a major issue. Was England to be allowed to tear up the Monroe Doctrine? The question was asked repeatedly in the Senate, while many newspapers warned President Taylor that the nation would not tolerate supine timidity in the face of British aggression. Among them was the New Orleans *Crescent,* with Walker as editor of foreign news.

III

Walker did not as yet know—only a few people in Washington then knew—just why the United States after so long had begun to challenge the presence of the British in Mosquito. The fact was that his life was becoming intertwined with great forces of which he was not even aware. The springboard from which he was to leap to fame was being secretly shaped and set by men occupied with vast affairs—peace or war, millions made or lost—in London, Washington, New York.

The central figure in the Nicaraguan situation was a man who in type, conditioning, outlook, and purpose stood so far apart from Walker that they might almost have belonged to different species. Cornelius Vanderbilt was tall, strong boned, physically powerful, loud and blunt of speech, domineering. In his middle fifties, although white-haired, he was still a man spectacularly virile, who had produced thirteen children, all of whom he bent ruthlessly to his will; whose wife, having once been confined by him in an institution for the insane, lived in mortal fear of his temper; and whose mistresses were open secrets in the gossip of New York City. But his ruling passion was money. He was the economic man personified—practical, realistic, impatient of theory and philosophical speculation, contemptuous of legalism and sometimes of the law—a man who believed that the one test of sound business was the size of the profit, and who regarded wealth and power as interchangeable terms. "What do I care about the Law?" he is quoted as saying. "Hain't I got the power?" When he took monetary risks, he sought not only to add to his fortune, but to prove his mastery over men and circumstances, to glory in his strength and cunning as he crushed competitors and raked in his gains. Far more than Walker he was the true type of the freebooter, ferocious in attack, merciless in conquest. One of his contemporaries, describing a Vanderbilt operation in cornering a stock, wrote: "The stock flies up from 20 to 200, and for seven days the torturing screws are turned down tighter and tighter till the Stock Exchange rings with the clamor of his victims. . . . When summoned before a court . . . his memory fades out so completely that he forgets . . . even his own signature.

There is something magnificent in a career in which a million dollars is like a ten-cent piece taken by a shoe-blacking gamin. . . . He strips the street of five millions with the same nonchalance as he would win a hundred dollars at cards."* In 1849, Vanderbilt had as yet acquired no more than five or six millions—in itself a reasonable success for the poor boy who at the age of sixteen had gone into business as a ferryman—to which he added steadily through the profitable operation of a large fleet of steamboats on the Hudson River and Long Island Sound. It was from this business that he took his favorite title, "Commodore."

Like many another tycoon, he had discovered naked power to be a witch-woman of surpassing beauty and no inhibitions, and he could no longer be content with the commonplace grapplings of business. One of his mortifications just then was that a former competitor on the Hudson River, a man of almost equal aggressiveness and sagacity, George Law, had stolen a march on him. Founding the United States Mail Steamship Company, Law had prevailed on the government in Washington to grant him a subsidy of $290,000, for which he agreed to provide steamships to carry California mail between New York and Panama. A similar grant had been made to a San Francisco ship owner, who was providing comparable service between Panama and San Francisco. What irked Vanderbilt, however, was not the governmental bounty these men received, so much as their luck. Their contracts with the government had scarcely been signed when California's golden news arrived. From that moment, with the gold fever raging on the east coast, the passenger service from New York to San Francisco became a bonanza. Law's steamships were the largest seen up to that time on the Atlantic coast, and a berth in a crowded stateroom to Panama could command as much as five hundred dollars. It was estimated that each trip of a Law steamship from New York to its Panama port netted a profit of over $100,000, and in 1849 the line made the run thirty times. Even the hardships of the overland crossing of Panama, by oxcart, mule, or foot, with ever-present danger of brigands, sunstroke, fever, and snakes, did not deter many "forty-niners" who knew that by this route they might be in California five months sooner than if they went overland. To add to Law's windfall, work had been begun on a railroad across Panama, in which he had

---

* J. K. Medbery, *Men and Mysteries of Wall Street*, 1879, p. 155.

an interest, and which would still further increase the popularity of his steamship line.

Hearing of Law's triumph with huge Atlantic steamships, while he himself owned nothing more than riverboats, Vanderbilt asked himself the inevitable question: how could he, a late-comer, overtake his rival? He began to study maps of Central America, and they disclosed to him a possibility that seized his imagination. Panama, obviously, was the narrowest part of the Central American isthmus, but did that make it the best point for transit? Why not instead use Nicaragua, which would take 500 miles off the route to California? Let the Panama Railroad be built; it would require six or seven years to complete the track over the mountains that ran down the center of the isthmus there. And the railroad would soon become obsolete, if there were a canal through Nicaragua which would enable passengers, freight, and mail to go from ocean to ocean without having to be disembarked. Although on the map Nicaragua at its narrowest point looked three times as wide as Panama, it actually seemed to offer the better route for a canal, for Lake Nicaragua permitted unimpeded ship travel for nearly half the distance, and use could be made of the San Juan River, which flowed from the lake to the Atlantic. Construction of a canal east of the lake, he estimated, would be comparatively easy, requiring few locks. Only in the strip between the lake and the Pacific would there be difficulties, and this was a mere eleven miles.

The plan took shape: he would form a company to build the canal, and while it was in the building, he would create a line of steamships from New York to Nicaragua, and another from Nicaragua to San Francisco, with an overland transit of passengers between; he would not only collect mail subsidies, but by offering passengers the shortest route to California, he would scuttle George Law's scheme and make millions.

IV

Vanderbilt realized that before anything could be done, England would have to be persuaded into cooperation. If she remained adamant, it might require nothing less than a war to bring her to reason. Early in 1849, one of his associates went to Washington to explore the matter with the new Taylor administration. Suddenly the capital buzzed with talk of Mosquito, the sanctity of the Monroe Doctrine, and the comparative strength of British and American arms.

It was a report of debate on Nicaragua in the United States Senate that caught Walker's attention. "If the war must come," he wrote enthusiastically in the *Crescent*, "then let it come!" Gone now were all pacifistic inclinations. "America will be found fighting where she has always been morally—at the head of the column of Progress and Democracy." He did not use the phrase "Alliance for Progress" but something similar was in his mind.

IV

THE ANGRY MAN

The death of Ellen Martin was a turning point in Walker's life.

A fever, followed by pneumonia—described by the attending physician as "congestion"—and all at once she was gone. The loss must have been the more shocking since by that time, April, 1849, the cholera epidemic had almost run its course, and she had appeared to be safe. Moreover he had just then begun to achieve the success which might have made their marriage possible. Only a few weeks earlier, his name had appeared on the *Crescent*'s masthead as one of the publishers.

A Nicaraguan writer who investigated his years in New Orleans declares, "Walker, who held in his heart the love of two women only, his mother and Ellen, returned from the cemetery a spirit shattered; and sick with loneliness, threw to the winds all that he had. So ended the first phase of his life." This judgment has a somewhat operatic sound, but all the available evidence supports it. The extent to which he was shaken can be read between the lines of the *Crescent*'s editorial page. For several weeks the characteristic Walker articles were missing from the paper, which in his absence almost ceased to comment on foreign affairs and the slavery issue. When he began to write again, his editorials sounded a new note of stridency and bitterness.

A month after Ellen's interment, the Mississippi rose and overflowed the levees, flooding the city's cemeteries. A wild and ranting editorial cried out at the municipal authorities for their failure to protect the dead from watery desecration. Let the living, it said, look to their own spiritual salvation—"If we live basely and ignobly, not all great Neptune's flood can wash the stain from out our souls." A similar feverishness appeared in articles on events abroad. An attack on Louis Bonaparte, then President of the French Republic, for perverting the French revolution, was followed by a defense of Italian revolutionaries which in its radicalism could only curdle the blood of conservative readers. Followers of Calhoun in New Orleans were alienated by an article condemning the views of the apostle of slavery. "We do not," it said coldly, "rank among his admirers."

It was almost as if Walker was obsessed by a wild and joyless purpose to destroy the *Crescent*'s circulation, and as if he had infected his associates with his rage. Gauntlets were thrown down right and left. A sharp attack on the municipal government for making no effort to arrest men known to have committed murder was followed by a sudden slashing indictment of the powerful *Picayune* and the *Delta,* because they had failed to condemn graft in the state capital. When these formerly courteous rivals replied in kind, they evoked a snarl of outrage against "a petty clique, to whom the *Crescent* is an object of jealousy and hate." This was journalism in a very different tone from that of a year earlier. And the mood of anger alternated with Hugoesque and mystical flights of the pen, which heralded the emergence of the new Walker. "Unless a man believes that there is something great for him to do, he can do nothing great. Hence so many of the captains and reformers of the world have relied on fate and the stars. A great idea springs up in a man's soul; it agitates his whole being, transports him from the ignorant present and makes him feel the future in a moment. It is natural for a man so possessed to conceive that he is a special agent for working out into practice the thought that has been revealed to him. . . . Why should such a revelation be made to him, why should he be enabled to perceive what is hidden to others—if not that he should carry it into practice?"

What was that revelation? With Ellen gone, he had begun to

dream of himself at the head of that "column of Progress and Democracy" of which he had written, riding in the name of America's Manifest Destiny, diverting the passions of the nation from civil commotion to the uplifting of peoples from whom the benefits of civilization were being withheld by European imperialists. He felt an evangelical mission in which the highest ideals of the America of his time were fused—the spreading of democracy—the enhancement of the national power—the uplifting of downtrodden peoples—the prevention of fratricidal war.

II

For a controversial journalist, the South then held special hazards. Offended readers brandishing horsewhips were a recurrent spectacle in newspaper offices, and in spite of laws against duelling, challenges from rival editors were to be expected whenever they regarded themselves as insulted—a frequent phenomenon, since their thresholds of tolerance were low. Nevertheless, Walker had come through the year 1848 unscathed, unchallenged, and uncompromised in conviction. Perhaps the boyish look of him turned away wrath.

The change that came over him with Ellen's death expressed itself in a sudden urge to personal as well as journalistic violence. Soon afterward he fought a duel with an editor named Kennedy, the cause unknown. (It is probably no more than a coincidence that the physician who had attended Ellen in her mortal illness was also named Kennedy.) Neither man was wounded. The duelists, says the account, "met with pistols at twelve paces, exchanged shots, and retired, satisfied." There was also a contemporary story to the effect that an anonymous New Orleans journalist had challenged a man who insulted him to "a duel with the cholera"—that is, exposure to the disease by nursing its victims. This has the sound of a Walkerism. Later in the year, he is known to have administered a severe flogging to the editor of the Spanish newspaper, *La Patria,* for printed remarks that he considered offensive.

It was a stormy time for the *Crescent.* In the summer of 1849, the Cuban issue boiled to a crisis, when the Spanish consul in New Orleans was accused of complicity in the kidnaping of an American citizen. The abducted man was a Cuban revolutionary named Garcia-Rey, who had taken out naturalization papers. His story was that a ship's captain, one McConnel, had brought him against his will to Havana, where he was held incommunicado and subjected to beatings until diplomatic representations by American officials effected his release. On learning of the charge, the Spanish Government recalled its consul, but McConnel was arrested and brought to trial. For his defense he retained J. C. Larue, one of the *Crescent*'s proprietors and a noted attorney.

Ever since the days of George Washington and the great quarrel with Spain over the navigation of the Mississippi, tempers had always run high in New Orleans when Spaniards were suspected of transgression. Garcia-Rey's story was dubious—there were contradictory affidavits by the score—but the essential political fact was that Southern expansionist leaders promptly took up his case as their own. Here at last, so it seemed to them, was a "legitimate" reason for the immediate invasion and seizure of Cuba. Their philosophy was crisply summed up by General John A. Quitman, one of the ardent proponents of the plan. "Our destiny is intertwined with that of Cuba. If slave institutions perish there, they will perish here. Thus interested, we must act. Our government, already distracted with the slavery question, cannot or will not act. We must do it as individuals."

The time seemed especially right for the purpose, because a suitable man to lead an expedition against Cuba was then available. There had recently come to the United States a famous fighter for Cuban independence, General Narciso Lopez, a Venezuelan by birth, who had just met with Calhoun and had received secret encouragement from the fountainhead of Southern wisdom. A group of New Orleans extremists proposed to Lopez that he raise a small army in their city, transport it to Cuba, rally the Cubans to his revolutionary banner, drive out the Spanish governors, set up his own administration in Havana (retaining the institution of slavery), and then apply for the admission of the island to the American Union.

Recruitment was no problem. New Orleans was crowded with veterans returned from Mexico, restless, roving fire-eaters as ardent for adventure as their descendants would be for security a century later. For them, the conquest of the Caribbean appeared a natural and proper sequel to the Mexican campaign. Money was available. Although Lopez was careful to keep in the background, his agents printed bonds on the Cuban treasury, to be redeemed at par as soon as Cuba should become independent; these were offered at a few cents on the dollar, and were snapped up by speculators. Management of the enterprise was in the hands of the so-called Cuban Junta, which, according to the New York *Sun,* included some of the South's most distinguished men.

The only problem was publicity, or rather, its avoidance. During the summer of 1849, shipping for the expedition was secretly assembled at an obscure island in the Gulf of Mexico, just off the delta. It was imperative that federal authorities in New Orleans remain unaware of the rendezvous, or at least look the other way, until Lopez and his troops were on the seas, and beyond the danger of interception by the United States Navy. Otherwise the Taylor administration would feel compelled to invoke the Neutrality Laws against the expedition.

The *Crescent* had thrown itself into the Rey case (as the newspapers called it) partly no doubt because of Larue's active role as lawyer for the defense, but also out of conviction. It reaffirmed its stand against violation of the Neutrality Laws, and by implication against the expansion of slavery. Long editorials appeared denying the right of American citizens to retaliate for the alleged kidnaping by intervening in Cuban affairs. But the paper was inviting more punishment than it could return. In opposing the Lopez scheme it stood alone among the journals of New Orleans. The owners of the *Delta* were intimately connected with the Cuban junta, and the *Picayune* was of the same persuasion. Theirs was the popular side, and they made the most of the advantage. Daily they blasted at the *Crescent,* until the sheer weight of their invective caused the city to respond, and the *Crescent's* circulation and advertising fell away.

Desperately, the *Crescent* fired its last remaining shot. In August, 1849, it published an article which made it impossible for Washington to ignore any longer the fact of the Lopez expedition. Under the heading "The Mysterious Expedition and the Laws," it described "mysterious gatherings designed for the invasion of the island of Cuba," and gave the exact location of the ships and encampments. Under such prodding, the Federal Marshals in New Orleans, with whatever reluctance, were compelled to act in support of the Neutrality Laws. Washington was notified, and United States Navy gunboats were ordered to prevent the Lopez expedition from sailing.

The intervention of the Navy was a victory, but a Pyrrhic victory for the *Crescent*. Torrents of abuse poured on its editors from all sides. They had, it was said, betrayed the South; they had befriended the Yankee abolitionists. Against attacks so virulent and sustained, the paper was defenseless. Hayes, the chief owner, had no illusions as to the outcome. To stay in business would have meant the putting up of more money and probably the fighting of more duels. Late in 1849 he suspended publication, and subsequently sold the name and the presses.

III

Now New Orleans no longer had any hold on Walker; he was loveless, jobless, and even friendless, for Edmund Randolph had succumbed to the spell of the Golden Fleece and had gone to California. In the autumn, Walker followed. Most of the wagon trains of the period assembled at Independence, Missouri, and took the Old Oregon Trail past Fort Laramie, Fort Bridger, and Salt Lake, over the Sierras to Sacramento and San Francisco; but references to the long journey are conspicuously absent from the the the Walker literature. The eight or nine months spent in crossing two thousand miles of plains and mountains, through the lands of the Comanches, the Sioux, and the Blackfeet, he must have regarded as so much time lost from the pursuit of his destiny. If there were hardships endured, fights with Indians, and strange sights seen, they apparently impressed him so little that he never mentioned them in the brief accounts of his career that he subsequently gave to his associates. All that is known of this passage in his life is that in June of 1850 he appeared in San Francisco, sunburned and weather-beaten, an unimpressive figure in dusty old clothes and a broad-brimmed black hat, and almost penniless.

V

THE HIGHER DIPLOMACY

Late in 1849, Cornelius Vanderbilt initiated the enterprise for control of which, a few years later, he would contend with the President of Nicaragua, Walker. A company with a resounding name—the American Atlantic and Pacific Canal Company—was incorporated, and Vanderbilt was careful to include in its management a lawyer, Joseph L. White, who had intimate ties with the country's leading politicians. White journeyed to Washington, and wheels began to turn.

A new minister to Nicaragua, George Squier, was appointed, Secretary of State John M. Clayton gave him a letter of instructions, the nub of which lay in a single sentence: "We are willing to enter into a treaty stipulation with the government of Nicaragua, that both governments shall forever protect and defend the proprietors who may succeed in cutting the canal and opening the water communication between the two oceans for our commerce." The "proprietors" whom Clayton had in mind were Vanderbilt and his associates. Soon Squier wrote that "Vanderbilt and Company has made a proposition to the Nicaraguan government which, if I am correctly informed of its details, is most extravagant."

The "extravagant" offer consisted of a promise to pay $10,000 on signing of a suitable contract; $10,000 a year thereafter until completion of the canal; $200,000 of stock in the enterprise; and 20 per cent of the net profits of the canal. It was enough. The Nicaraguan Congress ratified a contract with Vanderbilt, and in the autumn of 1849, Squier was able to write to Clayton: "I have the satisfaction of informing the department that I have succeeded in accomplishing the objects of my mission to this republic. The commissioner of the 'American Atlantic and Pacific Canal Company' has concluded his contract."

II

England's chief agent in Central America, Frederick Chatfield, had observed the activities of Squier and Vanderbilt's agents with misgivings. Letters from him to Lord Palmerston in London warned that the Yankees were seriously negotiating with Nicaragua for a canal route. The possibility was obvious that the United States, by invoking the Monroe Doctrine, might encourage Nicaragua to seize Greytown, to assure an Atlantic entry for the canal. Whether or not war resulted, England would be at a disadvantage; her claim to Greytown was undeniably weak, and the place was impossible to defend against assault from the interior.

Palmerston, who was known for his bold diplomacy, responded pugnaciously. England's first need, he decided, was to preempt the Pacific end of the proposed canal route. His eye was on an island known as Tigre, owned by Honduras. Occupying a dominant position in one of the world's great natural harbors, the Gulf of Fonseca, it could give England more obstructive power on the west coast of Central America than could any other single spot. What he wanted now was a diplomatic excuse to justify occupation of this island. The specialists of the Foreign Office obliged him. With just such a purpose in mind, they had been nursing an ancient claim against Honduras for alleged mistreatment of some of Her Majesty's subjects by Honduran officials. Orders went to Chatfield, and simultaneously the British admiralty was instructed to move strong squadrons of warships to both sides of the isthmus.*

---

* R. W. Van Alystyne, "The Central American Policy of Lord Palmerston," *Hispanic-American Historical Review*, Vol. XVI, pp. 352-7.

Chatfield wasted no time. Hastening to Truxillo, the chief Atlantic port of Honduras, he demanded immediate settlement of England's claim. When the Hondurans denied the validity of the claim, Chatfield called their attention to the British battleships which were by then standing off Truxillo, with their guns trained on the town.

The American minister in Nicaragua, Squier, was a man of ability and resource. Sensing England's intention, he rushed to Truxillo with the draft of a treaty under which the United States offered to pay Honduras generously for Tigre Island and for permission to fortify certain mainland stations on the Gulf of Fonseca. As between the free-spending eagle and the threatening lion in these circumstances there was little choice, and the Hondurans hastily signed the Squier treaty.

The frustration of the British was expressed by the naval squadron which, just before sailing from Truxillo harbor, fired a single indignant cannon ball at the town. Chatfield, however, had only begun to fight. Riding westward across Honduras, to the Pacific, he met with the admiral in command of the British fleet which was by then anchored in the Gulf of Fonseca, and authorized him to seize Tigre Island "for debt" in the name of the Crown, to hoist the British flag, and put down a garrison. This the admiral did on October 16, 1849.

The shadow of war was now dark over Central America, but still Squier did not hesitate to assume responsibility. A terse note went to Chatfield, stating that England had unlawfully taken possession of land belonging to the United States and must evacuate Tigre immediately. When Chatfield, with the diplomatic equivalent of a sneer, refused, Squier issued nothing less than an ultimatum, requiring the British to withdraw from Tigre within six days. Otherwise, he said, their occupation of the island would be regarded by the United States as an act of aggression, and dealt with accordingly. But the British stayed where they were, and with the Union Jack still flying over Tigre, Chatfield reported the situation to London, Squier to Washington.

This was the situation when Vanderbilt prodded Clayton to take a positive stand on the Nicaraguan question. Specifically the financier wanted to know what the British would say to his contract with Nicaragua. The problem confronting Clayton was thus two-pronged. On the one hand he wanted to prevent a war if he could. At the same time he felt the obligation to advance the cause of an American-controlled canal in Nicaragua. The best hope, as the Secretary saw it, lay in the time-honored diplomatic technique —a club in the right hand and a gift in the left. If England were plainly confronted with the danger of war, and at the same time were offered a chance to share in the Nicaragua canal, she might just possibly consent to a peaceful compromise. At any rate, the idea was worth trying. In this spirit, he sent a message to the British minister in Washington, John F. Crampton, requesting him to call.

III

In the weeks that followed, a series of extraordinary dispatches went from Crampton to Palmerston.*

Washington, September 15, 1849

My Lord: Mr. Clayton having requested me to call upon him at the Department of State, said that he wished to converse with me frankly and confidentially upon the subject of the proposed passage across the isthmus, by way of Nicaragua and the river San Juan, with regard to which he had long felt a great deal of anxiety. . . . You know, he said, that the government have no majority in the Senate . . . and you can form an idea of the eagerness with which the party opposed to the government will avail themselves of the opportunity of either forcing us into a collision with Great Britain on this subject, or of making it appear that we have abandoned, through pusillanimity, great and splendid advantages. . . . He begged me to communicate the substance of what he had said to me to your lordship.

Washington, October 1, 1849

. . . I am the more anxious to report accurately to your lordship the substance of Mr. Clayton's remarks from the circumstance that the President . . . joined in our conversation. . . .

The junction of the two oceans by a canal, Mr. Clayton observed, was an object so important to the whole of the commercial world that . . . it should be made a bond of peace and good understanding, by being brought about by a combined effort, and for the general benefit of mankind. . . .

What the United States Government would now propose, therefore,

---

* *Documents and Correspondence Relative to a Trans-Isthmian Canal.* Compiled from the archives of the British Foreign Office and the U. S. Department of State and privately printed by the law firm of Sullivan and Cromwell, New York, 1900.

was this: That the United States . . . should propose, simultaneously with Her Majesty's Government, [a] treaty to Nicaragua . . . the great object of which should be to guarantee the safety of a company of capitalists, to whom a charter should be granted by Nicaragua. . . .

Mr. Clayton then recurred to the embarrassing position in which the friends of this great enterprise would be placed if Her Majesty's Government continued to support the Mosquito claim in opposition to the arrangement now proposed. . . .

Mr. Clayton considered that this question could never be amicably settled unless both Great Britain and the United States withdrew all claim to the territory of Nicaragua. . . . General Taylor cordially concurred. . . .

Washington, November 4, 1849

My Lord: I had the honor of forwarding to your lordship . . . the copy of a contract between an American company and the Government of Nicaragua for the formation of an interoceanic canal by way of the river St. John and the Lake of Nicaragua. . . . Mr. Clayton, although he approved of the general tenor of the contract, thought that some of the articles were objectionable . . . particularly those which require that all directors of the company and a majority of the shareholders shall be American citizens. . . .

Mr. Clayton now informs me that he has had a conference with the two principal directors of the company in question [Vanderbilt and White]; and that as he anticipated, he finds that no objection will be raised on their part so to modify the provisions of the contract as to remove from it anything of an exclusive nature.

IV

All was now clear to Palmerston. The United States government, on behalf of Vanderbilt, was seeking to entice England with an offer of shares in a nonexistent canal, or to coerce her by the threat of war into giving up a strategic position of great potential importance to her future.

Peace or war, then? England's trade with the Orient, vital to her prosperity, was already feeling the competition of the Yankee merchant marine. Let the Americans open a passage for cargo through the Central American isthmus and they would gain a significant advantage of distance and time in reaching the profitable markets of China, Southeast Asia, and the East Indies. The British government would not tolerate the building of a Nicaraguan canal unless England herself could control the route. It was for this reason, more than any other, that the British had held so tenaciously to the swamps of Mosquito for over a century. To share such a canal with others would be to give away one of the chief assets of the Empire, the strategic scheme of trade routes dominated by English guns. The Cape of Good Hope was British; so were the Falkland Islands that lay on the route to Cape Horn; and if there was to be another way for ships to Asia, it would have to be under the flag of England.

In Palmerston's view, Vanderbilt's proposal that England share in ownership of his canal company was naïve. Did the Yankee actually expect to get the benefit of British capital for a project which, in the final test, was bound to be more beneficial to the United States than to any other country?

It was only the Nicaraguan route across the isthmus that concerned Palmerston. The possibility that the United States would seek to dig its canal in Panama struck him as remote. Surveys made for the Royal Geographic Society left no doubt that, with the construction techniques then in use, the Cordilleran range in Panama presented insuperable obstacles to a canal; and he himself had flatly said as much to Parliament. As he saw the situation, Nicaragua was worth a war. "The desirability of obtaining so desirable a spot in the commercial world and freeing it from the competition of so adventurous a race as the North Americans" had been stressed in reports from men whom he trusted. His conviction was in part due also to no less a personage than Louis Bonaparte, then President of the Second Republic of France, and soon to be Emperor Napoleon III. In a pamphlet written some years earlier and published in London, Bonaparte had proposed to form a company to be known as *La Canal Napoléon de Nicaragua,* and had presented such an array of supporting facts and figures as to have a profound effect on British opinion. "The State of Nicaragua," he had asserted, "can become . . . the necessary route of the great commerce of the world, and is destined to attain *an extraordinary degree of prosperity and grandeur."* For Palmerston, it was essential to make sure that the canal would not be dug unless England dug it, and that English businessmen would have an advantage in exploiting the Central American resources. If this policy meant war with the United States, then England would fight for her ocean supremacy as she had fought many times before.

Not that Palmerston wanted war. On the contrary, he was only too aware of its perils. The United States was now a far more formidable nation than it had been in 1812. Moreover, some of England's largest financial houses, notably the Rothschilds and the Barings, had large and profitable investments in American railroads, and were eager to see the peace preserved.

Palmerston had to consider, too, that a crisis with Russia over the spoils of the tottering Ottoman Empire was distinctly visible on the diplomatic horizon. If it should result in war between the western European powers and the Czar, and if the United States were to seize the opportunity to annex the Caribbean countries, England might be unable to do much more than protest. Consequently there was much to be said for finding a peaceful solution of the Central American problem. If diplomacy could serve to avoid war while keeping Greytown and Tigre under England's control, let the diplomats by all means have their chance.

What if England were to strike a conciliatory pose, perhaps sending a new minister plenipotentiary to Washington specifically for the purpose of negotiating with Clayton—and without giving up anything, yet keep the peace? It would be a master stroke, and it would take a master of diplomacy to bring it off. But it was not unthinkable. And Palmerston knew the very man to whom such a mission might be entrusted.

V

While Walker was somewhere on the trail to Fort Laramie (one can imagine him sitting alongside the driver of a wagon, his face impassive, his eyes on the bleak horizon, saying a few courteous words now and then in his low voice, but absorbed for the most part in his thoughts and dreams), another strand in the web of his destiny was being spun in Washington, where Palmerston's emissary, Sir Henry Lytton Bulwer, had arrived. Elder brother of the novelist, Bulwer-Lytton, he had a well-earned reputation as a wily and successful gambler, both in diplomacy and at the tables. On December 24, 1849, Bulwer, in full dress uniform, presented his credentials as Envoy Extraordinary and Ambassador Plenipotentiary to President Taylor—a glittering Christmas present, as it were, from Great Britain to the United States. His was a spirit completely attuned to the majestic hypocrisies of British statecraft. In a brief, eloquent address he spoke of the Anglo-American community of interest. "I have entire confidence, Sir, that our two governments will act with the most perfect concord in carrying out this great design, and for my own part I unfeignedly assure you that I could not have a duty more congenial to my feelings." To which the President replied, "I hope, Sir, that your residence in this country will prove as agreeable to you personally as you have given me reason for believing that it will be honorable and advantageous, both for Great Britain and America."

Almost at once Secretary Clayton and the ambassador went to work on the draft of a treaty covering the problem of the Central American canal, setting the stage on which Walker was triumphantly to leap five years later. One of Bulwer's convictions was that nothing has greater value in diplomacy than "seizing the important point in an affair, the peculiar characteristic of an individual, the genius and tendency of an epoch." The important point in this affair was the Vanderbilt contract with Nicaragua; the essential characteristic of Clayton was his frankness, for he made no attempt to conceal his anxiety for the canal; and the tendency of the epoch was the widening of the breach between North and South, which gravely hampered the United States in its conduct of diplomacy. That he could play on these three keys to sound "Rule, Britannia," Bulwer was confident. He lost no time in telling Clayton that he could participate in the drafting of a treaty only with the proviso that the *status quo* in Central America should not be changed. The Mosquito question could not be considered, he said, "except to the limited extent determined" by the needs of the canal. These qualifications Clayton accepted without demur.

Every advantage in the contest went to Bulwer. Not that Clayton was incompetent—on the contrary, he was a successful lawyer and had been a useful senator; he thought clearly and talked well. His disadvantage was inherent in the situation, in the fact that he was emotionally involved with the Nicaraguan canal project. His interest was more than political, more than a matter of commitment to Vanderbilt and White. The canal had long been a favorite dream of his. Shortly before Bulwer arrived in Washington Clayton wrote to another American official that the subject of the canal had attracted his attention twenty years earlier, "since which time it has never ceased to occupy my mind." To go down in history as the man who made the canal possible was his ambition. In consequence, he was eager—always a defect in diplomacy. He wanted something that only England could give him, the freedom of the Nicaraguan canal route, from a man who knew a dozen ways of denying a request while appearing to accede to it.

Six weeks later a draft of the treaty was complete. Its essence was the agreement of the two powers that neither would seek exclusive control of any canal built through Nicaragua, and a declaration that neither would "assume or exercise dominion" over any part of Central America. In sending the draft to Palmerston, Bulwer wrote, "I finally agreed to submit to your Lordship's sanction the enclosed project . . . its object being to exclude all questions of the disputes between Nicaragua and the Mosquitos . . . [except] as far as the ship communication between the Atlantic and Pacific was concerned. . . . As the matter now stands, it is clearly understood that Her Majesty's Government holds by its own opinions already expressed as to Mosquito."

As Bulwer saw the issue, it hinged on the meaning of the word "dominion." The treaty, he wrote, with his tongue unmistakably in his cheek, left England "protecting" Mosquito, "but forbade the protection to be used for the purposes of dominion." Where did the one end and the other begin? On this matter of definition, the treaty was silent. What then had Britain conceded? Nothing.

The United States, however, had conceded a good deal. At one point in their negotiation, Clayton conveyed to Bulwer, and without more distortion than is usual in diplomacy, that it would be comparatively easy to bring all Central America into the American Union. "There is not one of these five Central American states that would not annex themselves to us tomorrow, if they could; and if it is any secret worth knowing you are welcome to it—*Some of them have offered and asked to be annexed to the United States already.*"

Bulwer knew precisely how much value to place on this statement. He was well aware that, as matters then stood, the North was unwilling to let the Central American republics, any more than Cuba, join the United States under the domination of the South, while Southerners wanted them on no other terms. It was also obvious that Clayton wished to avoid a war for the isthmus, such as would almost certainly result if the United States were to force the issue at once. Immediate annexation was therefore out of the question. On the other hand, if the Americans bided their time until England became involved in difficulties with Russia, they might well be able to establish hegemony over the isthmus without war; and in such an inviting situation, North and South might work out an accommodation in the matter. Unquestionably, Clayton's threat had some basis in reality; so that, in agreeing not to seek dominion in Central America, the United States was yielding up a useful counter in the game.

Even better, from England's standpoint, was the treaty's provision that the United States could not proceed with a Nicaraguan canal without British assent and participation. Bulwer did, however, make a friendly gesture in the direction of Vanderbilt. "I should state to your Lordship," he wrote to Palmerston, "that . . . a gentleman of great weight . . . considered that it would be only fair that the two governments should give an open and avowed preference by name to an American company. . . . This I objected to. . . . A sort of compromise was effected. . . ." The compromise was a clause giving a "priority of claim" to any company that already had a contract for the construction of the canal, and that had "made preparations and expended time, money and trouble on the faith of such contract." The name of the "gentleman of great weight" never appeared in the correspondence.

Bulwer had fulfilled his mission. He had negotiated a treaty which, while committing the United States, left England uncommitted; and so he told Clayton graciously that "Her Majesty's Government would freely undertake to obtain the consent of Mosquito" for the canal. By March, 1850, both sides were ready to proceed with ratification.

VI

As soon as Clayton showed the draft approved by Bulwer and himself to members of the Senate Foreign Relations Committee, he was sharply challenged. Was England, said the senators, to retain Mosquito? If so, ratification by the Senate was unthinkable. Knowing that England could not be persuaded to abandon her protectorate in Mosquito, Clayton was in a quandary. At last, however, a possible way out occurred to him. When he next saw Bulwer, he had with him the draft of a new clause to the effect that neither nation would "make use of protectorates or alliances for the purposes of . . . occupying, fortifying or colonizing . . . any part of Central America." Clayton reasoned that if England agreed to this clause, she would be virtually abjuring the use of force in Central America; and if she abjured the use of force, was that not for practical purposes equivalent to eventual withdrawal from Central America? And would not the Senate be willing on these grounds to ratify the treaty?

Bulwer, of course, understood perfectly well what was in the Secretary's mind. Reading the proposed clause, it struck him as having little practical significance in the light of other sections of the treaty. The loopholes in the document as drafted were large enough to permit a British fleet to pass through them if necessary—and if the new clause would serve to assure ratification of the treaty, he would not reject it. But neither was he willing to accept it out of hand. His agreement had to be made to look like the large concession that Clayton wanted to report to the Senate. Assuming an air of injured innocence, the ambassador gently reproved Clayton for inconstancy. But when the Secretary, in considerable distress of mind, threatened to jettison the treaty, Bulwer appeared to capitulate. "It is no use our trying to get around each other," he wrote to Clayton, "and it is in neither of our characters. . . . I now agree to all you have asked."

Clayton was elated. Writing to the American ambassador in London he said triumphantly that thenceforth the Mosquito protectorate would stand only "as the shadow of a name." There was a note of satisfaction, too, in the presidential message which accompanied the treaty when it was formally submitted to the Senate: "I found Great Britain in possession of nearly half of Central America, as the ally and protector of the Mosquito king. It has been my object, in negotiating this treaty, not only to secure the passage across the isthmus . . . but to maintain the independence and sovereignty of all Central American republics. The Senate will judge how far these objects have been effected."

Popular opinion, as reflected in the press, was sharply divided. Some papers praised the treaty as a masterpiece of high-minded statesmanship, by means of which war with Britain had been averted. Others saw it as a repudiation of the Monroe Doctrine. The New York *Herald* went so far as to assail Clayton as "weak" and "ignorant," and alleged openly that the treaty had been "concocted" by Joseph White for the Vanderbilt interests. But Clayton remained confident that his efforts would be vindicated by time. England, he assured the Senate, had in effect abandoned her policy of encroachment in Central America. The two great Anglo-Saxon powers were to join hands fraternally in the interest of commerce and enduring peace. And the senators, responding perhaps less to the Secretary's eloquence than to Joseph White's lobbying, rushed the treaty to a vote, and ratified it.

This was the moment for Bulwer to play the winning trump concealed in his hand. It took the form of a short note simply stating that he did not "understand the engagements of the convention to apply to Her Majesty's settlement at Honduras or its dependencies." As Clayton read, the icy touch of reality must have shocked him. The treaty did indeed say that the British would not occupy, fortify, or colonize any part of Central America. But what was Central America? It was merely a loose geographic term, like the Orient, or the Levant. Did it comprise all of the isthmus or only the five independent republics? Nowhere in the treaty was it defined. Not that Clayton had ever seriously hoped to bring British Honduras, a long-established Crown Colony, under the restrictions of the treaty. If England chose to regard this possession as distinct from "Central America," the United States could hardly object. But the real menace of Bulwer's note came in the word "dependencies." Why was it now for the first time introduced into the dialogue? Here was a distinct implication that England had decided to make her other Central American holdings dependencies of British Honduras, and in this way remove them also from "Central America" and free them from the restrictions of the treaty. If Mosquito were to become such a dependency it could be occupied and fortified as England chose, without technical violation of the treaty. Moreover, since the boundaries of Mosquito were largely undefined, as were, indeed, those of the five republics, there would be nothing to prevent "the King of the Mosquitos" from claiming still more Central American territory as part of his ancestral lands, as had been done in the past.

Clayton could envisage the storm that would be stirred up in Congress and the press if the suspicion arose that the treaty had accomplished no more than this. The resulting anger and ridicule might prevent the promulgation of the treaty, destroy the prestige of the administration, put an end to all hope for the canal, injure the investors who had bought stock in Vanderbilt's new companies, and conceivably lead to war. On the other hand, the Secretary could not afford to ignore Bulwer's note. An evasive tactic was his only solution. Writing to the Chairman of the Senate Foreign Relations Committee, he asked for that gentleman's personal concurrence in the view that the treaty was not intended to apply to British Honduras; but he carefully omitted any mention of "dependencies." In this way he succeeded in extracting from the innocent senator agreement that "the Senate perfectly understood that the treaty did not include British Honduras."

Thus reinforced, Clayton wrote to Bulwer acknowledging that "British Honduras was not embraced in the treaty," but declining "to affirm or deny the British title to their settlement or its alleged dependencies." As to the boundaries of the Central American states, he admitted that no alteration could be made in the treaty for the purpose of defining them, "without referring the same to the Senate." But perhaps in the future something might be done to remedy the omission?

To this feeble effort Bulwer replied with scarcely veiled sarcasm. "I understand that you do not deem yourself called upon to mark out at this time the exact limits of Her Majesty's settlements . . . but that you fully recognize that Her Majesty's title thereto will remain just as it was. . . . I now deem myself authorized to exchange Her Majesty's ratification of the treaty . . . for that of the President of the United States."

Clayton had in effect agreed to an amendment of the treaty without consulting the Senate. His painful awareness of his predicament found expression in a memorandum that he wrote and secretly deposited in the vault of the Department of State, together with Bulwer's decisive letter. "The written declaration from Sir Henry Lytton Bulwer was received by me. . . . I wrote him . . . carefully declining to affirm or deny the British title" [to their Central American possessions]. "The consent of the Senate to the declaration was not required and the treaty was ratified as it stood."

With an eye to patriotic symbolism, the anxious Secretary had selected July Fourth as the date for the formal signing of the treaty by President Taylor and Bulwer. The President's comments as he took his pen in hand showed simple and unfeigned pleasure in the event, leading to the surmise that Clayton had not told him of the hidden letter from Bulwer. No event more memorable had occurred in Taylor's administration, nor would occur, for a few weeks later the well-meaning old soldier was dead of the cholera.

The British view of the transaction was as clear and unambiguous as that of the Americans was hazy and obscure. The London *Times* called it "a contest in the use of terms," and had no doubt as to the victor. As soon as the signed treaty was in Palmerston's hands, he ordered a warship to Greytown, where marines were landed to perform yet another flag-raising ceremony, and to reassert once more the authority of "the Mosquito King." It was as well to remind all concerned that England had given up nothing.

In this way, "the convention between the United States of America and Her British Majesty for facilitating and protecting the construction of a ship canal between the Atlantic and Pacific oceans" became law. Its immediate effect was to prevent America from asserting her power at a point of high strategic importance to her interests. The nation now had no way in which to control the situation in Nicaragua except by privately organized military expeditions. The moment that the treaty was signed, Walker's spectacular adventure became possible.

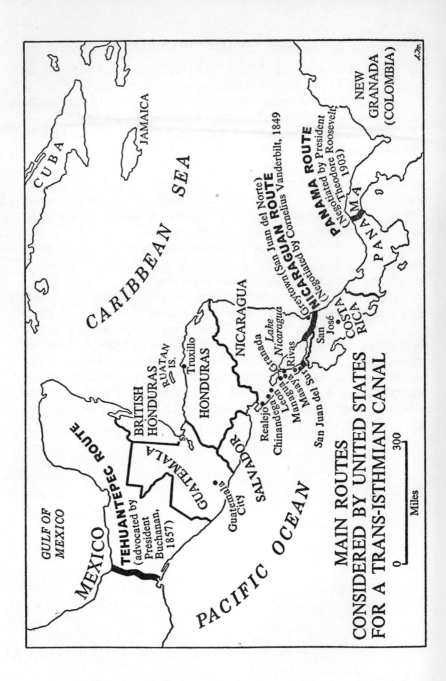

MAIN ROUTES
CONSIDERED BY UNITED STATES
FOR A TRANS-ISTHMIAN CANAL

GULF OF MEXICO

CUBA

JAMAICA

CARIBBEAN SEA

MEXICO

TEHUANTEPEC ROUTE
(advocated by
President Buchanan, 1857)

BRITISH HONDURAS

RUATAN IS.

Truxillo

HONDURAS

GUATEMALA

SALVADOR

Guatemala City

NICARAGUA

Granada
Lake Nicaragua
Rivas
Masaya
Managua
Leon
Chinandega
Realejo

San Juan del Sur

Greytown (San Juan del Norte)

NICARAGUAN ROUTE
(Negotiated by Cornelius Vanderbilt, 1849)

San José

COSTA RICA

PANAMA

PANAMA ROUTE
(Negotiated by President Theodore Roosevelt, 1903)

NEW GRANADA (COLOMBIA)

PACIFIC OCEAN

0   300
Miles

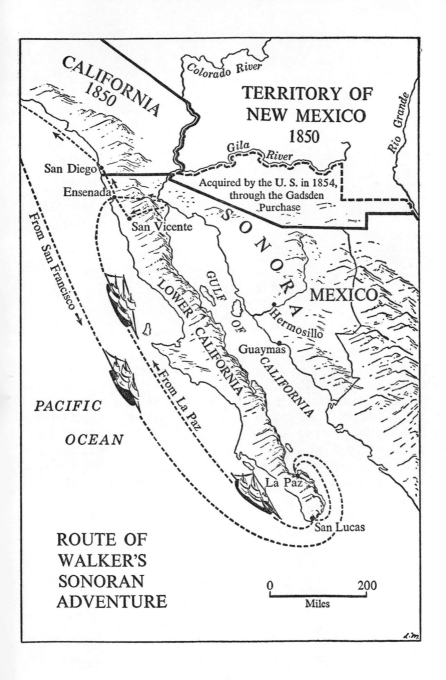

CALIFORNIA
1850

Colorado River

TERRITORY OF
NEW MEXICO
1850

Rio Grande

Gila River

San Diego

Acquired by the U. S. in 1854,
through the Gadsden
Purchase

Ensenada

S O N O R A

San Vicente

From San Francisco

MEXICO

GULF OF CALIFORNIA

Hermosillo

LOWER CALIFORNIA

Guaymas

PACIFIC

From La Paz

OCEAN

La Paz

San Lucas

ROUTE OF
WALKER'S
SONORAN
ADVENTURE

0   200
Miles

VI

THE MAN OF PRINCIPLE

Walker's first action on arriving in San Francisco was to seek out his old friend Edmund Randolph, who had by that time put down roots in the community; and through him he met John Nugent, the proprietor and editor of the youngest of the city's dozen newspapers, the *Herald*. Nugent gladly put him to work. The little paper was thriving, for every San Franciscan was avid for news. Like its bouncing competitors, the *Herald* charged twelve cents per copy, filled much more than half of its four pages with advertising, and published a "steamer edition," at one dollar per copy, for passengers on outgoing ships. Its chief problem was the shortage of newsprint, which had to be imported from the east, and which cost twenty times its price in New York. San Francisco's publishers had to accept what supplies they could get, however cheap, coarse, or discolored, and when ships failed to arrive on time, desperate printers would turn out editions on grey paper used to wrap Chinese tea, or on legal foolscap.

The *Herald*'s deficiencies of appearance, however, were more than offset by its vitality. It had a definite and usually liberal opinion about everything. It was for free trade and the right of divorce in unhappy marriages. It strongly opposed the introduction of slavery into California. It believed that the slavery issue in the Union as a whole could be settled without secession and civil war if extremists on both sides could be held in check. It quoted the London *Times*: "There can be no doubt that the anti-slavery feeling will eventually preponderate in the States to the extinction of the Southern institution; but the question will not be carried by the violence of the present agitators." It was eloquent on French culture and especially the theaters of Paris. It resented the American ambassador to England who, in an address in London, boasted that "We Americans are of the Anglo-Saxon race, reared in the Protestant faith." The *Herald* exploded into satire. "Wonderful! What geniuses we must be! Only think of it—to be of the Anglo-Saxon race!" What of the Celts and the French? What of the Catholics and the Jews? Were they not also Americans?

Two months after the Clayton-Bulwer Treaty was signed, news of it reached San Francisco and was published in the *Herald,* as in other newspapers. Taken at face value, it seemed a hopeful development, and editorial comment was favorable. But international diplomacy meant little to the San Franciscans of 1850. The great topic of the day was crime in their own midst. Wars and treaties were nothing by comparison. Even gold strikes had become secondary. Gangs of robbers and murderers, many of them from Australia's convict colonies, nightly roamed the city and made it a hell for the law-abiding. No respectable man, whatever arms he carried, could safely walk the street after dark. There was no room in the newspapers to deal with more than a few of the sensational murders, assaults, and burglaries that were committed every day. Most of the city's bars and taverns provided women as a sideline and, thus baited with liquor and lechery, served as traps for the unwary. As the *Herald* reported: "These ruffian resorts are the hot beds of drunkenness and the scenes of unnumbered crimes. Unsuspecting sailors and miners . . . are filled with liquor—drugged if necessary—until . . . they fall an easy victim. . . . Many robberies are committed which are not brought to light through shame on the part of the victim."

It could not be said that law enforcement had broken down, for it had never got started. In a few months of 1850 over one hundred murders were committed, without the execution of a single criminal. Worse: three times that year the city was devastated by fires which, it was shown, were deliberately started by the pestilential gang known as the Sydney Ducks to provide a rogues' festival of robbery and rape. The city was close to anarchy.

Shortly after Walker's arrival, the *Herald* began an anticrime crusade which made it a storm center, and which, as events showed, was largely his work. With his experience of the New Orleans courts, he quickly perceived that the essence of the terrifying situation lay in the alliance of the gangs with the crooked politicians who dominated the city, and who had the police and the judges under their venal thumbs. Nugent gave him a free rein. The first blast of the *Herald* was against the California Supreme Court, which from its seat in Sacramento set the tone of the entire judiciary of the state. "The Supreme Court," said an editorial, "has rendered itself ridiculous," by "flagrant stupidity," and by its toleration of "unprincipled and disreputable hangers-on" and "corrupt practitioners and pettifoggers." To this unexpected attack, the first of its kind to appear in the San Francisco press, the justices of the Supreme Court felt impelled to reply. Using the Sacramento City Council as their mouthpiece, they issued a strong diatribe against the *Herald,* as subversive of justice. Walker was now in his element. Happily he delivered an even harder thrust. On Christmas, 1850, he published an item headed "Personal," to express his feelings about the Sacramento Council. It began on a lofty note: "If an editor were to turn from his course to notice the abuse mouthed by corrupt officials . . . he would indeed be stooping". . . . However, to leave no uncertainty as to his opinions, he added that the Council was "a collection of knaves and blackguards."

For some weeks thereafter, under the heading of "Law Intelligence," the *Herald* published detailed accounts of miscarriages of justice in the courts, and seldom missed an opportunity to upbraid the authorities for failure to act against the criminals of the city. It had plenty of ammunition. The police force was an absurdity. Constables openly consorted with criminals. There was not even a jail in San Francisco. Even if the perpetrator of a crime was identified and brought to court he ran no risk. A little money or the right connection would always uncover a legal technicality to assure dismissal of his case. Or the jury would be packed with friends of the man on trial. Crime had become a way of life for hundreds of dangerous men and women, while the courts looked the other way.

It was a ringing editorial in the *Herald,* "A Way To Stop Crime," that first publicly advocated a Vigilante movement, although the word was not yet used. "A band of two or three hundred 'regulators,' composed of such men as have a stake in the town" was needed, said the *Herald*, "to drive the criminals from the city," if necessary with "a few examples of Lynch Law." Twice that week the advice was repeated, with full recognition of its dangers, and a somber warning: "Terrible is the retribution which our citizens will visit on the unworthy public servants who have reduced them to the necessity of defending themselves" against the criminal elements.

Other newspapers took up the idea of a Vigilante corps, until alarm at the prospect impelled the ruling politicians to make some gesture to public opinion. At the request of the district attorney, a Grand Jury of respectable citizens was impaneled to try to cope with the flood of crime. Taking itself seriously, it quickly found indictments against a number of known criminals, only to call forth a reprimand from the bench. The Chief Judge of the District Court, Levi Parsons, informed the Grand Jury that it could not indict except on evidence warranting conviction by a petit jury—which meant, for practical purposes, that it could not indict.

It was Parsons' misfortune that this instruction, which might have passed almost unnoticed in the scurry and cynicism of San Francisco life, fell under Walker's legally trained eye. Next day the *Herald* printed a little paragraph, signed "One of the People," and which said, "Whether his Honor, Judge Parsons, in this instance has laid down for the guidance of the Grand Jury, an incorrect rule of law, through haste, inadvertence or misapprehension it is immaterial to inquire." The fact remained, by every precedent of law a Grand Jury need not wait to indict until it had accumulated all the evidence required to convict in an ordinary court.

Judge Parsons, known for his pomposity, replied by an ill-advised blast from the bench. The *Herald*, he said, was a public nuisance and should be prosecuted as such by the county authorities. He then appeared personally before the Grand Jury and urged the indictment of the *Herald* for contempt of court; but the jurors refused to act. Walker seized the opening. In a biting editorial, "The Press A Nuisance," he said plainly that "the District Court instructs the Grand Jury to aid the escape of criminals. . . . No wonder that after laying down the law favorably to criminals the District Judge should declare

against the Press." This Walker concluded, was "judicial madness."
As for the charge of contempt, "The courts cannot be reduced much
lower than they have reduced themselves. If we were the Guardian
Angel of the District Judge we would whisper in his ear, Beware!"

A group of lawyers who were friendly to Parsons promptly held a
meeting at which the *Herald* was denounced on the ground that in
attacking the Judge it had attacked the courts and the process of
justice. Some even called for the paper's suppression. Thus fortified,
as he thought, Parsons took direct action. It was common gossip in
the city that the attacks on him had come from Walker's pen, and the
Judge issued a warrant for his arrest, on a charge of contempt of court.

I I

Walker's appearance before the court was reported in great detail by
the San Francisco press. The courtroom was crowded with partisans
both of the Judge and the accused. Edmund Randolph, already regarded as a leading light of the San Francisco bar, spoke for the defense. Handsome, impressive, combining aristocratic hauteur with a
touch of fire, he had the further advantage of being known as an
excellent shot—a significant asset in the profession of law in
the San Francisco of the 1850's. He began by requesting that the
charge against Walker be put into writing. Parsons said, "The objection is overruled," and so continuous were his interruptions thereafter that Randolph was unable to complete a sentence.

Finally he made himself heard, shouting that the Judge stood in
violation of the Bill of Rights of the California Constitution. "You are
liable to impeachment by the Legislature for your official conduct.
. . . The proceeding is monstrous!"

"Mr. Randolph!" yelled the Judge. "The Court cannot sit here to
hear itself abused and its proceedings characterized as monstrous!"

Randolph retorted, "I will then call your conduct monstrously
illegal, monstrously unjust—" An uproar arose among the spectators,
while Parsons, purple in the face, said that he could not tolerate
Randolph's "exceedingly disrespectful" language.

"I regret," said Randolph icily, "that the circumstances of the case
will not allow me to make an apology."

This was a word full of menace, for it brought the thought of a duel to every mind. Hastily Parsons said, "We do not ask for an apology."

The defense was then permitted to state its case—which was simply that Walker did not stand in contempt of court. If the Judge had a proper charge against him, it was libel, not contempt. "I admit that it" [the controversial editorial] "is a libel; there is pungency in it; and if the statements contained therein are true, the conclusion is inevitable that Levi Parsons is a corrupt man, a dishonest judge." The court rocked at this blast. A fist fight broke out among the spectators. Perceiving the danger of a riot, Parsons sought to terminate the hearing by demanding that Walker admit authorship of the editorial. The room quieted. "Yes," said Walker, "I wrote and published that article to promote—*and not obstruct*—public justice."

Parsons instantly replied, "Then I find you guilty as charged! The fine is five hundred dollars."

"I shall not pay it," Walker said quietly.

"Sheriff!" ordered the Judge. "This man is to be held in close confinement until the fine is paid."

The extraordinary excitement generated by the case reflected the public's awareness that for the first time the scandal of judicial corruption had been brought into the open. Walker had hardly been taken to a cell next to the Sheriff's office and locked up when placards began to appear all over the city: "Justice! Public Meeting! . . . to express opinions in regard to the decision of the Judge of the District Court." . . . That day 4,000 men gathered on the plaza before the court house and held a mass-meeting remarkable for its gravity and decorum. Edmund Randolph was the chief speaker. A great point of law was at stake, he said—the rights of Californians under the Constitution. Let there be no violence. "Mr. Walker has asked me to speak to you of the importance of avoiding violence. He said to me that he will not let himself be set free by violence."

Some of his listeners were disappointed. There were shouts: "Let's bring the Judge out here!" "Parsons resign!" "Set Walker free!" But Randolph maintained his calm and kept the crowd in check. A resolution condemning Parsons' action as "an unwarrantable exercise of power and violation of law" was formally proposed and carried in a voice vote. This resolution, it was agreed, would be delivered in writing to Parsons by a Committee of Ten. Meanwhile, Randolph would apply to the Superior Court of the city for a writ of *habeas corpus.*

Whatever else might be said of Parsons, he was a stern fighter for injustice, and he showed no sign of giving way to public pressure. For the following week, while the *habeas corpus* proceeding was being argued, most of the San Francisco newspapers allotted whole columns daily to the affair. The case was seen as a major test of the common law, as a defense of the public against judicial tyranny. Walker, from his cell, provided additional editorial matter for the *Herald,* referring to Parsons' "masterly inactivity" in dealing with crime, and adding, "The Judge is a stickler for contempt and he has succeeded in securing to himself an unstinted measure. . . . In trying to snuff out the *Herald,* his Honor has extinguished himself."

The judge of the Superior Court who had to consider Randolph's demand for a writ of *habeas corpus* was in an embarrassing position. To deny the writ would be to defy an aroused public opinion; to grant it would offend the powerful Parsons and his cronies. By this time, however, the case had attracted the attention of the entire state, and steps for the impeachment of Parsons were under way before the Legislature. Ten days after Walker's arrest, the writ was reluctantly issued by the Court, and he was set free. His first action was to publish "A Card" in the *Herald,* thanking those who had rallied to his cause, which was the cause "of the whole people of California." Of Edmund Randolph's arduous efforts he spoke with especial feeling. "It would be idle ceremony for me to return thanks"; this had been an unforgettable act of friendship. The recollection of that act would, five years later, profoundly affect not only Walker's destiny but that of a nation.

As the tumult died away, it appeared that the only real beneficiary of the affair was the *Herald.* Its circulation boomed; it enlarged its page size so as to accommodate more advertising and began to turn out a weekly newspaper in addition to the daily. But Walker was well aware that nothing had yet been accomplished for the city. Crime was unabated. The courts went on their accustomed way. The attack on Parsons and the judiciary, he felt, had to be pressed. Early in April, he appeared before a special committee of the Legislature in Sacramento to present a memorial on Parsons' instruction to the Grand Jury. The committee investigated the charge and recommended impeachment; and the impeachment proceedings moved as far as the floor of the Legislature. There, however, Parsons' political friends were able to intervene successfully; and after some desultory debate, the matter was dropped.

III

The San Francisco underworld had its own views on "the contempt case," as it was called, and it expressed them with ferocity. On the night of May 4, 1851, simultaneous fires broke out at a dozen points in the downtown business districts, producing a conflagration that totally destroyed twenty blocks of wooden buildings, among them the office and printing plant of the *Herald*. Under cover of the excitement the gangs swarmed into the city and robbed and looted to their hearts' content.

It was a night of terror and despair; and the hope that the Walker case had aroused went up in smoke. The *Herald* lost everything except its fighting spirit. A printing plant which had escaped the fire was put at Nugent's disposal, and he managed to resume publication three days after the fire, with anger bubbling from every page, calling for "a volunteer police." This time something was done, and men armed with rifles began to patrol the city. The entire press of the city was demanding action against the arsonists. The *Herald* went further. On June 5, it came out with an editorial headed, "The Organization of Crime in This State," in which it flatly asserted that the men who had set the fire were known to the authorities, and were receiving the protection of politicians, some of whom were Catilines aiming at nothing less than complete mastery of the city and the state. It was time, said the *Herald,* for "a general war on crime." The shocked and frightened public, however, was in no mood to harken to clarion calls. It was rumored that many respectable people were preparing to leave San Francisco.

The *Herald*'s charge of a major political conspiracy resting on a criminal base became more credible when, about three weeks later, with the rebuilding of the ruined district well under way, another great fire broke out, destroying even more of the city, again to the accompaniment of countless robberies. It was this devastating blaze that provided the immediate impetus for the formation of the first Committee of Public Safety, the Vigilantes, who would finally crush the gangs only to impose their own despotism.

IV

The *Herald* still held to its conviction that, before order could be established, the courts had to be freed from corrupt judges of the Parsons stamp. His docket was crowded with cases, yet he absented himself from the court for days at a time. "How long must we tolerate this man?" Walker demanded editorially. The same question, in reverse, was in Judge Parsons' mind, and he was in the better position to answer it. Among his friends was a notorious duelist, Graham Hicks, known for his deadly skill with the revolver. Several prominent San Franciscans had already fallen to his marksmanship. He was a small wiry man, not unlike Walker himself in build. Walker, said Hicks, had insulted "a friend of his," and would have to apologize or fight. Duelling was the most popular spectator sport in the city, and as soon as the challenge became known and the time of the meeting was set, a huge crowd turned out for the event.

The fact that Walker fought four revolver duels in his life without wounding a single antagonist led some to believe that his marksmanship was poor; but it would have had to be almost incredibly bad to achieve such a record, and other evidence points in the opposite direction. It is perhaps not unreasonable to believe that he had an aversion to this cold-blooded form of killing—that he deliberately shot into the air or the ground in the expectation that his opponents would follow his example. This practice was not unusual among the gentlemen of New Orleans, as a means of satisfying honor without bloodshed. In one of his duels, fought in San Francisco with W. H. Carter in the spring of 1855, at eight paces, Walker was wounded in the foot —an injury sufficiently unusual to suggest that Carter was shooting to miss or to inflict minimal damage after Walker had missed. In the Hicks duel, also fought at eight paces, Walker as usual got his shot off first, without effect. Hicks, however, felt no obligations to *noblesse*. His shot, intended to kill, went through the upper part of Walker's arm, near the shoulder, just missing the bone.

What followed made a great impression on the spectators. Showing no sign of pain, Walker motioned to Hicks that they should take a second shot, but before they could raise their guns again, the seconds intervened, and the duel was declared over.

Some later commentators on Walker's career professed to find in his several duels the signs of a bloodthirsty character, of a desperado, but it is safe to say that they misread both the man and his age. A contemporary of Walker's who sought to explain his outlook to a later generation stressed the atmosphere of the 1850's as an essential factor to be considered. "Men looked upon life from a more romantic viewpoint than they do now. There was more sentiment, more singing of songs . . . grace and gallantry. . . . Men had not outgrown the customs of their forefathers, and if they resorted to the *code duello* in defense of their honor, and the honor of women, they were moved by sincerity, and surrounded by traditions still too potent to be cast aside." The way in which a gentleman conducted himself in a duel in Walker's time was taken as a major test of character; the fortitude with which he bore the wound inflicted by Hicks and the anger that made him want to continue the duel gave him an instant reputation as a man among men. "A brave, highly educated and able man" with "a high moral and political position"* on all issues of the time, was the character attributed to Walker in the San Francisco of the 1850's. Men clustered around him.

* F. Soulé, J. H. Gihon, and J. Nisbet, *Annals of San Francisco*, 1855.

VII

⟨✦⟩

MR. VANDERBILT FORGIVES
GREAT BRITAIN

Walker in the San Francisco *Herald,* quoting the New York press, commented enthusiastically on Commodore Vanderbilt's great enterprise in Nicaragua. He saw the canal as the key to the Americanization of the Caribbean. The interests of the great capitalist had begun to touch those of the inconspicuous journalist. With the signing of the Clayton-Bulwer Treaty, two new Vanderbilt corporations had sprung into life: the Nicaraguan Canal Company, which was to dig the canal under Anglo-American management; and the Accessory Transit Company, which would carry passengers across Nicaragua until completion of the canal. Talk of war died away. Even the New York *Herald,* which had been virulently anti-British, discovered that in the matter of Nicaragua the United States as well as the British had been at fault, "but an influence of common sense arose from . . . the London Exchange on the one side and Wall Street on the other."

San Francisco heard nothing but favorable news of the venture. Already the Accessory Transit Company was constructing shallow-draft steamboats to operate on the San Juan River and Lake Nicaragua.

Yet another Vanderbilt company, the Nicaragua Steamship Line, had ordered ships of unsurpassed size and speed to make the runs from New York to Nicaragua and from Nicaragua to San Francisco. An eminent engineer, Colonel C. W. Childs, had agreed to go to Nicaragua for Vanderbilt to make a detailed survey for the canal and an estimate of cost. And finally it was announced that Vanderbilt would go forthwith to England to negotiate with British financiers.

The success of the canal scheme was taken for granted. How could America and England, acting together, fail? All hopes seemed confirmed when copies of the *Times* of London arrived, praising the Vanderbilt project, and stating, "There is every prospect of the undertaking . . . being pushed to a successful issue." Vanderbilt's talks with the Rothschilds and Baring Brothers, said the *Times,* had resulted in "a satisfactory financial arrangement."

Vanderbilt's next concern was to bring the Accessory Transit Company to life while Colonel Childs was making his survey of the canal. Here he ran into difficulties. Engineers whom he had sent to Nicaragua had reported that the San Juan River, contrary to expectations, was not passable by steamboat, owing to five dangerous rapids along its course. The only hope for the transit route, they said, would be to dig small canals around these rapids. With his accustomed energy, the Commodore decided to see for himself. The first of his new ocean-going steamships, the *Prometheus*, was ready for him. It was a fast boat, but on this first voyage made no attempt at a speed record, for it towed behind it, on the ten-day run to Greytown, a small shallow-draft steamboat, the *Director*, designed for use on Lake Nicaragua.

I I

"The presence of the enterprising and indefatigable Commodore Vanderbilt," wrote Walker in the *Herald,* "will insure the perfection of all arrangements to make the transit connection complete." The tribute was merited. When the *Prometheus* docked at Greytown and Vanderbilt proposed to take the *Director* up the San Juan to the lake, he found himself up against a solid front of pessimism among his own employees. The boat would be wrecked, warned his engineers. No one had ever succeeded in getting a steamboat through the San

Juan. Vanderbilt brushed objections aside. He had come to take a boat up the river and he would do it. What followed left his men awestruck. With Vanderbilt himself at the wheel, the *Director* headed upstream as if possessed of a devil. "The Commodore," reported one of the crew, "insisted on 'jumping' all the obstacles, and tied down the safety valves, put on all steam, and compelled the little steamer to scrape and struggle over the obstructions into clear water again." At one point where the river dropped appallingly and the water boiled around huge protruding rocks, Vanderbilt taught the crew another lesson, by using heavy rope tied around trees to warp the vessel, an inch at a time, past the rapids.

On New Year's Day, 1851, the *Director* completed the 119-mile course of the river and entered Lake Nicaragua. The remainder of Vanderbilt's trip was equally full of achievement. By the time that he returned to Greytown he had laid out the complete transit route. From Virgin Bay, on the west side of the lake, a road was to be cut through the jungle to the nearest usable harbor on the Pacific, San Juan del Sur. To the east, the San Juan River was to be improved by blasting, and where that would not suffice for the passage of boats, a portage around obstinate rapids would take care of the problem. The Commodore gave orders: construct wharves in all of the Transit's harbors on seacoast and lakeshore; purchase mules and stagecoaches to carry passengers and their baggage; please the Nicaraguans by painting the coaches in their national colors, blue and white; lay wooden planks all along the road through the jungle; buy land outside Greytown and put up company offices—move, act, build! Then he boarded the *Prometheus* and made a record-smashing run back to New York.

From this moment all went as if by magic. Ocean-going steamships designed to Vanderbilt's specifications were constructed and sent around Cape Horn to handle the run between San Juan del Sur and San Francisco. He also ordered two small iron-hulled steamers to be built especially for the rocky San Juan River, and he named these, not inappropriately, the *John M. Clayton* and the *Sir Henry Bulwer*. A somewhat larger boat was sent to join the *Director* on Lake Nicaragua. On July 3, 1851, one year precisely after the signing of the Clayton-Bulwer treaty, advertisements appeared in New York newspapers for the "New and Independent Line for California." All New York was excited. What could not Americans do when they put their minds to it? The New York *Herald* looked forward to the time "when the government and institutions of the United States will be extended over the whole of Mexico and Central America," as a result of the enterprise of such men as Vanderbilt and George Law. California was even more elated, if possible. The fastest ship-time from New York to San Francisco around Cape Horn had been fifty-one days. The new route through Nicaragua would shorten the trip to twenty-five days.

When the *Prometheus* sailed from New York for Greytown, Vanderbilt and a large party of guests were aboard her. Still his luck held. The passengers enjoyed the summer voyage, marveled at the lush scenery of the Nicaraguan coast, were hospitably received in Greytown, boarded the *Sir Henry Bulwer,* ascended the San Juan River with only minor difficulties, were transferred to the *Director,* crossed the lake to Virgin Bay, mounted mules (the stages being still undelivered), and rode eleven miles to San Juan del Sur, where one of Vanderbilt's big new ships, the *Pacific,* was waiting to take them aboard for the run to San Francisco. A letter received by the New York *Herald* from one of the passengers might almost have been written to Vanderbilt's order: "With good swift boats, gentlemanly commanders, and with scenery to attract the eye, studded with banana, orange, lemon, palm and a thousand varieties of trees, what shall deter the traveler from the United States in making a choice of this sure and practicable route?"

More steamships were coming from the ways for the Vanderbilt line, and by late 1851 it was in full competition with Law's Panama route. All the advantage now lay with the Commodore. California-bound passengers soon learned that they could save four days (days in which they might find a gold deposit before someone else got to it!) by traveling through Nicaragua. When Law tried to hold his position by warning the public in print against "melancholy detentions" on the Nicaragua route, Vanderbilt hotly countered with assertions that cholera was rampant in Panama. Law lowered his fares; Vanderbilt lowered his still more. On the early runs of the *Prometheus*, first-class passengers paid $400 per person, but month by month the price went down until at one point it stood at $150, while steerage passengers could make the voyage to San Francisco for only $45. At this stage, loud complaints were heard from passengers about crowded conditions, wretched food, and poor seamanship, but Vanderbilt could afford to shrug; his boats were traveling full, Law's half empty. Nothing could daunt the multitudes eager to reach the promised land of California by the shortest route, and the price war notwithstanding, Vanderbilt's profits were massive. The line was making three sailings a month out of New York, carrying up to 600 passengers at a time, while the San Francisco office was booking about 300 passengers per trip and obtaining large revenues from the shipment of eastbound gold. The gross revenues of the Nicaragua Steamship Line and the Accessory Transit Company in their first year of full operation were reported to be over $5,000,000, of which nearly 40 per cent was net profit. (Walker in that year of 1852 was lucky if journalism earned him a thousand dollars.)

I I I

San Francisco heard that the Commodore's Nicaraguan venture was dazzling Wall Street by its success and ingenuity. Accessory Transit did not even have to pay taxes to New York State, since, as its lawyers made clear to the courts, it was "a Nicaraguan enterprise." Where taxes were not concerned, however, the company was glad to wrap itself in the American flag. At one point friction arose with Nicaragua, whose government was so temerarious as to request the share of profits due it under its contract with the company. Vanderbilt claimed that there had been no profits, that a steamboat had been lost, that the outlook was bleak. This the Nicaraguans could hardly credit, since it was public knowledge that Accessory Transit had paid agreeable dividends to stockholders; and they sent two commissioners to New York to press their case. Vanderbilt refused to see them.

To every display of the Commodore's aggressiveness, the public responded with applause, and more than applause, with money. While the price of shares in Law's Panama Line was dropping on the exchange, Accessory Transit stock became a favorite of the bulls, rising in a few months from $18 to $50 per share. At this price, so it was later asserted, Vanderbilt disposed of most of his shares. But this was the least of his gains. It was the soaring of Nicaraguan Canal Company stock that set Wall Streeters agog. Coming on the market at $800 per share, it was first regarded only as an interesting speculation for the wealthy. Then, just at the time when the success of the

Accessory Transit Company had made Vanderbilt the darling of the financial community, came the awaited report from Colonel Childs. The sum of $32,000,000, said the colonel, would be enough to build a practicable lock canal on the Nicaraguan route; and what was more, his plans had been approved by engineers of the British and American governments. A wild rush for Nicaraguan Canal Company shares followed. Although the *New York Times* shook its editorial head, pointing out that the project still existed only on paper, and reminding its readers of the Mississippi Bubble, Wall Street paid no attention. Up and up went the price until in March, 1852, it stood at $3600 per share.

The precise details of the subsequent collapse were never revealed, but shrewd guesses were made. As soon as Colonel Childs returned from Nicaragua, Vanderbilt sent him with some financial advisors to London, to arrange for British capital in the venture. A few weeks later he held in his hands a letter, transmitted by Childs, from a partner of Baring Brothers, which knocked the props out from under his hopes. British finance would have nothing to do with the Nicaraguan Canal Company. As planned by Childs, the canal would be too narrow to accommodate large freighters, and the cost was excessive relative to the revenue that could be obtained from small passenger ships.

Whether or not the Barings' calculations were valid, whether or not Childs' plans for the canal could have been modified to meet their objections, hardly mattered. The fact, as George Squier, the American minister, plainly stated, was that all estimates of the cost of the canal were only guesses. He himself guessed $100,000,000 as being closer to the mark than Childs' figure. Any man of common sense, he said, could see that the canal's immense benefits would justify an outlay of $200,000,000, if necessary. Vanderbilt, too, understood this. He perceived between the lines of the British refusal its real significance. England simply did not want the canal. Her policy had not changed an iota; and since the Clayton-Bulwer Treaty, which bound her to nothing, effectively prevented the United States from proceeding without her, there would be no canal.

How long Vanderbilt knew of the Baring letter before he released it for publication no one could find out. The *Herald* made plain its conviction that he kept his information to himself until he had unloaded his shares at some $3600 each. With the announcement came panic. First by hundreds and then by thousands of dollars the price of the stock fell, until buyers could not be found at any price.

While regretting England's decision, Vanderbilt let it be known that he harbored no hostility toward her. Perhaps the reason for his forgiving attitude lay in the profit that he realized from his Wall Street transactions at this period. He was worth, so he told a friend, some eleven millions—which meant that he had doubled his fortune in three years. More, his money was so invested as to yield him a return of 25 per cent. He could afford to forgive those who had transgressed against him. In any event his original purpose was achieved. Nicaragua had replaced Panama as the favored route to California, and the stock of George Law's Panama Steamship Line was steadly dropping on the exchange.

Thus, after three years of high diplomacy and even higher finance, England and Vanderbilt were satisfied, but the American government found its position in Central America sadly worsened, and its hopes of a canal blighted. Senatorial inquiry to find out why the plan had foundered had a curious result, for it brought to light the letter from Bulwer that Clayton had hidden away, together with his secret memorandum. Aghast, Congress and the public realized how large Bulwer's diplomatic victory had been; and senator after senator arose to aver that he would never have voted for the treaty if he had known of this "outrageous betrayal." But betrayal or no betrayal, there the treaty stood, a firm barrier against closer relations between the United States and Central America. The one benefit that the nation had gained was the development of the Nicaraguan transit route, through which thousands of California-bound Americans continued to pour.

To Walker, as to many another American, the Clayton-Bulwer Treaty now seemed a terrible misfortune for the nation, an evil which it was the obligation of all men of spirit to resist and overcome. The fact that it may have served to avert a war with England was less important to him than the sharp limits which had been set on the expansion of American power to the south.

VIII

⟨₩⟩

"A RASH AND DESPERATE
UNDERTAKING"

A new opportunity had come Walker's way. A highly regarded lawyer, Henry P. Watkins, who had a practice in nearby Marysville and was involved in state politics, offered him a partnership. Walker was again restless. He had exhausted the possibilities of San Francisco journalism for challenge and recognition. Without much deliberation, he accepted Watkins' offer and moved to Marysville.

With Watkins looking after the business side of the practice, Walker was able to concentrate on the forensic battles which were the only aspect of legal practice that attracted him. A tribute to his rhetorical power came to him from Stephen J. Field, a colleague of the Marysville bar who later became a Justice of the United States Supreme Court, and who called Walker "a brilliant speaker." This was in his twenty-seventh year. It was not to be expected, however, that his temperament and ambition would permit him to take the slow, steady course to professional affluence and political preferment. Nor did anything in the society around him conduce to a settled life. "Those were the days when the ardor for adventure by land and sea was hot in the breasts of men." The one influence that might have made him give up his romantic dreams for conventional reality, the love of a woman, was absent. If there had been any chance of his finding a flesh-and-blood woman who could displace Ellen Martin's image for him, Marysville was the last place in which to seek her. The shortage of women there was even more acute than in San Francisco. Few newcomers to the town were able to find wives who had not first been prostitutes. Most men patronized the brothels; some became pederasts; more than one arrest was reported in the newspapers for "bestiality." In many instances, Walker's among them, the sexual impulse was suppressed—or rather, transmuted into other forms of action. His chance of emotional liberation had gone with the death of Ellen Martin. The extraordinary heat that he seemed to generate, so that every situation in which he found himself became incandescent and explosive, may well have had its psychological root in sexual abstinence. His maleness found its outlet in an assault, as it were, upon the political timidities of his environment. Frustration must nevertheless have tormented him. There is more than a hint in his life of the same psychic forces that caused Girolamo Savonarola, after a thwarted love affair, to become a monk, and by the intensity of his belief to make himself the master of Florence. One suspects that the tremendous outpouring of Walker's energy into work and the harsh monastic rigors and fatigues that he imposed on his waking life, and at which his friends marveled, were a way of exorcising the female images of night, and allaying the unresolved tensions of continence.

During his year in San Francisco he had met a remarkable personality who, in some ways, so much resembled him that they might almost have been brothers—a French nobleman, Count Gaston Raoul de Raousset-Boulbon. Raousset, like Walker, was a man with a chivalric and romantic stance toward life. Both were idealistic democrats in the French revolutionary tradition; both were imbued with and exalted by the idea of personal heroism. The Frenchman was some seven years older than Walker, similarly short and slender, and with a face distinguished by magnetic eyes. They also matched each other in energy, courage, education, and literary flair. Raousset while in Paris had founded and edited a radical newspaper, *La Liberté,* and had written an emotional novel, *La Conversion,* describing his transformation from aristocrat to democrat.

He had in fact tried his hand at even more professions than Walker: he had been a soldier in Algeria, and in California a miner, a fisherman, a hunter, a cattle dealer. It was in their attitude toward women that they differed most; if Walker was Galahad, Raousset was Don Juan. In France he had fought a number of duels over women, with a ferocity that earned him the sobriquet of *Petit Loup.* One of his literary fragments, a poem written on the eve of his departure from Paris as a penniless adventurer—he had dissipated a fortune on pleasure—caught the essential spirit of him. "My despairing heart runs from one to another; who knows if I shall live to be thirty, whether the future will be gay, or whether I shall be shot; only kiss me, Camille, kiss me."

Early in 1852, the California newspapers began to carry extraordinary news of Raousset. Despite his empty purse, he was the center of the French colony of San Francisco, where one man out of every ten was a Frenchman seeking adventure in adversity. One of their chief topics of conversation was the possibility of wresting from Mexico the southern region of Arizona, then part of the State of Sonora, and reputed to be rich in mineral wealth. A plan to this end quickly took shape in the Count's fertile mind. The population of Sonora was living in terror of the frequent raids southward from Arizona of the savage Apache Indians. It struck Raousset that if he went to Mexico City with the diplomatic support of the French government and offered to lead a French force into Sonora to suppress the Apaches, he might as a reward obtain from the Mexican government a concession to the gold and silver mines of Arizona. And after that, who knew what his power might become?

By the spring of 1852, it seemed that success was close. The rulers of Mexico were as well disposed to the French as they were resentful of Americans. A company was formed to operate the mines, with a suitable distribution of shares to certain Mexican officials; Raousset formally pledged himself to clear the Apaches out of Sonora; the government granted the new company rights to the Arizona mines; and all went with dreamlike precision. Hastening back to San Francisco, Raousset obtained the aid of the French consul in chartering a ship and raising an expeditionary force of 150 of his compatriots, and in May, 1852, sailed for Guaymas, the chief port of Sonora. Since they went nominally as "colonists," and at the invitation of the Mexican government, the American Neutrality Laws were not invoked to prevent their departure.

II

Walker viewed normal life, with its emphasis on security, with the impatience of a race horse hitched to a milk cart. Raousset's glamorous enterprise made the practice of law in Marysville seem insignificant and tawdry. Life in San Francisco had hardened Walker and the duel with Hicks had left more than a physical scar. His respect for the law had been corroded and cracked. The Neutrality Laws which, in his New Orleans days, had caused him to inveigh against General Lopez' filibustering designs on Cuba, now seemed to him merely a legalistic cover for the weakness and timidity of politicians in Washington, three thousand miles away. Were these ill-advised laws to be obeyed while France took Sonora? Was America, after winning the Mexican War, to stop short of one of the chief prizes of victory, the mines of Arizona? Confident of his vision of the American future, he regarded as ignorant and reactionary those laws which seemed to him to sacrifice the future to the present.

The fact that Raousset already had a contract with the Mexican government did not disturb Walker. It was generally thought that the Sonorans were disaffected and ripe for revolution. Why should not Sonora, like California, be given the benefit of American institutions? Why should not an American company, by making a contract with the Sonoran government, put itself in a position where it could either share Raousset's project or displace it?

Although Walker was for the most part soft-spoken, reticent, and thoughtful of demeanor, he was capable of flashing bursts of excitement that illuminated the projects in which he was interested, and made the people around him regard him as their natural leader. His enthusiasm for the Sonoran venture was so contagious that it won over his partner, Watkins, and several other prominent men. That spring of 1852 a group selected by Walker met to discuss the possibility of an American expedition to Sonora. Agreement was reached, money was found, and two of the men present were designated to go to Guaymas, their purpose to obtain permission from the Governor of Sonora to bring into the state a number of American "colonists." The hope proved futile. Before Walker's agents could reach Guaymas, Raousset had already come to terms with the Governor of Sonora. Owning a substantial block of shares in the French mining company, the Governor had no interest in any other expedition, and certainly not one composed of *gringos*. Walker's agents returned to Marysville disappointed, and he and Watkins had reluctantly to go back to their petty practice.

A few months passed and then the fever returned, as fresh news came of Raouset's expedition. It appeared that the military commander of Sonora, General Blanco, who had more actual power than the state's governor, had somehow been overlooked in the distribution of stock in Raousset's company. A San Francisco banking house, with its eye on the Sonora mines, hastily took advantage of the situation to bribe Blanco to its interest. If he would ignore the Mexican government's contract with Raousset, the bankers told him, he could sign one of his own with a new company to be formed for the purpose. Instantly it became Blanco's chief aim to wreck the French expedition. To this end he kept Raousset and his men dangling in Guaymas, on one official pretext or another, until idleness and disease began to take their toll, and supplies began to run short. When at last the Count was allowed to depart for the north his force was gravely enfeebled; and its situation was made worse by wholesale desertions of Mexican muleteers and guides. The wily Blanco then showed his hand by demanding that Raousset's company submit themselves to him and either become Mexican citizens or work as laborers at the mines under his command. Enraged, the French leader sought to organize a revolutionary movement among the Sonoran people, but without success. Finally in desperation he launched an attack against Sonora's capital, Hermosillo, a city of 12,000 where Blanco had a large garrison. In the battle that followed 243 Frenchmen stormed the adobe walls in the face of musket and cannon fire from 1200 Mexicans, took the town, and almost captured Blanco. But still unable to bring the natives to his side, and suffering from fever, Raousset was compelled at last to come to terms with the Mexican, and to leave Sonora.

If this was failure, San Francisco did not know it. On his return, Raousset was greeted as one of the heroes of the age. He further delighted his admirers when, in accepting the honors heaped upon him, he vowed to go back to Mexico. "I cannot live without Sonora," he said. With that he began to prepare for another and larger expedition.

Not to have been part of so stirring an adventure was more than Walker could bear. Early in 1853, he and his partner Watkins called on Raousset and offered their cooperation and services for the new attempt.

"Together," Walker told Raousset, "we would be far more than twice as strong. There are many in the United States who would stand with us and use their influence in our behalf."

Raousset listened courteously and with appreciation of Walker's intensity. "My friends," he replied, "what you say is perhaps true, but I cannot be associated with you. To be frank, Americans are so strongly detested in Mexico that your presence would destroy my chances."

Walker did not argue. With one of his rare smiles he said, "Then we must be rivals."

"So be it," said Raousset, and they shook hands warmly, while the prosaic Watkins looked on in admiration.

The Frenchman was basing his hopes on a report that a revolution had just brought to the Presidency of Mexico General Santa Anna, known to be friendly to France. This was the moment for another visit to Mexico City, to make a new and binding contract; and he would soon be on his way. Walker's plan was far more daring—nothing less than to introduce a force of Americans into Sonora, under the guise of colonists, and make himself master of the state, either with the cooperation of its politicos or without them. Sonora would then declare itself an independent republic, put itself under the protection of the United States, and give the mining concession to an American company, regardless of any contracts with the French signed in Mexico City.

This was also the reasoning of some of San Francisco's wealthy mining men, who were eager to speculate on the chance of a concession for the Sonora mines. Their need was for a leader who could dominate a fighting force recruited from among the adventurers of San Francisco, and at the same time outmaneuver the Frenchman, Raousset, and the Mexican Governor of Sonora. In the view of the San Francisco magnates, Walker's reputation for bravery, his burning conviction, his power of speech, and his legal and journalistic training outweighed his lack of military experience. They would provide him with the necessary backing and funds, they told him, if he would devote himself to the expedition. Money was raised by the sale of bonds "secured" by the land which Walker expected to obtain in Sonora.

The Independence Loan Fund [the bonds read] has received of ———— ———— the sum of $500, and the Republic of Sonora will issue to him or his assigns a land warrant for one square league of land, to be located on the public domain of said Republic.

Signed, this first day of May,
William Walker,
Colonel of the Independence Regiment*

Sold secretly to selected purchasers, the bonds provided enough money to permit recruitment, the purchase of guns and supplies, and the hiring of a ship. Walker had brought Edmund Randolph and another close friend, Parker Crittenden, also a lawyer, into the project, and together they organized the expedition. He felt, however, that before sailing he needed firsthand information on the conditions that he would have to face; and a few days after Raousset-Boulbon left for Mexico City, the self-created colonel boarded a ship for Guaymas.

Walker found the Sonoran port less than hospitable. The Mexican authorities would not even have permitted him to remain if the American consul had not come to his aid. When he sent a message to the Governor of Sonora, asking permission to call on him, no reply was forthcoming for days. His time had to be spent largely in the small American colony of the town. There several American women spoke of their fear of the Apaches, who had been raiding close to the city, and they begged Walker to bring enough men to Sonora to assure their safety. In this way they provided him with the one ingredient that had been missing from his enterprise—the need of defenseless womanhood for his knightly protection.

The effect that Walker made at Guaymas in 1853, as he appeared in his new role as soldier and liberator, is preserved in an eye-

---

* *Alta California,* Dec. 1, 1853.

witness account. "His appearance was anything else than that of a military chieftain . . . unprepossessing . . . insignificant. . . . But anyone who estimated Mr. Walker by his personal appearance made a great mistake. Extremely taciturn, he would sit for an hour in company without opening his lips; but once interested he arrested your attention with the first word he uttered, and as he proceeded, you felt convinced that he was no ordinary person. To a few confidential friends he was most enthusiastic upon the subject of his darling project, but outside of those immediately interested he never mentioned the topic."*

Presently a message came to him from the Governor: if Walker would come to the capital of Sonora, Hermosillo, they would discuss the matter of colonization and the suppression of the Apaches. Walker smelled a trap. Too much time had gone by. Almost certainly the canny Governor had learned the real purpose of the Americans, and would find a way to dispose of their leader if he once got him in his clutches. The desired land grant would have to be sacrificed. The expedition could no longer hope to mask itself as a group of peaceful colonists; it would have to sail from San Francisco in violation of federal law and fight for Sonora from the moment of its landing. The prospect in no way dismayed Walker. Hastening back to San Francisco, he prepared for action. One hundred men had been recruited, and the brig *Arrow* was in readiness, with a cargo of guns, ammunition, food, and other stores needed for a campaign.

The San Francisco press knew Walker's intention, and encouraged him. *Alta California,* reporting the murder in Sonora of eighty people by Apaches in a single week, declared, "They cannot protect themselves, and the government cannot protect them." But the American military authorities saw the matter otherwise. On September 30, 1853, Walker's plan came to a sudden halt when the United States Army general in command at San Francisco ordered the *Arrow* seized on suspicion that it was to be used to violate the Neutrality Laws.

With Edmund Randolph as his attorney, Walker instantly filed suit to have the vessel released; but the outlook was dark and he did not intend to submit to any lengthy legal process. Instead, he

---

* T. Robinson Warren, *Dust and Foam*, 1858.

had another brig, the *Caroline*, fitted out for his purposes and, with as many of his recruits as could be hastily rounded up, secretly boarded the vessel, weighed anchor and stood out to sea before they could be intercepted. Forty-five men were with him. The date was October 8, 1853. Before he sailed he received news which must have heartened him. French rivalry no longer was a threat. Count Raousset-Boulbon had fallen out with President Santa Anna, had been forced to flee Mexico for his life, and was back in San Francisco.

III

Walker was being driven by idealism and ambition together—an irresistible combination when their thrust is in the same direction. He believed with all his heart that the democratic institutions of the United States offered hope to the peoples of the world and that there was an obligation on Americans to bring the light of democracy to their benighted neighbors. At the same time he held in his heart the heroic dream of world fame. All his secret aspirations were centered on the overcoming of enemies and victory in battle—but in the name of right, justice, and the United States.

He was undismayed by the appearance of absurdity. There was in him just that touch of fanaticism required to ignore public opinion when it ran counter to his own convictions. His true profession was heroism. Like Raousset, another incurable romantic, Walker could no more resist an opportunity to risk everything for a high purpose than a dedicated surgeon could refuse a chance to pit his skill against death. He had become an addict of danger. Regardless of the practical purpose of the Sonoran enterprise as conceived by his backers, to him from the beginning it had always been a personal test, a feat of arms against great odds, by which a man might overnight enter the ranks of glory for the sake of his country. His failure on this, his first try at war and conquest, was abysmal, it was grotesque; and yet it had about it something that was not of the time, a hint of ancient quest and knightly fortitude, a touch of grandeur that men recognized, and that in time caused the laughter and the sneers to die away, and Walker to emerge a larger figure than ever in the eyes of the California public.

In a broad political sense as well, the expedition was by no means fruitless. Although commentators have called it "an inexcusable raid on an unoffending people" and "a rash and desperate undertaking which needs the pen of a Cervantes to do it justice," the fact remains that it played a considerable, if indirect, part in the acquisition by the United States of 45,000 square miles of Mexican territory, an area as large as the state of Pennsylvania, and containing the valuable minerals coveted by California interests, as well as a desirable railroad route. This was the so-called Gadsden Purchase, which a few months later was incorporated with the territories of Arizona and New Mexico.

Walker's original strategic plan called for a landing near Guaymas, but he was compelled to change it. With fewer than fifty men, he could not hope to contend with the strong Mexican garrison at Guaymas. A suitable base of operations was needed at which to assemble additional recruits, promote a native insurrection against the Sonoran government, and finally launch an invasion. For this purpose he decided that his first conquest had to be the sparsely populated peninsula of Lower California, less than a hundred miles across the Gulf of California from Sonora. The *Caroline* accordingly put in at La Paz, the capital, and Walker landed his force. Without firing a shot they quickly made a prisoner of the Governor of the state, put him on board the brig, hauled down the Mexican flag over his house and raised in its place the flag of the "Republic of Lower California."

To the natives he gave assurance that his purpose was to lead a successful revolution for them against the tyranny of Mexico. Lower California, he stated in a proclamation, was "free, sovereign and independent." Its people no longer owed allegiance to Mexico. He himself would serve as President of the new nation until it was firmly established.

Subsequently his men beat back an attack from a small Mexican force, and captured a Mexican revenue cutter. There was danger that a major expedition might sail against Walker from nearby Guaymas, and not as yet wishing to face such a risk, he sailed north. The port of Ensenada, only one hundred miles south of the American border, struck him as a suitable place at which to marshal the reinforcements that he expected, and from which communication could readily be maintained with the United States. He took possession of the town without bloodshed, and issued a statement for the American people, elaborating his aims. Lower California, he said, had been shamefully neglected by the Mexican government. His purpose in creating the new republic was to develop the resources of the peninsula and "to effect a proper social organization therein." To accomplish this, it was first necessary to achieve independence from Mexico. He had therefore established a government of Americans to begin to administer the country. A list of "cabinet appointments" of chosen officers followed.

This large declaration, coming from a man of twenty-nine years and no military experience, and whose minuscule force consisted in the main of dockside toughs, undisciplined and untried, struck many Americans as ridiculous when they read of it. But it was more astute than Walker's contemporaries realized. He was gambling on sustained support from his backers in San Francisco. To show anything less than complete confidence would have been folly. Everything depended on the reinforcements and supplies that Henry Watkins was supposed to bring him. If the San Francisco newspapers failed to carry word, and bold word, of his achievements and purpose, the entire project might collapse from inattention.

While he awaited Watkins, he had to lead his men in his first serious battle. Two hundred Mexican soldiers, advancing from the north, entered Ensenada and laid siege to a house which he had selected as a fort. The defense was strong and competent, and after three days of bloody fighting, a bold sortie routed the attackers. The elation of victory did not last long, however. One morning soon thereafter the ship *Caroline,* on which most of Walker's provisions were stored, was seen to be hoisting anchor and making sail. Incredulously Walker and his men saw it put out to sea on a southward course, ignoring all his signals. Later it appeared that the crew had succumbed to the bribes of their prisoner, the Governor of Lower California, who had been left on board.

A few days later, the brig *Anita* put into the harbor, carrying Watkins and 230 men, full of zeal and expectation. Walker's first question was, what supplies had Watkins brought? The answer bore out his fears. The *Anita* carried guns and ammunition, but little food. This was a terrible blow. As soon as the new men had disembarked, Watkins had to turn around and sail for California; everything depended on the speed with which he could return with a cargo of provisions. Meanwhile, with so many mouths to feed, Walker sought a way to obtain supplies without arousing the animosity of the rancheros by raids on their land. His scouts learned that a noted Mexican outlaw, Melendrez, whose camp was nearby, had considerable supplies of corn as well as cattle and horses; and in a surprise attack on Melendrez' camp, Walker seized this booty. His problem, however, remained acute. Reduced rations consisting entirely of beef and corn took a toll of his men's morale, already weakening from idleness and disease. They resented, too, the strict discipline that Walker enforced, especially his threat to shoot any man who robbed a house or raped a woman. The signs of impending mutiny were unmistakable.

IV

News of Walker's proclamation of independence had gone to Mexico City, and there it produced political consequences which were to deprive his venture, in American eyes, of its purpose. The Mexican government was then being pressed by the American minister, James Gadsden, to sell northern Sonora for $10,000,000 plus assurance that the Apaches would be prevented from raiding into Mexico. The price was felt by Mexican officials to be outrageously low, and the offer as a whole insulting, but they had to consider whether the United States, if balked, might not use force to compel submission. They had been shocked by Walker's raid on La Paz; now the news from Ensenada that Lower California had been declared independent under American rule seemed to presage disaster for Mexico. Fearing that Walker was secretly abetted by the American government, they came to the conclusion that if they did not consent to negotiate they might lose both the peninsula and Sonora, without compensation. The result was a provisional treaty hastily drawn and signed on December 31, 1853, in which Gadsden's terms were met. A separate letter from him assured the Mexican government that the United States regarded Walker as a violator of federal law, and would deal with him accordingly.

From this point, Walker's expedition lost its appeal for Americans. With the coveted mineral-bearing part of Sonora secured for the United States, who cared about Lower California, or about "effecting a proper social organization" in Sonora?

Adversity now multiplied its forms. A Mexican gunboat appeared off Ensenada and patrolled the coast to prevent further reinforcement of Walker's troops; and almost at the same time an American warship, the *Portsmouth*, anchored in the harbor. Its commander came ashore, met with Walker, gave him news of the Gadsden Purchase, and warned him: he could expect no further aid from his friends in San Francisco, and certainly none from the government of the United States.

The provisional treaty that Gadsden had signed with Mexico struck Walker as altogether unsatisfactory. Its chief defect was its failure to provide an outlet for the United States on the Gulf of California—a limitation certain to hamper the development of the American southwest, Mexico and Central America. The fact remained that Walker could do nothing about it. His military situation was desperate, and he admitted as much to his officers. The question was, had they any choice but to slink home to the jeers of San Francisco? Was there still a chance to convert humiliation into glory? If the venture was not to be abandoned, there was only one direction in which to move—Sonora. His staff agreed: any risk, however rash, was preferable to certain dishonor. So long as there was something still to try, self-respect demanded that they go on. Walker thought it barely possible, but nevertheless possible, that a Sonoran insurrection against Mexico could be fomented, would submit to his leadership, and bring the Gulf of California under American control. On this remote chance he now staked everything.

V

How does a foreigner make a revolution in a place where his countrymen are hated, where his motives are suspect, and when he is not even there? Walker conceived the idea of beginning with an assembly of disaffected elements in Lower California. Then, bolstered by popular support, he would cross the Colorado River into Sonora and try to win over enough natives to give momentum to his cause. In this hope, he issued another proclamation, asserting Sonora's independence from Mexico, with the status of an independent republic, like that of Lower California.

Food was a major consideration. This time there was no alternative to foraging. The regiment ranged the countryside around Ensenada, commandeering cattle and corn in the name of the revolution, and stirring up hot indignation among landowners. On the whole, there was little violence, and Walker's orders against pillage were respected. But the restrictions that he enforced on his men's behavior became increasingly aggravating to them as their situation deteriorated. Although his officers, who were in daily contact with him and felt the impact of his own conviction, remained steadfast, the morale of the soldiers in the ranks was cracking badly, and they needed only an excuse to show their resentment.

The crisis came when Walker, organizing the transport of supplies into Sonora, gave orders that horses which had been taken from the outlaw Melendrez were to be used for this purpose. A number of his men had come to regard these mounts as their own and they flatly refused to turn them over to their officers. Summoned to the spot, Walker was met by open complaints and even threats.

It appeared that the expedition was about to founder in turmoil and disgrace. Those of the men who were still loyal to Walker waited pessimistically to see what he would do. His response startled them. He ordered the bugler to blow assembly. Hesitantly, the men formed ranks and stood at attention. After a long moment of silence, he spoke to them in a ringing voice, and in courteous, restrained language.

"If any of you wish to leave the expedition, you are free to do so. I shall not compel anyone to remain who wishes to go. Those of you who wish to stay with me I shall ask to signify their loyalty by taking an oath of allegiance to the flag of Lower California. Let there be no misunderstanding. I shall expect the men who follow me to abide by the highest standards of military behavior. Those who wish to go can fill their pockets with rations and leave camp. I shall expect them to be gone within two hours. The American boundary is only a three or four days' march from here. Any of you who do not wish to take the oath of allegiance will step forward, put down your rifles, and go to the supply depot for rations."

About fifty of the men left the formation, and gathered in a group to one side, talking among themselves. Some were embarrassed and uncertain, others in a state of intense anger. Finally they decided on a course of action. Instead of accepting Walker's offer, they turned and began to walk away from the camp, their rifles still in their hands.

Walker's aide, Captain Timothy Crocker, known for his courage, rushed after the deserters and ordered them to drop their guns. When no one obeyed, he drew his pistol. A man snarled, "Go on, shoot, Captain. I dare you." Several rifles were aimed at Crocker. At this point, without waiting for orders, another of Walker's officers ran to a nearby howitzer, already loaded, and trained it on the mutineers, ready to fire if Crocker were shot. Walker shouted, "Hold your fire!" For a moment, no one stirred; then the sullen men turned their backs on Crocker and continued to walk away. Walker jumped on a horse, and rode after them. An eyewitness, reporting the subsequent scene, was astonished by the kindliness and calmness of his voice when he overtook them. "Men," he said, "you are going to need rations, and you had better go back for them. I shall not try to take your rifles from you, but you know as well as I do that they are badly needed, and they belong to the regiment. I ask you to leave them behind."

More than half of the men put their rifles down. Two or three expressed their frustration and rage by smashing the butts on nearby rocks before they turned away. Some went back for rations. The entire group crossed the American border safely, and were taken by steamer to San Francisco. It was largely from their bitter testimony that the American press formed its judgment of Walker at this time. He was accused of being excessively harsh with his men, and of believing that "might makes right." But better than anyone else, he had reason to know that might does not make right, for the might was always with others, not with him. In Lower California it was the men behind him who had the power, not he. All they had to do was snap their fingers at him, and he was finished. What he depended on, in the final test, was discipline, or the idea of discipline. In order to hold in check the self-assertive and unruly men who had volunteered for this adventure, he had to focus the full power of his personality on every breach of discipline. Boyish, slight, physically unimpressive, possessed only of an indomitable will and searching grey eyes, he held them by a thin thread. A single lapse in their respect for him would have been fatal. To command them, he had to make them fear, not so much himself, as the disciplined response of their comrades to his orders. In this he was surprisingly successful. After the mass desertion at Ensenada, he increased, rather than diminished the severity of his discipline, for he knew that the least relaxation would invite further mutiny from men to whom the least restriction was galling. The punctilio of military etiquette was not abated for an instant. Privates were expected to salute their officers. Men stood at attention when addressed by their superiors in rank. All were warned that the death sentence would be imposed on mutineers and deserters. In practice, however, this rule was modified. Of four men who subsequently deserted after having taken the oath of allegiance, only the leader was shot; the others were driven from the camp.

When he finally marched out of Ensenada Walker had to leave behind him many who had been wounded or were ill. His active force numbered only 130. Establishing temporary headquarters at San Vicente, some thirty miles south of Ensenada, he spent ten days in a diligent search for natives who might lend themselves to his revolutionary purpose. Finally he convened an assembly of 62 Mexicans, who were received in a setting as impressive as ingenuity, in that poverty-stricken land, could make it—complete with a guard of honor, a vestigial military band, and a display of the flags of the new republics of Sonora and Lower California. There were oaths of allegiance, cheers, the firing of field pieces. A written declaration of loyalty prepared by the assembly and addressed to Walker gave him sanction, as the leader of the revolution, for further foraging and requisitioning of provisions.

When at last, leaving a small garrison in San Vicente, he led his shrunken regiment on the 200-mile march eastward to the Colorado River, they drove a herd of cattle before them. It took two weeks of wearisome struggle to climb up the rugged trails of the Sierras and down again almost to the mouth of the Colorado. By this time they were in rags, and their boots were worn through; Walker himself had lost one boot, and had improvised a kind of sandal in its place, giving a special touch of the grotesque to his

emaciated little figure. Exhausted though they were, they had no
choice, he said, but to go on. Somewhere in that arid countryside
they found wood with which to build rafts. The great question was
whether the cattle could be made to swim across the river, which
ran wide, deep and swift. An hour later they had their answer;
the men and some bags of corn crossed safely, but such cattle as
could be driven into the river were swept away and perished.

They were, then, in Sonora, and finished; almost without food,
almost without shoe leather, totally without hope. Seventy miles
up the river, they knew, was Fort Yuma, under the American flag.
Half of the men did not stop for Walker's decision, but deserted
and started their northward trek at once. The others waited for
their commander to lead them in the same direction. To their
considerable resentment, he refused. A skinny hollow-eyed scarecrow standing among scarecrows, he maintained his military dignity,
saying that he would give his orders at the right time; and somehow he kept his hold on them.

Three days later he knew that he could expect no aid or comfort from the Sonorans. His half-starved, bearded men lined up
at his order, and in silence heard him say that they would march
back to San Vicente, for the comrades who had been left there
could not be abandoned to the Mexicans. From San Vicente they
would go north again across the desert to the United States. Grimly
they listened, and obeyed—recrossed the river, and laboriously began to climb the stony mountain trails behind their leader.

VI

May 8, 1854, was Walker's thirtieth birthday. This was the day
on which, with the thirty-four men who were all that remained
to him, he staggered toward the American military post across the
border in California. The last thirty miles had been under the hot
desert sun, without food and almost without water. Continuous
harassment by the Mexican outlaws commanded by Melendrez, and
who rode, jeering, just beyond bullet reach, added the final note
of irony to that march. But even now, with his exhausted, parched,
and starving little troop at its last gasp, the preservation of dignity
was important to Walker. Presenting himself to the American mili-

tary commander at San Diego, and holding himself erect, he said formally, "I am Colonel William Walker. I wish to surrender my force to the United States."

He was arraigned before the Federal Court in San Francisco on an indictment by a Grand Jury, charged with violation of the Neutrality Laws. His partner, Watkins, had already been tried under the same auspices, convicted and fined $1500—a light penalty, as the judge pointed out, since the chief interest of the court was vindication of the law. Filibustering, as seen by public opinion, was a doomed profession. Walker's rival, Count Raousset-Boulbon, had failed in yet another attempt to enter Sonora with a military force, and was soon to face a Mexican firing squad. Major General John E. Wool, newly appointed to the command of the Department of the Pacific of the United States Army, had made public an order from President Pierce: "You will, to the utmost of your ability, use all proper means to detect the fitting out of armed expeditions against countries with which the United States are at peace, and will zealously cooperate with the civil authorities in maintaining the Neutrality Laws." It was Wool's watchfulness that had brought Watkins into court. *Alta California* exulted in the demonstration that the courts of San Francisco had done "what New York and New Orleans failed, discreditably failed, to do"—upheld the federal law against filibustering. All the auguries seemed to be against Walker when, with Edmund Randolph again at his side, he heard the clerk of the court read the charges, and answered, "Not guilty."

The trial was put off for four months, and he was set free on Randolph's recognizance. In spite of his failure and the gibes of the newspapers, Walker's reputation, it appeared, was far from shattered. The loyal men who had returned with him from Mexico, whatever their resentments of him as a martinet, had no fault to find with him as fighting man, and the San Francisco press began to change its tune. Even his insistence on preserving his military dignity under conditions of despair was now seen in a sympathetic light. Everywhere he went he was a center of respectful attention. His friends, especially Watkins and Randolph, urged him to enter politics, and sufficiently persuaded him so that he returned to Marysville, as a base of candidacy for public office.

Delegates were then being chosen for the Democratic State Convention of 1854, and "Mr. Walker of Yuba County" was among those elected. When the Convention met in the Baptist Church of Sacramento, on July 18, he was one of its prominent figures, although still under indictment.*

VII

Nothing in which Walker participated was ever quiet, and the Convention was no exception. The chief issue of the time was the contest for control of the State Democratic Party between David C. Broderick, President of the State Senate, who came from New York City and was an ardent free-soiler and strong antislavery man, and United States Senator William M. Gwin, formerly of Mississippi, a Southern fire-eater who never stopped urging the introduction of slavery into California. Walker from the first was a Broderick man and, when he arrived at the Convention, his faction, which had a slight majority, at once made him Chairman of the Platform Committee, Chairman of the Committee to Nominate Permanent Officers, and Keynote Speaker. Nothing could more have outraged Gwin's followers. Not only did they refuse to let the Convention be organized unless the slavery interest was given equal representation, but they backed their refusal by setting up their own separate committees. Noisy confusion and turmoil prevented the Convention from making any progress on its first morning, and there were even threats of violence from Gwin's supporters, most of whom came from the South, and were quick to turn to guns when tempers flared. In their eyes Walker was a traitor to his Southern origin.

When, on the afternoon of the first day, he rose to speak, the hall was tense. He had hardly begun when a Gwin man yelled that he was nothing but a tool of Yankee abolitionists. Bedlam broke out while Walker waited quietly on the platform. Suddenly a shot was heard. Later it was reported that a nervous delegate had been handling his pistol to make sure it was loaded, and that it had accidentally gone off, but at the time it was believed the shot was aimed at Walker. The effect was cataclysmic. Several delegates

---

* H. S. Hoblitzell, *Early Historical Sketch of the City of Marysville and Yuba County*, 1876.

jumped out of the windows, others engaged in fist fights, while Broderick's men rushed to protect Walker. Eventually quiet was restored, but as soon as Walker tried to resume his speech, he was again hooted down by the Gwin element. Thus the first day's session ended.

Overnight an arrangement was made that the Gwin and Broderick factions would meet the next day in separate halls, and try to negotiate a compromise. Walker, never more mild and reasonable then when he was the center of turmoil, was appointed as chairman of a "Committee of Compromise and Reconciliation" for his group, and led his associates to a meeting with their opponents. The result was predictable. Gwin's people rejected all compromise; one man even went so far as to propose, in a formal motion, that Walker be thrown out of a window. On that note the Convention fell apart.

IX

THE OPENING OF THE GATE

Walker's first experience in practical American politics was his last. He never ran for office. For a time after the Convention he busied himself with political journalism, contributing regularly to the *Democratic State Journal* of Sacramento, a Broderick organ. But soon there entered into his orbit a new personality, who was to have a determining influence on his subsequent career. This was Byron Cole, a well-to-do, ambitious, and sophisticated young man, who had recently come to San Francisco from New England, and had bought control of a declining conservative newspaper, the *Commercial-Advertiser*, so as to have a vantage point from which to seek out greater opportunities. Cole, who had covered the Democratic Convention for his newspaper, saw in Walker's gift of leadership a magic ingredient which, in combination with his own connections, might achieve great things, and he invited Walker to return to San Francisco as editor of the *Commercial-Advertiser*. The post itself appealed to Walker less than other journalistic openings that were available to him, but Cole was able to add compelling inducements. From the first it was Manifest Destiny, rather than journalism, that linked the two men.

Cole's voyage to California had been by way of Nicaragua, and

93

what he saw there had convinced him that the country was ripe for American intervention. The alternative was sustained chaos. Civil war was almost continuous. The rapid alternation of dictatorship and revolt was like the pulse of a feverish patient, sick with despair. In a period of six years, fifteen presidents had held power, their capitals shifting between Granada in the south, where the aristocratic party known as the Legitimists had its base, and León in the north, the stronghold of the Democrats. The country was beautiful to look upon and rich in natural resources; it had valuable lumber—mahogany, cedar, Brazilwood—in inexhaustible quantities; it produced gold, silver, copper, lead, iron, sulphur; its plantations grew cacao, sugar, cotton, indigo, tobacco, maize, wheat, rice, and a hundred fruits, vegetables, and spices; cattle were abundant; but the people had been ravaged beyond endurance by poverty, war, and disease. Repeated conscription of males into the warring armies of the politicos was a major source of misery. Women outnumbered men three to two, in some villages five to one, while the population remained almost static, at some 250,000.

The current revolution was an attempt to oust from the Presidency Fruto Chamorro, the formidable leader of the Legitimists. Supported by wealthy rancheros and, behind the scenes, by the British government, Chamorro had forced his way to the Presidency in order to prevent the Democratic government from forming a new liberal federation with Honduras and San Salvador; and he had changed the Nicaraguan constitution to give himself dictatorial powers. The desperate Democrats, foreseeing their doom, had promptly set up a rebel government in León. Other Central American states, in which there was an almost identical division of parties, threw their influence into the struggle. Honduras, with a liberal administration friendly to the United States, supported the Democrats; while Costa Rica, where the British enjoyed great influence under a conservative government, gave active aid to Chamorro.

In the early months of 1854, the hopes of the Democrats had been lifted by a substantial military reinforcement from Honduras. But England's agents in Central America soon managed to reverse the trend. Their strategy was simple and effective. Guatemala, where there was a conservative regime, was encouraged to threaten neighboring Honduras with war, with the result that the Honduran government hastily withdrew its soldiers from Nicaragua in order to strengthen its own defenses. This was an almost mortal blow to the Nicaraguan Democrats. It appeared unlikely that they could long sustain themselves against the attack which the Legitimists could be counted on to launch as soon as their army was sufficiently strong.

The situation as outlined by Cole inflamed Walker's imagination, and revived in him the vision of the "column of Progress and Democracy" about which he had written in New Orleans. The United States and especially California, had a great stake in Nicaragua, with its overland Transit and its potentialities for a canal. If British domination of the isthmus was to be prevented, America could not afford to delay in asserting its democratic leadership. The indifference of President Pierce's administration to England's manipulation of the Central American governments was rapidly destroying the prestige of the United States among them. Neutrality Laws or no Neutrality Laws, the Democrats of Nicaragua deserved American support, and the United States could not afford to withhold it.

What if a band of privately organized American fighting men undertook the task? They might turn the tide of the Nicaraguan struggle, and compel action by Washington. An O'Higgins had rescued Chile from Spanish oppression; a Walker might save Nicaragua from native tyranny. Under friendly tutelage from the North, Nicaragua might set a shining example of economic creativity for the entire isthmus. She might even become the center of a Caribbean alliance with close ties with the United States.

The prospect, with its potentialities of glory and its idealistic aspect, was irresistibly attractive to Walker, as for more practical reasons it was to Byron Cole. If the Democratic effort failed, Cole was aware, the government of Honduras would almost certainly go down with it and be replaced by a pro-British regime. In that event American business interests in Honduras would be imperiled—and Cole was one of the owners of the Honduras Mining and Trading Company, which was about to exploit a large tract of mineral-bearing lands. He was eager for action to protect his interests, and no sooner had Walker accepted the proffered post on the *Commercial-Advertiser,* than the publisher embarked on a ship for Nicaragua, to explore the situation.

I I

It was autumn of 1854, and Cole had not yet returned, when Walker stood trial on charges of having violated the Neutrality Laws in his Sonoran enterprise. He came before the federal court as editor of a respectable newspaper and a figure of considerable prominence. Addressing the jury in his own behalf, he began with an appeal to their sense of fair play. The Neutrality Laws he believed to be injurious to the country, and probably unconstitutional, but if they were to be regarded as law, then the courts had an obligation to prosecute equally all who were believed to have violated them. Yet none of the Frenchmen who had gone to Mexico with Count Raousset-Boulbon had been brought to trial. Why should the government choose Americans for punishment? The point was particularly effective for the jury owing to the circumstance, perhaps prearranged, that some of the Frenchmen who had been associated with Raousset's ill-starred adventure were sitting in the courtroom, scot-free, as Walker spoke.

Primarily, however, Walker rested his belief that he was not guilty on the moral aspect of his case. The people of Sonora were notoriously oppressed by a corrupt government and were virtually without protection against the raids of the terrifying Apaches. When he had been at Guaymas, Mexicans as well as Americans, women as well as men had urged him to return. He had felt a call that transcended mere legalistic niceties. "It was then that I took my decision and made my plan, which, had it not been for the interference of the government, might have succeeded," he told the jury.

His failure he attributed to the federal authorities. When they prevented the sailing of the whole body of men who had volunteered to accompany him, when they deprived him of needful stores and field-pieces, all began to go awry. As a result, "I found myself at sea with only forty-five men, and with so few followers I was compelled to land in a sparsely settled region. Some sort of flag had to be raised to protect us." They had been able to sustain their long ordeal in Lower California and their nightmare marches across the mountains and desert only by the consciousness that "right and humanity" were on their side. "The Pilgrim fathers came to a savage land, rescued it from savages and made it an abode of civilization." Was there not always a moral sanction for men who sought to emulate them?

The federal prosecutor, District Attorney Inge, would have none of this. Scoffing at Walker's claim to a humane purpose, he said that regardless of whether he had intended to protect the Sonorans against Apaches or to loot the country, the expedition had violated the Neutrality Laws and Walker was guilty. The judge obviously shared this view of the case, for his summation of evidence and charge to the jury were distinctly unfavorable to Walker. The jury, however, consisted of men in whom the expansionist spirit of the age and the belief in America's Manifest Destiny were stronger than merely legal considerations. After only eight minutes of deliberation, they returned with a verdict of not guilty. Some of the San Francisco newspapers were concerned; Watkins, who was only an agent of Walker's, had been found guilty, while Walker himself was acquitted; was this justice? But the *Herald* replied that Watkins was Watkins, and Walker was Walker, and this seemed to be sufficient answer.

Walker's reputation, which five months earlier had been shattered by failure, now rose intact and brighter than ever. It was rumored that a new Walker expedition, its goal as yet unknown, was in the making, and men eager for adventure sought him out and offered their services in whatever project he might be planning.

III

By late October, Cole was back in San Francisco, bearing with him a signed letter from the Provisional Director of the Democratic rebel government, Francisco de Castellon. If Cole would bring three hundred men to Nicaragua to serve in the Democratic army, the letter said, they would receive regular pay and land grants after Castellon became head of the national government. To Cole's disappointment, Walker found the letter useless. To attempt to raise an expedition with no better legal ground than it contained would lay them open to immediate arrest for violation of the Neutrality Laws—and with little hope, this time, of escaping conviction. The need, he told Cole, was for a formal grant of a substantial tract of land in Nicaragua and for permission to colonize it—a contractual document which would say nothing of a military purpose. If Cole could obtain such a grant, "something might be done with it," Walker said. Even then, if the federal authorities insisted on probing beneath the surface of the contract, the expedition might not be allowed to sail.

Cole had begun to count heavily on Walker, and he was impelled to make another voyage to Nicaragua. By this time his connection with the *Commercial-Advertiser* had become so tenuous that he saw no purpose in maintaining his interest in the newspaper, and he sold it. Simultaneously, Walker resigned as editor and accepted a similar position in Sacramento, with the *State Democratic Journal*. He was still regarded as a promising political figure, for whom high public office in California was a distinct possibility. Two months passed. Then, early in 1855, Cole sent from Nicaragua a contract, signed by Castellon, and meeting Walker's specifications. This time his efforts bore fruit. On receipt of the contract, Walker at once gave up his post with the *State Democratic Journal* and returned to San Francisco to prepare for his next adventure. He had been given the key to political advancement, and he threw it away with a shrug, as a married man might throw away the key to a prostitute's room; he was in fact married to danger, and he regarded politics as prostitution.

The decisive question for him was whether, in view of President Pierce's recent proclamation against filibustering, Major General Wool would accept Castellon's colonization grant as sufficient justification for the sailing of an armed force from the port. The prospect was by no means hopeful. Wool had achieved much publicity by urging the prosecution of the French consul in San Francisco on the ground that he had aided the filibustering expedition of Raousset-Boulbon. Although a jury had failed to convict the consul, it seemed likely that the general's policy in respect to future expeditions would be stern. District Attorney Inge, still smarting from his defeat at Walker's hands in the trial resulting from the Sonora affair, was not likely to be cooperative. Nevertheless, having gone so far with Cole, Walker was obligated to try to convince Inge and Wool that the fighting men he planned to recruit would be no more than peaceful colonists on their way to a foreign land. Everything would depend on their willingness to let themselves be deceived.

IV

In the period when Walker was practicing law in Marysville, Commodore Vanderbilt had taken it into his head to go abroad; and the impulse that removed him from New York and from active supervision of his affairs introduced a radical change in the unfolding pattern of events, and gave a dramatic new turn to Walker's life story. The repercussions of Vanderbilt's decision were felt finally in the attitude of District Attorney Inge toward Walker's enterprise.

Between Vanderbilt and total success in life there stood, to his way of thought, only one obstacle—the social barrier. In spite of his great wealth, he and his family had not been able to escape the stigma of the *parvenu*, had never been able to penetrate the high society of the period. The invitations that they most desired were withheld from them, and they had to find their friends in families whose riches were as recent as their own. This was intolerable, and he conceived a plan for dealing with the problem. Believing that the surest key to the locked door of aristocracy is fame, and that the short cut to fame is publicity, he decided to generate such publicity as no mere millionaire before him had ever received. He would compel the bows of New Yorkers who professed to regard him as a vulgar money-man, by first compelling the respectful attention of the entire world.

For his instrument, he decided on a steam yacht, which was designed to his specifications in 1852. The *North Star,* 2500 tons, 270 feet long, cost him half a million dollars to build and half as much again to operate each year. Engineered to perfection, with an interior in which marble flooring, granite columns, rosewood paneling, and frescoed ceilings created the effect of a luxury hotel, it was by far the largest and most elaborate pleasure craft seen in American waters up to that time. Even before it was completed in 1853, Vanderbilt announced an intention that delighted New York's sensation-hungry newspapers. With his family and a few friends and retainers, he would take the *North Star* on a gala transatlantic voyage such as no American had ever previously undertaken. It was easy to envisage the stir his magnificent boat would make in the ports of England, France, Italy, Russia—tangible proofs for haughty European eyes of the potentialities of American enterprise. Everyone could imagine the brilliant receptions that would be given on board for the aristocracy of Europe, the enviable invitations received in return. Thereafter, the Commodore calculated, even the proudest New York homes would be open to the Vanderbilts—while the huge advertisement could hardly fail to benefit his business interests.

He had to consider, however, that the trip as planned would

consume the better part of half a year. What of the companies that he managed? On this score, as always, his decisions were bold, simple, and profitable. The subsequent deal, when its details became known, made other millionaires quiver with envy. By this time, Vanderbilt had got rid of those in Accessory Transit who were capable of offering resistance to his will, and a puppet board of directors obligingly met his terms. Almost overnight he sold to the company the ships of his Nicaragua Line for $1,500,000, resigned from the presidency, opened his own office as exclusive New York agent for the company, and took as his emolument no less than 20 per cent of the company's gross receipts—this for continuing to manage the ships—plus an agent's commission of 2½ per cent of all passenger fares.

At a later time, the arrangement was criticized as an outrage against business morality, but Vanderbilt calmly maintained that it was no more than his due as founder and moving spirit of the Transit. By this stroke he relieved himself of responsibility, added to his fortune and assured himself of an enormous income without giving up power. It was a neat, compact plan. He not only ate his cake and had it; he also sold it.

A problem remained—who could properly manage the affairs of Accessory Transit while he was abroad? Two strong and capable executives were needed—one in whose hands he could safely leave the New York headquarters, the other to look after the San Francisco end of the business. Searching his acquaintance, he turned to Charles Morgan, a prominent shipowner, almost as well-known as Vanderbilt himself, and whose Morgan Line dominated the traffic between New York and the ports of the Gulf of Mexico. When Morgan, in return for a share in the commissions earned by the New York agency, consented to serve as Vanderbilt's deputy, the Commodore was flattered. In addition, Morgan was able to settle the question of the California agency. He had formed a connection with a redoubtable man of business, Cornelius K. Garrison, who had made a fortune as a banker in Panama, and who was at that very time planning to establish a banking house in San Francisco. It was Morgan's suggestion that Garrison be invited to New York and induced to manage Accessory Transit's affairs on the West Coast. So it was arranged; Vanderbilt was impressed by Garrison; and a sufficient inducement was found for him in a contract at a salary of $60,000 per year, placing Garrison among the highest-paid men in the United States.

V

The cruise amply fulfilled Vanderbilt's hopes. While everything that Walker did was the wild gamble of a moneyless man, his only stake his life, Vanderbilt's least venture was expensively planned in detail. He did indeed experience one or two snubs from British aristocrats, but these were more than balanced in his eyes by a reception given in his honor by leading Americans in London. There he met many of the great political and social figures of England, and after that, the rest was easy. Admiring descriptions of his career and his yacht appeared in the British press and were circulated throughout the world. The London *Daily News* compared him favorably with Cosimo de Medici, and added, "It is time that *parvenu* should be looked upon as a word of honor. . . . It is time that the middle classes should take the place that is rightfully theirs in the world that they have made." In Paris, men of prominence respectfully approached Vanderbilt with business proposals; in Italy he sat for a portrait bust by America's most noted sculptor, Hiram Powers; in Russia the Czar himself took an interest in the *North Star* and gave Vanderbilt the use of one of the imperial carriages. From first to last, the cruise sparkled like the gem of self-assertion that it was. But it had its flaw. Letters from New York which came to Vanderbilt just before he sailed for home told of maneuvers by Morgan and Garrison to oust him permanently from control of Accessory Transit. Under Morgan's leadership, the company had canceled its contract with the Commodore's agency, on the ground that it had proved "impossible to obtain a statement of accounts" from Vanderbilt. There was even a suggestion that he had defrauded the company. A new agency, owned by Morgan, now handled all Transit business in New York, and took the commissions which the Commodore regarded as his own; while Garrison had allied the West Coast operation with Morgan.

In the last days of the voyage Vanderbilt burned with a desire for revenge. Knowing his temper, Wall Street held its breath as the *North Star* was reported steaming back to New York. When, in September, 1853, the *Herald* commented that "trouble is expected upon the return of Commodore Vanderbilt," the sophisticated chuckled at the dry understatement. A few days after his return, Vanderbilt addressed to Morgan and Garrison one of the shortest and most famous letters in the history of business. "Gentlemen," it said, "You have undertaken to cheat me. I won't sue you, for the law is too slow. I'll ruin you. Yours truly, Cornelius Vanderbilt."

To many, the threat, which was published, sounded like bombast. Morgan and Garrison were men of wealth, power, and driving energy comparable with Vanderbilt's own. Within six months of his arrival in San Francisco, Garrison had been elected Mayor of the city, while his administration of the company on the Pacific side was an unqualified success. Morgan had similarly proved an efficient manager of the business in New York. The service on the Nicaragua Line, everyone agreed, had never been so satisfactory, the profits of Accessory Transit had never been so high. The price of the shares had risen 50 per cent above what it had been at the time of Vanderbilt's retirement from the presidency, and the sentiment of the investment community was largely with Morgan.

The courts of New York soon swarmed with lawyers in *Vanderbilt vs. Accessory Transit Company, C. Morgan and C. K. Garrison.* So numerous were the charges and countercharges, so confused the records of account, so complex the issues uncovered, that the public soon came to agree with the *Herald*'s prediction that "no one would ever get at the bottom of this mysterious, mixed-up matter." Vanderbilt himself regarded the litigation merely as a harassing action against his enemies. It was on a direct, frontal attack that he was counting. Early in 1854, he organized a new line of steamships, which included the famous *North Star,* to carry passengers to San Francisco by way of Panama—the very route that he had formerly decried. His new service, called the Independent Line, was designed for one purpose only—to divert passengers from the Nicaragua Line—and it made much of the fact that the transisthmian railroad in Panama was almost completed. The Independent Line offered rates even lower than those which had marked Vanderbilt's earlier price war with George Law. For $100, plus the railroad fare, a man could travel "first class" all the way to California, while steerage cost no more than $30.

From the moment that the Independent Line's advertisements

appeared, saying flatly that "passengers will be guaranteed to arrive in San Francisco ahead of the Nicaragua Line," its ships were crowded. Whether it could make money with rates so low was debatable, but Vanderbilt knew more than one way to turn a dollar. Before Wall Street got wind of his scheme he sold short many thousands of shares of Accessory Transit stock. Never was a speculative profit more certain. The falling off of business on the Nicaragua Line was accompanied by a steady decline in the price of Accessory Transit shares on the exchange. To add to bearish sentiment, the New York press published reports of serious fighting in the latest of Nicaragua's long series of revolutions, further inclining passengers to look to Panama, and investors to sell their Accessory Transit shares. As a result Vanderbilt was able to buy in his "covering" shares at a substantial gain. Morgan and Garrison were his targets, but his hard thrusts at them were also damaging the Panama Line which Law had founded. Wall Street soon began to gossip that the Commodore had "done it again." All his enemies were in retreat.

Morgan and Garrison were particularly hard hit when, in the summer of 1854, the Accessory Transit Company, now their property, ran into trouble with obstructive British officials in the port of Greytown. In resentment, the company persuaded the American Navy to bombard the sleepy little town*, and the news caused a further diversion of the Caribbean passenger traffic to Panama.

The immediate beneficiary of the affair was Vanderbilt, for the price of Accessory Transit stock, already depressed, took a further drop. At this point, instead of selling, he began to buy the stock in large quantities. His purpose now was to regain control of the company; and Morgan and Garrison, alarmed, sought a compromise. Accessory Transit, they said, would pay Vanderbilt's claim for moneys due him under his agency contract, if he in return would sell his Independent Line to the company and agree to retire from isthmian shipping. "A settlement," reported the New York *Tribune,* "has been amicably arranged." "Amicably" was hardly the appropriate adverb. No victory that was less than complete could slake Vanderbilt's thirst for revenge. Morgan and Garrison still had the

---

* *Wheeler Scrapbooks,* Vol. II, p. 10, Congressional Library. W. O. Scroggs, *Filibusters and Financiers,* New York, 1916, Ch. 7.

Accessory Transit Company, which he had founded. Quietly he continued to accumulate the company's shares.

Mayor Garrison, still in charge of Accessory Transit's office on the West Coast, sensed that the Commodore would soon make another attempt to recapture the company. Garrison was a man of resource and daring, to whom defeat, especially public defeat, was as intolerable as it was to Vanderbilt. Like Vanderbilt, he had fought his way up in the world from lowly beginnings, and he too understood the techniques of power. San Francisco was under his thumb. He was the idol of the Vigilantes and the collaborator of Broderick, the state boss, in plucking the political plums of the time. Almost as much as he valued his $60,000 salary from Accessory Transit he valued his reputation as a consistent winner. His position was strong, for his contract with the company meant that Vanderbilt could not easily dispose of him; and through a San Francisco banking house in which he and Morgan were partners he had access to considerable financial resources. Given a weapon with which to fight, he could bring to bear enough money and influence to give pause even to Vanderbilt.

The hint that a weapon might be found came to Garrison late in 1854 from a Sacramento publisher who had a slight acquaintance with Walker. This man, Parker H. French, combined an almost total lack of scruple with a fertile imagination, enormous effrontery, and a persuasive tongue. He had learned of Walker's talks with Cole about Nicaragua; he knew of Garrison's struggle with Vanderbilt; and without Walker's knowledge, he appointed himself go-between.*

Garrison was interested, but he was too canny to act hastily or impulsively. He could not afford to have it said that he was in any way connected with a violation of the Neutrality Laws. If Walker could succeed in reaching Nicaragua and establishing himself there—in itself an unlikely assumption—that would be time enough to consider an approach to him. He dismissed French with a curt message. He wished "to have nothing to do with such enterprises as he supposed Walker to contemplate." Nevertheless, from this moment, he took a friendly if distant interest in Walker's plans; and his influence in San Francisco being what it was, the danger that District Attorney Inge would stop Walker from taking an expedition to Nicaragua became negligible.

---

* William Walker, *The War in Nicaragua*, Mobile, 1860, Ch. 5.

VI

An even more roundabout stream of circumstance, originating in Madrid, played on the mind of General Wool, who had the intention and the physical power at his command to prevent Walker from defying the Neutrality Laws. A few years earlier Spain had raised to aggravating heights Cuba's tariffs on American goods entering the port of Havana and had imposed onerous new rules on American shipping. At that time Cuba was America's third largest export market, taking large quantities of such products as flour, corn, pork, and dried fish; the drastic decline in exports, resulting from the new tariffs, was felt especially by Southern businessmen.

Secretary of War Jefferson Davis, who had inherited Calhoun's mantle as chief spokesman for the South, and who wanted to see Cuba annexed for political reasons, promptly demanded action against Spain, even at the price of war. He did not believe that, in the final test, England or France would stand by the Spaniards. Many influential Englishmen, in fact, were already reconciled to the annexation of Cuba by the United States. The London *Spectator,* speaking for a large segment of British opinion, had said openly that it would be "a fatal mistake" to pledge England "to uphold the perishing interests of Spain."

President Pierce, as was his habit, put the problem in the hands of his Secretary of State, William Marcy. A shrewd man, stronger and keener than Pierce, and allied to large business interests in New York, Marcy was noted for his frank defense of the spoils system which he had helped to introduce into American politics. For practical purposes, he and Davis ran the administration through a series of superficial compromises, while the fundamental cleavage between North and South grew steadily more dangerous.

The specific measure advocated by Davis with respect to Cuba was suspension of the Neutrality Laws. This move in his plan was to be followed by a new and this time powerful filibustering expedition, which, coinciding with a popular Cuban revolution, would drive out the Spaniards, without providing a pretext for British and French intervention. Thereafter a friendly Cuban regime would seek statehood in the Union. Davis' great fear was that, unless the island was quickly brought into the United States, Spain might abolish Negro slavery there—a development which could wipe out the political value of the acquisition for the South, and would intensify the agitation over slavery in the United States.

Marcy held back from the naked use of force, and urged that an attempt be made to purchase Cuba from Spain. The annexation would then appear to be a national, rather than a Southern solution of the problem. Reluctantly, Davis consented, stipulating only that the negotiation with Spain be entrusted to a Southerner. The assignment went to Senator Pierre Soulé of Louisiana, a Frenchman born, and a man of great personal charm, if otherwise unfitted for diplomacy. As minister to Madrid, he was instructed by Pierce and Marcy to offer Spain "a reasonable sum" for Cuba, up to $130,000,000. This much was known at the time; what was not discovered for another seventy-five years was that Soulé's orders contained also a secret clause, stating that if Spain proved unwilling to sell, "you will then direct your efforts to the next most desirable object, which is to detach that island from the Spanish dominion and from all dependence on any European power."*

VII

Soulé turned out to be a diplomatic disaster. Medieval notions of personal honor and a tendency to resort to arms at the least slight caused him to be regarded as the wild man of Madrid's diplomatic colony. Within a few months of his arrival in Madrid, he had seriously wounded the French ambassador in a duel, and had hopelessly antagonized Spain's Foreign Minister, Calderon, with whom he was supposed to negotiate. Under the circumstances, "to part with Cuba," Calderon told Spain, "would be to part with national honor." In Havana, Spanish authorities expressed Madrid's anger in action, by seizing an American ship, the *Black Warrior,* and confiscating its cargo, on the pretext that the vessel had violated technical regulations of the port.

A great diplomatic to-do followed. Marcy instructed Soulé to demand a $300,000 indemnity from Spain for the *Black Warrior,* but the fire-eating minister was not content to follow orders; he converted

---

* A. A. Ettinger, *The Mission to Spain of Pierre Soulé*, 1932, p. 412.

his note into an ultimatum, giving Spain forty-eight hours to comply. The effect was to revive the spirit of the Spanish government, which replied by sending 6000 soldiers to reinforce its garrison in Havana. By now most of the American press was demanding strong action by President Pierce—repeal of the Neutrality Laws, a blockade of Cuba, an invasion in force. "In the course of the thick-coming events Cuba is bound to be admitted to the Union," the *New York Times* told its readers. Southerners were so convinced that the Neutrality Laws would be suspended that General John Quitman of Mississippi openly began to organize a filibustering expedition of gigantic proportions. To add to American confidence, the Crimean War had begun; England and France were hotly engaged in Russia, and had veered away from support of Spain if it involved war with the United States. In Parliament the influential Richard Cobden made a stir when he plainly declared, "In the present state of feeling no great regret would be felt if the Americans were to get possession of Cuba."

In all the decades during which the eyes of America's leaders, from Jefferson on, had been fixed yearningly on "The Pearl of the Antilles," there had never before been so promising an opportunity for its annexation. That the moment was not seized was due to the peculiar political position in which President Pierce found himself. At the time of the *Black Warrior* crisis the Senate was being torn by strife over the Kansas-Nebraska bill,* and sectional animosities were inflamed to the kindling point. Pierce, who had to think about renomination by the Democratic Party in 1856, had chosen to conciliate Southern opinion by declining to take a firm stand against the dangerous measure, and in so doing had stirred up deep resentment in the North. Under the circumstances, if he had given way to the South on Cuba as well, he would have lost most of his Northern support in the next Democratic Convention.

At one point, in an effort to extricate himself from his dilemma, he tried to use Cuba as a bargaining point with Southern senators. Had they been content to see Kansas and Nebraska enter the Union as free states, under the terms of the Missouri Compromise, their reward might well have been the suspension of the Neutrality Laws

---

* Urged by Southerners, this bill left to the settlers of Kansas and Nebraska the decision as to whether slavery should be permitted in their territories. It was generally assumed that Kansas at least would become a slave state. The bill became law in the spring of 1854.

and the annexation of Cuba. They were, however, determined to have both the island and Kansas. This was their undoing, and Pierce's. The South's threat to secede from the Union, unless the rich lands of Kansas were opened to the slave trade and Southern domination, was met by firm determination on the part of most Northern senators not to move against Cuba.

While the debate raged, the opportunity passed. In May, 1854, Spain altered the entire complexion of the affair. Suddenly she announced that thenceforth the slave trade would be banned in Cuba, and hinted at eventual emancipation of the island's Negroes. No move could have been better calculated to harden the split in American opinion and paralyze the administration. Many in the North who had favored acquisition of Cuba so long as the move appeared to be directed against Spanish tyranny now became intensely aware of the moral problem involved, and took a fixed stand against any steps to annex the island.

Then, while Congress was trying to find its footing in the tangled affair, Havana announced that the *Black Warrior* and its cargo had been released. This done, the United States had no choice but to regard the incident as closed. The danger of war, President Pierce told Congress, had passed, and he warned that violations of the Neutrality Laws would be severely punished. At Marcy's orders, General Quitman was arrested and compelled to give bond to assure his compliance with the law.

The relation of the Cuban affair to the Kansas-Nebraska bill was well understood by the press. On June 1, immediately after the passage of the bill, the conservative Northern view of the matter was expressed by New York's *Courier and Enquirer*. "There was a time when the North would have consented to annex Cuba, but the Nebraska wrong has forever rendered annexation impossible." Marcy himself privately wrote, "The Nebraska question has sadly shattered our party in all the free states and deprived it of that strength which was needed and would have been much more profitably used in the acquisition of Cuba."

Walker, then editing the *Democratic State Journal* in Sacramento, also felt impelled to declare himself on the issue. In a revealing editorial he wrote, "Events are justifying the foresight of the Southern men who opposed the Kansas-Nebraska bill. The South . . . has lost instead of gaining by the act. . . . A few hot-headed and narrow-minded men have persuaded the South into a course she already begins to repent of. . . . It is now too late to repent. . . . Ultra-slavery men are the most active and efficient agents abolitionists can have in the Southern States. The true friends of the South are those who repudiate the ideas and acts of the South Carolina school."* At this stage, his views on slavery were identical with those which he had expressed while editing the New Orleans *Crescent* five years earlier— against its expansion and against secession.

VIII

President Pierce's political position was becoming hopeless, and the real party leaders, Marcy and Jefferson Davis, lost no time in seeking to assert their influence over the Presidential election to come in 1856. Both men recognized that James Buchanan was a strong candidate. As Secretary of State under Polk, he had cautiously avoided serious offense to cither Northern or Southern prejudices. Where slavery was concerned he professed to be neutral. Even if he was not a strong swimmer in the political currents of the time, he could tread water with the best.

Buchanan's fitness for the Presidency, as Davis saw it, would be determined largely by his willingness to declare himself favorable to the Southern aspiration for Cuba and Kansas. Marcy's position was less definite. He himself had a hankering for the Presidency. Nevertheless his interest as a leader of the Northern wing of the party and as its chief dispenser of patronage required a Democratic victory in 1856, no matter who the candidate. The first need was to make Davis feel that either Buchanan or himself, Marcy, might be acceptable to the South, in terms of Cuban policy. This seems to have been the main motive behind the extraordinary developments that followed.

The three chief American envoys in Europe, Buchanan, Soulé, and the minister to France, John Mason, were instructed by Marcy to meet on the continent and come to a joint recommendation for the administration's policy with respect to Cuba. The meeting took place in October, 1854, at Ostend, Belgium. Out of it came the notorious document known as the Ostend Manifesto. If Spain re-

* *Democratic State Journal,* Sacramento, Cal., Aug. 12, 1854.

fused to sell Cuba, said the Manifesto, and if the island in her hands constituted a threat to the United States, "then, by every law, human and divine, we shall be justified in wresting it from Spain if we possess the power."

Although the Manifesto was supposed to be secret, its contents became known to European journalists even before the official version reached Marcy in Washington. England's newspapers professed to be outraged by the flagrant immorality of the document. The London *Times* said that if the policy expressed in the Manifesto were seriously entertained by the American government, it would justify a declaration of war. America's antislavery press was equally loud in denunciation. The New York *Post* called the Manifesto "atrocious!" Horace Greeley's phrase for it in the influential *Tribune* was "a Manifesto of brigands," and he demanded its repudiation by Pierce.

The violence of the adverse Northern reaction shocked Marcy, and in self-protection he bluntly renounced the Manifesto that he himself had invited. Its first effect, however, was to revive the attack of Jefferson Davis and others on the Neutrality Laws. Although he had been thwarted on the Cuban issue, Davis now developed a strong interest in the possibility that one or more filibustering expeditions might head for Nicaragua. He saw that if a private military force should succeed in Nicaragua, the entire position of the United States in the Caribbean might be altered. The Neutrality Laws might be swept into the discard, and the government compelled after all to seize Cuba and fight Spain. As Secretary of War, Davis was officially committed to rigorous enforcement of the Neutrality Laws, but as a practical politician he knew how large the gap is between the avowal of a law and its implementation. To that gap he now directed his efforts. Rumors of a possible expedition from California to Nicaragua were already current. A remarkable letter from Davis to General Wool in San Francisco now made clear his wish that the general temper zeal with discretion where the Neutrality Laws were concerned.

"Doubtful questions," wrote Davis, "may arise in regard to the powers vested in the President to enforce our neutrality laws, and the extent to which he may devolve authority for that purpose upon military officers. These laws have not yet received at all points a full judicial consideration. It is understood from the language of the Supreme Court that the President may authorize a general in command to use his command directly against the violators of these laws, and without the interposition of the civil authorities. But the court were also of the opinion that this 'high and delicate power' ought only be exercised when 'by the ordinary process of exercise of civil authority, the purpose of the law cannot be effectuated,' and when military or naval force is necessary to ensure the execution of the laws."*

This letter was understood by Wool as implying that he was to invoke the Neutrality Laws against filibusters only if the civil authorities requested his intervention. Consequently, when Walker approached Wool early in 1855 to ascertain his views on the expedition, the general was suddenly all affability. He declared frankly that the instructions of the Secretary of War left him no authority to interfere unless San Francisco's District Attorney requested him to do so. Privately the old soldier went even further, grasping Walker by the hand, and saying, "Not only will I not place any hindrance in your way, but I wish you the greatest success!"

The civil power of the city, with Mayor Garrison setting its tone, was equally obliging. District Attorney Inge, after inspecting Walker's contract with Castellon, made no effort to probe beneath its surface. The contract in itself contained no violation of law, and he saw no reason to invoke interference by the Army with Walker's movements.

The train of great events that Commodore Vanderbilt had set in motion five years earlier, when he sought to construct a canal in Nicaragua, had at last intersected Walker's curious orbit. Through the instrumentality of Jefferson Davis and General Wool, through Cornelius Garrison and District Attorney Inge, he was being given a chance to make history.

---

* House Exec. Doc., 88, 35th Cong., 1 Sess., pp. 98-100.

PART TWO

The Shape of Destiny

《《 》》

"We have again and again called Walker a hero.
... We are obliged to recognize a persistence, an endurance,
a resolute heroism which merit a higher place in human
esteem that can be ceded to all the knights errant of history
and Faërydom. . . . The difference is that ours is a nineteenth century hero. . . . Who knows how soon he may
replace the laurel of the hero with the diadem of a king?"

Harper's Weekly, JANUARY 31, 1857

X

"THE IMMORTALS"

The failure of Walker's Sonora expedition notwithstanding, hundreds of the adventurers and soldiers of fortune in whom San Francisco abounded, as well as its derelicts, offered themselves for his service. From among them he chose with a shrewd eye for courage and endurance. His enthusiasm and conviction about his new venture were infectious. He had been studying a detailed description of Nicaragua's history, geography, and people, by the former American minister, George E. Squier, and it significantly aided recruitment. In addition to arresting facts, the book was full of charming little vignettes of Nicaraguan life. Squier had been especially susceptible to the charm of the lissome, glossy-haired native girls, "of all shades from white to ebon black, straight as arrows, lithe yet full-figured, with quick, mischievous eyes"—flirtatious, full of animal spirits, and dressed in vividly colored skirts and scanty blouses that often revealed as much as they concealed when the girls raised their arms to balance red water jars or baskets of fruit on their heads. One passage in his book was picked up by the newspapers—a scene in which Nicaraguan soldiers, seeing some girls swimming nude in a river, sought to scare them to the beach by shouting, *"Lagartos! Lagartos!"* ("Alligators!"). Another anecdote described the negotiation of an infatuated young Bostonian with a village priest for the hand of his "niece"— all unaware that it was customary to find in the household of many a *padre* a young and pretty girl designated as the *sobrina*—a niece only by courtesy. A little sketch by Squier of a bare-bosomed beauty rolling tortillas similarly attracted attention by its frankness. In woman-starved California, the sexual possibilities of Nicaragua must have excited almost as much masculine interest as the prospect of winning rich lands in Walker's service. Squier pointed out that the owners of the great Nicaraguan plantations, drawing princely incomes from the land, lived a life of feudal satisfactions such as could not be found in the United States. An aristocrat with a hundred thousand cacao trees or so might obtain from this crop alone some $30,000 per year, free of all taxes; master of his workmen, he would be impeded only by his own conscience in his access to their women folk.

To those who, like Walker, needed an idealistic purpose in any adventure, he was able to speak of the benefits that Nicaraguans themselves would gain from peace, democracy, and American civilization. A number of the men who joined him brought exceptional experience and abilities to the expedition. One was a physician, Dr. Alexander Jones, who had already tasted high adventure in a hunt for buried treasure in the Indian Ocean, and who yearned for further action in a world of danger. Another was Achilles Kewen, who had fought alongside General Narciso Lopez in his attempt to liberate Cuba, and whose brother Edward was prominent in California politics. Colonel C. C. Hornsby had served with distinction in the Mexican War, and had visited Nicaragua; he too threw in his lot with Walker. So did Major Frank Anderson, another noted veteran of the Mexican War, and Timothy Crocker who, as Walker's aide, had undergone the miseries of the campaign in Lower California, and was nevertheless still loyal to him. A high proportion of the other recruits were miners and prospectors who had been disappointed in the gold fields, and were ready to try their luck elsewhere.

The limiting factor in Walker's effort to prepare his expedition was money. His own meager resources were soon exhausted. Influential friends did their best for him, among them Edmund Randolph, now married and a pillar of San Francisco society. Another favorable voice was raised for Walker by California's favorite son, Colonel John C. Frémont, who, running against Buchanan in 1856, would be the first Republican candidate for the Presidency of the United States. But the funds at Walker's disposal fell far short of his need. A ship had to be chartered; arms, equipment, and food had to be bought. Each additional recruit increased the cost of the expedition—which, it was plain from the first, would have to travel on a shoestring. He was hampered, too, in raising money by the wound in his foot sustained in his latest duel, and which resulted in a painful if temporary limp. When all was done, Walker was unable to pay for many of his purchases; he could afford no better boat than an unseaworthy old brig named *Vesta*; he had no money with which to hire a crew; the only captain available to him was a drunken ne'er-do-well; and he could put aboard only fifty-eight men. It was these men who, a few months later, were celebrated by the entire press of the nation as "The Immortals."

II

The element of the absurd which was so often present in Walker's undertakings, and which generally arose from his refusal to admit the hopelessness of the odds against him, materialized on the *Vesta* just before it was due to weigh anchor. A revenue cutter, the *Marcy*, came alongside, and San Francisco's sheriff, with a party of deputies, boarded the *Vesta* and ordered it attached for debt. A storekeeper who had extended credit to Walker had changed his mind, and was demanding immediate payment. Until it was forthcoming, the brig might not leave port. To make certain of Walker's compliance, the sheriff seized the *Vesta*'s sails and carried them onto the dock.

One of the newspaper accounts of the incident stated that Walker showed "profound anger"—a display of emotion unusual for him. He suspected that the development was a stratagem of District Attorney Inge, who, while unwilling to block the expedition openly and thus incur the displeasure of Mayor Garrison, might well have resorted to a legalistic trick to express his enmity. Walker acted, however, with restraint and prudence. Cautioning his restive men not to interfere with the sheriff, he limped ashore, sought out the trouble-making storekeeper, and quietly pointed out the hazards that would be run by the man whom his recruits might hold responsible for the failure of the expedition to sail. It was a cogent argument, and the creditor hastily agreed to lift the libel on the ship.

But Walker's problem was far from solved. A more serious threat awaited him on the *Vesta*. The sheriff, in his absence, had prepared a bill of costs for his own part in attaching the brig, and wanted three hundred dollars before he would release it—a sum so far out of Walker's reach as to imply the end of the expedition. At this moment, only one thing was clear to him. The *Vesta* had to sail, and soon. Many of his men, irked by the delay, were becoming unruly and dangerous. Another day's idleness could mean violence, the disintegration of his force, and an end to all his hopes. The sarcasms of the newspapers, too, as they reported his plight, had to be cut short before they weakened the chances of raising future reinforcements.

"It is almost night," he said quietly to the sheriff. "I shall not be able to get the money until morning."

Pleased that Walker had not questioned his exorbitant demand, the sheriff said that he would wait.

"However," Walker went on, "you will not be paid unless the sails are brought back on board immediately. Legally, you had no right to remove them. If necessary, I shall ask the court for a ruling."

The sheriff, uncertain of his legal position, and with his mind fixed on the three hundred dollars, was not disposed to argue the point. The return of the sails seemed to him to involve no risk. Not knowing that the creditor's libel on the ship had already been lifted, he thought that the cutter *Marcy,* still alongside, would continue to guard the brig; and it did not seem likely that the *Vesta* would sail without a crew. He assented to Walker's request. A deputy, he said, would spend the night on the brig, and he himself would be around to collect the money in the morning.

With the sails once more on board and the sheriff gone, Walker courteously invited the deputy, one Purdy, to join him in a drink. Together they went to his cabin. Once inside, Walker fixed Purdy with a cold grey eye. "The *Vesta* is going to sail, Mr. Purdy," he remarked in the low-pitched drawl that, in him, always signified high tension. As the deputy gaped at him, he pointed to a table. "There, sir," he said, "are champagne and cigars." From his pocket he drew a pair of handcuffs which he placed alongside the bottle. "And there are handcuffs and irons. Pray take your choice."*

Purdy, who had been a member of the California legislature, was inclined to be philosophical; and he settled down in a chair with the bottle. Excusing himself, Walker locked the cabin door behind him and went aboard the *Marcy* to show its commander proof that the ship had been cleared to leave port. This done, and finding the officer friendly, he asked a favor of him. Would the *Marcy's* crew help in bending on the *Vesta's* sails—a task for which Walker's own men were untrained? Sailors from the *Marcy* came over the brig's side, and by midnight the work was completed.

As soon as the *Marcy* had gone, Walker signaled the shore. A steam tug for which he had previously arranged came alongside, took the *Vesta* in tow, and brought it to a point well outside the harbor. Just before the tug cast off, deputy Purdy was put aboard her, to raucous cheering from Walker's recruits. Then, spreading her sails, the *Vesta* stood out to sea.

III

Six weeks later (the *Vesta* had sailed a slow, stormy, and erratic course) Walker landed at Realejo, the northernmost port of Nicaragua, close to the revolutionary capital of León. The wild and piratical look of the bearded Americans did not prevent heartening displays of friendliness by the people who lined the streets of the shabby little town. Men cheered, women waved, everyone smiled at the newcomers who were to help the Democrats of the north against their enemies, the Legitimists. A formal welcome from an officer of the Leónese army was followed by the appearance of a gentleman of British birth, Charles Doubleday, who knew Nicaragua well and who offered his services to Walker—a valuable acquisition. Doubleday, who served thereafter as an officer in Walker's army and wrote a book about his experiences, described the impression that the American made on him: "He exercised a magnetic attraction . . . such as is rarely witnessed." Testimony to the same effect came from Joaquin Miller, who in one of his poems spoke of Walker as having "a piercing eye, a princely air, a presence like a chevalier." His

* *Harper's Weekly*, 1857, Vol. I, p. 332. New York *Herald*, June 2, 1855.

appeal for them was obviously much more than a matter of eyes and bearing. Their response and that of many another to Walker was of the kind that idealism alone is able to evoke in educated and sensitive men. Regarding himself as an apostle of American democracy and with unshakable faith in the justice of his cause, Walker radiated the intense glow of the true believer. There was already in him that touch of fanaticism, later to become more apparent, which all men respect as a source of power, and which, in so soft-spoken and courteous a personality, was all the more effective.

IV

From the first, Walker felt the fascination of the unique Nicaraguan landscape. He had read of the great green plain bordered in the far distance by low emerald hills and a belt of black towering volcanoes, by great blue lakes and a vast rain forest, but everything exceeded his expectation. The brilliant contrasts of raw color under the blazing sun and the dreamlike splendor of the soft tropic night generated in him a sensuous excitement that he never lost. "You felt," he wrote, "as if a thin and vapory exhalation of opium, soothing and exhilarating by turns, was being mixed at intervals with the common elements of the atmosphere." He was as infatuated with the country as if it had been a woman. There was languid music even in the names of the towns, which ran from north to south, on or close to the Pacific coast: Realejo, Chinandega, Corinto, León, Managua, Masaya, Granada, Rivas, San Juan del Sur. But his enthusiasm was held within himself. Outwardly he remained altogether the military man —crisp, definite, authoritative. His first order was a warning to his men of stern punishment if they disturbed the peace of Realejo. It is some measure of the respect in which he was held that those hard-bitten adventurers, who had been confined to a wretched little vessel for six weeks, and who were now quartered on the town, contented themselves with some drinking of *aguardiente* and a little singing in the taverns (which also served as brothels) and refrained from looting, rape, and street brawls.

The day after his arrival, Walker rode to León for his first interview with the Provisional Director of the revolutionary regime, Castellon. The first summer rains had come, and everything that grew was green. He had the sense of traveling in an ocean of verdure, through avenues of huge tropical trees meeting overhead, past high hedges of red-flowered cactus, and sudden clumps of coconut palm, mango, and banana trees. All around him the rich fields bespoke fertility, and mules laden with produce and browsing herds of cattle added to the picture of a bountiful land. On this ride Walker may have glimpsed the ageless and serene Indian villages where, among the thatch-roofed huts and green-fruited calabash trees, broad-hipped women, naked to the waist, smoked their *cigarros* as they went about their chores; where small boys ran naked except for straw hats and little cigars, and where only a dozing policeman, wearing a sword and with an old blunderbuss at his side, suggested the high civilizing influence of government.

León, a city one-third the size of San Francisco in 1855, was an impressive contrast to that wild boom town. Dignity and tradition were the essence of the Democratic capital. At the center of each municipal district was a church and a plaza, the core of community life and of the markets, while at the city's heart was a venerable cathedral, facing the grand plaza and the government buildings. As he passed the cathedral, Walker noted that its stone walls were heavily scarred with bullet pocks, marks of past revolutions in which the great building had been used as a fortress. A few days later, he would meet the dominant personality of León, the purple-robed Bishop, a man of exceptional intellect and experience, who was well disposed to Walker from the beginning. One of the Bishop's favorite remarks was, "Nicaragua needs only the aid of the United States to become an Eden of beauty and the garden of the world."

V

Walker could hardly have come at a more fortunate moment for his purposes. The hopes of the Democrats were waning fast. A strong Legitimist army under the most famous of Nicaraguan commanders, General Ponciano Corral, was preparing to march on León from the south. Castellon, grey and anxious, received the American as a drowning man clutches at a log. Through his embraces and compliments Walker perceived a faltering spirit and incipient despair, and he came at once to the conclusion that Castellon "was not the man to control a revolutionary movement or to conduct it to a successful issue." On the surface, however, they established an amicable understanding. Castellon proposed and Walker agreed that the Americans would be constituted a separate corps—*La Falange Americana*—the American Phalanx. To Walker's request that he be given an additional two hundred Nicaraguan soldiers there was no demur. His next and crucial demand, however, produced an immediate crisis. This was for authority to sail south in the *Vesta* and occupy the Transit route. As he himself later wrote in *The War in Nicaragua,* "It was a fixed policy with Walker to get as near the Transit as possible, in order to recruit from the passengers . . . and to have the means of rapid communication with the United States. . . . It was idle for them [the *Falange*] to waste their energies and strength on a campaign that did not bring them toward the Transit road."

It was not Castellon, but his military commander, General Muñoz, who objected. Muñoz was a tall, handsome, and haughty egotist, by no means incapable, but exceedingly jealous of his prerogatives. Resplendent in a blue uniform with red lining and much gilt, he eyed Walker's drab clothing and slight figure with unconcealed disdain. The *Falange*, he insisted, should remain in the vicinity of León to defend the capital against probable attack. Walker replied quietly that it would be unwise to submit his men to the corrosive temptations of garrison life. "Nothing so much tries the firmness of men like those in the *Falange* as inaction." They had to an extreme degree, he said, "the characteristic American thirst for action and movement."

An argument took shape. Muñoz' strategy was based on the traditional concept of war in Central America, in which victory went to the side that successfully stormed the enemy's capital. Usually the hard fighting took place at the very center of a besieged city, its grand plaza and cathedral. The defenders would sacrifice the countryside and outlying sections of the city in order to entice the enemy into its heart, where fortification and supply gave an advantage to the besieged. A decade earlier a Legitimist army, having failed to capture León, had sacked and burned a thousand dwellings on the outskirts—an atrocity the memory of which still inflamed the passions of the Leónese. Nevertheless, Muñoz saw no alternative but to prepare for another such campaign.

Walker barely concealed his impatience. The strategy of siege made for long, inconclusive, and highly destructive fighting, and was altogether at odds with his temperament. Swift attack, the seizure of lines of communication, the shattering of enemy morale, and the rout of his army were the essence of military success, his reading had taught him. The Americans had not come to Nicaragua to be cornered in a city. The victory could not be won by waiting for the enemy to come north. The Democratic army had to take the initiative, and he and his men were prepared to be the spearhead of the attack.

This line of reasoning left Muñoz cold. "I must first consider the safety of the capital," he said. "That is my responsibility."

"And my responsibility," said Walker, "is to maintain the fighting power of my men and win the war."

The Nicaraguan drew himself up. "It should be understood," he snapped, "that the decision lies with the Commander in Chief— subject, of course, to the wishes of the Provisional Director."

There was a moment's silence; then Walker turned to Major Kewen, who stood next to him. "Mr. Kewen," he said, "will you show the general, on this map, the plan of campaign that we have discussed?" Muñoz tried to brush Kewen aside, but the diversion served Walker's purpose; he was able to take Castellon slightly apart from the others and say to him in a low voice, "Let me speak frankly. If General Muñoz is to give me orders, I cannot serve you."

"But," Castellon protested, "he is the commanding general."

"Perhaps that explains the perilous position of your government," said Walker.

The merits of the case aside—and there was much to be said for Walker's stand—the urge to rebel against constituted authority was growing stronger in him. No man had ever commanded him. He had sprung directly to his colonelcy from the freedom of civilian life, without ever having served in an army. An order from another was a sting, arousing all his combativeness. His challenges were invariably aimed at the men who issued orders, men more powerful than himself. It had been Judge Parsons; now it was Muñoz; soon it would be Vanderbilt. It had once been his father.

One senses that power for Walker was more than a psychological, it had become a biological need. Like other ascetic romantics of exceptional energy, ability, and idealism—John Knox, Savonarola, Robespierre—men who cut themselves off from sexual womanhood and rejected possession of things—Walker had left himself only one direction in which to discharge his masculine potential—domination. The democratic cause was still his purpose and his justification, but the burning pressure within him was to rule. Although he had been in León only a day, already he had generated controversy. But his calculation was sound. Castellon did not dare risk the withdrawal of the Americans. Reluctantly, apologetically, the Provisional Director turned to Muñoz and said, "General, I think we should give Colonel Walker the opportunity he asks."

"As you wish," said Muñoz icily, and making a formal bow to Walker, left the room.

VI

A man who had made as many enemies as Walker could not be unduly disturbed at making another, but from this moment he sensed that Muñoz' influence would be used to destroy him, and he was right. Instead of the two hundred Nicaraguans promised him, he received, after a long interval, only half that number. Supplies needed at Realejo were so slow in arriving as seriously to delay the departure of the *Vesta*. By the time Walker landed his force near the Pacific end of the Transit road, valuable days had been lost, and he soon had reason to believe that advance word of his plan had gone to the enemy through an agent employed by Muñoz.

His first objective was the inland town of Rivas, a Legitimist base near Lake Nicaragua which had to be taken before the Transit could be held. Simple caution dictated that a surprise attack be made at night, but his native guides proved untrustworthy and the crucial hours of darkness were lost in following a circuitous route through the rain forest. A heavy downpour, with continuous flashes of lightning overhead and treacherous mud underfoot, further impeded the march. When the rain ended, and the moon could be glimpsed through the thick foliage, the spectral effect of the black gigantic tree trunks, the heavy branches, the creepers and vines, and a sense of the wild animal life around them made some of the men uneasy; and they began to sing, low-voiced, the favorite tunes of California: "Oh, Susanna" and "Hail, Columbia!" Walker always enjoyed the singing of his troops. Few as the men were, they made a formidable showing. "The felt hats of the *Falange*," he observed, "showed, in their drooping brims, the effect of the night's rain, and thick heavy beards gave to most of the body a wild and dangerous air." Wearing dark trousers and shirts, booted, carrying pistols and Bowie knives in addition to rifles, the Americans formed a sharp contrast to the barefooted Nicaraguans, who wore straw hats and once-white cotton pantaloons, and were armed with old-fashioned muskets and machetes. Their common purpose showed on their hats, where red ribbons signified their Democratic allegiance.

As a result of the delay, the *Falange* was compelled to advance on Rivas in broad daylight. Walker's own description of the march strikes an almost lyrical note. "Every now and then market-women, with baskets on their heads, and just come from Rivas, would gayly greet the soldiers. . . . Such of the men as spoke any Spanish would waste all the terms of endearment they could muster on the girls, who seemed pleased. . . . When, however, the command reached the summit of a hill . . . a scene of beauty and splendor drew them from everything else. Though the order was to march in silence an exclamation of surprise and pleasure escaped the lips of all. . . . The lake of Nicaragua lay in full view and rising from it, as Venus from the sea, was the tall and graceful cone of Omotepe. The dark forests of the tropics clothed the side of the volcano. . . . The beholder would not have been surprised to see it waken at any time. The first glimpse of the scene made the pulse stand still; and the *Falange* had scarcely recovered from its effects when the command was halted in order to prepare for the attack."

At noon on June 29, 1855, as the *Falange* advanced on Rivas for its first battle, it became evident to Walker that he had been betrayed. The enemy force awaiting him behind barricades was far larger than he had been given reason to expect, and it was under the command of a notorious Honduran general, Santos Guardiola, who had come to Nicaragua to aid the Legitimists. Guardiola was known—with reason—to all Central America as "The Butcher," and the terror of his name was enough to weaken the morale of Walker's Nicaraguan troops. At the first fire they fled without making even the pretense of a stand, leaving 55 Americans opposed to over 500 of the enemy.

In the first few minutes of fighting six of Walker's men were killed

—among them two of his chief aides, Crocker and Kewen. Hard-pressed, the *Falange* fought its way to a large house and held off the enemy by accurate rifle fire from the windows. The men's fighting spirit was heightened by rage, for they saw five of their wounded comrades, unable to reach the house, done to death on the streets by sadistic bayonets. After four hours of sporadic shooting, the enemy losses exceeded those of the *Falange* ten to one. Now, how-ever, the Legitimists received reinforcements, including a cannon, and with this advantage were able to approach the improvised fort-ress and set it on fire.

The last hope of the Americans who were still on their feet was to break through the enemy lines, and at Walker's signal, with a wild yell, they charged out of the house by an unguarded door. The move-ment was so unexpected and their marksmanship so effective that the nearest of the Legitimist troops turned and fled, while the rest were momentarily paralyzed. Retreating through the streets of Rivas, beating back their pursuers with deadly bullets, the Americans were able to make their way into the forest and at last back to the coast. A few hours later, weary and disheartened, they were again on the *Vesta*, sailing north.

Curiously, the defeat at Rivas did not diminish, but rather rein-forced, Walker's sense of destiny. Like many a soldier who comes unscathed from a stricken field, he may have gained a kind of strength from the simple fact that he was alive when so many were dead. It has often been noted that repeated survival of great dangers breeds a sense of invulnerability, a secret feeling that one is favored by the gods. After the battle his men saw in him, to their amazement, not chagrin and worry, but a confidence and assurance that sprang wholly from within him, for there was certainly nothing in their circumstances to warrant it. He spent the days of the voyage back to Realejo tending their wounds, seeing that they rested, reviving their morale, and drafting a report for Castellon.

The primary purpose of the report, which he sent by messenger from Realejo, was to break the hold of General Muñoz on the Demo-cratic army. The general, it said bluntly, had acted in bad faith; and he, Walker, would leave Nicaragua with his men at once unless Cas-tellon investigated the sources of the apparent treason which had led to the defeat at Rivas. The response was much as Walker anticipated.

Castellon, although unwilling to challenge Muñoz, begged Walker not to leave, but to bring his force to León, where fears of a Legitimist attack were thickening.

In the two weeks of fruitless correspondence that followed, Walker gave the appearance of sulking in his tent, but as soon as his men were fit to march he appeared to yield to Castellon's entreaties, and headed for León and a showdown with Muñoz. Fresh encouragement had come to him in the arrival of Byron Cole, who had just returned from Honduras, and who brought with him another valuable man. This was Bruno von Natzmer, a former Prussian cavalry officer, who knew Nicaragua as well as any foreigner. Their presence made Walker feel a little less the loss of Crocker and Kewen. Natzmer confirmed a point of considerable military importance that had begun to come home to Walker. The ordinary Nicaraguan, though he feared the North Americans, feared even more being conscripted into the armies of his own country, and would take far greater risks to escape the recruiting sergeant than he would ever run in battle. "There is scarcely any labor a Nicaraguan will not do," noted Walker, "in order to keep out of the clutches of the press-gang." He laughed at the Nicaraguan generals for their "inveterate habit of catching a man and tying him up with a musket in his hand to make a soldier of him." The only natives that he cared to have in his army, from this time on, were volunteers.

VII

Walker was beginning to sense the mercurial and wide-ranging temperament of the Central American, with his insistence on *dignidad* and his love of the flamboyant, with his religiosity and his superstition, with his hot courage and, in many instances, his cold treachery. Especially there was no mistaking the hostility that lay just beneath the surface of the Nicaraguan's formal courtesy to the *gringo*. It expressed itself in many ways, from the studied indifference of Nicaraguan aristocrats to the suppressed mockery of a guide, when, as Walker's men came through a forest, they were showered with excrement by a band of chattering monkeys. The monkeys, said the guide with a straight face, for some strange reason performed that trick only on North Americans.

Walker was not unduly surprised, on returning to León, to find that although Castellon's professions of friendship were unabated, he was willing to deliver the *Falange* to the mercies of Muñoz. The general had put forward a new proposal—let the American force be broken into small units and distributed among the Nicaraguan regiments. As soon as Walker became convinced that Castellon was about to support Muñoz on the issue, he decided to take his men out of León to a safer spot. But horses and oxcarts were needed, and when he sent a requisition for them to Castellon, it was ignored. An hour later Muñoz marched a strong Nicaraguan force into quarters directly opposite those of the Americans, as if daring them to attempt a move; and for a time it appeared that the *Falange* would have to fight its way out of León.

Walker then wrote an ultimatum to Castellon: "Remove your troops within an hour or we will consider them a hostile force and act accordingly." The threat succeeded. Rather than face the prospect of battle within his own ranks, Castellon agreed to exert his authority over Muñoz. The Nicaraguan troops were ordered away from the danger spot, horses and oxcarts were provided, and the Americans were allowed to leave the city.

There remained Muñoz to be dealt with. The plan in Walker's mind was open defiance of the general—in effect, a mutiny within the revolutionary army—supported by the populace of the countryside, where Muñoz, as a ruthless conscriptor of men, was highly unpopular. Chance, however, made this drastic action unnecessary. A small Legitimist force appeared south of León, and Muñoz, leading his troops in a raid against it, was mortally wounded. His death freed Walker to develop his own strategy.

He had selected the city of Chinandega, not far from León, as his headquarters, while he prepared his next move, for the Chinandegans were known to be dissatisfied with the do-nothing policies of Castellon. The people were hospitable enough, but the morale of his own men caused him serious concern. In their view, the expedition had come to a dead end. Supplies of cartridge metal were so low that they were compelled to range the countryside for objects made of lead—a futile search, which they could not even enliven by loot or women without incurring severe punishment. Their interest in Walker's purpose was fading fast. What they wanted was to enjoy such Lotus pleasures as the country afforded—to sprawl in the green tropic shade, pluck fruit from the trees, dally with the Indian girls who preened themselves under their hard masculine stares. Chinandega was one of the many Nicaraguan towns where the dearth of males made women exceptionally responsive. In such an atmosphere Walker's insistence on frequent drill, long hours of duty, and high standards of personal behavior provoked bitter feeling. Two of his men deserted.

Spirits began to revive, however, when a contest between Walker and an English merchant in Chinandega solved the ammunition problem. This gentleman, Thomas Manning, had been a former British consul; and he bore himself so proudly and at the same time was so shrewd a man of business that no Nicaraguan dared oppose him. He professed to regard Walker and his enterprise with contempt. When it was learned that he and he alone in the area owned enough lead to provide a fresh supply of bullets for Walker's men, and an officer went to his house and proposed to purchase the metal, Manning rebuffed him in strong language. Walker recognized that his reputation among the Nicaraguans and the Americans alike might hinge on the outcome of the matter, and he felt more tension than showed in his own report. "A small guard was sent with orders to take the lead, paying a reasonable price. Thereupon the Englishman declared . . . that if the guard entered his house he would run up the British flag and put his house under the protection of the British government. The officer, uncertain how to act, returned . . . for orders; and being told that no foreign resident, except the representative of the sovereignty of his country, had a right to fly a foreign flag, he was ordered to enter the house; and in case the British colors were shown over it, to tear them down and trample them underfoot, thus returning the insult offered to the Republic of Nicaragua by their display. The native authorities, accustomed to yield to the wishes not only of British consuls but even of British merchants, were utterly astounded at these orders. On the Englishman, however, the orders produced a wholesome effect; for he immediately gave up the lead . . . for the use of the Americans." Manning conceived a considerable respect for Walker, and a little later congratulated him warmly on his successes.

A more important result of this affair was its part in bringing Walker a potent new friend—José Vallé, a pure Indian of vast bulk, robust personality, and great influence, who had been a colonel in the Democratic army before a serious wound forced his retirement. Walker's boldness and vigor appealed to him; intensely loyal to the Democratic cause and a shrewd judge of fighting men, he saw in the American far more hope for his party than in the vacillating Castellon, and gave him undeviating allegiance. Walker on his part conceived a hearty liking for Vallé, whose vitality, keen intuition, and emotional force made him a natural leader of men. "With a certain rude eloquence," Walker described him, "he was accustomed to stir the hearts of the people with a recitation of the wrongs they had suffered from the Legitimist government." Nor was Vallé's influence confined to the men. He was a performer on the guitar, an instrument which, with its yearning sounds and female shape, was particularly satisfying both to the lusty player and the women who listened to him. The practical political value of Vallé's musical talent comes out in Walker's comment on his new ally. "When he took the guitar in hand he would carry the women away with his songs of love or of patriotism; and the control he exercised over the women was not to be despised in a country where they serve to some extent the use of newspapers, at the same time scattering news and forming opinion."

VIII

Vallé proceeded to recruit a force of Indian field hands and town workers—volunteers, for Walker barred conscripts—to serve under the American with himself as their captain. When word of this activity reached Castellon, he promptly sent Vallé a peremptory order to disband his troop. No one bothered to reply. Instead, Walker led his Americans to Realejo and boarded the *Vesta,* where they were joined a few days later by Vallé and his Nicaraguans. Hot on their heels came another message from Castellon: Walker was to bring the *Falange* back to León.

This was serious, for Castellon was one of those essentially weak public men who need occasionally to taste raw power, as a kind of political aphrodisiac. If disobeyed, he might well use the one effective weapon at his disposal—declare his contract with the Americans void, thus destroying their legal justification for being in the country, and reducing their status to that of mere freebooters. Walker decided that the *Falange* must leave Realejo before such an order could arrive. The moment was hardly propitious, for cholera had broken out on shipboard, and was taking a heavy toll of Vallé's men, but Walker, after imposing stringent sanitary regulations on the American troops, gave orders to sail. Not one of the *Falange* came down with cholera on this voyage, in spite of its presence all around them, and the epidemic among the Nicaraguans was held in check—facts suggesting that Walker's medical training was proving its military value. It was at this time that his men, impressed by his care for their welfare, took to calling their thirty-one-year-old commander—behind his back— "Uncle Billy."

Again the *Vesta* bore southward, and three days later was anchored in the harbor of San Juan del Sur. There Walker heard news which revealed the full extent of the trial that lay ahead. The Legitimists had not been deceived as to his purpose, and 600 of their best troops were approaching under the command of The Butcher, Guardiola, who had sworn a sacred oath to drive the *falanginos* into the sea. Walker had not read his military historians for nothing. It was essential to occupy a favorable strategic position, and one that would command the Transit, without delay. A forced march brought him and his men, now comprising 50 Americans and 120 natives under Vallé, to Virgin Bay, the Transit harbor on Lake Nicaragua. They were eating breakfast and spreading their blankets when the advance guard of Guardiola's army, which had found their trail, attacked their pickets. These pickets, Nicaraguans all, proved the courage and the reliability of the native volunteer, as distinguished from the native conscript. Their cool, disciplined, and staunch defense of their posts gave Walker time to deploy his troops in strong positions, on rising ground, with their backs to the lake, and in possession of the buildings owned by Accessory Transit.

With no retreat possible, and with the knowledge that they could expect no quarter from the enemy, the *falanginos* and Vallé's men made their bullets count. After hours of rifle fire, the Legitimists fled. Sixty of them were found dead after the fight, but not a single American was killed, and only two of Walker's Nicaraguan allies. He himself had a close call, for he was struck in the throat by a spent bullet, and another shot cut through a packet of letters from Castellon, which were in his coat pocket. His readiness to expose himself to enemy fire and the dash with which he led a charge won him unstinted admiration from his men. The Leónese troops were even more impressed, however, by the care that he took to preserve the lives of the enemy wounded—an innovation, for the stricken Nicaraguan soldier left behind in a retreat could usually count on being shot or bayoneted by his captors.

For Walker, the battle of Virgin Bay, his first military victory, was a turning point. He could not know how widely and with what enthusiasm it would be reported in the United States, but the effect in Nicaragua was all that his heart could desire. The country was deeply stirred by the Democratic triumph, which was enhanced by the fact that the dictator, Chamorro, had been stricken by cholera, and was dead—a passing which to many seemed an omen of Legitimist doom.

From León, too, came encouragement. There Walker was hailed as a hero, the man who had defeated The Butcher. Castellon also had fallen a victim to the cholera epidemic, and his successor wrote Walker that a company of Nicaraguan volunteers was on its way to serve as reinforcement. Even better, in American eyes, was the arrival of a Transit vessel from San Francisco, with 35 recruits for the *Falange;* while local representatives of the Accessory Transit Company, who had viewed Walker with distrust, were suddenly affable and cooperative.

His army now consisted of nearly 250 men—enough, he considered, for a major offensive. The audacity of his next move, if it had not succeeded, would have made him a laughing stock among military strategists. It was nothing less than the capture of the Legitimist capital, the old city of Granada. Using the tactics of surprise, he embarked his force on a steamboat of the Transit Company, landed at night at a point near Granada, advanced under cover of darkness, attacked at dawn, scattered the city's garrison within a few minutes, and took possession of the government offices. There was little bloodshed. "The encounter," said Walker lightly, "could scarcely be dignified with the name of an action." No triumph in battle could have been more effective. Overnight, from being a military adventurer at the head of a tiny force, he had become, for practical purposes, the dominant man of the nation; for the life of Nicaragua centered in the fertile lands that stretched from Granada to León, and to hold both cities was to hold the country.

His first order, as usual, was a warning to his men against looting, rape, and brutality. Resentment among the Americans was multiplied in his Leónese companies, most of whose men had seen their families suffer at Legitimist hands, and who dreamed of revenge. The heavy punishments with which he proposed to enforce his discipline caused mutinous murmurings, and for a time even his staunch comrade-in-arms, the Indian Vallé, was enraged at him.

IX

Shortly after entering the city, Walker paid his respects to the American minister to Nicaragua, John H. Wheeler, and at the legation found a large number of Granadan women and children who had sought the protection of the American flag. Amazed by his boyish appearance and gentle manner, they begged him for mercy, only to find, incredulously, that he regarded himself as their protector. Among the women to whom Wheeler presented him was one who particularly caught his attention—Doña Irena Ohoran, an unmarried woman of mixed Spanish and Irish blood (her name had once been spelled O'Horan), who was one of the leaders of Granadan society and a power in Legitimist politics. A few years older than Walker, diminutive, and with a face that radiated intelligence, she touched a responsive chord in him. When she offered her house, one of the finest in Granada, to serve as his headquarters, he instantly accepted. Under her guidance he glimpsed the beauties of Granada. It was a city of only 15,000, much smaller than León, but proud. Through green avenues of palm and orange trees one could see the vast blue sheet of Lake Nicaragua, stretching a hundred miles to the south, and where great seafish, the shark, the swordfish, the tarpon, were found in fresh water. Irena Ohoran pointed out volcanic islands in the distance, inhabited by idol-worshiping Indians, hostile to all whites. There was the beautiful Cathedral of Guadalupe, the grand plaza, and the market place— empty, now; but tomorrow, when the people understood that Colonel Walker intended them no harm, the shutters on the shops would come down and hundreds of market women would appear with their colorful baskets of fruit and vegetables. The shops were the best in Nicaragua, offering cottons from England, jewelry from Spain, silks and wines from France.

As for the social life of Granada, it was extremely active. The wide houses in the fashionable streets were more elegant than they looked from the outside. Built low in order to withstand earthquakes, almost every house had its patio and its garden of gay flowers, and many had rooms large enough for a ball. Granadans loved to dance, and orchestras of six, or even ten, violins and guitars were available. But the best entertainment of all was in the streets. In the cool of the evening the ladies, in their finery, would sit at their windows while in the wide avenue the *caballeros,* mounted on their best horses, would come in brilliant colors and wide-brimmed hats, guitars in hand, to serenade their favorite señoritas, display their horsemanship, and exchange gossip from house to house.

The horses and riders were as good as any in the world, and there was many a race in the Nicaraguan style. At the crack of a pistol, two young men would start out holding hands, and race until one was dragged from his horse: broken bones, sometimes broken necks resulted. Of other sports, too, there were plenty—especially cockfighting, the national pastime. Bullfighting was prohibited by law, but bull baiting was permitted—nearly as exciting, when ambitious youths tried to ride the maddened creatures. Men could gamble, too, at a casino, or in the billiard rooms. Theaters were lacking, but sometimes British variety acts—tumblers, singers, clowns—would appear, and one could occasionally ride out to the country to see villagers perform *una sagrada función*—a kind of morality play—very amusing to the sophisticates of the town. In no other small city in Central America did the gentry live so carefree a life. Servants were abundant and cheap. There was much wealth in Granada, derived largely from the great cacao and sugar estates nearby; and every year many Granadans went to Europe to study or travel.

Walker was well aware that the life described by Irena Ohoran was that of a few hundred families only. He did not need to be instructed in the condition of the poverty-ridden workers of the town, or the Indians of the countryside, serfs doomed to incessant labor and to premature death. He had seen their rickety hovels, usually shared with chickens, with dirt floors, mildewed walls, and beds consisting of the stretched hide of a cow. In those dwellings, the chief luxury was the candle. It not only gave illumination but also yielded soft balls of wax, which, when rubbed on the body were a reasonably efficient way of removing the ticks which bored into human skin and were regarded as a worse plague than the scorpions and the snakes.

Among the Granadans Walker became more popular with every hour, the more so because Legitimist propaganda had created an image of him as a bloodthirsty and lecherous buccaneer—and worse, a Democrat—from whom no mercy could be expected. When he set free a large number of political prisoners who had been chained in a medieval dungeon, crowds gathered in the streets to cheer him— crowds composed, it was noted, largely of poor folk who had made their way to the city's center, curious to see their new conqueror, a *gringo* and a Democrat. It was clear to everyone that he was much under Doña Irena's influence, which showed on the very day following his victory. This was a Sunday, and he attended eight o'clock mass at the Cathedral of Granada, where he listened to a sermon counseling "peace, moderation, and the putting aside of revolutionary passions." Afterward he called to his side the parish priest who had delivered the sermon, Padre Augustin Vijil (later to be minister to the United States), and publicly approved his sentiments.

This was the first move in Walker's policy of conciliation toward the Catholic Church. He needed, and knew that he needed, the great influence of the clergy on his side. His enemies abroad, as well as in Nicaragua, spread reports that he encouraged his men to desecrate shrines and churches; there was even a legend that he buried gold and jewels looted from the holy places of the country, but such stories were later found to be fabrications designed to discredit him. In his "Fifty-Three Articles of War By Which the Army of the Republic of Nicaragua Shall be Governed," Article I read: "It is earnestly recommended to all officers and soldiers to attend divine worship, and any officer or soldier who shall in any way behave with impropriety in any place of divine worship shall be punished according to his offense by sentence of a court-martial."

At one point, the Church authorities of Granada granted him a loan of 1000 ounces of silver bullion, certainly without expecting to be repaid. The reality of Walker's relationship to the Church in the early days of his regime is suggested by a letter written to him on November 26, 1855, by the Vicar-General of the See of Nicaragua: "I congratulate your excellency on the victory obtained in favor of liberal principles. . . . I congratulate my country, for she will now come out of the ruins in which she has been sunk for more than thirty years." At the time, the Vicar-General was under the impression that Walker was dissociating himself from the extreme Democratic partisans. Later, when Walker's political activity began to deviate sharply from the preferences of the Church, most of the clergy of the country turned against him, but the issues between them were those of political ideology, not of religion.

Even the British, it would appear, regarded him in those first months as a hopeful figure. A letter from Thomas Manning, with whom Walker had quarreled in Chinandega only a few weeks earlier, and who had been appointed England's Acting Vice-Consul in Nicaragua, said, "As an eyewitness of all the horrors and events which have occurred since May, 1851 [the outbreak of the current Nicaraguan revolution], nobody can better appreciate than myself the re-establishment of order and quiet. . . . Be persuaded, Sir, that the government of Her British Majesty will be disposed to sympathize with you." In London, the highly regarded *Economist* was even willing to concede all Central America to Walker and the United States. "We could not hinder the ultimate absorption by the Anglo-Saxon republicans of Central America if we would—and we are by no means certain that we should."

XI

〜〜

THE HOT SUN OF NICARAGUA

Whether or not Walker actually fell in love with Irena Ohoran, his men gossiped freely about them. Her popular nickname in Granada was La Niña, the little one, and by the time rumor had worked its way through the ranks of the American force, La Niña Irena had been distorted into "Nila Mairena." Under this name she later appeared as a figure of mystery in American writings about Walker. The men sensed, however, that this was no ordinary affair of the flesh. Between the lines of his own comments on La Niña much can be read. Initially he described her as "a quick and minute observer, with all the gravity and apparent indifference of the native race . . . fertile in resources for sending intelligence to her friends. She had rendered much service to the Legitimist party in days past; and even the stern nature of Fruto Chamorro owned her sway and yielded to her influence, when all others failed to move him."

There soon appears in his account, however, a strong hint of something more than respect for her political talents. He discovered that she had a highly placed lover. "The private relations," wrote Walker in a vein of extraordinary bitterness, "which it is said, and probably with truth, existed between her and D. Narciso Espinosa, a leading man among the Legitimists, enabled her to breathe her spirit into the party after the death of Chamorro." His feelings about Espinosa, whom he described as "a man without principle and without honor," were tinged with a personal resentment such as he displayed toward no other Nicaraguan. It took the form finally of an accusation of complicity in an alleged Legitimist plot against the new regime. What was the evidence against Espinosa? Walker himself admitted that it was only "vague and uncertain," yet he had the man forcibly deported from Nicaragua. Such unusual heat in him suggests emotions at work which were more than political. From this time, the connection between Walker and La Niña became merely formal.

Prior to the Espinosa incident, however, Irena helped to steer Walker through the maze of Nicaraguan politics and to indoctrinate him in the techniques of political warfare, Central American style. In so doing she may well have influenced fundamental decisions. A major strategic problem then confronted him—and more than strategic, for it touched the core of his philosophy. Was he a Democratic partisan, the role implied by his contract with Castellon, or was he seeking to reshape Nicaragua in a new way? There was a common impression in the United States that the partisan armies of Central America represented no more than the personal ambitions of the warlords who led them, and that party programs counted for little, but Nicaraguans knew better. The Democrats had espoused far-reaching reforms in land rents, peonage, and trade, and contemplated a revival of the old Central American Federation. The Provisional Government at León and the Leónese troops in Granada were counting on Walker to secure their control of the country. Anything less than total victory over the Legitimists, in their view, would be an invitation to a renewal of civil war. Similarly the Democrats and Liberals of the neighboring republics regarded Walker with high hope. The San Salvador newspaper, *El Rol,* on January 2, 1856, defended Walker against attacks by conservative elements, stating boldly that "this much-decried invasion of Nicaragua by the North Americans is but an invective and a calumny of the aristocratic party." It was the belief of many throughout the isthmus that unless Walker succeeded in re-establishing the Central American Federation under Democratic rule, nation would continue to fight nation, party would continue to fight party, and the people would be doomed to incessant warfare and inevitable retrogression.

The issue could not be long postponed. Already the Liberal regime in Honduras had been driven from power, and the ousted President, Trinidad Cabañas, who had unhesitatingly sent troops to fight alongside the Nicaraguan Democrats in their time of need, was asking Walker for similar aid. Could he, should he rescue Honduran democracy? This was the question Walker had to decide.

He fully accepted the view that the five Central American republics ought to be consolidated. The Great Seal of State that he designed for the Nicaraguan government showed five volcanoes in a close cluster, with the sun rising behind the first, and the legend *Dios—Union—Libertad*. In the flag that he adopted (two broad horizontal stripes of azure blue and a white stripe between) the center was dominated by a five-pointed red star. But a political conception was one thing, military reality another. He was less misled than the enthusiastic Democrats by the appearance of his triumph. The Legitimist power could not easily be broken. Its army, under General Corral, still occupied strongly fortified positions on the Transit route, and was much larger than the forces at Walker's command. And throughout Central America, behind the conservatives and the aristocrats, stood not only the prevailing influence of the Church, but also that of England.

Part of Walker's case against England was her indifference to the condition of the people. He pointed out that although her protectorate over the Mosquito Indians had lasted for over a century, "still they have not made any progress toward civilization." The British government did not forget for a moment, however, the interests of England's magnates in the mines of Guatemala and Honduras, and the mahogany of Nicaragua and Costa Rica. The Legitimists of Nicaragua were openly called "the British party," and Costa Rica's aristocratic government was reorganizing its army with the aid of a British Captain (later Colonel) John Cauty.

It was obvious to Walker that a successful democratic revolution in Central America could take place only if it were strongly supported by the United States. But the administration of President Pierce, far from encouraging the Nicaraguan Democrats, showed a strong bias in favor of the Legitimists; it had recognized Chamorro in spite of his flagrant suppression of democratic rights. The Accessory Transit Company, too, had been content with Chamorro, so long as he did not interfere with their operations. Against this background, Walker took it for granted that a strongly partisan position would invite an attack in overwhelming force from all sides.

In the upshot, the strategy that he chose was a painful disappointment to his Democratic friends. To bring peace to the country was his first purpose, he announced, and this could be done only by compromising the differences between the two parties and establishing a coalition government. His Leónese soldiers muttered, but for the Granadans this was pleasant news. All at once Walker was a favorite of the Legitimists. Receptions given in his honor by Irena Ohoran and others were attended by the wealthiest and most aristocratic families of the city, who now regarded Walker as the only barrier between them and the vengeance of the Democrats. Every honor was accorded him; when he entered a room men and women rose and applauded. The Granadans were in fact awed by his ability to control both the hotheaded Leónese troops and the bearded *gringos*. When one of the Americans in a drunken fog wantonly shot and killed a Nicaraguan boy, and Walker had him court-martialed and executed, the city felt that here at last was a military man dedicated to justice.

II

The American's driving energy also impressed Nicaragua. His working hours were from six o'clock in the morning until ten at night, his only recreation a daily horseback ride. Confronted with a thousand problems of the moment, he nevertheless found time to plunge into new and ambitious projects, among them the establishment of an official newspaper. One of his Californians had been a printer and editor; they imported a press and some fonts of type from San Francisco, and were able to improvise a remarkably competent weekly, *El Nicaragüense,* partly in English, partly in Spanish. From the beginning it was one of Walker's major tools, through which he interpreted his purpose to the Granadans and the world. Copies went regularly to the United States, inviting Americans to share in the exotic pleasures and bright future of beautiful Nicaragua; and the influence of the paper on the American press, which quoted it extensively, played a large part in bringing nearly one thousand recruits to Walker's service in the year that followed. Political opinion was similarly shaped. *El Nicaragüense* made it clear that Walker was no mere freebooter or dangerous revolutionary, but the "regenerator" of a much abused and unhappy nation. The effect showed in many American newspapers as skepticism steadily gave way to approval. The influential *Alta California,* which had for a time jeered at the filibuster ("What a hero Walker has become! William the Conqueror, Cortez and Pizarro are but the forerunners of a greater, the destined conqueror of Central America!"), soon was soberly admitting to San Francisco that "Walker, in his campaign in Nicaragua, has certainly exhibited a good degree of skill, perseverance, energy and a vast amount of policy," and complimented him on "the considerable degree of ability" shown in his newspaper.

He was especially successful in surrounding his name with an aura of predestination. There was an old legend among the Nicaraguan Indians, that the people would some day be brought into the light by a redeemer, who would be recognized by his grey eyes. Walker had come across this legend in his reading; under the circumstances, he may even have been inclined to believe it. *El Nicaragüense* left no doubt that he was "the grey-eyed man of destiny." "Last week," reported the newspaper, "we saw in Granada a delegation of Indians, who rarely visit the city, who desired to see General Walker. They were charmed by his gentle reception, and offered to him their heartfelt thanks for their liberation from oppression and for the present state of quiet of this country. They laid at his feet the simple offerings of their fruits and fields, and hailed him as 'Grey-Eyed Man' so long and anxiously awaited by their fathers." Newspapers throughout the United States seized on the story, and for a year it was a rare newspaper article about Nicaragua that did not refer to Walker's grey eyes.

Even the sophisticated European mind was caught by him. British periodicals, which then habitually shrugged at America's politics and public figures, felt constrained to report Walker's actions and statements with close attention, mentioning his name more frequently than they did the President of the United States. Spain's government made him the subject of repeated and anxious notes to its representatives in Washington, London, Paris, Mexico, and Havana. In France, Emperor Napoleon III requested a special memoir on Walker from his Minister of Foreign Affairs. The *Revue des Deux Mondes* published a major article on the significance of his achievements, ranking him among the great political figures of the age, "the rival of Washington." Other journals circulated the rumor that Walker was by birth a French aristocrat and a formidable lover of women, and for a time he was the talk of Paris.

Europe was fascinated not so much by the dramatic fact that, with a handful of men, Walker had swiftly conquered a country and become its dictator, as by the practical implications of his action. Was the United States entering on its imperialistic phase? Accustomed to the ways of their own governments, the statesmen of England, France, and Spain found it almost inconceivable that he could have undertaken such a project, not to say succeeded at it, without undercover support from Washington. The British especially could not believe that he stood alone, and expecting him momentarily to receive recognition and aid from Washington, were tentative and cautious in their first dealings with him.

III

As the strong man of a Central American republic, Walker suffered from the serious liability of a puritanical upbringing. Instinctively the Nicaraguans felt him to be at the polar extreme of temperament from themselves. He might sympathize with their sorrows, but could never enjoy their pleasures, the stronger force binding men together in daily life. Cockfighting, Granada's favorite sport, he privately considered detestable. He did not even laugh, he hardly smiled. That there was an ironic humor in Walker is shown by many passages in his writings, but to him ready displays of mirth were a sign of weakness. He had read Hobbes, who perceived that laughter at its core expresses a sudden feeling of superiority, and he chose to discipline that feeling within himself. His serious manner was not the pose of a man with a romantic sorrow, nor was it the dour style of his Scottish forebears: it expressed the ascetic determination to live at the highest level of self-control of which he was capable. To most Nicaraguans, this was incomprehensible. They respected his ability to control other men, but they were baffled by his insistence on controlling himself. In their feudal world, full of visible misery, imminent pain and sudden death, it was altogether sensible to conciliate those stronger than oneself, take advantage of the weaker, and freely indulge such pleasures of the flesh as were available, while one could. If North American civilization meant a way of life less sensuous than that to which they were accustomed, they wanted none of it. Even the style of Walker's dress struck them as bizarre. Who ever heard of a dictator who wore an ordinary blue coat with cheap dark pantaloons and a black felt hat with a partisan red ribbon, and who moreover carried no arms except in battle?

The chief problem that Walker faced, very simply, was that he wanted to regenerate Nicaragua, and that Nicaraguans did not wish to be regenerated—or, more precisely, the gentry and the clergy wished things to stay as they were, and the unschooled poor, the Indians and half-breeds, aspired to no more than a little more food and clothing. Long experience with Indian gods and Spanish rulers had destroyed hope. To most of the Nicaraguan people it seemed that the difficulties of their lives could only be made worse by radical change. Politically, they lived in a jungle world of passion without principle; they were not in favor of anything; they were merely against everything; their attitude might be described as anti-ism. They would follow a revolutionary leader to help him destroy an oppressive government, but as soon as the new government was established, it in turn became their enemy, for it represented the hated power of the law. Every attempt in the past to bring modern improvements to the country had been fiercely resisted. A few years before Walker's arrival in the country, a wealthy Nicaraguan plantation owner of singular progressivism and benevolence had imported from the United States machinery for the refining of sugar, with the consequence that the machinery was promptly wrecked and he was murdered by workers of the countryside, who had been told that their livelihoods would be destroyed by the new methods.

Temperament aside, Walker showed himself a shrewd judge of popular feeling. He said little about his plans for the country. When the municipal council of Granada drew up a petition urging him to assume the Presidency of Nicaragua, he reproved them in terms perfectly calculated to allay Legitimist anxieties. They had no right, he said, to make the offer, nor he to accept it; much more appropriate would be the election of such a man as the Legitimist Commander in Chief, General Corral, with a government drawn from the best men of both parties.

This move was highly approved by the Americans in Granada as well as by the Legitimists. Minister John Wheeler was so impressed by Walker's bearing that he offered to go to Rivas, where Corral had his headquarters and to serve as intermediary between the two—and this although Walker had no legal status in the United States. Wheeler was an amiable and impressionable man, himself a former soldier, who regarded Walker as a great man, a rare combination of military virtues and intellectual refinement. Presently his hero-worship would express itself in a remarkable collection of Walkeriana. But in attempting to negotiate with Corral, he exceeded both his authority and his talents. Corral, a man of personal force and conviction, regarded him as Walker's tool, insulted him, and declared his intention to pursue the war against the Democrats.*

More effective than Wheeler's intervention was Irena Ohoran's subterranean influence among the Legitimists. How she persuaded Corral is not clear, but just when the situation seemed most dangerous, a letter from him arrived at Granada, offering to receive Walker for private talks. Doubtless to Irena's surprise, Walker now resisted her. If Corral wished a meeting, he said, it would have to take place in Granada; for he sensed that the first overt move of conciliation on either side would be read as a sign of weakness.

Just when he needed it, a way to exert pressure on Corral was unexpectedly put into his hands by a twisting chain of events. A contingent of recruits from California had just arrived in Nicaragua, and its leaders, acting without Walker's knowledge, and even before they had reported to him, decided for their own aggrandizement to seek battle with Legitimist forces on Lake Nicaragua. Commandeering a Transit steamer, they fired on a fortress overlooking the lake, and controlled by Corral. The result was disastrous. Not only were they forced by bombardment to scurry back to safety, but they provoked the Legitimists to reprisals in which a number of innocent Transit passengers, including women and children, were massacred.

The crisis was the more serious because Walker needed the services of the American officers who had ordered the attack, and on whose cooperation depended the arrival of future reinforcements from California. With them he went no further than stern reproof; most of his wrath was directed at the Legitimists, on the incontestable ground that their assault on the Transit passengers had been cruel beyond

---

* Senate Exec. Doc. 68, 34th Cong., 1 Sess.

military need. In an angry pronouncement, he called for the punishment of those Granadans who, because of their opposition to the idea of a unified country, had urged General Corral to maintain his armed resistance. These Legitimist conspirators were "morally responsible" for the tragedy of the Transit passengers, Walker declared; and the guilt was especially heavy in the instance of one Mateo Mayorga, a former Legitimist cabinet minister. Mayorga, who had earlier been arrested on suspicion of treason but released on parole at the request of John Wheeler, and was actually living in Wheeler's home, had taken advantage of Walker's indulgence to intrigue against him and encourage Corral. Walker had him taken into custody, submitted the facts to a court-martial which quickly found Mayorga guilty of conspiracy to foment civil war, and turned him over to a firing squad.

When Mayorga was led to the plaza and publicly executed, the Leónese soldiers cheered, and Legitimists trembled. Who would be next? Was this the beginning of the Democratic reign of terror that they had feared? At the height of the agitation, Walker sent a message to Corral. From this moment, he vowed, all the Granadan families of officers of the Legitimist army would be regarded as hostages for the good behavior of Corral's soldiers. The effect was magical. With one voice Corral's officers urged him to make peace; and he went immediately to Granada.

IV

Outside Granada, Corral was met by Walker with a mounted escort, and at a stately pace they rode together to the city's center. Walker later recalled the enthusiasm of the Granadans at the spectacle. "As they passed, the doors and windows of the houses were filled with women and children, dressed in the bright colors of the country and smiling through tears at the prospects of peace." During the ride, the two men exchanged enough courtesies so that by the time they reached Government House the tension between them had been somewhat relaxed. In the ensuing conference, Walker allowed himself to appear at a disadvantage. Corral was empowered to speak officially for the Legitimist Party, but the American had been given no such authority by the Democratic regime at León, and he was careful to limit himself to such statements as befitted "the colonel commanding the forces occupying Granada." Accordingly, he let Corral "develop freely the terms he desired, saying little by way either of objection or of amendment. . . . The treaty, as signed, was nearly altogether the work of Corral."*

It was a reasonable document. Establishing a Provisional Government, naming as President an elderly and respected gentleman of conservative views, Don Patricio Rivas, making Corral Minister of War, it pleased the Legitimists; while the Democrats were to be satisfied by constitutional reforms, for which they had been contending; and Walker was given the post of Commander in Chief of the army. In the fact that he, who had been totally without military experience a year or so earlier, now assumed the rank of general, his critics in the United States later professed to find proof of unbridled vanity, but it is difficult to see how he could otherwise have commanded an army already loaded with generals.

A few days later word came from León approving the treaty and confirming the peace. All the bells of Granada rang out. The Legitimists especially were elated by what they felt to be a diplomatic triumph, for what, after all, was a mere constitution as compared with the power of administration? Corral was overheard to call out to Irena Ohoran, as he rode past her house one evening, "we have beaten them with their own game-cock!" This piece of gossip filtered back to Walker from his Leónese officers and widened the rift between him and La Niña.

Corral's jubilation, however, was premature. From the outset, he misread Walker's character. He had expected to find a bully who would attempt to dominate him, trick him, or even humiliate him, in order to gain ascendancy. Discovering instead a quiet and courteous little man, with a profound respect for law, he was unimpressed. He himself had a tall and majestic presence, and this fact may have contributed to his feeling that Walker could be reduced to a subordinate role. His error was soon made plain to him. Walker had based his calculation on the insights which he had recently gained into the mind of the Nicaraguan conscript, and events proved him right. With the announcement of peace, the Legitimist garrisons in the towns, consisting largely of Indians and *mestizos* longing for their homes,

* William Walker, *The War in Nicaragua*, p. 125.

melted away; and Walker, as Commander in Chief, did nothing to interfere with their desertion. Within a few weeks Corral's authority over the army had become merely nominal; the real power of compulsion now rested with the *Falange,* and Walker lost no time in exercising it.

A question arose as to the selection of a cabinet officer responsible for relations with the other Central American republics. To Corral's resentment, Walker insisted that the post go to the most celebrated and ardent revolutionary among the Democratic generals, Maximo Jerez, who was also an intellectual with a degree in law, and with whom Walker had conversed at length in León. Such an appointment meant to Corral a major threat to his control of the administration and to the gentry of the entire isthmus. If the extreme Democrats were to have control not only of the army but also of intergovernmental communications, they might well be able to promote revolutions in countries north and south. At all costs Jerez had to be kept out of the cabinet, and Corral said hotly and flatly that he would not serve in the same government with the Leónese. Walker replied simply, "Then we must refer the matter to the President." All Granada by this time was aware that President Rivas regarded the American as Nicaragua's only hope for peace, and never opposed him.

Corral awoke too late to Walker's force of leadership. Although he did not resign from the cabinet, he felt that the Legitimist cause was lost in Nicaragua. His misgivings were strengthened by the evident determination of the Leónese soldiery to maintain their partisan solidarity. Walker had issued an order requiring troops of both parties to remove from their hats the colors of their political faiths, the red ribbon of the Democrats, the white of the Legitimists, and to wear instead the blue ribbon of the nation, with the device, NICARAGUA INDEPENDENTE. The Legitimists obeyed, but the red ribbon remained on most of the Democratic hats. This persistence of the revolutionary spirit Corral considered an evil augury. It was, he felt, only through the intervention of other countries that he and his friends could now be saved.

In that conviction, he wrote an impulsive letter to the new dictator of Honduras, and sent it off by secret messenger. Coming from the Minister of War of the Nicaraguan government to the head of another state, this letter was the stuff of treason unmistakable. "My esteemed friend: It is necessary that you write to friends to advise them of the danger we are in, and that they work actively. If they delay two months, there will not then be time. Think of us and of your offers . . . Nicaragua is lost; lost Honduras, San Salvador and Guatemala, if they let this develop. Let them come quickly, if they would find allies here."

Some historians have seen in this letter a warning against seizure of the isthmus by Walker for the United States, but there is more reason to believe that Corral's great fear was the triumph of the Democrats throughout Central America. Unfortunately for him, the messenger whom he chose to carry this dangerous missive had strong grievances against the Legitimists. Instead of taking the letter out of Granada, he promptly put it into the hands of a Leónese officer, and within the hour it was being read by Walker, together with two other notes of the same kind penned by Corral. The situation thus created, while in one way to Walker's advantage, also confronted him with an ugly problem. That Corral had to be exposed and punished was evident, but the man was much loved in Granada. Imprisoned, he would be a center of conspiracy; executed, a martyr to whose memory thousands would rally; while a light penalty would stir bitter resentment among the Leónese troops, who might even suspect Walker of supporting the Legitimists against them.

In a grim mood, Walker notified President Rivas that an emergency demanded an immediate cabinet meeting, and Corral, not scenting danger, attended. To the assembled ministers Rivas said, "General Walker has something of grave consequence to tell us." Walker put the fatal letters in front of Corral and asked, "Did you write these, General?"

Corral turned pale, but bearing himself with dignity, admitted authorship of the letters, which were then read aloud to the cabinet. "President," said Walker to Rivas, "I charge General Corral with treason, and request you to order his arrest." Rivas nodded unhappily; a Leónese officer who had been waiting outside the door was summoned; Corral gave up his arms and was placed in confinement.

V

Corral's crime, committed as a civilian official, called for a civilian trial. The new government, however, had not yet established a civil court, and it was apparent, moreover, that no Nicaraguan could be

William Walker in 1857 (from an old print)

(Courtesy of New Orleans *Times-Picayune*)

Walker's great love, Ellen Galt Martin, "in costume for a fancy dress ball" (from a portrait in oils)

Walker leading the final charge at the first battle of Rivas (from *Leslie's Illustrated Newspaper*)

Cornelius Vanderbilt

One of Vanderbilt's Lake Nicaragua steamboats (from *Leslie's Illustrated Newspaper*)

This issue of Walker's official newspaper, appearing before he became President, sought to reassure American opinion as to the stability and pro-American character of his regime. It states that Walker, although not President, "is the government of Nicaragua as Louis Napoleon is the government of France."

A serial biography of Walker, "The Man of Destiny," was featured in New Orleans shortly after his election as President of Nicaragua.

Victory of Walker's schooner *Granada* over the Costa Rican warship *Once de Abril* (from *Leslie's Illustrated Newspaper*)

The Transit route, on a map prepared at Walker's instructions to show Nicaraguan ownership of territories in dispute with Costa Rica and Honduras.

One of the bonds issued by Walker in 1856, after he became President of Nicaragua

Captain Callender Irvine Fayssoux, Commander of Walker's "Navy"
(from *Leslie's Illustrated Newspaper*)

Major General Charles
Frederick Henningsen
(from an old print)

Pierre Soulé
(from a portrait)

Rivas Jan. 16th 1857

Capt. C. J. Fayssoux :

Come to this place as
soon as possible. I wish to consult
you on an important matter.

Your obt. servt.
Wm. Walker

A military order, written by Walker to Captain Fayssoux of the warship *Granada* at

Walker's draft of his response to an irresponsible challenge to a duel from a former officer in his army, Col. S. A. Lockridge, who felt himself insulted by a passage in Walker's book, *The War in Nicaragua*. The note, addressed to Lockridge's second, says, ". . . I did not intend to impugn the honor or courage of Mr. Lockridge. When I aim to make charges against the character of any man, let me assure you it shall be in words not easily misunderstood."

Full pages of leading newspapers devoted to Walker's exploits were not uncommon in the late 1850's. The *New York Times* saw in Walker's victory at Rivas, in 1857, a major change in his fortunes. The New York *Herald*, in 1860, sent a special correspondent to accompany Walker on his last expedition.

President James Buchanan (from a daguerreotype)

THE BEWILDERED OLD WOMAN.

A famous cartoon of the year before the outbreak of the Civil War.
Lost in a graveyard, Buchanan protests, "Sakes alive! I know no North,
no South, no East, no West—no Nothing!"—and tries to conceal the
Ostend Manifesto.

expected to be impartial in the matter. The Cabinet therefore decided on a court-martial to be composed entirely of American officers. No time was lost; the trial was conducted fairly, the verdict was guilty, the sentence "death by shooting." But the court was unanimous in urging Walker to show clemency to the prisoner.

The burden was now altogether his. No matter what the decision, it could only harm him; that was evident. In the end he fell back on the principles of John Knox and his Scottish forebears, on belief in the value of the cautionary example. How could the treaty of peace which he and Corral had solemnly sworn to uphold "continue to have the force of law if the first violation of it—and that by the very man who had signed it—was permitted to pass unpunished? . . . Mercy to Corral would have been an invitation to all Legitimists to engage in like conspiracies."

The word went out—Corral was to be shot. Immediately there was a great outcry in the city. Priests and notables begged Walker to remit the sentence. "The night before the fatal day," he himself related, "the daughters of Corral, accompanied by many of the women of the city, came with sobs and anguish and tears" to plead for their father's life. At such a moment a man of Latin blood, a Bolívar or a San Martín, might have let himself be carried away by pity, might have commuted the sentence, and endeared himself, at least briefly, to the populace. But Walker, congenitally averse to emotional displays, sought to remain detached. "He who looks only at present grief, nor sees in the distance the thousand-fold sorrow a misplaced mercy may create, is little suited for the duties of public life," he wrote in self-justification. Nevertheless, he was deeply disturbed by "such entreaties as the daughters of the prisoner pressed," and he "closed the painful interview as soon as kind feeling permitted." An effort on Corral's behalf by Irena Ohoran was equally fruitless.

The execution of the Legitimist general, on November 8, 1855, left Walker the undisputed master of the Nicaraguan government. But locks of hair from Corral's corpse and handkerchiefs dipped in his blood were preserved in many a Granada home, symbols of a revenge to come. Where Walker had been feared, he was suddenly hated. A people accustomed to the hot cruelty of rage could not be expected to comprehend the lucid and cool cruelty of reason. If Walker had shrieked out a denunciation of Corral and personally stabbed him they would have understood him better and felt closer to him; but they could not forgive his dispassionate and unshakable judgment that the man had to die.

VI

So long as Corral lived, the dominant conservative groups of Central America had reserved judgment on the Rivas regime, but with his death they concluded that Rivas was a mere figurehead for the revolutionary Democrats led by the Americans. Walker made earnest efforts to allay their animosity. A circular letter went to all four of the other isthmian republics, declaring Nicaragua's peaceful purposes, and asking for their friendship. Only little San Salvador replied in kind. In Guatemala, Honduras, and Costa Rica the letter was ignored, while their official newspapers made unbridled attacks on the Rivas government. At this stage, hundreds of Nicaraguan Legitimists began to cross into Costa Rica, seeking asylum and offering their services in a war against the Americans; and the equivalent party in Costa Rica, the *Serviles,* demanded that their nation mobilize.

A new decision faced Walker—attack, or wait to be attacked? General Jerez, whose presence in the cabinet had precipitated the Corral crisis, urged him to seize the initiative. Central American democracy was indivisible, he told Walker, and he outlined a bold plan. Rally the Democrats of the entire isthmus. Mobilize a large Democratic army. Send troops, Americans among them, to restore Cabañas to power in Honduras. Move swiftly against the Costa Ricans. Remove the Nicaraguan government to León. Begin to fight. Walker was tempted but unconvinced. To recruit a substantial force of volunteers would take months; he had no faith in Nicaraguan conscripts; he had only a few hundred Americans behind him; and with so small a force he saw only one way to win a simultaneous war against Costa Rica, Honduras, and the Nicaraguan Legitimists. That was to persuade the United States government to cooperate in sending him recruits and supplies in quantity. "Let the enemy strike the first blow," he told Jerez, for if he appeared to be the aggressor he might alienate the sympathies of the American people, on whom he counted for final victory.

To one concession he agreed. Cabañas was invited to Granada to present his case in person, and was received with all respect. He was one of those dedicated revolutionaries who, out of love for humanity, was ready "to embrace Liberty upon a pile of corpses." But Walker remained adamant in the face of the Honduran's plea—a decision that would later rise to haunt him. The high-minded Cabañas and the fiery Jerez felt betrayed. It seemed to them, as Jerez later wrote, that Walker was seeking not a Democratic victory, but personal power, and in this conviction they left Granada angrily and rode north to the protection of León.

Walker was learning some bitter truths of power: that every significant decision of the ruler makes a new enemy, and that every significant enemy imposes a new decision; that although support at best grows only arithmetically, opposition may well grow geometrically. In spite of the confusion of forces around him he saw his situation more clearly than did most of his advisers and critics. In the end, everything would depend on the aid, the men and the money, coming to him from the United States. If that aid were sufficient, he would be able to federate the republics of the isthmus, bring them under "the civilizing influence of the American people," and introduce democratic institutions. Otherwise Central American democracy was a lost cause.

The British government shared this view. As the London press made clear, the big question at the Foreign Office about Central America was whether Walker, in addition to popular and Congressional support, had the backing of President Pierce. If so, it would be difficult to prevent Walker from succeeding. London noted that President Pierce had asked Congress for a discretionary fund of three million dollars to be used in the event of a rupture with England, and that a bill calling for construction of ten new warships was being sped through the Senate. Untimely British intervention in Central America might trigger a costly and undesirable war, at a time when England's taxpayers were still groaning over the expense of the Crimean muddle.

Fortunately, from the British standpoint, the American minister in London, James Buchanan, seemed almost eager to support England's position and was using his influence in Washington to that end. His attitude was especially significant because he was bound to be a strong candidate for the American Presidency in 1856. As an astute politician, he was aware that behind the scenes British influence would be a weighty factor in the presidential preference of the wealthy, conservative and powerful businessmen of New England and New York. In a private letter to Lord Clarendon, the British Foreign Minister, in whose friendship Buchanan took great satisfaction, the American had written that "the friendly offices of the two governments will be required to put things to rights in Central America," and his only worry over his stand seemed to be "What will Mrs. Grundy say? . . . That Buchanan has made a capitulation."*

The Foreign Office judged that it would be wise to watch and wait and strengthen the Costa Rican army until the signs of Washington's intentions could be read more clearly, or until Buchanan became President. Instructions to that effect went out to England's diplomatic agents in Central America, while a secret shipment of British guns was sent to Costa Rica. Although that nation's dominant political figure, President Mora, was eager to move on Granada, his British advisers counseled delay. For the time being Mora had to confine himself to statements denouncing the American Phalanx—or Rangers, as Walker had renamed them. "They have come to Central America to seek in our wives and daughters, our houses and our lands, satisfaction for their fierce passions, food for their unbridled appetites." When this diatribe was read in Granada by Walker's men, who were growing more and more restive under his strict discipline, it provoked a good deal of satirical laughter.

---

* *Buchanan Papers,* Pennsylvania Historical Society, Philadelphia (Holograph letter of Jan. 2, 1855).

XII

MEPHISTO AS ENVOY

Two months before Corral's execution, just prior to the battle of
Virgin Bay, when Walker's star was flickering uncertainly, an old
acquaintance had boarded the *Vesta* in the harbor of San Juan del
Sur—the former Sacramento publisher and promoter, Parker French
—he who claimed to have the ear of Cornelius Garrison. French had
something to say that arrested Walker's attention. If Walker would
give him the necessary authority, he would return to San Francisco,
recruit seventy-five men, and bring them to Nicaragua on an Accessory
Transit steamer, at the company's expense.

Although Walker was aware of a cloud around French's reputation, he knew nothing specific to his discredit—and San Francisco
was a city full of forgotten pasts. Whatever else the man might be,
he was a personality. One-armed—he had lost the other years before
in a Mexican adventure—he cultivated the style of a soldier of
fortune. He had a handsome, Mephistophelean head, and wearing
a beard like that of Napoleon III, whom he somewhat resembled, and
talking with the glib charm of a P. T. Barnum, he evoked so much
interest that one almost forgot to distrust him. Dubious though he
was of the man, Walker saw no reason to refuse his offer. French

thereupon returned to San Francisco, while Walker went on to victory at Virgin Bay.

For some weeks there was no communication between them. Soon after the conquest of Granada, however, French landed in San Juan del Sur at the head of a company of volunteers, as promised. In addition, he brought tidings so hopeful as to make all else secondary. The friendship of Garrison for Walker's enterprise, he said, was not to be doubted, even though it could not appear on the surface. The Transit Company, eager to see the situation in Nicaragua stabilized, stood ready to carry without charge as many as 500 additional recruits to Nicaragua. What was more, money was available to meet Walker's pressing needs. The new General Agent of the company in Nicaragua, C. J. McDonald, who had just arrived from San Francisco, could put $20,000 at Walker's disposal.

These were magical words in Walker's ears. The problem of pay and supply for his men gave him no peace, for the Nicaraguan treasury was empty. They spoke of French's reward for bringing the company's aid to Walker. If the promised cooperation from Accessory Transit materialized, French said, he would hope to be made Nicaragua's minister to Washington.

Walker was taken aback. He knew how much depended on his selection of an envoy to the United States. His intention was to send a trustworthy Nicaraguan, who might appear to speak for his people. The fact remained that French seemed able to speak for Garrison. Without his good offices the Provisional Government might collapse from sheer inability to pay and feed its troops. Putting first things first, he agreed to French's demand.

Mephistopheles, bargaining for Faust's soul in return for his favors, insisted on a pledge signed in blood, but French, surer of his man, accepted Walker's spoken word. Together they went to McDonald, who turned out to be a cautious Scot, carrying credentials signed by Garrison. He confirmed French's statements. The company, he said, wished success to Walker because it wished to see the Transit route kept open. A loan was perfectly feasible. There was at the moment in Nicaragua, on the way to New York, a large shipment of privately owned California gold bullion. If Walker could provide reasonable security, $20,000 worth of the bullion would be extracted from the shipment, and turned over to him. The owners of the bullion would receive instead drafts for $20,000 on Charles Morgan, the Transit Company's agent in New York, whose credit was unimpeachable. As for security, that presented no problem. Under the terms of its charter, the company owed the Nicaraguan government certain sums, the amount still in dispute. Let the $20,000 borrowed be subtracted from that debt. Thus the loan would be instantly repaid.*

A few days later, the necessary papers had been signed, and the gold was turned over to Walker. That it was tendered him in the interest of Garrison and Morgan was obvious, but no effort had been made to commit him. No one could say that he had been bought. There had been no dishonorable bargain. The initiative remained with him, to act as the best interests of the Nicaraguan government demanded. As if to assert this view, he dispatched two Nicaraguan emissaries to New York, to demand that the company settle all remaining obligations due his government.

Now there was French, waiting for his reward. There was only one honorable way for Walker to extricate himself from his pledge— by giving the man a post even more attractive to him than that of envoy. A cabinet seat was open, the Ministry of *Hacienda,* with authority over landed estates and responsibility for finding revenue. This French consented to accept in lieu of the Washington mission. Almost at once he distinguished himself by confiscating property and goods on a scale that aroused nationwide resentment. "His rapacity," Walker commented ruefully, "made him dreaded by the people," and it became urgent to get him out of the country without delay. Thus, although beset by doubts about him, Walker was forced back to his original promise.

His hope was that the Pierce administration, even if less than happy with the appointment of French, would be well disposed. American newspapers were highly encouraging as to Marcy's intentions. Although he was being urged by Nicaragua's neighbors to ban shipments of arms to Walker, he had resisted them, saying that he "would not infringe the sovereign rights" of Nicaragua. How could this be interpreted, if not as a hint that the Rivas government would soon be recognized? All that French would have to do would be to present his credentials, keep quiet, and stand by.

---

* William Walker, *The War in Nicaragua,* Ch. 5.

The American press and the people as a whole were unmistakably on Walker's side, regarding him as the avatar of the nation's destiny. Wherever he looked in the autumn of 1855, the horizon was rosy with hope. He felt sufficiently secure so that he invited his younger brothers, Norvell and James, to join him and share his success.

II

Some common-sense perceptions that men need in order to function in a commercial society were markedly lacking in Walker. He had no talent for the small and continuous compromises that are the building blocks of security. He did not hesitate to make enemies of those who might have helped him, if their conduct failed to conform to his code of gentlemanly behavior. He felt obliged to fulfill his promises, no matter how inconvenient. The claims of friendship he regarded as taking precedence over his own interests. It is no wonder that many practical men of affairs were outraged by him. Wherever his large strategic requirements came into conflict with his personal code of honor, the strategic requirement was sacrificed, and not because he was blind to it. This was not so much bad judgment as antijudgment. He was often called ambitious, but it would have been more correct to say that he was not ambitious enough, or perhaps that his ambition, like Caesar's, should have been made of sterner stuff. Whether any statesman has the moral right to put personal honor ahead of the needs of his government is a moot question, but Walker did, or tried to. He actually seemed to take seriously the views which he had put forward in his address on *The Unity of Art,* seven years earlier—to regard heroic behavior as a form of the aesthetic in life, more important than mere success.

This attitude, which showed in his unwillingness to break his word to French, almost immediately afterward led him deeper into danger. Not long before, another expedition had left the United States for Nicaragua, commanded by Colonel Henry Kinney of Texas. The colonel claimed the right to colonize a piece of Nicaragua about the size of the State of Maine, and including Greytown and most of Mosquito. This claim was based on a deed which the former Mosquito "King," Robert Charles Frederick, had granted to an American trader, and which Kinney had acquired. Persons close to President

Pierce were backing him financially, and worked to have the Neutrality Laws suspended in his favor. The Accessory Transit Company, which was counting on Walker to protect its interests, regarded Kinney as a potential nuisance, and tried to prevent his sailing, but without success; and it fell to Walker to deal with the problem.

Kinney was anathema to Walker—partly because he sought to colonize Nicaraguan territory on the basis of a claim which had no legality in Nicaraguan eyes; partly because Kinney, in Greytown, had power to interfere with Walker's Atlantic communications; partly because his venture, clearly heading for failure, was likely to discredit American influence among Nicaraguans. Kinney was ill, the ship on which he had set out from the United States had been wrecked, and he himself lacked essential qualities of leadership. With a few followers he had gone through the motions of establishing a "government" in Greytown, but its emptiness was evident from the beginning. The hopelessness of his situation was plain to everyone but himself. Finally, his men urged him to seek an alliance with Walker, and the unhappy colonel sent three of them to Granada for the purpose.

Walker greeted them courteously, but on hearing the proposal that he join forces with Kinney, he let his indignation show. Kinney, he told them, had no right to be in Nicaragua. He could only be regarded as an enemy of the Nicaraguan government. "Tell Governor Kinney, or Colonel Kinney, or Mr. Kinney, or whatever he chooses to call himself, that if I ever lay hands on him on Nicaraguan soil I shall surely hang him!"

The threat snapped the slender cord of loyalty that linked Kinney's men to him. They conferred briefly, and then they said, "General, we have no wish to return to Greytown. We would like to join your army."

It seemed to everyone that Walker had scored an effortless triumph. But impotent as Kinney was, he yet had one thing that Walker needed. He could count on the friendship of the White House, and especially of Sidney Webster, President Pierce's private secretary. Another of his financial backers was Caleb Cushing, the Attorney General of the United States. Two of Walker's high-ranking officers, who had known Kinney in the States, came to the conclusion that the interests of both men required an accommodation, and in this belief they made a journey to Greytown, and urged the Texan to go to Granada himself and talk with Walker. They would, they told him, pledge their honor for his safety. Under the impression that their invitation had Walker's approval, Kinney accepted.

Meanwhile, Walker had prepared a decree declaring all of Mosquito, including the lands claimed by Kinney, to belong to Nicaragua. Just after this document had been made public he heard, to his astonishment, that Kinney was in Granada. His first impression was that the Colonel had come to surrender and seek a place in the Nicaraguan government and on this assumption he agreed to a meeting.

When Kinney entered his office, Walker was cold but not hostile. It came to him as a shock to hear the proposal that their two governments mutually recognize each other, and that he use his army, if need be, to protect Kinney in his possessions. Incredulous, he merely stared. But tenacity was Kinney's strong point, and long experience in fighting Indians and bamboozling settlers on the Texas frontier had given him a certain shrewdness and crude verbal power. "He had acquired," Walker said of him, "that sort of knowledge and experience of human nature derived from the exercise of the mule trade." Sprinkling his talk with profanities of which he himself was unconscious, unaware of the disdain with which he was being listened to, he ignored Walker's rejection of him. He had a right to be in Mosquito, he asserted. His claim had been paid for in hard cash. His syndicate had so far spent over a hundred thousand dollars on the colonization project. How could Walker reasonably expect them to abandon it?

This argument Walker shrugged aside. "You can't survive another month," he pointed out, "without the protection and aid of the Nicaraguan government. Why should I help you? What do you offer in return?"

Kinney's reply was definite. He could bring to Nicaragua a large number of American colonists; he was in a position to negotiate a loan in the United States; and most important, he could do more than anyone else to secure American recognition for Walker.

These were cogent points, and despite his prejudice against the man, Walker hesitated, adjourning the meeting until next day. For some hours it appeared that an alliance of sorts might after all materialize between them. But Kinney was a man who could not even sniff the fumes of the heady brew of power without losing his common sense. Flushed with hope and lacking in sensitivity, he committed an offense which, in Walker's eyes, was unpardonable. He had hardly left Walker when he sought a private meeting with President Rivas and set about to discredit his rival. Walker's army, he told Rivas, would eat up the country like a plague of locusts. Himself he presented as a man of peace and of business, without political ambitions. Colonization—agriculture—new blood—these were the needs of Nicaragua. One American colonist was worth five soldiers to the country.

Rivas, unimpressed, answered that Nicaragua, faced with the threat of invasion, looked to General Walker. He dismissed Kinney; and to assure that Walker, if he heard of the meeting, would not misunderstand its nature, he sent him a detailed report of Kinney's remarks and his own replies.

Even now, if Walker had chosen to dissemble he might easily have kept Kinney dangling without a commitment, until he had made use of the man's connection with Pierce, but this he could not bring himself to do. When the optimistic Kinney presented himself the next morning, Walter's voice and words were soft and restrained, but deadly. "I wish no further communication with you, Mr. Kinney," he said. "You have used improper methods in discussing government affairs."

Kinney, a big man, stood for a moment speechless before the slight figure of his adversary, and Walker added, "I have ordered your arrest."

"Arrest!" shouted Kinney. "You can't do that! I came here on a guarantee of safe-conduct."

This was news to Walker, but on inquiry, he found that such a pledge had actually been given. Thereupon he changed his order from one of arrest to deportation, and Kinney was taken back to Greytown ignominiously, under armed guard. He left the country soon afterward.

III

News of the breach between Kinney and Walker reached Washington some little time before French arrived to present his credentials to

Secretary of State Marcy. He came with a great fanfare of personal publicity. Walker was then the darling of the American press, and French was able to bask in his light. People believed, erroneously, that he was one of the fifty-eight Immortals, a one-armed hero, a paladin. His name was heard everywhere. Newspapers in New York and Washington urged Marcy to receive him promptly and with honor. But the ambassadors of England, France, and Spain were making strong representations against recognition of the Walker government, and Marcy felt it advisable to wait. When French requested an audience he was told that "those who were instrumental in overthrowing the government of Nicaragua were not citizens belonging to it." Marcy's view was that the country should be represented by one of its own nationals. He went on to convey that a free election showing that Rivas and Walker were supported by the Nicaraguan people might influence the attitude of the United States.

Leading publicists at once rallied to French and berated the administration. The New York *Daily News* contended that Marcy's alleged reason for denying recognition to Walker was meretricious on the face of it. The real reason, said the *News,* lay in the investments made by members of the Pierce administration in the Kinney claim. In California, another motive was found—the fact that Walker had supported antiadministration candidates for high office. In Ohio, Marcy was accused of playing England's game. Walker's own reply, when the news of Marcy's action reached him, was a vigorous editorial in *El Nicaragüense,* praised by the *New York Times* as "reasoning sustained to a high degree of ability." Its essence was a reminder that American independence had been won with the aid of foreigners— Lafayette, De Kalb, Steuben. The Rivas government, Walker said, represented the only hope of Nicaraguan independence and democracy, and was entitled to American aid. As for a free election, the Provisional Government was prepared to hold one in the very near future.

A number of newspapers pressed home the argument, and there were signs that Marcy was beginning to weaken under Congressional prodding. It was plain that the American public cared little about the merits of the Nicaraguan revolution. They regarded it as a kind of athletic competition, and they wanted the Americans to win; that was all.

Marcy had, in fact, left a door open for retreat, in the event that public opinion forced his hand. If the promise of a free election had been coupled with a modicum of discretion on the part of French, the issue could quickly have been resolved in Walker's favor. But French's ego made him indifferent to his obligations. He set up such an anti-Marcy clamor in the Press that the Secretary in self-respect could not modify his stand. The Kinney story especially was French's stock in trade. His accusations were so open that Webster and Cushing, not to say Pierce and Marcy, had to counter them with blows of their own. Cushing, as Attorney General, set in motion an investigation of French's past as the best means to justify Marcy's rejection of him.

Still exuberant, French went to New York, where he found the welcome that had been denied him in Washington. His suite at the St. Nicholas Hotel was a favorite gathering place of reporters, for he was lavish of champagne and cigars, and every day he had something new and exciting to tell about the iniquities of the Pierce administration, the bravery of the Immortals, and the importance of his own contributions to Walker's success. In one respect only did he serve Walker. He obtained a promise from Charles Morgan to transport recruits for Nicaragua from New York, as from San Francisco. With an eye on the Neutrality Laws, "emigrants" would be shipped for only twenty dollars per head, and no cash would be demanded. As in the case of recruits carried from San Francisco, the cost would simply be deducted from the company's debt to the Nicaraguan government. This policy was continued after Vanderbilt ousted Morgan from the Accessory Transit Company.

So far as the Commodore was concerned, there was every reason to assist Walker to stabilize Nicaragua. French was encouraged to place advertisements of a seemingly innocuous nature in New York's newspapers—"Wanted: ten or fifteen young men to go a short distance out of the city. Single men preferred. Apply at 347 Broadway, corner of Leonard Street, Room 12, between the hours of ten and four. Passage paid." The same newspapers carried glowing reports from Nicaragua and excerpts from *El Nicaragüense* on the opportunities awaiting Americans there—the beauty, fertility, and resources of the country, the broad lands available to settlers, the low cost of living, and the charm of the señoritas—until the imagination of Manhattan's footloose males had been thoroughly aroused. Nothing was said of cholera, dysentery, mosquitoes, flies, or the chiggers that burrowed into human flesh and were the torment of Walker's troops. Hundreds of men were interviewed by French and accepted as "emigrants." Soon all New York knew what was in the wind. Newspapers reported that in California Walker's agents were swamped by volunteers. A riot broke out at San Francisco's docks, when so many passengers sought to board a Transit steamer for Nicaragua that nearly 300 had to be left behind. New Orleans also was bursting with enthusiasm. There a distinguished Cuban fighter for independence, Domingo de Goicuria, was busily recruiting 250 men, many of them Cubans, for service in Nicaragua, and Vanderbilt had assured him of a Transit ship to carry them to Greytown.

IV

The federal government felt compelled to make another effort to enforce the Neutrality Laws. Attorney General Cushing demanded that the District Attorneys of the great ports put an immediate stop to the recruitment and transportation of men for Walker. To assist them, he gave the press his accumulated facts about French's past. A startled public learned that French had been incontestably guilty, not many years before, of forgery and embezzlement. Worse, in the days of the gold rush, he had defrauded and victimized thousands of emigrants en route to California by wagon train. A Senate report bore evidence to his misdeeds, and a pamphlet called *The Sufferings and Hardships of Parker H. French's Overland Expedition* had been privately printed in 1851.

Newspapers which had been lauding French were silenced. The New York *Mercury* spoke the disgust of many when it said, "In bitterness of spirit, let us exclaim, with Sir Harcourt Courtly, 'Will nobody take this man away?' " The abuse heaped on French was as pungent as former praise of him had been saccharine. Heavy criticism was aimed at Walker also for having chosen such a man as his envoy. Nevertheless, to the extent that French was Walker's representative, he still had support. The *New York Times* reminded Marcy that "it is not Captain French, of questionable antecedents, who solicits the ear of our government, but the agent of a sovereign power," and the *Sun* commented that "eminently bad men, morally, hold high places in the governments with which we maintain friendly relations. International morals are not so pure that there need be any squeamishness in admitting Colonel French to the diplomatic circle."

French employed all the tricks his ingenuity could conceive, and they were many, to put Nicaragua-bound recruits on board the Transit steamships without giving the government firm legal grounds for interference. A favorite device was to have the men come on board singly, and mingle with California-bound passengers, of whom there were always a considerable number, and who were always glad to pretend that Walker's men were their sons and brothers. The frustration of federal officers, who knew the filibusters were there and yet were unable to distinguish them from their companions with any certainty, was compounded by the open derision of the passengers. Steamer after steamer was able to sail from New York loaded with "emigrants" to Greytown, while crowds on the dock cheered the name of Walker and booed any mention of Pierce. New York's District Attorney obtained Grand Jury indictments against French; he even had him put under arrest, but this move proved so unpopular that the order was hastily rescinded.

French, however, had not reckoned on the depth of Walker's anger over his behavior, and especially over his statements about Pierce and Marcy. A curt letter came to him from Granada. His commission as minister was revoked. A new envoy had been appointed to Washington—the Nicaraguan priest, Augustin Vijil, who had steadfastly supported Walker from the beginning. With this news, French lost his hold on all that remained to him of public approval, and when he left New York the newspapers hardly bothered to dust their editorial hands of him. He went to Nicaragua, to hear from Walker's own lips that there was no place for him in the country. French was wise enough not to argue, and boarded a ship for New Orleans. There he gave out that he was on secret business for Walker, and roamed the South, delivering lectures on Nicaragua to large audiences. Returning to New York, he sought to promote a new steamship venture, asserting that in spite of everything he was still Walker's trusted friend. So persistent was he that *El Nicaragüense* was finally compelled to publish a statement by Walker that "French has no connection whatever with this government; . . . he is at present engaged in doing the [Nicaraguan] administration all the injury his genius is capable of."

XIII

MR. VANDERBILT IS OUTRAGED

In November, 1855, Cornelius Garrison, reading letters from Morgan in New York, knew that the moment of crisis was at hand. Wall Street sources left no doubt that Vanderbilt's purchases of Accessory Transit stock were rapidly bringing the company under his thumb, and that at the next stockholders' meeting he would take over.

Although Garrison's contract with the company had some years to go, he was highly vulnerable, not only because of past opposition to Vanderbilt, but perhaps even more because of certain irregular transactions of the company's San Francisco office—transactions which he was unwilling to submit to Vanderbilt's scrutiny. But in Garrison's philosophy there was always more than one way to skin a tiger, even if his name was Vanderbilt. He and Morgan had sketched out a plan by which the Commodore might be made the butt of Wall Street for a change, instead of its hero, and some of his millions squeezed out of him.

Everything now depended on one man, Walker. Experience as a politician and banker had made Garrison a shrewd judge of character. It was clear to him that Walker's motivations differed sharply from those of the run of men. Conversations in Nicaragua reported by C. J. McDonald and Parker French had so far brought nothing more from Walker than formal appreciation of Garrison's aid. The time had now come to get a definite commitment from him.

With such a man, Garrison sensed, a crude appeal to the pocket-book would not serve. You cannot bribe a knight-errant. But you can always appeal to his knightliness. Garrison accordingly began his campaign by retaining the services of two of Walker's oldest friends, Edmund Randolph and another well-known San Francisco attorney, Parker Crittenden, offering them shares in large future profits if they would go to Nicaragua on his behalf. Their specific assignment was to persuade Walker to seize the properties of the Accessory Transit Company in the name of Nicaragua, and turn them over to Randolph, who would form a new company to be headed by Garrison and Morgan. A legal justification for such a move could be found in the fact that Accessory Transit over the years had refused to admit its sizable debt to Nicaragua.

It was the plan of Morgan and Garrison, if they could win Walker's consent, to sell the stock of Accessory Transit short in huge quantities and make a Wall Street killing when the news broke. But nothing of this was to be said to Walker. Randolph and Crittenden were to emphasize that the new company would accept a charter far more favorable to Nicaragua than that held by Vanderbilt, a contract that would assure frequent and regular shipping service from the United States; and that cooperation in providing the recruits and supplies needed by Walker would be unstinted. He was to be told, further, that if he would not agree, Morgan and Garrison would no longer feel an obligation to make efforts on his behalf. With so cogent an argument, Randolph and Crittenden saw no reason why they should not accept the mission. At the last moment, the Mayor suggested that they take with them his son and trusted aid, W. R. Garrison.

II

In December, 1855, Cornelius Vanderbilt, once more at the helm of Accessory Transit, was feeling expansive. Having accumulated all the necessary stock, he had ousted Morgan from the company and regained the presidency. The company's shares had thereupon bounded upward and had added at least a million to his wealth. With Walker in Nicaragua, the Transit route was secure; and his success might open up not only Nicaragua but the entire Caribbean to American capital. There could be no doubt that the independence of Cuba was one of Walker's major objectives. Why else was the noted Cuban revolutionary, Domingo de Goicuria, recruiting for him in New Orleans? One of Vanderbilt's first actions after assuming command at Accessory Transit had been to confirm an order previously issued by Morgan to send a company ship to New Orleans to transport Goicuria and his men to Greytown without asking cash payment. Vanderbilt expected to begin negotiations with Walker soon over the amount of the Transit's debt to Nicaragua, and he anticipated that his bill for the ocean fares of Walker's recruits, plus the filibuster's gratitude, would offset most of the obligation. Goicuria's gratitude could be expected to have similar dollar value if and when he and Walker succeeded in wresting Cuba from Spain.

At Granada, Walker received a message from Goicuria, who said that if Walker and he were in agreement on future strategy, he would bring to Nicaragua 250 fighting men. One thing only the Cuban wanted to determine. Could he count on aid not only in the overthrow of the Spanish tyranny in Cuba, but in support of Cuban independence against any aggressive tendencies that the United States might display?

Walker was able to reply, with complete truth, that to aid in the liberation of Cuba had always been one of his dreams. He believed that the best interests of the United States would be served by the independence of the Caribbean nations, which, under efficient and honest administration, would benefit from the availability of American capital, business enterprise, and trade.

A memorandum of agreement was drawn up and signed. Goicuria was to aid Walker in "consolidating the peace and the government of the Republic of Nicaragua." Walker on his part would "assist and cooperate with his person and his various resources, such as men, in the cause of Cuba and in favor of her liberty."*

---

* W. O. Scroggs, "William Walker's Designs on Cuba," in *Mississippi Valley Historical Review*, 1914, Vol. I, p. 199.

III

While Goicuria and Walker were negotiating for the future of Cuba, Randolph, Crittenden, and young Garrison arrived in Granada, together with a hundred new recruits. It was a joyous moment for Walker, able to receive his oldest friend against a background of power and fame. That evening he entertained the three San Franciscans at a dinner attended by President Rivas and the entire cabinet; and the next day he met privately with Randolph.

Subsequently reporting Walker's action in seizing the Transit, some American newspapers said that in accepting Garrison's offer he displayed impulsiveness and ignorance verging on idiocy. Walker himself made no defense of his action. But his decision was far from impulsive or ignorant. Several weeks earlier word has come to him from San Francisco that some kind of stock-rigging deal was in the wind.* There was nothing in this to tempt him. No one could read the New York newspapers, as he had done for years, without being aware of Vanderbilt's tremendous power. That he was wary of any commitment to Garrison and Morgan shows in their recourse to Randolph. He appreciated the aid he had received from Garrison, but he did not misunderstand it or overvalue it. Sooner or later it would all be paid for by Nicaragua through reductions of Accessory Transit's debt.

New York newspapers telling of Vanderbilt's bid for recapture of Accessory Transit reached Granada before Randolph's arrival. The practical question that Walker had to consider was whether he would be better off to cooperate with the legal head of the company, Vanderbilt, or to throw in his lot with the men whom Vanderbilt had defeated. While only that question was before him, he remained neutral. He wanted the good will of the company regardless of the identity of its head. The dangers that would follow defiance of Vanderbilt were unmistakable. But when Randolph came to him, the situation suddenly changed. This was the man of all men to whom he was devoted, the friend who had more than once come to his rescue, helped him, saved him.

A realist, a Napoleon, would have had no hesitation in sacrificing

* William Walker, *The War in Nicaragua*, p. 149.

the friendship to political advantage—would have played for time, put off the decision until Randolph grew tired of waiting. Not so Walker. The saying that "a friend in power is a friend lost" did not apply to him. Given his attitude toward life, he could deny Randolph nothing—the point on which Garrison counted. Walker's motivation in the matter was described enigmatically by himself. "The friendship between Randolph, Crittenden, and Walker was of a character not to be expressed by words; but the existence of such a sentiment between these three is essential for an understanding of the perfect confidence which marked their acts in reference to the Transit."

The press was mystified by what seemed to be a totally irresponsible action on the part of a man who, until then, had conducted his affairs with considerable skill. What it could not know was that, reasoning from Walker's special premises, his decision was in fact entirely logical. His life had never been guided by the canons of success, but by the canons of personal honor, in which the claim of friendship was paramount.

He was not unaware of the economic motivations of politics. Rather he rejected them. It was this apparent indifference to the realities of American life that prompted Horace Greeley to call him "the Don Quixote of Central America." The Knight of La Mancha did not seem more wrong-minded and absurd to his contemporaries than Walker in the eyes of the great magnates of the 1850's. It was not merely that he dared to defy Vanderbilt. He was defying the onset of a new age. He was tilting at the unshakable windmill of the money-power.

His own description of his private meeting with Randolph, while formalized, hints at the forces at work in him. "Randolph informed Walker that he and Crittenden had carefully examined the charter of the Accessory Transit Company, and were both clear and decided in the opinion that it had been forfeited. . . . After due reflection, Walker was entirely satisfied . . . that the agreement with Garrison was the means, and at that time the only means, for carrying out the policy vital to the Rivas administration. True, neither the President nor the cabinet knew of the means whereby their objects were accomplished; and it was in fact highly necessary to the success of the measures that they should be known to as few persons as possible. After Randolph and Walker had agreed on the terms of a new transit grant, a copy was sent to Garrison at San Francisco, McDonald being the bearer of it. W. R. Garrison went to New York for the purpose of informing Charles Morgan of the arrangements which had been made, and were about to be made, while Randolph remained at Granada. Nothing was said to Rivas of the new transit contract."

Walker's failure to fulfill his responsibility to Rivas was heavy on his mind. When the President was informed of the affair, he exclaimed indignantly that Walker had consented to "the sale of the country." This Walker did not deny. Instead, ruefully, he said, " 'The sale of the country,' in Rivas' use of the term, was a foregone conclusion . . . the only way to get into the country a force capable of protecting it, not only from domestic but from foreign enemies. . . . Whoever desires to hold Nicaragua securely must be careful that the navigation . . . is controlled by those who are his staunchest and most reliable friends." He did not, however, attempt to explain why he had broken with Vanderbilt when the latter was cooperatively providing free passage for recruits.

As Richard III for a kingdom, so for friendship Walker was ready to "set his life upon a cast," and "stand the hazard of the die."

IV

At the end of February, 1856, the stock of the Accessory Transit Company sold at $23 a share, in a rising market. Early in March, the *New York Times* reported that Morgan, "lately in the administration of the company, was selling the stock [short] much as Vanderbilt had done after the latter had lost control." Vanderbilt eagerly grasped what seemed to him a heaven-sent opportunity to corner the stock and squeeze a fortune out of his enemy, and he bought as heavily as Morgan was selling, holding the price close to its peak level. Then, on March 12, news from Nicaragua that Walker had annulled the Accessory Transit charter, and had issued a new charter to Edmund Randolph, precipitated a wild rush on Wall Street to sell Transit shares. That day the price of the stock dropped four points, and it continued to fall until the shares were selling at $13 each. At this price Morgan covered his short sales, for a profit estimated at close to a million.

Incredulous at the first reports of Walker's action, once Vanderbilt was sure of the facts he let out his rage in private and public. The great question in New York's financial community was: what had possessed Walker to do such a thing? Regretfully the well-informed *Herald* remarked that "the great mass of the American people deeply sympathize with the present government of Nicaragua and will regret that its gallant head has perilled its hitherto bright prospects. It will be seen that it is in Mr. Vanderbilt's power to kill off the new government by opening another route and thus cutting off Walker's communications with San Francisco and New York."

The accuracy of this forecast soon became evident. Morgan had neglected to organize the new line of steamships on which Walker was counting, and for six vital weeks no steamers sailed from New York with the men and supplies essential to Walker's security. Efforts made by Garrison to keep Accessory Transit steamers running from San Francisco to Nicaragua proved fruitless when a Vanderbilt agent arrived with orders that all of the company's ships out of California were to be routed to Panama, where their passengers would be transferred to the Atlantic side by railroad. The Commodore was moving simultaneously on many fronts. When his letters demanding intervention by the United States brought only a cold reply from Secretary of State Marcy, the millionaire promptly turned to England. His agents rushed to London and to the Caribbean to invoke the aid of British diplomacy and warships in blocking the Transit entry at Greytown. Still another agent went to Granada, where he talked secretly with President Rivas, in an effort to produce an open break between him and Walker. Simultaneously Vanderbilt brought suit for $500,000 against Garrison, on a charge of fraud, and another, for $1,000,000 against Morgan, Garrison, and Walker, alleging trespass, conversion, and dispersal of the company's goods, and fraudulent conspiracy to interrupt and molest the corporation.

The force of these moves produced a prompt effect on Morgan and Garrison. Content with their stockmarket killing, they had gone through the form of purchasing the new transit charter from Randolph; now they offered to sell the new charter, with its privileges, to Vanderbilt. He flatly refused. His duty, he replied, was to protect the stockholders of the old company, and he wrote a letter to the New York *Herald* to explain his virtuous stand. "Mr. Garrison called on me and ... intimated that if I would participate with him and Charles

Morgan . . . we could make a good business of it to the exclusion of the Transit Company. I told him he must clear up his character as regards his conduct toward the company. . . ." This was no doubt accurate, but it was far from being the truth. The great financier had in fact found it possible to extract a cash profit from the situation. His order to withdraw his ships from Nicaragua and enter the Panama run created consternation among the other Panama lines. Recognizing his nuisance value, Vanderbilt promptly offered to withdraw his ships from competition, on payment by the Panama lines of a monthly "subsidy" of $40,000 (later, $56,000) a month. The agreement was too close to blackmail to be put into writing, but it was made orally, and carried out.*

---

* *Harper's Weekly*, 1859, Vol. III, p. 114.

XIV

⟨✤⟩

"YOU STAND ALONE"

Walker, in 1856, stood at a focal point of history, where great political
and economic forces converged: the need of the United States for a
short ocean route to California—the determination of England to
prevent the Americans from building an interoceanic canal that
would give them an advantage in trade with the Orient—the drive of
New York capitalists to control the Central American isthmus—
the dream of Manifest Destiny shared by millions of Americans—the
urge of the South to annex Cuba and the Caribbean lands—the
unending struggle of Central America's peons against feudal serfdom.
The importance that the world attributed to his venture is suggested
by the enemies that he made. These included, in addition to Vanderbilt, the conservative wing of the American Congress; the Nicaraguan
Legitimists; the governments of Costa Rica, Honduras, and Guatemala; England; and less overtly, Spain and France. In the immensity
of their power he found a wry satisfaction. He still hoped for victory,
but a defeat by hostile forces of such magnitude would at least be
no disgrace.

Almost at the moment when his defiance of Vanderbilt was shocking informed circles in New York, a number of speeches sharply

critical of him were made in the United States Senate, while British enmity was not confined to words. The chances of intervention on Walker's behalf by the Pierce administration had diminished, England calculated, to the point where her Central American friends need no longer be restrained. State papers which were not made public until many years later revealed that Great Britain's War Office at this time arranged a grant of arms to Costa Rica to combat "the troops under Mr. Walker, against whom you may have to defend yourselves."

These British arms included, in addition to 2,000 rifled muskets equipped with sights and superior to those used by Walker's men, a million rounds of ammunition and much other equipment.* This became known to Walker when a messenger carrying official mail to San José was intercepted and letters from the Costa Rican consul in London were found containing evidence that the British Foreign Secretary, Lord Clarendon, had personally authorized the shipment of arms which emboldened Costa Rica to go to war. "When I was telling Lord Clarendon," wrote the consul, "that Costa Rica already had an army of eight hundred men on the frontier, he was much pleased, and said that was a proper move . . . and that is the reason for their giving us the muskets."

To a letter from the Costa Rican government requesting naval support as well, the Foreign Office replied that a cruiser would visit Costa Rica "to protect British interests." Actually, a large squadron comprising some of England's finest warships began to range both coasts of Central America. Reported the New York *Daily News,* a pro-Walker organ, "The British Ambassador at our Federal Capital, having been in due form interrogated regarding the aggressive posture of the . . . British fleet off San Jan del Norte declines communicating any explanation."

Thus encouraged, at the beginning of March, 1856, President Mora of Costa Rica issued an order of mobilization calling for an army of 9000 men "to take up arms for the republic of Nicaragua" against what he maintained was an American invasion; and without waiting for a formal declaration of war, a substantial force equipped with British guns advanced into Nicaragua. Advising Mora, it subse-

---

* British State Papers, Vol. XVI, pp. 784-5, 794-6.

quently became known, were agents of Spain and France, as well as of England.

To this invasion the Nicaraguan government responded with a declaration of war. Let the world note, said President Rivas, that his country had been attacked without provocation. More to the point was a statement personally issued by Walker—the affirmation of political principles that Jerez had earlier urged him to make. Throwing off all claims to impartiality as between Democrats and Legitimists, he made a frank appeal to the revolutionary elements of the entire isthmus. He had been invited to Nicaragua by the Democrats, he said, and he and his men had never ceased to struggle for the principles of the revolution. True, he had held his Democratic friends in check, he had sought to conciliate the Legitimists, he had tried to establish friendly relations with the antidemocratic governments of neighboring countries, but all his advances for the sake of peace had been repulsed with scorn. Now the country was being attacked. Let it be so. He and his American followers were joined with Nicaraguan Democrats in eternal opposition to *Servile* governments throughout Central America, and they would resume and wear forever the red ribbon of democracy.

Walker's belief in democracy was by no means inconsistent with his urge to power. For him, as for the world of his time, the institutions of the United States could be equated with democracy. To extend these institutions to another people, as he hoped eventually to do in Central America, was to serve the democratic cause. His opponents assumed that his professions of democratic faith were dictated by cold expediency. To the conservatives his aim seemed to be "absolute and exclusive domination of the country" in the interest of the United States.* The fact remained that in 1856 Walker's reaffirmation of democratic allegiance was accepted by many Nicaraguans. Native volunteers continued to serve in his army. His popularity among the poorer classes was noted more than once. The most dedicated of the Democratic leaders, Maximo Jerez, agreed to join the new Rivas cabinet as Minister of War.

For all the turbulence he created, one comes at the core of his thinking to a sudden quiet perception of a truth to which America

---

* R. Obregon Loria, *La Campaña del Transito,* San José, 1956, p. 58.

did not awaken until he had been dead a century—that a great power best serves its own interest by lifting poor and primitive peoples into the light of productive civilization. At a time when economic assistance to other countries on a national scale was unheard of, it was only by capitalistic enterprise and the introduction of equitable institutions that exploiting nations could help the exploited make progress, as the United States later did in the Philippines. It is not to be mistaken that, left to their own devices, the Central American peoples experienced a lowering of their standards of living and social condition after Walker's day, not an advance.*

Horace Greeley might consider him a power-hungry pirate, Wall Street an agent of cunning capitalists, but he thought of himself as the head of a revolutionary army, fighting against the feudal owners of the isthmus in the name of democracy. As proof of his Democratic good faith he not only brought Maximo Jerez into the government, but gave two other cabinet posts to Democrats of Jerez' choice; he authorized the transfer of the seat of government from Granada to León; and he had the government announce an early presidential and congressional election, to be held by popular vote.

To him the shocking thing was that although England did not hesitate to support her reactionary aims in Central America with arms and supplies, the government of the United States, calling itself democratic, refused to see the significance of the struggle that he was waging. *Harper's Weekly* remarked that the treatment of Walker by the American government was very like that of John Knox and John Wesley by the Church of England. It was a comparison the more apt because of the psychological similarity of Walker to the great religious reformers. Like them, he never complained about the injuries inflicted on him by enemies, but the calumnies of his own countrymen left a scar. He had ridden out under the banner of democracy into a world full of danger, seeking dragons to slay, and his feelings about the castigation of him by Marcy and Buchanan were like those of a knight who, while on a great quest, heard that he had been blackballed and barred from the Round Table.

---

* A. G. Frank, "The Economic Development of Nicaragua," in *Inter-American Affairs,* 1955, Vol. VIII, No. 4.

II

In the ensuing military campaign, which comprised only two battles, Walker's forces lost both, and his reputation as a general was permanently damaged, yet he emerged as the victor and a greater hero than ever in the eyes of the American public. The first battle took place at Santa Rosa, south of Lake Nicaragua, where the enemy vanguard was encamped, and where the Costa Ricans swore death to every American on whom they could lay hands. Walker's situation was deteriorating rapidly. Another cholera epidemic, then in its initial stage, coupled with widespread dysentery and fevers, had reduced his American effectives to only 600. He himself was down with fever and a painful swelling of the face. In an effort to conserve his men for what he could not doubt would be a long struggle, he determined to send against the Costa Ricans initially a battalion of four companies: one composed entirely of Frenchmen recently arrived from San Francisco; one of German immigrants out of New York; one of Nicaraguans, and one of raw American recruits. A question immediately arose: who was to command this polyglot force? Walker's choice could hardly have been worse if he had been delirious with fever, as some thought he was. His attention centered on a German named Louis Schlessinger, an educated and plausible man whom he had previously used on diplomatic missions, and who spoke all of the four essential languages. Totally untrained and psychologically unfit for military leadership, Schlessinger failed to scout the territory into which he was advancing, and was surprised by the enemy in force. At the first fire the undisciplined company of Germans broke and fled, followed by the French, with Schlessinger himself among them. For a few minutes the Nicaraguans and Americans held back the enemy but, after a hundred men had fallen, joined the rout, leaving their wounded to summary execution at the hands of the jubilant Costa Ricans.

News of this shocking defeat came to a Granada already unnerved by the terrors of cholera, and was followed closely by rumors that a Honduran army was about to join in the attack on Walker. The resulting wave of panic swept up many Americans as well as Nicaraguans. Scores of recent arrivals from New York who had not yet enlisted in Walker's force begged to be sent home. Even his veterans were dispirited, especially since a number of his best officers had been stricken by cholera. Efforts to revive morale were unavailing before the despondency evoked by the spectacle of half-starved fugitives from Santa Rosa straggling in with reports of Schlessinger's incompetence and Costa Rican savagery. Schlessinger himself was arrested, court-martialed and condemned to be shot as a coward, but managed to escape, some thought with the secret connivance of Walker, whose own responsibility in having selected so untried a man for a military command was manifest. To his friend and most stalwart defender in the United States Congress, Senator John Weller of California, Walker wrote in a vein of grim realism: "We have great moral odds against us. . . . I may not live to see the end . . . but if we fail, we feel that it will be in the cause of honor."

Most imminent and acute of all the dangers confronting Walker was the likelihood that the enemy, now numbering 4,000, would occupy the all-important Transit route and block the way for American reinforcements. To forestall this move, although he was still weak from his illness, he took personal command of the 500 Americans left to him, and led them south to the town of Rivas, the scene of his defeat a year earlier, astride the western segment of the route. There he put all his energy into a revival of the health, morale, and discipline of his troops.

"Woe betide the luckless wretch who unfitted himself for duty in that dread presence on the eve of battle," wrote one of his officers. It was at this time that Walker publicly reprimanded his brother Norvell, and reduced him from a captaincy to the ranks, for having participated in an all-night carouse against orders. Thereafter he paraded his restive men in the plaza of Rivas, and briefly addressed them. It was a typically Walkerian performance. Thinner than ever, pale and feverish, his drab clothing hanging from him like a scarecrow's slops, he sought to give his men a vision of themselves as heroes.

"Let me try," he said, "to place before you the moral grandeur of the position that you occupy. You stand alone in the world, without a friendly government to give even its sympathy, much less its aid. You have nothing to support you in this struggle except the consciousness of the justice of your cause. Those who should have befriended you have maligned you. . . . I would not conceal from you the great peril and the urgency of the danger in which you stand." They heard him in silence. But "the words . . . had the desired effect and created a new spirit among them," Walker wrote. "It is only by constant appeals to the loftier qualities of man that you can make him a good soldier; and all military discipline is a mere effort to make virtue constant and reliable by making it habitual."

III

The news grew worse. President Rivas reported from León that in spite of his efforts to conciliate the Hondurans, they were about to invade Nicaragua and attack Granada. Walker now had to consider whether he dared do battle with the Costa Ricans on the Transit route; for even if he won against the heavy odds confronting him, his losses were almost certain to be large, and his army would be unfit to meet the Hondurans. His decision was to return to Granada until Nicaraguan reinforcements then being organized in León could reach him.

No sooner had he reached Granada than further word came: the rumors from Honduras were false. An invasion from the north was not anticipated in the near future. Shaken by this disclosure of the weakness of President Rivas as a source of intelligence, Walker turned back toward the Transit, but too late; the Costa Ricans had taken advantage of his withdrawal to occupy the towns of Rivas and Virgin Bay, where they seized the buildings of the Transit Company and wantonly killed nine of its American employees.

In such a situation, failure to attack would be equivalent to slow suicide. As Walker saw it, his only hope lay in forcing the Costa Ricans out of their strong position in Rivas. Despite the small size of his force and his lack of artillery, he determined on an immediate assault. The first hours of the battle went well for him. Driving into the streets of Rivas in an unexpected circular movement, his men trapped and shot down large numbers of the enemy, and forced the rest, nearly 2000, into the center of the town. There for a time the exchange of fire continued heavily in favor of the Americans, with five Costa Ricans falling for every one of Walker's soldiers. But he lacked the manpower needed to maintain his advantage, and his casualties, killed and wounded, rose to 120, one quarter of his total command. The fall of night enabled him to withdraw his men, the movement being carried out in utmost silence, and when with daylight the Costa Ricans prepared to resume the battle they found to their astonishment that the Americans were gone, carrying their wounded with them.

Some of Walker's own associates thought the end had come, as they again retreated northward toward Granada, but they did not reckon on the imponderables of war. Costa Rica soon began to hear the truth about her heavy losses at Rivas, and after General Mora's bombast the long casualty lists came as a shock. Even worse was the appearance of the cholera in his army, in an especially virulent form. It was not to see thousands of its young men destroyed within a fortnight that his nation had heeded the call to arms; and the epidemic, which had begun to spread throughout Costa Rica itself, was blamed on the war. When a spontaneous demonstration demanding the return of the army and verging on revolt broke out in San José, Mora decided to hasten back to his capital with such troops as were fit to march.

Suddenly, amazingly, the Americans heard that Rivas, Virgin Bay, and the Transit once more lay open to them. There came a note from the commander whom Mora had left in Rivas, begging the indulgence of Walker for the stricken hundreds of Costa Ricans whom he would find there. The first reaction in Walker's camp was a roar of protest; was the shooting and bayoneting of wounded Americans to go unrequited? Nevertheless, when Walker issued an order that the troops respect the conventions of war among civilized peoples, it was obeyed. The enemy sick were tended; those who recovered were repatriated, and those who died were given formal burial. Even the most anti-American of Costa Rican historians had to admit, "In regard for the truth, we must say that Walker treated with humanity the soldiers whom he found in Rivas."*

This display of humanitarianism in the midst of despair and horror caught the imagination of the American people, and proved to be Walker's most effective political instrument, more than offsetting his

* J. Perez, *Memorias,* II, p. 51.

loss of military prestige. Nation-wide approval greeted reports of scenes in the improvised hospitals of Rivas, where he personally inspected the wounds of enemies and provided them with such care as could be found. The press, which had begun to grow cool at news of his defeats, took him again to its editorial heart, praised him for his forbearance and generosity, rejoiced in the fact that the tide had turned for him, and even saw in the ravages of the cholera, which had brought Mora's campaign to its abrupt end, the beneficent favor of Providence for Americans, recalling the fate of the Assyrian when he came down like a wolf on the fold.

"*Los Yankis,*" exulted the *Daily News* of New York, "are not monsters of rudeness and cruelty, as the designing slanders of European bureaucracy describe us, but . . . have burst their way like a fertilizing torrent through the barriers of barbarism. . . . Nicaragua is at peace." British journals too were impressed, the London *Post*, no friend to Walker, going so far as to see in him "a certain resemblance to the chivalry of the middle ages . . . the Normans in their palmy days"; while the influential *Saturday Review* told England that "if Walker . . . should eventually annex Central America to the United States, it may be doubted whether European statesmen have any longer a motive for interfering."

In May, 1856, Walker, regarded as doomed two months earlier, was again in full command of the situation. Costa Rica and Honduras appeared to have lost their stomach for war. Legitimist insurrectionists had been put down by Nicaraguan troops under the command of Vallé and Goicuria. Some reinforcements and supplies from America were again reaching Greytown on a steamer belatedly supplied by Morgan. And most important, American sentiment for Walker was making itself heard more and more loudly in political circles. A speech in the Senate on May 1, 1856, by Senator Weller of California was widely reported. "There is no man whose character has been more shamefully misrepresented in this country than General Walker. I have known him for several years on the Pacific Coast as a quiet, unobtrusive and intelligent gentleman of uncommon energy and de- cided character. His integrity—his honor—was never impeached in any quarter. After being invited, he went to Nicaragua—not as a 'freebooter'; he did not go there for plunder. He neither coveted their lands nor their money, for no one has less of the sordid feeling than General Walker. He was actuated by a high and honorable ambition —a patriotic desire to aid in establishing free institutions in Nicaragua, and ultimately confederate, in a peaceable manner, the Central American states into one great republic. This was his ambition—this was the object he sought to accomplish. Many gentlemen of the highest character residing on the Pacific, actuated by the same motives, rallied under his banner. It is a great mistake to suppose these men are desperadoes and freebooters!"

IV

Like any political man, Walker was perpetually striving to make rational decisions in an irrational framework. Whether his judgment was good or bad in a given instance mattered less than the ever-changing and unpredictable pattern of circumstance in which he worked and which more than anything else determined the outcome of his actions. A man shooting from the hip at a mile-high eagle had as good a chance of hitting his target as Walker to overcome the hostility of the Pierce administration by anything that he might purposefully do. Only great luck, some favorable concatenation of events could change the President's attitude toward him. That luck was his in the spring of 1856, when his mercy to the Costa Ricans at Rivas was affecting American sentiment. The Platform Committee of the Democratic Party was then at work drafting the principles on which the party's choice of a presidential nominee would presumably be made. Prominent in the Committee was Pierre Soulé, who had never forgiven Marcy and Pierce for their "betrayal" of him in the matter of the Ostend Manifesto. Regarded as a leading light of the American expansionists, he was determined to revive the spirit of the Manifesto in the Democratic platform. The soaring of Walker's reputation—"the noble Walker," Soulé called him—provided the former ambassador with precisely the opportunity he sought; and almost singlehanded he drafted a plank for the platform that, he hoped, would alter the nation's policy not only toward Walker's effort in Nicaragua, but with respect to Spanish and British provocations throughout the Caribbean.

"The time has come for the people of the United States to declare themselves in favor of free seas, and progressive free trade throughout the world. . . .

"Resolved, That the great highway . . . marked out for free communication between the Atlantic and Pacific oceans . . . would be secured by a timely and efficient exertion of the control which we have the right to claim over it. . . . No power on earth should be suffered to impede or clog its progress. . . .

"Resolved, That, in view of so commanding an interest, the people of the United States cannot help but sympathize with the efforts which are being made by the people of Central America to regenerate that portion of the continent which covers the passage across the inter-oceanic isthmus."

Soulé in effect was saying that only a candidate who would agree to back Walker and the Ostend Manifesto would get the majority of the Southern delegations at the Convention which was to assemble in Cincinnati in June—a warning to Buchanan, and an invitation to other hopefuls. Buchanan was playing a subtle game. To Southerners he spoke of his satisfaction in his part in the Manifesto, to which he had made considerable contributions. But in the North and in British circles he let it be known privately that Soulé, "a regular bird-charmer," had hypnotized him into signing the document, and that he was in fact out of sympathy with it. No one could be sure precisely where he stood in the matter.

The first candidate to yield to Soulé's pressure was President Pierce, who still dreamed of succeeding himself in the White House. For once overriding Marcy, and ignoring protests from Costa Rica, Honduras, and Cornelius Vanderbilt, on May 14, 1856, he recognized the Rivas government of Nicaragua, in the person of its new minister, Padre Augustin Vijil.

No one could have been more surprised by the new turn of events than Padre Vijil himself, who from the moment of his appearance in Washington had been subjected to insults and vilification. A gentle and idealistic soul, a former lawyer turned priest, eager to serve the cause of peace and the popular welfare, he was dismayed by the intensity of feeling against Walker that he encountered wherever the influence of Great Britain, the Central American conservatives, or the Catholic hierarchy was felt. Most of Washington's diplomats ignored him, the Vanderbilt-oriented press abused him, and the Archbishop of Baltimore rebuked him: "Is it possible that a Catholic priest should come to this country to labour against his Church and his native land?" It took the President's acceptance of his credentials to make Vijil realize that Walker's strength lay not in Washington but in the country at large.

In New York City a mass meeting, attended by thousands, was held to celebrate the recognition of Walker, with gigantic signs reading NO BRITISH INTERFERENCE ON THE AMERICAN CONTINENT! and ENLARGE THE BOUNDS OF LIBERTY! At this meeting, another contender for the Democratic nomination joined the pro-Walker camp—Lewis Cass, United States Senator from Michigan. In a letter read to the cheering crowd he said, "I am free to confess that the heroic effort of our countrymen in Nicaragua excites my admiration. . . . The difficulties which General Walker has encountered and overcome will place his name high on the roll of distinguished men of his age. . . . A new day, I hope, is opening upon the states of Central America. Our countrymen will plant there the seeds of our institutions, and God grant that they may grow up into an abundant harvest of industry, enterprise and prosperity."

These developments were not lost on the British, who supposed that recognition of Walker would be followed by open American aid to him. It was the easier for England to believe this, since she herself was secretly aiding his enemies. As evidence of the seriousness with which he viewed the situation, Lord Palmerston ordered 20,000 troops to Canada, and staged a great naval review, to which the American minister in London was pointedly invited. A wave of war talk rose again on both sides of the Atlantic. The London *Post* warned that "no one can tell to what consequences the success of filibustering in Central America may lead. . . . We must be prepared to defend our possessions." Advocates of a direct American challenge to England, over Nicaragua, were prominent at the Democratic Convention in Cincinnati. There, after hot debate, Soulé's Nicaraguan plank was incorporated in the party platform to loud cheers.

Most of the Southern delegates at the convention gave their votes to Cass or Pierce. The Northern states, however, felt safer with the always-uncommitted and exquisitely cautious Buchanan, and as many had foreseen, he emerged with the nomination. With the ineffectual

Millard Fillmore as the American Party (Know-Nothing) candidate, and the newly born Republican Party gambling wildly on General Frémont of California, it was not difficult to foresee where the victory would lie in the coming November. At this stage there was still a widespread impression that once Buchanan was in the Presidency he would reveal himself as an expansionist, call what was generally assumed to be Palmerston's bluff, and give Walker all possible aid and encouragement.

XV

〜✦〜

THE PRESIDENT

In Nicaragua, too, 1856 saw a presidential contest, and it achieved a degree of turbulence remarkable even for Latin America. In the early spring, when southern Nicaragua was in the throes of war, there was an election in the region around León. A head of state was chosen from among three candidates—Rivas, standing as a moderate, Jerez, representing the radical wing of the Democratic party, and Mariano Salazar, a wealthy merchant turned army officer, who had achieved considerable popularity by fiery speeches and judicious expenditure. The returns favored Salazar by a slight margin. After Walker had re-established order in the south, however, Rivas demanded that Granada and the districts to the east and southwest of Lake Nicaragua, where most of his own strength lay, be polled. Instantly trouble began.

The Granadans were agitated by the realization that no matter which of the three candidates was elected, they would be subordinate to hated León. Even Rivas was committed to the northern center as Nicaragua's capital. The alarms of war had not abated the rivalry of the two cities by an iota. They had been brought into uneasy truce only by the American, Walker. If there was to be a new

President, said many in Granada, let him too be a candidate. Let there be a completely new election.

Against this proposal Rivas, Salazar, and Jerez all three took a firm stand. They had no doubt as to the outcome of an election in which Walker was a contestant. Not only the Granadans but even some of the Leónese could be expected to vote for him. Withdrawal of the Costa Rican troops had made him a national hero. In Granada he was followed by cheering crowds wherever he went. When he visited León with some of his American troops the city went wild with enthusiasm. Feasts were given, songs were written in his honor, "women of every age and condition" thronged around him with blessings for having protected their homes. News of Padre Vijil's recognition by President Pierce added to his stature in the public eye. He was the successful man, and the people, realizing that further attacks on their country from south and north were probable, looked to him and his *gringos* to protect them.

The intensity of feeling with which Rivas opposed the idea of a new election took Walker aback. He came to the conclusion that pressure from Vanderbilt's agents and from the British-dominated Guatemalan government had begun to sway Rivas. In no other way could he account for the proposal that the elderly President blurted out during their meeting in León—that Walker, in order to appease Nicaragua's neighbors, reduce by half the size of his American force. Sensing conspiracy in the air, he replied only that he would consider such an idea when Nicaragua was able to pay the men discharged, in accordance with their contract, which promised them substantial grants of money and land at the end of their service.

Walker noted, too, that "the face of Jerez had a cloud over it." One evening Jerez came to Walker's residence in León to discuss the future of the Nicaraguan legation in Washington, for Father Vijil had asked to be relieved of the post. Thinking that Jerez wanted the appointment for himself, Walker promptly offered his approval, and Jerez seemed pleased when he took his leave. Within the hour he returned, however, to ask uneasily, "My appointment to the United States is then decided on?" Walker caught the intimation. The offer, Jerez felt, might be designed to get rid of him. To reassure him, Walker said, "I will support the appointment, Don Maximo, only if you desire it." But Jerez still showed suspicion, and Walker realized that no words of his could restore their former amity.

Salazar also became a potential source of trouble, for it transpired that he had used his army position to make profitable contracts for himself as a merchant, at the expense of the state. Walker, calling him to account, turned him into a powerful enemy. "There were many," he wrote of this period of tension, "desirous of exciting popular passions and prejudices against the Americans . . . to destroy the confidence of the people in the naturalized Nicaraguans." He and most of his men had long since become citizens of their adopted state.

II

At a cabinet meeting, when Rivas' ministers debated whether or not to call a new election, all except one of them stood opposed. Walker listened in silence. Central American historians, dealing at length with this moment in his career, concluded that he was animated wholly by ambition, but this view misses the fact that he could have made himself President long since had he so chosen. He himself had established and maintained the Rivas government in power. The Presidency, for him, was certain to be an embarrassment, giving fresh ammunition to his enemies in Washington. There is no reason to doubt his own statement that his motive in insisting on a new election with himself as a candidate was to assure the protection of his American followers. "All things tended to show that in case Nicaragua was invaded . . . the Americans might find the machinery of the government they had created and sustained turned against themselves," he wrote. "Hence, unless disposed to carry Rivas off a prisoner—and thereby the whole moral force of his government would have been lost —it was necessary for the welfare of the Americans that a new election should be called." He could no longer control the government from behind the scenes—and not to control it would have been to betray the army that had loyally fought for him.

At the decisive cabinet meeting, having listened patiently to every opinion, he turned to Rivas and quietly requested him to decree a new election. Threats were unnecessary; all knew that the issue had been reduced to a test of power, and there could be no doubt as to where the power lay. Yielding, the President signed the decree.

The next day, leaving an American garrison under Natzmer in the city, Walker rode south toward Managua, midway between Granada and León. Rivas went to considerable lengths to convey that he was reconciled to Walker's policy. "The President and many others of the chief citizens . . . accompanied him [Walker] several miles on his journey; and at parting Don Patricio [Rivas] affectionately embraced the general-in-chief, remarking with moist eyes that he could be depended on in any emergency." But Walker had not gone twenty miles when the political storm hanging over León broke. Suddenly the unfounded rumor spread that the entire cabinet was about to be arrested by Natzmer, and as if convinced of its truth the President and several of his ministers took horses and fled northward. Chief fomenter of the trouble was Salazar, who rode through the city proclaiming that the Americans were about to assassinate the Nicaraguan leaders. The unfounded accusation was especially effective in the poorer sections of the city, where the poverty-ridden were easily stirred to demonstrations and riots. Large numbers of ragged and perpetually hungry men came out of their huts, some of them armed, and began at Salazar's urging to throw up barricades in the streets near an arms depot guarded by American troops.

The crisis mounted fast. Natzmer, believing his soldiers were about to be attacked, ordered his small force to occupy the towers of the Cathedral of León, and prepare to defend themselves. Promptly an order came to him from Jerez, as Minister of War: the Americans were to evacuate the Cathedral, and would be replaced by Nicaraguan troops, who would maintain order in the city. Natzmer hesitated. Disobedience might be construed as mutiny, but he feared to expose his men to attack in the streets. Hastily he sent a fast rider to Walker with Jerez' order and a request for guidance.

As Walker saw the matter, "the designs of Rivas and Jerez were now apparent . . . Jerez had given the order to Natzmer, supposing it would not be obeyed, thereby hoping to make the movement against the Americans turn on their disobedience to a lawful authority." Unwilling to have the breach between himself and the Leónese occur on such an issue, he ordered Natzmer to withdraw his men from León immediately, and join him on the road to Granada.

III

In a bitter proclamation Walker told Nicaragua that Rivas had betrayed his faith as President by inviting the troops of other nations, Guatemala and San Salvador, into Nicaragua. Of this there was factual evidence. "Conspiring against the very people it was bound to protect, the late Provisional Government was no longer worthy of existence. In the name of the people I have therefore declared its dissolution." A new Provisional President was appointed—a Nicaraguan who had held responsible government posts and whose headquarters were in Granada. Rivas, from León, replied in kind, calling Walker a traitor, depriving him of his command and summoning the country to take arms against the Americans.

Sunday, June 29, the election was held. As tabulated in *El Nicaragüense,* the ballots gave Walker an overwhelming majority— almost 16,000 out of a total vote of 23,000, and out of some 35,000 eligible to vote in the entire nation. These figures were obviously incredible, since no ballots were cast in the heavily populated area in and around León. In this respect, the Granadans who ran the election for Walker followed the national custom. Nicaraguan elections were traditionally almost as dishonest as those held in New York or San Francisco at the same period. Of the country's small male population only a small fraction had the qualifications and the interest needed to vote. Most of those who did vote were townsmen of the middle class, shopkeepers and artisans, for few in the rural districts would make the tedious journey to town merely to replace one politico by another. The total vote was generally too small to be convincing, and the standard procedure of the controlling party was to inflate the size of its victory, so as to create the impression of a popular choice.

To the Granadans the outcome of the election was a relief; what would have happened if a Leónese had become their ruler? The city turned out *en masse* for the inaugural, and the streets were filled with cheering multitudes. *"Viva el Presidente! Muerte a los enemigos del orden!"* To the splendor-loving Latin American multitude Walker's drab personal appearance must have been sadly disappointing. The thirty-two-year-old undersized President was dressed in a rusty black coat, baggy trousers, and a black felt hat—looking, in the words of a reporter for the New York *Tribune,* like "a grocery keeper from one of the poorer localities of the Sixth Ward." Nevertheless, there was a sufficiency of pomp—a parade, martial music, flags, a church service, a solemn ceremonial oath. Later Walker addressed a great crowd assembled in the plaza of Granada. A rumor that he would utilize the occasion to seek to annex Nicaragua to the United States had been widely circulated, and representatives of the press and consuls of the great powers were present in considerable numbers. To the general surprise, the crux of the speech was a warning of Nicaragua's intention to control her own destiny at any cost, and a denial of the rights of other powers, "either neighboring or distant," to occupy or dispose of any part of her territory. The firing of a twenty-one-gun salute put exclamation points after this proud asseveration.

An inaugural banquet, attended by fifty leading Nicaraguans and Americans was equally a success. In deference to Walker's personal preference, all toasts were drunk in light wines—a sensible precaution, since no fewer than fifty-three were offered. Walker himself proposed a toast to President Pierce, but the most enthusiastic response greeted a toast by one of his officers to "Uncle Billy." It brought a hearty laugh from Walker—a phenomenon sufficiently rare to cause comment in the press.

IV

Two days later he announced the formation of his cabinet, consisting entirely of Nicaraguans—who were backed, however, by American deputies. As reform followed reform, it was quickly seen that his intention was to Americanize the country, even while retaining its independence. English was introduced into the courts as a legal language "of equal value" to Spanish. Currency values were brought into line with the American dollar. Bonds bearing six per cent interest were printed, to be offered for sale through agents in the United States. Military scrip in dollars was issued to meet current expenses. But the most important changes came in fiscal policy. The Nicaraguan government had in the past drawn its chief revenue from high tariffs on imported staples, such as cloth, wines, knives, plows, and the like, an arrangement which had made prices oppressive for the poor. These commodities Walker put on the free list, while duties on other items were sharply limited in order to encourage trade.

The government, Walker declared, must henceforth look for income to sources which previously had been exempt from taxes. All retailers were to be licensed, and to pay a licensing tax to the government. Manufacturers (the chief, almost the only "manufactured" product of Nicaragua was the national alcoholic beverage, *aguardiente*) were similarly required to pay heavily for the privilege of doing business. Lands which had been in the possession of disloyal persons—those who had assisted the enemies of the Republic—which meant Nicaraguan Legitimists who had supported the Costa Rican invasion—were to be confiscated and sold. Of such estates there were several score, including some of the richest in the country. These announcements, reminiscent of measures introduced by Robespierre in the radical years of the French Revolution, brought howls of pain from Nicaragua's conservatives, and considerable criticism in the United States.

The seizure of the large estates was a major element in Walker's program of Americanization. It was the only way, he believed, to attract American capital to Nicaragua. Every piece of land which the government believed itself justified in taking was to be appraised by a Board of Commissioners, and unless the owner appeared within forty days to show cause why it should not be sold, the sale would be made to the highest bidder. The first of these auctions, held in Granada late in September, 1856, comprised over forty estates. Properties listed—ranches, houses, crops, and animals—were appraised at $753,000, and the auction was publicized by newspapers in New York, New Orleans, and San Francisco.

The seizure of the estates outraged Nicaragua's propertied class, but it also deeply disturbed the tenant farmers and hired hands of the countryside. Whatever the hardships of their lives, they had no desire to exchange their familiar masters for strangers and *gringos*. The unpopularity of Walker's land policy was evident from the first. He was not in a position, however, to alleviate the blow. Time was running out. With the Leónese against him and troops from San Salvador and Guatemala likely to join them at any time, and with England prodding Costa Rica to a resumption of the war, prompt American support more than ever was his only hope. If money, men, and supplies were not soon forthcoming from the United States in quantity, defense against the impending odds would be hopeless. The rich farms of Nicaragua were bait which he deliberately dangled before the eyes of Americans in order to lure them to Nicaragua and the defense of his government. "It may be," he later wrote, "that the reorganization in Nicaragua was attempted too soon, but . . . the Americans were driven forward by the force of events."

V

He was seeking to strengthen his army, and he even established a rudimentary navy. This initially consisted of a single schooner, owned by Walker's Leónese enemy, Salazar, who had begun to trade with Costa Rica under an American flag to which he had no claim. When the schooner put into the harbor of San Juan del Sur, Walker's men promptly seized it. Two small cannon were put on board, it was renamed the *Granada,* and was placed under the command of a remarkable young sailor of fortune, Lieutenant Callender Fayssoux, a handsome, bearded young Missourian who had distinguished himself with the Cuban expeditions of Narciso Lopez five years earlier. Resembling Walker in pride of bearing and determination, Fayssoux quickly justified Walker's faith in him. A British man-of-war, the *Esk,* hailed him on the seas, and its captain, Sir Robert McClure, ordered him to come aboard and exhibit the commission under which he sailed the *Granada,* "flying a flag unknown to any nation." Fayssoux bluntly refused, and threats to sink his ship could not make him obey McClure's order.

Walker, reading Fayssoux's report of this incident, resolved not to let it pass. Some days later McClure visited him in Granada to arrange for the safe departure of some British subjects then in the city. Walker did not rise or even suggest that the Englishman be seated. Instead, looking at him coldly, he said, "I hope, sir, that you have come to apologize for that affair of the schooner. Your conduct to Lieutenant Fayssoux was unbecoming an Englishman and a British officer. I shall make a report of it to your government, demand an investigation, and insure an explanation."

McClure found that he would be unable to transact his business until he apologized, and he finally consented to do so. From this time on, Fayssoux was Walker's favorite among his officers.

Another temporary lift to Walker's prestige came from the American minister in Granada, Wheeler. A belated letter from Secretary Marcy informed Wheeler that the credentials of the Nicaraguan minister Vijil had been accepted, and instructed him to establish diplomatic relations with the Nicaraguan government. So far as Marcy knew when he wrote this letter, the President of Nicaragua was Rivas. Wheeler did not bother to wait until the Secretary could reconsider the matter in the light of Walker's assumption of the Presidency. Instead, he hastened to Walker with the news that he would immediately recognize his government on behalf of the United States. At a subsequent ceremony, Wheeler took it on himself to threaten Great Britain, by implication, with war. "The government of the United States," he told Walker, "hopes to unite cordially with you in the fixed purpose of preventing any foreign power that may attempt to impede Nicaragua's progress by any interference whatever. The great voice of my nation has spoken. Its words must not be unheeded."

VI

The hopes kindled by Wheeler's action soon fizzled out. Its chief effect was to precipitate an open break between the Pierce administration and Walker. Pierce, now a lame-duck President, no longer had any motive to support Walker against Marcy's wishes. Marcy was thus able to rebuke Wheeler in caustic terms, and recall him to Washington; and he was equally sharp in denying an interview to the new minister whom Walker had sent to replace Vijil.

So far as the American government was concerned, Walker was now an outlaw whose head was forfeit to any one of his myriad enemies who could capture him. Was there then any hope? One man on Walker's staff thought there was—the Cuban, Domingo de Goicuria, then a brigadier general in Walker's service. Nearly sixty years old, a man of broad experience and common sense, he was impatient of Walker's romanticism. He himself cut a romantic figure— he wore a flowing grey beard which he had vowed never to shave until his country should be free from Spain—but the idea of compromise did not disturb him. Walker's willingness to fight Vanderbilt and his determination to make no concessions to British power struck Goicuria as unreasonable in a man whose own country had abandoned him. Why should Walker not abandon the United States? It seemed possible to Goicuria that England could be made to see Nicaragua under the new regime, not as an American bastion, but rather as a buffer against any move by the United States into the Caribbean. Only a month earlier Benjamin Disraeli had made a speech in the House of Commons, suggesting that England might cease to contest the Americanization of Nicaragua if the United States would give up the aspiration to Cuba—an idea full of encouragement for the Cuban independence movement.

Walker believed that if he could hold out for some eight or nine months, until Buchanan won the Presidential election and assumed office, all might yet go well. He had received no indication that Buchanan would ignore the plank in the Democratic platform calling for support of the American effort in Nicaragua. His need was for time, and any expedient that might win him time was worth trying. In this frame of mind, he agreed to let Goicuria make a diplomatic effort on his behalf, and appointed him minister to England with a twofold mission: first, to negotiate a loan in the United States; and thereafter to proceed to London to see what he could do. In furtherance of his approach to England, he gave the Cuban a letter carefully concocted to produce the impression that, as between England and America, he was neutral. "Make them [the British] see that we are not engaged in any scheme for annexation. You can make them see that the only way to cut the expanding and expansive democracy of the north is by a powerful and compact southern federation based on military principles."

This was one of those letters, familiar in diplomacy, which, while ostensibly containing secret instructions, are actually intended to be shown privately to statesmen on the opposite side, in order to carry conviction—a card in the diplomatic game, accepted by Goicuria in this sense. Walker evidently felt the need to reassure Goicuria's Cuban friends as well as the British of his intentions with regard to Cuba, for he added, "Cuba must and shall be free, but not for the Yankees. Oh, no! That fine country is not fit for those barbarous Yankees.

What should such a psalm-singing set do in the island?" This was the tone in which Latin Americans were accustomed to talk of the *gringo;* the style is curiously inconsistent with Walker's, and it is not unlikely that the idea and phrasing were suggested by Goicuria.

VII

In his first port of call, New Orleans, Goicuria was badly jolted. The public might feel enthusiasm for Walker, but Southern men of means felt none whatever for Nicaragua's bonds. Aside from the precariousness of Walker's situation, they could not overlook his unsatisfactory stand on slavery. Such hope as remained of raising money on the requisite scale lay in New York, and Goicuria went north without delay. But there the situation was even more disillusioning. Financiers merely smiled at the suggestion of a loan for Walker. With Vanderbilt to contend with? And with Morgan and Garrison already backing away from their contract to supply ships for the Nicaragua run? No one would touch the proposition. The men with whom he talked showed moreover a distressing cynicism about Walker's motives. It was well known in Wall Street that Randolph stood to gain a personal fortune from the deal with Morgan and Garrison. Would anyone in his right mind doubt that Walker himself was to be similarly paid? Goicuria defended his chief against the imputation; on this ground, at least, he knew his man. Walker might be corruptible in other ways, it might be that the need to hold power was already corrupting him, but no one cared less for personal wealth.

The Cuban was seized by a tremendous idea. Since Walker's government could not survive without a loan, and since a loan could not be obtained against the weight of Vanderbilt's enmity, there was only one way out. He would approach the Commodore. Impetuously, without waiting for instructions from Granada, he called on the millionaire and boldly stated his proposition—restoration of Vanderbilt's privileges in the Transit route, in return for a loan.

The Commodore was interested—more, amenable. The destruction of Walker was turning out to be a costly business—and his admiration had been stirred by the man's courage and persistence. All he wanted was Walker's capitulation; that assured, he was disposed to be generous. A loan of a quarter of a million dollars to Walker was discussed—one hundred thousand to be paid on the day when Vanderbilt restored ship service to Nicaragua, the balance within a year thereafter.

Overjoyed, Goicuria hastened to write Walker the great news. He could not resist, however, adding to his letter the reports that he had heard of Randolph's personal stake in the deal with Morgan and Garrison. This proved a fatal error. He did not understand that where Randolph was concerned Walker would hear no criticism. A month of uncertainty followed while the letter went to Granada and was answered. The reply when it came was like a whip across Goicuria's face. "You will please not trouble yourself further about the Transit Company. As to anything you say about Mr. Randolph, it is entirely thrown away on me."

So curt a rebuff the Cuban could not endure, and he wrote Walker in terms which put them still farther apart. It was evidently useless, he said, for him to proceed to England. If the comparatively friendly American government had refused to receive Walker's envoy, there could hardly be hope of British recognition—until at least the present Nicaraguan government had proved its stability by a decisive victory over its military enemies. In icy language, Walker responded that if Goicuria chose to resign from his mission, another would go in his place; and he spoke bluntly of his concern over rumors that the Cuban had become an agent of Vanderbilt's.

At the same time, Walker revoked Goicuria's commission as a brigadier general in the Nicaraguan army, and an item to that effect appeared in *El Nicaragüense.* New York's newspapers, especially the *Herald,* pressed Goicuria to explain, and unable to contain his anger, he released for publication that part of his correspondence with Walker which bore on his attempt to regain the good will of Vanderbilt. The entire nation focused on the controversy. The Vanderbilt faction gleefully cited the letters as proof that Walker was either a fool or a hireling of Morgan and Garrison's, while friends of Walker denounced Goicuria as Vanderbilt's cat's-paw. Edmund Randolph, who was then seriously ill and confined to his bed in the Washington Hotel on Broadway, published in the *Herald* a paid notice which delighted readers: "In the Transit business Don Domingo de Goicuria is an intruder, with a dishonest and treacherous intent, and knowing the import of the language I use, I shall remain here until one o'clock tomorrow and longer if it is the pleasure of Don Domingo de Goicuria."

The duel of pistols was averted, but the duel of words went on. It was at this stage that the wrathful Cuban scored his most telling blow, by publishing Walker's secret letter of instructions for his mission to England. Readers of the *Herald* learned that, contrary to the general expectation, Walker had no intention of bringing Nicaragua and Cuba into the United States—that he intended rather to bar the way to American expansion—that he regarded Yankees as "a psalm-singing set" not fit to control the Caribbean lands. The purpose for which the letter had been written was not explained.

Some years later the Cuban privately expressed regret at having allowed the Walker correspondence to be published, for its effect on Walker's reputation was enduring and deadly. The floodgates were opened to vicious abuse of Walker from American, as well as from British and Central American sources. He was condemned as unpatriotic and false to the interests of the United States. He was called a cold-blooded martinet indifferent to human suffering. The *Atlantic Monthly* published a savage piece by a deserter from Walker's army, who, writing under a pseudonym, complained that General Walker, "instead of treating us like fellow-soldiers and adventurers in danger . . . bore himself like an Eastern tyrant—reserved and haughty—scarcely saluting when he met us, mixing not at all." A scurrilous pamphlet called "The Address of the Seven Prisoners," ostensibly written by seven of Walker's soldiers "captured by the Costa Ricans at Santa Rosa," received wide attention. As Mora's captives, asserted the authors, they had been freer and better treated than as Walker's soldiers. Later it was learned that only three of the seven signatories were Americans, and that one of these, a drummer boy, knew no more of the document than that it had been shown to him by a deserter, that he had refused to sign it, and that his name had been used without his knowledge.

XVI

THE MOMENT OF FALSEHOOD

With the November election coming closer, James Buchanan, as the candidate of the Democratic Party, had to make up his mind about Walker and Nicaragua. The scope of the decision went far beyond American interests in Central America. In the words of an authoritative interpreter of the diplomacy of Buchanan's administration, the President recognized that "the only way to avert civil war . . . was to unite North and South by a common foreign policy of a nature to arouse national feeling."* There was one means by which he might hope to rally North and South to a common cause—abrogation of the Clayton-Bulwer Treaty and reassertion of the Monroe Doctrine. This was precisely the policy for which Walker stood. But it was not easy to predict how the British would react to such a challenge; and Buchanan, aside from his anglophilia, was temperamentally incapable of taking the risks inherent in an adventurous foreign policy.

There was also another reason, one which came to light only later, why he preferred to adopt a hands-off policy toward Nicaragua. His close friend and political manager, Senator John Slidell of Louisiana,

---

* L. Einstein, "Lewis Cass," in *American Secretaries of State*, (S. F. Bemis, ed.), Vol. VI, p. 302.

and the junior Senator from Louisiana, the financier Judah P. Benjamin, were actively interested in promoting an interoceanic railroad and canal route across the Tehuantepec Isthmus of Mexico. Buchanan himself certainly had no financial interest in this venture. He was a wealthy man, scrupulous in the observance of proprieties, patriotic in every ordinary sense. He had a habit, however, of convincing himself that expedients comfortable for himself coincided with the nation's benefit. With Slidell and Benjamin opposed to governmental support for Walker and the Nicaraguan Transit, it was not to be expected that Buchanan would move in the opposite direction.

To Soulé, Buchanan's attitude was a crass betrayal, and he wrote the President-to-be an incredulous letter. "It could not be that one so high as you in the estimation of your country . . . has thus belied what I shall not cease to consider one of the proudest acts of his life" [the Ostend Manifesto]. But the ardent Creole recognized that his party's nominee would do nothing to give pain to his friends in Washington or London. Walker consequently stood in the gravest peril. The London *Times* shared this view, for it contentedly commented that if Buchanan had not been nominated, "Walker's government, founded upon the strongest anti-British feeling, would have been able to . . . set the current of feeling [in the United States] against us. As it is . . . we may look forward to an early and satisfactory settlement of the dispute."

Only one card remained in Soulé's hand, and he now played it. Announcing that he was going to Nicaragua to confer with Walker, he boarded ship in New Orleans and on October 20, 1856, arrived in Granada. The main reason for his visit, as stated in *El Nicaragüense,* was to advise Walker as to methods of floating a loan in the United States. So far as it went, this statement was accurate. It was Soulé's advice, which Walker accepted, not to attempt to combat Vanderbilt's influence in New York, but to handle the loan entirely through agents in New Orleans. Twenty-year bonds, paying six per cent, in the amount of $500,000, and secured by one million acres of public lands would be issued; and at the same time Walker put on the market other public lands at low prices for purchasers in the Southern states. It was obvious, however, that these formal moves in themselves meant nothing. The wealthy men of the South, the great majority of whom were plantation owners, had no interest in acquiring lands or making investments in a country which excluded slave labor. In their view efficient cultivation of the tropical crops which Nicaragua produced was possible only with slaves, either Negroes brought into the country, or Nicaraguan Indians. The burden of Soulé's message was that if Walker wanted Southern support, he would have to pay for it in the one form which the South's aristocracy would accept—the introduction of slavery in Nicaragua. This was the only door of survival still open to him—"the only way in which he could secure the countenance and aid of the Southern politicians who . . . dominate in the government of the United States."*

If Parker French was Mephisto to Walker's Faust, Soulé was Lucifer himself. A man of fiery temperament, vivid imagination, and great verbal power, he had a gift for evoking dreams and inspiring visions. The temptations that he put before Walker must have been grand of scope and eloquent of description. Anyone could foresee that the South would separate from the Union before long. On which side would Walker be? From which country, the Northern rump of the United States or the Southern confederacy could he expect support? To which would he, a Southerner, want to give support? Nicaragua and the Caribbean might well become the key to the survival of Southern civilization.

In his journalistic days Walker had taken what was then termed the "conservative" position on slavery—against its expansion, and less overtly, in favor of its gradual elimination by law and economic measures. When he had been a small boy, advocates of this stand were numerous even in the South. Of some 125 antislavery societies in the United States in the 1820's, nearly three fourths were south of the Mason-Dixon line. Many Southerners hoped to prevent the frightful economic and social problems of sudden emancipation by encouraging state-by-state abolition. In the North, too, gradualism had vigorous support. Several prominent businessmen urged that Northern capital be used to construct railroads and factories in the South, to demonstrate the benefits of free labor while breaking down dependence on a plantation economy. Others (including a radical Whig Congressman named Abraham Lincoln) thought that Congress should authorize the government to compensate slaveholders who emancipated their

---

* Congressional *Globe*, Jan. 14, 1858. Speech of the Hon. Frank P. Blair, Jr., of Missouri, on Soulé and Walker.

slaves. Dr. William Ellery Channing, the noted Boston minister, urged Daniel Webster to reassure the South that "we consider slavery as your calamity, not your crime, and we share with you the burden of putting an end to it." Unfortunately, this view had little appeal for the Northern taxpayers who would have had to contribute funds to share the burden of emancipation. Although as late as 1848 it was thought that the border states would soon abolish slavery, and the New Orleans *Crescent,* with Walker as editor, openly made such a prediction, no practical steps to this end were taken. In Washington, shrewd politicians professed to be "neutral" on slavery. Inertia sat in the White House, term after term. When all the pious oratory was vaporized, it could be seen that the residual choice offered the South was in reality no choice at all—or, more accurately, a choice of evils so appalling that rational selection between them was impossible. Southerners could sacrifice themselves for the higher morality and the nation by giving up their slaves and voluntarily plunging into bankruptcy and social chaos, or they could continue to oppose the entire trend of world thought and eventually fight against the superior military force of the North. The human paradox was—and is—that men so closely identified their own survival with the persistence of their institutions, that they preferred to die rather than submit to changes in their way of life. The institution, becoming a symbol of life, invited death for its sake. As usual when the only chance of peace depended on the willingness of men to give up an institution that they had been taught to revere, there was no chance of peace.

The voices of peace and good will grew faint. By 1856 the Southern "ultras" and the militant Northern abolitionists were dominating public opinion. It was becoming rare to find any informed American who did not grimly believe that the time had passed for a peaceful solution. As the threat of civil war came closer, Southern gradualists were faced with the wrenching need to choose between beloved Dixie and the claims of an uneasy social conscience. For most of them loyalty to the homeland was the stronger emotion, and they found themselves struggling to preserve an institution that in their secret thoughts they regarded as an evil and a misfortune.

In Walker's case the issue was even more painful. His last hope of success in Nicaragua was at stake. The situation as Soulé presented it must have been crystal clear. Walker could maintain an antislavery stand and go down with his men to sure disaster, or he could flee Nicaragua and seek discreditable asylum abroad, or he could abjure his former political views, link himself to the land of his origins, and perhaps rise to further triumphs with the aid of his own people.

II

He was being torn apart by the same forces that were tearing apart his country. He had to fight the Civil War within himself five years before it began. His effort to preserve his intellectual integrity showed in the weeks that it took him to make up his mind. His first response was an attempt at compromise. Early in September he issued a decree which, in effect, established a system of forced labor for all Nicaraguans who were adjudged guilty of vagrancy, or who failed to fulfill the terms of their labor contracts with employers. This decree did not in fact materially change the status of the Nicaraguan farm worker, who while technically free lived actually in a state of feudal serfdom. In effect, Walker was reassuring American purchasers of Nicaraguan estates as to the availability of workers.

If he hoped to avoid further concessions, he was mistaken. A change in the military situation forced his hand, when word came that a strong army, representing Guatemala, San Salvador, Honduras, and the Leónese Nicaraguans was being mobilized for attack on him. At this time, Walker had not yet committed himself on the slavery issue. Several days went by in which he must have been close to despair. Later there were those who said that as a matter of cold reason, such as he had brought to bear on the fate of Corral, he should have taken his own life rather than sacrifice a principle under duress. But the urge to triumph over adversity was still strong in him, and in any event, suicide in his view was morally unthinkable, a coward's solution, especially when the survival of his American soldiers was involved with his own. He could not abandon his men, whatever political convictions he might be compelled to abandon.

On September 22, he issued the decree which was to brand him as a slavery man. It did not mention slavery. Its essence was a declaration that certain provisions of the Nicaraguan Constitution were null and void. One of these had prohibited the introduction of slaves into the country.

The thing being done, he had to find a justification with which he could live. The poorest and most numerous class in Nicaragua, the Indian workers of the Nicaraguan plantations, he wrote in a letter to an American Congressman, had been exploited by the great landowners and the town tradesmen until their economic and social condition was worse than that of most slaves in the United States. Slavery under the American system would actually be a step upward for them, the best way of freeing them from perpetual indebtedness. In Nicaragua, he conveyed, slavery would not be the end of democracy, for there was no democracy there. His decree provided a practical means, as he saw the matter, by which Americans could be induced to come to Nicaragua as planters and to introduce the democratic institutions required to begin the regeneration of the country.

But when all was said, he knew what he had done to his moral position in the eyes of the Nicaraguan people. He had been popular among the Indians largely because he spared them from the horrors of military conscription. Now he was bound to lose them. One of his letters to Congressmen admitted that in revoking Nicaragua's decree of freedom he "was opposed by the whole body of native inhabitants."

Some of his antislavery admirers were loath to believe that their hero could overnight shift his position so radically. The former American minister to Nicaragua, George Squier, wrote a letter to the London *Times* denying that Walker really intended to introduce slavery in Nicaragua. But from this time on, Walker's chief allies were Southern ultras. He who had refused to be served by conscripts and who had never owned or wished to own a slave could find support only among the slavery men.

It was later rumored that he had from the first been an agent of the slavery interest, and he deliberately lent credence to this notion. Rather than admit that he had changed his politics and chosen survival at the expense of principle, he preferred to appear as a man who had always been secretly dedicated to the Southern cause. Once he made his fundamental concession, he went to extremes to have it thought that in his heart he had never doubted the virtues of slavery, and so had no need to be convinced by Soulé. To his earlier writings on the subject he never referred.

In a long and tortured chapter in *The War In Nicaragua,* written just before the outbreak of the Civil War, he sought to find some solid intellectual ground on which to stand before the peoples of the Americas as a proslavery man and avowed racist; but in spite of himself, his inner doubts showed through. In one strange, confessional passage, he implied that if he had realized how resentful the Northern reaction to the slavery decree would be, he might not have issued it. "It is true the author of the slavery decree was not aware, at the time it was published, of the strong and universal feeling which exists in the Northern States against Southern society. He did not know how thoroughly anti-slavery sentiments prevail in the free-labor states." Again, he could not bring himself actually to denounce the anti-slavery position. Apropos of a speech by Senator Seward on the unsound economics of slavery he wrote, "It is impossible not to approve the force and vigor of his thoughts and language. The writer deems it a great error, on the part of Southern men, to attempt to belittle the intellect, or depreciate the motives of the leaders of the anti-slavery party."* His efforts to convey that the establishment of slavery in Nicaragua had been his intention from the first may have deceived some; but one of his officers, who observed him closely during the crucial period of his decision, had no doubt that "the subject [slavery] took root and form in the mind of General Walker in the summer of 1856."

III

The concerted attacks on Walker in the United States, resulting from his slavery decree and the Goicuria affair, came at a time when his military position was rapidly worsening. Over 2,000 troops had been put into the field by the alliance of the Northern republics. Costa Rica was preparing to renew her war on Walker from the south. Thirteen British warships manned by 2500 men had arrived in the harbor of Greytown. Against these forces Walker had only one ally —the cholera, which, while it depleted his own ranks, took a much heavier toll from enemy troops, and temporarily paralyzed them. In every other respect—with only 600 men, with no new recruits to be expected, facing serious shortages of food and ammunition—he was

---

* William Walker, *The War in Nicaragua,* p. 264.

at a hopeless disadvantage. For readers of American newspapers the allied advance toward Granada in September and the first reports of the fighting presaged his imminent doom. At Masaya, on the allied route to Granada, his troops suffered a severe repulse, and had to fall back on the capital; but before he could reach the city, a strong Guatemalan column had invested it, murdered a number of American civilians, and seized all the munitions and food supplies they could find.

Everyone thought he was finished. It came both to Nicaragua and to the United States as a stunning surprise when, in a battle on October 13, exactly one year after his original seizure of the city, he drove the enemy out of Granada, inflicting heavy losses, and re-established his authority in the capital.

XVII

MR. VANDERBILT TAKES HIS
REVENGE

After Walker's unexpected recapture of Granada, a strange rumor began to circulate in the financial district of New York. Behind the scenes a powerful and unexpected well-wisher was working for him—the only man perhaps capable of coping with Walker's enemies at home—the great "Liveoak" George Law, Panama shipping magnate, railroader, multimillionaire, and a man who harbored heavy personal grievances against Vanderbilt. It had struck Law that neither the Garrison-Morgan combine nor Vanderbilt's company any longer had a firm legal hold on the Nicaraguan Transit route. If aid initiated by himself were to enable Walker to win his war, would he not reward his benefactor with the privileges of the Transit, and would not Vanderbilt writhe? This appears to have been the reasoning behind the moves made by Law in the summer of 1857.

He knew, or thought, he knew, how to rescue Walker from his dark military situation. Among Law's friends in New York was one of the world's most renowned soldiers of fortune—the Swedish-born Charles Frederick Henningsen, a blond Viking of a man, scarcely forty years of age, who had distinguished himself in wars in Spain, in Russia, and notably in the Hungarian revolution, where he had become one of the chief officers and close friends of the famous Kossuth. The author of several much-praised books on military strategy, his talents went still further: he was an able journalist, a novelist of wit and repute, and the husband of a wealthy and aristocratic Georgian beauty. Henningsen had from the first taken a deep and admiring interest in the youthful Walker's struggle and had come to the belief that with a few hundred more men, some mortars and howitzers, better rifles, and adequate supplies, the American could yet beat back his foes and conquer the isthmus. When he mentioned his views to Law, the financier instantly proposed that they join forces. It was the kind of adventure that Henningsen could not resist. Law had bought several thousand army muskets with a view to their use in Nicaragua, and he offered these to Henningsen together with $20,000 for the purchase of artillery and ammunition.

Henningsen's first move was to supervise the conversion of Law's muskets into Minié rifles, the most advanced body-arm of their time, and which had never before been produced in the United States. When this news reached Vanderbilt, he countered by having Goicuria, whose connection with him was still not generally known, approach Law and ask, as if on Walker's behalf, for part of the accumulated arms, ostensibly to be taken to Nicaragua by himself. For a time Law believed in the Cuban's good faith, but on making inquiries he perceived Vanderbilt's shadow in the background, and brushed the proposal aside.

The landing of Henningsen in Greytown early in October, 1856, was widely acclaimed by the American press as a possible turning point in Walker's fortunes. Boats of the Accessory Transit Company brought him and his armament to Granada, where they were joyfully welcomed by Walker and his men; and within two weeks the Swede had organized and trained two effective companies of artillery and one of sappers and miners. His impact on the little army was considerable, and Walker wrote that he "never had reason to regret the confidence" that he placed in Henningsen. From the first his knowledge, skills, and competence were so manifest that even when his commission as Major General put him above other veteran commanders in rank, jealousy was diluted with respect.

Henningsen willingly accepted Walker's leadership, and later wrote articles for New Orleans and Nashville newspapers, paying high tribute to Walker's intelligence, modest bearing, and force of character. The curious composition of the little army also impressed the Swedish adventurer. In explaining the ability of Walker's soldiers to sustain battle against appalling odds, he wrote, "Such men do not turn up in . . . everyday life. I was on the Confederate side in many of the bloodiest battles of the late [Civil] war, but I aver that if at the end of that war I had been allowed to pick 5000 of the bravest Confederate or Federal soldiers I ever saw, and could resurrect and pit against them 1000 of such men as lie beneath the orange trees of Nicaragua, I feel certain that the thousand would have scattered and utterly routed the 5000 within an hour. All military science failed, on a sudden field, before assailants who came on at a run, to close with their revolvers, and who thought little of charging a battery, pistol in hand." He calculated that for each 100 men in Walker's army, 137 wounds had been received in the course of their 1856 campaign, without diminishing their fighting spirit. The extraordinary number of educated men who were risking their lives in Walker's service similarly surprised him. "I have heard two greasy privates disputing over the correct reading and comparative merits of Aeschylus and Euripides. I have seen a soldier on guard incessantly scribbling strips of paper, which turned out to be a finely versified translation of the Divina Commedia." Products of American universities fought side by side with famous duellists and adventurers, among them the legendary Colonel Thomas Henry, one of the original "Immortals," and Frederick Townsend Ward, later a general of the Chinese army.

The very same qualities that made practical men of affairs turn from Walker drew to him the idealistic youths, the poets, and the soldiers of fortune. The small band of Americans who followed him to Nicaragua produced no fewer than six books about his venture, as well as numerous articles and a considerable amount of poetry. Although his men found it hard to understand his motivation, one thing at least was clear—he was indifferent to material reward, not interested in having, owning, or getting.

The army's morale was remarkable, and contrary to statements by Walker's Northern critics, he was revered by his men, who recalled an occasion on which he had given his horse to a wounded soldier, while he himself trudged thirty miles on foot. Similarly, Henningsen praised the discipline of the army, and discounted frequent charges of pillage and rape against Walker's troops. Much of the adverse criticism aimed at the Americans on this score was due to the depredations of thirty men, who in July, 1856, arrived from Texas in a body, and who turned out to be a robber gang urgently wanted by United States authorities. Deserting almost immediately after arrival, and wearing the uniforms of Walker's Rangers, they wandered through the Nicaraguan countryside in search of loot, leaving a trail of misery behind them, and carefully avoiding Walker, who had sworn to hang them if they fell into his hands.

Another striking feature of Walker's operation observed by Henningsen was the good will shown him by the poorer folk of the countryside. Even the "slavery decree" did not materially affect the attitude of the Nicaraguan Indians toward Walker in the first months of his war with the allies. Their feeling was undoubtedly due mainly to the fact that, unlike their native commanders, he never conscripted them for military service—a dispensation which filled them with gratitude amounting almost to reverence. The company of Nicaraguans who remained in his service to the end, and whom he regarded as equal to any of his troops in courage and loyalty, were all volunteers.

It was the propertied and their retainers, the *calzados,* the wearers of shoes, numbering perhaps one tenth of the Nicaraguan people, who regarded Walker as their natural enemy. The change that took place in the popular attitude toward him came only in the late stages of the war, when appalling shortages of food compelled his men to forage. Unlike Walker himself, who ate sparingly and almost indifferently of whatever rations came to hand, they were accustomed to consume far more provender than did the typical Nicaraguan. Not content with a diet of *tortillas* and plantains, they seized grain, cows, horses, mules, and chickens as they found them, ravaging the countryside for miles around their camps. Word of such depredations spread quickly, and before the war's end country folk and town dwellers alike had come to regard the appearance of Walker's bearded Rangers as a disaster. When Henningsen first came to Nicaragua, however, his chief's reputation among the common folk was considerably higher than that of any Central American general.

II

Three weeks after Henningsen's arrival, a strong Costa Rican army crossed into Nicaragua and moved north to occupy the Transit route west of Lake Nicaragua. Simultaneously a Leónese column marched south to join the Guatemalans and Salvadoreans for another attack on Granada. With 600 men Walker had to fight a war on two fronts against nearly 5000. A sudden attack drove the Costa Ricans out of San Juan del Sur, but this did not help him much. Compelled to leave a garrison of 250 men to hold the Transit route, he had only 300 effectives with which to resist the northern allies, who were strongly fortified in the town of Masaya, some twenty miles north of Granada.

The allied army had every advantage except one—artillery. The great question for Walker was how far mortars and howitzers could offset weakness in numbers. His only hope lay in a bold strategy. The enemy had to be shattered in a single battle. He and Henningsen wasted no time before beginning the attack on Masaya. Within an hour, however, they realized that their main asset was hollow. The fuses of their mortar shells were too short, and the explosions were taking place harmlessly in the air, instead of on the ground. To retreat would have invited pursuit in force; they had no choice but to try to take Masaya by assault, relying on Henningsen's trained sappers and miners to dislodge the allies from their strongholds. For a time success seemed possible. In three days of sleepless effort they pushed the Central Americans into the center of Masaya, and pressed them hard. A few hundred fresh troops, had they been available, could conceivably have compelled the surrender of the entire allied army, and made Walker the master of Central America. But exhaustion was taking its toll. With a third of his men killed or wounded, and the rest staggering from weariness, there was nothing for them to do but abandon the attack and drag themselves back to Granada. A strong sortie by the enemy would have finished them. It was their good fortune that the losses of the allies were so heavy, and their commanders so shaken by their close call, that they did not follow up their advantage.

There was worse to come. Although a few days of recuperation somewhat restored the morale of Walker's men, their extreme fatigue and the primitive conditions of their hospitals, where flies and vermin abounded, made them excessively vulnerable to the most dangerous enemy of all, cholera. An epidemic broke out, raging at a new peak of mortality, and claiming as one of its victims Lieutenant James Walker, the filibuster's youngest and favorite brother. As each day took the lives of two or three per cent of his force, Walker's surgeons warned him that unless he evacuated Granada every American there would be dead within six weeks.

Granada had to be abandoned, and under Walker's personal direction the sick were moved across Lake Nicaragua, first to one desolate place, then to another, in an effort to find safety and tolerable conditions. Their miseries and fatalities increased with each day. The horrors of this hopeless flight from disease shook Walker as had nothing before in his experience, for among the evacuees were a number of women, some of them wives of Americans who had come to Nicaragua as to a promised land. He, the defender of womankind, had no internal defense against their sufferings and reproaches—any more than he could forget that he had lured his brother to his death.

It was at this point of psychic turmoil that he had to make a decision which was bound to confirm to the outside world his reputation for ferocity. The allies, anyone could foresee, would soon occupy Granada, and the moral, as well as the military effect of the move would be disastrous. Holding both Granada and León, they would hold the core of Nicaragua. No hope would remain for Walker's army. To destroy the city would be to send up cries of horror from all Central America, but to leave it intact would be suicidal. So, at least, Walker and Henningsen reasoned. It fell to Henningsen, with 300 men, to undertake the task of razing Granada after first evacuating the native population. Amid further scenes of misery and tragedy, the shocked and wretched Granadans, such as still remained in the city, were removed by boats of the Transit Company to points along the shores of Lake Nicaragua, while the grim work commenced.

Part of Granada was still intact when the allied army surrounded the city and commenced a three-sided assault on Henningsen's small force. Through four days of incessant fighting, firing from adobe houses and public buildings, the Americans stood them off, their marksmanship taking a great toll of life. An illustration of the battle in an American magazine suggests the scene: the plaza under the pale blazing sky, everything starkly outlined in sunlit white and angular black shadow, a wretched rubble of buildings in the background, puffs of musket smoke coming from the few that remained standing, and white-clad Guatemalan corpses sprawled in the tawny dirt.

Henningsen's problem was complicated by the fact that the strongest position in the city, Guadalupe Cathedral, had been seized by the enemy. To leave it in their hands, he realized, would be fatal. It had to be taken by storm; but could he afford the resulting losses? To make matters more difficult, his men uncovered in one of their improvised fortresses a large store of liquor, and their discipline, already faltering from exhaustion and desperation, disintegrated. In the middle of the battle, half of them were stupefied by drink. Nevertheless, at a lull in the fighting the tireless and inspired Henningsen was able to rally enough volunteers to drive the enemy out of the cathedral. A few hours later he had crowded into it his entire force, now reduced to 200 men able to fight, together with the mutilated, the sick, the drunk, and some scores of women and children, many of them Americans, who still remained in the city. Their ordeal, marked by instances of extraordinary heroism and self-sacrifice on the part of women as well as men, provided sensational material for American journalists.

Presently General Zavala, the Guatemalan commander, realized that Henningsen was depending on supplies brought to the wharves of Granada by Walker's lake boats, which were also his only means of escape. For a time Zavala was deterred from attacking the wharves by uncertainty as to the size of the force which had been left to protect them, and which was strongly barricaded. Then fortune played into his hands. One of the defenders of the all-important area was a Venezuelan whom Walker had rescued from a Granadan dungeon a year earlier. Since then his gratitude had thinned away, and now he deserted and revealed to Zavala that there were only 27 men between him and command of the lake front. The storming action that followed wiped out the Americans in the little garrison to a man, and isolated the remainder of Henningsen's force.

With Walker's boats unable to reach the city, food supplies in Guadalupe Cathedral soon ran so low that men and women had to subsist on small rations of mule meat and decayed flour. Ammunition reserves also were dwindling fast. To provided shot for their field pieces Henningsen's artillery officers made holes in the sand, filled them with scraps of iron, and poured melted lead over them to form an approximate ball. Their situation seemed beyond hope. Zavala, however, was not in a position to follow up his advantage. His losses had been staggering, and in order to regroup his forces he temporarily broke off the attack. Instantly Henningsen ordered his men to proceed with the firing of Granada. Their effort culminated in a final explosion of powder trains which demolished the center of the city. Simultaneously a successful attack by Walker regained command of the wharves, and Henningsen was able to withdraw his troops and the noncombatants under his protection. His flair showed in his last gesture on leaving the ruined city, when he raised an improvised flag in the rubble, bearing the legend AQUI FUÉ GRANADA—"Here was Granada."

The unexpected success of the Americans in sustaining the siege, the burning of the city, the terrible mortality among the allies, the rejoining of Henningsen's force with Walker's, and the continued ravages of disease so shook Zavala that he hastily ordered a retreat to Masaya. The Costa Ricans also thought it wise to pull back, relieving the pressure on the Transit route. Quarrels between the allied commanders still further diminished the possibility of an effective attack on Walker. All at once his generalship, which had been sharply questioned by the American press, seemed vindicated.

Of major importance was word from San Francisco that a hundred well-armed recruits were on the way to join him. At this stage, he had to meet a new threat, when a large and well-armed brig of British origin appeared outside the harbor of San Juan del Sur, flying the Costa Rican flag, and manned by a large Costa Rican crew. Its obvious purpose was to blockade the port and prevent the landing of reinforcements. Walker's hopes rested on the little schooner *Granada,* with its 28 men and two guns. A two-hour sea fight ensued, in which Captain Fayssoux, by brilliant seamanship and accurate gunnery, sank the enemy vessel, and added compassion to victory by rescuing from the Pacific nearly half of the brig's 114 sailors. Almost immediately afterward, the ship from San Francisco arrived with Walker's recruits.

The Americans were further heartened by word that several hundred fighting men were on their way to Greytown from New Orleans. In spite of everything that England, Vanderbilt, and the Central American coalition had done to destroy him, it still appeared possible that Walker might re-establish control over Nicaragua.

III

To Vanderbilt it was unthinkable that his aims should be frustrated by a few hundred Americans led by the man who had dared to confiscate his property, and who was supported by his commercial foes. In his opinion Walker's Central American enemies had failed to grasp the strategic realities of their situation. To try to defeat the man's army of daredevils in direct battle would take too long and cost too much. The way to break Walker's resistance, he was certain, was simply to cut his lines of communication across the isthmus. So long as the filibuster held the Transit route and the boats of the San Juan River and Lake Nicaragua, he could be supplied by Law or by Morgan and Garrison; but without the route and the boats, he could soon be starved out and put at the mercy of the Central Americans.

Late in November, 1856, two of Vanderbilt's men traveled on his fastest ship to Costa Rica, where they held secret talks with President Mora. One of them was an American, Sylvanus Spencer, an old-time employee of Vanderbilt's, eminently suited to the task before him. He had at one time served as engineer on the Transit boats, understood every detail of their operation, knew their crews personally, and had navigated the San Juan River many times. With Spencer was an enigmatic Englishman, William R. C. Webster, an agent of the British government who apparently was assigned to Vanderbilt for the mission to Costa Rica, and who coordinated Spencer's operations with those of Captain Cauty, the chief British military officer in Costa Rica, and with the Central American army in the north.

In their arrangement with Mora, Spencer and Webster agreed to aid him to recapture and hold the Transit route while the northern allies destroyed Walker's army. In return, Vanderbilt would expect Mora's influence on the next Nicaraguan administration to be used to grant him anew the title and privileges of the Transit. Word of the agreement went to Vanderbilt from Spencer, and on December 25, 1856, the financier gave a Christmas remembrance to stockholders of the Accessory Transit Company, in the form of a notice in the

New York *Herald:* "Present appearances indicate a realization of my hopes that the company will be speedily restored to their rights, franchises and property upon the isthmus of Nicaragua."

Action followed swiftly. Within two days, Costa Rican troops led by Spencer, in a series of cleverly planned surprise attacks, had seized most of the Transit steamers and Spencer had assured the loyalty of the boats' officers and crews for his service by judicious use of a fund provided by Vanderbilt. Another Costa Rican column under the command of Captain Cauty invested a key fortress on the eastern shore of Lake Nicaragua, where Walker had not been able to leave more than a skeleton garrison. At Greytown, a British man-of-war prevented 400 well-armed American recruits who had arrived from New Orleans from recapturing one of the riverboats and steaming upstream to join Walker. Across the isthmus, at San Juan del Sur, British ships bottled up the harbor where the ship *Granada* rode at anchor. The joy of the Costa Rican government over these events spilled into a proclamation to its army: "The main artery of filibusterism has been cut forever. The sword of Costa Rica has severed it."

Under the Costa Rican flag, the Transit steamers swiftly concentrated the forces under Spencer and Cauty near the Transit route and they seized the crucial lake town of Virgin Bay before Walker, in his camp at nearby Rivas, had even been informed of the invasion. At the same time, the allied army at Masaya again advanced southward to form the upper jaw of the pincer movement in which he was now almost trapped. But in spite of their enormous advantage in manpower, they did not attack in force. The new plan was to bring the Americans to their knees by starvation. For four bitter months the siege continued, while hunger, thirst, disease, and boredom sapped the strength of Walker's men. And this was not the whole tally of his burden. He was concealing from his men two pieces of disastrous news. A letter from California had revealed that Garrison and Morgan had surrendered to Vanderbilt, and would no longer provide any aid for Nicaragua; and the effort of one of his trusted officers, Colonel S. A. Lockridge, to bring in the Americans stranded at Greytown had been conclusively thwarted by the British.

Walker fell sick of a fever, and to his sickbed came word, in March, 1857, that 160 of his men, who might in other days have fought off a thousand of the enemy, had been routed by a body of only 200 allied troops on the road west of Rivas. This demonstration of the extent to which the army's morale had deteriorated was more than he could bear. Dragging himself to his feet, he assembled his men on the plaza of Rivas and tried with words to revive their courage. "We are engaged in no ordinary warfare. . . . We have come here as the advance guard of American civilization. . . . Are we to be driven from the country merely because we were not born on its soil? Never! Never!"

His hold on them was still strong, for a few days later 400 of them followed him into a desperate attack on 2000 Guatemalans. In this battle his wild and reckless exposure of himself to enemy fire awed even those who thought they knew him. He seemed to be saying, with Marc Antony, "I'll make death love me!" But the bullet that might have honorably extricated him from his dilemma did not strike. In spite of feats of extraordinary valor on the part of his men, the attack failed, and Walker had to move back swiftly to Rivas. At one point during the retreat he was thought to be wounded, when a burst of musket fire from a house made his horse rear; but he relieved the alarm of his troops when he brought the horse under control, and drawing his revolver, fired a few deliberate and, as it were, symbolic shots at the window from which the bullets had come. Then with a wave of his hand, he motioned the column forward.

Twice his troops repulsed attacks by the Costa Ricans, but the victories were empty. The situation worsened from day to day. Rumors of the Garrison-Morgan betrayal had begun to spread among his men. Provisions were steadily diminishing, and foraging raids on the countryside had become unproductive. Henningsen, looking at the small hunk of mule meat that was counted as dinner, remarked "A little more of this and we'll have to eat the prisoners." Walker's own mood had become fatalistic. He no longer cared to submit his men to pitched battles which, even if won, could not save them; and daily exchanges of fire with the enemy were producing more casualties than he could stand. In a letter to Edmund Randolph, Walker told him that of some 800 men in Rivas, only 332 were fit for duty, and 224 were sick or wounded.

The last battle came on April 11, 1857, when Zavala, having learned of conditions in Rivas, grew overconfident, and mounted a surprise assault with nearly 2000 men, most of them raw conscripts from the farms of Guatemala. The result proved that Walker was still to be reckoned with. The open advance of the enemy was met with such withering rifle fire from behind barricades that 700 of the attacking force were killed or wounded, as against 9 American casualties. "It was with a feeling almost of pity for these forced levies," wrote Walker, "that the Americans were obliged to shoot them down like so many cattle. The Guatemalan officers cared no more for their men than if they were sheep."

Even now he still nourished a last secret hope of victory. The cholera, which had saved him before, was again decimating the enemy. Both the Guatemalan and the Costa Rican troop camps were daily losing scores of men to the disease. He felt that in another few weeks panic might yet compel them to lift the siege. Everything depended on such spirit as remained in his own army. It was dwindling fast. No longer was Walker "Uncle Billy" to his troops; many, especially among the recent arrivals, had begun to see him as a heartless fanatic, forcing them to fight in a lost cause that was meaningless for them. Eating their repulsive mule meat, they muttered to each other, where was the high adventure, where the rich lands, where the beautiful women for which they had journeyed to Nicaragua? In the period of inaction that followed the slaughter of the Guatemalan conscripts, morale steadily sank.

It was at this stage that General Mora of Costa Rica executed his most telling stroke. Recognizing that the struggle had become one of morale in both camps, he proclaimed that his former "no quarter" policy had been abandoned. Instead, he offered protection, food, liquor, and free passage home to any American who would come across the lines and give up his arms. Nothing could have more painfully shaken Walker's men. Not only a number of soldiers in the ranks but several officers stole away from their quarters on the very night of Mora's proclamation. One of the officers even appeared the next day on the enemy barricades, calling to his former comrades to join him and share in the meals, tobacco, and *aguardiente* that Mora was providing.

Daily the wave of desertions mounted until as many as twenty men a day were being lost. What followed was pure Walker. Calling his remaining force together, he told them that any soldier who wished to leave his service would be given his passports, so that he could cross the enemy lines without being regarded as a deserter. Probably no other tactic could have stiffened the backs of those unhappy men. Five soldiers among them who asked for their papers were hooted by their comrades as they left; and one who tried to turn back was intercepted by Walker himself, and was made to go on. The remaining troops, fewer than 200, laughed, cheered, and returned to their weary routines and wretched rations.

IV

Early in 1857, President Buchanan found himself under increasing pressure to bring the Central American embroilment to an end. Senator Benjamin and his associates were eager to begin active negotiations with Mexico for the Tehuantepec route, and were handicapped by the uncertainties over Nicaragua. Commodore Vanderbilt was disturbed by indications that the Costa Rican government, having put its flag on the Transit steamers, had no intention of letting them go. Action was needed, and it took the form of the arrival at San Juan del Sur of a powerful American sloop-of-war, the *St. Mary's,* and Commander Charles N. Davis, with official instructions to "take such steps as circumstances required for the protection of American citizens" in Nicaragua, and perhaps unofficial instructions to put an end to the war by any means that came to hand.

A shrewd man, Davis began by negotiating with General Mora to allow the removal of American women and children from Rivas under the protection of the American flag. A truce was declared for this purpose, and while it was still in effect, he suggested to Mora and the northern allies that they permit at the same time the departure of Walker's army. They were delighted to comply. Subsequently Mora admitted that in another twenty days his losses resulting from cholera would have compelled a cessation of the war. The only stipulation that he made was that he was to receive all of Walker's artillery and munitions. On April 30, Davis wrote Walker a letter, carried to him under a flag of truce by one of Mora's officers. Its essence was that the situation was hopeless, and that Walker would be well advised to surrender himself and his men to the United States, represented by Davis. If this offer were not accepted, Davis went on, he would seize the *Granada* at San Juan del Sur, thus cutting off the last marginal hope of escape.

The threat infuriated Walker; at the same time it made him see the futility of further resistance, and he replied that he was ready to negotiate the terms of capitulation. Conferences followed, distinguished chiefly by his determination to assure the safety of those Nicaraguan soldiers who had continued to serve in his army; he would sign no agreement that did not allow them to go peacefully to their homes. Nor did he have any intention of letting the Costa Ricans benefit from his artillery. The articles of surrender, while calling on him to deliver his field pieces, did not say that they had to be in firing order; and Henningsen and his officers proceeded systematically to wreck all mortars and howitzers, as well as an arsenal that they had constructed.

On May 1, 1857, at five o'clock in the afternoon, Walker addressed his men for the last time. His brief remarks were in a vein not likely to give much comfort to his dispirited and hungry followers. The tone was defiant, the ideas remote from their present miseries. One suspects that it was only by remoteness and detachment that he had been able to sustain his own morale during the siege; if he had identified himself with his men, their misery would have destroyed him. Now he told them that he and they must part "for the present." They had "written a page of American history which it is impossible to forget or erase. From the future, if not from the present, we may expect just judgment." He then thanked the officers and men who had served under him, and stood aside while General Henningsen explained the terms of the surrender and the order of march. Walker and his staff would go to San Juan del Sur, and deliver themselves to Commander Davis aboard the *St. Mary's*. The remainder of the army and the noncombatants would be taken over the Transit route to Greytown, to board another United States warship, the frigate *Wabash,* Commodore Hiram Paulding in command.

The fact that Walker and his higher officers were Davis's prisoners apparently did not come home to many of his men. Nor were they interested in the plans already in his mind for the future, and which required his return to the United States at the earliest moment. To the newer recruits especially, those who knew him least and had not felt the impact of his personality, the overriding fact was that he was leaving them at the low point of their lives. His departure, abrupt and seemingly unemotional, was to them the climax of a nightmare. From the moment when they saw him ride away their accumulated resentments gathered force. They felt toward him as the remnants of Napoleon's Grand Army felt when he left them on the retreat from Moscow. High politics meant nothing to the disheartened men in the ranks of Walker's army. They had endured hunger, festering wounds, fevers, flies, chiggers, lice, dysentery; they had lived in a miasma of blood, foul smells, fear, and disease; they had seen their friends, and even American women and children, suffer and die in Nicaragua; and now their leader, the man for whom they had risked everything, had deserted them: so they felt. He and his officers rode horses; they had to walk—or hobble, if they were wounded—the miles that lay between Rivas and Lake Nicaragua. He was in the hands of Americans; they were left to the mercies of the Costa Ricans. Rage grew in them on the slow boat journey across Lake Nicaragua and down the San Juan River to Greytown. Although Mora's troops refrained from obvious violence, they missed no opportunity to pilfer such belongings as the Americans still had, and to humiliate them; and such food as was offered them was barely edible. When at last they staggered on board the *Wabash,* the ship's officers were shocked and filled with pity by their plight, and the voyage home, through a stormy sea, was a long hymn of hate to Walker.

V

A crisis developed after Walker boarded the *St. Mary's,* for Commander Davis insisted on the surrender of the *Granada.* This had not been provided for in the articles, but when both Walker and Fayssoux demurred, Davis threatened to sink the vessel then and there, and trained his guns on the little ship. After a bitter protest, Walker wrote an order to Fayssoux—"Deliver the *Granada* to the United States." The sense of injury that he felt was compounded when Davis turned the vessel over to the Costa Ricans, and he subsequently expressed grim satisfaction when incompetent seamanship under the Costa Rican flag caused the doughty little schooner to be wrecked and lost.

In all, 2500 American fighting men had served under Walker in Nicaragua—never more than 800 in any one engagement—against enemy forces estimated by Henningsen at 17,000. Of the total American enlistment, 1000 had died of wounds or disease, 700 had deserted, 250 had been discharged, and 80 had been captured by the enemy. Henningsen, a trained military observer, believed that about 5800 Central Americans must have been killed or wounded in battle during the war, but how many had died of disease he could not guess. The press of the world made much of the surrender. The London *Times* regretted that Davis had not left Walker and his "armed rabble" to be exterminated by the Costa Ricans, and Greeley's *Tribune* echoed the sentiment. But Walker had his defenders. Senator Toombs of Georgia expressed outrage at the administration's behavior in the matter, telling the Senate that Walker "had been driven out of the Presidency of Nicaragua . . . by a foreign invasion, aided by Commander Davis of the United States Navy." *Harper's Weekly* took the position that Walker's defeat was due primarily to Vanderbilt and Spencer, and surprised its readers by implying that it would be a good thing for Central America if Walker could come to terms with the Transit Company and assume again the Presidency of the country.

VI

The next moves on the Washington chessboard were predictable. The Costa Rican minister announced that his country had a legitimate claim to the Nicaraguan Transit, and planned to participate in its future control. Vanderbilt protested. Buchanan said that legality must be observed. Senator Benjamin and an associate left Washington for Mexico City, with the intention of concluding a contract for the Tehuantepec Transit route.

At this point, as so often during his administration, Buchanan's hopes of achievement collapsed at the first challenge. Neither he nor Benjamin expected that Pierre Soulé would forestall them in Mexico. Savagely indignant at the wrecking of his hopes for Nicaragua, the father of the Ostend Manifesto was determined to frustrate Buchanan by every means at his disposal. The Mexican officials responded to his political skill and eloquence, and Benjamin's negotiation swiftly lost momentum and came to a stop.

Here was a new embarrassment for the President. If an American transit could not be established in Tehuantepec, then the Nicaraguan route took on renewed importance. Belatedly he raised the question of its future with England. An almost plaintive letter went to his friend Lord Clarendon. "I think you ought to keep your protégés in Central America in better order. I wish I could induce you to believe that the interest of the United States in that region is the very same with your own. Your special favorite Costa Rica is now endeavoring to convert her patriotic assistance to her sister state against the filibusters into a war of conquest, and she modestly claims the right to sell the Transit route to the highest bidder."

Buchanan then added, in his first draft of the letter, as preserved in his files, the sentence, "To this I shall never submit." However, he characteristically struck out the word "never," and the letter as it went to Clarendon read merely, "To this I shall not submit." Then, on a sighing note, the President lamented, "Both of our countries and the world would have been better off if the Clayton-Bulwer treaty had not existed."

PART THREE

All or Nothing

《《 》》

"That his success would have inured to the benefit of civilization, few, perhaps, in view of the present condition of Central America, will be so rash as to deny."

W. O. SCROGGS ON WALKER,
in *Filibusters and Financiers*

"Had he been successful, the Civil War might have been postponed, might never have been fought, or might have had another result."

LAWRENCE GREENE ON WALKER,
in *The Filibuster*

XVIII

A NAME TO CONJURE WITH

He had gone to Nicaragua in the name of democracy and the Nicaraguan Democrats had turned against him. He had begun with a sense of America's mission to the world, and the government of the United States had rejected him. He had stood for the gradual elimination of slavery, and now the world knew him as a slavery man. His purpose had been twisted until all the idealistic essence had been wrung out of it. He could no longer hold on to his Byronic conception of himself. But to the average American he was still the hero of heroes. This fact first came home to Walker in the wild welcome that awaited him at New Orleans, where he landed on May 27, 1857. Word had come from Washington that, on order of the President, no charges would be preferred against him for violation of the Neutrality Laws; he was a free man. A cheering crowd was on the wharves; men surrounded him, lifted him to their shoulders, bore him to a waiting carriage, formed a procession, and marched behind him to the sumptuous St. Charles Hotel, where rooms had been reserved for him. So numerous and persistent were the people in the street outside that he was compelled to appear on the balcony of his apartment and make a short speech. This was not enough; his admirers entered the hotel and refused to leave until they saw him again.

He came down to the rotunda, mounted a table, spoke of his pleasure in being back in New Orleans, and promised that he would give a full account of his experiences at a mass meeting then being organized. Finally the crowd dispersed, to read newspapers which blazoned the hero's return over their front pages. When adjectival journalism gave out, editors filled their columns with panegyrics from readers in prose and verse. One lady of the city provided fifteen stanzas on the theme of Walker's greatness: "All hail to thee, Chief! Heaven's blessing may rest on thy battle-scarred brow" . . . and so forth. Women especially found irresistible the combination of his fame and his boyish appearance. Letters written to him by one enamored girl were still extant a century later. When one night he arrived late to see a play and was recognized, female throats accounted for a large share of the frenzy with which he was greeted. The show stopped, actors and audience applauded him, the orchestra struck up the Star-Spangled Banner, and he was cheered for ten minutes. "Never," commented a French writer, "was a monarch returning from victory more acclaimed by a people delirious with happiness."

At the mass meeting, held in the open two nights later, he stood on a platform surrounded by flags of the United States and Nicaragua, and spoke for two hours, making no secret of his intention to return to Central America and complete the task he had begun. The New Orleans press reported his oration as a *tour de force,* an oral history of his career on the isthmus, and an explanation—pointing bluntly at Secretary Marcy, Commodore Vanderbilt, and the British government —of the reasons why he had not succeeded. In speaking of President Buchanan, however, Walker was reserved; already arrangements were being made for a talk between them at the White House. One newspaper wondered whether he was planning on a political future in the United States. If so, the popular base for it was established. His was a name to conjure with.

II

Walker could not have been unmindful that all the cheering was being done by men whose politics he had opposed a few years earlier. Like others whose guiding principle has crumpled under pressure, he could achieve forgetfulness only by doubling the intensity of his new con-

viction, and hypnotizing himself with its repetition. Journeying northward, he asserted in every speech not only that the introduction of
American civilization in Central America was the road to salvation
for the United States, but that Southern institutions had to prevail
there. Memphis took him to its heart. In Louisville, where he visited
his sister, Mrs. Alice Walker Richardson, the press accorded him the
tributes reserved for the mighty. In Cincinnati, Democratic politicians
made much of him. Even in cynical Washington, where he arrived
on June 12, he generated extraordinary interest. Newspapers reported
that in a long and private conference at the White House he had given
the President his version of events in Nicaragua, and had strongly protested the actions of Commander Davis, especially with respect to the
seizure of the *Granada*. It was Walker's position that if it had not
been for Davis's interference, the Central American armies would have
disintegrated; while the morale of his own men would have been sustained by the knowledge that a route of retreat was open to them. He
made these charges first orally, then in writing.

Some months later, in a speech at Mobile, Walker said that the
President in this meeting had not only heard him with attention but
had actually encouraged him to make another attempt to conquer
Nicaragua. Friends of Buchanan's scoffed, and accused Walker of
outright fabrication; yet it would not have been out of character for
the President to make remarks which Walker could have interpreted
as encouragement. Buchanan was not the man to offend a visitor who
had so strong a hold on public opinion as Walker had in the summer
of 1857. According to an Assistant Secretary of State who served
under him and had frequent opportunities to observe him, the President was far from being the amiable weakling so often portrayed.
Rather he was "cold and calculating, with a clear head but no heart
. . . with a habit of indirectness that at times became almost falsehood
and a wariness that sometimes degenerated into craftiness."* It would
have been nothing for Buchanan to drop hints of sympathy and
understanding without actually committing himself—hints that would
have been the more effective because Walker as yet knew nothing of
the President's commitment to the Tehuantepec project.

With a strong revival of inner confidence, Walker went on to the

* "Narrative of W. H. Trescott," in the *American Historical Review*, Vol.
XIII, p. 547.

culminating point of his triumphal tour, New York. There even New Orleans' hullabaloo was exceeded. A committee of admirers met him in New Jersey and escorted him by boat to Battery Park, where in spite of rain a large crowd awaited him, and where he accommodated them with a short speech. At his hotel, hero-worshipers and reporters besieged him from dawn to midnight. It was his intention to spend his time conferring with members of his Nicaraguan staff who had assembled in New York, but his schedule was torn apart. When he went to Wallack's Theatre as the guest of General and Mrs. Henningsen, the ensuing uproar was quieted only when the orchestra struck up "Hail, Columbia." Walker was compelled to speak to the audience from the Henningsens' box, and beg their attention for the play they had come to see. At its end, the press of people outside the theater was so thick and persistent that he and the Henningsens could hardly reach their carriage. When he finally got to his hotel, it was to discover a brass band waiting for him, and he had to submit to an hour-long serenade.

So ruthless an invasion of his privacy was more than he could bear. Three days after his arrival he secretly left the hotel and secluded himself in a friend's house, the address of which was known only to a few intimates. There he set about the business on which he had come. This was nothing less than the formation of a secret "Central American League," with branches in the main American cities, each under the charge of a trusted officer, to raise funds, recruits, and supplies for a second expedition to Nicaragua. Henningsen was in charge of the New York branch. One after another his key men took their instructions from Walker, as from the general of an actual army, and departed. "We meet again at Philippi," Henningsen was reported as saying to them.

Walker's decision to hide himself from New York's reporters did him no good in their eyes. Perhaps he had forgotten that the fury of a journalist frustrated exceeds that of a woman scorned. During the preceding days, most of the city's newspapers had written of Walker with respect. Notwithstanding his quarrrels with Vanderbilt and Goicuria and his slavery decree, he had been credited with extraordinary talents. Now the press readily seized the first opportunity to turn against him. Several newspapers criticized him sharply for impugning the motives of Commander Davis, who after all "had saved him." A more serious attack followed, when Commodore Paulding's frigate *Wabash,* carrying 140 refugees from Nicaragua, including 13 women and 5 children, arrived in New York harbor. Many were sick; all were gaunt from long privation, and desperate with uncertainty as to the future. The reporters who visited the *Wabash* came away with enough in their notebooks to wreck a dozen reputations. As seen by the poor wretches on the *Wabash,* Walker was cruel and heartless. Paulding added a touch greatly appreciated by the press when he said that Walker's men were so covered with lice when they left Greytown that the ship had become infested, and its personnel had to "bathe in rum." This was a story to kindle the eyes of an editor. A dozen acidulous articles ate away Walker's prestige. The *Herald* admitted that the woes of the refugees might have been dictated by events beyond his control, but it was up to him to prove it. The press accused him of lack of compassion, of cold cynicism, and finally of moral cowardice, for reporters had been unable to locate him. He had "sneaked away," said the *Tribune.* The fact was that he had become indifferent both to popular praise and journalistic condemnation. Events would speak for him, or nothing would.

III

It was not a good time in which to raise money. A financial panic which had shaken the City of London was suddenly echoed in Wall Street; stock prices collapsed, credit tightened, business fell off, men lost their jobs, and a cloud of pessimism settled over the country. The Dred Scott decision and reports of violence between slavery men and free-soilers in Kansas added to the general disquiet. Many promises of support came to Walker, but they were seldom backed with cash. Nevertheless, he made some progress. He had gone to New Orleans, where, keeping out of the public eye, he found enough money to enable one of his secret agents to purchase a steamship, the *Fashion,* and a cargo of arms and military stores. Recruiting was no problem; many young Southerners were eager to serve under Walker, despite all the hardships his previous army had endured. The essential question was that which he had faced two years earlier in California— whether the Neutrality Laws would be enforced against him. It was soon answered. Buchanan's administration showed every sign of antagonism. Particularly significant was the fact that the new Secretary of State, Lewis Cass, who a year earlier, when he hoped for the Presidency, had backed Walker and "the rights of Americans to emigrate and take their arms with them," had reversed his stand. In subservience to Buchanan, Cass now ordered federal authorities in all port cities to be on guard against the departure of any filibustering expeditions.

On November 10, 1857, federal marshals appeared at Walker's house and arrested him. He made no protest. In the court hearing that followed, the New Orleans federal attorney showed evidence that the *Fashion,* which was advertised to depart for Nicaragua, had taken on board an extraordinary quantity of supplies such as would be required in a military campaign. That the passengers would be filibusters recruited by Walker was the prosecution's case, and the judge thought it good enough to remand Walker for trial, setting bail in the amount of $2000. There was no actual proof, however, that the *Fashion* had violated any law. Walker being ashore, and none of his men on board, the ship was allowed to weigh anchor and steam away.

With Pierre Soulé as his lawyer, Walker found bail and, released from custody, proceeded to execute a plan carefully devised for that very situation. Mobile, even more than New Orleans, was sympathetic to his cause, and it was unlikely that any federal officer there would seriously seek to stop him. Ignoring the fact that he was on bail, he and a few members of his military staff boarded the daily mail boat from New Orleans to Mobile. At every stop they were joined by additional small groups who had quietly left New Orleans well in advance, and by the time they reached Mobile Bay the boat was crammed with Walker's men. Among them were six of the original Immortals.

They found the *Fashion* anchored far out in Mobile Bay, where it had taken on a cargo of arms, and they boarded her without interference. The final test lay ahead. A cutter drew alongside and federal officers came on board. They had been instructed, they said, to inspect the steamer, its passengers, and the cargo. Solemnly they performed their duty, but carefully managed to see no arms, no sign of Walker or his officers, no suspicious circumstance of any kind. With 270 men on board, including such famous veterans as Colonels

Hornsby, Anderson, Natzmer, and Henry, and Commander Fayssoux, the *Fashion* was given her clearance for Nicaragua; and a telegram from Washington, ordering pursuit of the ship, was mysteriously lost before it reached the federal officer to whom it was addressed.

IV

Buchanan was then engaged in an attempt to persuade England to scrap the Clayton-Bulwer Treaty—something that England was determined not to do. Walker's flaunting of the Neutrality Laws not only made the President look foolish, but was interpreted by the British ambassador, Lord Napier, as proof that the United States had imperialistic designs in Central America, and stood in violation of the treaty. Otherwise would Walker not have been prevented from sailing? Buchanan hastily assured Napier that he intended to uphold the treaty until it was abandoned by mutual agreement. He then declared war on Walker. An order went to his Secretary of the Navy, Isaac Toucey: intercept the *Fashion*. Soon afterward, Buchanan sent his first annual message to Congress, and urged the enactment of legislation which would "be effectual in preventing our citizens from committing such outrages" as Walker had perpetrated. Walker's expedition could "do no possible good to the country" but was certain to "injure its interests and its character."

The unaccustomed vigor of the President's attack on Walker had a shrewd political purpose. Although Buchanan professed personal aversion to slavery on moral grounds, he had found it politically expedient to favor the slavery interest in Kansas. To justify his policy, the President had arrived at a strict and sterile interpretation of the Constitution which enabled him to maintain that the slavery problem in Kansas and elsewhere could be dealt with simply by "proper administration of the law." His position in Kansas had excited unrealistic expectations in the South and extreme abolitionist agitation in the North. Irreconcilables on both sides were increasing their power. But having won over the Southerners in Congress with his Kansas policy, Buchanan had to deal with the heavy fire then being aimed at him by the Northern press. His need was to show himself to the North, if he could, as, after all, neutral on slavery. Walker provided the perfect instrument. He was backed by slavery men; in attacking him, therefore, the President seemed to be attacking slavery, a position calculated to mollify Northern critics. And it was a safe tactic in the South, for Southern leaders in Congress were so eager to keep Buchanan's Kansas policy unchanged that they were unwilling to make a strong effort on Walker's behalf. It was politic and it was easy for Buchanan to condemn him unrestrainedly.

But the wording of Secretary Toucey's order to the Navy's Caribbean Squadron, calling for Walker's interception, was so vague as to create uncertainty in every officer who received it. One of them went so far as to request enlightenment from the Secretary: was he to "seize a suspicious vessel in a foreign port?" Or, rather than risk so illegal a proceeding, should he merely prevent the passengers from going ashore? And what if the passengers claimed to be only peaceful travelers? Toucey's reply doubled the doubt. A naval officer could not act, of course, merely on suspicion. There must be no interference, of course, with lawful commerce. Of course, there should be no violation of the soil of other nations. But if a vessel "was manifestly engaged" in filibustering, it should be intercepted and prevented from landing its men and arms. How this was to be done the Secretary did not say, but the sloop-of-war *Saratoga,* Commander Frederick Chatard, was ordered to the harbor of Greytown.

Walker, who foresaw that some such move would be made, seemed to his companions on the *Fashion* strangely unconcerned, as if he had an inner knowledge of events to come. So certain was he of success that he had even brought with him the editor of *El Nicaragüense,* John Tabor, several new fonts of type, and the Great Seal of Nicaragua, which he had carried away with him. The nine days of the voyage from Mobile were spent in organizing his force and drilling his men. His strategy had been thoroughly worked out. The first essential was the capture of the Transit steamers on the San Juan River and the small fort, Fort Castillo, which dominated the entry from the river into Lake Nicaragua. To try to move up the San Juan from Greytown, however, was hopeless; the Transit boats would be forewarned and would simply escape to the lake. Surprise was of the essence, and Walker knew how to achieve it. A fork of the San Juan known as the Colorado, which reached the sea at a desolate spot some miles south of Greytown, was known to be unguarded. Before attempting to land at Greytown, the *Fashion* would put down a company of picked men under Colonel Anderson at the Colorado, with three boats; this force would row upstream, seize the first Transit vessel encountered, capture the other steamers as they came down the San Juan, disembark at Fort Castillo under cover of the Costa Rican flag, and disarm the unsuspecting garrison. The steamers would then be sent back to bring the rest of Walker's troops up the San Juan and across Lake Nicaragua. Before an army could be mobilized against them they would take Virgin Bay, Rivas, and San Juan del Sur. By that time reinforcements already being organized by Henningsen in the United States would have arrived, they would sweep north to Granada, Masaya, Managua, and León, and Nicaragua would once more be in American hands.

True to this plan, the *Fashion* skirted Greytown harbor and in a drenching rain reached the mouth of the Colorado unobserved. After seeing Anderson and his men on their way, Walker ordered the ship to stand out to sea, and cruise slowly along the coast through the night, timing its approach to Greytown for broad daylight the next morning—an hour when, presumably, no filibustering ship would dare to run the *Saratoga*'s guns.

V

At seven o'clock on the morning of November 24, 1857, Commander Chatard of the *Saratoga* saw the steamship *Fashion* come into Greytown harbor, with fifteen passengers or so on deck. When he hailed the ship, an officer on the vessel called back something that could not be distinctly heard, except for the word "transit." Knowing that the Vanderbilt interests intended to reclaim the Transit property, Chatard came to the conclusion that this was the purpose of the party on board the *Fashion,* and he made no effort to interfere with its progress. A few minutes later, when the steamer tied up at a wharf, he had the shock of his life. All at once the *Fashion*'s decks were crowded with laughing men, carrying rifles, and leaping ashore.

Chatard's orders gave him no right to use force against the filibusters once they had landed. Only if they offered violence against members of his ship's company could he justify the use of his guns to coerce these Americans on foreign soil. To provoke some hostile action by Walker now became the purpose of the humiliated Commander, and in this he showed considerable ingenuity. Sailors went ashore to prevent Walker's men from occupying the buildings of the Transit Company, thus compelling them to bivouac in the open, exposed to the steady tropical rain. Officers of the *Saratoga,* disregarding Walker's sentries, strolled through his camp, some of them not even in uniform, inviting a challenge. More malevolently, the ship's gunners were ordered to use an area only a few yards from Walker's camp for cannon practice.

Understanding Chatard's strategy, Walker ordered his restive men to ignore all provocations, and quietly moved his camp to safer ground while awaiting news from Anderson. He was not, however, submissive under Chatard's pressure. The commanding officer of the *Saratoga*'s squadron, Commodore Paulding, was known to be at his Panama station on his flagship, the *Wabash,* and Walker sent the *Fashion* off to find him, with a letter detailing Chatard's offenses. Almost at the same time, a fast British mail boat put into Greytown, and Chatard took advantage of her presence to write Paulding on his own account. With his official report went a personal and highly emotional note which later figured in a Congressional investigation. He could not explain how he had allowed Walker to dupe him. "Somehow or other I was spellbound. . . . I beg you, Sir, in the most earnest manner, to come here and advise me. I am in a very cruel state of mind, and look gloomily to the future." He had reason for his gloom; Secretary Toucey, on hearing of his lapse, suspended him.

At Walker's camp, days of incessant rain passed with no word from Anderson. Mud, insects, boredom, and anxiety were telling on the men. Walker himself began to sit up of nights at a campfire, waiting for a signal from the river. On the afternoon of the twelfth day, when confidence was ebbing fast, a native canoe appeared on the San Juan, with one of Anderson's men sitting comfortably in the stern with a rifle, while two Costa Ricans, his prisoners, worked the paddles. The news that he brought sent the camp into a wild demonstration of joy. Anderson's expedition had been a total success. Without the loss of a single man, he had captured the river steamers and Fort Castillo; and although navigational problems had delayed the steamers, they were on their way to Greytown. In a day or two Walker and all his men would be able to start up the river.

The revival of spirits did not last long. Before a river boat could arrive, the frigate *Wabash* steamed into the bay, and anchored as close as it could to Walker's camp. Shortly it was joined by another American ship, the *Fulton,* and by two British men-of-war. With the *Saratoga* these ships among them carried over 200 guns. Pinnaces plied back and forth and the commanders were entertained at dinner by Commodore Paulding aboard the *Wabash.* The Commodore, a large, robust, and ambitious man, had been excessively aggravated by the thought that a United States Navy vessel, and a ship of his own squadron to boot, should be held up to derision. When British officers suggested that the ships of both nations join in taking Walker prisoner, he refused; he wanted Walker's scalp for himself.

His first move was to have small boats from the *Saratoga* go up the San Juan, ostensibly for fresh water, but actually to establish a blockade of the river. When two of Walker's chief aides, Hornsby and Fayssoux, arrived on board the *Wabash* to make a formal protest against this proceeding, he shrugged their words aside, and gave orders that they were not to be allowed to leave ship. They would be joined, he told them, by Walker and all his men, whom he would shortly make his prisoners.

Three hundred marines were sent ashore to take up a position that would prevent the filibusters from moving inland, and the ships swung their broadsides toward the camp. Walker could clearly see the gunners take their battle stations and train their cannon. Some of his men, unable to bear their disappointment, begged him to fight, but he refused to permit so senseless a sacrifice of life. He still bore his head high; no one observing him could have guessed that all his hopes had become ashes in his mouth. When a boat put off from the *Fulton,* in it one of Paulding's officers, Captain Engle, Walker went courteously to meet him. They shook hands, and Walker listened quietly while Engle read a note from Paulding. He and his men would board the Navy ships and be taken back to the United States, or they would be fired upon by sea and by land. As a sign of his surrender he was to lower the Nicaraguan flag that flew over his camp.

Walker merely said to Engle, "I surrender to the United States," and ordered his men to break camp. Of the two, Engle appeared the more emotional. "General," he said to Walker, "I am sorry to see an officer of your ability employed in such a service. Nothing would give me greater pleasure than to see you at the head of regular troops."

The cup of Walker's bitterness ran over when, at that very moment, one of the delayed river steamboats appeared with some of Anderson's men aboard, ready to begin the movement of his troops upstream. He had to watch while the boat was seized by Paulding's marines, and the men taken prisoner.

Having carried the day without opposition, Paulding was disposed to be considerate. Another officer came ashore to reassure Walker that, once on board, he and his officers, instead of being treated as prisoners, would have quarters suited to their rank. A polite oral reply from Walker acknowledged this gesture, and added that he did not seek privileges beyond those given his men. This message, garbled in transmission, came to Paulding as a blunt rejection—"General Walker asks no special benefits"—and deeply offended him. His next communication was a sharp command to Walker to embark immediately on the *Fulton,* to which the Commodore had transferred his flag.

A few minutes later Walker stood in Paulding's quarters, hearing himself addressed in a tone and in terms that no man had dared to use to him since he had been a boy in his father's house. He and his men were a disgrace to the United States. They had dishonored their country. They were no better than pirates and murderers. For the first time Walker's self-control cracked under the edge of suppressed rage and the weight of failure. With a curious mingling of satisfaction and sympathy, the tall, handsomely uniformed Commodore saw tears come to the eyes of the shabby little man whom all the world knew. So much, at least, is suggested by a letter that Paulding wrote to his wife. "This lion-hearted devil, who had so often destroyed the lives of other men, came to me, humbled himself, and wept like a child. You may suppose it made a woman of me, and I have had him in the cabin since as my guest. We laugh and talk as though nothing had happened, and you would think, to see him with the captain and myself, that he was one of us. He is a sharp fellow and requires a sharp fellow to deal with him. I have taken strong measures in forcing him from a neutral territory. It may make me President or may cost me my commission."

Paulding's uneasiness at the possible consequences of his actions grew when the *Fulton* arrived at its Panama base. He had accepted Walker's pledged word to proceed to New York by passenger ship and give himself up to the United States marshal there; and his desire to conciliate his prisoner before they parted expressed itself in numerous courtesies. Pointing out that five days would elapse before the next steamer would leave for the United States, he invited Walker to remain for this period in his comfortable cabin on the *Fulton,* rather than take up quarters in a flea-infested hotel of the town. Walker declined; he would not even share another meal with his captor. It was too much to expect that he could forgive the only man who had pierced the armor of his self-control. From this moment they resumed their enmity.

VI

Two distinguished lawyers and an Army general, all friends of Walker's, accompanied him when he offered himself for arrest to the United States marshal in New York. An ironic aspect of the situation lay in the fact that the marshal himself was one of Walker's great admirers—Captain Isaiah Rynders, a leader of Tammany Hall who had taken a large part in organizing public support for Walker. An arrest, Rynders said, was out of the question, since he had neither warrant nor official instructions. A conference followed, and out of it came a decision that he and Walker would go to Washington and present the problem to the administration. By that time impatient reporters were pushing their way into the marshal's office and demanding a statement from Walker. He gave them one that made headlines the next day. Paulding had invaded the territory of a friendly nation and insulted its flag. The government of the United States had an obligation to remedy his gross error. This it could do by returning him, Walker, and his men to the place from which they had been forcibly removed. On this note, leaving the reporters agape, he departed with Rynders for Washington.

Walker's departure had infuriated Buchanan; his return embarrassed him. Paulding had unmistakably exceeded his authority. Southern indignation promptly flared into mass meetings where Paulding was denounced in passionate terms and his condign punishment demanded. A resolution passed in New Orleans urged that the government not only return Walker's expedition to Nicaragua but indemnify it for losses "sustained from capture, detention and privation of liberty and property," and several senators volunteered to initiate Congressional action to that effect.

Increasingly the issue took the form of a personal contest between Walker and the President. As always, Buchanan moved with great caution. When the filibuster appeared in Washington, Cass quickly announced that there was no reason to keep him in custody. Walker staked his case on a long letter to the President, which he made public. His expedition had been justified, he insisted, in law and morality. He was the president-in-exile of a foreign government which had been recognized by a former President of the United States. It was his right and his duty to Nicaragua to seek to re-establish that government in power, with or without the aid of the United States. "Some have told you, I know, that I am a man 'without faith and without mercy'; but from the beginning to the end of my career in Nicaragua, I challenge the world to produce a single violation of public faith."

For Paulding's methods he expressed not so much resentment as disdain. "Far more grievous than the surrender . . . was it to be told that we were there to the dishonor of the United States. . . . There were men on that sandy beach, Mr. President, who had carried your flag aloft [in Mexico] amidst the thickest of the foe . . . who had led your soldiers across the continent in the path of duty and honor. . . . I call for the justice it is your high prerogative to bestow.

"But permit me to conclude by adding that . . . no extreme of illegal interference—no amount of hard words and unjust epithets—can deter us from following the path which is before us."

The day on which this letter appeared, January 4, 1858, the Senate passed a resolution calling on the President for "the correspondence, instructions and orders to the United States naval forces on the coast of Central America, connected with the arrest of William Walker and his associates." Buchanan was now compelled to reply, and he did so in a communication of considerable ingenuity. "In capturing General Walker and his command . . . Commodore Paulding has, in my opinion, committed a grave error. It is quite evident, however . . . that this was done from pure and patriotic motives." The President, having thus made clear his intention to let the Commodore off lightly, quickly moved to safer terrain. On a note of reassuring, if empty, prophecy, he said, "The tide of emigration will flow to the South. . . . Central America will soon contain an American population which will confer blessings and benefits upon the natives and their respective governments." Therefore, he implied, Walker and his methods were not needed. He went on to say he believed in the "Manifest Destiny" of the American people to dominate in the Western Hemisphere, but "no administration can successfully conduct the foreign affairs of the country in Central America . . . if it is interfered with at every step by lawless military expeditions set on foot in the United States."

A tumult of debate followed in both Senate and House. Conflicting resolutions were introduced, one calling for official punishment of Paulding, another for the presentation to him of a gold medal for his action in Nicaragua. For days all other business stood still while Walker and Paulding were each roundly criticized and staunchly defended. Fifteen senators made speeches, covering every aspect of the controversy. The question was raised, how was it that Paulding, if he regarded Walker and his men as "outlaws who had . . . left our shores for the purpose of rapine and murder"—the Commodore's words in his own defense—how was it that he had made Walker his close companion on the *Fulton,* taken meals with him, addressed him always as "general," and accepted his parole of honor for his return to New York? The question went unanswered.

The hardest attack on Walker came from Senator Slidell of Louisiana, Buchanan's great friend, who asserted at great length that Walker was a bloodthirsty pirate who merited no consideration from his country. In the end, the weary senators and the President arrived at a compromise. All resolutions were dropped. While Paulding was mildly censured by the Secretary of the Navy and temporarily relieved of his command, Walker was given no encouragement. When all was done, the administration still stood firmly against him; the Congress was divided as before.

VII

From the reception that he received as he journeyed South from Washington, one would have thought that Walker came with renewed laurels of conquest, instead of as a man who had twice failed of his purpose and had been roundly castigated by the President and many senators of his country. In Richmond and Montgomery, where every honor was heaped on him, he reminded his audiences that before leaving New Orleans for Nicaragua he had been arrested and put on bail; he was returning now to insist that he be tried for violation of the Neutrality Laws. At Mobile, he made a major address on the issue between Buchanan and himself. It was in this speech, delivered on January 25, 1858, that he brought into the open Buchanan's support of the Tehuantepec scheme, and Soulé's part in thwarting it.

The style of the Mobile speech and of the letters which Walker wrote on the Davis and Paulding affairs suggests the profound psychological change that had taken place in him. The former note of high-mindedness, the alleviating flashes of ironic humor have given way to hot indignation and cold legalism. While he regarded himself as a missionary for Americanism and democracy, his personality had color and warmth, but he seemed motivated now mainly by a demonic drive to fulfill "his destiny." At the age of thirty-three the only possibility of life that interested him was his return to Nicaragua.

But perhaps for that very reason his power to lift an audience to its feet was never greater. The Mobile speech was an immense success, a devastating exposure of Buchanan's inconsistency. The President's stand, Walker asserted, had nothing to do with principle. Surely the co-author of the Ostend Manifesto was not the man to defend the Neutrality Laws! It was not filibustering as such that aroused Buchanan's wrath, said Walker. What the President really resented was his, Walker's, alliance with Soulé, who had blocked the Tehuantepec project. The administration was perfectly willing to encourage filibustering attempts elsewhere than in Nicaragua. The Secretary of War, John B. Floyd, had actually urged Henningsen to aid a revolution in Mexico and incite a war with Spain, so as to provide a pretext for the annexation of Cuba. Therefore Buchanan's attacks on Walker had nothing to do with principle. They were to be understood simply as a matter of low politics to serve the interests of the President's friends in Tehuantepec; and Walker was fully justified in his defiance.

The public seized excitedly on this revelation. Floyd, who could not deny that he had met with Henningsen, contended that the statements attributed to him were false. The abolitionist North believed him; the South preferred to believe Walker, and became even more convinced that he had spoken truth when Henningsen went to Mexico to offer his services to a revolutionary movement in that country.

The practical result of the Mobile speech promptly showed in the Alabama legislature. Deeply impressed by Walker's arguments, the state granted a charter to the Mobile and Nicaragua Steamship Company, known to have been incorporated by Walker's supporters. Simultaneously the Central American League was revived, under the name of the Southern Emigration Society, and its branches throughout the South again took up the task of raising funds and finding recruits for Walker. Contributions were at first slow, for even ardent supporters now understood the weight of the odds against Walker. He had finally to undertake an extensive lecture tour, and this proved more successful. Listening to him, Southern audiences became convinced that Nicaragua was the key to their future security, and they responded with substantial donations to the cause. "General Walker," declared a newspaper after one of his speeches, "could raise a million dollars in Dallas County [Alabama] to Americanize Central America."

Even after two failures he still retained his luster. It was not the sad loyalty for a fallen idol, not the loyalty of nostalgia, that Southerners gave him, but a vibrant faith that he would yet achieve his purpose. When he stood trial in New Orleans he made the federal prosecutor appear feeble. An impassioned speech in his own defense outweighed in the minds of the jury both the evidence against him and an adverse charge by the judge; ten jurors out of twelve voted for acquittal. Intent on complete vindication, he demanded a new trial, but the government declined to prosecute further. On leaving the courtroom he declared openly that he would soon return to Nicaragua and "eat Christmas dinner in Granada."

XIX

THE DARK LIGHT OF HOPE

The strategic moment, Walker felt, could not be far away. Knowing Central American politicians, he was convinced that it would not be long before Costa Rica, holding the Transit, and the new Nicaraguan government were at daggers' points, and that a determined invasion would find only faltering and feeble resistance. In the early months of 1858, the press was astir with rumors of another Walker expedition, and this time it seemed that Buchanan would be unable to stop it. The President's hold on the Southerners in Congress had been seriously weakened by events in Kansas. In spite of his inclination to favor the Southern interest in the territory, resistance to slavery by "free-soil" settlers from the North had become so vigorous and so much blood was being shed, that Southerners had begun to lose hope. Kansas was no longer an effective lever with which Buchanan could push the South into acceptance of his anti-Walker measures. A major split in the Democratic Party and a revolt in Congress threatened the President if he sought to interfere with the new and powerful Walker expedition which, as widely rumored in the press, was in preparation. Walker himself went to Washington, where, after conferring with senatorial supporters, he wrote enthusiastically in a pri-

242

vate letter that the administration would either "yield to the voice of the country in regard to our affairs," or face catastrophic Congressional reprisals.*

Buchanan, however, had by no means exhausted his repertory of political devices in his contest with Walker. There was yet one way in which criticism of his Nicaraguan policy could be silenced and Walker frustrated once and for all. That was to send to Nicaragua, with the consent of its new government, a strong force of American marines, who would occupy the Transit route and render meaningless and hopeless any attempt by Walker to land an expeditionary force. To this end Buchanan, through Secretary of State Cass, now addressed himself. The fact that his new policy ran counter to everything he had said and done in connection with Nicaragua since taking office did not trouble him.

The first step in Buchanan's plan was to aid an American company to gain control of the Transit concession. No one was any longer sure where legal title to the Transit lay. Nicaragua owned the route, Costa Rica held it; but the positions of Vanderbilt, and of Morgan and Garrison were obscure. The latter two made a bold effort to reassert their claim. It seemed to them that since Costa Rican troops held the boats and occupied most of the route, the key to the outcome lay with President Mora, and their problem was only to find an agent who could exert the necessary pressure on him. W.R.C. Webster, who had been instrumental in organizing the alliance against Walker, was an obvious choice; he had the advantage of being British and had a claim of sorts on Costa Rican gratitude. The fact that he was in Vanderbilt's employ was not a serious deterrent for Morgan and Garrison, who knew the uses of money. Webster broke with Vanderbilt, entered their service, traveled to Costa Rica with ample funds at his disposal, and within a short time was able to report success. Mora, always generous with his signature on documents that could be repudiated, had given him the desired contract.

Buchanan, however, did not trust Morgan and Garrison, largely owing to their previous connection with Walker. He quickly wrote to Lord Clarendon in London that Costa Rica "had got hold of the greatest scamps as purchasers" of the Transit route and plainly conveyed his feeling that Mora should be discouraged from any thought

* Fayssoux Collection (ms.) No. 66, Jan. 5, 1858.

of executing the contract he had given Webster. England cooperatively intervened, and from this time Morgan and Garrison ceased to
be serious contenders for the prize.

Vanderbilt had bitterly, hotly, and publicly protested the Morgan-
Garrison contract, and it was generally thought that their failure
would be his success. He, after all, controlled Accessory Transit Company, which held a contract with Nicaragua for the route; but with
his innate contempt for the law, he was unwilling to take his stand
on a merely legal claim. He wanted to get physical control of the
Transit first, and argue about legality later. To this end he began a
secret intrigue with a high-ranking Costa Rican general. This proved
a poor tactic. Agents of the State Department reported the plot to
Washington, and Buchanan was incensed to the point where he refused to give the Commodore diplomatic support. Instead he turned
to a new contestant for the Transit—Vanderbilt's former associate,
Joseph L. White, godfather of the Clayton-Bulwer treaty, and a
political manipulator of great skill and experience. With some wealthy
associates, White had accumulated the worthless shares of the old
Atlantic and Pacific Ship Canal Company. Thus he had acquired the
original canal concession granted by Nicaragua, which gave his claim
to the Transit a certain air of legality. More important, he had persuaded the new Nicaraguan government to grant him secretly a provisional contract covering both overland transit and canal. Here was
the opportunity that the President sought to put an end to filibustering and regain popularity among the expansionists. He set Secretary
of State Cass to work negotiating a treaty with Nicaragua under
which the United States would have the right to use military force, if
necessary, to protect "persons and property conveyed over the
route," as operated by White. Objections from Vanderbilt were disregarded.

To Lord Clarendon, Buchanan wrote that British interests would
be protected, that the new treaty, known as the Cass-Irissari Convention, in no way threatened her rights or violated the intent of the
Clayton-Bulwer treaty, and that the Costa Ricans would have no
cause for complaint. "Great Britain and the United States, while
treating them [the Costa Ricans] justly and even liberally, ought to
let them know that this transit shall be kept open and shall never
again be interrupted."

II

At this juncture the Nicaraguan kaleidoscope was shaken again, and a totally new pattern emerged. To Buchanan's consternation, Nicaragua at the last moment rejected both the Cass-Irissari Convention and the White contract, and announced that the concession for the canal and Transit route had been granted, not to an American, not even to an Englishman, but to a Frenchman, one Félix Belly; and that in this grant Nicaragua and Costa Rica had acted in concert, as joint owners of the route.

The American press and Congress howled with anger. The weakness of the American government had lost the greatest prize in the Western Hemisphere, the isthmian canal route, to a European power —with all that that implied for the Monroe Doctrine and the future of the United States. There was talk of war with France. Was it for this that the President had rejected Walker? Buchanan was scourged even by newspapers which had been friendly to him. To make matters worse for the President, the tone of the Nicaraguan announcement was offensive in the extreme. Monsieur Belly, who represented a Parisian syndicate, was trading on the anti-*gringo* sentiment of the isthmus. Fluent in Spanish, vivacious, eloquent, with a talent for bravura, he was able to excite and persuade the Central American mind as could no Anglo-Saxon. He knew how to convey, without actually saying, that he was a trusted agent of Napoleon III, and that the wealth and arms of imperial France stood behind him. Why, he asked President Mora of Costa Rica, and the new president of Nicaragua, Martinez—why should they yield the Transit to the *gringos*? Instead, let them confer the rights to the route on a company of Europeans who shared their religion and their culture. Assured of protection by the French, and of a large share in the profits, their countries could grow rich, put an end to American pressure, and be free at last of William Walker.

This last point especially carried great weight with Mora and Martinez, who lived in dread of Walker's return. With a shrewd eye for theater, the Frenchman brought them together in the bullet-pocked town of Rivas, on the Transit route, to work out an agreement, and the resulting documents were made public on May 1, 1858, the first anniversary of Walker's surrender to Commander Davis. Most sensational of their productions was a joint Manifesto declaring the belief of the two Presidents that a new filibustering expedition against Central America was being organized in the United States, and requesting England and France not to leave them "at the mercy of barbarians." A separate declaration empowered Belly to arrange for the stationing of "European vessels of war" on the Central American coast.

Buchanan protested in language which for him was surprisingly strong. The Manifesto was an insult, he told Nicaragua and Costa Rica. The United States would not permit Nicaragua's contract with Belly to interfere with rights to the Transit already acquired by American citizens. If a canal were built, it would have to be a free and safe passage for all nations, and controlled by no one nation. The American government under no conditions would tolerate the stationing of French warships at the entry points of the canal or in it. To this the Central American presidents replied with much polite reassurance, but without in the least changing their minds; while Belly took ship for Paris, expecting to return with the approval of Emperor Napoleon III and all the necessary funds.

But like everyone else in the tangled business, he was doomed to disappointment. The French government shrugged him aside, partly because it was then deeply involved in a European crisis, partly because Belly's backers were out of favor at the imperial court, and partly because Napoleon was thinking vaguely of promoting his own long-dreamed-of Nicaraguan canal company. The one hope for Belly now lay in the possibility that American financiers and the Buchanan administration, recognizing his hold on the Central American leaders, would overlook his previous attacks on the United States, come to terms with him, and give him support. In this feeble hope he embarked for New York; but at the very moment of his arrival, the *Herald* was running a front-page dispatch from Paris under the headline DISAVOWAL OF M. BELLY. The myth of his power was exploded, and with it went all expectation that he would ever dig his canal.

III

With Belly's failure, every advantage in the contest for the Transit reverted to Vanderbilt. The bewildered Nicaraguan government was easily persuaded by his agents to declare invalid all previous contracts for the route, and to restore the concession to the original owner, the Accessory Transit Company. General applause greeted this news in the American press. Several newspapers confidently predicted that the Commodore would promptly move with his much-admired energy to reopen the Nicaraguan route and bring peace and prosperity to Central America. Buchanan himself now favored the Vanderbilt cause. The Commodore could at least be counted on to oppose Walker's return to Nicaragua.

But weeks went by, and Vanderbilt took no action. When queried as to the causes of the delay, he referred gravely to the physical deterioration of the Transit route. New steamboats would have to be built and bridges restored. Silting at the mouth of the San Juan River had seriously impaired the channel at Greytown harbor. The road west of Lake Nicaragua was in need of repair. Large new sums of capital would have to be invested—and the company was already in debt to Vanderbilt personally for loans made in the past. He would of course do what he could, but it was all very, very difficult.

Then, in June, 1858, light dawned on the press and the public, when word leaked out of Vanderbilt's arrangement with the Panama lines. Merely for withholding his ships from competition on the Panama run, he had been receiving $480,000 a year. Now he had yet another lever, the threat of renewed service to Nicaragua, with which to squeeze the Panama shipping magnates even harder. Rather than compete again with the Nicaraguan Transit, they had agreed to raise their payment to Vanderbilt by 40 per cent, to $56,000 a month.

Gone was any hope that the Accessory Transit Company would resume business—this despite the fact that the Commodore had urged the stockholders of the company to hold on to their shares. Over a million "blackmailing" dollars had gone into the Commodore's private pocket, more than he had lost on Accessory Transit stock two years earlier, and he was not a man to relinquish lightly so good a deal.

In the United States Senate, Robert Toombs of Georgia, one of Walker's staunch adherents, brought out the facts. "You give $900,000 a year to carry the mails to California," he told his fellow-senators, "and Vanderbilt compels the contractors to give him $56,000 a month to keep quiet. . . . He is the Kingfish that is robbing those small plunderers that come about the capital." The *New York*

Times compared Vanderbilt with "those old German barons who, from their eyries along the Rhine, swooped down upon the commerce of the noble river."

Prodded by the government and by public opinion, the Panama lines finally terminated their arrangement with the great financier. Only then did his interest in the Transit revive. Presently he wrote a letter to Buchanan: he understood that a new minister to Nicaragua, Alexander Dimitry, had been appointed, and would like to see him before he left the country, to discuss the reopening of the enterprise. "The route cannot be put into operation unless I do it myself." Evidently thinking it best to allay any suspicion that he might be planning further blackmail of the Panama lines, the Commodore added, "The only object I have in this matter is to further the wishes of your administration and to gratify my own feelings, as I have been heretofore so much identified with this particular route." Buchanan's reply was immediate and courteous. "Mr. Dimitry will be in New York tomorrow night. . . . I commend him to your kind attention."

A few months later, Vanderbilt informed Washington that he was planning a trip to Nicaragua, and Buchanan provided him with a personal letter addressed to Dimitry. "This letter will be delivered to you by Commodore Vanderbilt. He is about to . . . open the Nicaragua route. . . . I know no man in the United States who is so able and so willing to open it speedily as he is himself. This is an object the accomplishment of which I have much at heart. . . . This is in my opinion the wisest and most advantageous course the government of Nicaragua can pursue. . . . It is my desire therefore, that you should, as a private individual, exert yourself . . . for Mr. Vanderbilt."

The trip, however, never materialized. It was plain to Vanderbilt that the importance of the Nicaragua overland route was diminishing. Its troubles had created public suspicion of it, and California-bound travelers had become accustomed to the Panama service. Accessory Transit could never again be the bonanza it had been a few years earlier. As for a canal, the chances that it could be dug in the face of British opposition, and with the Clayton-Bulwer treaty still in effect, were as poor as they had ever been.

Besides, Vanderbilt's own interests were shifting. Now in his mid-sixties, he was still eager to prove his powers, and his mind was turning to great new ventures—transatlantic ocean liners, the railroads of the northeast, Wall Street warfare on a grand scale. He was through with Nicaragua. Those who continued to dream of a Nicaraguan canal and of the Transit route's revival recognized that everything would depend on Walker's next expedition.

IV

The leaders of Central America had come to believe the legends they had helped to create, in which Walker was seen as another Tamerlane, combining an insatiable thirst for blood with military genius—the implication being that they, having triumphed over this "military tactician of epic proportions," were the more deserving of their people's gratitude. In Nicaragua especially dread of Walker had been so sedulously cultivated by officials and priests that the prospect of his return evoked a nation-wide shudder. When the New Orleans *Delta* erroneously stated that Walker was in San Francisco, recruiting a thousand men for an invasion of Nicaragua's west coast, President Martinez was seized by panic. Bitter against America and disappointed in France, he turned to England for aid. Would she provide naval protection for Nicaragua's coasts and cope with Walker if he landed? The British were glad to comply. The opportunity was ready-made to extend their control of Central American resources and markets at the expense of the United States. All that was necessary was to keep the Clayton-Bulwer treaty in operation, Buchanan in his customary permissive state, and Walker out of Nicaragua, while British diplomats made the necessary arrangements.

The new British strategy hinged on an ostensible act of generosity, a voluntary yielding up of Central American territory. The first move in their gambit was an interview with Buchanan, solicited by Lord Napier, the British ambassador. The insight of the British into Buchanan's psychology had been shown in their selection of Napier as minister to his administration. He was an aristocrat of great astuteness and much charm; and the President was highly susceptible to displays of friendship by England's titled diplomats. With a light and delicate touch, Napier shaped Buchanan's mind to the views of Whitehall. He began by referring to the agitation in Congress for unilateral abrogation of the Clayton-Bulwer treaty. What were the President's views in the matter? Buchanan replied that he considered the treaty "a fruitful source of misunderstanding" but on the other hand it was a binding agreement, and "no attempt by Congress against it would have any countenance from him."

So far, so good; Napier now advanced another pawn. In recognition of the purport of the treaty, his government contemplated certain territorial concessions, long urged by the United States, to the republics of the isthmus. England was prepared at last to give Mosquito back to Nicaragua, and to return to Honduras certain islands off her Atlantic coast, seized by the British years earlier. Assuming that the President would welcome these moves, London would like to send out a special commissioner "to carry the Clayton-Bulwer treaty into execution . . . by separate negotiation with the Central American republics, in lieu of negotiation with the federal government" [of the United States].

Buchanan now stood at a crossroads of decision, but he chose not to see it. He could not have been oblivious to the ulterior motives that lay behind England's unusual philanthropy. It was apparent that the British no longer needed to maintain and pay for protectorates in Mosquito and the Bay Islands. They had been seized primarily to prevent the Nicaraguan canal from being dug; with the Clayton-Bulwer treaty in effect, they added little to England's position. Far more important to the British were valuable mining, forestry, and commercial rights (some of them formerly held by Americans), which the grateful Central American governments could be counted on to grant England in return for these territories; and long-range strategic benefits which would accrue from the establishment of pro-British governments up and down the isthmus.

Buchanan, if he felt a touch of skepticism within him, was not so inconsiderate of Lord Napier's feelings as to voice it. Instead, he expressed satisfaction at England's attitude. He said that "to him it was indifferent whether the concessions contemplated by Her Majesty's Government were consigned to a direct engagement between England and the United States, or to treaties between England and the Central American republics. The latter method might in some respects be even more acceptable to him."*

Napier doubtless understood the willingness, even eagerness, with which the President accepted his proposal. Although both houses

---

* *The Buchanan Papers,* ms. letters from Napier to Clarendon, Oct. 22, 24, 1857.

of the Congress were Democratic, antagonism to Buchanan was then so intense as to threaten the collapse of his legislative program. He urgently needed to be able to show the Congress and the country some constructive result of his statesmanship that would restore his prestige. If the people would accept England's concessions as a retreat on her part, the President would receive credit for it, and be strengthened accordingly.

In further recognition of England's gesture, Buchanan assured Napier that the United States had no territorial designs on Central America. "What could we do with such a people? We could not incorporate them; if we did, they would tear us asunder."

Napier said he could understand the President's view, but he believed "some Americans did contemplate the creation of colonies or dependencies" on the isthmus.

"That could not happen," insisted Buchanan. "We can only annex vacant territory." He had evidently forgotten his signature on the Ostend Manifesto, and he could not of course foresee the annexation of Hawaii, the Philippines, and Puerto Rico forty years later.

It was not long, however, before Buchanan was smitten by misgivings, for the British in Central America negotiated treaties so favorable to themselves as gravely to prejudice American interests. Disturbed, the President protested to Clarendon in a private letter that the new agreements were not "in the spirit of the Clayton-Bulwer treaty." He disliked especially a pledge given by England to "the great and mighty Republic of Nicaragua," assuring her of protection against filibusters. Buchanan felt that Nicaragua should have asked the United States to provide such protection. Soon afterward, the naval officer in command of America's Caribbean squadron informed Nicaragua, in a pride-swallowing note, that he would be glad to patrol her harbors to prevent filibusters from landing. The invitation was not forthcoming. A systematic patrol of Nicaragua's coasts by British warships went into effect, without American participation.

V

Walker's hopes of landing another expedition in Nicaragua were gone. Commanders of American warships might be reluctant to fire on a ship of his on the high seas, and lacking authorization from Nicaragua, might find it difficult to prevent him from landing or to pursue him, once landed; but the British, it was safe to say, would not be so inhibited. In view of Buchanan's attitude, they would feel no qualms in destroying filibusters at sea or on land. If there was to be another Walker expedition, it would have to be based on a new strategy, and this he began to work out in the autumn of 1858. He would aim not immediately at Nicaragua, but at Honduras, where he would not be expected; and having made a landing there, would establish a strong base. A revolt by Honduran Liberals was then gathering force; he would collaborate with it, defeat the existing regime, establish the Liberals in power, and with a friendly government at his back, drive south into Nicaragua.

He still had enough funds at his disposal to charter a ship and take an expedition out of the country. The question now was, would he be able to clear a ship from a Southern port? Could Washington exert enough influence on port officials in Mobile and New Orleans to prevent his sailing? The answer came in the curious indirect way of politics.

At that moment all Latin America shared and enjoyed the feeling that the United States was, after all, a paper eagle. This feeling was intensified when British warships in the Gulf of Mexico began to stop American merchantmen suspected of being slavers, and even fired on one or two which disobeyed their orders. Not since 1812 had so much humiliation been heaped on vessels flying the flag of the United States. The British, who were apparently testing the extent of Buchanan's tolerance, this time touched its limit, for he found the courage to lodge a protest and to send naval vessels to protect the country's shipping. Thereupon England acknowledged that her navy had no right to search American vessels in time of peace, and discontinued the practice.

If England had deliberately tried to revive Buchanan's prestige in the United States, she could have found no better means. The American public was all at once delighted with him, for had he not compelled perfidious Albion to respect the American flag? Was this not proof, after all—especially when taken together with England's return of Mosquito to Nicaragua—of bold and forceful statecraft on the part of the administration? A number of senators who had been extremely annoyed with Buchanan once more veered to his side. Without opposition he was able to staff the Gulf ports with federal officers on whom he could rely not to connive with Walker at evasions of the Neutrality Law.

The effect of this move by the President was fully felt by Walker late in 1858, when he assembled 300 men and a cargo of munitions at Mobile, and chartered a steamship to take them to Nicaragua as "peaceful emigrants." The new Collector of the Port, Thaddeus Sanford, flatly refused clearance, and the District Attorney summoned Walker before a Grand Jury, charged with conspiracy to violate the law. As usual, Walker spoke to the jurors in his own defense, and the old magic held. Gazing into the teeth of the evidence, the Grand Jury solemnly adjudged them false teeth, and exonerated him. But the expedition had been irretrievably damaged. His men, warned by United States marshals of their impending arrest, scattered to their homes, his ship was seized, and its cargo of munitions was confiscated.

Buchanan's campaign against Walker had turned out to be the single most successful effort of his administration.

THE EASING OF PAIN

Close to the end of his resources, and with his chances of success steadily diminishing, Walker could not afford a long delay before trying again. Within a few days of his Grand Jury appearance, his veteran officers were scouting the Southern states to find yet more recruits and money for him. This time only about 100 men agreed to serve, and their quality, it was noted, was poorer than in the past. One of his chief aides, Doubleday, described them as "mostly of the class found about the wharves of Southern cities, with here and there a Northern bank cashier who had suddenly decided to change his vocation." Men of schooling or political conviction were few among them.

He had no money with which to charter a steamship, and this time his hope of taking an expedition out of Mobile centered on a sailing vessel, the schooner *Susan,* owned by one of his friends. On a December day the *Susan* put into harbor, and her owner asked for clearance, not to Central America, but merely to Key West. It was refused. Port Collector Sanford had no doubt of the true destination and purpose of the voyage, and he could not be budged. For a day or two it appeared that this expedition too would disin-

tegrate before it could sail. One move alone was still open to Walker
—defiance of the federal government—and he was desperate enough
to try it. The *Susan* left Mobile without clearance papers. Walker's
intention was to follow on another boat. But the *Susan* came to
grief on a reef off British Honduras, and its company were brought
back to Mobile by a British warship. Their return, on New Year's
Day, 1859, struck a curious note of triumph. The people of Mobile were so pleased by the British action that the failure of the
filibusters' mission was almost ignored. The city's leading men tendered a banquet to the officers of the warship and lauded them in
warm speeches, with toast after toast to Anglo-American, or more
correctly, Anglo-Southern friendship. Walker was not present. The
changing mood of Mobile, the last stronghold of filibusterism, could
not have been lost on him.

II

There was no reason to believe that another effort to take an armed
force to Central America would prove more successful than the
last. On the contrary, the barriers against him were rising fast. Was
he so committed to his dream as to rule out every other possibility
of a career? If he had been willing to forego military adventures
and enter politics, he might still have opened up new and impressive possibilities for himself. But to Walker the current excite-
ments that were provoking the South to secession and war—the
bloodshed in Kansas—John Brown's slave-liberating raids into Virginia—the agitation in the North for higher tariffs inimical to Southern interests—all this was the shadow of doom. As before, the one
hope that he could see was the conquest of Central America in
the face of European opposition, as a rallying point for the entire
nation. All his efforts were still concentrated on this last declining
chance, which was linked to his inner need to regain the power
he had lost. For him the remaining alternatives were success or
death.

A new strategy for outwitting the federal government occurred
to him, and he and Henningsen obtained George Law's backing
for it. A hundred men would be placed on board a schooner, the
Granada, and cleared for Panama by way of Cuba with California

as their eventual destination. The port authorities at New Orleans could not deny the right of American citizens to go from state to state. He himself meanwhile would travel to Cuba, wait for the *Granada* to put into Havana harbor, and board it. The expedition would proceed to Panama and cross the isthmus. A steamship would be waiting for them on the Pacific side. Since there were comparatively few British warships patrolling the west coast of Nicaragua, Walker had no doubt that he could effect a landing there, and maintain a strong position until reinforcements, to be recruited in California, could join him.

A single aide, Colonel Bruno von Natzmer, was with him when he embarked on one of Law's Panama Line steamships, for which Havana was a port of call. His departure was observed, and a newspaper reporter, guessing part of the truth, concocted a story to the effect that Walker was going to Panama, and would proceed to California in order to recruit an army there. This report, published the very day of Walker's sailing, was a deadly misfortune for the plan. Federal authorities were alerted to the danger of permitting any vessel bound for Panama to carry what might be a filibustering expedition, and refused clearance to the *Granada*. Walker hastily tried to overcome the effect of the news story, by telling Havana correspondents that he was indeed going to Panama, but only "to take the English steamer for Southampton, intending to try what I can do in Europe." But it was too late to draw red herrings across his trail. On learning that his men had been taken off the *Granada* and dispersed, he returned to New Orleans.

If the piece of paper, a clearance certificate with an official signature on it, that stood between him and his purpose could not be obtained in one way, then it would have to be got in another. Fayssoux concentrated on winning over key officials in the office of the port of New Orleans, and finally reported success. Elated, Walker took the next step, a journey to New York, where he and Henningsen persuaded George Law to provide the funds needed for yet another expedition. By September, 1859, all was ready. A hundred Southerners were again waiting for the word to take ship with him. A Panama Line steamer, the *Philadelphia,* left New York for New Orleans with cases of guns and ammunition in its hold, and in a secret compartment an even larger quantity of arms. A second ship, the *St. Louis,* was to follow with 200 recruits from New York in the familiar guise of "emigrants." The expedition, as planned, was the largest ever assembled for Walker.

As soon as the *Philadelphia* docked in New Orleans, requesting clearance for Panama, most of the New Orleans contingent left the city on a small boat, intending to board the steamer unnoticed, just before it entered the Gulf. At first, all went well; the port inspectors examined the *Philadelphia,* found no contraband, and approved the sailing. At the last moment, however, high federal officials, including Buchanan's Secretary of the Treasury, Howell Cobb, took a hand, and formal clearance was refused. A company of soldiers from the garrison at Baton Rouge were sent down river to arrest Walker's men; the *Philadelphia* was twice searched until all the arms aboard had been found and confiscated; the ship itself was seized; and its sister-vessel, the *St. Louis,* was not permitted to leave New York. Cobb wrote to Buchanan: "You will be gratified to learn that the Walker expedition has *in all probability* been frustrated by the energy of our officers." It is some indication of the alarm still created by Walker's name in official quarters that even with the ships sequestered and the men under arrest, the Secretary was not quite sure that the expedition had been thwarted.

III

The loyalty that Walker evoked from the men who knew him best was a strange, if not a unique, phenomenon. He had managed to instill into his veterans—Henningsen, Anderson, Natzmer, Doubleday, Thomas Henry, Fayssoux, and others—his own feeling that to fight again in Central America was the only goal worth striving for. Those hard-bitten soldiers of fortune no longer sought fortune, for there was obviously none to be won in Walker's service. The ideals of democracy and Manifest Destiny with which some of them had begun had drained out through their wounds, but like him, they still believed that the future of the South and the prevention of civil war depended on the expansion of American institutions into the Caribbean. And there was still in them a determination, such as many a soldier has known, not to be thwarted by politicians and speculators. They had not yet had their fill of adventure. They wanted to fight again at the side of a man whom, for all his failures, they regarded as a great hero and a high-minded gentleman. So long as ships, guns, and recruits could be found, they would not desert him. After the dangers that they had survived with Walker, what else could they hope to do in life that would not seem pale and trivial by comparison?

The former sources of Walker's funds had dried up. George Law had concluded that the firmness of the federal government and the strength of British naval patrols in the Caribbean made the chance of taking another expedition to Central America too small to consider. To Southern magnates it also was evident that contributions to Walker's cause could no longer be regarded as a sound investment. He had, however, an invisible asset—his journalistic talent. In the autumn of 1859 a publisher offered him a contract for a book based on his experiences, and he spent the winter writing it. His hope for its success is suggested by a letter that he wrote to Fayssoux, reporting that the book was to be published in New York and Mobile simultaneously, and that the publisher expected to sell 20,000 copies in Alabama alone.

The haste of the writing shows repeatedly in the 430 pages of the volume, yet it is in many ways a remarkable production. Modeled in its third-person narrative after Caesar's *Commentaries,* it describes in clean and vigorous prose, with touches of classical scholarship, his adventures in conquest and the purposes that motivated him. Factually, the book is so accurate that even Central American historians to whom Walker was the great enemy accepted it as a reliable source of data. But Walker's passion for truth was at odds with the practical need to raise money for a new expedition, and much of the book was an effort to reaffirm his devotion to the South and to convince readers of the importance of Nicaragua to the future of Southern institutions.

The most remarkable feature of *The War in Nicaragua* is its impersonal restraint, which stands in sharp contrast to the highly emotional quality of his writing ten years earlier. It is as if Walker had deliberately censored every word that might reveal his feelings. The only expressions of pleasure come in his descriptions of landscape and of the bravery of his men in battle; the only regrets are for comrades lost; the only contempt is for the pusillanimity of American politicians. His attitude toward enemies is that of a gentleman whose hat has been accidentally knocked off by a passer-by—a slightly disdainful acceptance of an unpleasant fact. Probably his sharpest barb is a Dantesque reference to President Mora, who had just been banished from Costa Rica by a rival. "Let us pass Mora in exile, as Ugolino in hell, afar off and in silence."

Only a man habituated to monastic self-control could have written so exciting a story in so reserved a style. As he wrote, images full of pain must have come to his mind. He had been close to a world-shaking triumph, and where was it? Recollections of his own errors, of the bravery of his comrades, and the treason of those whom he had believed friends must have filled his heart, but only a cool and proud distillation of them reached paper. It seems a reasonable presumption that no writer of a personal memoir could suppress so much of himself unless he was seeking at a deeper level to suppress some unbearable admission. For Walker no admission could have been more bitter than that of failure. He had set out to be a Galahad, a Byron, a Bolívar—and he found himself at the age of thirty-five regarded as a tool of the slavery ultras, a fanatic with a lost cause.

He had been totally defeated, but he could not bring himself to say so. For him, failure was guilt—a guilt which overshadowed all the other guilts of his life, and they were many: the guilt of the hero who had betrayed his ideals, of the commander who had spilled the blood of others uselessly, of the man who had failed to use his procreative powers, perhaps of the boy who, loving his mother too much, had rejected his father. One of the mementos of this passage of Walker's life is a little note scrawled by his father about the time the book was published, and in which the relationship between them can perhaps be sensed. Addressed to Captain Fayssoux, it reads: "When you hear from my son, any information in regard to his health and movements will be acceptable to me—with kind regards to yourself, I remain very truly yours, James Walker."

As Walker wrote his story, and exposed himself to the terrors of memory, the need to be forgiven must have grown in him, for he could not forgive himself. It is not surprising that he turned that winter to religion, the one source from which he might yet win forgiveness. Significantly, the religion to which he gave himself was not that of his father, but Roman Catholicism, the faith which strict Tennessee Protestants of the 1850's most feared and hated.

The name of the priest who indoctrinated and prepared him was not revealed by the press. Some thought that the impulse to Catholicism had taken root in him years earlier in Nicaragua, under the inspiration of his gentle friend, Father Vijil. Following the news of his conversion, he was widely accused of cynical pretense. Was it not obvious, newspapers asked, that he hoped by becoming a Catholic to placate the Church in Central America and win new adherents there? Or perhaps to extract more money for his expeditions from the Catholic community of New Orleans? This view presupposes a naïveté in Walker that goes beyond credibility. He knew only too well how high the odds against him had become. The forces working in him at this stage of his life went far beyond ambition. Friends who were with him during the period of his conversion had no doubt of his sincerity. This was perhaps the logical conclusion for the man who had taken pride in his "unconquerable will." Only the religion of absolution could ease his pain.

XXI

ALL OR NOTHING

In April, 1860, the last springtime of peace before the great holocaust, Walker went to Louisville to visit his sister Alice, the one
living member of his family to whom he was close. On his return
to New Orleans, he found the bearded Fayssoux waiting for him
in a state of excitement, with hopeful news. An Englishman had
come from the Caribbean to seek Walker out, and in his absence
had confided his mission to Fayssoux. He spoke, he said, for most
of the British community on the large island of Ruatan, in the
Bay of Honduras, where he was a substantial merchant. Ruatan
was one of those islands which England had arbitrarily appropriated years earlier, and which she now proposed to turn over to
Honduras in return for commercial concessions on the mainland.
The transfer was to be consummated late in July, 1860; but many
Englishmen on the island had agreed that, rather than submit to Honduran rule, they would seize the government office as soon as the
British flag was lowered, set up an independent government, and
defy Honduras. Would Walker assist them?

The prospect of action had a tonic effect on Walker. At once
he began to conceive a grand scheme in which the liberation of

261

Ruatan was only the first step. With the island at war with Honduras, he would be justified in attacking the mainland and allying himself with the country's Liberals, who were in revolt under the leadership of the former president, Trinidad Cabañas. To be sure, Cabañas had no reason to feel friendly toward Walker, who in his Nicaraguan days had refused to help him; but four years had elapsed since then, and the necessities of war could be counted on to bridge the rift between them. There would be no more talk of slavery. Together they would overthrow the Honduran dictatorship and establish Cabañas as president. Walker would then recruit an American army, descend on Nicaragua and Costa Rica, appeal to the democratic elements, call for aid from the United States, and make a last attempt to achieve the great goal, Central American federation.

Within a week a small party of chosen men were on the way to Ruatan, traveling as ordinary passengers on a cargo boat, to study the situation. Walker himself, under the name of Williams, went to the island in June. After conferring with his Ruatanese allies, he established a secret supply depot on an uninhabited island not far away, with the fairy-tale name of Cozumel—this to avoid British interference with the landing of cargo on Ruatan. A message was sent to Cabañas, then said to be recruiting a rebel army of Hondurans in Salvador, to alert him to the new prospect, and to urge him to join forces with Walker in eastern Honduras in late August.

Returning to New Orleans, Walker took charge of the main body of the expedition, nearly a hundred men, who were to sail from Mobile in a schooner, the *Taylor,* with port clearance arranged by Fayssoux. Another schooner, loaded with supplies, sailed from New Orleans with a party under the command of a noted Alabama soldier, Colonel A. F. Rudler. But the plan had a fatal flaw— it could not be kept secret. The British sponsors of the intended coup disclosed it to friends in the government, in the futile hope of enlisting their cooperation, and from that moment Walker's chances of taking Ruatan were negligible. England was intent on completing her deal with Honduras, in which the island was a minor item; and she did not intend to let Walker return to Central America if she could help it. To block him was an easy matter. All that was necessary was to postpone the transfer of Ruatan to Honduras.

It was a safe assumption that so long as the Union Jack flew over the island, Walker would not attempt to land there. The strategy of delay was proposed to the Honduran government and eagerly accepted, as the best way to keep Walker out of their country.

Walker, as yet unaware that he had been outmaneuvered, ordered the *Taylor* to head for his supply base on Cozumel. The little island was by no means paradise, for the rainy season had begun early, but the men believed that they would have only a few days to wait before the British colors were struck on Ruatan. They would then take to their boat, make a landing, seize the government, and prepare for the invasion of Honduras. At Cozumel they were joined by a correspondent for the New York *Herald* who had got wind of the enterprise. He was greatly impressed; the expedition he described as "a fine-looking set of men," and Walker as "a silent, thoughtful man," "a wise leader"—"gentlemanly," with "cool determination."

A dull, wet week passed—and England still held Ruatan, with a warship in the harbor and a battalion of marines ashore. Walker's chief concern at this point was that Rudler's boat, which carried most of their ammunition, had failed to appear. Seeking to find Rudler and to maintain morale, Walker ordered the expedition onto the *Taylor* and sailed the surrounding seas. The blows of fate now became heavier. When finally Rudler and his men appeared off Ruatan, it was in a vessel other than the schooner in which they had set out. Their boat, together with its all-important cargo, had been seized by the British when necessity compelled a stop at a British port on the way to Ruatan.

With the entire expedition now aboard the *Taylor,* Walker continued to cruise off the Honduran coast. After a few more days, the painful truth became obvious: the British were determined to outwait him. Before Honduras took possession of Ruatan, his supplies would be gone.

He was trapped. The Ruatan project was finished. To return ingloriously to the United States would invite only mockery. What was left? Cabañas. True, without Ruatan Walker had little to offer the Honduran revolution—but that might be remedied. A wild scheme took shape in his mind—a way of making a grand gesture of defiance to the powers that were frustrating him, and at the same time, if he were lucky, of gaining enough military power to make an alliance with him worth Cabañas' while. He shared his idea with his men. The chance of success was slight, the risks were mortal; he would have no man follow him except by free choice. None refused. The extent to which his faith in his destiny and his urge to live had dwindled was known to no one but himself.

His proposal was nothing less than to storm and capture a great stone fortress, dating from the days of Cortez, that guarded the busy Honduran port of Truxillo. This done, they would take the town, join Cabañas, and win the country. Sailing in darkness, they made a landing three miles north of Truxillo and before daybreak were on the march. But some fishermen saw them, and before they reached the fort the alarm had been given. The fort's garrison was small, consisting only of some thirty Hondurans, but they had the advantage of artillery and walls, and once they were alerted, everything seemed to favor a successful defense.

II

Walker's tactics at Fort Truxillo were based on his intuition of the Central American soldier, who usually shot at the nearest target and found it a strain to reserve his fire. Six men, willing to face the probability of death, volunteered to go forward to draw the first cannonade. If the Hondurans could be decoyed into firing their artillery prematurely, the main assault would be made from another direction before the guns could be reloaded and reaimed.

At dawn, the action began. It was one of those heavy, wet, dispirited tropical mornings in which even the birds and the monkeys are still. The hill leading to the fort was covered with slippery grass, and the grey stone walls above, with the mouths of the cannon visible in the embrasures, looked huge and formidable. Walker gave the signal. As the six volunteers broke from cover and ran forward, yelling and beckoning to an imaginary force behind them, every Honduran cannoneer discharged his load of grapeshot and canister at them. Three of the men were instantly killed, the other three badly wounded. Under the haze of smoke, the rest of Walker's force rushed the fort, ignoring a few panicky rifle shots. To hoist each other over the walls the Americans formed human pyramids, and as they jumped down on the other side the Hondurans took to their heels and fled.

Citizens of the town of Truxillo, who had climbed a hill nearby to view the battle, as at a spectator sport, saw with amazement the lowering of the Honduran colors hardly fifteen minutes after the first shots had been fired. Over the fort Walker raised the flag he had brought with him—the colors of the old Central American federation, symbolizing union and democracy. He was determined that the victory be recognized as the first battle in a democratic revolution, not as an act of piracy. Within an hour he was in Truxillo, reassuring the people that they would not be molested.

One of the first buildings in Truxillo occupied by Walker's men was the customhouse of the port, through which Honduras received most of its imports. Since the customs in most Central American countries were the main source of revenue for their governments, Walker believed that by cutting off the Truxillo duties he could inflict serious injury on the Honduran regime. With this end in view, he declared Truxillo a free port—an action also calculated to please local merchants. What he did not realize, however, was that England had an agreement with Honduras, under which all customs revenue from Truxillo was assigned to the British government for payment of an old debt.

When one of Walker's officers and a squad of men entered the building, the Honduran customs officials had already disappeared. There disappeared also, at this time, some $3000 which had been kept in a locked box, awaiting transfer to the British inspector who periodically visited the port. Whether the Hondurans had taken this money with them when they fled, or whether it had been misappropriated by the Americans could never be ascertained. The one certainty was that its removal provided the British with a legitimate pretext for intervening with military force.

Unaware as yet of the trouble which the seizure of the customhouse invited, Walker set himself to win the confidence of the local population. A proclamation to the citizens of Truxillo told them that he had not come to make war on the people of their country, but only on their government, "which stands in the way of the interests, not only of Honduras, but of all Central America." The people could rely on him to protect their rights, "both of person and of property." The tone of his statement was mild and placatory.

III

News of the victory at Truxillo, in spite of the tiny force engaged, produced a stir in the United States. An entire page of the New York *Herald* was headed: THE WALKER EXPEDITION—SUDDEN DESCENT ON HONDURAS—CAPTURE OF TRUXILLO. Much was made of the fact that Walker had established a hospital in Truxillo, and was himself assisting his surgeon in caring for the soldiers wounded in the battle, Hondurans as well as Americans. It seemed that the press was about to revive his heroic glamor. The American public was led to believe that he was well on his way to the conquest of the isthmus. Exultant Southern newspapers told readers that Walker and a hundred Americans in a fort with cannon and plenty of ammunition were equivalent to a Central American army of thousands.

Walker himself held no such illusion. He knew that, cannon or no cannon, unless supplies came to him promptly he could easily be starved out. Already it was reported that a strong Honduran force was approaching Truxillo. Everything would depend, as it had depended from the beginning, on his success in joining Cabañas, and making the revolution their common enterprise. There were rumors in Truxillo that the old Liberal was not far away, but no one could say where.

To try to locate Cabañas' camp, Walker chose the most experienced jungle fighter on his force, Colonel Thomas Henry, who set out with a Honduran guide, and was gone for several days. On his return, before reporting to Walker he stopped at a Truxillo tavern for a few drinks to offset his fatigue. He was by nature a pugnacious man—the survivor of a dozen duels, twenty battles, and many wounds—and liquor invariably accented his belligerence. When he climbed the hill to the fort, his mood was dangerous. Unable to find Walker in his quarters, he waited briefly, smoking a cigar, and then began to search the fort. The door to one room—the powder magazine—was closed, and he pushed it open. Inside was a squad of men preparing charges for the fort's cannon, and loose gunpowder was scattered on the floor. The young lieutenant in charge pointed to Henry's cigar and ordered him out. Nothing more was needed to inflame the wrath of a man spoiling for a fight. Cursing, Henry struck the lieutenant and tried to grapple with him. In a panic, the young man leaped back and pulled a pistol from his belt, and when the colonel rushed him, fired blindly. The bullet struck Henry in the jaw, carrying away the lower part of his face, a wound so hideous that even the most hardened veterans of battle were shocked by the sight.

In great pain, Henry was taken to the hospital, where the surgeon gave him morphine, before sending for Walker. The message on which Walker's hopes rested now lay in the mind of a drugged man, whose wound made it certain that he would never be able to speak again. Walker waited at the bedside and himself performed such surgery as might help to save Henry's life; but the lack of needed antiseptics made for a dark prognosis.

While Walker was waiting for Henry to regain consciousness, he was faced by still worse trouble, with the arrival at Truxillo of the British warship *Icarus,* Captain Norvell Salmon. Within a few hours a sailor brought Walker a curt message: he was to surrender, lay down his arms, and restore the money which had been in the customhouse when his men took possession of it, and which was the property of the British crown. This was Walker's first intimation that the money had been stolen.

The problem now was to prevent Captain Salmon from shelling the fort and landing marines. Still hoping for news of Cabañas from Henry, Walker played for time. His hastily written reply to Salmon said, "I cannot, under the circumstances, regard it as dishonorable to lay down my arms to an officer of the British crown"; but he asked Salmon to particularize his terms for a surrender, and to investigate the facts surrounding the alleged theft.

Henry had meanwhile opened his eyes and recognized Walker. A slate was put into the hands of the voiceless man, and he managed to scrawl a few words, apparently enough to convey some faint notion of Cabañas' whereabouts. Walker's choice was painfully clear. On the one hand, there was the will-o'-the-wisp chance of finding the jungle encampment of the Liberal rebels, who might or might not be willing to accept him. On the other hand, there was the opportunity to surrender safely to the British. Salmon's second note, which arrived some days later, was specific, if supercilious: the Americans would have the protection of the British flag when they laid down their arms. They would then leave the country on a schooner; and Walker himself would have to make good the money stolen from the customhouse by someone in his service. The note also pointedly remarked that 700 Honduran government soldiers had taken up a position just outside Truxillo.

Salmon's haughty tone may have influenced Walker's decision. Three times before in his life he had been compelled to surrender to officers of the American Army or Navy, and once he had wept at the necessity, but to bow to an Englishman was an even more crushing prospect. Consulting with his officers, he found them ready to follow him in a last desperate effort. Word went to Salmon, postponing until the next day a final reply to his demand for surrender.

While his men were spiking the guns of the fort and destroying all munitions they could not carry with them, Walker visited the hospital to say goodbye to the wounded and to leave a message for Salmon, asking that they be protected against Honduran vengeance. One of the filibusters later described Walker's farewell to the dying Colonel Henry. The gangrene in Henry's wound was spreading rapidly, maggots had appeared in the rotting flesh of his wound, and his voiceless suffering was agonizing for the men around him to see. There was a cup near him, and when Walker, after a few words, turned to go, he squeezed Henry's shoulder, and left alongside the cup a full bottle of morphine. Then, turning abruptly, he strode away. The others watched as Henry painfully reached for the cup, emptied the bottle into it, and forced the drug down his gullet. Before dying, he pulled his blanket over his graveyard face.

IV

Silently, before dawn, the men left the fort and, with a Honduran guide, followed a jungle track not far from the Atlantic coast, moving southeast toward the place in which Cabañas had last been seen. As soon as their flight became known in Truxillo, a strong force of Honduran soldiers set out after them. Twenty-four hours later, as the filibusters were about to ford a stream, the pursuers caught up with them and opened fire, wounding twenty men at the first volley.

Walker rallied the rest, and they managed to beat off the attack. In this engagement he sustained a flesh wound in his cheek, his first injury in all the battles in which he had fought in Central America. Carrying their wounded with them through narrow, twisting jungle trails they pushed on, until they came to the banks of a broad river, the Rio Negro, where a friendly tribe of Carib Indians provided shelter for them. Here their guide, after conferring with the Caribs, gave Walker an encouraging report. A day's journey toward the coast, on the banks of the Negro, they would find Cabañas and his men.

With Walker's long experience of treason in all forms, suspicion must have hammered at him and become near-certainty when the guide disappeared. Nevertheless, he decided to make the indicated move, for his men were subsisting entirely on bananas, the wounded men were in distress, and nothing was to be gained by tramping aimlessly through the jungle. He commandeered the Caribs' canoes, and they drifted downstream, until a few miles from the coast they saw signs of a deserted encampment. Whoever had been there, Cabañas or another, had long since gone.

As they got out of their canoes, they were attacked by waiting Honduran snipers. What saved them was the presence of some rotting barricades, from behind which they were able to defend themselves. A week of sleepless nights and hopeless days ensued. The camp was located in a swampy region, and the insects, the fetid odors, the drenching bursts of rain, the burning sun, and the incessant rifle fire reduced the hungry little band to a state of misery in which the only relief was an occasional successful shot at a Honduran. Several of the men were killed, others wounded. Walker himself came down with fever, which he tried to ignore. Moving from man to man behind their defenses, guiding their rifle fire, shifting their positions as necessity required, tending the wounded, he did what he could, until fatigue began to close down on them, like a fog. It was with a sense of mingled despair and relief that, nine days after the fighting began, he saw two British boats coming up the river, manned by British sailors, with Captain Salmon sitting stiffly in the bow of the lead boat. As the Hondurans ceased firing, a sailor got out of the boat, advanced to the camp, and gave Walker a message. The Captain wished him to come at once to his boat, prepared to surrender his force.

The last military decision of Walker's life was in some ways the easiest. His urge to resist was gone. The only gesture that he made to his reputation as he walked to the shore was a conscious straightening of his shoulders and lifting of his head.

Salmon was a big man, with a ruddy complexion and a booming voice—almost a caricature of his type. "Sir," he began, "I demand that you surrender to me immediately."

"To whom do I surrender?" asked Walker.

"To an officer of Her Majesty's Government. And you may thank me, too"—pointing at the Honduran soldiers in the distance —"that you have a whole bone in your body and that your men leave here alive."

Something in Salmon's manner must have aroused Walker's distrust, for he repeated his question in a slightly different form. "Do I understand you to say, sir, that my surrender would be to a representative of Her Majesty's Government?"

"Yes," said Salmon, "to me."

"Under these circumstances," Walker replied, "I surrender to you, Captain." He handed his sword and pistol to Salmon, and turning, ordered his men to deliver their guns and knives to the British marines. That was all.*

He and Colonel Rudler were taken immediately to the *Icarus,* the rest of the men following in other boats. As soon as all were on board, Salmon ordered the ship to proceed at full steam to Truxillo. There, he announced, they would be handed over to the Honduran authorities. Walker's men would be protected by the British flag, but the fate of Walker himself, and Rudler, would be left to the Hondurans.

Walker was at first incredulous, then disdainful. The correspondent of the New York *Herald* boarded the *Icarus* at Truxillo, and before leaving the ship Walker dictated a short statement to him.

* New York *Herald*, Sept. 28, Oct. 4, 1860. *Harper's Weekly*, Vol. IV, p. 647.

On board the Steamer *Icarus*
Sept. 5, 1860

I hereby protest before the civilized world that when I surrendered to the captain of Her Majesty's Steamer *Icarus,* that officer expressly received my sword and pistol, as well as the arms of Colonel Rudler, and the surrender was expressly made in so many words to him, as the representative of Her Britannic Majesty.

William Walker

That was the last flicker in him of the urge to survive. He was ripe for death and knew it. At thirty-six, he had exhausted the possibilities of romantic heroism; knights-errant must die young. Asceticism had deprived him of the best reason for enduring the pain of failure—the woman and the child. He knew that the world was tired of him, and he was tired of himself. The Hondurans who took him to the fort that he had stormed not long before and put him in an improvised cell found him courteous and tractable. He did not really wish to resist the end that he could foresee. His only request was that a priest be sent to him. The priest, later interviewed by Joaquin Miller, said that Walker told him, "I am prepared to die. My political career is finished."

His chief concern was to have the priest intercede with the Honduran government for the security of his men. "I alone made the decision to attack Truxillo. They knew nothing of it." It was, he felt, altogether unfair that Colonel Rudler should share his fate. When after a few days a Honduran officer came to him to say that he would be executed the next morning, he asked at once about Rudler, and was relieved to hear that the Colonel's sentence had been commuted to a limited imprisonment.

Many concocted versions of Walker's execution appeared in the American press, including "last words" which it is virtually certain that he never uttered. What is known is that at eight o'clock on September 12, 1860, flanked by two priests, he was led by a company of soldiers to a ruined wall, on the outskirts of Truxillo, followed by a large and jubilant crowd of Hondurans. He ignored the laughter and jests around him. His bearing was calm and resolute, and he seemed to give his attention wholly to the words of the priests. The soldiers formed a line around the square in front of the wall, as the last rites were administered. When the priests had concluded and withdrew, Walker stood erect, facing the soldiers impassively and without speaking. A squad of Hondurans stepped forward, aimed, and at an officer's command, fired. Walker was apparently dead when he fell. A second squad then advanced and fired another volley at the body, after which the officer walked forward, put his pistol to the head of the corpse, and pulled the trigger, mutilating the face beyond recognition. The crowd cheered, the troops marched off, and the priests removed the body, with the help of some Americans who had come off a ship in Truxillo, and who paid for a coffin. The interment was conducted with a Catholic service at an isolated spot. Afterward the Tennessee Historical Society, of which Walker was an honorary member, attempted to bring the remains to Nashville for burial, but the Honduran government refused permission. Captain Salmon, with a shrewd eye for British relations in Central America, gave Walker's sword to Nicaragua. There was considerable criticism of him in the United States for his mortal deception of Walker, but the British government winked at the episode and it did not interfere with his subsequent career.

V

The blaze of interest that centered on Walker while he lived contrasts curiously with the oblivion that overtook him in the grave. As abruptly as he had come to the world's notice, he dropped out of it. Perhaps the same thing would have happened to Napoleon if he had been trapped in Egypt, or to Clive if he had been defeated at Plassey. But the speed with which Walker's fame evaporated had something of the same phenomenal quality that marked him all his life. The coming of the Civil War, with its new crop of heroes, was no doubt mainly responsible for the country's readiness to forget him, but there may have been also another, more subtle reason—the way of thinking and feeling for which he stood. Men of business had then begun to take possession of the United States; their special outlook and mentality was becoming dominant throughout the North and in parts of the South; and their standards of judgment were more and more regarded as identical with law, morality, and good government. Walker's entire career was a romantic challenge to economic man, his personality wholly antithetic to the great powers then about to reshape the Ameri-

can way of life. By his enemies is a man known, and Walker contended with the money-master, Cornelius Vanderbilt, was abandoned
by the artful friend of wealth, Buchanan, and was castigated by the
leading advocate of the economic virtues, Greeley.

A concerted and final attack on his reputation by the abolitionist
press was in the making when he died. Its tone was set by Greeley
in the New York *Tribune*. A long editorial, which appeared before
news of the execution had reached the United States, called Walker
"impudent" — "imbecilic" — "idiotic" — "insane" — "cowardly" —
"contemptible" — "a vagabond" — "pestilent creature" — and found
it "inexplicable that men should follow him." His death, the editorial
plainly conveyed, would be a godsend. Even in that age of easy
slander, this was remarkable. President Buchanan echoed Greeley's
sentiments. In a message to Congress in December, 1860, when the
nation was rocking toward civil war, he took time to express pious
satisfaction in Walker's disappearance from the national scene. "I
congratulate you on the public sentiment which now exists," he told
Congress, "against the crime of setting on foot military expeditions
within the limits of the United States, to proceed from thence and
make war upon the people of unoffending states with whom we are at
peace. In this respect a happy change has been effected since the
commencement of my administration." Buchanan had chosen to forget that he himself had once advocated the forcible annexation of
Cuba, that he had been elected on a Democratic platform which called
on the administration to support Walker, and that he had received him
at the White House with every civility and courtesy. His remarks
were in fact an echo of statements made by the press of England,
where Walker's death was regarded with unalloyed pleasure. On both
sides of the Atlantic, official opinion took the stand that he had
been simply a troublemaker; and the Northern interpretation of history
which dominated American thought after the Civil War accepted this
view.

The *New York Times* saw Walker otherwise. "Whatever hard things
may have been said of General Walker—and much, we doubt not,
would have been left unsaid had his fortune been more propitious—
he was at least no vulgar adventurer, either by birth, habits, or education, or the honourable purposes with which he set out in life. His
parentage was unsullied, his private walk and temperance unques-

tioned, his learning profound, and his original aims, however subsequently misdirected by an unchastened ambition, such as commended him to success, while enlisting the esteem of numerous friends. Even those who deny him all claim to military skill or political sagacity as a leader, pay the highest compliment to his moral force and personal integrity. Without these his first failure as an adventurer must inevitably have been his last."

Until the flame of his natural genius was quenched by despair, Walker had the glow of an idealist as well as the heat of a hero. *Harper's Weekly* observed that he failed because, instead of seeking to win support from the wealthy and influential, he relied only on himself. The real tragedy, *Harper's* commented, lay in the rejection of him by the American government. "Had William Walker been an Englishman or a Frenchman, he would never have become a 'filibuster,' but would have found ample scope for his extraordinary talents in the legitimate service of his country."* It was the kind of epitaph that Walker himself might have desired.

---

* It is impossible not to wonder what would have happened in Central America if President Pierce or Buchanan had chosen to support Walker in the first flush of his conquest, and before he made his fatal concession to the South. Would the flow of American capital and enterprise to the isthmian republics have enabled them to make more progress in the century that followed? It seems safe to say that they could hardly have made less. Would England have gone to war with the United States over Nicaragua in 1856? There is considerable reason to doubt it. Would American concentration on Central America and the construction of a canal there have eased the internal schism in the United States? Would Walker have been justified in his belief in the possibility of averting civil war by rallying the nation to an expansion of democratic institutions and productivity overseas? It may be noted that echoes of the idea persist in mid-twentieth-century politics. At a time when, as Adlai Stevenson has said, the world itself is threatened with civil war, there are not a few who feel that the most realistic hope of peace lies in the diversion of the energies of the great powers away from direct confrontation and to an effort to bring underprivileged peoples into "the column of Progress and Democracy" of which Walker wrote.

BIBLIOGRAPHY

Among manuscript collections consulted in the writing of this book two were of especial importance: the *Fayssoux Collection,* at the Middle American Research Institute of Tulane University, New Orleans, and the *Buchanan Papers,* Pennsylvania Historical Society, Philadelphia. The *Clayton Papers* in the Congressional Library and manuscript archives of the United States Department of State and the United States Navy Department dealing with Central America in the 1850's also provided valuable data.

Documents and Correspondence Relative to a Trans-Isthmian Canal, privately printed by the New York law firm of Sullivan and Cromwell in 1900, contributed greatly; and the *Wheeler Scrapbooks,* a large collection of newspaper clippings in five volumes, at the Library of Congress, were a significant source of material.

Contemporary newspapers in every city in which Walker stayed for an appreciable time were consulted. Among the more essential were: for the years 1848–49, the *Crescent, Delta,* and *Picayune* of New Orleans; for 1850–55, the San Francisco *Herald, Alta California,* and the *State Democratic Journal* of Sacramento; for 1856–60, the *Herald, Tribune,* and *Times* of New York, the *Delta* and *Picayune* of New Orleans, and *El Nicaragüense.* For official views of Walker between 1855 and 1860, the *Congressional Globe,* and for Anglo-American Relations, the *London Times* were indispensable.

Fresh insights into Walker's psychology were afforded by his published address, *The Unity of Art,* in the Library of the Tennessee State Archives at Nashville. Prior to 1962, this pamphlet was incorrectly attributed. Among the books listed below, *Filibusters and Financiers,* by W. O. Scroggs, by the thoroughness of its documentation greatly aided the search for useful sources and provided numerous interpretive clues. Walker's own book, *The War in Nicaragua,* is, of course, a primary source.

BOOKS

Adams, James Truslow, *America's Tragedy,* New York, 1934.

Alemán Blaños, G., *Centenario de la Guerra Nacional de Nicaragua contra Walker,* Guatemala, 1956.

Alfaro, Olmedo, *El Filibustero Walker en Nicaragua* (Pamphlet), Panama, 1932.

Alvarez, Miguel, *Los Filibusteros en Nicaragua,* Granada, 1944.

"An Officer in the Service of Walker" (Anon.), *The Destiny of Nicaragua,* Boston, 1856.

Andrews, Wayne, *The Vanderbilt Legend,* New York, 1941.

Asbury, Herbert, *The Barbary Coast,* New York, 1933.

———, *The French Quarter,* New York, 1936.

Atkinson, E., *Cheap Cotton and Free Labor,* Boston, 1861.

Atlantic and Pacific Ship Canal Company, *Terms of the Contract Between the State of Nicaragua and the Company* (Pamphlet), New York, 1849.

Bailey, Thomas A., *A Diplomatic History of the American People,* New York, 1944.

Bancroft, H. H., *History of Central America,* San Francisco, 1887.

———, *History of Mexico,* Vol. IV, San Francisco, 1888.

Bass, J. M., *William Walker* (Pamphlet), Nashville, 1898.

Belly, F., *A Travers l'Amérique Centrale,* 2 vols., Paris, 1860.

Belt, Thomas, *The Naturalist in Nicaragua,* London, 1874.

Bigelow, John, *Breaches of Anglo-American Treaties,* New York, 1917.

———, *Retrospections of an Active Life,* New York, 1909.

Bonaparte, Louis Napoleon, *A Project to Connect the Atlantic and Pacific Oceans* (Pamphlet), London, 1846.

Bulwer, Sir H. Lytton, *Historical Characters,* London, 1867.

Caldwell, R. G., *The Lopez Expeditions to Cuba,* Princeton, 1915.

Chase, H. and Sanborn, C. W., *The North and the South: A Statistical View,* New York, 1856.

Choules, J. O., *The Cruise of the North Star,* New York, 1854.

Christy, D., *Cotton Is King,* New York, 1856.

Claiborne, J. F. H., *Life and Correspondence of John A. Quitman,* 2 vols., New York, 1860.

Clapp, Theodore, *Autobiographical Sketches,* Boston, 1858.

Comegys, J. P., *Memoir of John M. Clayton,* Wilmington, 1882.

Croffut, W. A., *The Vanderbilts and the Story of Their Fortune*, New York, 1882.

Crowe, Frederick, *The Gospel in Central America*, London, 1850.

D'Auvergne, E. B. F., *Envoys Extraordinary*, London, 1937.

Davis, Richard Harding, *Real Soldiers of Fortune*, New York, 1906.

Doubleday, C. W., *Reminiscences of the "Filibuster" War in Nicaragua*, New York, 1886.

Einstein, L., "Lewis Cass," in *American Secretaries of State* (S. F. Bemis, ed.), New York, 1928.

Ettinger, A. A., *The Mission to Spain of Pierre Soulé*, New Haven, 1932.

Field, S. J., *Personal Reminiscences of Early Days in California* (Privately printed), 1893.

Gámez, J., *Historia de Nicaragua*, Managua, 1889.

Gándara, M. M., *El Gobernador y Commandante General de Sonora a Sus Habitantes* (Broadside), Hermosillo, 1853.

Greeley, Horace, *The American Conflict*, 2 vols., Hartford, 1864–66.

Greene, Lawrence, *The Filibuster*, Indianapolis, 1937.

Hall, A. H., *The Manhattaner in New Orleans*, New Orleans, 1851.

Hittell, J. S., *California*, 3 vols., San Francisco, 1878.

Hoblitzell, H. S., *Early Historical Sketch of the City of Marysville and Yuba County*, 1876.

Jamison, J. C., *With Walker in Nicaragua*, Columbia, Mo., 1909.

Keasbey, L. M., *The Nicaragua Canal and the Monroe Doctrine*, Philadelphia, 1896.

Lambertie, R., *Le Drame de la Sonore*, Paris, 1856.

Lane, Wheaton J., *Commodore Vanderbilt*, New York, 1942.

Learned, H. B., "William Marcy," in *American Secretaries of State*, New York, 1928.

Letts, J. M., *California Illustrated*, New York, 1852.

Lévy, Daniel, *Les Francais en Californie*, San Francisco, 1884.

Manning, William R. (ed.), *Diplomatic Correspondence of the United States*, vol. 4, Washington, 1932.

Meade, Rebecca Paulding, *Life of Hiram Paulding*, New York, 1910.

Medbery, J. K., *Men and Mysteries of Wall Street*, New York, 1879.

Melendez Ch. Carlos, *Ideario politico de Walker*, San José, 1956.

Montúfar, L., *Walker en Centro America*, 2 vols., Guatemala, 1887.

Naval Affairs Committee (House), "Arrest of William Walker by Commodore Paulding" (Pamphlet), Washington, 1858.

Neumann, Alfred, *Strange Conquest*, New York, 1954.

———, *Gitterwerk des Lebens*, Los Angeles, 1951.

Nicaise, Auguste, *Les Filibustiers Américains*, Paris, 1860.

Nichols, R. F., *Franklin Pierce*, Philadelphia, 1931.

Obregon Loria, Rafael, *La Campaña del Transito, 1856–57*, San José, 1956.

Oliphant, Laurence, *Patriots and Filibusters*, London, 1860.

Olmstead, F. L., *The Cotton Kingdom,* New York, 1862.

O'Meara, James, *Broderick and Gwin,* San Francisco, 1881.

Perez, J., *Memorias . . . de la guerra contra los Filibusteros,* Managua, 1857.

Perkins, Dexter, *The Monroe Doctrine, 1826–67,* Baltimore, 1933.

Polk, James K., *Diary of James K. Polk,* 4 vols., New York, 1910.

Powell, E. A., *Gentlemen Rovers,* New York, 1913.

Ratterman, Elleanore, *Documents* (ed. by W. O. Scroggs), Nashville, 1916.

Rauch, Basil, *American Interest in Cuba, 1848–1855,* New York, 1948.

Rhodes, J. F., *History of the United States, 1850–4,* Vols. 1-2, New York, 1902.

Ripley, E. M., *Social Life In Old New Orleans,* New Orleans, 1921.

Rippy, J. F. *The United States and Mexico,* New York, 1926.

Roche, J. J., *The Story of the Filibusters,* London, 1891.

———, *Byways of War,* Boston, 1901.

Rollins, Clinton (Arturo Ortega, trans.) (Sp.), *William Walker,* Managua, 1945.

Scroggs, W. O., *Filibusters and Financiers,* New York, 1916.

Shuck, O. T., *Representative Men of the Pacific,* San Francisco, 1870.

Smith, J. H. *The War with Mexico,* New York, 1919.

Soulé, E.; Gihon, J. H.; and Nisbet, J., *Annals of San Francisco,* San Francisco, 1855.

Squier, E. G., *Nicaragua,* 2 vols., New York, 1852.

Stout, P. F., *Nicaragua, Past, Present and Future,* Philadelphia, 1859.

Sullivan and Cromwell, *Documents and Correspondence Relative To A Trans-Isthmian Canal* (Privately printed), 4 vols., New York, 1900.

Thomas, Jane H., *Old Days in Nashville,* Nashville, 1897.

Tinker, E. L., *Gombo—The Creole Dialect* (Pamphlet), Worcester, 1910.

Truman, Ben C., *The Field of Honor,* New York, 1884.

U. S. Senate, *Speeches on William Walker* (Pamphlet), 1858.

Walker, William, *The War in Nicaragua,* Mobile, 1860.

———, *Letters of General Walker* (Pamphlet), New York, 1858.

———, *Mexico and Central America: The Problem and Its Solution* (Pamphlet), New Orleans, 1858.

Warren, T. Robinson, *Dust and Foam,* New York, 1859.

Weller, J. B., *Remarks on Nicaraguan Affairs,* Washington, 1856.

Wells, William V., *Walker's Expedititon to Nicaragua,* New York, 1856.

———, *Explorations and Adventures in Honduras,* New York, 1857.

Wencker, Friedrich, "William Walker, der Diktator von Nicaragua," in *Ungekrönte Könige,* Vienna, 1934.

Williams, M. F., *History of the San Francisco Vigilance Committee of 1851,* San Francisco, 1911.

Williams, M. W., "John Middleton Clayton," in *American Secretaries of State* (S. F. Bemis, ed.), New York, 1928.

Wilson, Edmund, *Patriotic Gore,* New York, 1962.

PERIODICALS

The following periodicals contain articles of exceptional value relating to Walker, his times, or the later course of Central America's development:

Academia de Geografia e Historia de Nicaragua (Revista), Managua, 1946, t. 8, no. 3. ("William Walker trata de explicar por qué se esforzó en renstabler la esclavitud en Nicaragua").

American Historical Review, Vol. VII, pp. 709-750 (L. M. Sears— "Slidell and Buchanan").

Vol. X, pp. 792-811 (W. O. Scroggs—"William Walker and the Steamship Corporation in Nicaragua").

Vol. XLII, p. 497 (R. W. Van Alstyne, ed.,—"Anglo-American Relations 1853–59").

Annual Report of the American Historical Association, 1911, Vol. II, p. 447 ("The Correspondence of . . . Howell Cobb").

Arizona Historical Review, 1935 ("William Walker's Invasion of Sonora").

Atlantic Monthly, Vol. IV, p. 665 ("A. Absalom").

Blackwood's Magazine, 1856, Vol. LXXIX, pp. 314-316 ("The Destiny of Nicaragua").

Harper's Weekly, 1857–60 (frequent editorial comment, 1857–60, in Vols. I, II, III).

Hispanic-American Historical Review, Vol. XVI, pp. 352-357 (R. W. Van Alstyne—"The Central American Policy of Lord Palmerston").

Huntington Library Quarterly, 1944, Vol. VII, pp. 153-166 ("Bandini's Account of William Walker's Invasion of Lower California").

Inter-American Affairs, 1955, Vol. VIII, No. 4 (A. G. Frank—"The Economic Development of Nicaragua").

Journal of Modern History, Vol. XI, pp. 157-161 (R. W. Van Alstyne— "British Diplomacy and the Clayton-Bulwer Treaty").

Mississippi Valley Historical Review, Vol. I, p. 199 (W. O. Scroggs— "William Walker's Designs on Cuba").

Pacific Historical Review, 1933, Vol. II, pp. 194-213 (R. K. Wyllys— "The Republic of Lower California").

Political Science Quarterly, Vol. VIII, p. 22 (S. Webster—"The Ostend Manifesto").

Proceedings of the South Carolina Historical Assn., 1947, p. 9 (W. H. Patterson).

Putnam's Magazine, April, 1857, pp. 425-435.

Revue des Deux Mondes, August, 1856 (A. Assolant—"Walker et les Aventuriers Américains").

Sociedad de Geografia e Historia de Guatemala (Revista), 1957, t. 30, No. 1-4, pp. 7-92 (V. Rodriguez Beteta—"Transcendencia de la guerra nacional de Centro America").

Sunset Magazine, Vol. XVI, p. 564 (Poem and article by Joaquin Miller).

ACKNOWLEDGMENTS

I am deeply indebted to several friends who read the manuscript of this book at various stages of its development and provided helpful criticism: Phyllis Duganne (Mrs. Eben Given), O. Rudolph Johnson, and Richard Johnson. Dr. Sandor Rado generously reviewed my findings on Walker's psychology and made a number of stimulating suggestions. I must express, too, my gratitude to the staff of the Boston Athenaeum for many valuable services during the final year of research.

A.Z.C.

INDEX

Academy of Sciences (Paris), 29
Accessory Transit Company, 66, 67, 70-71, 100 ff, 132, 139, 156, 161, 165, 169, 214-15, 221, 244, 247
  See also Buchanan, James; Vanderbilt, Cornelius; Walker, William
"Address of the Seven Prisoners, The" (pamphlet), 197
Alta California (newspaper), 79 n, 80, 90, 141
American Historical Review, 227 n
American Phalanx. *See Falange Americana, La*
American Secretaries of State (book), 198
Anderson, Colonel Frank, 116, 231, 233-34, 236, 257
Anita (brig), 83
Annals of San Francisco (1855), 65 n
Arrow (brig), 80
Atlantic and Pacific Ship Canal Company, 244, 427
Atlantic Monthly, 197

Baring Brothers, 67, 71
Belly, Monsieur, 245-46
Benjamin, Judah P. (statesman), 199, 218, 221
Black Warrior (ship), 106-8
Blanco, General, 77
Bolívar, Simón (revolutionist), 29, 149
Bonaparte, Louis. *See* Napoleon III, Emperor Louis Bonaparte
British Foreign Office, 29
Broderick, David C. (politician), 91

Brown, John (abolitionist), 255
Buchanan, James, President of the United States, 31, 109, 151-52, 175, 182, 184, 194, 218, 221-22, 226-27, 238, 240-53, 257, 273 n
  criticizes Clayton-Bulwer treaty, 229-31
  plan to send marines to Nicaragua, 243 ff
  plan for reassertion of Monroe Doctrine, 198-99
Buchanan Papers, 152 n, 250 n
Bulwer, Sir Henry Lytton, 48-55 *passim,* 57, 66, 68, 71
Bulwer-Lytton, Edward (novelist), 48

Cabañas, Trinidad, President of Honduras, 139, 150 ff, 262, 264, 267-69
Calderón, Foreign Minister, 106
Calhoun, John C. (statesman), 18, 24, 37, 39, 105
Calvin, John (theologian), 7
Campaña del Transito, La, 174 n
Canal Napoléon de Nicaragua, La, 47
"Card, A" (newspaper editorial), 62
Caroline (brig), 81, 83
Carter, W. H., 65
Cass, Lewis (statesman), 183, 230, 243-44
Cass-Irissari Convention, 244-45
Castellón, Francisco de, 97-98, 111, 120, 122 ff
Cauty, Colonel John, 139, 214-15
Central American Federation, 29, 138

About the Author

The nature of power and its impact on the men who wield it have long been a major interest of Albert Z. Carr. Previous books of his have dealt with Napoleon Bonaparte, Joseph Stalin and John D. Rockefeller.

Trained as an economist, during World War II Mr. Carr was assistant to the Chairman of the War Production Board and subsequently a White House adviser, serving on missions to England, China, Japan and other countries. After the war, as a director of the Inter-Allied Reparation Agency, he worked on the problem of German reparations. He also served as a consultant to President Truman during his 1948 campaign for re-election.

Mr. Carr's literary career began with short stories and articles contributed to leading magazines. A number of his stories have been made into motion pictures. In the fields of history and biography he has published eight books, which include *Juggernaut: The Path of Dictatorship, The Coming of War,* and *Men of Power.*

UNITE[D]

Rio Grande

MEXICO

*PACIFIC
OCEAN*

WILLIAM WALKER

0   300

Miles

Mautner